RKO Radio Pictures
Horror, Science Fiction and
Fantasy Films, 1929–1956

RKO Radio Pictures
Horror, Science Fiction and
Fantasy Films, 1929–1956

Michael R. Pitts

McFarland & Company, Inc., Publishers

Jefferson, North Carolina

LIBRARY OF CONGRESS CATALOGUING-IN-PUBLICATION DATA

Pitts, Michael R.
RKO radio pictures horror, science fiction and fantasy films, 1929–1956 /
Michael R. Pitts.
p.   cm.
Includes bibliographical references and index.

ISBN 978-0-7864-6047-2 (softcover : acid free paper) ∞
ISBN 978-1-4766-1683-4 (ebook)

1. RKO Radio Pictures—History.   2. Motion pictures—United States—
History—20th century.   I. Title.

PN1999.R3P58 2015   384'.80979494—dc23   2015002999

BRITISH LIBRARY CATALOGUING DATA ARE AVAILABLE

Cover images © iStock/Thinkstock

Printed in the United States of America

*McFarland & Company, Inc., Publishers
Box 611, Jefferson, North Carolina 28640
www.mcfarlandpub.com*

To the memory of my cousin,
Bernadine Herkless Morgan
(1909–2010)

Table of Contents

Preface

From 1929 to 1956, RKO Pictures released more than 140 feature films dealing with horror, science fiction and fantasy themes. Today, the company is mainly remembered in these genres for the classics *King Kong* and *The Thing from Another World*, but RKO also did a number of other memorable features like *The Most Dangerous Game, The Phantom of Crestwood, She, The Hunchback of Notre Dame, Experiment Perilous, The Enchanted Cottage, The Spiral Staircase* and *It's a Wonderful Life*. RKO is also known for a series of atmospheric psychological horror thrillers produced by Val Lewton, including *Cat People, I Walked with a Zombie, The Seventh Victim, The Curse of the Cat People* and *The Body Snatcher*. In the realm of fantasy, RKO served as the feature film distributor for Walt Disney Studios between 1938 and 1954, releasing the classics *Snow White and the Seven Dwarfs, Fantasia, Pinocchio, Dumbo, Bambi, Cinderella, Alice in Wonderland* and *Peter Pan*.

While RKO only made horror, science fiction and fantasy movies in the sound era, its roots date back to the silent days with these genres. RKO Radio Pictures came into being in 1929 with the merging of Film Booking Offices of America (FBO) with Radio Corporation of America's Keith-Albee-Orpheus (KAO) theater circuit. Thus the studio had the production facilities of FBO and the Keith-Albee-Orpheum theaters needed to exhibit its product. The merger was facilitated by the head of Radio Corporation of America (RCA), David Sarnoff, who wanted an outlet for RCA Photophone, a sound-on-film process. FBO was owned by Joseph Kennedy, who had bought it in 1926; prior to 1922 it had been known as Robertson-Cole. In 1927 KAO merged Pathé Exchange and Producers Distributing Corporation (PDC), which was owned by Cecil B. DeMille, and this conglomerate also became a part of RKO Radio Pictures. RKO bought Pathé from Kennedy in 1931, obtaining its Culver City studio and backlot.

Pathé had a fairly lengthy involvement with horror-related features and serials. A production and distribution company from 1921 to 1927, it was founded in 1910 by Pathé, a French company that had been distributing its films stateside since 1900. By 1914 the U.S. operation was known as Pathé Frères and it became independent in 1921, calling itself Pathé Exchange. Between 1915 and 1930, Pathé was involved in the production of some 475 titles.

One of Pathé's first genre-related features was *The House of Fear* (1915), the third in a series based on John T. McIntyre's short stories about sleuth Ashton-Kirk, played by Arnold Daly. This outing had the famed detective trying to unravel mysterious happenings in an old house, eventually finding a series of tunnels used by counterfeiters. Veteran serial villain Sheldon Lewis co-starred and the leading lady was future Broadway star Jeanne Eagels. In 1917 Pathé distributed Thanhouser Film Corporation's production of Wilkie Collins' *The Woman in White*, starring Florence LaBadie and Richard R. Neill. The next year Pathé issued the Anderson-Brunton Company feature *The Ghost of the Rancho* in which a dissipated young man (Bryant Washburn) redeems himself by pretending to be a ghost and protecting the woman he loves (Rhea Mitchell) from Mexican bandits. The year 1918 saw Pathé releasing another Anderson-Brunton film, *The*

Bells, starring Frank Keenan and Lois Wilson. It told of an innkeeper (Keenan) murdering a wealthy man and years later being driven mad by the sound of bells after fearing a mesmerist will make him confess to the crime. Chadwick did another version of the Henry Irving story in 1926 starring Lionel Barrymore with Boris Karloff as the mesmerist. In 1919 Pathé issued the first of three screen versions of Bayard Veiller's play *The Thirteenth Chair*. Starring Yvonne Delva and Creighton Hale, it was an involved tale of murder and blackmail featuring a clairvoyant and séances. MGM remade it in 1929 and 1937.

The House of the Tolling Bell, a J. Stuart Blackton Feature Pictures production, was released by Pathé in 1920. Blackton directed this old house thriller in which May McAvoy and Bruce Gordon agree to spend a year in a spooky mansion in order to receive an inheritance from a rich relative (Anthony Cole). Another relation (William R. Dunn) plans to do them in for the money but the supposed deceased rises from his coffin, scaring off the villain, and blessing the soon-to-be-betrothed young people, who become his heirs. The same year Pathé co-distributed (with W.W. Hodkinson) Robert Brunton Productions' *The House of Whispers*, headlining J. Warren Kerrigan and Fritzi Brunette. Kerrigan played a man who moves into his uncle's apartment in an house that is plagued by strange noises, including screams and whispering. He finds the place is riddled with secret passages and eventually uncovers a plan by a supposedly dead man (Fred C. Jones) to drive his wife (Marjorie Wilson) mad so he and his first wife (Claire DuBrey) can get her money.

Pathé was also involved in the production and distribution of a number of serials with horrific elements. Pearl White starred in the most famous of all movie serials, *The Perils of Pauline* (1914), a 20-episode affair. Following this immensely popular, but somewhat crude, production, Pathé teamed with the Star Company to make a trio of serials starring White, *Exploits of Elaine* (1914), *The New Exploits of Elaine* and *The Romance of Elaine* (both 1915), with Arnold Daly as Arthur B. Reeve's scientific detective Craig Kennedy and Creighton Hale as his associate, Walter Jameson. These chapterplays introduced the menace of the super-villain, which became a standard fixture in the serial genre. With Balboa Feature Film Corporation, Pathé made *The Red Circle* (1915) about a young woman (Ruth Roland) who is cursed to commit crimes, but is redeemed by the love of a detective (Frank Mayo). *The Mysteries of Myra* (1916) is an all-out horror cliffhanger starring Jean Sothern as a young woman terrorized by a cult of magicians, the Black Order, who dwell in an underground city, practice the occult arts, and use a female vampire and a thought monster to carry out their schemes. The masked hero character first appeared in *The Iron Claw* (1916) with White as a young woman in the clutches of the title villain and saved by the mystery man. There was a science fiction element to the plot of Pathé–Astra Films' *The Shielding Shadow* (1916) with the hero (Ralph Kellard) becoming invisible via a mysterious pellet; Grace Darmond was the leading lady. Invisibility courtesy of an ancient Egyptian violet diamond was the central plot ploy of *The Fatal Ring* (1917) starring Pearl White and Earle Fox, with Warner Oland as the villain. The title character of the 15-chapter *The Hidden Hand* (1917) used a claw glove to dispatch his victims; Doris Kenyon, Mahlon Hamilton, Sheldon Lewis and Arline Pretty starred and the scenario was co-written by Arthur B. Reeve. The masked phantom first appeared in *Mystery of the Double Cross* (1917) with Mollie King, Leon Bary and Ralph Stuart. While phantoms were usually villainous, sometimes they were heroic as in *Hands Up* (1918) starring Ruth Roland, George Chesebro and George Larkin. In *The House of Hate* (1918), headlining Pearl White and Antonio Moreno, the Hooded Terror was out to destroy a munitions factory. An outlaw who wears a wolf's head is opposed by a government agent (George Larkin) in the seven-chapter *The Terror of the Range* (1919), top-lining Betty Compson. Ruth Roland tries to keep a gold mine in *The Tiger's Trail* (1919) but is opposed by crooks as well as a cult of tiger

Advertisement for *The House of the Tolling Bell* **(Pathé, 1920).**

worshipping Hindus. *The Phantom Foe* (1920) had the power to suddenly disappear; this one starred Warner Oland and Juanita Hansen.

Starting in 1921 Pathé Exchange made serials without co-producing them with Astra Films as it did between 1916 and 1920. It was not until 1923 that the studio returned to horrific themes. Ruth Roland starred as a woman out to stop a gang from stealing her father's formula for substitute coal in *Ruth of the Range* (1923). Roland starred in her eleventh and last cliffhanger as a landowner in *Haunted Valley* (1923); she is at odds with a crook who wants her land and uses television and a three-dimensional invention to his advantage. Also ending her serial starring career, Pearl White did *Plunder* (1923), a horror tale about buried treasure, a mad scientist and his 12-foot creation.

The leading man was Warren Krech, later known as Warren William. Lots of underground tunnels, trap doors and an ancient tomb add to the adventure in *The Fortieth Door* (1924) in which Allene Ray is promised to an Arab scoundrel (Frank Lackteen) but loves an American archeologist (Bruce Gordon). It was also released as a six-reel feature. Pathé made a number of cliffhangers based on the works of Edgar Wallace, including *The Green Archer* (1925) starring the popular serial team of Allene Ray and Walter Miller. It had the mysterious title character at odds with an evil millionaire (Burr McIntosh). Charlie Chan (George Kuwa) was introduced to the screen, albeit in a small role, in the ten-chapter mystery thriller *The House Without a Key* (1926), also starring Ray and Miller. Finding a lost gold mine, and saving the young woman (Dorothy Phillips) who inherited it, was the plot of *The Bar-C Mystery* (1926), with Wallace MacDonald as the mysterious hero. A five-reel feature version was also released. Cullen Landis was a Secret Service agent on the trail of a smuggling gang leader called the Ghost in *The Crimson Flash* (1927). *The Masked Menace* (1927) top-lined Larry Kent and Jean Arthur in the story of a young woman lusted after by an occultist, her father's killer. Ray and Miller were the leads in *The Man Without a Face* (1927) with the title character trying to cheat two sisters out of an inheritance. The Secret Service must stop smugglers from stealing an aircraft engine silencer in *Eagle of the Night* (1928) with Frank Clarke, Shirley Palmer and Maurice Costello. Edgar Wallace's novel *The Fellowship of the Frog* was made into the ten-chapter serial *Mark of the Frog* (1928), starring Donald Reed

Walter Miller, Frank Lackteen, Allene Ray and George Kuwa in *The House Without a Key* (Pathé, 1926).

and Margaret Morris; the masked Frog and his gang are out to retrieve a million dollars stolen two decades before. A black cowl–wearing figure with a hairy, clawed hand wants revenge when a forger is executed for murder in *The Terrible People* (1928), another cliffhanger based on the works of Edgar Wallace. In *The Yellow Cameo* (1928), a mysterious stranger and his dog (Cyclone) help a young woman (Allene Ray) in the story of a cameo which holds the key to a treasure buried on a remote ranch. Devil worshippers and a wolfman-like villain contend with Mountie (Walter Miller) in *Queen of the Northwoods* (1929) with Ethlyne Claire playing the title character; it was Pathé's penultimate cliffhanger. Following *The Black Book* (1929), starring Allene Ray and Walter Miller, Pathé closed its serial unit with the coming of sound.

When RKO Radio Pictures first came into being in 1929, Pathé, Radio Pictures and RKO were separate entities but within a year they merged and the studio quickly became known for its top-notch pictorial quality. With ornate sets and location backgrounds, along with highly capable cinematographers, editors, composers, art directors, sound technicians and wardrobe people, RKO offered a polished product as good as that of any other Hollywood studio. Along with Metro-Goldwyn-Mayer, Warner Bros., Paramount and 20th Century–Fox, RKO Radio Pictures was considered one of the top Hollywood studios from the 1930s into the 1950s.

Unfortunately RKO was not stable financially during its existence. There were years when the studio made big profits but there were many others with financial losses. One of its major problems was a constant change in heads of production. Between 1931 and 1948 this post was held at various times by David O. Selznick, Merian C. Cooper, B.B. Kahane, Samuel Briskin, Pandro S. Berman, George Schaefer, Charles Koerner, Peter N. Rathvon and Dore Schary. Industrialist Howard Hughes acquired the studio in 1948 and sold it to General Teleradio, Inc., in 1955. William Dozier was head of production from 1955 until the studio ceased making films in 1957. It continued as a releasing company into 1960.

In 1956 General Teleradio released RKO's films to television under the C&C Television banner. A C&C logo replaced the studio's logo on TV prints. After a number of turnovers, beginning in 1971 when C&C's successor TransBeacon went bankrupt, Turner Broadcasting bought the rights to the RKO movies in 1985, making them available for television. Time Warner has controlled and distributed most of the RKO library since 1996 although a number of features, including the Disneys, are governed by other entities or are in public domain. Trademarks, logos, story rights, etc., for the studio are owned by RKO Pictures LLC.

Although mainly known for its feature films, RKO Radio Pictures also produced and distributed hundreds of short subjects, including cartoons, two-reel comedies, sports series, documentaries, musicals and the popular "March of Time" and "Pathé News" series. While this volume mainly covers features, there is a section on short subjects, mostly made up of "spook comedies" which were popular two-reel fare from the 1930s into the early 1950s.

In regards to horror, science fiction and fantasy feature films, the company kicked off its genre releases late in 1929 with the hugely successful *Seven Keys to Baldpate*, starring Richard Dix. The next year it struck gold again with Amos 'n Andy in *Check and Double Check* and Betty Compson in *Midnight Mystery*. The year 1931 saw only two genre outings under the RKO Distributing Corporation banner, the British import *The Perfect Alibi* and Richard Dix's *The Public Defender*. In 1932 RKO Radio Pictures released nine such features, including *Ghost Valley*, *Bird of Paradise*, *The Most Dangerous Game*, *Thirteen Women*, *The Phantom of Crestwood* and *Secrets of the French Police*. The year 1933 was even more prolific with 11 releases, including the box office blockbuster *King Kong* in addition to *The Monkey's Paw*, *Deluge*, *Tomorrow at Seven*, *Before Dawn* and *The Son of Kong*. Nine more genre efforts came out in 1934, among them *The Lost Patrol*, *Murder on the Blackboard*, *Their Big Moment* and *Dangerous Corner*. The pace kept up in 1935 with seven releases, including *The Nitwits, She, The Return of Peter Grimm* and a second version of *Seven Keys to Baldpate*. As the popularity of the horror film cycle of the 1930s began to diminish, only four such films came out in 1936, including the Hildegarde Withers mysteries *Murder on a Bridle Path* and *The Plot Thickens*, plus Bert Wheeler and Robert Woolsey's comedy *Mummy's Boys*. The years 1937 and 1938 were also lean, although the latter did have Walt Disney's classic fairy tale fantasy *Snow White and the Seven Dwarfs*. There were only three genre releases in 1939, one of them a profitable artistic achievement, *The Hunchback of Notre Dame*.

With a horror revival in the 1940s, the studio had a half-dozen releases in 1940, including two Disney classics, *Fantasia* and *Pinocchio*, plus the fantasy *Beyond Tomorrow* and the teaming of Boris Karloff, Bela Lugosi and Peter Lorre in the Kay Kyser comedy *You'll Find Out*. The year 1941 had only four releases, with *Dumbo* and *All That Money Can Buy* both released in October. Of the studio's five 1942 genre releases, the most important horror-wise came at the end of the year: producer Val Lewton's *Cat People*. The year 1943 saw an upsurge with ten releases, including *I Walked with a Zombie, The Leopard Man, The Ghost Ship* and *The Seventh Victim*, all from Lewton. The genre output of 1944 included *The Curse of the Cat People*, another Lewton, and *Experiment Perilous*. RKO's most prolific year genre-wise was in 1945 with 14 features, including *Zombies on Broadway, The Enchanted Cottage, The Body Snatcher, Isle of the Dead, The Brighton Strangler* and *The Spiral Staircase*. Eight more genre-related films came out in 1946, including *Bedlam* and *Genius at Work*, and the pace kept up in 1947 with seven outings, including *It's a Wonderful Life, The Secret Life of Walter Mitty* and a third version of *Seven Keys to Baldpate*. Five peripheral genre films were issued in 1948, such as *The Miracle of the Bells* and *The Boy with Green Hair*, and 1949 saw four releases, including *Mighty Joe Young* and *The Adventures of Ichabod and Mr. Toad*.

For RKO the 1950s was the most sparse decade for horror, science fiction and fantasy films with the most profitable of four 1950 releases being *Cinderella*. The classic *The Thing from Another World* was issued in the spring of 1951 and among the year's four other films was *Alice in Wonderland*. Coming at the end of 1952, *Angel Face* was the most noted of a trio of genre releases. Another three came out in 1953 with *Peter Pan* topping the list. The year 1954 had another three issues, starting with the tacky *Killers from Space* and closing with the animated feature *Hansel and Gretel*. In 1955 RKO briefly released the Japanese import *Rodan* before it was taken over by Distributors Corporation of America. RKO acquired distribution rights to *From the Earth to the Moon* (1958) and *The Mysterians* (1959) but then stopped distributing films; both features were being picked up and released by other companies.

RKO Radio Pictures played an important part in making horror, science fiction and fantasy films from the early 1930s into the mid–1950s. While not as recognized as Universal or as prolific as some other studios, RKO placed many genre features on the market for appreciative audiences. Television revived interest in many of these films in the 1950s and 1960s and with the coming of the video age in the 1980s, the RKO genre efforts were reborn yet again. It is my hope you will enjoy reading about these movies which without doubt will continue to entertain for generations to come.

Thanks to James Robert Parish, Gary Kramer and Ray White for their help in preparing this volume.

Feature Films

Adventure Girl (1934; 69 minutes)

SUPERVISOR: Ashton Dearholt. DIRECTOR: Herman Raymaker. SCREENPLAY: Ferrin Frazier. Based on the novel *The Cradle of the Deep* by Joan Lowell. PHOTOGRAPHY: Harry Squire. EDITOR: Sam B. Jacobson. MUSIC: Winston Sharples. SOUND: Larry Lynn & Al Sinton.

CAST: Joan Lowell (Herself/Narrator), Captain Nicholas Wagner, Bill Sawyer, Otto Siegler (Themselves), Ula Holt (Princess Maya), Manola (Village Chief), Captain Jack (dog).

Big game hunter Frank Buck became a screen favorite when RKO released *Bring 'Em Back Alive*, one of the studio's top moneymakers in 1932. Produced by the Van Beuren Corporation, that well-done documentary had Buck narrating his adventures in Central America. Its success led to the follow-ups *Wild Cargo* (1934), *Fang and Claw* (1935) and the compilation feature *Jungle Cavalcade* (1941).

RKO re-teamed with Van Beuren to release another adventure set in the Mayan Peninsula, *Adventure Girl*, based on the 1929 novel *The Cradle of the Deep* by Joan Lowell, who had earlier acted in silent films like *Souls for Sale* (1923), *Branded a Thief* and *His Own Law* (both 1924) and *The Gold Rush* (1925). Lowell starred in *Adventure Girl* as well as narrating it. While hardly up to the entertainment standards of the initial Frank Buck feature, this re-enactment of Lowell's adventures is fast-paced and fairly exciting with the added plus of a comely heroine. Unlike the Buck documentaries, the Lowell feature is more fiction than fact and includes plot elements such as the worship of ancient gods, a fabled temple of ivory and an emerald so big that people would die from looking at it. The *San Antonio* (Texas) *Express* reported that the feature "contains several jungle episodes which are said to rival anything before recorded for the screen." *Harrison's Reports* revealed that the Detroit Council of Catholic Organizations considered the film to be defective or offensive in spots and not suitable for children or adolescents.

As a 76th birthday present for her sea captain father Nicholas Wagner (himself), Joan Lowell (herself) and sailors Bill Sawyer and Otto Siegler (themselves) set sail from New York City to the Caribbean on the *Black Hawk,* her 48-foot ship. At sea they are hit by a hurricane and Bill falls overboard with Joan coming to his rescue. The next day brings calm seas and they find themselves in a ships' graveyard where Bill and Otto obtain a mast to replace the one that split off their vessel during the storm. Joan and her father board a derelict Spanish galleon and on it she finds a chest containing the map to the location of a huge emerald the captain hid a century before. Since her father believes in the seafaring superstition about not claiming a dead man's treasure, Joan keeps the map to herself. She changes the course of their voyage to the Mayan Peninsula and then, without drinking water, drifts in calm seas for three days. They sight a windjammer but the vessel will not help them. Joan and Bill get into a rowboat and try to find land. Eventually the boat drifts to an island where Joan is saved from a deadly fer-de-lance by a mongoose before being given life-saving cocoanut milk by a native. She revives Bill and with many

7

cocoanuts and a water supply they head back to the boat and save her father and Otto. The ship lands near a village not far from the ruins where the emerald is supposedly hidden. Joan and Bill meet the local ruler, Princess Maya (Ula Holt). Joan tells the princess she is looking for rich minerals and will turn over all the profits to Maya's people. Although the village chief Manola (himself) warns Maya not to trust the strangers, she agrees to lead Joan and Bill to the hidden city. They journey up the Rio Dolce in a motor-powered raft and make their way to the lost city, encountering vultures, alligators, snakes and a stone frog god. After finding a hidden tunnel, the trio emerge in the ruined city, the Temple of the Sun, and Joan finds the idol in which the emerald is supposedly hidden. Manola and his men have secretly followed on foot. When Joan has Bill try to divert Maya's attention, she digs for the emerald and causes the stone idol to collapse. Maya accuses Joan and Bill of desecrating the gods of her ancestors. Manola and his cohorts show up and capture Joan but Bill manages to escape. They use the raft to carry Joan back to the ruins of San Martine, a Spanish fort, where Maya orders her burned alive. At the last minute Bill rescues Joan and they use the raft to try and escape. Maya, Manola and the natives follow in their boats. Using gasoline, Joan and Bill set the river on fire but find themselves surrounded by flames. Bill cuts a hole in the bottom of the boat and he and Joan swim to the safety of the *Black Hawk* with Joan vowing never again to pursue a dead man's treasure.

Naturally, the scenery and the wildlife are among the highlights of *Adventure Girl* as are the various Mayan ruins and Spanish architecture, including the stone arch at Chichicastinago. Some of these locales also are featured in the serial *The New Adventures of Tarzan* (Burroughs–Tarzan Pictures, 1936). Also filmed in Guatemala, that cliffhanger's leading lady was Ula Holt, who played Princess Maya in *Adventure Girl*. The serial was produced by Tarzan's creator, Edgar Rice Burroughs, and his friend and business partner, silent screen actor Ashton Dearholt. At the time the Joan Lowell feature was produced, Dearholt was RKO's representative in Guatemala and supervised her film. During the dangerous and difficult production of the serial, Dearholt and Holt fell in love and were later married. Dearholt's ex-spouse, actress Florence Gilbert, wed Burroughs, who was recently divorced from his first wife.

In 1935 Lowell instigated a lawsuit against producer Amadee van Beuren and his studio for an accounting of the film's box office gross, asking for the 15 percent of the profits guaranteed to her. Van Beuren countersued Lowell for $300,000, claiming his studio lost that amount on the production due to her supplying them with an inferior product that was "improperly acted and performed."

Following *Adventure Girl*, Lowell worked as a writer and in radio before launching a Brazilian coffee plantation.

Motion Picture Daily called *Adventure Girl* "a good outdoor action picture for family audiences" and noted the final escape scenes were hand-colored by Gustav F.O. Brock and "are very effective pictorially." *Photoplay* wrote, "Though some of the incidents in this account of Joan Lowell's adventures in the tropics are quite beyond belief, the film offers to thrill-seekers an hour packed with action. Some very beautiful camera work, and interesting narration by Miss Lowell." *Variety* was dubious: "It's a long-winded account of things that couldn't be, presented as though they were facts. It won't fool customers anywhere, and it won't get many customers to fool.... Even in the old days of the wild and woolly adventure serials the stuff would have been too tough to dish out for credulous customers." *The* (Sandusky, Ohio) *Register* declared, "[T]he story is stranger than fiction and wilder than dreams of the adventures of Joan Lowell...." *The Film Daily* stated, "For adventure film fans, and those who enjoy pictures of dangerous pursuits, this one will fit the bill.... Scenery is beautiful. Properly exploited, the film should draw them in."

The Adventures of Ichabod and Mr. Toad (1949; 68 minutes; Color)

PRESENTER: Walt Disney. DIRECTORS: James Algar, Clyde Geronimi & Jack Kinney. ANIMATION DIRECTORS: Franklin Thomas, Oliver Johnston, Jr., Wolfgang Reitherman, Milt Kahl, John Loundsbery & Ward Kimball. CHARACTER ANIMATORS: Fred Moore, John Sibley, Marc Davis, Hal Ambro, Harvey Toombs, Hal King, Hugh Fraser, Don Lusk. SCREENPLAY: Erdman Penner, Winston Hibler, Joe Rinaldi, Ted Sears, Homer Brightman & Harry Reeves, from "The Legend of Sleepy Hollow" by Washington Irving & "The Wind in the Willows" by Kenneth Grahame. EDITOR: John O. Young. MUSIC DIRECTOR: Oliver Wallace. ORCHESTRATOR: Joseph Dublin. VOCAL ARRANGER: Ken Darby. MUSIC EDITOR: Oscar Teeter. SONGS: Don Raye, Gene de Paul, Frank Churchill, Charles Wolcott, Larry Morey & Ray Gilbert. SOUND: Robert O. Cook & C.O. Slyfield. VISUAL EFFECTS: Jack Boyd, Ub Iwerks & George Rowley. PRODUCTION SUPERVISOR: Ben Sharpsteen.

VOICE CAST: Bing Crosby, Basil Rathbone (Narrators), Eric Blore (Mr. J. Thaddeus Toad), Pat O'Malley (Cyril Proudbottom), John [McLeish] Ployardt (Prosecutor), Colin Campbell (Mole), Campbell Grant (Angus McBadger), Claud Allister (Water Rat), The Rhythmaires (Singers), Oliver Wallace (Winky the Bartender).

In October 1949, RKO released the Walt Disney production *The Adventures of Ichabod and Mr. Toad*, an animated feature about two great literary characters taken from Washington Irving's story "The Legend of Sleepy Hollow" (1820) and Kenneth Grahame's "The Wind in the Willows" (1908). Leonard Maltin wrote in *The Disney Films, 3rd Edition* (1995), "In the late 1940s Disney admirers were seriously worried that the filmmaker was slipping into a pattern of mass-audience mediocrity. The first film to really reassert Disney's staff as the leading exponents of animated film was *The Adventures of Ichabod and Mr. Toad*.... [It] is one of Disney's most beguiling animated features: *The Wind in the Willows* in particular has some of the finest work the studio ever did." Filmed as *Two Fabulous Characters*, the movie was also shown as two separate featurettes, *The Legend of Sleepy Hollow* (34 minutes) and *The Wind in the Willows* (30 minutes). The feature was sometimes titled *Ichabod and Mr. Toad*.

Basil Rathbone tells the story of the unbridled J. Thaddeus Toad (voice of Eric Blore) and his friends Water Rat (voice of Claud Allister), Mole (voice of Colin Campbell) and Angus McBadger (voice of Campbell Grant). While having tea together, Water Rat and Mole are asked to come to Toad Hall by Angus, the trustee of Toad's estate. He informs them that Toad is on the brink of bankruptcy due to his extravagant ways. After staving off Toad's creditors, Angus announces Toad's latest mania is a yellow gypsy cart and its horse, Cyril Proudbottom (voice of Pat O'Malley). When Toad arrives, his three pals manage to subdue him but he quickly becomes obsessed with a motor car so they lock him in his room and takes his clothes. Managing to get away, Toad find a car and drives off in it but is soon arrested for theft. The prosecutor (voice of John Ployardt) claims Toad stole the auto from a gang of weasels but Water Rat and Mole testify their friend has no funds. Toad's defense is that he traded Toad Hall to bartender Winky (voice of Oliver Wallace) for the auto. Winky lies, saying that Toad tried to sell him a stolen car. Toad is sent to prison but on Christmas Eve Cyril shows up in disguise and helps him escape. Toad steals a locomotive and is chased by the police. After jumping into a river, he goes to Water Rat's den where Angus arrives, saying that the weasels and Winky have taken over Toad Hall and are drunk. The four friends go there to find Toad's bill of sale to Winky and, finding him passed out, they manage to get the paper. They waken the drunken weasels and barely escape after a frantic chase. A reformed Toad promises his pals he will be good but soon comes under the spell of an airplane.

Bing Crosby narrates the story of lanky, ill-framed schoolmaster Ichabod Crane, who comes to the hamlet of Sleepy Hollow, New York, near Tarrytown, to teach. The superstitious Ichabod is soon under the spell of lovely coquette Katrina van Tassel, daughter of the richest farmer in the county. Ichabod not only covets the girl but also dreams of inheriting the farm and its riches. Rowdy Brom Bones loves Katrina and wants to marry her but she plays his affections against those of Ichabod, whom Brom dislikes. At a Halloween party, Ichabod easily shows up Brom when he dances with Katrina. Brom relates the story of the Headless Horseman who rides at night in the Sleepy Hollow vicinity. After midnight the frightened Ichabod rides home on an aged horse and soon finds himself being stalked by the headless phantom. A chase ensues and after many attempts to get away, Ichabod manages to ride across a covered bridge where the ghost's powers end. Getting to the other side, Ichabod turns and sees a fiery pumpkin hurtling toward him. The next day only the burst pumpkin is found with no sign of the schoolmaster. Katrina and Brom are soon married. Rumor has it that Ichabod escaped and later wed a wealthy widow. Many of the locals, however, believe the teacher was a victim of the Headless Horseman of Sleepy Hollow.

Whether taken as a whole or in its two parts, *The Adventures of Ichabod and Mr. Toad* is a delight for audiences of all ages. As narrator of the "Ichabod" segment, Bing Crosby sings a trio of songs, "Ichabod Crane," "Katrina" and "Headless Horsemen," and even briefly kids his image by having choir master Crane start a singing lesson with three damsels by crooning "boo-boo-boo." In the "Mr. Toad" sequence, narrator Basil Rathbone is satirized by having Water Rat wearing a deerstalker and smoking a pipe, *a la* the actor's signature character, Sherlock Holmes. For horror fans, the Headless Horseman in the "Ichabod" segment is realistically conceived and frightening.

Variety reported that the feature "ranks among the best full-length cartoons turned out by the Walt Disney studios.... The dialog and narration are impeccably tailored to match the animation.... The tinting of both yarns is skillfully keyed to the tone of each yarn. While 'Mr. Toad' is drawn in soft pastels, the Ichabod yarn is swept by full, contrasty colors. In both cases, it pars Disney's standard for excellence." *Boxoffice* enthused, "Walt Disney's animated wizardy is at its best in this thoroughly delightful and amusing twin-bill.... [T]his has strong marquee draw and entertainment value for young and old alike. The animated characters in the British fairy tale are among Disney's most appealing and imaginative...." Centering on the two main characters in the feature, Bosley Crowther wrote in *The New York Times* that they "make [the film] blithely amusing entertainment because they're cracky but genuine."

"The Wind in the Willows" was filmed several times after the Disney effort, with animated versions in 1983, 1987, 1988 and two in 1995 plus the 1996 series *The Adventures of Toad* from England's Channel 4 Television. There were also live action versions released in 1996 and 2006.

The Washington Irving classic story was first filmed in 1908 as a one-reeler by Kalem as *The Legend of Sleepy Hollow* and again in 1912 under that title by the Motion Picture Distribution and Sales Company, starring Alec B. Francis as Ichabod Crane. Perhaps the most faithful adaptation of the work was *The Headless Horseman*, released in 1923 by W.W. Hodkinson with Will Rogers as Ichabod. *The Headless Horseman* was also the title of a ten-minute 1934 ComiColor cartoon takeoff. Released by Celebrity Productions, it was directed by Ub Iwerks, who worked on the visual effects for the 1949 Disney feature. Since the Disney version, there have been several other screen efforts, none of them nearly as good. In 1972 John Carradine narrated the animated short *The Legend of Sleepy Hollow* for Pyramid Films and in 1980 Jeff Goldblum starred in a sub-par feature version for NBC-TV. The year before, the Amazing Kreskin had the title role in the Canadian Broadcasting Corporation telefilm *The New Misadventures of Ichabod Crane*. The year 1999 saw a trio of screen versions: two animated features, *The Legend of Sleepy Hollow* and *The Night of the Headless Horseman*, plus the hugely disappointing *Sleepy Hollow*, directed by Tim Burton and starring Johnny Depp as Ichabod Crane.

Alice in Wonderland (1951; 75 minutes; Color)

PRODUCER-PRESENTER: Walt Disney. DIRECTORS: Clyde Geronimi, Wilfred Jackson & Hamilton Luske. SCREENPLAY: Winston Hibler, Ted Sears, Bill Peet, Erdman Penner, Joe Rinaldi, Milt Banta, Bill Cottrell, Dick Kelsey, Joe Grant, Dick Huemer, Del Connell, Tom Oreb & John Walbridge, from the novels *Alice in Wonderland* and *Through the Looking Glass* by Lewis Carroll. EDITOR: Lloyd Richardson. MUSIC: Oliver Wallace. MUSIC & VOCAL ARRANGER: Jud Conlon. SONGS: Mack David, Al Hoffman, Jerry Livingston, Don Raye, Gene De Paul, Sammy Fain, Bob Hilliard, Oliver Wallace & Ted Sears. SOUND: C.O. Slyfield, Robert O. Cook & Harold J. Steck. EFFECTS ANIMATORS: Josh Meador, Dan Macmanus, Blaine Gibson & George Rowley. ANIMATION DIRECTORS: Milt Kahl, Ward Kimball, Franklin Thomas, Eric Larson, John Lounsbery, Oliver Johnston, Jr., Wolfgang Reitherman, Marc Davis, Les Clark, Norman Ferguson. CHARACTER ANIMATORS: Hal King, Judge Whitaker, Hal Ambro, Bill Justice, Phil Duncan, Bob Carlson, Don Lusk, Cliff Nordberg, Harvey Toombs, Fred Moore, Marvin Woodward, Hugh Fraser & Charles Nichols. SPECIAL PROCESSES: Ub Iwerks. PRODUCTION SUPERVISOR: Ben Sharpsteen.

VOICE CAST: Kathryn Beaumont (Alice), Ed Wynn (The Mad Hatter), Richard Haydn (Caterpillar), Sterling Holloway (The Cheshire Cat), Jerry Colonna (The March Hare), Verna Felton (Queen of Hearts), Pat O'Malley (Tweedledee/Tweedledum/Walrus/Carpenter), Bill Thompson (White Rabbit/Dodo), Heather Angel (Alice's Sister), Joseph Kearns (Doorknob), Larry Grey (Bill/Card), Queenie Leonard (Tree Bird/Flower), Dink Trout (King of Hearts), Doris Lloyd (Rose), James MacDonald (Doormouse), The Mellowmen (Card Painters), Don Barclay, Ken Beaumont (Cards), Pinto Colvig (Flamingoes), Ed Penner (Baglet).

Walt Disney first made short subjects featuring Lewis Carroll's literary character Alice in 1923, mixing animation and live action. Starring Virginia Davis in the title role, the series "Alice in Cartoonland" ran until 1926, encompassing 57 shorts. A decade later Disney planned a feature film in the same vein, to star Mary Pickford, and in the 1940s it was announced that Ginger Rogers, and later Luana Patten, would play Alice. In 1949 Margaret O'Brien was considered for the role, but after she turned it down, Walt Disney Productions began *Alice in Wonderland* as an animated feature budgeted at $5 million. After it was promoted in the 1950 Christmas Day special "One Hour in Wonderland," the film was issued theatrically in the summer of 1951. Just before it premiered, a British-French *Alice in Wonderland*, a puppet-live action version of the story, debuted; Disney and RKO unsuccessfully sought an injunction to halt its release.

On a summer day, while being read to by her sister (voice of Heather Angel) and playing with her cat Dinah, Alice (voice of Kathryn Beaumont) daydreams of her own special world where all is nonsense and everything would be what it is not. Spotting a White Rabbit (voice of Bill Thompson) wearing a vest and toting a clock while claiming he is late, Alice runs into a cave and falls down a long brick tunnel. After going through several doors she reaches one that is too small and the doorknob (voice of Joseph Kearns) suggests she drink from a bottle on a nearby table; this causes her to become small enough to go through his door but it is locked. The key is on the table but she's now too small to reach it. The doorknob then suggests she eat some crackers which turn her into a giant. Alice begins to cry and her tears flood the room. When a bottle floats by, she drinks from it and it makes her small enough to go through the keyhole. She finds a group of creatures parading around a Dodo (voice of Bill Thompson). She follows the White Rabbit into the woods where she meets two odd twins, Tweedledee (voice of Pat O'Malley) and Tweedledum (voice of Pat O'Malley), who recite to her the story of the Walrus (voice of Pat O'Malley) and the Carpenter (voice of Pat O'Malley). Sneaking away from the pair, Alice finds the White Rabbit in his home. While helping him look for a lost glove, she eats a biscuit and grows so big she fills the abode. The Dodo tries to use a lizard to get her out of the house and when that fails he plans to set it on fire. Alice eats a carrot from a nearby garden and becomes three inches tall. She runs into a bed of talking and singing flowers who soon decide she is a weed. Alice finds a hookah-smoking Caterpillar (voice of Richard Haydn) who corrects her speech and tells her that eating mushrooms will make her bigger and smaller. She eats one and returns to her own size and then is confronted by a Cheshire Cat (voice of Sterling Holloway) who says nearly everyone here is mad. Next she encounters the Mad Hatter (voice of Ed Wynn), March Hare (voice of Jerry Colonna) and Dormouse (voice of James MacDonald) having an unbirthday party. They invite her to join them but make her continually switch chairs. When she mentions her cat, Dormouse has a nervous fit. The White Rabbit, still thinking he is late, shows up and the Mad Hatter tries to repair his clock with butter and jelly, causing it to go crazy. When the White Rabbitt leaves, Alice walks to Tulgey Wood which has musical instrument animals and the flower-like Mome Raths who put her on a path that is soon swept away by a dog with a brush for a chin. Wanting to go home, Alice cries and says she gives herself good advice but seldom follows it. The Cheshire Cat directs her to a tree where a door opens into a maze where she finds a trio of playing cards (voices of the Mellowmen) painting roses red. The ruler of the area, the Queen of Hearts (voice of Verna Felton), marches in with her army of playing card soldiers and orders the painters to lose their heads. She then asks Alice to play croquet in which the mallets are flamingos who hit hedgehogs. The game is fixed so the queen always wins. When the Cheshire Cat causes her to expose her white and red underpants, she blames Alice and orders her beheaded. The tiny, henpecked king (voice of Dink Trout) wants Alice to have a trial at which the March Hare, Mad Hatter and Dormouse are witnesses. Alice eats a mushroom and becomes a giant and then shrinks to her normal size. She runs from the kingdom, chased by the queen and her card army. Retracing her steps past all the beings she met along the way, Alice comes to the Doorknob and sees herself asleep through the keyhole. Crying for herself to wake up, Alice is roused by her peeved sister, who takes her home to tea.

While pictorially satisfying, *Alice in Wonderland* is mostly slow going with a bevy of mediocre songs. It lacks the ingratiating atmosphere of most Disney animated features although it does have some delightful sequences such as "The Walrus and the Carpenter," Alice's game of croquet with the Queen of Hearts and the musical teakettles at the unbirthday party. Overall, though, the feature leaves the viewer unenthused at its finale. It simply lacks the magic that resonates from the pages of Lewis Carroll's 1865 *Alice in Wonderland* and 1870's *Through the Looking Glass* on which it is based.

Boxoffice wrote that Disney "successfully surmounted what must have been difficult and exacting artistic and technical problems to bring to the screen the true whimsical flavor of the Lewis Carroll story with a minimum of distortion and without altering the characters. That it will be a must-see item for movie patrons of all ages is a foregone conclusion." On a more highbrow note, Adam Garbica and Jacek Klinowski opined in *Cinema, The Magic Vehicle: A Guide to Its Achievement, Journey Two: The Cinema of the Fifties* (1979), "This time Disney had things to draw! He could not claim merit in the past for modernizing or developing the run-of-the-mill didacticism of such age-old fairy tales as 'Cinderella,' but when it came to 'Alice in Wonderland,' this classic of children's literature, he transplanted it to the screen beyond reproach. Although of course many political references must have got lost in the process, the film is as rich in ideas as the book, and is maintained in the same spirit of a perhaps cool, but imaginative Surrealist romp." More on the mark was Leonard Maltin in *The Disney Films, 3rd Edition* (1995), who noted, "In all, *Alice in Wonderland* is a very flashy and generally entertaining film, but it lacks that essential thread that made Disney's best features hang together, and, moreover, it lacks *warmth*.... Once over, it can be dismissed, and though one wouldn't have wanted Disney to turn the story into a Grimm's fairy tale, there should have been some way to give the audience more empathy with its heroine."

Despite its multitude of fantasy elements, *Alice in Wonderland* has rarely made a successful transition to films, either live action or animated. The first screen adaptation was a 1903 one-reel Cecil Hepworth production from England with Mabel Clark as Alice. Edwin S. Porter directed the 1910 Edison short *Alice's Adventures in Wonderland*; in 1915 Viola Savoy played the title role in a Nonpareil six-reeler; and five years later Mabel Taliaferro starred in still another version. In 1928 Pathé released the four-reel *Alice Through a Looking Glass*, directed by Walter Lang. The initial sound version of *Alice in Wonderland* starred Ruth Gilbert and was directed and edited by Bud Pollard. This 1931 Unique Foto Films release used an Irving Berlin song. Perhaps the best-known live-action version of the novel was the 1933 Paramount production *Alice in Wonderland* starring Charlotte Henry in the title role supported by an all-star cast that could not save it from being mediocre at best. The previously mentioned British-French puppet–live action version starred Carol Marsh; it was made in 1948 but not released stateside until 1951. *Alice in Wonderland in Paris* was a 1966 Childhood Productions animated release that interpolated several other stories with Lewis Carroll's characters. In 1972 the British made the dreary *Alice's Adventures in Wonderland* with Fiona Fullerton; like the 1933 feature, it had a supporting cast of major players. Irwin Allen produced a two-part version of *Alice of Wonderland* for Columbia-TV in 1985 starring Natalie Gregory and an all-star cast with lyrics by Steve Allen. Tina Majorino was Alice in a Hallmark–NBC television production of *Alice in Wonderland* in 1999.

Kathryn Beaumont and most of the supporting players from the 1951 Disney feature redid their roles on the December 24, 1951, broadcast of NBC's *Lux Radio Theatre*. The other cast members heard in this episode were Ed Wynn, Jerry Colonna, Sterling Holloway, Bill Thompson, Verna Felton, Joseph Kearns and Doris Lloyd, with the remaining character voices provided by Gale Gordon, Jack Kruschen, Gil Stratton, Norma Varden, Jonathan Hole, Margie Liszt and Eddie Marr. The feature itself was telecast on November 3, 1954, on ABC-TV's *Disneyland*, only three years after its theatrical showings. A box office dud, it did not get reissued until 1974.

While she never appeared on film as Alice, Ginger Rogers did a studio cast recording of "Alice in Wonderland" for Decca (DL-5040) in 1949, and the film's soundtrack was released by RCA on a ten-inch LP (LY-1) coupled with Disney's "Treasure Island" in 1951. A studio track was put out on the Disneyland (ST-3909) and reissued on the label in 1958 (WDL-4015) and 1959 (DQ-1208).

All That Money Can Buy (1941; 106 minutes)

PRODUCER-DIRECTOR: William Dieterle. ASSOCIATE PRODUCER: Charles L. GLETT. SCREENPLAY: Dan Totheroh & Stephen Vincent Benet, from the story "The Devil and Daniel Webster" by Stephen Vincent Benet. PHOTOGRAPHY: Joseph August. EDITOR: Robert Wise. MUSIC: Bernard Herrmann. ART DIRECTORS: Van Nest Polglase & Al Herman. SOUND: James G. Stewart & Hugh McDowell, Jr. SET DECORATIONS: Darrell Silvera. COSTUMES: Edward Stevenson. SPECIAL EFFECTS: Vernon L. Walker. DIALOGUE DIRECTOR: Peter Berneis. ASSISTANT DIRECTOR: Argyle Nelson.

CAST: Edward Arnold (Daniel Webster), Walter Huston (Mr. Scratch), James Craig (Jabez Stone), Anne Shirley (Mary Simpson Stone), Jane Darwell (Ma Stone), Simone Simon (Belle), Gene Lockhart (Squire Slossum), John Qualen (Elijah Stevens), H.B. Warner (Justice Hathorne), Frank Conlan (Sheriff), Lindy Wade (Daniel Stone), George Cleveland (Cy Bibber), Jeff Corey (Tom Sharp), Carl Stockdale (Van Brooks), Alec Craig (Eli Higgins), Sonny Bupp (Martin Van Buren Aldrich), Eddie Dew, Jim Toney (Farmers), Sarah Edwards (Lucy Slossum), Walter Baldwin (Hank), Patricia Doyle (Dorothy), Harry Humphrey (Minister), Stewart Richards (Doctor), Ferris Taylor (President), Robert Strange (Court Clerk), Robert Dudley (Lem), Harry Hood (Tailor), Bob Pittard (Clerk), Eddie Borden (Poker Player), Frank Austin (Spectator), Charles Berzinger (Old Farmhand), William Alland (Guide), June Preston (Blonde Girl), Bob Burns (Citizen), Horace B. Carpenter, Tex Cooper (Party Guests).

Poster for *All That Money Can Buy* (1941).

Stephen Vincent Benet co-authored the screenplay adaptation of his short story "The Devil and Daniel Webster," which was produced by William Dieterle Productions. Two years earlier, Benet's story had been the basis for a Broadway play, "The Devil and Daniel Webster," that only ran for six performances. It was staged by John Houseman and starred Lansing Hatfield as Webster and George Rasely as Mr. Scratch.

The motion picture was previewed in August 1941 as *Here Is a Man* and saw final release as *All That Money Can Buy* three months later. The reception was mixed. RKO also showed it under the titles *A Certain Mr. Scratch* and *Mr. Scratch* as it lost over $50,000 in its initial run. In 1952, Astor Pictures reissued it as *The Devil and Daniel Webster*, with 21 minutes of footage removed.

In 1840 near the New Hampshire town of Cross Corners, Mr. Scratch (Walter Huston), the Devil, has his sights set on hard luck farmer Jabez Stone (James Craig). Jabez, his young wife Mary (Anne Shirley) and his mother, Ma Stone (Jane Darwell), are optimistic about the coming of spring after a hard winter although the Stone farm is mortgaged to miser Elijah Stevens (John Qualen), who is demanding full payment. Farmers Tom Sharp (Jeff Corey), Van Brooks (Carl Stockdale) and Eli Higgins (Alec Craig) ask Jabez to join them in forming a Grange, a farmers' association. He agrees to think about the matter but soon realizes he cannot pay his mortgage and in a moment of gloom says he will sell his soul to the Devil for two cents. Overhearing the comment, Mr. Scratch offers Jabez money and prosperity for seven years in return for his soul at the end of that time. Jabez signs a document agreeing to Mr. Scratch's terms. When he shows Mary and Ma his newfound wealth, supposedly lost Hessian treasure, they are not pleased.

Jabez pays off the mortgage and buys seed for his farm, a bonnet for Mary and a shawl for Ma. He also helps other farmers about to lose their homesteads to Stevens. Daniel Webster (Edward Arnold), the Massachusetts Senator fighting for the Grange movement, comes to Cross Corners and Jabez gives a speech supporting him, winning him still more friends in the community. When he finds out that Mary is going to have a baby, Jabez tries to chop down the tree on which Mr. Scratch has inscribed the date on which Jabez will lose his soul. This results in a hail storm that destroys all the area crops except those on Jabez's farm. At harvest time, Mr. Scratch gives the destitute area farmers one dollar each in advance, plus wages, to bring in Jabez's harvest, but this causes the men to resent him. To celebrate the harvest, Jabez gives a dance and that night Mary gives birth to their son Daniel, who she names after Webster, his godfather and an old friend of her family. That night the mysterious Belle (Simone Simon), sent by Mr. Scratch, arrives to be the baby's nurse and is quickly distrusted by Mary and Ma. Jabez soon lusts for Belle and he turns away from the scriptures, even playing poker with his cronies while Mary and Ma are at church.

During the next seven years, as his son (Lindy Wade) grows, Jabez becomes obsessed with money as Belle continues to turn him against Mary. To celebrate his riches, Jabez has a grand house built and plans a huge party. He asks Squire Slossum (Gene Lockhart), who owes him gambling debts, to invite only the "best" people. As Belle tries to come between Mary and her son, Mary goes to see Webster about Jabez and he agrees to come home with her and talk with him. Webster arrives in Cross Corners on the night of the party but is delayed by the farmers, who complain to him about Jabez's behavior. No one except Stevens comes to the party, and he tells Jabez he is worried about the fate of his soul. A group of spectral visitors arrive, eating and dancing. While waltzing with Belle, Stevens collapses and dies. Webster reprimands Jabez about his avarice but Jabez blames Mary and tells her and Webster to leave his house. Mr. Scratch shows Jabez a moth he has wrapped in a handkerchief and tells him it is Stevens' soul. He also says it's time for Jabez to pay his debt, as per their bargain, but says he will extend the agreement in return for young Daniel. Realizing the error of his ways, Jabez runs to see Mary but finds she and Daniel have departed with Webster. He follows them, ignoring Belle, whom he passes along the road. Jabez asks Webster to help him fight Mr. Scratch and the Senator assents, although defeat will also cause the loss of his own soul. At midnight Mr. Scratch agrees to a trial, but only if he can choose the jury. From Hell he invokes the spirits of past American traitors like Benedict Arnold, Captain Kidd, Simon Girty and Walter Butler, along with Salem Witch Trial Justice Hathorne (H.B. Warner) to preside. The judge is hostile but allows Webster to address the jury. Webster appeals to their patriotism and sense of freedom and reminds them they sold their souls to the Devil and asks them to reprieve Jabez for making the same mistake they did. The jury finds for Jabez, tearing up the contract. Webster throws Mr. Scratch out of the barn; the Devil tells him he will make sure that Webster will never be president. Jabez burns his new house, tears up the farmers' mortgages and joins them in the Grange. Reunited with his family, Jabez looks forward to a new life without greed. Undeterred, Mr. Scratch seeks new victims.

There is much to like about *All That Money Can Buy* but it also has many deficits. The best thing about the film is the performances. Edward Arnold does some of the best work of his long career as Daniel Webster, and Walter Huston was nominated for an Academy Award as Best Actor for playing Mr. Scratch. He manages to imbue the character with equal parts of evil and humor while making him always repulsive. The film launched James Craig to stardom. Anne Shirley is a standout as his loyal wife, as is Jane Darwell playing his stolid mother. Although only seen in a small role, H.B. Warner is particularly effective as the spectral Justice Hathorne, a real character from the Salem Witch Trials and an ancestor of Nathaniel Hawthorne. Thomas Mitchell began the filming as Daniel Webster but he and child actor Lindy Wade were involved in a carriage accident. Mitchell received a skull fracture and had to withdraw from the production although some sources claim that footage of him in long shots remain in the finished film.

The movie's chief deficit is that it is too long and often has dry stretches. From the odd opening credits, in which the main participants both in front of and behind the camera are identified but not their roles, the film has an unreal feel to it. While many of the characters are very human (Mary, Ma and many of the rustic locals, to name a few), one has a hard time feeling much compassion for James Craig's wide eyed Jabez. Even more unbelievable is Simone Simon's character of the Devil's servant, Belle. The character adds almost nothing to the plot and could easily have been eliminated without tarnishing the work's moral. The next year, Simon scored a major success starring for RKO in producer Val Lewton's *Cat People*.

Bosley Crowther opined in *The New York Times* that *All That Money Can Buy* is "a pleasantly provocative and slyly humorous film," adding that it "should have made a fine, simple film. It should never have been elaborated out of proportion of its original modest frame. It should have been told as a fireside story without a lot of sounding brass. And it should have been directed by someone who understood New England." *Photoplay* said, "Here is a picture that for sheer novelty takes its place among the best of its kind.... [T]he film has been given a strong cast, a weak title and superb direction by William Dieterle." (The reviewer saw the film as *Here Is a Man*.) Also reviewing the picture under that title, the *Film Daily* reviewer wrote, "One of the year's best; is tops in all departments and should click solidly with all audiences." Regarding producer-director Dieterle's work, William Tolbert Leonard wrote in *Theatre: Stage to Screen to Television* (1981) that "the flavor and Yankee substance of Benet's fantasy appeared to escape him. Backgrounds for the picture were obvious painted stage backdrops and Dan Totheroh's script appeared caught in limbo between reality and fantasy."

Bernard Herrmann's score received an Academy Award. The music was later issued on the Unicorn label (UNS-237) performed by Herrmann and his orchestra as "The Devil and Daniel

Webster." Herrmann also conducted the National Philharmonic Orchestra's rendition of the score on "Music from Great Film Classics" (London SP-44144). A studio cast version of the 1939 play was issued on Desto Records (SE-6450).

On April 2, 1950, Walter Huston repeated his role of Mr. Scratch on radio's *Theatre Guild of the Air* when the drama was broadcast as "All That Money Can Buy." The ABC program co-starred Cornel Wilde and Martha Scott. Edward G. Robinson played Webster, David Wayne was Mr. Scratch and Tim O'Connor was Jabez Stone in NBC-TV's *Sunday Showcase* production of "The Devil and Daniel Webster," telecast February 14, 1960, and hosted by Edgar Bergen. It was repeated two years later on CBS-TV.

Angel Face (1952; 91 minutes)

PRESENTER: Howard Hughes. PRODUCER-DIRECTOR: Otto Preminger. SCREENPLAY: Frank Nugent & Oscar Millard. STORY: Chester Erskine. PHOTOGRAPHY: Harry Stradling. EDITOR: Frederick Knudtson. MUSIC: Dimitri Tiomkin. MUSIC COORDINATOR: C. Bakaleinikoff. ART DIRECTORS: Carroll Clark & Albert S. D'Agostino. SOUND: Clem Portman & Earl Wolcott. SET DECORATIONS: Jack Mills & Darrell Silvera. COSTUMES: Michael Woulfe. MAKEUP: Mel Berns. HAIR STYLIST: Larry Germain. UNIT MANAGER: Edward Killy. ASSISTANT DIRECTOR: Fred A. Fleck.

CAST: Robert Mitchum (Frank Jessup), Jean Simmons (Diane Tremayne), Mona Freeman (Mary Wilton), Herbert Marshall (Charles Tremayne), Leon Ames (Fred Barrett), Barbara O'Neil (Catherine Tremayne), Kenneth Tobey (Bill Crompton), Raymond Greenleaf (Arthur Vance), Griff Barnett (Judge), Robert Gist (Mr. Miller), Morgan Farley (Juror), Jim Backus (District Attorney Judson), Larry J. Blake (Detective Ed Brady), Frank Kumagai (Igo), Brick Sullivan (Deputy Sheriff Kelly), Max Takasugi (Chiyo), Lewis Martin (Police Sergeant), Alex Gerry (Mr. Lewis), Jeffrey Sayre (Court Clerk), Buck Young, Roy Darmour (Assistant District Attorneys), Gertrude Astor (Matron), Herbert Lytton (Doctor), Robert Haines (Court Reporter), Jack Ellis (Jury Foreman), Theresa Harris (Nurse Theresa), Frank O'Connor (Bailiff), Morgan Brown (Diner Owner Harry), Bess Flowers (Shirley), Charmienne Harker (Miss Preston), Marvin Jones, Jim Hope, Peter Kellett (Detectives), Mike Lally, Bob Peoples, Clark Curtiss (Reporters), Doreen Tryden, Cora Shannon, Charlotte Portney, Mary Lee Martin (Patients), Lucille Barkley (Waitress), George Sherwood, Jack Chefe, Carl Sklover, Sammy Shack (Men), Mary Jane Carey (Woman).

Released late in 1952, *Angel Face* is a slick psychological horror melodrama supposedly based on an actual 1947 California case when a young couple was accused of the murder of the girl's parents since she would inherit a large fortune. (They were tried and acquitted.) The leading female character is not only psychotic and deadly but also appears to have an Electra complex. Some sources claim that an uncredited Ben Hecht contributed to the script.

When Beverly Hills ambulance drivers Frank Jessup (Robert Mitchum) and Bill Crompton (Kenneth Tobey) make a run to the posh Tremayne estate, they find wealthy Catherine Tremayne (Barbara O'Neil) recovering from inhaling gas. She claims someone tried to kill her but the authorities tell her husband, novelist Charles Tremayne (Herbert Marshall), she must have accidentally turned on the gas in her bedroom fireplace. As he is leaving, Frank hears Charles' daughter Diane (Jean Simmons) playing the piano and tells her that her stepmother is all right. When Diane goes into hysterics, he slaps her and she slaps him back and then says she is sorry. Diane tells Frank she is almost 20. When the ambulance leaves, Diane follows in her sports car. After work, Frank goes to Harry's Diner to call his fiancée, nurse Mary Wilton (Mona Freeman), and when she does not answer, he is surprised to see Diane there. Fascinated by the girl, Frank nixes a planned dinner with Mary to go out with Diane. She relates that her father is a famous novelist who has not been able to write since marrying her stepmother and Frank says he was a race car driver before the war and is driving an ambulance to get enough money to open his own auto repair shop. Later they go dancing.

The next day Diane invites Mary to lunch and tells her about the evening before and offers to give her one thousand dollars for the garage fund. Mary informs her that she has been successful in shaking her faith in Frank. When he goes to pick up Mary that night, Frank again lies about the night before and Mary rejects him in favor of Bill, who also loves her. When Diane returns to Harry's Diner, Frank berates her for talking with Mary. He soon forgives the girl when she offers to let him race her car in an upcoming Pebble Beach contest. The next day Diane proposes to her father and stepmother that they hire a chauffeur and that night she convinces Frank to take the job, so he can live on the estate and make more money. Diane tells Frank to draw up a proposal so her stepmother will invest in his garage; Catherine later tells him she will consult her lawyer, Arthur Vance (Raymond Greenleaf), who is leaving on a trip to San Francisco. Charles and Catherine have an argument about his spending $300 on a new dress for Diane and she complains about him not working. Diane informs Frank she found his proposal in the trash and if Catherine finds out they are lovers, she will take it out on her father. That night Diane comes to Frank's garage apartment and says her stepmother tried to kill her by turning on the gas in her bedroom. He finds the story hard to believe and tells Diane to go back to bed. Early the next morning Frank goes to see Mary and says he is thinking about leaving his new job because the Tremayne family is a weird outfit. He asks to see Mary that evening and then returns to the estate to pack his belongings. Diane goes to his apartment with her own suitcase. When he tells her he is leaving, she cries and implores him to take her with him. He says he will stay a few more days but warns Diane that the hatred she has for Catherine may cause her to end up killing her stepmother. The next day Catherine borrows Diane's car to drive to a bridge game and Charles asks to come along and be dropped off downtown. As Catherine presses the accelerator, the car shoots backwards over a bluff and she and her husband are killed. Frank is questioned by his friend, Detective Brady (Larry J. Blake), who informs him that Diane's suitcase was found in his room. The policeman advises him to get a good lawyer since Diane has been arrested as she will inherit Catherine's estate. Suffering a breakdown, Diane is placed in a prison hospital while Vance gets famous trial lawyer Fred Barrett (Leon Ames) to defend her. Barrett tells Frank's lawyer (Alex Gerry) that motive, means and opportunity link his client to Diane and he suggests the defendants marry so they can use the defense that her suitcase was in Frank's apartment as they planned to elope. Frank and Diane are married in the psychiatric ward. During the trial, the district attorney (Jim Backus) brings in an expert witness (Robert Gist) who testifies the engine and shift mechanism on the wrecked car had been tampered with. The slick Barrett manages to mitigate the testimony and proclaims that any damage was done by the vehicle's falling 150 feet and bouncing off rocks. In his summation, the district attorney charges that Frank and Diane premeditated the murders so she could get a half-million dollar inheritance but Barrett proclaims their only guilt is being in love. The jury finds for the defendants. Back home, Frank tells Diane he wants a divorce and she tries to convince him she is sorry about what happened and how troubled her life has been since her mother was killed in an air raid when she was ten. Frank says he is going back to Mary; Diane bets him her sports car she will not have him. When Frank goes to see Mary, he finds Bill there and learns the two are engaged. Mary says he never believed him to be guilty. Depressed over Frank's leaving, Diane goes to Barrett and confesses to the murders but he tells her double jeopardy prevents her from a second prosecution. He also says if she sticks with her confession, she will end up in an insane asylum. Back at the estate, Diane learns that Frank is going to Mexico and she asks to go with him. He refuses but takes her up on her offer to drive him to the bus station. In the car, Frank starts to open a champagne bottle when Diane puts the vehicle in reverse and sends it speeding backward over the bluff, with both of them being killed.

Poster for *Angel Face* (1952).

Jean Simmons dominates *Angel Face* with her terrific portrayal of the mentally unbalanced Diane. Her dark-haired beauty and winning ways mask an unhinged personality who longs to be rid of her hated stepmother in order to have her weak-willed father to herself. It is one of the actress' finest performances. On the other hand, Robert Mitchum appears to be miscast as the ambulance driver who comes under her spell, a part more suited for Burt Lancaster or Edmond O'Brien; the latter had been considered for the part when Belsam Pictures optioned the story in 1947. The rest of the cast is very good, especially Mona Freeman as the level-headed nurse, Leon Ames as the defense attorney and Jim Backus as the prosecutor. Herbert Marshall and Barbara O'Neil handle their roles ably although their screen time is limited.

"Overcoming a slow start, employed to establish background and characters, this yarn of murder and punishment gathers plenty of speed about mid-footage and winds up as an exciting, engrossing film," proclaimed *Boxoffice*. *The New York Times* complained that the film "is an exasperating blend of genuine talent, occasional perceptiveness and turgid psychological claptrap that enhances neither RKO, which should know better, nor the participants...." *Variety* determined *Angel Face* to be "a fair suspense melodrama," adding, "Producer-director Otto Preminger tackles the Frank Nugent-Oscar Millard screenplay too deliberately, and the result is a slow pacing that prevents any really sharp suspense as the rather grim Chester Erskine story is unfolded." In *Robert Mitchum* (1976), John Belton called it "one of Otto Preminger's bleakest and most uncompromising films."

Mitchum and Simmons re-teamed for another RKO feature, *She Couldn't Say No*, released in 1954.

Bad Lands (1939; 71 minutes)

PRODUCER: Robert Sisk. EXECUTIVE PRODUCER: Lee Marcus. DIRECTOR: Lew Landers. STORY & SCREENPLAY: Clarence Upson Young. PHOTOGRAPHY: Frank Redman. EDITOR: George Hively. MUSIC: Roy Webb. ART DIRECTORS: Feild Gray & Van Nest Polglase. SOUND: Earl A. Wolcott.

CAST: Robert Barrat (Sheriff Bill Cummings), Noah Beery, Jr. (Chick Lyman), Guinn Williams (Billy Sweet), Douglas Walton (Bob Mulford), Addison Richards (Rayburn), Andy Clyde (Henry Cluff), Francis Ford (Charlie Garth), Paul Hurst (Dogface Curly Tom), Robert Coote (Eaton), Francis McDonald (Manuel Lopez), Carlyle Moore, Jr. (Cavalry Lieutenant), Jack Payne (Apache Jack), Billy Wilkerson (Indian).

Filmed near Victorville, California, *Bad Lands* is a reworking of *The Lost Patrol* (1934) (q.v.), itself a remake of the 1929 silent British production of the same title. While not a scene-for-scene rehash of the 1934 John Ford film, which is set in the Mesopotamian desert, *Bad Lands* is often compared to it, and nearly always in an unfavorable light. In reality the feature can stand on its own as an out-of-the ordinary B Western with a literate script, good direction, fine performances and excellent character delineation. Like its predecessor, it is included here because of its element of "fear of the unknown," in this case marauding, deadly Apaches. As with the later Val Lewton thrillers, in *Bad Lands* it is not what they can see that spooks the protagonists, it is not knowing whether or not they will survive against their unseen, bloodthirsty adversaries.

In 1875, Arizona Sheriff Bill Cummins (Robert Barrat) organizes a posse of diverse characters to go after renegade Apache Jack (Jack Payne), who has abducted and murdered the young wife of Manuel Lopez (Francis McDonald). Riding into the desert, they come across the body of a murdered scout and continue their pursuit of Apache Jack, who appears not to try to cover his tracks. Soon animosities begin to develop between the men. The sheriff says there will be not fighting but Rayburn (Addison Richards) claims he wants to find out how tough the lawman is. After traveling nearly 100 miles and needing water, the party locates a water hole but it is dry.

The sheriff believes Apache Jack is headed for the dragoons, 50 miles away. New Yorker Bob Mulford (Douglas Walton) collapses from lack of water and has to cling to his saddle horn.

Smoke signals are visible to the posse and it is feared they may be from Geronimo. At last they find water; Dogface Curly Tom (Paul Hurst) sees skeletons lying among some nearby rocks. Old-time prospectors Henry Cluff (Andy Clyde) and Charlie Garth (Francis Ford) declare it is a rich silver deposit and the posse members begin to lose interest in finding Apache Jack. The sheriff tells them that when their job is done they can do what they want with the silver. Eaton (Robert Coote), a disgraced British soldier with a facial scar, is assigned to stand guard that night but the next day he and the horses are missing. Cluff and Garth celebrate finding a rich silver vein in a nearby wash, but Cluff is shot and killed. Mulford declares himself a "Jonah," bringing bad luck to anyone he meets. When more smoke signals are seen, Garth says it is a sign the Apaches are calling other braves to join them. The sheriff's horse returns carrying the dead body of Eaton, who is buried alongside Cluff. Billy Sweet (Guinn Williams) and Garth draw cards to see who will go for help; the sheriff tells them there is a regimental outpost 25 miles due north. Lopez loses his reason, thinking he hears voices calling him, and he heads out to kill Apache Jack. When Dogface Curly Tom tries to stop him, he is stabbed. Rayburn goes after Lopez, who is shot by the Apaches, and he brings back his body, saying he dispatched two of the attackers. When Rayburn decides to go into the hills and fight the Indians, the sheriff knocks him out and takes his guns. The lawman finds the dead bodies of Sweet and Garth while Bob fights with another posse member, cowboy Chick Lyman (Noah Beery, Jr.). Later Chick knocks out Bob, who is on guard duty, and steals the sheriff's horse. Dogface Curly Tom tries to stop him but is too weak and dies from the exertion. Chick is killed by the Apaches as he tries to escape. The three survivors bury their dead comrades and Rayburn declares he will fight off the Indians so the sheriff and Mulford can make it to a nearby wash to make a stand. After the sheriff puts up eight crosses to fool the Indians, Rayburn leaves but is soon killed. The sheriff and Mulford take cover as the Apaches converge on their camp. Apache Jack is shot and killed, as are most of the other Indians. When the sheriff and Mulford emerge to survey the scene, a wounded warrior (Billy Wilkerson) shoots Mulford. Nearly insane from the loss of his comrades, the sheriff is rescued by a platoon of cavalry who were patrolling nearby and heard the shooting.

Besides the cat-and-mouse game the posse plays with the Apaches, the most interesting aspect of *Bad Lands* is the individual characters. The group is held together by the strong-willed sheriff, who in desperation near the end of the siege recites "The Lord's Prayer." At one point he questions how they can "hold out against something you can't even get a good look at." The adversary relationship between the lawman and Rayburn is compelling, as is the good-natured verbal jabbing of partners Cluff and Garth, the latter especially well delineated by Francis Ford. Douglas Walton, who had a different role in the 1934 *Lost Patrol*, is effective as the Easterner trying to prove his worth, and Robert Coote does well as the dishonored British soldier whose disgrace was a result of protecting his younger brother. Interestingly, all the characters except the lawman talk of the future yet he is the only one to survive.

Comparing *Bad Lands* to *The Lost Patrol*, Frank S. Nugent wrote in *The New York Times*, "It measures up neither in caliber of its performance nor in the skill of its writing and direction. But regarded simply as a horse opera, inexpensively produced and fired pointblank at the action-story trade, it can be let off gently as being a notch or two above most of the sagas about the boys from Bloody Gulch and Dry Mesa." *Boxoffice* opined that, compared to *The Lost Patrol*, "it can classify only as a he-man western, in which category it will probably serve satisfactorily." *Variety* reported the feature "should do fairly well.... [It] is strictly a man's dish, and as such, particularly among sagebrush fans, will pass muster. There isn't a single shot of a woman in it.... Action figures rather than dialog and some of the harrowing experiences of the trapped men out in the blistering desert are brought forth very effectively.... Performances go a long way toward making *Bad Lands* suitable western entertainment. [Robert] Barrat is excellent as the sheriff.... Noah Beery, Jr., unsympathetically cast, also comes through resoundingly." *Photoplay* complained, "When you walk out of this you'll be pretty bewildered." On the other hand, *The Film Daily* declared, "Strong dramatic story is suspenseful and filled with action."

Bad Lands was novelized in the January 27, 1940, issue of the British magazine *Boy's Cinema*.

Bambi (1942; 69 minutes; Color)

PRODUCER: Walt Disney. SUPERVISING DIRECTOR: David D. Hand. SEQUENCE DIRECTORS: James Algar, Bill Roberts, Norman Wright, Sam Armstrong, Paul Satterfield, Graham Heid. STORY: Felix Salten. STORY DIRECTION: Perce Pearce. STORY ADAPTATION: Larry Morey. STORY DEVELOPMENT: George Stallings, Melvin Shaw, Carl Fallberg, Chuck Couch & Ralph Wright. MUSIC: Edward Plumb & Frank Churchill. MUSIC CHORAL ARRANGER: Charles Henderson. ART DIRECTORS: Thomas H. Codrick, Robert C. Cormack, Lloyd Harting, David Hilberman, John Hubley, Dick Kelsey, McLaren Stewart & Al Zinnen. SUPERVISING ANIMATORS: Franklin Thomas, Milt Kahl, Eric Larson, Oliver M. Johnston, Jr. ANIMATORS: Fraser Davis, Bill Justice, Bernard Garbutt, Don Lusk, Retta Scott, Kenneth O'Brien, Louis Schmidt, John Bradbury, Joshua Meador, Phil Duncan, George Rowely, Art Palmer, Art Elliott. BACKGROUNDS: Merle Cox, Tyrus Wong, Art Riley, Robert McIntosh, Travis Johnston, W. Richard Anthony, Stan Spohn, Ray Huffine, Ed Levitt & Joe Stanley. CHARACTER MODELS: Jane Randolph & Donna Atwood.

VOICE CAST: Peter Behn (Young Thumper), Hardie Albright (Adolescent Bambi), Ann Gillis (Adult Faline), Thelma Hubbard (Pheasant/Bunny/Mother Quail), Sterling Holloway (Adult Flower), Will Wright (Friend Owl), Sam Edwards (Adult Thumper), Marion Darlington (Bird Sounds), Donnie Dunagan (Young Bambi), John Sutherland (Adult Bambi), Bobby Stewart (Baby Bambi), Fred Shields (Great Prince), Paula Winslowe (Bambi's Mother), Otis Harlan (Mr. Mole), Cammie King (Young Faline), Clarence Nash (Bullfrog), Mary Lansing (Aunt Ena/Mrs. Possum), Stan Alexander (Young Flower), Tim Davis (Adult Thumper/Adolescent Flower), Eddie Holden (Chipmunk), Margaret Lee (Thumper's Mother).

Released in August 1942, the Technicolor production *Bambi* is dedicated to film director Sidney A. Franklin, from whom Walt Disney acquired the rights to Felix Salten's serialized 1922 story. Costing over $2 million, the project was in the works for five years, beginning in 1937. A small zoo was kept at Disney's Burbank, California, studio, so his artists could photograph and later animate the story's animals. As the movie was being made, other films were also in production and Bambi can be spied briefly in *The Reluctant Dragon* (q.v.). For the film's ice skating sequence, actress Jane Randolph and skater Donna Atwood modeled for the characters of Bambi and Thumper. *Bambi* received three Academy Award nominations, including one for the tune "Love Is a Song" by Frank Churchill and Larry Morey. *Bambi* did not turn a profit until its first re-release in 1947. Unlike most Disney productions, the feature did cause some controversy when hunters objected to Bambi's mother's death scene.

In the spring in a great forest, a young fawn named Bambi is born to the Great Prince of the Forest and his mate. After watching Bambi takes his first unsteady steps, young rabbit Thumper goes with him on a walk, teaching him to talk and enjoy the beauty around them. As he grows up, Bambi is happy living with his mother, who takes him to a beautiful meadow but warns him to always stay under cover. Bambi shyly meets a little female fawn, Faline. When gunshots are heard near the meadow, the Great Prince gets Bambi and his mother to safety. His mother warns Bambi about men with guns. During the winter Bambi and Thumper ice skate on a frozen pond as Bambi's mother tries to keep them fed during the rough season. When spring arrives, Bambi and his mother return to the meadow but are soon hearing gunshots. After Bambi runs for cover in a thicket, his father tells him his mother will never be with him again. As the days pass, Bambi plays with Thumper and another friend, Flower, and he again meets Faline, to whom he is attracted. When another young deer also wants Faline, Bambi does battle with him and wins. Alerted by the sound of hunting horns, the Great Prince urges the deer to retreat into the forest, but Faline is separated from Bambi and soon cornered by a pack of hunting dogs. Bambi returns and fights the dogs as Faline gets away. As he jumps a ravine, Bambi is shot. The hunters' campfire causes a blaze that spreads through the forest. The Great Prince finds the unconscious Bambi and helps him get to safety, where he finds Faline. The next spring the forest begins to recover from the fire with Thumper and Flower now having their own families. Bambi and Faline are the proud parents of twins and Bambi, standing with his aging father, becomes the new forest prince.

Boxoffice wrote, "Herewith is added another bright and lustrous gem to the crown worn by Walt Disney as a symbol of his leadership in the realm of animated cartoon production...." *Photoplay* enthused, "There is such soul in *Bambi* it is difficult to imagine this is a cartooned and not a photographed film.... [A]lthough lacking the humor of *Snow White* and the novelty of *Pinocchio*, [*Bambi*] stands as a monument to the men who conceived it." In *The Disney Films, 3rd Edition* (1995), Leonard Maltin said, "*Bambi* is the gentlest of Disney's animated features, a delicate rendering of Felix Salten's classic story. It stands unique among the Disney cartoons in its style and atmosphere, and indeed, it would be quite some time before the studio would again go to such lengths to achieve the realistic detail found in this film.... [It] is a beautiful film, and the extraordinary effort that went into making it shows in the finished product.... It remains one of the Disney studio's loveliest works, dealing in qualities of nature and life that will keep it young and fresh forever."

Bedlam (1946; 79 minutes)

PRODUCER: Val Lewton. EXECUTIVE PRODUCER: Jack J. Gross. DIRECTOR: Mark Robson. SCREENPLAY: Carlos Keith [Val Lewton] & Mark Robson, from the engravings "The Rake's Progress" by William Hogarth. PHOTOGRAPHY: Nicholas Musuraca. EDITOR: Lyle Boyer. MUSIC: Roy Webb. MUSIC DIRECTOR: C. Bakaleinikoff. ART DIRECTORS: Albert S. D'Agostino & Walter E. Keller. SOUND: Terry Kellum & Jean L. Speak. SET DECORATIONS: Darrell Silvera. SET DESIGN: John Sturtevant. GOWNS: Edward Stevenson. SPECIAL EFFECTS: Vernon L. Walker. ASSISTANT DIRECTOR: Doran Cox.

CAST: Boris Karloff (Master George Sims), Anna Lee (Nell Bowen), Billy House (Lord Mortimer), Richard Fraser (William Hannay), Glenn Vernon (Gilded Boy), Ian Wolfe (Sidney Long), Jason Robards (Oliver Todd), Leyland Hodgson (John "That Devil" Wilkes), Joan Newton (Dorothea the Dove), Elizabeth Russell (Kitty Sims), Victor Holbrook (Tom the Tiger), Robert Clarke (Dan the Dog), Larry Wheat (Clerk Podge), Bruce Edwards (Warder), John Meredith (Maniac Inmate), John Beck (Solomon), Ellen Corby (Betty, Queen of Artichokes), John Ince (Judge), Skelton Knaggs (Varney), Harry Harvey (John Gray), John Goldsworthy (Chief Commissioner), Polly Bailey (Scrubwoman), Victor Travers (Sims' Friend), James Logan (Bailiff), Foster Phinney (Lord Sandwich), Nan Leslie, Donna Lee (Young Cockney Women), Tommy Noonan, George Holmes, Jimmy Jordan (Stonemasons), Robert Manning (Footman John), Frankie Dee (Pompey), Hamilton Camp (Voice of Pompey), Betty Gillette (Woman).

Bedlam was Boris Karloff's third RKO production for producer Val Lewton and while advertised as a horror film it is really a hard-hitting exposé on the conditions in British mental institutions in the 1760s. Still the feature contains enough horrific elements to appeal to genre followers. Karloff holds the film together as the smooth-talking, erudite sadist Master Sims. While the character is totally evil, Karloff manages to imbue it with touches of droll comedy, such as the scene in which he tries to entice rotund Lord Mortimer (Billy House) to take an interest in his crass, gin-imbibing niece, beautifully played against type by Elizabeth Russell. There are a number of memorable scenes in *Bedlam*, including the death of a young patient (Glenn Vernon) whose body has been gilded and the amused reactions of most of the revelers at the event; the filthy and appalling conditions in the asylum; and the characters of the various inmates, including Dan the Dog (Robert Clarke), Tom the Tiger (Victor Holbrook), the Queen of Artichokes (Ellen Corby), semi-mad solicitor Sidney Long (Ian Wolfe), and author Oliver Todd (Jason Robards), whose family houses him in Bedlam so he cannot drink and therefore can write and support them. The film also hints that Sims took erotic advantage of another inmate, the beautiful Dorothea the Dove (Joan Newton). While not the best of Lewton's RKO horror efforts, *Bedlam*, despite its depressing storyline, is good viewing.

During the "Age of Reason," in 1761 London, an inmate of St. Mary's of Bethlehem Asylum, commonly known as Bedlam, is intentionally killed as he tries to escape. Rotund Lord Mortimer (House) and his protégé, 23-year-old Nell Bowen (Anna Lee), are driving by and Mortimer is notified that the dead man, a poet named Colby, was known to him. The next day Mortimer calls in the Apothecary General and warden of the asylum, Master George Sims (Karloff), and queries him about the incident. Claiming it was an accidental death, Sims suggests that the poet, who was his rival, be replaced by some of his inmates as entertainment at Mortimer's upcoming festivity. Nell is appalled by Sims and his proposal but decides to follow Mortimer's advice and visit Bedlam. At the asylum, clerk Podge (Larry Wheat) informs Sims that a Quaker stonemason, William Hannay (Richard Fraser), is waiting to see him. Sims tries to bribe the man as Nell arrives and pays a tuppence to see the inmates. She is horrified at the condition of the place and its denizens and as she is leaving she hits Sims in the face with her riding crop. Seeing the incident, William tells Nell she showed pity for the unfortunates, but she denies it. At the dinner, Sims has a young man (Vernon) gilded in paint do a recitation and one of the guests, Tory Mortimer's political Whig rival John Wilkes (Leland Hodgson), known as "That Devil," says that a person must be able to breathe through their skin pores in order to live. The young man collapses and dies, causing Sims to be the recipient of more of Nell's ire. When she again meets William, Nell agrees to his suggestion that she try to get Mortimer to help Bedlam's inmates. Mortimer agrees and informs Sims of his plans, but backs down when the warden says it will cost him 500 guineas. Nell flies into a rage and tells Mortimer she does not want to be with him. Mortimer has her evicted from her house and takes all its furniture. She is left only with her valet, Varney (Skelton Knaggs), and a white parrot, Polly. Sims brings his uncouth niece, Kitty (Russell), to see Mortimer, hoping she will be chosen to replace Nell. To get revenge, Nell offers the bird for sale in the public square as it repeats an unflattering poem about Mortimer. Sims sees Nell with Wilkes at the shop of a printer (Harry Harvey) and warns Mortimer, suggesting he get of writ of seizure on the parrot. When Nell refuses a large amount of money for Polly, Sims and Mortimer try to bribe her and she shows contempt for them by taking a bite out of the currency and slapping Sims. Although Mortimer earlier refused Sims' suggestion that Nell be placed in Bedlam, he signs a warrant to do so and she is brought before a lunacy tribunal. Since Mortimer sits on the commission, he influences the others, and Nell is committed to Bedlam.

When he cannot find Nell, William goes to Mortimer, whose new employee, Varney, informs him of her whereabouts. Although Sims refuses him admission, William manages to get inside the asylum and he finds Nell. She tells him to go to Wilkes for help and implores him to give her his masonry trowel so she can use it to defend herself. She joins the "people of the pillar," lawyer Sidney Long (Wolfe), writer Oliver Todd (Robards) and Dan the Dog (Clarke), in playing cards and then gives aid to a prisoner in pain. As she is doing so, the trowel is stolen. Sims taunts Nell for only associating with the saner inmates and asks why she is not showing compassion for the

Lobby card for *Bedlam* (1946).

others. She decides to provide better treatment for the inmates and Sims places her in a cell with a usually chained madman, Tom the Tiger (Holbrook). Nell uses kindness to calm him. William locates Wilkes, who arranges a new sanity hearing for Nell. When Sims learns of the new hearing, he decides to get rid of Nell. She realizes he plans to kill her and urges the inmates to take him prisoner. With the help of Tom, who lifts her onto a roof, she escapes while Long presides over Sims' trial by the inmates. Upon questioning by Todd, Sims claims he did not want to torment his charges but had to do so in order to keep his position. He is found to be sane but as he backs away to escape he is stabbed by the trowel, wielded by Dorothea the Dove (Newton). Nell locates William in a Society of Friends meeting house and he tells her they must go back and help Sims because he too is mad. The inmates, afraid they will be punished for Sims' murder, take his body and seal it up in a wall unfinished by the stonemasons. When William and Nell arrive with Wilkes and members of the lunacy commission, they cannot locate Sims. Although Nell and William realize what happened to the warden, they agree to silence. They also are aware that they are falling in love.

Released in May 1946, *Bedlam* was made as *Chamber of Horrors* and *A Tale of Bedlam*. The asylum set was a re-dressing of the church from *The Bells of St. Mary's* (1945). Budgeted at $350,000, *Bedlam* was the most expensive feature producer Val Lewton did for RKO although co-star Anna Lee later recalled some of the costumes she wore came from others features, including *Experiment Perilous* [q.v.] and *Gone with the Wind* (1939). Lee and Boris Karloff had already worked together in the British film *The Man Who Changed His Mind* (1936). Richard Bojarski noted in *The Films of Boris Karloff* (1974) that RKO "was short-sighted as to the film's qualities and did not give it the distribution it deserved." In *Karloff: The Man, the Monster, the Movies* (1973) Denis Gifford reported the feature "so shocked the British Censors that to this day a certificate has not been granted."

Boxoffice called *Bedlam* "a sordid and depressing subject, which solid production, skillful direction and sincere performances were unable to mitigate." *The New York Times* opined, "This is a production several cuts above the average run of so-called horror films.... While the film has a tendency to wander into unadulterated Hollywoodisms in spots, it is a generally straightforward and imaginative estimate of a two-century-old sociological theme." *The Motion Picture Herald* termed it "a powerful, manifestly painstaking account of conditions" in the asylum, adding: "Prepared with great care for historical accuracy [, it] is not to be confused with the routine horror picture, but proves more important than any of them." According to *Time*, "[S]incere, artful and scary as the best of *Bedlam* is, its horror and high-mindedness don't always blend smoothly." *Variety* pegged it as "a horror film in a more actual sense of the phrase than most of the tame concoctions advertised in that category.... Although RKO's picturization touches on the sociological question lamely and superficially, film succeeds in its avowed purpose—shock."

To complete his four-picture contract with RKO, Boris Karloff was next scheduled to star in *Bluebeard* for producer Lewton but the disappointing box office returns from *Bedlam* halted the project and the actor eventually filled out his studio commitment with *Dick Tracy Meets Gruesome* (q.v.).

Before Dawn (1933; 60 minutes)

EXECUTIVE PRODUCER: Merian C. Cooper. ASSOCIATE PRODUCER: Shirley Burden. DIRECTOR: Irving Pichel. SCREENPLAY: Garrett Fort, from the story "Death Watch" by Edgar Wallace. PHOTOGRAPHY: Lucien Andriot. EDITOR: William Hamilton. MUSIC DIRECTOR: Max Steiner. SETTINGS: Carroll Clark & Van Nest Polglase. SOUND: Philip J. Faulkner, Jr.

CAST: Stuart Erwin (Special Investigator Dwight Wilson), Dorothy Wilson (Patricia Merrick/Mlle. Mystera), Warner Oland (Dr. Paul Cornelius), Dudley Digges (Horace Merrick), Gertrude W. Hoffman (Mattie), Oscar Apfel (Chief of Detectives John F. O'Hara), Frank Reicher (Joe Valerie), Jane Darwell (Mrs. Marble), Stanley Blystone, Max Wagner (Police Car Cops), Pat O'Malley (Detective Brady), Tom Brower (Detective Schultz), Ed Brady (Paddywagon Officer), Ted Oliver (Sergeant Hamilton), Irving Pichel (Police Radio Caller).

Before Dawn was based on the story "Death Watch" which Edgar Wallace penned in Hollywood as part of a six-month contract with RKO. The famed author died not long after its completion. Ginger Rogers and Betty Furness were both considered for the role of the fortune teller before it went to Dorothy Wilson. Garrett Fort's screenplay adaptation of the Wallace work is a polished effort that contains a number of horror elements, including an impressive, spooky old house, clairvoyance, a white-faced specter and a cursed treasure. As handled by director Irving Pichel, the feature is fast-paced and thrilling. A compact cast delivers the acting goods, especially Warner Oland as the repulsive psychopathologist, Dudley Digges as the heroine's slimy father and Gertrude W. Hoffman's as the obtuse, superstitious housekeeper. This August 1933 Radio release is one of the studio's better genre outings of the early 1930s.

At a hospital in Vienna, gangster Joe Valerie (Frank Reicher) tells Dr. Paul Cornelius (Warner Oland) the hiding place of a million dollars in gold he and his gang stole from a bank 15 years before. At the remote mansion where Valerie hid the money, a newspaper arrives with the news of his death and Mrs. Marble (Jane Darwell) announces to her housekeeper Mattie (Gertrude W. Hoffman) that she plans to retrieve it to travel and buy nice clothes. Mattie tells her the gold is cursed. When Mrs. Marble goes upstairs, she sees a ghostly face and falls to her death. Leading an investigation into the city's fake fortune-telling racketeers, detective Dwight Wilson (Stuart Erwin) asks pretty Mlle. Mystera, really Patricia Merrick (Wilson), to find his Aunt Minnie. She tells him he is an unwilling customer and her father, Horace Merrick (Digges), will return his three dollars. Dwight tries to get the money and when Horace refuses he arrests both the Merricks. At police headquarters Horace attempts to get out of the rap by telling Police

Poster for *Before Dawn* (1932).

Chief O'Hara (Oscar Apfel) that his daughter worked with three Midwest police departments using clairvoyance in solving crimes. When Dwight sits with Patricia outside the chief's office, she says he entrapped her and slaps him. She then uses her powers to recall images of Dwight's deceased younger sister. Dwight convinces O'Hara to give Patricia a chance and she tells them a gangster they are after is dead. O'Hara is ready to send both Patricia and her father to jail when word comes the gangster has just been shot. When Dwight suggests to O'Hara that Patricia work on the Marble case, she recounts the old woman's fall and says there was something in the dark at the top of the stairs with a white, horrible face. The detectives take Patricia and her father to the Marble house and asks Mattie to describe the night her employer died. As Mattie goes to the top of the stairs, everyone hears footsteps and she says it is Valerie come back from the dead. When no intruder is found, Patricia announces that someone is coming near and there is a knock at the door. The visitor is Cornelius, who informs O'Hara that Valerie told him the two women were the custodians of his hidden fortune and that the gangster and Mrs. Marble were married.

At police headquarters, Cornelius asks O'Hara to let him stay at the Marble house and try to get the truth out of Mattie using the ruse that he is interested in Patricia's psychic abilities. At breakfast the next day, Horace tells Patricia he is suspicious of Cornelius. Dwight arrives with tools needed to find the money. Cornelius informs Mattie that people think she killed Mrs. Marble and is liable to be hanged. He gives her 24 hours to tell him the truth about the gold. Horace informs Cornelius that Dwight is there in search of the fortune and then tries to get Patricia to concentrate on its hiding place but she refuses. Mattie is awakened by a white face. Her screams bring the others to her room and she says she saw Valerie but refuses to divulge the money's whereabouts. Patricia announces that Valerie was never there. After Dwight leaves in search of the patrol car cops he left to guard the house, Horace hears Cornelius tell Mattie the money is hidden in a secret room. Trying to find it, Horace discovers a hidden passage and a white death mask. Cornelius finds Horace looking for the money and kills him. He then informs Patricia that her father has gone for help and that Mattie is dangerously deranged. Telling Patricia to remain downstairs while he gives Mattie a hypo, Cornelius returns to the old woman's room and she agrees to lead him to the gold. Patricia sees a vision of her father's face in a lamp. Mattie takes Cornelius to the cellar after he informs her he killed Horace in self-defense. On the cellar steps, Mattie tries to trick Cornelius, who throws her into a deep well at the foot of the passage. Patricia finds her father's body and Cornelius says Mattie killed him; she does not believe him. Dwight and two patrol car cops (Stanley Blystone, Max Wagner) return to the house and hear Patricia scream. Dwight breaks into the secret passage. When Patricia calls to him, he finds the entrance to the cellar stairway. He fights with Cornelius, who falls down the stairs and drowns in the well. At police headquarters, Patricia tells O'Hara she wants Dwight to have the reward for finding the money. As she is about to sign an affidavit to that effect, she sees it is a marriage license and she and Dwight kiss.

Mordaunt Hall wrote in *The New York Times,* "Like most of [Edgar Wallace's] works, this particularly ruddy specimen is blessed with vigor and imagination. Mr. Wallace was not content with the ordinary stock props of murder mysteries. There are enough killings and accidental deaths to satisfy the most ardent enthusiasts of such thrillers." *Motion Picture Daily* thought the film's title a bit tame but added, "Story, cast and action make a good picture of its kind; offering suspense, thrills and romance and the lighter touches of Stuart Erwin's sleuthing and wooing for a good measure of entertainment." *New England Film News* decreed, "This one will really give you goose-flesh and cold chills.... The scene of the action is an old haunted house and no detail which might give you another shiver-up-the-spine is omitted. Too scary for children." *Photoplay* concurred, saying, "Not for the kiddies." The *El Paso* (Texas) *Herald-Post* wrote, "A delightful love story intersperses the excitement of the mystery adventure," and *The Bakersfield* (California) *Californian* called it "a thrilling murder mystery." Reviewing the film under its working title *The Death Watch*, *The New Movie Magazine* opined, "[A] competent cast has made a fair picture out of it.... [T]here is rather less action than in the usual Wallace story.... If you want to see something that will take our mind off your troubles, catch a load of this and you'll be sitting up nights to figure it out." In another review, the same publication complained, "This film has been taken from a horror tale by Edgar Wallace and all of the original author's dexterity has been left behind. Whatever it was in print, on celluloid it sounds just plain silly." Regarding the cast, the reviewer stated, "Assembling them for *Before Dawn* is rather like asking the architects of the Empire State Building to knock together a woodshed."

Beyond Tomorrow (1940; 84 minutes)

PRODUCER: Lee Garmes. ASSOCIATE PRODUCER–SCREENPLAY: Adele Comandini. DIRECTOR: A. Edward Sutherland. STORY: Mildred Cram & Adele Comandini. PHOTOGRAPHY: Lester White. EDITOR: Otto Ludwig. MUSIC: Frank Tours. SONGS: Stephen Foster, Harold Spina & Charles Newman. ART DIRECTOR: Stephen Goosson. SOUND: William Wilmarth. PRODUCTION MANAGER: Joseph H. Nadel. SPECIAL EFFECTS: Jack Cosgrove & Ned Mann. INTERIOR DECORATOR: Babs Johnstone. GOWNS: Edwina. MONTAGE: Howard Anderson. CASTING: Jack Murton. ASSISTANT DIRECTOR: Robert Stillman.

CAST: Harry Carey (George Vale Melton), C. Aubrey Smith (Major Allan "Chad" Chadwick), Charles Winninger (Michael O'Brien), Richard Carlson (James "Jimmy" Houston), Jean Parker (Jean Lawrence), Alex Melesh (Josef), Maria Ouspenskaya (Madame Tanya), Helen Vinson (Arlene Terry), Rod La Rocque (Phil Hubert), J. Anthony Hughes (Officer Johnson), Robert Homans (Police Sergeant), Virginia McMullen (Radio Station Secretary), James Bush (Jace Taylor), William Bakewell (David Chadwick), Nell Craig (Stenographer Suzie), Gino Corrado (Cook Alfonso), Hank Worden (Visitor with Flowers), Ruth Warren (Arlene Terry's Maid), Cyril Ring (Messenger), Gertrude Sutton (Clinic Nurse), Frank Wilcox (Waiter), Dan White (Gas Station Attendant), Sam McDaniel (Driver).

Filmed as *And So Goodbye*, the May 1940 release *Beyond Tomorrow* was the first feature made by cinematographer Lee Garmes' Academy Productions. A whimsical fantasy, it mixes romance, music and benign ghosts in equal portions. The result is either heartwarming or cloying, depending on one's perspective. It is a handsomely mounted production with fine performances by the leads, although Richard Carlson seems a bit out of place as a radio crooner. Whoever dubbed him singing "I Dream of Jeanie" and "It's Raining Dreams" possessed a fine voice. Overall, the film is entertaining but it relies more on its cast than storyline, which gets more and more convoluted as Carlson's character falls under the spell of a soulless vamp.

On Christmas Eve in New York City, stern and bitter George Vale Melton (Harry Carey), jovial British military veteran Major Allan "Chad" Chadwick (C. Aubrey Smith) and good-natured Michael O'Brien (Charles Winninger) find themselves alone after their dinner guests cancel. The three businessmen live in a mansion and are watched over by their Russian émigré housekeeper Madame Tanya (Maria Ouspenskaya) and butler Josef (Alex Melesh). Madame Tanya tells Josef that although she once had riches, she now lives to serve others and be needed. With nothing else to do, Michael comes up with the gag of throwing three gift wallets containing their individual business cards and ten dollars into the street to see if anyone will return them. He says someone will and George bets him a dinner he is wrong. At seven o'clock, Texan James "Jimmy" Houston (Carlson), who has been stranded in town after arriving with a rodeo, returns one of the wallets. Another is found by radio star Arlene Terry (Helen Vinson) and theatrical producer Phil Hubert (Rod La Rocque), with the money given to their driver (Sam McDaniel).

After Jimmy accepts a dinner invitation from the three business partners, pretty New Englander Jean Lawrence (Jean Parker) arrives with the third wallet and they invite her to join them. The five people spend the evening together and Jimmy sings "I Dream of Jeanie." Jean, an assistant at the Wayne Foundation Children's Clinic, and Jimmy are attracted to each other. During the next week, the two young people and the three men spend time together, including New Year's Eve at the Waldorf Hotel, visiting the school, going to an ice hockey game and bowling. George, Chad and Michael are summoned to Pittsburgh to test a new alloy and take a private plane, with Madame Tanya pleading with them to go by train. That night Jimmy proposes to Jean and they run to the mansion to tell Madame Tanya, only to be informed by Josef that the engineers died when their plane crashed.

The dead men's spirits return to the house and are felt by Madame Tanya, who asks Jimmy to live with her and Josef. Michael willed some bonds to the two young people and Jimmy uses his share to further his singing career, which garners newspaper publicity. At a radio audition he meets singing star Arlene, who finds him attractive. Jimmy becomes an overnight singing sensation and Arlene and Phil, her theatrical producer, decide to promote him. George warns Michael and Chad that Jimmy will get mixed up with people who will turn his head. During a thunderstorm, George is called below to atone for his past deeds. Jimmy signs with Phil to co-star with Arlene in a new musical comedy but neglects Jean. Arlene makes a play for Jimmy, much to Michael's disgust. Chad hears a bugle call and his war hero son David (William Bakewell) comes for him and he sees the old days in Simla and they go there. Michael pleads with Jean, who cannot see or hear him, to go to Jimmy, who is

Maria Ouspenskaya, Harry Carey and C. Aubrey Smith in *Beyond Tomorrow* (1940).

infatuated with Arlene. The singer's ex-husband (James Bush) shows up drunk, has a confrontation with Jimmy and promises revenge. Arlene asks Jimmy to spend three days in the country with her. When Jean goes to see Jimmy, he tells her things have gone too fast and she leaves. Michael attempts to signal both Jean and Madame Tanya to stop Jimmy from going away with Arlene. Madame Tanya informs Jimmy that George lost his home and reputation over a woman like Arlene but he refuses to listen. Unknown to them, Michael rides in the back seat of their car as Jimmy drives Arlene to the Pinewood Inn. They are also unaware that her ex-husband is following them. At the inn, Michael is called to Heaven but he refuses to go so he can stay and help Jimmy. A voice tells him he will linger in the shadows of the earth for all time. While Jimmy and Arlene are dining, her ex-husband shows up and shoots both of them. Jimmy dies on the operating table and meets Michael. He also sees Jean crying for him. Michael informs Jimmy that his success came too suddenly and the young man tries to tell Jean he is sorry. As Michael and Jimmy walk away, a bright light emerges and Michael is called to Heaven to be with his mother. He asks that Jimmy be given another chance and the request is granted. Jimmy comes back to life to be with Jean while Michael is greeted by George, who has repented and found eternal peace.

Variety felt the feature was "lacking in punchiness in its dramatic attempts.... [It] proves both ineffectual in its attempts to get over a dramatic premise, and rather dull in its unfolding. Stilted script, filled with long and uninteresting dialog passages and unimportant direction, proves major handicap here." On the other hand, *Boxoffice* said it "makes for pleasing entertainment." *The New York Times* took aim at the picture's three spirits: "For its first half it is a latter-day *Christmas Carol*, told with a gamin tenderness and warming as a hot toddy. But when its three elderly good Samaritans return from a plane crash as celluloid chimeras, its mystical peregrinations are more preposterous than moving.... Even a hot toddy wears off when one travels into the chilling interstellar spaces." *Photoplay* wrote, "This is a study in sweetness and light, as enervating a sermon upon what will happen to you if you aren't good as ever went under the guise of entertainment.... The piece displays naivete." *The Film Daily* opined that the film would prove interesting to audiences and commended the "very fine cast that does a workman-like job. Although there are no big names in the cast, there are a number of well known names that can be used on the marquee and the supernatural theme of the film lends itself readily to exploitation."

Beyond Tomorrow was reissued in 1946 by Astor Pictures and it later became a perennial television Christmas favorite. An alternate title for the film on DVD is *Beyond Christmas*.

Bird of Paradise (1932; 81 minutes)

PRODUCER-DIRECTOR: King Vidor. EXECUTIVE PRODUCER: David O. Selznick. SCREENPLAY: Wells Root, Wanda Tuchock & Leonard Praskins, from the play by Richard Walton Tully. PHOTOGRAPHY: Clyde DeVinna, Edward Cronjager & Lucien Andriot. EDITOR: Archie F. Marshek. MUSIC: Max Steiner. ART DIRECTOR: Carroll Clark. SOUND: Clem Portman. PHOTOGRAPHIC EFFECTS: Lloyd Knechtel. CHOREOGRAPHY: Busby Berkeley. PRODUCTION SUPERVISOR: John E. Burch.

CAST: Dolores Del Rio (Luana), Joel McCrea (Johnny Baker), John Halliday (Mac), Richard "Skeets" Gallagher (Chester), Bert Roach (Hector), Creighton Chaney [Lon Chaney, Jr.] (Thornton), Wade Boteler (Skipper Johnson), Arnold Gray (Walker), Reginald Simpson (O'Fallon), Napoleon Pukui (The King), Agostino Borgato (Medicine Man), Sofia Ortega (Mahumahu).

Richard Walton Tully's 1912 play *Bird of Paradise* first starred Laurette Taylor in the role of native girl Luana with a supporting cast that included Theodore Roberts, Lewis Stone and Guy Bates Post. Other actresses to portray Luana on stage include Lenore Ulric, Bessie Barriscale and Calotta Monterrey, who later married playwright Eugene O'Neill. The perennial stage favorite was reworked into a 1930 Broadway production called *Luana,* with music by Rudolf Friml and lyrics by J. Keirn Brennan. It starred Ruth Alexander in the title role with a cast that included Harold Whalen, Lillian Bond, George Nash, Joseph Macauly, Harry Jans, Harry C. Bradley, William C. Gordon, Doris Carson, Harold Ten Brook and Diana Chase. The play ran for 21 performances (September 17 and October 4, 1930). RKO then bought the rights to the Tully work for $375,000, announcing that the film version would be shot in Technicolor. With King Vidor borrowed from Metro-Goldwyn-Mayer to produce and direct the picture, *Bird of Paradise* began filming in Hawaii early in 1932 in black and white but costs soon ballooned due to unfavorable weather conditions with most of the footage eventually being lensed on Santa Catalina

Island and the Culver City, California, RKO Pathé lot. The resulting film proved to be pleasing to the eye with its lovely underwater photography (including star Dolores Del Rio swimming nude), native dances well staged by uncredited Busby Berkeley, and quite a bit of underplayed humor, such as Joel McCrea using a tennis racquet to swat at flying fish and using it again as a guitar while humming "Where the Blue of the Night Meets the Gold of the Day," then a popular recording by Bing Crosby. The horror aspects of the feature involve a native medicine man (Agostino Borgato) using his mental powers to wilt flowers and the curse of the volcano god Peli, who can only be appeased by the sacrifice of Luana (Del Rio).

Johnny Baker (McCrea) is a member of a party roaming the South Seas on a yacht owned by Mac (John Halliday) and captained by Skipper Johnson (Wade Boteler). Also on board are tippler Chester (Richard "Skeets" Gallagher), rotund Hector (Bert Roach), athletic Thornton (Lon Chaney, Jr.), Walker (Arnold Gray) and O'Fallon (Reginald Simpson). At a small island they are greeted by playful natives. When Johnny tries to spear a shark, his foot gets caught in a rope and he is pulled into the lagoon. Beautiful Luana (Del Rio) cuts the rope, saving his life. At a native luau, Mac explains to the men that a maiden must be sacrificed to the volcano god Pele to keep it inactive. Johnny is entranced by Luana and watches her dance but is told by her father (Napoleon Pukui), the island's king, that she is promised to a prince, making her taboo. That night she swims nude near the yacht and Johnny follows her to the shore, where they kiss. He decides to spend a few weeks on the island and, after biding farewell to his comrades, takes

Joel McCrea, Dolores Del Rio and Agostino Borgato in *Bird of Paradise* (1932).

his speedboat and joins the natives in catching flying fish. Luana tows his boat to shore where they kiss on a bed of roses but they are caught by her father and his men and she is flogged. A native woman, Mahumahu (Sofia Ortega), informs Johnny that Luana is about to be married. He follows Luana but is tied to a tree. Mahumahu sets him free and he gives her his phonograph in return for a canoe. Using berry juice to darken his skin, he follows the wedding party to a nearby island. During the wedding fire dance, Johnny carries off Luana and they escape to the secluded island of Lani. There they lead an idyllic romantic existence with Johnny building them a thatched hut and telling Luana he wants to take her with him when he returns to San Francisco. She replies that she must go to the volcano because he will die from its curse if she does not. After several weeks, the volcano erupts and the scared natives go after Luana for a sacrifice. Johnny returns to their hut to find Luana gone and their goat killed. He spies the native boats returning to Luana's village and follows them but nearly drowns in a whirlpool caused by the volcano before swimming to shore. There he sees a huge lava flow and has to swing over a gorge using vines before getting to the village where he is wounded by a spear. Tied to a wooden bier, Johnny finds Luana in the same situation but the two manage to kiss and proclaim their love before being carried to Peli. Unknown to the islanders, Johnny's friends have returned; the natives flee after Mac shoots two of them. Back on board the yacht, Mac tends to Johnny's wounds and tells Luana that her lover will survive. As the men debate taking the girl with them, the natives come to the boat and demand she go with them. Her father says Johnny will die from the volcano's curse unless Peli is appeased by Luana's sacrifice. Overhearing the conversation, Luana announces she will go with her people and bids farewell to Johnny. Luana returns to the island to die for the man she loves.

Reviews of *Bird of Paradise* were mixed. According to *The New York Times*, "King Vidor has produced a languid film with many beautifully photographed scenes. This story in its modernized form is frequently unconsciously humorous and even though much is made of the volcano on a South Sea isle exacting its annual human toll, there is here hardly anything akin to suspense." *The Film Daily* commented, "They went to a lot of expense and trouble to reproduce this old stage classic, and emerged with a picturesque and beautiful film, but the story lacks any sense of realism and shapes up as a rather fanciful and idealistic romance...." *The International Photographer* commented, "Pictorially the picture stands out.... For lovers of the romantic as well as of beautiful and picturesque in backgrounds there are many warm if attractive moments." *Picture Play Magazine* commented, "It enchants the eye and lulls the senses with the drenching loveliness of the tropics. Sad to say, it does not satisfy the mind and it falls short of being a noteworthy dramatic composition such as we expect from King Vidor."

"Lavish settings, gorgeous photography and the spirited musical score, plus good acting by Dolores Del Rio and Joel McCrea, give this a good rating. Young moderns will thrill to the love scenes, as romantic and daring as any recent film has offered, but the story about a native princess and a white boy will seem out of date," opined *Photoplay*. *Movie Classic* reported, "It is refreshing in its simplicity, in its glorification of those good, old primitive emotions, and its lack of weary sophistication. Its plot pattern is an old one, but is woven in new, more vivid colors, now that the screen can talk." The reviewer also touches on the racial differences in the two lovers, noting, "Joel *doesn't* forget the brown girl for a white girl."

RKO claimed *Bird of Paradise* cost over one million dollars to make but most sources put the figure at around $750,000. Whatever the expense, the film may have brought the studio a modicum of prestige but no profit. RKO sold the story to 20th Century–Fox, which filmed a listless color remake in 1951 starring Louis Jourdan, Debra Paget and Jeff Chandler.

The Black Abbot (1934; 53 minutes)

PRODUCER: Julius Hagen. DIRECTOR: George A. Cooper. SCREENPLAY: Terence Egan, from the novel *The Grange Mystery* by Philip Godfrey. PHOTOGRAPHY: Ernest Palmer. EDITOR: Lister Laurence. ART DIRECTOR: James A. Carter. SOUND: Carlisle Mounteney. COIFFEUR: Charles. ASSISTANT DIRECTOR: Fred Merrick.

CAST: John Stuart (Frank Brooks), Judy Kelly (Sylvia Hillcrest), Richard Cooper (Lord Jerry Pilkdown), Ben Welden (Charlie Marsh), Edgar Norfolk (Brian Heslewood), Farren Soutar (John Hillcrist), John Turnbull (Inspector Lockwood), Cyril Smith (Alf Higgins), Drusilla Willis (Aunt Mary Hillcrist), Earle Green (Phillips), Davina Craig (Jane).

Beginning in 1932, RKO began distributing (and sometimes co-financing) British films under the auspices of Radio Pictures (headquartered on Dean Street, Soho, London), with the majority being produced by Julius Hagen's Real Art Productions. One of these was *The Black Abbot*, which was not based on Edgar Wallace's 1926 novel of the same title but derived from *The Grange Mystery* by Philip Godfrey. The title character supposedly haunted a deserted monastery connected to a remote country estate. With scenes of a stalking figure wearing a black cowl and the mysterious disappearance of the lord of the manor, this compact thriller proved to be a flavorful horror-mystery-comedy.

At the country home of John Hillcrist (Farren Soutar), architect Frank Brooks (John Stuart) proposes marriage to John's pretty daughter Sylvia (Judy Kelly) and she accepts. Frank has been hired by his future father-in-law to revamp Monk's Hall, a long-deserted monastery connected to the grange which John and his sister Aunt Mary (Drusilla Willis) want to have for another room. Brian Hazelwood (Edgar Norfolk), who also wants to marry Sylvia, arrives and she tells him about her engagement to Frank. Later, another houseguest, Lord Jerry Pilkdown (Richard Cooper), congratulates the young couple. That evening the group is playing cards when they hear a scream: The maid, Jane (Davina Craig), thought she saw a ghost while in the Monk's Hall with her suitor, gardener Alf Higgins (Cyril Smith). The two are reprimanded by Phillips (Earle Green), the butler, who later tells his employers the figure may have been the Black Abbot, a monk condemned to haunt the old rectory because he dabbled in sorcery. Brian, who sold the grange to John to pay off his debs, scoffs at the legend and Frank suggests they all stay in Monk's Hall that night to see if the ghost reappears. At midnight John and Brian see the phantom and as they try to catch it, John is abducted by two men. Sylvia hears her aunt scream as Alf finds Brian unconscious in the garden. When it is evident that John is missing, Frank calls the police. Inspector Lockwood (John Turnbull) arrives with the news that a man named Pearson, who suffered severe financial losses, may be responsible for John's disappearance. Brian introduces Sylvia to his American friend, detective Charlie Marsh (Ben Welden), who volunteers to help. He thinks John has been kidnapped for a ransom but Lockwood laughs at the idea. Sylvia gets a letter from her father saying he will be killed unless she gets £10,000 for his release. Marsh tells her to get the money. Frank takes Sylvia to London but they are followed by Brian and the detective. That night Sylvia informs Marsh that her father's lawyer is bringing the money the next day and he announces he believes Frank is part of the kidnap plot. When Frank gets a phone call from Pearson, Sylvia overhears the conversation on an extension phone and begins to doubt her lover. Aunt Mary tells Jerry she also suspects Frank. Sylvia finds Frank at the entrance to Monk's Hall and he asks her to trust him. Lockwood sets a trap to catch the crooks, who are forcing John (held prisoner in a hidden room beneath the monastery) to sign another letter. The inspector and his men see a robed figure in a cowl emerge through a hidden panel in the monastery and it turns out to be Phillips. They then find the hidden room where John is being held prisoner and after a shootout they capture the other two crooks, Brian and Marsh. Lockwood says it was Frank who found the hidden room and Sylvia tells her fiancé she is sorry she did not trust him.

A running gag in *The Black Abbot* has Cockney gardener Alf romancing maid Jane, who has a perpetual cold. Unfortunately some of the dialogue between the two is difficult to decipher due to their thick accents. Alf is amusingly played by Cyril Smith, a Scottish music hall star who appeared in several genre films including *Transatlantic Tunnel* (1935), *The Frog* (1937), *The Torso Murder Mystery* (1939), *Meet Sexton Blake* and *The Echo Murders* (both 1945), *Daughter of Darkness* (1948), *Stolen Face* and *Old Mother Riley Meets the Vampire* (both 1952), *Svengali* (1954) and *The Brain Machine* (1956) [q.v.]. He also played Merlin in the 1956–57 TV series *The Adventures of Sir Lancelot*. Perhaps his greatest claim to fame is providing the vocals on the best-selling 1937 record "The Old Sow Song/With Her Head Tucked Under Her Arm" (Bluebird 7078), backed by Rudy Vallee and His Connecticut Yankees.

Top-billed John Stuart had a lengthy involvement in genre outings such as *The Hound of the Baskervilles* and *Mistress of Atlantis* (both 1932), *The Pointing Finger* (1934) [q.v.], *The Claydon Treasure Mystery* (1938), *Old Mother Riley's Ghost* (1941), *House of Darkness* (1948), *Four Sided Triangle* (1953), *Alias John Preston* and *Quatermass II (Enemy from Space)* (both 1957), *The Revenge of Frankenstein* and *Blood of the Vampire* (both 1958), *The Mummy* (1959), *Village of the Damned* (1960), *Paranoiac* (1963) and *Superman* (1978). He also starred in the BBC-TV series *The Lost Planet* (1954) and *Return to the Lost Planet* (1955).

In *British Sound Films: The Studio Years 1928–1959* (1984), David Quinlan called *The Black Abbot* a "weakish thriller."

The Black Ghost (1932; 70 minutes)

ASSOCIATE PRODUCER: Fred J. McConnell. DIRECTORS: Spencer Gordon Bennet & Thomas L. Storey. SCREENPLAY: George Plympton & Robert Hill. STORY: Courtney Riley Cooper. PHOTOGRAPHY: Edward Snyder & Gilbert Warrenton. EDITOR: Thomas Mallory. ART DIRECTOR: E.E. Sheely.

CAST: Creighton Chaney [Lon Chaney, Jr.] (Tom Kirby/The Black Ghost), Dorothy Gulliver (Betty Halliday), Francis X. Bushman, Jr. (Jeff Maitland), William Desmond (General Custer), Judith Barrie (Rose Maitland), Mary Jo Desmond (Aggie), Joe Bonomo (Joe), LeRoy Mason (Buck), Pete Morrison (Hank), King [Slim] Cole (Uncle Happy), Yakima Canutt (Wild Bill Hickok), Richard Neill (Lige Morris), Claude Peyton (General Halliday), Frank Lackteen (Chief Pawnee Blood), Ben Corbett (Ben), Fritzi Fenn (Nita), Fred Burns (Henchman), Bill Nestell (Tex).

The Black Ghost, the feature version of the 1932 RKO serial *The Last Frontier*, is not a horror film but it is included here because genre great Lon Chaney, Jr. (billed under his real name Creighton Chaney), essays the title role, a black-clad avenger who tries to halt gunrunning to Indians. *The Last Frontier*, RKO's only cliffhanger and Chaney's first starring vehicle, was a remake of the 1926 Metropolitan Pictures Corporation of California's feature of the same title that was issued theatrically by Producers Distributing Corporation (PDC), directed by George B. Seitz and starred William Boyd, Marguerite De La Motte, Jack Hoxie and Mitchell Lewis. The 12-chapter serial used much footage from the silent and both films featured Frank Lackteen as the Pawnee chief. It was distributed by RKO and produced by the Van Beuren Studios with co-direction by chapterplay ace Spencer Gordon Bennet and Thomas L. Storey. Besides the extensive use of stock footage from the 1926 version, the serial was heavily padded with lots of shooting and chase sequences.

The area near Placer City is Indian Territory and supposedly upstanding citizen Lige Morris (Richard Neill) wants to keep out settlers because he covets the gold buried there. Morris, his henchmen Buck (LeRoy Mason), Hank (Pete Morrison) and Joe (Joe Bonomo) and their gang

Advertisement for the serial *The Last Frontier* (1932), which was also issued as a feature called *The Black Ghost*.

have been supplying guns to the Indians. General Custer (William Desmond) orders local Army post commander General Halliday (Claude Peyton) to stop them. Also trying to combat the lawlessness is newspaper editor Tom Kirby (Chaney) and his printer Happy (King Cole). Tom, who is attracted to Halliday's daughter Betty (Dorothy Gulliver), takes on the guise of the phantom-like Black Ghost. The outlaws try to steal guns they have hidden in settler Jeff Maitland's

Dorothy Gulliver and Creighton Chaney—later renamed Lon Chaney, Jr.—in *The Black Ghost* (1932), feature version of the serial *The Last Frontier*.

(Francis X. Bushman, Jr.) wagon. Maitland is working with Morris but is traveling incognito with his wife Rose (Judith Barrie), who pretends to be his sister. When Tom tries to expose the gunrunners and save Betty from them, he becomes a fugitive but eventually Betty exonerates him. Fed up with Morris' greed, Maitland tries to quit the gang and is shot after a holdup and says he will give evidence against the crooks. The Indians, led by Chief Pawnee Blood (Lackteen), attempt to wipe out the settlers but the cavalry comes to the rescue. Morris tries to pass himself off as the Black Ghost and kidnaps Betty but is pursed by Kirby and trampled in a buffalo stampede.

The Last Frontier was reissued theatrically in 1940 by Commonwealth Pictures Corporation with new title cards billing the star as Lon Chaney, Jr., in order to cash in on his popularity from *Of Mice and Men*, released the previous year. The 12-chapter serial runs three hours and 31 minutes but when RKO fashioned it into a feature for theaters that did not exhibit chapterplays, *The Black Ghost* ran 70 minutes. Its running time was further reduced to 55 minutes for TV showings. Both feature versions are muddled affairs with the action piling on so fast that nothing makes sense and most of the supporting players make fleeting appearances.

The complete serial does include a scene in which a black sentry (Nicodemus Stewart) is scared by ghostly sounds made by Happy in a successful attempt to get Tom sprung from the brig after he is arrested for allegedly being a gunrunner. Kirby's adopted daughter Aggy is portrayed by Mary Jo Desmond, the daughter of silent star William Desmond, who appears briefly as General Custer.

In reviewing the first three chapters of *The Last Frontier*, *The Film Daily* wrote, "Here is a real old-fashioned serial that will have the kids sitting on the edge of their seats, and waiting breathlessly for the next chapter. The frontier atmosphere is very colorful and realistic. Where ever they like serials, here is a sure bet."

The Last Frontier was RKO's only serial. The studio advertised two more cliffhangers to be made with Van Beuren Productions, *Airplane Express* and *Lost in the Malayan Jungle*, but they were never filmed.

The Body Snatcher (1945; 78 minutes)

PRODUCER: Val Lewton. EXECUTIVE PRODUCER: Jack J. Gross. DIRECTOR: Robert Wise. SCREEN-PLAY: Philip MacDonald & Carlos Keith [Val Lewton]. PHOTOGRAPHY: Robert De Grasse. EDITOR: J.R. Whittredge. MUSIC: Roy Webb. MUSIC DIRECTOR: C. Bakaleinikoff. ART DIRECTORS: Albert S. D'Agostino & Walter E. Keller. SOUND: Bailey Fester & Terry Kellum. SET DECORATIONS: Darrell Silvera & John Sturtevant. COSTUMES: Renie. ASSISTANT DIRECTOR: Harry Scott.

CAST: Boris Karloff (John Gray), Bela Lugosi (Joseph), Henry Daniell (Dr. "Toddy" MacFarlane), Edith Atwater (Meg Camden MacFarlane), Russell Wade (Donald Fettes), Rita Corday (Mrs. Marsh), Sharyn Moffett (Georgina Marsh), Donna Lee (Street Singer), Robert Clarke (Richardson), Aina Constant (Tavern Girl), Mary Gordon (Mary McBride), Bill Williams (Service), Milton Kibbee (Dan the Bartender), Jim Moran (Angus), Carl Kent (Gilchrist), Jack Welch (Boy), Larry Wheat (Street Salesman), Ethan Laidlaw (Tavern Customer), Ted Billings (Citizen), Bobby Burns (Mourner), Sammy Blum (Waiter).

In 1944 Boris Karloff made *The Body Snatcher*, his second of three features for producer Val Lewton. Based on the 1884 story by Robert Louis Stevenson, it was filmed between the making of the actor's first Lewton, *Isle of the Dead* (q.v.), which was started in the summer of 1944 with the production being halted due to the star's back problems. *The Body Snatcher* was lensed in October–November 1944 and production of *Isle of the Dead* resumed in December of that year. Although given solo star billing, Karloff's part is secondary to that of the doctor played by Henry Daniell, who dominates the film, and his associate, portrayed by Russell Wade. Second-billed Bela Lugosi has only a small role although in the film's advertising he was given equal billing with Karloff. *The Body Snatcher* was released theatrically in May 1945, three months ahead of *Isle of the Dead*.

In 1831, Donald Fettes (Wade) sits in an Edinburgh, Scotland, cemetery contemplating his future and meets Mary McBride (Mary Gordon), who tends her son's grave which is guarded by his loyal dog. She complains of grave robbers and worries about security in the place. Donald is a student at a medical school run by famous surgeon Dr. MacFarlane (Daniell), who is visited by a young widow, Mrs. Marsh (Rita Corday), and her little daughter Georgina (Sharyn Moffett). The child is unable to walk, having been in a carriage accident that killed her father. After examining the child, MacFarlane says she needs an operation but he refuses to do it, saying it is too dangerous and he does not have the time because of his teaching duties. After the woman and her daughter leave, Donald informs MacFarlane he cannot continue his studies because of lack of funds, and the doctor makes him his assistant. Later MacFarlane tells Donald that not all the cadavers they use for dissection are those of paupers provided by the local morgue. During the night Donald is awakened by the arrival of cabman John Gray (Karloff), who brings the corpse of a young boy and demands £10 in payment.

The next day Mrs. Marsh asks Donald to intercede with MacFarlane on her daughter's behalf and he agrees to do so. He also sees a crowd at the cemetery and finds Mrs. McBride holding the dead body of her son's dog, which Gray had killed the previous evening while robbing the boy's grave. Donald tries to give up his job but MacFarlane refuses his resignation, saying laws have made it nearly impossible for doctors to have cadavers for research. That night the two men dine at the local inn and there they find Gray who taunts MacFarlane by calling him Toddy and telling Donald he once saved the doctor's skin. When Gray hears the doctor will not operate on the Marsh child, to whom Gray has taken a fancy and treated kindly, he dares MacFarlane to do it, but the doctor says he does not have a spinal column for experimentation. Donald visits Gray's quarters and asks him to acquire a specimen. When Gray does so, Donald sees that the body is that of a blind street singer (Donna Lee) to whom he had earlier given alms. After showing MacFarlane the girl's body, Donald tells him that Gray murdered her and he wants to go to the police. MacFarlane warns him to remain silent or he might be implicated in her death. The two are overheard by the doctor's workman, Joseph (Lugosi). MacFarlane agrees to do the surgery but warns Mrs. Marsh and Georgina the child will experience great pain during the operation. The young mother is comforted by the doctor's housekeeper, Meg Cameron (Edith Atwater). Following the surgery, MacFarlane informs Gray there will be no more business between them but the cabman tells the doctor he will never be rid of him. Although the operation went smoothly, Georgina still cannot walk. The disgruntled MacFarlane goes to the inn to drown his sorrows in drink and there he is tormented by Gray, who reminds him of their past association. When Gray goes home he is confronted by Joseph, who tells him he knows he has committed murders and demands hush money. Gray agrees to pay and tells Joseph they can work together to provide the doctor with cadavers. He says they will "Burke" the victims and relates to him the story of notorious resurrection men Burke and Hare, who were responsible for the deaths of 18 victims. After getting Joseph drunk, Gray suffocates him and takes his body to MacFarlane's laboratory. Donald shows MacFarlane Joseph's body. Meg tells Donald to go away and then recounts how the doctor, who is really her husband, was mixed up with Dr. Knox, who used the services of Burke and Hare. Gray worked for MacFarlane and withheld the truth about him during the grave robbers' trial. MacFarlane goes to Gray's abode and offers him money to go away but the cabman says he gets more satisfaction in lording over the great doctor. The two men fight and after Gray nearly gets the best of MacFarlane, the doctor breaks a chair over Gray and beats him to death. MacFarlane takes Gray's body back to his laboratory, planning to use it for dissection, and Meg tells him he will never be rid of the cabman. Later Donald talks with Mrs. Marsh as she and Georgina take air near a bridge. As the two converse, the little girl thinks she hears Gray's cab coming and stands up and tries to look over the ramparts. Donald is thrilled that the child can stand and begin to walk and runs to MacFarlane, but is informed by Meg that the doctor has gone to sell Gray's horse and carriage. Donald finds the doctor at an inn, where he has just completed the sale, and tells him of the success of the operation. Heartened by the news, MacFarlane sees mourners arrive and learns of a recent burial. He takes Donald and heads to a remote cemetery where they dig up the newly buried body of a woman. They place the cadaver between them in their carriage and drive home in a blinding thunderstorm. MacFarlane starts hearing Gray call to him and eventually he stops and has Donald adjust the light on the carriage so he can see the face of the corpse. He sees Gray's face and screams. This startles the horses and they take off, causing the carriage to crash off a hill. When Donald runs to the scene, he finds MacFarlane dead and near him a woman's body.

The Body Snatcher is a slick, well-made production that does not catch fire until its final five minutes, which provide terrific horror entertainment. As noted, Henry Daniell dominates the feature with his strong portrayal of MacFarlane, a brilliant physician and teacher under the cloud of having been associated with the infamous Burke and Hare. Karloff's cabman–grave robber is well modulated, the character ranging from a tender scene with the crippled child, to his bullying of MacFarlane and numerous homicides. Russell Wade's assistant is bland and surprisingly

Boris Karloff and Bela Lugosi in *The Body Snatcher* (1945).

the script makes little effort to link him romantically with the attractive young widow played by Rita Corday. Edith Atwater is quite good as MacFarlane's housekeeper, who is really his wife. As medical students, future stars Robert Clarke and Bill Williams have brief roles, while the always wonderful Mary Gordon seems a bit old to be the mourning mother of a young boy. Robert Wise's direction keeps the feature moving at a fair pace and Philip MacDonald's script, which was revised by producer Lewton under the name Carlos Keith, tries to balance the elements of Robert Louis Stevenson's story with executive producer Jack J. Gross' demands for horror content. The result is a passable effort that finishes with a flourish.

Scriptwriter MacDonald had a long career beginning in 1920 and continuing into the television era. His 1927 novel *Patrol* was the basis for RKO's *The Lost Patrol* (1934) [q.v.], also with Karloff, and he authored screenplays for the "Charlie Chan" and "Mr. Moto" series as well as the suspense classic *Rebecca* (1940).

Despite grave robbing and several killings, *The Body Snatcher* is fairly staid until the last five minutes when MacFarlane and Donald rob a grave in a creepy cemetery at night and then carry the corpse with them on their carriage ride home. As they drive through a heavy rainstorm, the cadaver keeps leaning against MacFarlane, who becomes more and more distraught until he thinks he hears Gray calling his name. When Donald shines a light on the cadaver, the medical man sees the face of Gray and goes completely mad, causing the stampede that takes his life. Few horror films have ended on a more fearful or exciting note.

The Film Daily called *The Body Snatcher* "a special treat for those who seek entertainment of the hair-raising variety.... Aimed at better-than-average audience appeal, a better-than-average budget for this type of film is evident, and the direction is noteworthy for its lip-biting suspense." *Boxoffice* opined, "It is an intelligently produced, rather artistic screen version of the Robert Louis Stevenson book [*sic*]...." That doesn't mean the picture isn't sufficiently ghoulish and horriferous to raise some neck-hairs. *The New York Times* claimed it "is certainly not the most exciting 'chiller-drama' ... but it is somewhat more credible than most and manages to hold its own with nary a werewolf or vampire." James Agee in *The Nation* termed it "a little dull and bookish" while *Harrison's Reports* said, "Skillfully produced and directed, this horror melodrama should more than satisfy those who like their screen entertainment weird and spine-chilling." When it was premiered in Great Britain in December 1945, it was cut by four minutes. *The Cinema* noted, "The unswerving devotee of the traditional spine-chiller will find plenty to absorb him there.... It must be admitted from the outset, however, that in striving too hard for effect the treatment degenerates at times into sheer absurdity, thereby lessening the total dramatic impression." *Variety* stated, "Containing horror in large doses, *The Body Snatcher* is a gruesome, low-budget chiller.... Denouement is really something to be remembered."

Bela Lugosi fans often are disappointed by his small part in *The Body Snatcher* and claim he was badly used by the producers. It should be noted that the part was written for him due to his box office potential and his performance is a good one, underplaying the role in a concise and entertaining manner. As noted, Lugosi shared equal billing with Karloff in the film's advertising, again pointing out his strong audience appeal. It was the last time the two titans of terror would work together.

The Boy with Green Hair (1948; 82 minutes; Color)

PRODUCER: Stephen Ames. EXECUTIVE PRODUCER: Dore Schary. DIRECTOR: Joseph Losey. SCREENPLAY: Ben Barzman & Alfred Lewis Levitt. STORY: Betsy Beaton. PHOTOGRAPHY: George Barnes. EDITOR: Frank Doyle. MUSIC: Leigh Harline. SONG: eben ahbez. ORCHESTRAL ARRANGEMENTS: Gil Grau. ART DIRECTORS: Ralph Berger & Albert S. D'Agostino. SOUND: Clem Portman & Earl Wolcott. SET DECORATIONS: Darrell Silvera & William Stevens. MAKEUP: Gordon Bau. GOWNS: Adele Balkan. COLOR CONSULTANT: Natalie Kalmus. ASSISTANT DIRECTOR: James Lane.

CAST: Pat O'Brien (Gramp Fry), Robert Ryan (Dr. Evans), Barbara Hale (Miss Brand), Dean Stockwell (Peter Fry, The Boy), Richard Lyon (Michael), Walter Catlett (The King), Samuel S. Hinds (Dr. Knudson), Regis Toomey (Milkman Davis), Charles Meredith (Store Owner Piper), David Clarke (Barber), Billy Sheffield (Red), John Calkins (Danny), Teddy Infuhr (Timmy), Dwayne Hickman (Joey), Russ Tamblyn, Curtis Jackson (Classmates), Charles Arnt (Mr. Hammond #2), Peter Brocco (Mr. Hammond #1), Ann Carter (Eva), Howard Brody (Eva's Brother), Al Murphy (Janitor), Anna Q. Nilsson, Lynn Whitney (Citizens), Charles Lane (Man on Street), Eula Guy (Mrs. Fisher), Dayle [Dale] Robertson, Brick Sullivan, Kenneth Patterson (Policemen), Carl Saxe (Plainclothes Policeman), Don Pietro (Newsboy), Carol Coombs, Cynthia Robichaux, Georgette Crooks, Donna Jo Gribble, Patricia Byrnes (Girls), Wendy Oser (Frail Girl), Sharon McManus (Crying Girl), Diana Graeff (Small Girl), Billy White, Baron White, Michael Losey, Speer Martin (Boys), Roger Perry (Small Boy), Ray Burkett, Warren Shannon (Old Men), Max Rose (Man).

One of RKO's most controversial features, *The Boy with Green Hair* was released theatrically in November 1948, with tepid box office results, after a somewhat convoluted production history. It was originally to be a diatribe against racial discrimination, a follow-up to the studio's successful anti–Semitic feature *Crossfire* (1947). Adrian Scott produced that film and was assigned *The Boy with Green Hair* as he and debuting director Joseph Losey helped work on the script. Scott was fired by RKO because of his failure to cooperate with the House Committee on Un-American Activities (HUAC), then investigating communist subversion in Hollywood. Stephen Ames took over as producer, thus helping the studio to make the production in color, since Ames was a

Trade advertisement for *The Boy with Green Hair* (1948).

major stockholder in Technicolor. Howard Hughes took over RKO in the spring of 1948 and wanted *The Boy with Green Hair* to reflect preparedness, instead of tolerance and pacifism. With retakes, new footage and various revisions, the film cost nearly $900,000 and ended up in the red.

The title character may have had green hair, but the production has often been labeled as "red," being cited as an example of communist infiltration in Hollywood in the post–World War II era. Not only did initial producer Scott go to prison in 1951 after being identified as a communist, but director Losey was blacklisted that year for the same reason. Thus in the late 1940s, with Soviet leader Josef Stalin's bellicose promise of Marxist world conquest, the anti-war and pacifistic messages of *The Boy with Green Hair* appeared to many to undermine American freedom. Thus the sad saga of a hard luck little boy became a battleground between right and left.

A young boy (Dean Stockwell) sits in a police station, refusing to give his name or to reveal why his head has been shaved. Dr. Evans (Robert Ryan) uses food to get the hungry boy to talk. He gives his name as Peter Fry and mentions a letter. Evans asks him to start at the beginning and Peter relates how he grew up in a happy family environment with his parents, who left him behind while they went to Europe to do war relief work. After many months a letter arrived and Peter was boarded with a series of relatives until he finally came to live with Gramp Fry (Pat O'Brien), a once-famous entertainer now reduced to working as a singing waiter. Peter does not know his parents are dead while Gramp introduces him as his grandson. Going to school, Peter is taken with his pretty teacher, Miss Brand (Barbara Hale), and soon makes friends with other children. When the school participates in a clothing drive for war orphans, Gramp borrows a car and helps Peter and his pals in their efforts. While stacking the clothes, a classmate unintentionally informs Peter that he is a war orphan since his parents are dead and the two boys fight. Gramp talks to Peter about dying and tells him his late wife was killed in a trapeze accident and how she loved to grow green plants, which to her were the sign of the hope of spring. Before he goes to bed, Peter is promised a surprise the next day by Gramp. After bathing that morning, the boy discovers he has green hair. He thinks this is a trick caused by Gramp, who is also a magician, but learns the surprise was a magician's scarf. Dr. Knudson (Samuel S. Hinds) tells Peter to either dye or cut off his hair. Not wanting to do either, the boy begs to stay home from school until his natural hair color returns. After several days he gets bored and he and Gramp go for a walk and he draws the attention of other citizens. Peter is soon an outcast and tormented by his peers. At school Miss Brand tries to point out that people have different color hair but this only makes Peter feel more ostracized. After tearing up a letter his father left for him to read when he turns 16, Peter runs into the forest and while crying hears his name being called. The war orphans on his school's posters are there and one of them suggests he use his green hair to show that war is horrible and fruitless. Peter takes hope and tries to inform adults he has green hair because he is an orphan of war. This causes further trouble since many of the townspeople think his condition is caused by tainted milk, thus damaging a milkman's (Regis Toomey) livelihood. When the citizens tell Peter to cut off his green hair, he refuses and returns to the forest hoping to find the war orphans but is chased by several boys who want to shave his head. Running back home, Peter is told by Gramp he should have his hair removed in order to be happy again. He cries as the barber (David Clarke) shaves his head and this shames Gramp and the townspeople. After Gramp tells Peter he is sorry for his suggestion, the boy runs away but is caught by the police. After hearing Peter's story, Dr. Evans tells the boy to have faith in himself and takes him to the waiting Gramp, Miss Brand and Dr. Knudson. Gramp reads to Peter the torn letter and it informs the boy that he was loved by his parents and for him to always remind others of the awfulness of war. A now proud Peter returns home with Gramp, hoping his hair will grow back green.

The fantasy elements of *The Boy with Green Hair* deal not only with the title condition, but also the scenes in the forest where Peter is confronted by the war orphans and a rather amusing, but tacky, sequence where Gramp meets an admiring King (Walter Catlett) and performs the old Irish ditty, "Tail O' Me Coat." The feature contains several well-etched character performances (Regis Toomey's milkman, Samuel S. Hinds' kindly doctor, Charles Meredith's store owner) while Robert Ryan and Barbara Hale are wasted in roles designed to add to the film's limited marquee appeal. Albert Sharpe was originally cast as Gramp but studio executives insisted he be replaced by contract star O'Brien. Dale Robertson and a young Russ Tamblyn made their screen debuts in the feature. The opening credits song "Nature Boy," composed by eben ahbez (who used only small letters in his name for religious reasons), became a hit record for Nat (King) Cole on the Capitol label.

Variety reported, "RKO has turned out an absorbing, sensitive story of tolerance and child understanding.... [T]he social significance, the tolerance and anti-war themes, are served up palatably, to make this a superior, and very moving film." Bosley Crowther in *The New York Times* opined, "A novel and noble endeavor to say something withering against war on behalf of the world's unnumbered children who are the most piteous victims thereof is made in the RKO picture, *The Boy with Green Hair*.... But the fact that the effort is earnest is no surety of its success. For all its proper intentions, the gesture falls short of its aim." *Harrison's Reports* enthused, "A fine human-interest drama.... It is a picture with a message—that of children being the real sufferers of warfare—told in terms that are most unusual but fascinating and profoundly moving.... While the film is primarily a preachment against war, it makes a poignant plea for more tolerance and child understanding.... Suitable for the entire family." *Independent Exhibitors Film Bulletin* declared it "an unconventional and gratifying motion picture. Everyone should see it. For seldom has there been such a movie, to combine delightful fantasy with vital timeliness, a movie with intelligence—and with heart. A legacy from the Dore Schary regime at RKO.... It is a picture RKO can be proud to have on its list.... It is completely acceptable as enjoyable entertainment, despite the 'message' that has been so painlessly injected—a plea against war."

The Brain Machine (1955; 84 minutes)

PRODUCER: Alec Snowden. DIRECTOR-SCREENPLAY: Ken Hughes. PHOTOGRAPHY: Josef Ambor. EDITOR: Geoffrey Muller. MUSIC DIRECTOR: Richard Taylor. ART DIRECTOR: George Haslam. SOUND: Ronald Abbott & Dick Smith. COSTUMES: Alice McLaren. MAKEUP: Jack Craig. CONTINUITY: Angela Allen. TECHNICAL CONSULTANT: Frederick Wilson. ASSISTANT DIRECTORS: Jim O'Connolly & Fred Ruff.

CAST: Maxwell Reed (Frank Smith), Elizabeth Allan (Dr. Phillipa Roberts), Patrick Barr (Dr. Geoffrey Allen), Russell Napier (Inspector Durham), Gibb McLaughlin (Spencer Simon), Neil Hallett (Detective Superintendent John Harris), Mark Bellamy (Louie), Bill Nagy (Charlie), Edwin Richfield (Henry Arthur Ryan), Clifford Buckton (Edward Jarritt), John Horsley (Dr. Richards), Donald Bisset (Major Gifford), Vanda Godsell (Mabel Smith), Hilda Barry (Mrs. Wright), Anthony Valentine (Tony), Marianne Stone (Technician), Thomas Gallagher (Bates), Gwen Bacon (Matron), Cyril Smith (Prison Warder), Henry Webb (Janitor), Joan Tyrrell (Woman in Hallway).

Psychiatrist Dr. Phillipa Roberts (Elizabeth Allan) wants a trial separation from her husband Geoffrey Allen (Patrick Barr), a physician, and takes a position at a hospital that utilizes the Electroencephalograph, a machine that studies brain waves. After using the apparatus on a maniac killer, Phillipa does the same with Frank Smith (Maxwell Reed), who is suffering from amnesia. She is surprised when both readings turn out to be very similar. She again uses the machine on Smith and it makes him recall being worked over by a gangster (Mark Bellamy) but he later denies the confession. Smith is a black market cortisone drug dealer and upon his release realizes that Phillipa knows too much about him and kidnaps her. At his hideout, she uncovers a truck full of contraband cortisone. Geoffrey begins looking for Phillipa and goes to see Smith's wife Mabel (Vanda Godsell). When gunmen employed by a dishonest chemical business murder Mabel, as revenge for Smith taking the drug, he realizes he is next and a gun battle ensues in which he avenges his wife's killing but is wounded. Geoffrey locates Smith and removes a bullet as the fugitive is captured by the police. Phillipa is freed and she and Geoffrey plan to give their marriage a second try.

The use of the title device is the sci-fi hook on which *The Brain Machine* is based. Other than that, it is the story of a crook on the run abducting a hostage who knows too much about his past, that knowledge having been attained by a futuristic invention. Written and directed by Ken Hughes, the feature, a competent "B" outing, is rather tedious in its early stages detailing the intricacies of the Electroencephalograph but starts building suspense once the drug dealer kidnaps the psychiatrist. In 1955 Hughes also directed another minor sci-fi effort, *Timeslip*, released in the U.S. as *The Atomic Man*. Co-star Elizabeth Allan appeared in other genre features like *The Lodger* (1932), released in the U.S. as *The Phantom Fiend*; *The Shadow* (1933), *Mark of the Vampire* (1935) and *Grip of the Strangler* (1958), shown stateside as *The Haunted Strangler*.

The Brain Machine was issued in Great Britain in 1954 by Anglo-Amalgamated and RKO released it in the U.S. in February 1956. *Boxoffice* opined, "The intriguing title of this British-made action melodrama is a better selling point than the English players in the cast.... It can play the lesser action spots or make a satisfactory supporting dualler generally.... [It] builds steadily to a suspenseful climax which has considerable excitement." In *British Sound Films: The Sound Era 1928–1959* (1984), David Quinlan wrote, "[S]ituations are familiar but directed with zest and ingenuity."

Breakaway (1955; 75 minutes)

PRODUCERS: Robert S. Baker & Monty Berman. DIRECTOR: Henry Cass. SCREENPLAY: Norman Hudis. STORY: Manning O'Brine. PHOTOGRAPHY: Monty Berman. EDITOR: Anne Barker. MUSIC: Stanley Black. ART DIRECTOR: Norman G. Arnold. SOUND: George Burgess.

CAST: Tom Conway (Tom "Duke" Martin), Honor Blackman (Paula Grant/Paula Jackson), Michael Balfour (Barney), Brian Worth (Johnny Matlock), Bruce Seton (Webb), Freddie Mills (Pat), Alexander Gauge (MacAllister), John Horsley (Michael Matlock), Paddy Webster (Diane Grant), John Colicos, Larry Taylor (Kidnappers), Arthur Lowe (Mitchell), Frederick Schrecker (Professor Dohlmann), Marianne Walla (Freda Dohlmann), Russell Westwood (Man from Berlin).

In 1955, Tom Conway starred as suave private eye Tom "Duke" Martin in the Associated Artists Productions feature *Barbados Quest*, which RKO issued in England under that title and in the U.S. as *Murder on Approval* (q.v.). He was teamed with a sidekick called Barney (Michael Balfour) in an attempt to recreate the screen chemistry between the Falcon and his buddy Goldie Locke in RKO's Falcon series of the 1940s. The film proved successful enough to warrant a sequel, *Breakaway*, which RKO released in England but not in the U.S. Its minor sci-fi plot element dealt with a formula for solving the problem of metal fatigue. Thus this lesser effort, which did not produce any follow-ups, was a combination mystery, science fiction and espionage thriller.

Johnny Matlock (Brian Worth) manages to go from East to West Berlin where he meets Freda Dohlmann (Marianne Walla) who takes him to her brother (Frederick Schrecker), a dying scientist who gives him a formula he has invented to reduce metal wear. Johnny is set upon by enemy agents at his hotel but manages to board a flight to London, the passenger next to him being private detective Tom "Duke" Martin (Conway). At the London air terminal, Johnny is greeted by his girlfriend Diane Grant (Paddy Webster), who works as the secretary for his brother Michael (John Horsley). Tom is met by his pal Barney (Balfour) and they are behind Johnny and Diane as they drive away. When Johnny and Diane stop to help a motorist whose car has broken down, two men (John Colicos, Larry Taylor) abduct Diane and knock out Johnny. Tom and Barney arrive on the scene and Tom finds the young woman's purse, which contains the formula, and promises her safe return.

　　　Learning that the victim frequents a club called the Crystal Jug, Tom goes there and meets beautiful Paula Jackson (Honor Blackman), who he later takes to her home. Tom realizes she is really Diane's sister. He trails her to Diane's house and back at his apartment he is assailed by the kidnappers, who take the purse. The following day, the club owner, Webb (Bruce Seton), comes to see Tom and tries to buy the formula. After he departs, Tom goes to see Michael. Webb and the two kidnappers again try to get the formula from Tom, but fail. Along with Barney, Tom talks with their friend Pat (Freddie Mills), a former boxer, the club's bartender. Johnny shows up and, after an altercation, tosses Barney into the Thames. Tom receives a telephone call telling him to go to Paula's apartment where he will find Diane but when he gets there the place is empty. He later learns that MacAllister (Alexander Gauge), a gangster, is involved and through him learns that Michael is the brains of the operation. Tom locates Diane and saves her from Webb, who runs away. Police arrest him after his car crashes. Tom and Diane locate the formula, which was concealed in her lipstick, as the gang is rounded up.

　　　Breakaway did not get shown in the U.S. until the 1960s when it was distributed to television by Warner Bros. TV. No doubt viewers were drawn to the film as it toplined Tom Conway and Honor Blackman, who had just scored as Pussy Galore in *Goldfinger* (1964), but were probably disappointed with its lack of romantic interest and Blackman's minor role. The producers' attempt to recreate the aura of the Falcon series resulted only in a tepid drama, lacking both the slickness and humor of the earlier Conway vehicles. Among the supporting players was Freddie Mills, who played an ex-boxer turned bartender. After a professional boxing career that spanned from 1936 to 1950, Mills operated a London night club. He was the world light heavyweight boxing champion from 1948 to 1950, British Empire light heavyweight title holder from 1942 to 1944 and European light heavyweight champion from 1947 to 1948.

　　　In *British Sound Films: The Studio Years 1928–1959* (1984), David Quinlan wrote of *Breakaway*, "Tedious thriller with regulation car chases."

The Brighton Strangler (1945; 67 minutes)

　　　PRODUCER: Herman Schlom. EXECUTIVE PRODUCER: Sid Rogell. DIRECTOR: Max Nosseck. SCREENPLAY: Max Nosseck & Arnold Phillips. ADDITIONAL DIALOGUE: Hugh Gray. PHOTOGRAPHY: J. Roy Hunt. EDITOR: Les Milbrook. MUSIC: Leigh Harline. MUSIC DIRECTOR: C. Bakaleinikoff. ART DIRECTORS: Ralph Berger & Albert S. D'Agostino. SET DECORATIONS: Harley Miller & Darrell Silvera. SOUND: Roy Meadows & James G. Stewart. SPECIAL EFFECTS: Vernon L. Walker. GOWNS: Renie. MONTAGE: Harold Palmer. ASSISTANT DIRECTOR: Lloyd Richards.

　　　CAST: John Loder (Reginald "Reggie" Parker), June Duprez (April Manby Carson), Michael St. Angel (Lieutenant Bob Carson), Miles Mander (Chief Inspector W.R. Allison), Rose Hobart (Dorothy Kent), Gilbert Emery (Dr. Manby), Rex Evans (Leslie Shelton), Matthew Boulton (Inspector Graham), Olaf Hytten (Banks), Lydia Bilbrook (Mrs. Manby), Ian Wolfe (Lord Mayor Herman Brandon R. Clive), Gavin Muir (Captain Perry), Colin Kenny (Inspector Higgins), Stanley Mann, Milton Owen, Robert R. Stephenson, Frank Baker (Police Inspectors), Frank Mayo, Alan Ward, Tom Burton, Steve Winston (Policemen), Wheaton Chambers (Clerk), Dorothy Stone (Miss Kent's Maid), Mary McLeod (Pamela), David Thursby (Fireman), Ellen George Ferguson (Mrs. Shackleton), George Broughton, George Atkinson, Frank Benson (Bellboys), Alec Harford (Ticket Clerk), Norman Ainsley, Joe North (Passengers), Florence Wix (Mrs. Kent), Victor Cutler, Harry Clay (Pilots), Lilyan Irene (Emily), Herbert Evans (Manby's Butler), Connie Leon (Mrs. Clive), Robert Cory (Chauffeur), Alec Craig (Bellhop with Vacuum Cleaner), Lillian Bronson (Hotel Maid), Joy Harington (Pub Barmaid), Robin Sanders Clark (British Pilot), Tom McGuire (Bartender), Audrey Manners (Cashier), Sherry Hall (Hotel Desk Clerk), Elaine Riley (Young Woman), Eric Wilton (Luggage Clerk), Gus Taillon (Newsboy).

　　　"See It All and Stay Awake for a Week!" proclaimed RKO's advertisement for *The Brighton Strangler*, issued in the fall of 1945 on a double bill with *The Body Snatcher* (q.v.). According to the hype, it "presents one of the screen's most unique treatments of murder mysteries. Suspense mounts in intensity because the audience knows the murderer but the cast does not.... [It] adds up to a superior thrill-film as modern as tomorrow's headlines." Unfortunately the ballyhoo could not cover up a deficient dramatic product that did not scare and only barely entertained. John Loder, in a part far better suited for Tom Conway, is bland as a decent man who becomes a homicidal maniac due to a head injury. June Duprez (in a role Jean Brooks should have played) hardly registers as the leading lady and she is matched by Michael St. Angel (who later changed his name to Steven Flagg) as her secret husband. The title character commits two murders, both victims public officials, but the light-colored gloves he uses in dispatching his victims are more comical than horrifying. The most realistic part of the film is its use of air raid footage and its aftermath of a devastated London. Overall, it was a slick, well-made production without chills or thrills.

Stage star Reginald "Reggie" Parker (Loder) has grown tired of playing the title role in the stage success *The Brighton Stranger,* written by his fiancée Dorothy Kent (Rose Hobart). The play's producer, Leslie Shelton (Rex Evans), wants him to continue in the part for another year but he refuses since he and Dorothy plan to wed when the play closes in a week. Dorothy travels to Canterbury, where she and Reggie are to marry, and after the last performance of the play Reggie thanks the cast and gives his valet Banks (Olaf Hytten) a Christmas present. The Mayfield Theatre, where the play was staged, is bombed by German planes and Reggie is hit on the head by a falling beam. When he awakens in a bewildered condition, he finds a luggage ticket in his pocket and goes to Victoria Station. There he gets in line behind WAAF April Manby (Duprez) and, hearing her speak dialogue from the play, Reggie thinks he is Edward Grey, the character he portrayed in the production. Aboard a train, April tends to his head wound, and when they reach Brighton she introduces him to her parents, Dr. Manby (Gilbert Emery) and Mrs. Manby (Lydia Bilbrook). He tells them he is writing a book and they invite him to their home for a Christmas Eve party. Dorothy is mistakenly informed of her fiancé's death. Grey realizes he must murder the town's mayor (Ian Wolfe), as in the play, and goes to his home that night in a snowstorm and strangles him with a cord. He sets the victim's watch ahead and then breaks it. He attends the Manby party where April confides in him that she is married to American Lieutenant Bob Carson (St. Angel), who Grey met at the train station when he came to see April. She asks him to keep their secret since her mother has not yet gotten over the death of her brother, a pilot who was shot down a few weeks before. Chief Inspector Allison (Miles Mander) investigates the mayor's murder and has his men question all strangers in town; Grey has an alibi since he was at the Manby party. When April learns her husband is coming to Brighton, Grey offers to meet him at the station. At their hotel, Grey and Bob agree to meet for a drink but when Bob goes to Grey's room he hears him talking in his sleep. At the Manby home, Grey is introduced to Allison and later the sound of a vacuum cleaner causes him to believe he has to kill the inspector, as in the play. Several days later Grey spots Allison going into a movie theater and follows him. When he is about to strangle the inspector, he is disturbed by newsreel footage of the bombing of the Mayfield Theatre. Allison sees Grey in the theater lobby and the two agree to meet at the policeman's home later in the evening to discuss criminology. Bob informs April he does not trust Grey but she tells him he is jealous and they need this new friend to help conceal their marriage. April asks Grey to pretend to take her to a concert while she really meets Bob. Grey then goes to Allison's home and, after seeing his collection of weapons used in murder cases he solved, Grey admits killing the lord mayor and then strangles the inspector. Allison's blind neighbor, Captain Perry (Gavin Muir), arrives to return a record he borrowed and is unaware of the homicide. Bob is called back to his base and April goes to the concert but does not find Grey. Later she meets

Advertisement for *The Brighton Strangler* (1945).

Grey at his hotel and asks him why he was not at the concert. He suggests they go for a walk along some nearby cliffs and as he starts to strangle her she mentions New Year's Eve, a clue to the final act in the play. Grey becomes dizzy and April assists him back to his hotel, where he invites her to travel with him to London to celebrate the new year with Bob. At a London pub, Bob sees a poster featuring Grey and the barmaid (Joy Harington) informs him the actor was killed in an air raid. Bob takes the poster to Inspector Graham (Matthew Boulton) and tells him it is the picture of a man he knows in Brighton. Since Grey's body was never found, Graham and Bob go to see Dorothy. During their visit with her, a radio broadcast announces the murder of Allison. Dorothy realizes Reggie is living the part of Grey and says the play ends at a hotel roof garden. The trio go to the nearest such spot and find Reggie and April already there. They see Reggie try to strangle April and as Graham is about to shoot him, Dorothy says to applaud, which halts Reggie's actions. He looks at his audience, takes a step back to acknowledge their applause and falls backward onto the concrete floor. Dying, Reggie regains his senses as Dorothy tells him the play has ended.

In a snide two-paragraph review of *The Brighton Strangler* in the *New York Times,* Bosley Crowther ridicules it without really saying much about it. *Boxoffice* said it lacked "suspense and movement—usually found in successful offerings of its ilk. John Loder, in the title role, is about as menacing as a bowl of mush."

The reviewer also noted, "Picture's best assets are its production values and the exploitability of the story's unusual twist." *Variety* thought it "a neatly grooved psychological melodrama.... Mood is well-sustained in building to climax and Max Nosseck's direction restrains the playing for realistic effects. John Loder's lead spot is excellently treated, character maintaining sympathy despite wanton killings." *The Film Daily* wrote, "Boasting unique opening sequence for a good mystery thriller, the film then takes a nosedive on imagination; and its obvious lack of suspense plus the incredible casting of John Loder as a victim of shock who turns killer takes the edge off the purpose of this film." In *B Movies* (1973), Don Miller noted, "The nucleus of the plot was gainfully used by Ruth Gordon and Garson Kanin for Ronald Colman later on in *A Double Life* (1947), with great difference in details; the present item was nothing more than humdrum horror...."

Bunco Squad (1950; 67 minutes)

PRODUCER: Lewis J. Rachmil. DIRECTOR: Herbert I. Leeds. SCREENPLAY: George Callahan. STORY: Reginald Taviner. PHOTOGRAPHY: Henry Freulich. EDITOR: Desmond Marquette. MUSIC: Paul Sawtell. ART DIRECTORS: Albert S. D'Agostino & Walter E. Keller. SOUND: Frank Sarver & Clem Portman. SET DECORATIONS: Darrell Silvera & James Altwies. MAKEUP: Fred Phillips. HAIR STYLIST: Stephanie Garland. PRODUCTION MANAGERS: John Burch & Walter Daniels. ASSISTANT DIRECTOR: John E. Pommer.

CAST: Robert Sterling (Detective Sergeant Steve Johnson), Joan Dixon (Grace Bradshaw/Madame Bradshaw/Movie Bride), Ricardo Cortez (Tony Weldon/Anthony Wells), Douglas Fowley (Detective Sergeant Mack McManus), Marguerite Churchill (Barbara Madison), Elisabeth Risdon (Jessica Royce), John Kellogg (Fred Reed), Bernadene Hayes (Princess Liane), Robert Bice (Swami Drake), Vivien Oakland (Annie Cobb), Dante (Himself), Tol Avery (Captain Edwards), Frank Wilcox (Dr. Largo/Mike Finlayson/Benjamin Lazetti), Rand Brooks (Robert), Pauline Garon (Mary), John Hamilton (Lawyer), Dick Elliott (Realtor), Elizabeth Flournoy (Beautician), Richard Irving (Danny Bowman), James Craven (Swami Swenson), Earle Hodgins (Professor Markett), Harry Lauter (Disabled Veteran), Don Dillaway (Bible Salesman), John Parrish (Detective Rand), Fred Aldrich (Desk Detective), Robert F. Hill (Preacher), Art Dupuis (Golfer), Eddie Rochelle (Gangster), Al Murphy (Cab Driver), Ann Tyrrell (Miss Dilby), Donald Kerr (Film Bunco Artist), Forbes Murray (Film Bunco Victim), Thomas Martin (Waiter), Marie Osborne (Laundry Clerk), Jack Chefe (Maitre d'), James Conaty (Movie Bride's Father), Victor Cutler (Movie Bridegroom), Jack Gargan (Movie Director), Jewel Rose (Young Widow).

A re-working of 1938's *Crime Ring* (q.v.), *Bunco Squad* was released theatrically in September 1950, and like its predecessor dealt with exposing the spiritualist racket. Outside of a couple of spooky séances utilizing astral voices and ectoplasm, there is little of the supernatural in this version although it is a compact, fast-paced effort filled with delightful cameo performances, such as Earle Hodgins as numerologist Professor Markett, Rand Brooks and Pauline Garon as séance participants and Ann Tyrrell as a bunco victim. Robert Sterling and Douglas Fowley handle the hero parts in good fashion, as does Joan Dixon as the actress wheedled into helping them expose the murderous operation. Ricardo Cortez, as the leader of the gang, is at his most polished, oily best and he gets great support from those playing his cohorts: Bernadene Hayes, John Kellogg, Vivien Oakland and Robert Bice. Elisabeth Risdon comes across well as the wealthy intended victim as does Marguerite Churchill as her doubting secretary. Dante the Magician, who also appeared in the Stan Laurel-Oliver Hardy feature *A-Haunting We Will Go* (1942), has some good

Lobby card for *Bunco Squad* (1950) picturing Douglas Fowley, Robert Sterling and Joan Dixon.

moments, especially in the scene where he and Fowley, dressed in black robes, rough up Bice, who gets punchy swinging at phantoms in the dark.

At a society meeting, bunco squad Detective Sergeants Steve Johnson (Sterling) and Mack MacManus (Fowley) show a film about swindle artists and their methods. They are called back to headquarters by their superior, Captain Edwards (Tol Avery), who informs them that, at the scene of recent suicide by a banker bilked by a crooked racket, astrology magazines were found. He assigns them to see if there is any connection and they question a variety of fortune tellers, spiritualist racket swindlers, taro card readers and numerologists, including Professor Markett (Hodgins) and mediums Annie Cobb (Oakland) and Liane (Bernadene Hayes). Liane's former partner, Anthony Wells (Cortez), now known as Tony Weldon, meets wealthy widow Jessica Royce (Risdon) and her attractive secretary Barbara Madison (Churchill) on a train and later takes Barbara to dinner. When he finds out that Jessica sees consulting psychologist Dr. Largo (Frank Wilcox), Wells visits Liane and wants to bury the hatchet over taking a three-year prison rap while he went free. He tells her they should unite with Annie, Swami Drake (Bice) and con man Fred Reed (Kellogg) to bilk Jessica out of her two million dollar fortune. They form the Rama Society, a religious organization dealing with the science of the occult. When Steve takes his aspiring actress girlfriend Grace Bradshaw (Joan Dixon) to dinner, he spots Liane with Drake. Tony has his minions learn all they can about Jessica's dead war hero son Philip and then has Reed force Largo, under the threat of revealing his past, to call Jessica and suggest she attend a society function. Going with Barbara, Jessica observes as Liane, now called Madame Liane, calls Jessica's son from the beyond and hears him call her by the pet name Sicca. Convinced of Liane's powers, Jessica asks for another sitting the next day. When Steve finds out that Liane, Annie and Drake have disappeared, he traces Liane to a laundry and follows her to the society's mansion headquarters. They refuse to talk to him and, since he does not have a search warrant, he leaves. Then he sees Jessica as she arrives and takes down the license plate number on her car. He later tries to convince her the society is a fake. Jessica refuses to listen but as they are talking, Reed tampers with the brakes on Steve's car. He later loses control of the vehicle and ends up in the hospital. Tony tells his cohorts they need to convince Jessica to make the society the beneficiary in her will and afterward they will eliminate the woman and get away since Rama is a registered corporation and their names will not be revealed. As he is getting out of the hospital, Steve is informed by McManus that Liane and Reed were once involved with Tony. Steve suspects he is behind the phony operation. Needing someone to act as a rival medium in order to trap the gang, Steve convinces Grace to do it and he takes her to retired magician Dante (played by himself), who teaches her the tricks of the trade. A convalescing soldier (Harry Lauter) who knew Philip tells Steve to see the dead man's best friend Danny Bowman (Richard Irving), who lives in Kansas City. From Bowman, Steve obtains the last letter Philip wrote to his mother, one that was never mailed. Jessica has her lawyer (John Hamilton) change her will, making the Rama Society her beneficiary. Barbara, who has never believed in Liane's abilities, attempts to call Steve but when she fails to locate him she confides in Tony and he suggests they go to the police. The next day, newspaper headlines report that Barbara has been killed in an auto accident. Realizing Barbara has been murdered, Steve threatens to expose Dr. Largo's past unless he gets Jessica to see Grace, now set up as a medium at Dante's home and using the name Madame Bradshaw. Jessica consults Grace and is told of Philip's letter and decides to change her will. Tony tells Drake to rough up Grace but he is stopped by McManus and Dante. Steve follows Drake back to the society's headquarters and locates a secret room with recordings of Jessica's sessions. Tony and Reed go to Dante's house and knock out the magician and McManus. Reed cuts the brake line on their car so they can kill off Jessica. When she arrives to see Grace, the two crooks force Jessica out of the house at gunpoint but Steve arrives and shoots Reed. Tony attempts to make a getaway in the car but loses control on the highway and dies in a fiery crash. The rest of the society's members are taken into custody. After Grace finishes a movie wedding scene, McManus informs her that Steve has been promoted to lieutenant.

Variety wrote, "As a programmer for lowercase bookings, *Bunco Squad* will get by. There's nothing out of the ordinary in its makeup.... Plot could have been less complicated and Herbert I. Leeds' overall directorial pace faster.... Lewis J. Rachmil has handled the budget production capably to get the best physical values for money spent."

Boxoffice stated, "Considering its budgetary classification and the exhibition niche at which it is aimed, about the only criticism that can be made of this constable-and-crooks drama is that the writers undertook to contain too many elements in the script, including a semi-documentary approach to the yarn's spinning. Producer Lewis J. Rachmil made every production dollar count and the direction of Herbert I. Leeds extracts everything possible from the story and performers."

Captive Women (1952; 64 minutes)

PRODUCERS-SCREENPLAY: Jack Pollexfen & Aubrey Wisberg. ASSOCIATE PRODUCER: Albert Zugsmith. DIRECTOR: Stuart Gilmore. PHOTOGRAPHY: Paul Ivano. EDITOR: Fred R. Feitshans, Jr. MUSIC: Charles Koff. SOUND: Frank McWhorter. PRODUCTION DESIGNER: Theobold Holsopple. SET DECORATIONS: Clarence Steenson. SPECIAL PHOTOGRAPHIC EFFECTS: Jack Rabin & Irving Block. MECHANICAL

EFFECTS: Rocky Cline. COSTUMES: Yvonne Wood. MAKEUP: Steven Clensos. ASSISTANT DIRECTOR: Ken Walters.

CAST: Robert Clarke (Rob), Margaret Field (Ruth), Gloria Saunders (Catherine), Ron Randell (Riddon), Stuart Randall (Gordon), Paul Dorety, Chili Williams (Norm Captives), Robert Bice (Bram), William Schallert (Carver), Eric Colmar (Sabron), Douglas Evans (Jason), James Guilfoyle (Eric), John Close (Danbridge), Jason Robards, Marshall Bradford, Jack Baston (Mutate Councilmen), Tom Daly (Durk), Lia Waggner (Mutate Woman), Barbara Hill, Cathy Qualen, June Jeffrey, Barbara O'Brien (Norm Women), George Bruggeman, Theodore Lynch (Norm Hunters).

Producers Jack Pollexfen and Aubrey Wisberg wrote the screenplay for a futuristic science fiction film called *3000 A.D.*, following the success of their initial outing *The Man from Planet X* (United Artists, 1951). After signing a three-picture contract with RKO, Pollexfen and Wisberg filmed *3000 A.D.* with *Planet X* leads Robert Clarke, Margaret Field and William Schallert, plus composer Charles Koff and editor Fred R. Feitshans, Jr., who also worked on the 1951 production. Albert Zugsmith joined the Pollexfen-Wisberg team as associate producer. The feature was not released for nearly 18 months and when it was, the title was changed to *Captive Women* upon the insistence of RKO chief Howard Hughes, who thought it was more exploitable.

The film opens with a dry prologue expounding on the use of atomic energy for good and then jumps a thousand years into the future with the planet a dark, murky world as a result of a nuclear war. Overall, *Captive Women* is little more than a mediocre cardboard drama. This is lamentable considering the talent involved, including cinematographer Paul Ivano, production designer Theobold Holsopple and set decorator Clarence Steenson. There is very little horrifying in the feature as the Mutates are not repulsive and there are no monsters. Even its post-nuclear barren world is no more littered than most large city ghettos. While *Captive Women* is an ancestor of the later sci-fi subgenre of a war-torn, bleak post-nuclear holocaust world, it is still only a very minor effort at best.

A thousand years after the final atomic war, a trio of tribes try to survive in what was once the New York area. In a dry and burned-out land, the Norms are devil worshippers while the scarred Mutates follow Christianity. A third group, the Up-River Men, are brutal scavengers. On his wedding day, Rob (Clarke), son of Norm leader Eric (James Guifoyle), hunts with his friend Bram (Robert Bice) and they see the chief of the Up-River Men, Gordon (Stuart Randall), murder a captured Mutate. As he is about to kill Riddon (Ron Randell), a second captive, Rob intervenes and the Mutate is set free. Gordon and his men are on their way to Rob's wedding, although they are not trusted by the Norms. Unknown to Eric, tribesman Jason (Douglas Evans) is the lover of Rob's treacherous fiancée Catherine (Gloria Saunders), the daughter of a high priest. After arriving at the Norms' camp, the Up-River Men plot with traitorous Jason to overthrow Eric. As the wedding ceremony dance takes place, Gordon murders Eric and the Up-River Men battle the Norms, with Rob and Bram escaping. In a wooded area, the two Norms are captured by Riddon and his band but because they earlier spared him, Riddon takes them into a hidden cave and they cross the Hudson River through an abandoned subway tunnel. There they are tried by three councilmen (Jason Robards, Marshall Bradford, James Baston). Riddon, who is only slightly scarred, comes to their defense. The captives are ordered never to return to their people or reveal the Mutates' hideout. At the Norms' compound, Gordon performs a wedding ceremony for Catherine and Jason and then declares Jason the new leader of his tribe. As Jason sits in the leader's chair, he is strangled by Gordon's henchman Danbridge (John Close) while Gordon takes the Norm women for himself and his men. One of the Norm women, Ruth (Field), spurns the Up-River Men and is punished when she defies Catherine, who has allied herself with Gordon. At the Mutate camp, jealous Carver (Schallert) foments trouble and tries to take over

Poster for *Captive Women* (1952).

Riddon's position as leader. With the help of tribesman Sabron (Eric Colmar), Carver challenges Riddon to combat but is defeated and exiled. After another Mutate baby is born deformed, Riddon and his men capture several Norm women for breeding purposes, including Ruth. Carver tries to ally himself with Gordon by agreeing to lead the Up-River Men to the Mutates' camp in return for becoming his tribe's leader. Ruth tries to get away from the Mutates but is recaptured by Riddon, who kisses her. Carver leads the Up-River Men through the tunnel and they attack the Mutates but he is killed as the Norm women are retaken by the Up-River Men, who also capture Riddon. Having escaped from the Up-River Men, Rob and Bram plot to free Riddon and meet Catherine, who says she has fled from the brutal Gordon. Rob forgives Catherine for her treachery and she agrees to lead him and Bram to the Norm conclave. As they near the locale, Rob turns on Catherine and tells Bram she is faking. They tie her up and use a sewer pipe to get into the underground tunnel. Catherine escapes her bonds and runs to Gordon, who kills her, and then takes his men to the Mutates' river cave. Rob and Bram have the Mutates loosen the pilings holding up the roof of the tunnel as Ruth takes food to the imprisoned Riddon and the two confirm their love for each other. Rob and Bram find Riddon and Ruth, Bram uses a large rock to loosen the prison bars and Riddon is able to escape. As Gordon and his men invade the cave, Rob, Bram, Riddon and Ruth climb out of the tunnel. The Mutates knock down the pilings and water comes rushing into the tunnel, drowning Gordon and his men. With a new alliance between the Norms and the Mutates, Riddon and Ruth are married, thus beginning a new freedom for both tribes.

The Hollywood Reporter termed Captive Women "a pretentious, long-winded dissertation" on the future of the human race, while Boxoffice felt it "a provocative and thoughtfully developed science fiction opus.... Within the limitations of its modest budget, the offering ... carries considerable dramatic impact...." Variety declared it "an elongated cliffhanger," adding, "All imaginative touches are kept hidden as the plot ploddingly relates the efforts of a New Jersey tribe to bear offspring who will not possess their hideous features.... Most of the acting is in the serial film tradition although Ron Randell occasionally shows himself as a first-rate actor."

After Captive Women, Robert Clarke next starred for producers Jack Pollexfen, Aubrey Wisberg and Albert Zugsmith in the swashbuckler Sword of Venus, a 1953 RKO release. In 1956 Captive Women was re-titled 1000 Years from Now and was reissued alongside the Zugsmith production Invasion U.S.A. (Columbia, 1953) on a double bill. When released in the United Kingdom, Captive Women reverted to its original title, 3000 A.D.

Cat People (1942; 73 minutes)

PRODUCER: Val Lewton. DIRECTOR: Jacques Tourneur. SCREENPLAY: DeWitt Bodeen. PHOTOGRAPHY: Nicholas Musuraca. EDITOR: Mark Robson. MUSIC: Roy Webb. MUSIC DIRECTOR: C. Bakaleinikoff. ART DIRECTORS: Albert S. D'Agostino & Walter E. Keller. SOUND: John L. Cass. SET DECORATIONS: Al Fields & Darrell Silvera. GOWNS: Renie. ASSISTANT DIRECTOR: Doran Cox.

CAST: Simone Simon (Irena Dubrovna Reed), Kent Smith (Oliver Reed), Tom Conway (Dr. Louis Judd), Jane Randolph (Alice Moore), Jack Holt (Commodore), Alan Napier (Doc Carver), Elizabeth Dunn (Miss Plunkett), Elizabeth Russell (Strange Woman), Mary Halsey (Blondie), Alec Craig (Zookeeper), Betty Roadman (Mrs. Hansen), Dot Farley (Mrs. Agnew), Charles Jordan (Bus Driver), Donald Kerr (Taxi Driver), Theresa Harris (Waitress Minnie), John Piffle (Café Owner), Murdock MacQuarrie (Zoo Sheepman), Eddie Dew (Policeman), Connie Leon (Neighbor), Henrietta Burnside (Sue Ellen), Stephen Soldi (Organ Grinder), Dynamite (Panther).

In the early 1940s, RKO attempted to emulate the box office profits of Universal by forming a unit to make modestly budgeted horror features. Hired to head the team was Val Lewton, one-

Simone Simon and Tom Conway in *Cat People* (1942).

time editorial assistant and story editor for producer David O. Selznick. While RKO demanded exploitable titles, Lewton wanted to make psychological horror films that stressed fear of the unknown instead of fiends and monsters. With the assistance of cinematographer Nicholas Musuraca, Lewton used lighting and shadows to create fright effects that amplified horrors in the minds of the audience in his first effort, *Cat People*. Released late in 1942, the film was budgeted at around $150,000 and grossed more that twice that amount, leading to further Lewton productions at RKO. In many ways, *Cat People* is a seminal entry in the horror film field in that it not only has horrific aspects but also permits the viewer to decide whether or not the character of Irene (Simone Simon) is really capable of transformation into a feline or if it is all in her mind.

Fashion illustrator Irene Dubrovna (Simon) is sketching a panther at a zoo when she meets maritime engineer Oliver Reed (Kent Smith). They strike up an acquaintance and Irene invites Oliver to her apartment for tea, telling him he is the first friend she has made since arriving in town. As they leave the zoo, she throws away the sketch she made, that of a panther with a dagger through it. As evening comes on, Irene tells Oliver she likes living near the zoo because the sounds of the animals calm her. When he asks her about a statue she owns, Irene says it is King John, who overcame the invaders of her homeland of Serbia and cleansed her village of witches, the most evil of whom fled to the mountains. Oliver wants to see Irene again and she agrees. The next day he buys her a kitten which he takes to work at the C.R. Cooper Ship and Barge Company. There the kitten catches the attention of his boss, the Commodore (Jack Holt), and fellow engineers Alice Moore (Jane Randolph) and Doc Carver (Alan Napier). That evening Oliver gives Irene the kitten but it is afraid of her so they take it back to the pet shop where all the animals become agitated by Irene's presence. Miss Plunkett (Elizabeth Dunn), the owner, tells Irene and Oliver that some people cannot be around animals and Oliver trades the kitten for a small song bird.

Oliver asks Irene to marry him but she says she is afraid of her animal instincts, which he claims are based on her ancestors' folklore. Irene accepts Oliver's proposal and at their wedding celebration, the Commodore confides to Carver that he thinks Irene is a bit strange. Also at the restaurant is a feline-looking woman (Elizabeth Russell) who approaches Irene and calls her "sister" in Serbian, causing the new bride to cross herself. That night Irene pleads with Oliver to be patient with her as they sleep in separate rooms. When she goes back to the zoo to see the panther, its keeper (Alec Craig) says the animal is evil. Irene later accidentally kills the song bird and takes its body to the zoo and feeds it to the big cat. After a month, Irene is still afraid to consummate their marriage and asks Oliver to find her a good psychiatrist. She goes to see Dr. Louis Judd (Conway) and under hypnosis reveals that she fears she has the capability to kill because of passion and that her mother was called a witch. Returning to the apartment, Irene finds Oliver talking with Alice and learns it was Alice who suggested that Irene consult Dr. Judd. Humiliated that Alice knows of her marital problems, Irene asks her to leave. Later that night she returns to see the panther. When she comes home Oliver apologizes and she pleads with him not to quarrel with her again. The next day at work, Alice tells Oliver she loves him. At the zoo, Irene runs into Dr. Judd, who informs her that the panther can be used as an instrument of death. When Oliver learns from Alice that Irene has not been seeing Dr. Judd, he confronts her and says he fears their marriage is failing. Oliver leaves to return to work. Irena later spies her husband sitting in a café with Alice. After Oliver informs Alice of his continuing troubles with his wife, she tells him he will have to solve his own problems and walks home but fears she is being followed. As she takes a bus home, a number of sheep at the zoo are found mutilated. That night an upset Irene dreams of cats and a key, with Dr. Judd becoming King John of Serbia. After stealing the key from the panther's cage, Irene goes with Oliver and Alice to a ship model exhibit but feels ignored and leaves. At Alice's apartment house, Alice decides to go swimming in the basement pool but becomes frightened when she hears a growl and sees a panther's shadow. Alice jumps into the water and screams but Irene turns on the lights and says her she is searching for her husband. When the desk clerk (Mary Halsey) gives Alice her robe, she finds it has been shredded. An agitated Alice asks Dr. Judd to come to her apartment house and she tells him she believes Irene can turn into a panther. He dismisses her story until he sees the tattered robe. When Irene goes to see the doctor again, she informs him she has lapses of memory and is afraid she will transform into a cat and kill Oliver if they make love. Judd says he cannot help her and that her actions approach insanity and he could have her put away for observation. He pleads with her to forget

Advertisement for *Cat People* (1942).

the legends of her country and try to lead a normal life. That night when Oliver returns home, Irena tells him she is no longer afraid but he confesses he loves Alice and wants a divorce. Distraught, Irene tells Oliver to leave. Oliver meets with Alice and Dr. Judd and they decide to have Irene committed for observation. That night the trio wait for Irene at the apartment but when she fails to show, Oliver and Jane go back to work as Dr. Judd fixes the front door lock so he can return. While they are working, Oliver and Jane hear a cat growl and fear they are being stalked by Irene. Backed against a wall with Jane, Oliver orders Irene to leave and uses a T-bar as a crucifix and its shadow causes the menace to depart. When Irene returns home, she finds Dr. Judd there. As he attempts to seduce her, he is attacked by a large cat which he wounds with a saber concealed in his cane. Oliver and Alice return to the apartment and hear Judd's screams and find him murdered as the injured Irene goes to the zoo. She opens the panther's cage and the cat leaps at her and then runs away, only to be run over by a taxi. When Oliver and Alice arrive at the zoo, they find a dead body in front of the cage.

Cat People is one of the earliest examples of RKO re-utilizing the mansion set constructed for *The Magnificent Ambersons*, released earlier in 1942, and it belies the horror film's modest budget. In some respects, the feature has a dream-like quality about it, especially in the scenes with the panther supposedly afoot. The sequence where Alice walks home at night with the feeling of being stalked is hair-raising, as is the sequence where she is cornered in the basement swimming pool by her feline tormenter. Equally harrowing is the dark office scene where Oliver and Jane are pursued by the big cat, with the sign of the cross used to scare off the creature.

All of this, however, is problematic since the story leaves it up to the viewer to decide if the horror is real or imagined. Even the last shots at the zoo are vague since a black figure is seen lying dead in front of the panther cage but the camera is too far away for viewers to tell if the body is human or animal.

Over the years *Cat People* has become a cult classic but at the time of its release it got a mixed critical reaction. *Variety* reported, "This is a weird drama of thrill-chill caliber, with developments of surprises confined to psychology and mental reactions, rather than transformation to grotesque and marauding characters for visual impact on the audiences.... [Director Jacques Tourneur] does a fine job with a most difficult assignment." *Boxoffice* complained, "Grim and unrelenting, this is a dose of horror best suited to addicts past the curable stage [and is] definitely not for children, young or old.... Potent stuff, straight from the psychopathic clinic." Bosley Crowther's snippy one-paragraph review in *The New York Times* said the heroine's predicament was "pursued at tedious and graphically unproductive length," adding it was "a labored and obvious attempt to induce shock. Miss Simon's cuddly little tabby would barely frighten a mouse under a chair." *Photoplay* judged, "It will give you icy jitters, but it's kinda fun at that."

In 1944 Lewton produced a sequel called *The Curse of the Cat People* (q.v.), again written by DeWitt Bodeen, with Simone Simon, Kent Smith and Jane Randolph repeating their roles although this time in a fantasy–fairy tale setting. While the character of Dr. Judd was killed in *Cat People*, Tom Conway reprised the character in Lewton's *The Seventh Victim* (q.v.) in 1943. *Cat People* was reissued theatrically by RKO in 1952. With far more emphasis on eroticism, *Cat People* was remade in 1982 by director Paul Schrader, starring Nastassia Kinski, Malcolm McDowell, John Heard and Annette O'Toole. It was poor compared to the original.

Check and Double Check (1930; 76 minutes)

PRODUCER: William LeBaron. ASSOCIATE PRODUCER: Bertram Millhauser. DIRECTOR: Melville Brown. SCREENPLAY-STORY: Bert Kalmar & Harry Ruby. ADAPTATION: J. Walter Ruben. PHOTOGRA-

PHY: William Marshall. EDITOR: Claude Berkeley. MUSIC: Bert Kalmar, Harry Ruby, Duke Ellington, Joseph Carl Breil, Clarence Lucas, Irving Mills & James "Bubber" Miley. SOUND: George D. Ellis. SCENERY-COSTUMES: Max Ree.

CAST: Freeman F. Gosden (Amos), Charles J. Correll (Andy), Sue Carol (Jean Blair), Irene Rich (Mrs. Blair), Ralf Harolde (Ralph Crawford), Charles S. Morton (Richard Williams), Edward Martindel (John Blair), Rita La Roy (Elinor Crawford), Russ Powell (Kingfish), Roscoe Ates (Brother Arthur), Duke Ellington & His Cotton Club Orchestra (Themselves), Robert Homans (Butler Mason), Pat Conway (Henchman), G. Pat Collins (Policeman), Bud Flanagan [Dennis O'Keefe], Larry Steers (Guests), The Rhythm Boys [Bing Crosby, Harry Barris, Al Rinker] (Vocalists).

Freeman F. Gosden and Charles J. Correll created the characters of black Harlem cabbies Sam and Henry on Chicago's WGN radio in 1926 and changed the characters' names to Amos and Andy when they joined WMAQ in 1928. The next year *Amos 'n' Andy* was broadcast on NBC and remained on that network for a decade until switching to CBS in 1939. By 1943 the show was back on NBC but reverted to CBS in 1948. In 1954 its title was changed to *Amos and Andy Music Hall* and it remained on the air until late in 1960. The program was one of radio's all-time popular shows with a listening audience of 40 million during the 1930s and 1940s.

Radio Pictures signed Gosden and Correll to repeat their radio roles in the film *Check and Double Check* with the two actors appearing in black makeup. Two other white actors, Russ Powell as Kingfish and Roscoe Ates as Brother Arthur, also appeared in blackface in the film.

Check and Double Check was a big moneymaker for Radio Pictures but despite their radio popularity, Amos and Andy did not have staying power on film. Their only other feature was *The Big Broadcast of 1936* (1935) in which they made a guest appearance. Once viewers had witnessed the novelty of their radio favorites in theaters, the feature failed to draw in second runs or reissues. Overall, it is quite amusing with the radio stars adapting well to the film medium and giving viewers lots of laughs with their adventures. The horror aspect of the movie takes place when the duo visits a supposedly haunted house at midnight during a thunderstorm as part of a lodge ritual. Another plus for the feature is the appearance of Duke Ellington and His Cotton Club Orchestra, including Barney Bigard, Sonny Greer, Johnny Hodges, Freddie Jenkins and Cootie Williams. They perform "Old Man Blues," "East St. Louis Toodle-O" and "Three Little Words," the latter composed by Bert Kalmar and Harry Ruby, who also wrote the film's script. The vocal on "Three Little Words" is sung on the soundtrack by the Rhythm Boys, made up of Bing Crosby, Harry Barris and Al Rinker. The *Amos 'n' Andy* radio theme, "The Perfect Song," is played over the opening credits.

A traffic jam takes place in New York City as wealthy John Blair (Edward Martindel) and his wife (Irene Rich) are on their way to Grand Central Station to meet Richard Williams (Charles S. Morton), the son of a late family friend. The problem is caused by the breakdown of an old flivver belonging to Freshair Taxicab Company operators Amos (Gosden) and Andy (Correll). After much commotion, a policeman (G. Pat Collins) gets the car started but by now Richard has taken a taxi to the Blair home in Westchester County. There, conniving Ralph Crawford (Ralf Harolde) proposes to the Blairs' daughter Jean (Sue Carol), who is anxious to see Richard since they were once sweethearts. Jean sends Ralph back to her house to get a new strap for her horse. When Richard's cab agitates his horse, Ralph tries to beat the animal and Richard stops him. The two men have words but Jean comes along and decides to ride home with Richard, much to Ralph's chagrin. At their cab office in Harlem, Amos and Andy make a date with Madame Queen and Ruby Taylor to take them to a dance that night following a meeting of their lodge, the Mystic Knights of the Sea. Lodge president Kingfish (Powell) offers the cabbies the job of driving Duke Ellington and His Cotton Club Orchestra to a dance at the Blair home that night. He promises twelve dollars for the job and manages to get two dollars of the fee for himself. At

Trade advertisement for *Check and Double Check* (1930).

the party, the Blairs realize that Jean and Richard have fallen in love, and Richard informs Mr. Blair that he needs to obtain the never recorded deed to his grandfather's vacant house in Harlem so he can sell it and have the money to marry Jean. He plans to go to the property since he thinks the deed is hidden there. Ralph overhears the conversation and tells his social-climbing sister Elinor (Rita La Roy) about the deed, saying he will find it first. Amos and Andy arrive with the Ellington Orchestra and after the dance begins, Jean tells Richard she will meet him later at a nearby lake. After Amos and Andy fix a flat tire on their cab, Richard recognizes them as having worked for his father in Georgia. He tells them his father has died and the two cabmen say he was the best friend they ever had. After Amos and Andy start their drive back to Harlem, Jean and Richard go canoeing on the lake and kiss. At the lodge meeting, the Kingfish announces that a member will be chosen for the annual trek to a vacant house in honor of the lodge's founder, who was lost at sea doing night duty. The chosen one must stay in the house for one hour, beginning at midnight, and find a paper with the words "Check and Double Check." He is to take someone with him, leave another paper to be found the next year, and return with the "Check and Double Check" document as proof that he carried out the assignment. Andy draws the number seven and chooses Amos to go with him to the supposedly haunted house. During a thunderstorm, Amos and Andy arrive at the vacant house, not knowing Ralph and a henchman (Pat Conway) are also there looking for the deed. All four men hear noises with Andy locating the needed paper and Amos finding the deed which they plan to use for next year's participants. Ralph and his pal get the drop on Amos and Andy and mistakenly take the "Check and Double Check" paper, thinking it is the deed. Richard also searches the house without finding the deed and the next day says farewell to Jean and heads to New York to catch a train. Amos and Andy lament losing their girlfriends, who dumped them when they did not show up to take them to the dance after the lodge meeting. Andy finds the deed in his jacket pocket and when Amos reads it he realizes they need to take it to Richard. After phoning the Blair estate and being told by the butler (Robert Homans) that Richard has gone to Grand Central Station, Amos and Andy rush there in their cab and give him the deed. After several days pass, Amos and Andy get a package containing a part of Richard and Jean's wedding cake in thanks for finding the deed. The two cabmen make up with their girlfriends and plan to share the cake with them but as they run out of their office, Andy drops the cake in the street and a truck comes by and crushes it.

Released in November 1930, *Check and Double Check* was Radio Pictures' biggest moneymaker of the year. It also found favor with the critics. *The New York Times* noted, "The scenes in which Amos 'n' Andy appear aroused hearty laughter, but when the picture is concerned with a romantic villain who beats his horse the film is not so effective. Neither is the hero ... of any great importance to the sketchy story. While the villain is plotting and the hero is bemoaning his ill-luck, this cinema work is amateurish, but the moment Amos 'n' Andy come to its rescue, the merriment starts again." *Exhibitors' Forum* opined, "Amos and Andy are the whole show working every minute to keep the laughs at a steady flow. Should be a moneymaker anywhere." "This story, which is rather slight, gives the lads a fine background for their comedy. They do not force any of the gags and the laughs come naturally—and often.... The acting of Amos 'n' Andy is at a par. Neither one outdoes the other, and the honors are even. Their voices are very good and the dialogue is clear—when the audience stops laughing long enough to hear it," wrote *Motion Picture News*. *Picture Play Magazine* claimed Amos and Andy, "like other radio stars, are good for ear appeal only, in their husky arguments about nothing." *Photoplay* summed it up: "Dis am entertainment!" *Variety* termed it "the best picture for children ever put on the screen.... The curiosity value of this Amos and Andy picture is tremendous, probably more so than any other, if not all others. As to the picture itself, it's sufficient.... Amos and Andy are funny in screen person."

Gosden and Correll brought their characters to television in 1951 when *Amos 'n' Andy* was broadcast on CBS where it ran for two seasons. An additional third season was filmed for syndication. Alvin Childress played Amos, Spencer Williams was Andy and Tim Moore portrayed Kingfish. During the 1951–52 season it was #13 in the ratings. The show remained a popular syndicated item until 1966 when it was withdrawn by CBS and has not been on the air since due to the political correctness crowd.

Cinderella (1950; 74 minutes; Color)

PRESENTER: Walt Disney. PRODUCER: Amy Bailey. DIRECTORS: Clyde Geronimi, Wilfred Jackson & Hamilton Luske. SCREENPLAY: William Peed, Erdman Penner, Ted Sears, Winston Hibler, Homer Brightman, Harry Reeves, Kenneth Anderson & Joe Rinaldi, from the story by Charles Perrault. EDITOR: Donald Halliday. MUSIC DIRECTOR: Oliver Wallace. MUSIC ARRANGER & VOCALS: Lynn Murray. MUSIC EDITOR: Al Teeter. SONGS: Mack David, Al Hoffman & Jerry Livingston. ORCHESTRATIONS: Joseph Dubin. SOUND: Robert O. Cook, Harold J. Steck & C.O. Slyfield. PRODUCTION MANAGER: Ben Sharpsteen. EFFECTS ANIMATORS: Josh Meador, Jack Boyd & George Rowley. SPECIAL PROCESSES: Ib Iwerks. ANIMATION DIRECTORS: Eric Larson, Ward Kimball, Norman Ferguson, Marc Davis, John Lounsbery, Milt Kahl, Wolfgang Reitherman, Les Clark, Oliver Johnston, Jr. & Frank Thomas. CHARACTER ANIMATORS: Marvin Woodward, Hal Ambro, George Nicholas, Fred Moore, Hugh Fraser, Hal King, Judge Whitaker, Phil Duncan, Cliff Nordberg, Ken O'Brien, Harvey Tombs & Don Lusk. BACKGROUNDS: Dick Anthony, Merle Cox, Ralph Hulett, Brice Mack, Ray Huffine, Art Riley & Thelma Witmer. LAYOUT: A. Kendall O'Connor, Thor Putnam, Charles Philippi, Tom Codrick, Don Griffith, McLaren Stewart, Lance Nolley & Hugh Hennesy. COLOR & STYLING: Claude Coats, Mary Blair, Donald Da Gradi & John Hench. LIVE ACTION MODELS: Eleanor Audley, Rhoda Williams, Helene Stanley & Claire Du Brey.

VOICE CAST: Ilene Woods (Cinderella), Eleanor Audley (Lady Tremaine), Verna Felton (Fairy Godmother), Rhoda Williams (Drizella), James MacDonald (Bruno/Gus/Jaq), Luis Van Rooten (King/Grand Duke), Don Barclay (Doorman), Lucille Bliss (Anastasia), William Phipps (Prince Charming), Mike Douglas (Singing Voice of Prince Charming), June Foray (Lucifer), Marion Darlington (Birds), Earl Keen (Bruno), Lucille Williams (Mouse Perla), Helen Seibert, Clint McCauley, June Sullivan (Mice), Thurl Ravenscroft, John Woodbury, Jeffrey Stone (Various Voices), Betty Lou Gerson (Narrator).

Cinderella is one of Walt Disney's most successful animated features, grossing over $4 million when RKO issued it in March 1950, and earning many times that since in various reissues. Disney first filmed the 1697 Charles Perrault fairy tale classic in 1922 as part of the Laugh-O-Grams short series and in 1930 he planned to re-do it as a Silly Symphony. A decade later Disney proposed an animated feature version of *Cinderella* but it did not go into production until 1949. Following its successful U.S. debut, the feature was dubbed into various languages for foreign release. It remained in theaters well into the 1980s and in 1990 was issued on home video. In 2002 the Disney organization did a direct-to-video sequel, *Cinderella II: Dreams Come True.*

Wealthy Lord Tremaine, who has a small daughter, Cinderella (voice of Ilene Woods), remarries following the death of his wife. His new bride, Lady Tremaine (voice of Eleanor Audley), has two girls, Drizella (voice of Rhoda Williams) and Anastasia (voice of Lucille Bliss), who are about the same age as Cinderella. After Lord Tremaine dies, Lady Tremaine proves to be cold and cruel and slights Cinderella in deference to her own children, eventually forcing her stepdaughter to become their scullery maid. As she grows up, the beautiful Cinderella finds hope in each new day and through her kindness makes friends with various animals and birds, including a horse, Major; a dog, Bruno (voice of Earl Keen); and Jaq (voice of James MacDonald), a mouse. When Jaq tells Cinderella that a rotund vole has been caught in a trap, she rescues the little fellow and dubs him Gus (voice of James MacDonald). At breakfast that day, Lady Tremaine's evil cat Lucifer (voice of June Foray) almost captures Gus but Jaq drops a broom on him. The escaping Gus hides in a teacup which Cinderella serves to Anastasia, who tells her mother. Lady Tremaine punishes Cinderella by making her clean the carpets and other hard work. At the same time, the domain's king (voice of Luis Van Rooten) wants grandchildren and orders his grand duke (voice of Luis Van Rooten) to hold a ball that night with all the eligible females in the kingdom in attendance so his son, Prince Charming (voices of William Phipps and Mike Douglas), can pick a bride. Cinderella wants to attend but Lady Tremaine, knowing her stepdaughter will upstage her own two ugly and gangly offspring, says she can go only if she finishes her work and has the proper attire. Cinderella's animal friends pilfer material from the two sisters and make her a lovely dress but when she tries to go to the ball, Drizella and Anastasia tear it apart. In the garden, the crying Cinderella is comforted by her Fairy Godmother (voice of Verna Felton) who turns a pumpkin into a grand coach and her mice friends into horses. She makes Major a coachman and Bruno the footman. Cinderella is given a beautiful gown replete with glass slippers but her Fairy Godmother warns her to leave the ball before midnight when her spells will end. Cinderella arrives at the ball and catches the eye of Prince Charming, and they spend the evening dancing. Midnight approaches and the king goes to bed, happy that his son has found a girl to marry, and warns the grand duke not to let anything spoil his plans. As Cinderella and Prince Charming are about to kiss in the garden, the clock begins chiming midnight and Cinderella hastens back to her coach, losing a glass slipper along the way. The prince and his men follow but the spell has been broken and Cinderella and her animal friends return to the Tremaine chateau. When he finds out the girl he expected his son would marry has vanished, the king orders the grand duke to take the glass slipper to every home and try it on all maidens until he gets a perfect fit. Cinderella hears Lady Tremaine tell her daughters about the king's order and retrieves the other glass slipper. When she hears Cinderella singing a song from the ball, Lady Tremaine realizes the girl in question is her stepdaughter and, to prevent her from trying on the slipper, she locks her in the attic. The grand duke and his footman (voice of Don Barclay) arrive at the chateau but after many tries neither Drizella or Anastasia can fit into the slipper. Jaq and Gus manage to steal the key to the attic from Lady Tremaine and drag it to Cinderella. Just as the grand duke and the footman are about to leave, Cinderella calls to them and asks to try on the slipper. Lady Tremaine objects but the grand duke orders the footman to bring him the slipper. As he does so, the wicked stepmother trips him and the slipper is broken. The grand duke becomes upset until Cinderella produces the other glass slipper, which fits her perfectly. Cinderella and Prince Charming are married and live happily ever after.

Variety had mixed feelings about *Cinderella*. The reviewer wrote it "has far more success in projecting the lower animals than in its central character ... who is on the colorless, doll-faced side as is Prince Charming.... The musical numbers woven into the fantasy are generally solid.... There's enough finesse and fun in *Cinderella* to make it universally entertaining." *Boxoffice* was much more upbeat: "Here is Walt Disney at his all-time best.... The Disney technique has progressed considerably since he made cartoon history with *Snow White and the Seven Dwarfs*, and on almost every count the new venture is superior to its illustrious predecessor. The music, an outstanding asset, contributes to the film's vast overall exploitability, and such ultimate in entertainment values and tremendous merchandising possibilities add up to stratospheric commercial potential." In *The Disney Films, 3rd Edition* (1995), Leonard Maltin opined, "It is a work of genuine charm, thanks to skillful characterizations and story work, and, most importantly, an especially winning score.... The film's strongest point is its ability to elicit emotional response from its audience."

Ilene Woods, Eleanor Audley and Verna Felton repeated their voice parts on radio's *Screen Directors' Playhouse* when "Cinderella" was broadcast on April 7, 1950, on the NBC network. The film received three Academy Award nominations, including "Bibbidi-Bobbidi-Boo" for Best Song.

The Crime Doctor (1934; 73 minutes)

EXECUTIVE PRODUCER: David O. Selznick. ASSOCIATE PRODUCER: David Lewis. DIRECTOR: John S. Robertson. SCREENPLAY: Jane Murfin, from the novel *The Big Bow Mystery* by Israel Zangwill.

PHOTOGRAPHY: Lucien N. Andriot. EDITOR: William Hamilton. MUSIC DIRECTOR: Max Steiner. ART DIRECTORS: Van Nest Polglase & Al Herman. SOUND: D.A. Cutler. SPECIAL EFFECTS SUPERVISOR: Harry Redmond, Sr. TECHNICAL DIRECTOR: Captain Don Wilkie.

CAST: Otto Kruger (Dan Gifford), Karen Morley (Andra Gifford), Nils Asther (Eric Anderson), Judith Wood (Blanche Flynn), William Frawley (Fraser), Donald Crisp (District Attorney), Frank Conroy (Martin Crowder), J. Farrell MacDonald (Kemp), Fred Kelsey (Bloodgood), G. Pat Collins (Walters), Samuel S. Hinds (Ballard), Ethel Wales (Miss Farnum), Wallis Clark (Judge Mallory), Tom London (Airport Detective), Willie Fung (Wah-Sing), Pat O'Malley, Lee Phelps (Detectives).

Criminologist Dan Gifford (Otto Kruger) learns that his wife Andra (Karen Morley) has been seeing Eric Anderson (Nils Asther), a Swedish mystery author. He confronts his wife and she tells him she wants a divorce so she can marry the writer. Dan begs his wife to take a week to reconsider and she agrees to do so. Giving up his position on the police force, Dan starts his own detective business and hires ex-convict Blanche Flynn (Judith Wood) to spy on Eric. Dan has Blanche take an apartment in the same building as the mystery writer and observe his female visitors. After seeing Andra at Eric's apartment on several occasions, Blanche tries to blackmail him and demands $10,000. Eric agrees to pay the sum but tells Andra. Not realizing her husband set up the scheme, figuring Blanche would try to blackmail Eric, Andra asks him to help Eric. Dan agrees and tells Eric to come to his office before making payment to Blanche. While Eric is at his office, Dan goes to the man's apartment and steals a gun from his collection of old weapons. Facing Blanche with her duplicity, Dan forces her to write a letter in which she not only admits blackmailing Eric but doing so out of jealousy. Using the stolen gun, Dan murders Blanche and then partially burns her missive in a fireplace. Dan leaves the apartment, meeting Eric who has arrived to pay the ransom. Blanche's body is found; between the note and the fact she was killed with Eric's gun, Eric is arrested and stands trial for murder. Found guilty, he is sentenced to be hanged. Andra remains loyal to him and leaves Dan to move near her lover. Wanting to keep Andra, Dan tells her if she gives up Eric, he will get the evidence necessary to exonerate him. Andra agrees and Dan signs a confession, then commits suicide. Andra finishes reading Dan's newest novel, entertained by his having used her and their friends in its murder mystery plot.

The twist ending, revealing *The Crime Doctor* to be a fantasy, was hardly novel; RKO used a similar plot device of dual endings the same year in *Dangerous Corner* (q.v.). *The Crime Doctor* bears no relationship to the popular Columbia Pictures series of the 1940s starring Warner Baxter, which was based on the CBS radio program that aired from 1940 to 1947. Richard Dix was initially announced to star in the feature with Wynne Gibson, Mary Astor and Corinne Griffith at various times touted to co-star. Griffith did begin filming but left the production after what she claimed were bullying tactics by Otto Kruger.

The New York Times felt *The Crime Doctor*'s plot about a perfect crime "is engineered with such skill and imagination by a criminologist, who is also a jealous husband, that it becomes a fascinating thing to watch." Regarding Kruger's work as the killer, the reviewer called it a "venomously exciting performance" but apparently was let down by the ending: "It seems such a shame to excuse a crime so expertly managed." *The Hollywood Reporter* noted, "*The Crime Doctor* is something new to murder mysteries. The audience is in on the whole thing from the start, and, with the exception of one lone clue near the beginning of the picture, is able to predict pretty well the general working out of the plot. But there's a surprise every minute, and you watch the darned thing, utterly intrigued and fascinated all along the way. And then the ending comes and you find that you have been thoroughly fooled after all.... [It's] an above average murder mystery." *Picture Play Magazine* complained, "A rather weak ending, one of those which insist that a murder is only make-believe after all, dulls the dramatic point of this picture. But it is engrossing until the let-down, due in large part to the brilliant acting of Otto Kruger, and his associates, Nils

Asther, Karen Morley and particularly Judith Wood, who grows more depraved in each picture and makes you admire her for it."

"This is one of the murder mysteries in which none but the audience knows who killed the victim. It is well staged and directed. Mr. Asther and Miss Morley do fine, sensitive work, and Mr. Kruger performed less finely with a regrettable tendency to express emotions by making faces. Judith Wood is more than satisfactory as the little so-and-so who is killed and the everlasting courtroom scene is well done," opined *The New Movie Magazine*. *The New York American* wrote, "One of the best murder yarns recently wrought into a picture. The story is keenly suspenseful from the very first sequence, and it holds gripping interest right through to the thrilling denouement. Otto Kruger is superb." *The New York Herald-Tribune* declared, "The work achieves horror and suspense, while remaining always credible—an excellent film celebration of homicide. Most of the credit for the mood must go to Otto Kruger in the title role." "Highly entertaining and splendidly played" is how the *New York Mirror* summed it up, while *The New York Sun* opined, "Never very exciting, it still manages to hold the interest until that faked ending." *The New York World-Telegram* chimed in: "An ingenious and irresistible tale of homicide that is full of excitement. The cast is precisely right and the direction is so restrained that the film becomes a fascinating game of wit and out-wit." The Detroit Council of Catholic Organizations declared the film unsuitable for children or adolescents. *Harrison's Reports* deemed the picture's box office take to be "Good to Fair."

The Crime Doctor was the second of three screen versions of Israel Zangwill's 1892 novel *The Big Bow Mystery*. It was first made by Film Booking Offices in 1928 as *The Perfect Crime*, starring Clive Brook and Irene Rich, with direction by Bert Glennon. Ethel Wales, who played the title character's secretary in the second version, also appeared in the FBO release. Warner Bros. did the story again in 1946 as *The Verdict*, directed by Don Siegel, with Sydney Greenstreet, Peter Lorre and Joan Lorring.

Crime Ring (1938; 76 minutes)

PRODUCER: Cliff Reid. DIRECTOR: Leslie Goodwins. SCREENPLAY: J. Robert Bren & Gladys Atwater. STORY: Reginald Taviner. PHOTOGRAPHY: Jack MacKenzie. EDITOR: Desmond Marquette. MUSIC: Roy Webb. ART DIRECTORS: Van Nest Polglase & Feild Gray. SOUND: John E. Tribby. GOWNS: Renie.

CAST: Allan Lane (Joe Ryan), Frances Mercer (Judy Allen), Clara Blandick (Phoebe Sawyer), Inez Courtney (Kitty), Bradley Page (Lionel Whitmore), Ben Welden (Nate), Walter Miller (Jenner), Frank M. Thomas (District Attorney Thomas Redwine), Jack Arnold [Vinton Hayworth] (Moe Buzzell), Morgan Conway (Ray Taylor), George Irving (Clifton), Leona Roberts (Alice Wharton), Charles Trowbridge (Marvin, the Sightless Wonder), Jack Mulhall (Detective Brady), Bryant Washburn (Swami), Vivien Oakland (Madame Jarman), Byron Foulger (George Myles), Helen Jerome Eddy (Mrs. Myles), Fern Emmett (Alice), Rollo Lloyd (E.J. Goshen), Tom Kennedy (Dummy), Paul Fix (Slim), Jonathan Hale (Bank President), Edward Earle (Psychiatrist), Selmer Jackson (Ernie), Alphone Martell, Dorothy Adams (Fortune Tellers), Chuck Hamilton (Policeman), Wolfgang Zilzer (Hans), Stanley Blystone (Trooper), Bob McKenzie, Eva McKenzie, Harry Depp (Phoebe Sawyer's Relatives), Sherry Hall (Marvin's Receptionist), Jim Farley (Turnkey), Jack O'Shea (Stock Trader), Bob Reeves (Intern), Jack Rice (Goshen's Worker), Sumner Getchell (Newsman with Black Eye), Harry Tyler (Peddler).

Crime Ring, released in the summer of 1938, masks a complicated plot under a routine gangster film title. While the overlong feature deals with the extortion and stock manipulation rackets, it also delves into fake spiritualism and fortune-telling and does a good job exposing them. Among the tricks of the trade revealed in the production are reverse writing which reveals a client's name, the use of research files to get background information on potential suckers, and stock-in-trade spook gimmicks like fake voices, ectoplasm and strange noises (moaning, chain-rattling, etc.).

The well-staged production has an excellent cast and moves along well under Leslie Goodwins' steady direction. He also helmed the genre outings *Mexican Spitfire Sees a Ghost* (1942) [q.v.], *Murder in the Blue Room* and *The Mummy's Curse* (both 1944, both for Universal), and *Genius at Work* (1946) [q.v.].

Newsman Joe Ryan (Allan Lane) investigates fake fortune tellers like Madame Jarman (Vivien Oakland), who has to pay protection money to crooked private detective Buzzell (Jack Arnold) to stay in business. While covering a story about a group of show girls ending up in jail following a raid, Ryan gets the idea to use two of them, actress Judy Allen (Frances Mercer) and ventriloquist Kitty (Inez Courtney), to set a trap for both group of crooks. He sells the idea to District Attorney Thomas Redwine (Frank M. Thomas) but Judy refuses to cooperate until Joe agrees to get the case against all the chorus girls dismissed. He and Redwine set up Judy in an apartment with a séance room, which includes a hidden camera and microphone, with Kitty acting as her spectral voice. Judy will operate under the name Haidee. After she opens for business, Buzzell sends his henchman Jenner (Walter Miller), who demands a $500 fee and ten percent of her take. Joe is friends with wealthy widow Phoebe Sawyer (Clara Blandick), who believes her greedy relatives are after her $40 million estate. Her maid, Alice (Fern Emmett), suggests she consult Marvin, the Sightless Seer (Charles Trowbridge), to find what happened to her long-lost son. Although skeptical, Phoebe goes to the spiritualist, who uses trickery to convince her of his sincerity. Marvin then plots with mob lawyer Ray Taylor (Morgan Conway) and corrupt stock manipulator Lionel Whitmore (Bradley Page) in sending the old lady on a wild goose chase to the South Pacific so that Taylor can liquidate her finances. After businessman George Myles (Byron Foulger) is cheated in a stock deal with Whitmore's stooge E.J. Goshen (Rollo Lloyd), he threatens to go to the law and Goshen has thugs Dummy (Tom Kennedy) and Slim (Paul Fix) beat him up. Myles dies from his injuries. In trying to break this racket, Joe takes an assumed name and pretends to consult Haidee, who advises him on a stock purchase. He buys one thousand dollars worth of stock from Goshen and when the deal falls apart he takes Buzzell and Jenner to Haidee and accuses her of robbing him. Jenner recognizes Joe as a reporter and orders Dummy and Slim to bump him off but Joe manages to run their car into a light pole and is rescued by police Detective Brady (Jack Mulhall) and his men. To keep the two thugs in custody, Redwine has them placed in a psychiatric hospital where the doctor (Edward Earle) says Dummy may soon crack under the strain and turn states evidence. Taylor gets handwriting expert Hans (Wolfgang Zilzer) to forge Phoebe's power of attorney over to him. Joe visits Phoebe and learns about her proposed trip as well as her consultations with Marvin. He is forced to tell her that Marvin is a fake and she agrees to help him break up the fortune-telling racket. Phoebe and her maid pretend to get on a steamer but Joe gets them off before it sails. They then join Brady and Redwine in a meeting with the president (Jonathan Hale) of the woman's bank. When Taylor shows up with the forged document, he is arrested. Whitmore has his chauffeur Nate (Ben Welden) murder Trowbridge and then learns that his accomplices have disappeared. He tells Buzzell that Haidee is to blame and sends Jenner to investigate her apartment. Whitmore and Nate stage a wreck and abduct Judy and Kitty while Joe finds their operation has been ransacked. Whitmore offers the two women $10,000 to find out how much the police know about his million-dollar-a-year racket. Joe and Richwine get Dummy and Slim sprung and takes them to Buzzell's office but he has already warned Whitmore, who takes the women to Phoebe's mansion. Whitmore sends his henchmen away in his limousine, which has a scratch from getting too close to the hitching post in Phoebe's front yard, and they wreck it. Joe and Richwine go to the scene of the accident and, when Joe sees the scratch, he knows where Judy and Kitty have been taken. As Joe, Richwine and the police break into the house to rescue the women, Nate gets the drop on them. Judy throws her voice and imitates Trowbridge talking from beyond the grave and the superstitious chauffeur faints. Whitmore and his gang are led away by Brady and his men as Joe and Kitty realize they have fallen in love.

Variety felt that, "as entertainment, the film badly misses its mark.... Main trouble ... is the meandering course of the plot.... Dialog is lukewarm and ekes interest and laughs largely from bright work of cast." The reviewer did like star Allan Lane's "bangup interpretation of the reporter" but added, "Leslie Goodwins' direction is jerky and has no original touches. Some first-rate production visible, but photography is ordinary." On the other hand, *Boxoffice* opined, "Liberally garnished with laughs and new plot twists, this contribution to the racketeering school is above par in its budget class and should please the customers. A generally good cast is headed by Allan Lane and Frances Mercer, plus smooth direction by Leslie Goodwins, are among the assets in a fast-moving exposé of the fortune-telling racket." The *Carroll* (Iowa) *Daily Herald* wrote, "The gripping story endeavors to reveal the dishonest methods employed by unlicensed and illegitimate 'psychics' who annually milk millions of dollars from innocent people, and in this respect the picture strikes a new note to racket-busting dramas." According to the *Hutchinson* (Kansas) *News-Herald*, "This is a dramatic exposé of the unholy alliance between fortune tellers and phony stock dealers. It is one of those things, and if you like 'em, it's swell." *The Film Daily* dubbed it a "fast-moving crime story.... Leslie Goodwins directed the picture with a neat touch, keeping it moving and never letting the characters get out of hand."

Publicity for *Crime Rang* claimed co-star Frances Mercer, daughter of Gotham sports writer Sid Mercer, visited three Hollywood psychics in preparing for her role and that all of them predicted film stardom and marriage for her within one year. Reginald Taviner's original story was later reworked by the studio as *Bunco Squad* (q.v.).

Top-billed Allan Lane appeared in 13 features for RKO in 1938 and 1939 before going to Republic where he starred in Westerns until 1953, including a stint as Red Ryder. He was billed as Allan "Rocky" Lane. Besides being a cowboy film hero, Lane was the voice of the talking horse *Mr. Ed* on CBS-TV from 1961 to 1965.

The Curse of the Cat People (1944; 70 minutes)

PRODUCER: Val Lewton. DIRECTORS: Gunther V. Fritsch & Robert Wise. SCREENPLAY: DeWitt Bodeen. PHOTOGRAPHY: Nicholas Musuraca. EDITOR: J.R. Whittredge. MUSIC: Roy Webb. MUSIC DIRECTOR: C. Bakaleinikoff. ART DIRECTORS: Albert S. D'Agostino & Walter E. Keller. SOUND: Francis M. Sarver & James G. Stewart. SET DECORATIONS: Darrell Silvera & William Stevens. MAKEUP: Mel Berns. GOWNS: Edward Stevenson. ASSISTANT DIRECTOR: Harry D'Arcy.

CAST: Simone Simon (Irena), Kent Smith (Oliver Reed), Jane Randolph (Alice Reed), Ann Carter (Amy Reed), Eve March (Miss Callahan), Julia Dean (Julia Farren), Elizabeth Russell (Barbara Farren), Erford Gage (State Police Captain), Sir Lancelot (Edward), Joel Davis (Donald Miller), Juanita Alvarez [Nita Hunter] (Lois Huggins), Charles Bates (Jack), Gloria Donovan, Ginny Wren, Linda Bieber (Little Girls), Sarah Selby (Miss Plumett), Mel Sternlight (State Trooper), Edmund Glover (Card Player).

In the aftermath of the box office success of *Cat People* (q.v.), both RKO and producer Val Lewton wanted to do a sequel. The *Cat People* script writer, DeWitt Bodeen, was engaged to develop the scenario based on a storyline conceived by Lewton. Production began on the sequel in August 1943, with Lewton wanting to call it *Amy and Her Friend*. The studio demanded a title connection to the initial film and it became *The Curse of the Cat People*. Simone Simon, Kent Smith and Jane Randolph appear in the roles they had in *Cat People* although the focus of the sequel is on the little girl, intelligently portrayed by Ann Carter. The acting highlight of the picture, however, is Julia Dean, a veteran stage star, who plays a once-famous actress, now confined to her old dark house and madness. Short subject director Gunther V. Fritsch made his feature debut with *The Curse of the Cat People* but he got behind schedule and was replaced by Robert Wise, the editor of *Citizen Kane* (1941). Filming was not totally finished until November 1943, at a production cost of over $200,000. Released theatrically in February 1944, *The Curse of the Cat People* was not as successful as its predecessor. RKO later placed it on a double bill with *Cat People*.

Poster for *The Curse of the Cat People* (1944).

A kindergarten class of teacher Miss Callahan (Eve March) is playing in the New York village of Tarrytown, near Sleepy Hollow. One of the children, Amy Reed (Carter), slaps a playmate (Joel Davis) for accidentally killing a butterfly she was chasing because she thought it was her friend. Her parents, boat builder Oliver Reed (Smith) and his wife Alice (Randolph), consult with Miss Callahan about Amy's behavior; Oliver confides to Alice that Amy reminds him of his first wife Irena (Simon) because of her fantasies. That afternoon Amy awaits the arrival of school friends for her sixth birthday party. When they do not come, Oliver investigates and finds Amy placed the invitations in a tree, which he once told her was a mailbox. Although Amy promises her father she will play with the other children, they shun her. Following three girls (Gloria Donovan, Ginny Wren, Linda Bieber), Amy finds herself in front of a large, foreboding house and hears a voice calling to her. A handkerchief with a ring tied to it is thrown to her but the handkerchief is then taken away from her by a stern woman, Barbara Farren (Elizabeth Russell), although Amy keeps the ring. She shows it to her parents' servant Edward (Sir Lancelot), who says it may be a real wishing ring. Amy goes to her father's workshop and tells him about the mysterious voice but he

Poster for *The Curse of the Cat People* (1944).

thinks it is another of her fantasies. Oliver and Alice argue over his not believing the child. In the garden, Amy wishes on the ring for a friend; Oliver and Edward later see her dancing happily around the yard. As Alice is getting Amy ready for bed that night, she sees the ring and tells her daughter she must return it. The next day, Amy sets out for the mysterious house while Miss Callahan visits with Alice, who tells her about Irena, who she sometimes thinks haunts their house. At the old mansion, Amy meets once-famous actress Julia Farren (Dean), now a recluse, who claims that her daughter Barbara is not really her daughter but a lying imposter. As Edward arrives to take Amy home, Julia enthralls the child with the local legend of the Headless Horseman of Sleepy Hollow. When Amy has a nightmare about the ghost that night, she wishes for her friend and is comforted by a soft breeze. Finding a picture of Irena the next day, Amy calls to her in the garden and she appears. Irena and Amy becomes fast friends with Irena telling the child she comes from great darkness and deep peace and that she must promise never to tell anyone about her. The months pass and on Christmas Eve, while her parents are singing with visiting carolers, Amy goes to the snow-covered garden and gives Irena a holiday gift, a dazzling broach. Amy also gives Julia a ring and the old lady shuns Barbara's present in deference to it, causing Barbara to hate the child. While Miss Callahan is visiting with them, Amy finds a picture of Oliver and Irena together and she tells him that Irena is her friend. Oliver takes his daughter into the garden and asks her if Irena is there. When the child says she is, he takes her to her bedroom and spanks her for lying to him. Irena appears before the crying Amy and tells her goodbye and fades away. Amy leaves the house and goes into the woods in search of Irena. A distraught Oliver tells Miss Callahan about having been married to Irena, who died from self-deception, having killed a man and then herself. She counsels him to be Amy's friend and not judge her fantasies. When he goes to check on his daughter he finds she has disappeared. Miss Callahan calls the state police as Amy wanders through the woods. She is badly frightened by what she thinks is the sound of hoof beats but it turns out only to be a tin lizzy. As snow begins to fall, the child becomes exhausted and falls asleep in a snow drift but is awakened by the sound of barking dogs—part of a search party led by state troopers and her parents. Amy runs to the Farren home where she is admitted by Julia. Since Barbara hates the child and has promised to kill her, Julia attempts to hide Amy in an upper room, but as they climb the stairs the old lady dies of a heart attack. Barbara finds Amy beside Julia's body and accuses her of stealing her mother's last moments. The frightened child calls for Irena and sees her in place of Barbara. Amy rushes to embrace Irena and in doing so causes Barbara to lose her hatred for the child. Oliver and Alice arrive with the state police and they take Amy home. Oliver promises his daughter he will be her friend and that he too sees Irena in the garden as her specter fades away.

Since *The Curse of the Cat People* is basically a fantasy, it captured the attention of critics usually condescending toward horror films. James Agee in *The Nation* called it "a brave, sensitive, and admirable little psychological melodrama" and Bosley Crowther in *The New York Times* termed it "a quite wistful and appealing little story of a small girl's fantasies.... [I]t makes a rare departure from the ordinary run of horror films and emerges as an oddly touching study of the working of a sensitive child's mind." *Boxoffice* reported, "The film is characterized by an eerie atmosphere, but there is an apparent lack of story incident. Certain scenes may tend to frighten some younger children; the older ones should be unaffected, however." The reviewer also proclaimed, "Ann Carter gives an authentic and sincere performance." *Variety* compared it to its predecessor and concluded it "highly disappointing because it fails to measure up as a horrific opus.... Chief trouble seems to be the over-supply of palaver and concern about a cute, but annoying, child." Noting the picture credited two directors, the reviewer stated, "Pair has turned out a strange cinema stew that is apt to make audiences laugh at the wrong places. Many episodes are

Lobby card for *The Curse of the Cat People* (1944).

unbelievably bad, with hardly anything happening in the first three reels." *The Film Daily* called the film "a strange compound of the real and the fantastic that won't draw more than mild attention from audiences, which are apt to be puzzled by it all. Given a fragile story that is stretched to the breaking point, the film has chiefly in its favor a sense of tenderness induced by the fact the main character is an abnormally sensitive young girl with an elf-like personality who lives in a dream world from which her parents have a hard time luring her. The child, as played by Ann Carter, gives the production some merit as a woman's picture.... Miss Carter runs away with the acting honors, giving an extremely appealing performance."

The Curse of the Cat People went over budget partly because two different endings were filmed. In DeWitt Bodeen's screenplay, the old actress' crazed daughter tries to kill Amy but Irena locks a door to keep her away from the child until her parents and the police arrive. Irena also tells Amy that she (Irena) is dead, thus giving the child closure to their relationship. In the version written by Val Lewton, which is used in the film, the child's goodness makes the daughter change her mind about wanting to kill her. In this ending, Amy does not learn that Irena was a ghost. In some ways, however, the Lewton version ends the curse of the cat people in that Elizabeth Russell played Simone Simon's nemesis in *Cat People* and here it is her character who is de-clawed by the goodness of an innocent child. Apparently actor Erford Gage suffered most from the deletion of the original ending. In the film's credits he is given eighth billing, in front of Sir Lancelot, who has a bigger role. In the released film Gage is barely evident as the state police captain, a part apparently much larger in the Bodeen screenplay. It should also be noted that the story has some similarities to Conrad Aiken's 1934 short story "Silent Snow, Secret Snow."

Dangerous Corner (1934; 66 minutes)

ASSOCIATE PRODUCER: B.P. Fineman. DIRECTOR: Phil Rosen. SCREENPLAY: Anne Morrison Chapin & Madeleine Ruthven, from the play by J.B. Priestley. PHOTOGRAPHY: J. Roy Hunt. EDITOR: Archie Marshek. MUSIC DIRECTOR: Max Steiner. ART DIRECTORS: Perry Ferguson & Van Nest Polglase. SOUND: John L. Cass. DIALOGUE DIRECTOR: Arthur Sircom.

CAST: Virginia Bruce (Ann Beale), Conrad Nagel (Robert Chatfield), Melvyn Douglas (Charles Stanton), Erin O'Brien-Moore (Fred Chatfield), Ian Keith (Martin Canfield), Betty Furness (Betty Chatfield Whitehouse), Henry Wadsworth (Gordon Whitehouse), Doris Lloyd (Maude Mockridge).

Based on J.P. Priestley's 1932 play, *Dangerous Corner* was "the story of what really happened and what might have happened." Its fantasy aspect is that it features two endings, with the pivotal point being the finding of a radio tube thus sending the plot back in time. Without the tube, the story descends into tragedy and with it the drama ends happily. In reality, it is simply a story about a group of people who talk too much. Basically a filmed stage production, *Dangerous Corner* is well acted but rather perplexing. One almost has to have a scorecard to keep track of who loves who in spite of the fact they are either married to someone else or may have stolen a bond that is the crux of the story.

Publishing house assistant Ann Beale (Virginia Bruce) invites bestselling British author Maude Mockridge (Doris Lloyd) for breakfast at her apartment. Ann's fellow worker Charles Stanton (Melvyn Douglas), who wants to marry Ann, arrives first with the excuse of bringing an unread manuscript. Maude suspects Ann and Charles are lovers. He returns to his office where

Henry Wadsworth, Melvyn Douglas and Virginia Bruce in *Dangerous Corner* (1934).

he reminds his boss, Robert Chatfield (Conrad Nagel), that today is the fifth anniversary of his marriage to Freda (Erin O'Brien-Moore). Charles plans an office party for the couple and that afternoon they are joined by another partner, Gordon Whitehouse (Henry Wadsworth), who is married to Robert's sister Betty (Betty Furness). A third brother, Martin Chatfield (Ian Keith), fails to arrive. Robert gets a telegram asking him to cash a bond being held for one of the company's authors but he is unable to find it in his office safe. The next day Charles goes to Martin's cottage to bring him to an office conference on the matter and finds he has been shot. A grand jury inquest brings in a verdict of suicide and everyone believes the motive was the bond theft by Martin. Several months later, Robert and Freda give a party for Maude, who has signed a three-book contract thanks to Ann, at their country home. Also present are Ann, Charles, Gordon and Betty. During the evening a radio tube breaks and without music to listen to, the group discusses Martin's suicide and the bond theft. When Freda and Ann have conflicting stories on the origins of a cigarette box, Gordon accuses Freda of taking it to Martin. She admits seeing him shortly before his death but Robert wonders why she never told him. Ann says she was at Martin's cottage the night he was killed as she thought he took the bond. After Maude, Charles, Gordon and Betty depart, Ann asks Robert if the took the bond. He replies that Martin was the thief. Freda informs Robert that Ann is in love with him and he admits his and Freda's marriage has not been a happy one. Wanting to get to the bottom of the theft, Robert calls Charles and asks him to return, and he does so with Gordon. Charles admits taking the bond because he needed the money and Robert accuses him of driving Martin to suicide. Charles dismisses the charge while Freda says she loved Martin, even before her marriage to Robert. Ann recounts going to Martin's cottage and how he started playing games with a gun; when he tried to force himself upon her, the weapon fired, killing him. Both Charles and Robert agree Ann is not to blame for Martin's death and Charles says he suspected what had occurred. Unable to sleep, Betty returns to the house and declares her marriage to Gordon is a sham and that she loves Charles, who sent her away when she went to his home. Finding out that Charles took the bond, Betty realizes it was to give her money to pay off gambling debts. Robert orders Charles out of the house and soon Betty and Gordon go home. Drinking too much, Robert tells Freda and Ann that he has lost everything, goes into the next room and shoots himself. Earlier Gordon finds a radio tube and dances with Betty while Robert and Freda talk with Maude. Charles and Ann go into the garden and she accepts his marriage proposal.

Motion Picture Daily wrote, "This mystery carries entertainment value, but is likely to confuse any but the most sophisticated audiences.... Director Phil Rosen handles this tricky story deftly, highlighting drama and suspense. Good performances are rendered by the cast...." *Photoplay* called it an "interesting experiment" and complimented the cast on "superior performances." *Variety* reported, "*Dangerous Corner* undertakes to mix a problem play with a mystery drama. The result makes for occasional excitement but more often for intentional confusion. It's not the sort of film fare that will appeal to the average fan to any great degree. The two endings given the script may be of some help in dissipating the morbid effect of the earlier situations, but to the general run of picturegoers this touch may appear more bewildering than novel." *The* (Connellsville, Pennsylvania) *Daily Courier* claimed the film "introduces a new story structure treatment. This revolutionary twist, plus excellent acting contributions by each member of the cast, makes this unusual production an outstanding entertainment."

"A unique contribution to the structural fabrication of motion picture" is how Massillon, Ohio's, *Evening Independent* described the film. *The Film Daily* noted, "Because of its intricate construction, putting somewhat of a tax on the mental faculties, and the fact that the dialogue is so far in excess of action, this murder drama looks best for the more intelligent class audience." Regarding the film's box office performance, *Harrison's Reports* declared it was "poor."

A Date with the Falcon (1942; 63 minutes)

PRODUCER: Howard Benedict. DIRECTOR: Irving Reis. SCREENPLAY: Lynn Root & Frank Fenton. PHOTOGRAPHY: Robert de Grasse. EDITOR: Harry Marker. MUSIC: Paul Sawtell. MUSIC DIRECTOR: C. Bakaleinikoff. ART DIRECTORS: Albert S. D'Agostino & Al Herman. SOUND: John L. Cass. GOWNS: Renie. ASSISTANT DIRECTOR: William Dorfman.

CAST: George Sanders (Gay Lawrence, The Falcon), Wendy Barrie (Helen Reed), James Gleason (Inspector Mike O'Hara), Allen Jenkins (Jonathan "Goldy" Locke), Mona Maris (Rita Mara), Edward Gargan (Detective Bates), Victor Kilian (Max Carlson), Frank Moran (Dutch), Russ Clark (Needles), Hans Conried (Desk Clerk), Earle Ross (Adolph Meyer), Eddie Dunn (Detective "Grimesy" Grimes), Selmer Jackson (Mr. Wallis), William Forrest (Mr. Ward), Leo Cleary (Detective Brody), Roxanne Barkley (Florist Jill), Frank Martinelli (Louie), Art Dupuis (Bartender Joe), Eddie Borden (Bribed Taxi Driver), Jack Carr (Taxi Driver), Dick Rich (Desk Sergeant), Malcolm "Bud" McTaggart, Harry Lee (Thugs), Elizabeth Russell (Airplane Passenger), Mickey Simpson, Eddie Hart, Al Sullivan, Anthony Blair (Policemen), Douglas Spencer (Accident Witness), Frank O'Connor (Accident Policeman), Paul Newlan (Hotel Policeman), Eddie Arden (Bellhop), Amarilla Morris, Aline Dixon, Youda Hayes (Street Spectators), Bobby Barber (Short Street Spectator), Helen Kleeb (Bystander).

A Date with the Falcon, issued by RKO early in 1942, has a minor sci-fi ploy of a scientist (Alec Craig) inventing a formula for the almost perfect synthetic diamonds. The rest is light-hearted mystery focusing on Gay Lawrence, the Falcon, a character created by Michael Arlen. From 1939 to 1941, George Sanders portrayed Simon Templar in a quintet of RKO features about Leslie Charteris' debonair detective "The Saint," but the studio dropped the series after problems with the author and they cast Sanders in exactly the same mold as "The Falcon." *The Gay Falcon* launched the series in 1941, followed by *A Date with the Falcon* and *The Falcon Takes Over* (1942), based on Raymond Chandler's 1939 novel *Farewell, My Lovely* with Gay Lawrence replaced Philip Marlowe as the sleuth. Sanders wanted out the series but RKO placated him by casting his older sibling, Tom Conway, opposite him in *The Falcon's Brother* (1942), killing off Gay with Tom Lawrence (Conway) becoming the crimefighting Falcon. Conway proved so successful in the part he went on to play the Falcon in nine more outings, culminating with 1946's *The Falcon's Adventure* (q.v.), a remake of *A Date with the Falcon*.

As New York City Police Inspector Mike O'Hara (James Gleason) observes, scientist Waldo Sampson (Craig) demonstrates to gem experts Wallis (Selmer Jackson) and Ward (William Forrest) his success in manufacturing synthetic diamonds as good as real ones. Sampson does not want to ruin the diamond industry and announces that his formula is only for the manufacture of diamonds for the defense industry. O'Hara tells Sampson not to leave his laboratory until he sends Detective Bates (Edward Gargan) to guard him. When the scientist gets a telegram from his brother Herman, he goes to the train station to meet him and is abducted by hoodlums Needles (Russ Clark) and Dutch (Frank Moran). At the Jack and Joe cocktail lounge, O'Hara shows one of the synthetic diamonds to playboy detective Gay Lawrence (Sanders), the Falcon, who is amazed at its quality. Gay is about to meet his fiancée Helen Reed (Wendy Barrie) but is attracted to pretty customer Rita Mara (Mona Maris), who tells him they met seven years before in Bucharest. When his house man Goldy Locke (Allen Jenkins) arrives, Gay informs him that Rita is involved with Sampson, who O'Hara told him is missing. Rita calls her cohort, Max Carlson (Victor Kilian), who tells her to get Gay out of the way. When Gay stops at a florist shop to buy flowers for Helen, Dutch tries to shoot him but misses. At his apartment, Gay calms Helen by telling her he was detained by meeting Rita, whom he describes as an old hag. When Rita shows up, Helen angrily goes into another room and Needles forces Gay to leave with him and Rita at gunpoint. Finding Rita's purse, Helen gets her address and goes there to confront Gay, who is taken for a ride by Rita, Needles and Dutch. Pretending to be drunk and belligerent, Gay causes the car to be stopped by the police and he slugs an officer in order to get arrested. After paying his bail, Gay returns home where Goldy informs him that Helen has gone to Rita's apartment. Following her to the Federal Hotel, Gay observes from the register that Sampson is staying there. After a confrontation with Helen, who runs off, Gay goes to Sampson's apartment and finds him dead. He goes through the man's belongings and finds a picture resembling Sampson in his watch. The suspicious desk clerk (Hans Conried) calls the police and Gay takes sanctuary on a ledge outside the dead man's room window, only to attract the attention of the returning Helen and a large crowd. Gay is arrested but gives Bates the slip and goes to Sampson's laboratory where he finds the telegram the scientist received from his brother. Calling Helen and telling her to meet him at the airport so they can fly to see her family, Gay is arrested by O'Hara at the rendezvous but then gets him to promise a 12-hour time allowance to find Sampson's killer. After telling Goldy to have Helen meet him at Jack and Joe's, Gay is taken at gunpoint there by Rita to see Max at his waterfront import office. There he learns Max has forced Sampson to reveal his synthetic diamond formula and that the murdered man was the scientist's twin brother, Herman Sampson (Craig). Goldy, who has trailed Gay, tips off O'Hara as to his boss' whereabouts and Bates is sent to arrest him. Telling Rita to get rid of Gay, Max goes to sell the formula to spy Adolph Meyer (Earle Ross) and is followed by Goldy, who forces his car off the road but ends up being arrested for drunk and reckless driving. When Bates and two officers arrive at the warehouse, they set Gay and Sampson free. Gay gets the drop on Bates and leaves with Rita, who is convinced that Max has double-crossed her. Rita and Gay go to the house where Max is meeting with Meyer and after confronting Max, Rita kills him and knocks out Gay. O'Hara and his men show up and arrest Gay for killing Max. Sampson, Helen and Goldy are also in custody. Bates arrives with Rita, Dutch and Needles, and Gay informs O'Hara as to the real identity of the victim, Sampson' brother. As Rita and her cohorts are taken to jail, Goldy produces a paper he took from Max that contains the formula. Gay and Helen, accompanied by Goldy, fly to see her parents only to be interrupted by another passenger (Elizabeth Russell), a pretty girl from Gay's past.

Bosley Crowther in *The New York Times* analyzed George Sanders' transformation from the Saint into the Falcon: "In all fairness, one must say that 'The Falcon' is doing better than 'The Saint.' The routine is the same, but a new producer, director and writers have pepped it up. The dialogue has a bit more luster, the situations are more brightly contrived, and an admirable cast [plays] it with somewhat more verve." *Boxoffice* reported, "Unless they be extremely rabid detective-film fans, it will probably be a matter of total indifference to average patrons whether or not they keep this date with the 'Falcon' ... George Sanders is still the 'Falcon' and does as well as can be expected with the material furnished him.... Attempts to inject the comedy elements which are standard equipment in the foregoing plot prove to be another stultifying factor." While declaring it "another interesting crime adventure," *The Film Daily* also complained, "For a detective yarn, the script fails to generate enough suspense and build-up situations." Far more upbeat were Karl and Sue Thiede in "The Falcon Saga" (*Views & Reviews,* Fall 1971), when they declared, "[T]he mystery is enjoyable with excellent musical scoring by Paul Sawtell."

Wendy Barrie played the same role in *A Date with the Falcon* as she did in the earlier *The Gay Falcon*; she was also George Sanders' leading leady in his last "Saint" outing, *The Saint in Palm Springs.* Irving Reis directed *The Gay Falcon* and *A Date with the Falcon* and Howard Benedict produced both. Besides Sanders, Allen Jenkins was Goldy Locke and Eddie Dunn appeared as Detective "Grimesy" Grimes in both ventures. James Gleason would play Inspector O'Hara again in *The Falcon Takes Over. A Date with the Falcon* was Edward Gargan's first of seven appearances as thick-headed Detective Bates.

Deluge (1933; 70 minutes)

PRODUCERS: Samuel Bischoff, Burt Kelly & William Saal. DIRECTOR: Felix Feist. SCREENPLAY: Warren Duff & John F. Goodrich, from the novel by S. Fowler Wright. PHOTOGRAPHY: Norbert Brodine. EDITORS: Martin G. Cohn & Rose Loewinger. MUSIC: Val Burton & Edward Kilenyl. ART DIRECTOR: Ralph M. DeLacy. SOUND: Corson Jowett, Hans Weeren, Martin Jackson, Gil Polleck & Alf Burton. PROPERTY MASTERS: Charles Hanley & Bob Murphy. VISUAL EFFECTS: Russell Lawson, Ned Mann & William N. Williams. ELECTRICAL EFFECTS: Al Cohen & Donald Donaldson. ASSISTANT DIRECTOR: Eric Stacey.

CAST: Peggy Shannon (Claire Arlington), Lois Wilson (Helen Webster), Sidney Blackmer (Martin Webster), Matt Moore (Tom), Fred Kohler (Jephson), Ralf Harolde (Norwood), Edward Van Sloan (Professor Carlyle), Samuel S. Hinds (Chief Forecaster), Lane Chandler (Jack), Fred "Snowflake" Toones (Black Sculptor Bidder), Ronnie Crosby (Ronnie Webster), John Elliott (Minister), Edward LeSaint (Passerby), William Norton Bailey, Henry Otho, Harry Semels, Philo McCullough, Billy N. Williams (Gang Members), Edwin Stanley (Radio Announcer), Albert J. Smith (Bellamy), Edna Marion (Edna), Dell Henderson (Navy Officer), Eddy Chandler (Ship Captain), Frank O'Connor, Charles Sullivan (Townsmen).

First shown theatrically by RKO in the spring of 1933, *Deluge* was thought to be a lost film until a copy, dubbed in Italian, was found in Rome in 1981. For decades prior to that, only a small piece of the feature could be seen: footage showing the destruction of New York City in *S.O.S. Tidal Wave*, a 1939 Republic release. Republic had purchased the sequence from RKO to use in this feature and later in the serials *Dick Tracy vs. Crime, Inc.* (1941) and *King of the Rocket Men* (1949). The special effects were done by Russell Lawson (mattes), Ned Mann (miniatures) and William Williams (photographer). They are very impressive, especially the crumbling buildings and the immense tidal wave. Following the destruction, *Deluge* settles down to become the precursor of both the post-apocalypse and disaster film genres. It even throws in a *ménage à trois* involving one male and two female survivors.

At a weather observatory in New York City, Professor Carlyle (Edward Van Sloan) and his chief forecaster (Samuel S. Hinds) monitor worldwide weather conditions with the barometer continuing to plunge. Violent storms cause all ships to be brought to port and aircraft grounded. Following an unexpected eclipse of the sun, four days of unending earthquakes shake the planet. Millions are killed along the West Coast and soon the entire western part of the country is demolished. Lawyer Martin Webster (Sidney Blackmer), his wife Helen (Lois Wilson) and their two children take shelter in a rock quarry after falling trees destroy their home, 40 miles from Gotham. An earthquake topples all the structures in New York City which is then washed away by a tidal wave. Martin is separated from his family. When the storm subsides he finds himself on an island. On another nearby islet, thugs Jepson (Fred Kohler) and Norwood (Ralf Harolde) find beautiful championship swimmer Claire Arlington (Peggy Shannon) unconscious on the beach. They carry her to their shack and in a few days both men lust for her. When Norwood tries to rape Claire, Jephson strangles him. Claire runs away and swims to Martin's island. He finds her exhausted on the beach and takes her to his shelter near a tunnel where he has collected provisions. Jephson follows in a boat and lands on the island. Martin trails him to a cave, the hideout of a murderous gang led by Bellamy (Albert J. Smith), and nearby he finds the body of a young woman they have killed. Jephson stays with the gang but tells them he wants Claire for himself. Claire wakes up and Martin gives her dry clothes and she agrees to remain with him after he tells her about the gang and the murdered girl.

In a settlement 20 miles away, Helen and her children are among 200 survivors led by Tom (Matt Moore), who wants Helen to marry him. She refuses, saying she believes Martin is still alive although Tom informs her of a new rule saying all unmarried women must wed. Believing his family is dead, Martin falls in love with Claire but Jephson knocks him out and takes her to the gang's cave. Martin rescues her and they return to his shelter and spend the night in the tunnel as man and wife. The next day Jephson and the gang surround the tunnel while Tom and the village men set out to destroy the marauders. The gang members rush the tunnel from both ends. Martin manages to shoot several of them, including Bellamy, but Jephson gets inside and the two men fight. The townsmen destroy the rest of the gang. As Jephson tries to kill Martin, Claire runs him through with a spike. Martin introduces Claire to Tom as his wife but when they go back to the village he is reunited with his children and is told that Helen is still alive. Claire and Tom are distraught by the revelations. Martin says he loves both women but is soon elected the leader of the community after he puts an end to fighting over goods by holding an auction. Helen tries to talk with Claire, who says she will not give up Martin for her or their children. After Martin makes a speech about the importance of working together for the future of the settlement's youngsters, Claire leaves the village and jumps into the sea. Realizing what she has done, Martin stands on the beach watching as she swims away.

Advertised as "An Adventure in Speculation," *Deluge* is particularly strong in its early scenes of destruction but manages to hold attention throughout. The production is surprisingly explicit in dealing with rape, murder and a love triangle. Peggy Shannon is especially fetching as Claire, the object of lust in a world in disarray. Lois Wilson too is quite attractive as her romantic rival and Sidney Blackmer makes the most of his role as the lawyer placed by nature in a spot that would make him the envy of most men. Fred Kohler contributes another fine portrayal of a homicidal ruffian as does Ralf Harolde as his weak cohort. Matt Moore is likable as the village leader and genre veteran Edward Van Sloan has a few good scenes early on as the head meteorologist. The production's rather mildewed look fits perfectly with its post-disaster setting which utilizes Bronson Canyon as the site of Martin's tunnel. Made by Admiral Productions in cooperation with RKO, *Deluge* cost over $170,000 with much of the expense going to its special effects.

Motion Picture Daily wrote, "A fantastic theme, that of the destruction of New York by a deluge, is employed to supply situations which provide a fair measure of action, suspense and romance, despite the almost incredible background against which the story is pictured." *Photoplay* opined, "Earthquakes, tidal waves, the end of the world provide the thrills here. Cast and story alike thwarted by the catastrophe." Mordaunt Hall in *The New York Times* referred to the film as a "rumbling and gurgling thriller" and noted, "It is remarkable how soon the few remaining mortals regain their composure after the world disaster and become quite interested in living in caverns and shacks." The (Jefferson City, Missouri) *Sunday News and Tribune* pointed out, "*Deluge* deserves special plaudits for its excellent photographic effects. The camera crew created ingenious devices to picture the earth's destruction, the earthquake and the action of raging waters." *The Hammond* (Indiana) *Times* concurred, "*Deluge* vividly depicts the end of the world by an earthquake and tidal wave spectacularly effected by modern photography." *Variety* said that the film "starts as a spectacle and winds up a western."

The Devil and Miss Jones (1941; 92 minutes)

PRODUCER: Frank Ross. DIRECTOR: Sam Wood. SCREENPLAY: Norman Krasna. PHOTOGRAPHY: Harry Stradling. EDITOR: Sherman Todd. MUSIC DIRECTOR: Roy Webb. ART DIRECTORS: Van Nest Polglase & Albert S. D'Agostino. SOUND: John L. Cass. PRODUCTION DESIGN: William Cameron Menzies. SPECIAL EFFECTS: Vernon L. Walker. COSTUMES: Irene. ASSISTANT DIRECTOR: Argyle Nelson.

CAST: Jean Arthur (Mary Jones), Robert Cummings (Joe O'Brien), Charles Coburn (John P. Merrick), Edmund Gwenn (Hooper), Spring Byington (Elizabeth Ellis), S.Z. Sakall (George), William Demarest, Charles Irwin (Detectives), Walter Kingsford (Allison), Montagu Love (Harrison), Richard Carle (Oliver), Charles Waldron (Needles), Edwin Maxwell (Withers), Edward McNamara (Police Sergeant), Robert Emmett Keane (Tom Higgins), Florence Bates (Customer), Matt McHugh (Sam), Julie Warren (Dorothy),

Ilene Brewer (Sally), Regis Toomey, Pat Moriarty (Policemen), Brooks Benedict (Mr. Felspar), Pat Flaherty (Officer Mark), Carol Dietrich (Blonde), Garry Owen (Drug Store Clerk), Suzanne Ridgeway (China Department Clerk), Minta Durfee, Fern Emmett, Kenner G. Kemp, Edna Hall (Shoppers), Walter Tetley (Stock Boy), Victor Potel, Frank Mills, William Elmer (Bath House Attendants), Mike Lally (Luggage Clerk), Lucio Villegas (Picket), Jack Gargan (Coney Island Man), Nicholas Soussanin (Man on Rooftop), Will Stanton (Pickpocket).

Hardly a horror film, *The Devil and Miss Jones* does contain one brief scene where Charles Coburn is shown as Satan in the environs of Hell while Jean Arthur is pictured as a halo-wearing angel. This impressive opening credits sequence was fashioned by William Cameron Menzies, one of the screen's great production designers, who co-directed *The Spider* (1931) and *Chandu the Magician* (1932) and solo-helmed *Things to Come* (1936), *The Whip Hand* (1951) [q.v.], *Invaders from Mars* and *The Maze* (both 1953). Otherwise, *The Devil and Miss Jones* is a delightful comedy that pokes fun at wealth, business and labor while giving Arthur one of her best screen roles. Miss Arthur's husband, Frank Ross, produced the feature with script writer Norman Krasna, and RKO distributed it in the spring of 1941. Coburn nearly steals the film as the world's richest man, netting an Academy Award nomination as Best Supporting Actor; Krasna was nominated for Best Original Screenplay. Coburn repeated the role in two radio adaptations, first on CBS's *The Screen Guild Theatre* on June 7, 1943, with Laraine Day and George Murphy, and on the same network's *Academy Award Theatre* on October 23, 1946, with Virginia Mayo. When "The Devil and Miss Jones" was broadcast on NBC's *Lux Radio Theatre* on January 19, 1942, Lana Turner, Lionel Barrymore and Fred MacKaye took over the lead roles. The same series did it again on March 12, 1945, with Linda Darnell, Frank Morgan and Gordon Oliver. On August 12, 1946, *The Screen Guild Theatre* did a second adaptation of *The Devil and Miss Jones* headlining Van Johnson, Donna Reed and Guy Kibbee.

Employees at a big department store have hung an effigy of multi-millionaire owner John P. Merrick (Coburn). Members of his board of directors are distressed by the event. Merrick fires a detective (Robert Emmett Keane) he hired to find the culprits and assumes the guise of a children's shoes sales clerk Higgins to investigate first hand.

A haughty manager, Hooper (Edmund Gwenn), debases him but he is treated kindly by another clerk, Mary Jones (Arthur); she gives him lunch money. Merrick meets employee Elizabeth Ellis (Spring Byington) and they dine together. That evening Mary invites Merrick to eat with her at an automat and then takes him to a store employees meeting where her boyfriend, Joe O'Brien (Robert Cummings), tries to get the workers to unite against Merrick, who he hung in effigy. While discussing the lack of job security, Mary tells the group how the new employee was treated by Hooper. That night, Merrick tells George (S.Z. Sakall), his butler, to bring a little girl to his department the next day so he can sell her shoes. George and Sally (Ilene Brewer) are about to purchase five pairs of expensive shoes when Hooper muscles in on the sale. Just as Merrick is about to fire Hooper, Mary talks him into going with her, Joe and Elizabeth to Coney Island. Merrick feels Joe is a bad influence on Mary but at the beach the next day she tells him she loves Joe. Later in the day Merrick gets lost and cannot find the bath house where he left his clothes and offers a clerk (Victor Potel) his gold watch for a nickel to make a telephone call. The clerk calls the police and Merrick is taken to jail, followed by Mary. Joe shows up with Elizabeth and uses his knowledge of the law and individual rights to get his friends released. Back at the beach, Merrick and Elizabeth, who are falling in love, relax in the sun. Mary asks Joe to marry her but he refuses, saying he is leaving town because of his failure to unionize the store workers. When Mary dubs him a coward, Joe throws away a list of 400 employees he talked with. Merrick finds it and tries to give it to Mary but she refuses to take it. On the train back to town, Elizabeth comments she could never marry a wealthy man and Merrick's reply makes Mary suspicious. Mary finds Merrick's ID card and checks on him, learning that "Higgins" is a private eye working for Merrick. Mary finds Joe at her apartment and they reconcile. She informs him that Higgins works for Merrick and has his employee list. Joe tells Mary to get Merrick in the storage area the next day so he can get the list but when they try to do so, they are taken to the office of the general manager, Allison (Walter Kingsford). Mary calls Merrick a Benedict Arnold. Merrick blames Allison for doing a poor job. Allison says he will meet with employees to discuss their grievances and takes the list. He then calls them morons. Mary takes back the list and she and Merrick tear it up and swallow it. Allison promises to fire all fifth floor employee but Mary uses the PA system to get the workers to unite. When his employees picket his mansion, Merrick tries to get away but they see him and dub him a hero. Merrick then brings Mary and Joe into his home where they are surprised to find him treated with deference. When they learn Merrick's real identity, Joe faints and Mary screams. Merrick agrees to make things better for his workers and treats them to a vacation in Hawaii. Joe and Mary and Merrick and Elizabeth have a double wedding and on the ship to Honolulu, Merrick is serenaded by his employees.

An alternate ending was filmed for *The Devil and Miss Jones* in which Merrick's board of directors identify the store's troublemaker as a wanted fugitive. He fires them and makes plans for a party where he will promise his workers improved conditions. He proceeds to picket his own mansion with Mary, Joe and Elizabeth and takes possession of his effigy. Following selected previews of the film, this ending was junked and a new one lensed.

Considered one of the top comedies of 1941, *The Devil and Miss Jones* garnered fine reviews. *Boxoffice* termed it "a fairy tale, spun in ultra-modern tempo and sprinkled with a sauce of sociological significance. It is far from the dour document its title might indicate, but, rather, a brightly concocted comedy which adroitly tempers with a multitude of laughs whatever preachment its script imparts." Bosley Crowther in *The New York Times* dubbed it "a fable which clicks off laughs like the ticking of a clock." He summed up the picture as "delightfully piquant." *Variety* termed it "a light and fluffy tale," adding, "At times, the script tends to over-dialog passages that tend to slow down the otherwise neatly paced tempo, but this is a minor shortcoming in the overall content of the picture." *Photoplay* summed it up as "riotous ... a honey." *The Film Daily* called *The Devil and Miss Jones* "a swell job on all scores.... Audiences should like it immensely and should be solidly entertained by it.... On the production side, there is nothing lacking. Director Sam Wood also deserves a full share of the laurels."

Dick Tracy (1945; 61 minutes)

PRODUCER: Herman Schlom. EXECUTIVE PRODUCER: Sid Rogell. DIRECTOR: William Berke. SCREENPLAY: Eric Taylor, from the comic strip by Chester Gould. PHOTOGRAPHY: Frank Redman. EDITOR: Ernie Leadlay. MUSIC: Roy Webb. MUSIC DIRECTOR: C. Bakaleinikoff. ART DIRECTORS: Ralph Berger & Albert S. D'Agostino. SOUND: Terry Kellum & Jean L. Speak. SET DECORATIONS: Darrell Silvera. ASSISTANT DIRECTOR: Clem Beauchamp.

CAST: Morgan Conway (Dick Tracy), Anne Jeffreys (Tess Trueheart), Mike Mazurki (Alexis "Splitface" Banning), Jane Greer (Judith Owens), Lyle Latell (Pat Patton), Joseph Crehan (Chief Brandon), Mickey Kuhn (Junior), Trevor Bardette (Professor Lindwood J. Starling), Morgan Wallace (Steve Owens), Milton Parsons (Deathridge), William Halligan (Mayor), Edythe Elliott (Mrs. Caraway), Ralph Dunn (Detective Manning), Tommy Noonan (Johnny Moko), Jason Robards, Wilbur Mack (Motorists), Alphonse Martell (Jules), Tanis Chandler (Miss Stanley), Mary Currier (Dorothy Stafford), Jack Chefe (Headwaiter), Robert Douglas (Busboy), Edmund Glover (Radio Dispatcher Joe), Franklyn Farnum (Murder Scene Bystander), Bob Reeves, Sam Ash, Frank Meredith, Jack Gargan, Carl Faulkner (Policemen), Harry Strang, George Magrill (Interrogation Officers), Bruce Mitchell (Bald Policeman), Bruce Edwards (Police Sergeant), Jimmy

Jordan, Carl Hanson (Pedestrians), Mike Lally (Mayor's Assistant), Harold Miller (Club Customer), Gertrude Astor, Florence Pepper (Women), Ken Carpenter (Voice of Radio Announcer).

Chester Gould's perennially popular comic strip "Dick Tracy" debuted in 1931 and he continued to do it until 1977 when he retired and it was taken over by Max Allan Collins and Rick Fletcher, a longtime Gould assistant. Dick Tracy's popularity extended to other media, including books, radio and movies. Ralph Byrd became typed as the character after playing him in four Republic serials, *Dick Tracy* (1937), *Dick Tracy Returns* (1938), *Dick Tracy's G-Men* (1939) and *Dick Tracy vs. Crime, Inc.* (1941). When RKO acquired the rights to Dick Tracy in 1945, instead of casting Byrd as the character, they had studio contract player Morgan Conway essay the role. While obviously comfortable as Tracy and somewhat looking the part, Conway did not click with audiences and after a second effort, *Dick Tracy vs. Cueball* (q.v.), RKO wisely brought in Byrd to wrap up the series with *Dick Tracy's Dilemma* and *Dick Tracy Meets Gruesome* (qq.v.). Anne Jeffreys, who played Tracy's girlfriend in the first two efforts, is a knockout as Tess Trueheart.

Released late in 1945, but carrying a 1946 copyright date, *Dick Tracy* is a stout, fast-paced detective yarn focused on Gould's fanciful characters and a mad killer known as Splitface (Mike Mazurki). Trevor Bardette plays a slimy mystic who uses his powers to predict the murders of several people, one of whom turns out to be him. Lyle Latell plays Tracy's sidekick Pat Patton, as he did in all four RKO-Tracy features, and Mickey Kuhn makes a solo appearance as Tracy's ward, Junior, and Edythe Elliott plays Mrs. Caraway, Tracy's housekeeper. Joseph Crehan makes the first of three appearances as Tracy's superior, Captain Brandon. All four features were produced by Herman Schlom. The RKO films have Dick Tracy working for the Gotham police department, as he did in the comic strip, in deference to the Republic serials which presented him as a G-man. Professional wrestler Mike Mazurki makes the powerful Splitface a formidable foe for Tracy, and his menacing presence dominates the picture. Mazurki scored a major success the year before as Moose Malloy in RKO's *Murder, My Sweet*.

Getting off a bus at night on Lakeview Road, Dorothy Stafford (Mary Currier) has her throat slit by a large man, Splitface (Mazurki), with her body being found by Miss Stanley (Tanis Chandler). Police detective Dick Tracy (Conway) is notified of the killing by his partner Pat Patton (Latell) and has to delay a dinner date with his frustrated girlfriend Tess Trueheart (Jeffreys). At the murder scene, a bystander (Franklyn Farnum) tells Tracy and Detective Manning (Ralph Dunn) that the attack was the work of a fiend. At his office, Tracy goes through the dead woman's belongings and finds a note signed "Splitface," demanding $500. Chief Brandon (Crehan) summons Tracy and Pat to the mayor's (William Halligan) office, where they are informed that Splitface has sent the mayor a missive demanding $10,000. Pat finds the name Wilbur Thomas in Dorothy's records but when he and Tracy go to interrogate the man, they find that he too has had his throat slit. Seeing a tall man running into the next yard, Tracy follows and questions the property owner, Steven Owens (Morgan Wallace), proprietor of the Paradise Club. Tracy becomes suspicious of Owens when a card from his club is found on Thomas' body. Wanting to survey Owens' club, Tracy takes Tess there for dinner and meets the owner's beautiful daughter Judith (Jane Greer), who has just returned from out of town. She informs Tracy she came immediately to the club after seeing a stranger in the garden of her home and gives him a key to the place. Tracy and Tess go there but find the electricity is off. While Tracy tries to locate the fuse box, Splitface attempts to stab Tess, who sees him and he runs away when the lights come on. Splitface escapes in his car but is followed by Tracy and Tess. Abandoning his vehicle, Splitface slips into a brownstone followed by Tracy. On the roof, Tracy finds Professor Linwood J. Starling (Bardette) observing the stars through a telescope; he is an astrologist and a doctor of the occult sciences.

Tracy searches Starling's room and finds a knife under his mattress. Starling looks into his crystal ball and says he sees blood dripping from two knives, with a dozen more murders to be committed. Pat takes Starling to headquarters to be questioned. On the chance the killer's scar may be makeup, Tracy returns with Tess to the Paradise Club so she can see Owens but Judith says her father is missing. Tracy takes Judith to stay at his home, for protection, with his housekeeper, Mrs. Caraway (Elliott), and his ward, Junior (Kuhn). A jealous Tess goes along to keep Judith company. Pat learns that the knife Tracy found at Starling's came from a surgical supply store that sold three of them to Deathridge (Milton Parsons), an undertaker. The two detectives interview Deathridge, who claims

Anne Jeffreys, Mike Mazurki and Jane Greer in *Dick Tracy* **(1945).**

that all three of his knives were stolen. At headquarters, Tracy interrogates Starling and feels the star gazer knows the undertaker. At his house, Judith complains to Tracy that she is being kept a prisoner. The undertaker is the killer's next victim.

At headquarters, Captain Brandon informs Tracy that Starling has been released on a writ of habeas corpus. Starling returns home and hurriedly packs but is summoned to the building's roof by Splitface, who accuses him of a double cross. Starling, who knew Splitface in prison, admits blackmailing his murder victims for easy money. Splitface throws him through a skylight into his apartment. Tracy arrives to find the man dying and then questions the mayor, learning he once was on a jury with the murder victims. They sent Alexis Banning (Mazurki) to prison for stabbing his sweetheart to death and he promised to kill them all. An all points bulletin is issued for Splitface. When Judith decides to leave Tracy's house, Tess calls her boyfriend to let him know. While she is talking to him, Splitface abducts Tess and drives her to an abandoned houseboat, unaware that Junior is riding on the back of the car and leaving clues to their destination by throwing off his hat and coat. Tracy and Pat follow them to the houseboat, where Splitface ties up Tess and Junior. As he attempts to escape, Splitface engages in a grueling fight with Tracy, who finally knocks him out. Pat handcuffs the killer and takes him to jail. With the case wrapped up, Tracy prepares to take Tess and Junior to dinner, but Pat announces that a cab driver has been shot and Tess is left to take Junior home.

The Film Daily's reviewer apparently was unaware of Dick Tracy's previous movie serial history: "With the potency of the Dick Tracy name as a come-on, RKO has been able safely to risk the choice of a well-worn, uninspired story and a pedestrian production in fashioning the screen debut of the comic-strip hero." *Boxoffice* said that *Dick Tracy* "is ably produced and directed and the performances leave little room for criticism. It's a fast-moving cops-and-robbers melodrama.... In the title role, Morgan Conway is convincing...." *Variety* declared, "Nifty action melodrama.... Chester Gould's comic strip of same title lends itself handily to screen melodrama.... Cast is excellent and bring the Gould characters alive without the grotesqueness that features the newspaper strip." James Van Nise opined in *Calling Tracy!: Six Decades of Dick Tracy* (1990), "From the beginning, this feature is film noir all the way. Not only are all the sets moody and evocative, but it is set at night.... Morgan Conway is interesting to watch and brings subtlety to the Tracy role, supported by a tight script by Eric Taylor."

During the time the RKO-Tracy films were being released, the character was very popular on radio in the *Dick Tracy* series. The program began early in 1935 on CBS, switching to Mutual later in the year. In 1938 it was sponsored by Quaker Oats on NBC. It moved to ABC in 1943 where its sponsor was the Sweets Company. The series left the airwaves on July 16, 1948. Among the actors portraying Tracy in the series were Ned Weaver, Matt Crowley and Barry Thompson.

Dick Tracy Meets Gruesome (1947; 65 minutes)

PRODUCER: Herman Schlom. DIRECTOR: John Rawlins. SCREENPLAY: Eric Taylor & Robertson White. STORY: Robert E. Kent & William H. Graffis, from the comic strip by Chester Gould. PHOTOGRAPHY: Frank Redman. EDITOR: Elmo Williams. MUSIC: Paul Sawtell. MUSIC DIRECTOR: C. Bakaleinikoff. ART DIRECTORS: Albert S. D'Agostino & Walter E. Keller. SOUND: Jean L. Speak & Terry Kellum. SET DECORATIONS: Darrell Silvera & James Altweis. MAKEUP: Gordon Bau. SPECIAL EFFECTS: Russell A. Cully. ASSISTANT DIRECTOR: James Lane.

CAST: Boris Karloff (Gruesome), Ralph Byrd (Dick Tracy), Anne Gwynne (Tess Trueheart), Edward Ashley (Dr. Lee Thal), June Clayworth (Dr. I.M. Learned), Lyle Latell (Pat Patton), Tony Barrett (Melody), Skelton Knaggs (X-Ray), Jim Nolan (Dan Sterne), Joseph Crehan (Chief Brandon), Milton Parsons (Dr. A. Tomic), Richard Powers [Tom Keene] (Dr. Frankey), Harry Harvey (Bank Guard Humphrey), Lex Barker (Ambulance Attendant), Sean McClory (Officer Carney), Robert Bray (Police Sergeant), Robert Clarke (Chemist Fred), Suzi Crandall (Blonde Bank Customer), George Cooper (Bank Teller Stone), Ernie Adams (Bar Waiter), George Lloyd (Bar Proprietor), Jason Robards (Mr. Fax), William Gould (Hospital Desk Sergeant), Robert Malcolm (Dr. Carver), Harry Strang (Policeman Tim), Bert Roach (Mr. Crandall), Lorin Raker (Broke Bank Customer), Phil Arnold (Sneezing Bank Customer), Eddie Borden (Bank Customer), Ben Hall (Luke), Lee Meehan, Bruce Mitchell, Lee Phelps (Police Car Officers), Tex Swan (Policeman).

Boris Karloff finished a four-picture contract with RKO by appearing as the title villain in *Dick Tracy Meets Gruesome*, released in late September 1947. This is one of the few times in movie history where the bad guy gets billing over the hero, in this case Ralph Byrd in his second and last appearance as Tracy in an RKO feature. John Rawlins, who previously directed Byrd in *Dick Tracy's Dilemma* (q.v.), helmed the production with Lyle Latell and Joseph Crehan reprising their roles of Pat Patton and Chief Brandon from the three previous Tracy outings. Anne Gwynne, who along with Karloff was in Universal's *Black Friday* (1940) and *House of Frankenstein* (1944), is Tess Trueheart. Working titles for the feature were *Dick Tracy Meets the Gruesome Guy*, *Dick Tracy Meets Karloff* and *Dick Tracy vs. Dr. Nerves*. In Great Britain it was issued as *Dick Tracy's Amazing Adventure*. Under any title, it is a slick, fast-moving and entertaining program feature, dominated by Karloff as the murderous Gruesome. Its sci-fi angle is a gas bomb that causes people to freeze for 15 minutes. Among its supporting cast, Skelton Knaggs and Milton Parsons contribute fine performances as eccentric characters, X-Ray and Dr. A. Tomic. Among the other Chester Gould comic strip character names are Dr. Lee Thal (Edward Ashley), Dr. I.M. Learned (June Clayworth) and bank president Mr. Fax (Jason Robards).

After escaping from prison, notorious criminal Gruesome (Karloff) heads to the Hangman's Knot Bar to see a cohort, Melody (Tony Barrett), who plays piano there. Melody takes him to see the head of Wood Plastics, Inc., about pulling off a big-time robbery. Upon their arrival, Melody goes to talk with the boss while Gruesome is warned by assistant X-Ray (Knaggs) not

Anne Gwynne, Ralph Byrd, Boris Karloff and Skelton Knaggs in *Dick Tracy Meets Gruesome* **(1947).**

to touch any of the chemicals in the room. After X-Ray leaves, Gruesome explores a cabinet and opens a vile which releases a gas which causes him to become disoriented. He stumbles back to the Hangman's Knot and passes out in front of the bar. A beat cop (Sean McClory) finds him and calls headquarters. Pat Patton (Latell) arrives, thinks Gruesome is drunk and drives him to the police hospital. Upon arrival, Dr. Carney (Richard Powers) pronounces the man dead and Pat contacts Dick Tracy (Byrd), believing it is now a homicide case. Tracy and Chief Brandon (Crehan) are in the middle of talking with physicist Dr. A. Tomic (Parsons), who says he has seen figures lurking in the shadows near his home and claims that he was nearly hit by two cars. As Pat is filling out a report on the dead man, Gruesome revives, knocks out the detective and takes his gun. When Pat tells Tracy he was hit from behind and the corpse is missing, Tracy says he simply had a drunk that woke up. Returning to Wood Plastics, Gruesome tells X-Ray to inform the boss that they are now partners. The next afternoon, just at its 3:00 closing, the First National Bank's staff and customers are frozen by the activation of one Tomic's gas bombs. Only customer Tess Trueheart (Gywnne), Tracy's girlfriend, escapes paralysis because she is in a telephone booth. Gruesome and Melody steal over $100,000 while Tess manages to sneak to a desk telephone and call Tracy. As X-Ray drives the escape car, Melody shoots and kills a policeman (Tex Swan).

Tracy and Pat arrive at the bank just as everyone revives. Back at headquarters, Chief Brandon tells Tracy that if the story of the robbery gets out, there will be a run on every bank in town. To complicate matters, newspaperman Dan Sterne (Jim Nolan) gets wind of the occurrence and Tracy makes him promise not to break the story until his final edition, ten hours away. Tracy wants to question Tomic about the mysterious gas, but learns from Tomic's assistant I.M. "Irma" Learned (Clayworth) that the doctor has gone missing. Tracy asks for a sample of a formula in one of the doctor's test tubes, which Irma drops. Managing to get a bit of the liquid, Tracy has it analyzed. At the Hangman's Knot, Pat spots Gruesome; he and Melody escape in a car, followed by Pat and Tracy. Gruesome escapes but Melody is injured and apprehended. At the police hospital, Melody is identified as one of the bank robbers by bank customer Dr. Lee Thal (Ashley). Irma meets Thal in a park and tells him she does not want to darken Tomic's reputation. When she returns to her apartment, Irma finds Tracy there and he informs her she may be an accessory to murder. After he leaves, Irma calls Thal, who promises to take her away and says to meet him at the corner of 6th and Park. Gruesome confronts Thal and demands his car keys so he can drive Irma to the distant cabin where the doctor plans to hide her. Tracy follows Irma as she goes to meet Thal. She finds Gruesome waiting and he shoots her. When he learns that Melody has died, Tracy sets a trap for Gruesome. Back at the laboratory, Gruesome informs

Boris Karloff, Ralph Byrd and Skelton Knaggs in *Dick Tracy Meets Gruesome* (1947).

Thal that Irma is dead. When the doctor and X-Ray try to use one of the paralyzing bombs on Gruesome, he shoots Thal. Just as he is about to do in X-Ray, Gruesome hears a radio broadcast saying Melody is alive and will be able to talk by morning. After incinerating Thal, just as he did Tomic, Gruesome steals an ambulance and he and X-Ray, dressed as hospital attendants, go to get Melody, who is being impersonated by Tracy, whose face is covered in bandages. They manage to get Tracy out of the hospital but Gruesome has a confrontation with an ambulance driver (Lex Barker), knocks him out and steals his vehicle. Gruesome takes Tracy, who he thinks is Melody, to Wood Plastics where he plans to incinerate him. As X-Ray is starting the fire, Gruesome searches for more bombs and Tracy tries to get Thal's gun, which is lying behind his body. He overpowers X-Ray but Gruesome spots him and traps Tracy in a store room where he activates one of the bombs. Tracy escapes through a skylight, gets the gun and shoots and kills Gruesome.

Dick Tracy Meets Gruesome was dubbed a "chiller-diller" by *Variety* with the reviewer adding, "Karloff, per usual, thefts every scene in which he appears. Byrd is acceptable as Tracy, even to resemblance to the square-jawed detective…. Director John Rawlins employs serial-type action but with surprisingly good results." *Boxoffice* wrote, "In story, situations, nomenclature and dialog this comes closer than its predecessors to capturing the tongue-in-cheek aura of the widely printed Chester Gould comic strip…. [T]he feature is as good as earlier chapters and is dependable to fare as well in attracting and pleasing customers." *Independent Exhibitors Film Bulletin* said, "The addition of Boris Karloff to the cast of this latest Dick Tracy movie adventure atomically endows it with greater box office value than any of the previous entries in the series…. [It] is superior on other counts, too…. [It's] all done in amusing tongue-in-cheek style, with ample excitement for those who want to take it straight…. This is topflight for action houses and a good supporting dualler elsewhere." The British publication *The Cinema* opined, "The principal artistes in this farrago are [Byrd and Karloff], both boisterous exponents of unblushing burlesque."

Harrison's Reports stated *Dick Tracy Meets Gruesome* did only "fair to poor" business at the box office, probably the main reason the studio did not renew its rights to the Dick Tracy character. That same year RKO ceased its Falcon series, another indication that the detective film cycle of the period was coming to an end.

Byrd returned to the Gould character in 1950, appearing in 24 episodes of the ABC-TV *Dick Tracy* series. Produced by Snader Television, the series ran from September 30, 1950, to February 12, 1951, with reruns each Saturday from February 17 to March 31, 1951. The next year plans were underway to have Byrd back on TV as Dick Tracy in a series produced by Rudy Vallee's company, Vallee-Video. Just as a deal was about to be signed with NBC-TV, Byrd died of a heart attack on August 18, 1952.

Dick Tracy vs. Cueball (1946; 62 minutes)

PRODUCER: Herman Schlom. EXECUTIVE PRODUCER: Sig Rogell. DIRECTOR: Gordon Douglas. SCREENPLAY: Dane Lussier & Robert E. Kent. STORY: Luci Ward, from the comic strip by Chester Gould. PHOTOGRAPHY: George E. Diskant. EDITOR: Philip Martin, Jr. MUSIC: Phil Ohman. MUSIC DIRECTOR: C. Bakaleinikoff. ART DIRECTORS: Albert S. D'Agostino & Lucius O. Croxton. SOUND: Roy Granville & Robert H. Guhl. SET DECORATIONS: Darrell Silvera & Shelby Willis. SPECIAL EFFECTS: Russell A. Cully. DIALOGUE DIRECTOR: Leslie Urbach.

CAST: Morgan Conway (Dick Tracy), Anne Jeffreys (Tess Trueheart), Lyle Latell (Pat Patton), Rita Corday (Mona Clyde), Ian Keith (Vitamin Flintheart), Dick Wessel (Cueball), Douglas Walton (Percival Priceless), Esther Howard (Filthy Flora), Joseph Crehan (Chief Brandon), Byron Foulger (Simon Little), Jimmy Crane (Junior), Milton Parsons (Higby), Skelton Knaggs (Rudolph), Phil Warren (Coroner), Harry V. Cheshire (Jules Sparkle), Jason Robards (Captain Mason), Max Wagner (Bartender), Lee Frederick

(Ship's Purser), Bill Wallace (Hotel Doorman), Jimmy Clemons (Butch), Robert Bray (Steve), Trevor Bardette (Lester Abbott), Eddie Borden, Frank Mills, Kit Guard (Bar Customers), Perc Launders (Police Sergeant), Ralph Dunn (Accident Policeman), Jack Cheatham, Raoul Freeman (Policemen).

Released late in 1946, *Dick Tracy vs. Cueball* is the second of four features RKO made based on Chester Gould's popular comic strip. Morgan Conway as Tracy, Anne Jeffreys as Tess Trueheart, Lyle Latell as Pat Patton and Joseph Crehan as Chief Brandon repeat their roles from the initial entry *Dick Tracy* (q.v.). A straight police thriller, *Dick Tracy vs. Cueball* contains only slight genre elements, mainly the character of the bald, grotesque Cueball, well played by Dick Wessel, and the use of such oddball names as Jules Sparkle, Percival Priceless and Filthy Flora. The film marked the first of two appearances by Ian Keith as ham actor Vitamin Flintheart, a very broad takeoff of John Barrymore in his later years. It was the second and last time Conway enacted the role of Dick Tracy. While more than competent in the part, Conway did not catch on with the public and exhibitors, who demanded the return of Ralph Byrd (who earlier stamped the role as his own in four Republic serials) as Tracy. Byrd took over the role in *Dick Tracy's Dilemma* (q.v.), issued five months later. *Dick Tracy vs. Cueball* was also Anne Jeffreys' second and final venture as Tess Trueheart.

Ex-convict Cueball (Wessel) sneaks aboard the *S.S. Palomar,* docked at Pier 30 at Gotham Harbor. He confronts Lester Abbott (Trevor Bardette), who is carrying $300,000 worth of stolen diamonds, and strangles him with a leather hat band when Abbott tries to shoot him. Dick Tracy (Conway) is called after Abbott's body is found; he and his partner Pat Patton (Latell) rush away from a birthday celebration just as his girlfriend Tess Trueheart (Jeffreys) and pal Vitamin Flintheart (Keith) bring in his cake. Tracy and Pat interview Abbott's boss, diamond dealer Jules Sparkle (Harry V. Cheshire), in his office at the Coburn Building. Sparkle tells Tracy that Abbott was bringing him a gem shipment. Tracy asks Sparkle's secretary, Mona Clyde (Rita Corday), to provide a list of the company's employees. While there, the two detectives are also introduced to Sparkle's diamond cutter, Simon Little (Byron Foulger); Tracy has Pat follow him home. When Little arrives at his apartment, his assistant Rudolph (Skelton Knaggs) says that Cueball is waiting for him in his basement workroom. Cueball informs Little he wants $10,000 for the diamonds and the lapidary says he will have to consult with his boss, antique dealer Percival Priceless (Douglas Walton). Leaving Little's abode, Cueball knocks out Pat, who has been standing guard. Tracy tails Mona to Priceless' shop where she slips a note under the door. He confronts the antique dealer, who informs him he was expecting Mona two hours earlier; her note dealt with his having found some rare candle holders for her.

Needing a place to hide, Cueball goes to the Dripping Dagger saloon and talks with the proprietor, Filthy Flora (Esther Howard), with whom he used to work. Seeing a newspaper story about the stolen diamonds, Flora offers him a hidden room for $500 a night and he accepts. Learning from the coroner (Phil Warren) that Abbott was murdered with a leather strap, Tracy gets Vitamin to pretend to be an eccentric antique collector and has him check out Priceless' shop, generally annoying Priceless' assistant, Higby (Milton Parsons). Vitamin reports to Tracy that Mona came to the place and met secretly with Priceless. Tracy and Pat follow Priceless to Flora's bar after she informs the antique dealer that Cueball is there. Priceless refuses to give Cueball the money he demands and when the ex-convict spots the two policemen, he thinks Priceless has double-crossed him and he uses his hat band to strangle him. The fleeing Cueball again knocks out Pat. Tracy and Pat chase Cueball, who has stolen an auto, but Pat ends up wrecking their squad car and finds himself arrested for drunk driving by a street cop (Ralph Dunn). Flora tries to locate the diamonds in her room and is observed by Cueball, who strangles her. At Tracy's house, Tess arrives to take Junior (Jimmy Crane), Tracy's ward, and his friend Butch (Jimmy

Clemons) to a rodeo; Tracy notices Butch's leather hat band and later learns it was made at the Rocky Mountain Penitentiary. As a result, the police are able to identify Cueball and an all points bulletin is put out for him. Tracy decides to trap Cueball by having a policewoman pose as a society girl interested in buying the diamonds. When none of the recruits are suitable, Tess offers to do the job and Vitamin coaches her in social deportment. Pretending to be wealthy heiress Blythe Belmonte, Tess meets with Sparkle and Mona, who promise to help her get the diamonds. Mona goes to Little's apartment where they offer Cueball slightly over $4,000 for the gems while planning to sell them to Tess for a larger sum. Cueball overhears Mona's phone call to Tess, unaware that Tracy and Pat are at her apartment. When Little tries to pay off Cueball and get the diamonds, he finds the ex-convict has disappeared. Little goes to Mona's apartment to inform her about Cueball, who poses as a cab driver taking Tess to see Mona. Tracy and Pat confront Mona and Little as Cueball drives Tess to Little's apartment. There they are seen by Rudolph, who phones Mona. Tracy intercepts the call and he and Pat go to rescue Tess. Cueball demands the money for the diamonds from Tess, and when she refuses to pay him he goes through her wallet and finds a picture of her with Tracy. Realizing he has been set up, Cueball tries to strangle Tess but Dick and Pat show up and Cueball drives off in the taxi. Tracy follows Cueball to a train yard where they play a game of cat and mouse until Cueball gets his foot stuck in some tracks and is run over by a train. Mona and Little are arrested and Dick finally gets to have his birthday party, only to have it interrupted when a shoot-out occurs in front of his house.

Dick Wessel was very good as Cueball and others in the supporting cast give equally fine performances, particularly Esther Howard as floozie Filthy Flora, Rita Corday as the beautiful Mona Clyde, Douglas Walton as the slimy antique dealer Percival Priceless, and Byron Foulger as the mousy diamond cutter, Simon Little. Also of interest were two eccentric characters, antique store clerk Higby and Little's associate Rudolph, nicely played by Milton Parsons and Skelton Knaggs.

"Hot action celluloid that's bang-up and bang-bang from start to finish," is how *Variety* enthusiastically reviewed *Dick Tracy vs. Cueball*. *Boxoffice* reported, "Thrills, suspense and sudden death saturate this second of the series…. As imitators of newspaper drawings the actors are better at times than the original characters. Good jobs of makeup have been done on the principals." *The Film Daily* enthused, "There's not a dull moment from start to finish and the conclusion is a rousing gun battle, probably one of the noisiest this season. This is solid thrill entertainment with mayhem from start to finish, quite in keeping with the general trend of the strip."

Dick Tracy's Dilemma (1947; 60 minutes)

PRODUCER: Herman Schlom. DIRECTOR: John Rawlins. SCREENPLAY: Robert Stephen Brode, from the comic strip by Chester Gould. PHOTOGRAPHY: Frank Redman. EDITOR: Marvin Coll. MUSIC: Paul Sawtell. MUSIC DIRECTOR: C. Bakaleinikoff. ART DIRECTORS: Albert S. D'Agostino & Lucius O. Croxton. SOUND: Terry Kellum & Jean L. Speak. SET DECORATIONS: Darrell Silvera. MAKEUP: Gordon Bau. SPECIAL PHOTOGRAPHIC EFFECTS: Russell A. Cully.

CAST: Ralph Byrd (Dick Tracy), Lyle Latell (Pat Patton), Kay Christopher (Tess Trueheart), Jack Lambert (Steve "The Claw" Michel), Ian Keith (Vitamin Flintheart), Bernadene Hayes (Longshot Lillie), Jimmy Conlin (Sightless), William B. Davidson (Peter Premium), Tony Barrett (Sam), Richard Powers [Tom Keene] (Fred), Charles Marsh (Mr. Humphries), Al Bridge (Cudd), Wade Crosby (Jigger), Jay Norris (Morgue Attendant Bill), Sean McClory (Officer Dillon), Jason Robards (Night Watchman Hawks), William Gould (Collins), Phil Warren (Police Sergeant Johnson), Harry Harvey (Officer Donovan), Harry Strang (Warehouse Foreman), Elena Warren (Policewoman), Roger Creed (Taxi Driver), Jack Perrin, Tom London, Frank O'Connor (Squad Car Policemen), Eddie Borden (Drunk), Frank Mills (Sailor).

Ralph Byrd returned to the role of Dick Tracy in *Dick Tracy's Dilemma*, which RKO released theatrically in the spring of 1947. Although Morgan Conway had been acceptable as Tracy in the studio's first two features *Dick Tracy* and *Dick Tracy vs. Cueball* (qq.v.), Byrd was preferable, having already established himself as the comic strip hero in the Republic serials *Dick Tracy* (1937), *Dick Tracy Returns* (1938), *Dick Tracy's G-Men* (1939) and *Dick Tracy vs. Crime, Inc.* (1941). It is too bad his feature reprisal of Tracy is basically a reworking of the previous series entry, *Dick Tracy vs. Cueball*. Both films have homicide detective Tracy and his dense pal Pat Patton (Lyle Latell) after a grotesque killer involved in a big heist. In the previous film it was stolen jewels and here it is furs. Both films even have some of the action centered around sleazy dives. Both also have the same type of finale: *Dick Tracy vs. Cueball* has the hero chasing the mad killer to a railroad yard where the bad guy meets a bad end, while *Dick Tracy's Dilemma* follows the same routine, only ending up in a junkyard housing a high voltage generator that does in the villain. *Dick Tracy's Dilemma* provides Tracy's love interest, Tess Trueheart (Kay Christopher), even less to do than in the previous outing, and Ian Keith again chews up the scenery as ham actor Vitamin Flintheart, once more carrying out an assignment that helps corner the killer. Like Dick Wessel as Cueball, Jack Lambert is impressive as the Claw, an unkempt killer with a hook for a right hand.

Gimpy giant Steve Michel (Lambert), known as "The Claw" because he has a hook instead of a hand, breaks into the Flawless Furs Warehouse and knocks out the night watchman, Hawks (Jason Robards). His henchmen Sam (Tony Barrett) and Fred (Richard Powers) drive a truck into the building and the trio open the safe and haul out $200,000 worth of furs. When Hawks revives and tries to stop them, the Claw kills him and they later dump his body. A beat policeman (Sean McClory) finds Hawks is missing and puts in a call to Dick Tracy (Byrd). Tracy and Pat Patton (Latell), who have been checking out the Blinking Skull bar and its owner, Jiggers (Wade Crosby), investigate and are met at the warehouse by its owner, Mr. Humphries (Charles Marsh), along with Honesty Insurance Company's Peter Premium (William B. Davidson) and his investigator Cudd (Alan Bridge). Humphries opens the safe and sees that the furs are missing. Premium wants the furs recovered or his company will have to cover the loss within 24 hours. Hawks' body is found and taken to the morgue where the attendant (Jay Norris) finds a note on the corpse. At the forensics lab, the technician (William Gould) is able to enlarge the writing, leading Tracy and Pat to surmise that three thieves made a getaway in a truck emblazoned with the word "Daisy." At their junkyard garage, Sam and Fred change the name on the truck to Rosebud Delivery and with the Claw go to the Blinking Skull where they contact their boss. Sightless (Jimmy Conlin), who pretends to be blind in order to beg for money, overhears the robbers but makes so much noise he is nearly done in by the Claw before escaping in a taxi cab. Since he works undercover for Tracy, Sightless goes to the detective's home where actor Vitamin Flintheart (Keith) is reciting lines from Hamlet to Tess Trueheart (Christopher), who is awaiting the return of her boyfriend, Tracy. Appalled by Sightless' appearance, Vitamin takes his message and sends him away. When Tracy and Pat return, Tess tells them about Sightless being there and Vitamin manages to recall that the message indicated that stolen furs were to change hands at a rendezvous on Hemp Street. Tracy and Pat go there and see gambler Longshot Lillie (Bernadene Hayes), who they find is carrying $20,000. They take her to headquarters for questioning and she finally admits getting a call from a stranger offering to sell her furs at a cheap price. As she is being interrogated, the Claw goes to Sightless' room and kills him. Tracy and Pat go to talk with Sightless and arrive just as the Claw is starting to make a call on a pay phone in the hall. After finding Sightless murdered, Tracy contacts headquarters and Pat is knocked down by the Claw. Pat revives and gives chase, managing to wound the Claw before he uses the fire escape to get to his car and escape. Finding that the Claw left scratch marks while making his call, Tracy assigns Pat to find the number. Officer Donovan (Harry Harvey) brings Tracy police documents that identify the Claw as Steve Michel, a former rum runner. Tess informs Tracy that Vitamin is brokenhearted over Sightless' murder and the detective gives him an assignment. Tracy then interrogates Priceless and Cudd, who deny stealing the furs. Pat arrives with the news that the phone number is that of Humphries. Tracy stays with Priceless while Pat and Cudd go to see Humphries. Sam and Fred find the wounded Claw passed out in their truck and decide to double-cross him, not knowing he has overheard them. Humphries calls Priceless and tells him he will sell the furs for $50,000 and to bring the money to the Blinking Skull. Fred and Sam go to the bar to wait for Humphries as Vitamin stands out front pretending to be a blind beggar. He sneaks into the back of the bar and sees the Claw confront his cohorts. During a fight, Fred accidentally shoots Sam and is then killed by the Claw. The Claw telephones Humphries, who is guarded by Pat and Cudd, but realizes there has been a frame-up and starts to leave when Vitamin backs into a bucket, arousing his suspicion. As the Claw is about to do in Vitamin, Tracy shows up and the Claw escapes. Vitamin tells Tracy the furs are at a junkyard on Primrose Street and the detective follows the Claw there. Badly wounded, the Claw tries to get away from Tracy and stumbles into a fenced area housing a high voltage generator. As he is about to use his hook to kill the detective, it comes in contact with the generator and he is electrocuted.

Critics did not seem to notice the similarity between *Dick Tracy's Dilemma* and its predecessor, *Dick Tracy vs. Cueball*, although they were released only five months apart. Regarding *Dick Tracy's Dilemma*, *Boxoffice* wrote, "Those who are ardent followers of the exploits of Chester Gould's indomitable pen-and-ink hero will love this episode, which ranks high among the best of the series. Furthermore, it has plenty of action, suspense and excitement for average seekers of cops-and-robbers films.... Ralph Byrd again demonstrates that he was a happy choice for the title role and delivers a characteristic square-jawed, rugged performance." *Variety* declared, "Thrills are backed up with good budget production values by Herman Schlom.... Ralph Byrd is an okay Tracy, with enough resemblance to the fictional character to carry off the role." *Independent Exhibitors Film Bulletin* wrote, "[A] compact action programmer [with] more than its share of suspense and thrills, [it] is certain to be enjoyed especially by juveniles.... It will serve as a good dualler.... Rawlins' tight direction, plus a workmanlike script, aid in maintaining a fast pace throughout." *The Film Daily* noted, "Pumped full of melodramatic fiction that will not for one moment be taken seriously by anyone in their right mind, this new number in the series generates murder, dirty work, ugly characters being very ugly and justice triumphing."

Filmed as *Dick Tracy vs. the Claw*, it was issued in Great Britain as *Mark of the Claw*.

Dumbo (1941; 64 minutes; Color)

PRODUCER: Walt Disney. SUPERVISING DIRECTOR: Ben Sharpsteen. SEQUENCE DIRECTORS: Norman Ferguson, Wilfred Jackson, Bill Roberts, Jack Kinney & Sam Armstrong. ANIMATION DIRECTORS: Vladimir Tytla, Fred Moore, Ward Kimball, John Lounsberry, Arthur Babbitt & Wolfgang Reitherman. SCREENPLAY: Joe Grant & Dick Heumer, from the book by Helen Aberson & Harold Pearl. STORY DIRECTION: Otto Englander. STORY DEVELOPMENT: George Stallings, Webb Smith, Joe Rinaldi & Bill Peet. MUSIC: Frank Church & Oliver Wallace. SONGS: Frank Church, Ned Washington, Oliver Wallace, Arthur Quenzer, Mildred J. Hill & Patty Smith Hill. ORCHESTRATIONS: Edward H. Plumb. ART DIRECTORS: Don Da Gradi, Dick Kelsey, Ernest Nordli, Ken O'Connor, Charles Payzant, Herb Ryman, Terrell Stapp & Al Zinnen. CHARACTER DESIGNERS: John P. Miller, Martin Provensen, John Walbridge, James Bodrero, Maurice Noble & Elmer Plummer. ANIMATORS: Hugh Fraser, Howard Swift, Harvey Toombs, Don Towsley, Milt Neil, Les Clark, Hicks Lokey, Claude Smith, Berny Wolf, Ray Patterson, Jack Campbell,

Grant Simmons, Walt Kelly, Joshua Meador, Don Patterson, Bill Shull, Cy Young & Art Palmer. BACKGROUNDS: Claude Coats, Albert Dempster, John Hench, Gerald Neivus, Ray Lochrem & Joe Stahley. LIVE ACTION MODELS: Arthur Treacher, Eugene Jackson & Freddie Jackson.

VOICE CAST: Edward Brophy (Timothy Q. Mouse), Sterling Holloway (Stork), Herman Bing (Ringmaster), Cliff Edwards (Jim Crow), Verna Felton (Eldest Elephant/Mrs. Jumbo), Billy Bletcher, Eddie Holden, Billy Sheets (Clowns), James Baskett, Nick Stewart, Jim Carmichael (Crows), Sara Selby (Prissy the Elephant), Dorothy Scott (Giddy the Elephant), Noreen Gammill (Cathy the Elephant), Margaret Wright (Casey, Jr.), Malcolm Hutton (Skinny), Chuck Stubbs, Tony Neil, Harold Manley (Boys), The King's Men (Choral Effects), The Hall Johnson Choir (Choral Sounds), Betty Noyes (Singer), John Fraser McLeish (Narrator).

Made for slightly under one million dollars over a span of eighteen months and filmed as *Dumbo the Flying Elephant, Dumbo* was released theatrically in the fall of 1941. A critical and audience success, it has proved to be one of Walt Disney's most endearing, and enduring, cinematic efforts. This Technicolor animated fantasy about a flying baby elephant has delighted audiences for over seven decades and remains a favorite with all ages. It was declared one of the ten best features of 1941 by the National Board of Review and *The New York Times* and it won Best Music score Academy Award. Six years later it was cited at the Cannes Film Festival as best animated feature.

Storks bring infants to various animals that are part of a Florida circus train, but elephant Mrs. Jumbo (voice of Verna Felton) receives none. A lost stork (voice of Sterling Holloway) finally locates the train as it leaves its winter quarters and brings her a bundle, a baby she names Jumbo, Jr. All of the other female elephants think he is cute until he sneezes, revealing oversized ears. They laugh at the little fellow and dub him Dumbo. When a group of boys taunt her little son and pull his ears, Mrs. Jumbo goes into a rage and is chained in a circus car by the ringmaster (voice of Herman Bing). Lonely Dumbo is snubbed by the other elephants but befriended by Timothy Q. Mouse (voice of Edward Brophy), who declares he will make him a star act. When Timothy overhears the ringmaster describe a new act using an elephant pyramid, he whispers the idea of having Dumbo at its top in the sleeping man's ear. During the first performance the clumsy Dumbo trips over his ears, causing the pyramid to fall. As punishment he is made to take part in a comedy act, falling from the top of a burning building into a tub of plaster. Timothy takes the depressed Dumbo to see his mother but their visit is all too short. They accidentally become intoxicated by drinking water containing liquor from a bottle dropped into it by one of the circus clowns. The next morning Dumbo and Timothy find themselves in a tree, surrounded by Jim Crow (voice of Cliff Edwards) and his mocking pals. They fall from the tree and start back to the circus when Timothy realizes Dumbo must have flown into the treetop. Timothy then works with the crows to convince Dumbo he can fly and they give him a magic feather and push him off a bluff. The young elephant uses his ears to fly. During the next performance, Dumbo jumps off the façade but loses the feather. Just as he is about to crash, Dumbo flies over the arena and takes revenge on his tormentors by shooting peanuts at them. Dumbo becomes world-famous and his mother is set free. She is given a special train car as Dumbo flies with Timothy and the crows to their next engagement.

Highlights of *Dumbo* include the detailed sequence in which the drunken young calf and Timothy have visions of pink elephants in various guises and the scenes with the crows, which is highlighted by Cliff Edwards, the voice of Jim Crow, singing "When I See an Elephant Fly." His recording of the song was issued on Victor Records (27662) in 1941 and later on several Disney and Disneyland long-playing record albums.

Variety reported, "Walt Disney returns in *Dumbo* to the formula that accounted for his original success with shorts cartoons—simple animal characterization. The result is topnotch

Advertisement for *Dumbo* (1941).

and should prove highly profitable all around." *Boxoffice* reported, "Unlike most creations from Walt Disney's inkwell, whose appeal is as strong to adults as to children, this new venture into the feature-length cartoon field will undoubtedly find its most popular acceptance among the juvenile element." According to *Photoplay*, "All the whimsical charm that Walt Disney as showered on his past fantasies is embodied in this heart-touching story.... It's appealing, funny and tragic, in turn and drawn to beautiful perfection." *The Film Daily* declared *Dumbo* "Disney at his best.... The story itself is delightful, and along the line is found a wealth of those gloriously tickling touches of grand showmanship, humanness, artistry and ingeniousness for which Disney is renowned."

The Enchanted Cottage (1945; 92 minutes)

PRODUCER: Harriet Parsons. EXECUTIVE PRODUCER: Jack J. Gross. DIRECTOR: John Cromwell. SCREENPLAY: DeWitt Bodeen & Herman J. Mankiewicz, from the play by Sir Arthur Wing Pinero. PHOTOGRAPHY: Ted Tetzlaff. EDITOR: Joseph Noriega. MUSIC: Roy Webb. MUSIC DIRECTOR: C. Bakaleinikoff. MUSIC ARRANGER: Gil Grau. ART DIRECTORS: Carroll Clark & Albert S. D'Agostino. SOUND: Richard Van Hessen & James G. Stewart. SET DECORATIONS: Harley Miller & Darrell Silvera. SPECIAL EFFECTS: Vernon L. Walker. GOWNS: Edward Stevenson. ASSISTANT DIRECTOR: Fred Fleck.

CAST: Dorothy McGuire (Laura Pennington), Robert Young (Oliver Bradford), Herbert Marshall (John Hillgrove), Mildred Natwick (Abigail Minnett), Spring Byington (Violet Bradford Price), Hillary Brooke (Beatrice Alexander), Richard Gaines (Freddy Price), Alec Englander (Danny "Taxi" Stanton), Robert Clarke (Embarrassed Marine Corporal), Josephine Whittell (Canteen Manager Annette), Mary Worth (Harriet Stanton), Rusty Farrell (Mildred), Eden Nicholas, Carl Kent (Soldier), Larry Wheat (Mailman), Walter Soderling (Taxi Driver), Virginia Belmont, Martha Holiday, Nancy Marlow, Patti Brill (Canteen Girls), Sherman Sanders (Dance Caller).

The Enchanted Cottage has a somewhat involved history. It was written by Sir Arthur Wing Pinero and first staged in 1922. It was allegedly done at the urging of the government of Great Britain as a solace for the shell-shocked veterans of the First World War. Associated First National Pictures filmed *The Enchanted Cottage* in 1924 starring Richard Barthelmess, May McAvoy and Holmes Herbert; it was directed by John S. Robertson. In 1929 RKO purchased the play's rights and planned to star Helen Twelvetrees in it and a decade later it was considered for Ginger Rogers. In the early 1940s Harriet Parsons picked the property as her initial RKO outing as a producer but she was replaced by Dudley Nichols, who planned to write the screenplay with Jean Renoir directing. That projected collaboration failed to materialize. Later Parsons again took over the reins, with DeWitt Bodeen and Herman J. Mankiewicz doing the screenplay, which changed the story's locale from World War I London to a remote New England town a quarter of a century later.

Well-made and well-directed, *The Enchanted Cottage* is a heartwarming fantasy that relies heavily on the emoting of its leads, Dorothy McGuire and Robert Young. Both handle well the difficult roles of two people who are physically ugly yet project inner beauty. The fairy tale of their seeing only beauty in each other is nicely handled and at no time becomes maudlin or comic. The other players are quite good, especially Herbert Marshall, who relates the story in the form of a tone poem. Interestingly, Marshall's character was blinded in the First World War and in reality the actor lost a leg in that conflict. Roy Webb's music score was nominated for an Academy Award. The feature proved to be one of RKO's top six moneymakers in 1945. *The Enchanted Cottage* was re-released theatrically by RKO in 1954 and 1957.

Pianist-composer John Hillgrove (Marshall), who is blind because his airplane was shot down over France's Argonne Forest in World War I, is about to perform his latest tone poem,

Poster for *The Enchanted Cottage* (1945).

"The Enchanted Cottage," for a select group of guests. When Oliver (Young) and Laura Bradford (McGuire), the inspirations for the piece, are late, he plays it, telling the group their story. He recalls how he often passed an old New England home, once a wing of a great estate that had been destroyed by fire. The house had been remodeled and rented to honeymooners for over a century until the present housekeeper, widow Abigail Minnett (Mildred Natwick), came there 25 years before. John is accompanied by his young nephew "Taxi" (Alec Englander). While John talks with Mrs. Minnett, "Taxi" meets unattractive Laura Pennington (McGuire) and tells her the house is haunted and its housekeeper is a witch. John is introduced to Laura and is impressed with her. She has come to see Mrs. Minnett about working there as a maid after being away from the area for nine years. Laura is told a young couple has rented the place and the housekeeper, who lost her husband during the last war, hires her. The couple, Oliver Bradford (Young) and Beatrice Alexander (Hillary Brooke), arrive and although Beatrice is not taken with the place, she agrees to live there. Over the years newlyweds who have resided in the cottage have etched their names in the window panes but when Oliver attempts to do so he breaks the diamond out of Beatrice's engagement ring. Mrs. Minnett feels this is a bad omen. Before he and Beatrice can marry, Oliver is called into the Army Air Corps and he has Beatrice send Mrs. Minnett a check and cancel their lease. Mrs. Minnett, who feels a kinship with Laura because both of them are lonely, asks her to stay on at the cottage and the young woman takes a job working at the local canteen. At a Halloween dance she is ignored by all the servicemen and returns home in a melancholy state. After more than a year passes, Oliver returns to lease the cottage, but he arrives alone. During the conflict his plane was shot down over Java, leaving him with a paralyzed right arm and a scarred face. Depressed, he does not want to see anyone and refuses to talk with his mother (Spring Byington), stepfather (Richard Gaines) and Beatrice when they come to see him. That night Laura stops Oliver from shooting himself and tells him he is not repulsive to her. Oliver and Laura become friends. John meets Oliver and tells him to have faith in himself. Oliver's newfound happiness is shattered when his mother writes to say she and her husband plan to move in with him and bring a nurse. Oliver proposes to Laura and they are married although both feel the ceremony is a sham. But they soon find they are in love and their physical abnormalities have disappeared. When John returns from a concert tour he visits the newlyweds and they inform him of the miracle. Laura says they think the cottage is a living thing filled with the thoughts and memories of those who lived there before and John tells them to accept what has happened to them. Their newfound happiness is short-lived when Oliver's mother and stepfather show up and comment on their ugliness. John tells the newlyweds he wanted to spare them the truth but Mrs. Minnett says a man and woman in love have a sight not given to others. As John finishes his recital, Oliver and Laura arrive, their looks restored.

The Film Daily reported, "Under the sensitive direction of John Cromwell, the film delivers an emotional wallop that makes it a heart-smasher with the women.... [It has] rare preciousness and a distinction beyond the ordinary." *The Motion Picture Daily* enthused, "Add *The Enchanted Cottage* to the ever-growing list of fine Hollywood efforts. By its own merits, this attraction carves itself a splendid niche.... Here is a film which rests heavily on the believability and the integrity of its principal performers and the steady, yet understanding, hand in its direction. It is a happy circumstance to report that this proves the case." *The Motion Picture Herald* called the film "a natural, both as box office and entertainment," and *The Hollywood Reporter* dubbed it a "rare jewel." Bosley Crowther in *The New York Times* complained that "the deep and studied poignance of this elaborately heart-torturing film appears not only unreasonable but very plainly contrived.... This story might be most affecting if intelligently and delicately told. As it stands, it is more of a horror film than a psychological romance." *Variety* termed *The Enchanted Cottage* "an artistic production which will catch both critical praise and plenty of audience attention.... Cromwell's direction deftly motivates the drama in top style.... [Producer Parsons] has turned in a most able job. Production mounting is fine, accentuated by the excellent photography of Ted Tetzlaff."

Dorothy McGuire and Robert Young reprised their *Enchanted Cottage* roles on CBS's *Lux Radio Theatre* on September 3, 1945. Peter Lawford and Joan Lorring starred in another radio version on CBS's *Academy Award Theatre*, broadcast December 11, 1946, and Richard Widmark headlined when CBS radio again did it on *Hallmark Playhouse* on May 19, 1949. NBC-TV presented "The Enchanted Cottage" as an episode of *Lux Video Theatre* on September 29, 1955, starring Teresa Wright and Dan O'Herlihy with support from Sara Haden, Lester Matthews, Mary Castle, Isobel Elsom and George Baxter.

Excess Baggage (1933; 59 minutes)

PRODUCER: Julius Hagen. DIRECTOR: Redd Davis. SCREENPLAY: H. Fowler Mear, from the novel by H.M. Raleigh. PHOTOGRAPHY: Sydney Blythe. EDITOR: Lister Laurence. SOUND: Carlisle Mounteney. ASSISTANT DIRECTOR: Fred V. Merrick.

CAST: Claud Allister (Colonel Murgatroyd, RSVP), Rene Ray (Angela Murgatroyd), Frank Pettingell (General Booster, SOS), Sydney Fairbrother (Miss Troop), Gerald Rawlinson (Clive Worthington), Viola Compton (Martha Murgatroyd), O.B. Clarence (Lord Grebe), Maud Gill (Duchess of Dillwater), Finlay Currie (Inspector Toucan), Minnie Rayner, Ruth Taylor, Charles Groves, Syd Crossley.

Apparently a lost film, *Excess Baggage* was one of 35 features Radio Pictures released in England during the 1930s, made with producer Julius Hagen's Real Art Productions. A horror comedy, it headlined Claud Allister, who portrayed Algy Longworth in *Bulldog Drummond* (1929), *The Return of Bulldog Drummond* (1935) and *Bulldog Drummond at Bay* (1937). He was also in *Three Live Ghosts* (1929) and *Dracula's Daughter* (1936) and provided character voices in Walt Disney's *The Reluctant Dragon* (1941) and *The Adventures of Ichabod and Mr. Toad* (1949) [qq.v.]. Leading lady Rene Ray appeared in *High Treason* (1928), *When London Sleeps* (1932), *The Passing of the Third Floor Back* (1935) and *The Return of the Frog* (1938). She later wrote the novel and teleplay for *The Strange World of Planet X* (1958), issued in the U.S. as *The Cosmic Monster*.

While on the trail of a ghost, addled Colonel Murgatroyd (Allister) accidentally shoots his superior, General Booster (Frank Pettingell). Thinking he has killed the man, he puts his body in a trunk and plans to drop it in a river. The trunk gets mixed up with one belonging to the Duchess of Dillwater (Maud Gill), who takes it to her country estate where one bedroom is said to be haunted. Murgatroyd attempts to locate the supposed corpse, only to run afoul of the duchess and other "ghosts."

In *British Sound Films: The Studio Years 1928–1959* (1984), David Quinlan called it an "acceptable 'spook' comedy."

Experiment Alcatraz (1950; 57 minutes)

PRODUCER-DIRECTOR: Edward L. Cahn. SCREENPLAY: Orville H. Hampton. STORY: George W. George & George F. Slavin. PHOTOGRAPHY: Jackson Rose. EDITOR: Philip Cahn. MUSIC: Irving Gertz. ART DIRECTOR: Boris Leven. SOUND: John R. Carter. SET DECORATIONS: Otto Siegel. MAKEUP: Ted Larsen & Lela Chambers. WARDROBE: Esther Krebs & Frank Tait. PROPERTY MASTER: George Bahr. SCRIPT SUPERVISOR: Meta D. Rebner. ASSISTANT DIRECTOR: Frank Fox.

CAST: John Howard (Dr. Ross Williams), Joan Dixon (Lieutenant Joan McKenna), Walter Kingsford

Poster for *Experiment Alcatraz* (1950).

(Dr. J.P. Finley), Lynne Carter (Ethel Gantz), Robert Shayne (Barry Morgan), Kim Spaulding (Duke Shaw), Sam Scar (Eddie Ganz), Kenneth MacDonald (Colonel Harris), Dick Cogan (Dan Stanley), Frank Cady (Max Henry), Byron Foulger (Jim Carlton), Ralph Peters (Bartender), Lewis Martin (Assistant District Attorney Walton), Harry Lauter (Dick McKenna), Raymond Largay (Warden Keaton), Myron Healey, Don Brodie (Wire Service Correspondents), Kit Guard (Abner Smith), Joe Ploski (Paul Willewitz), George Humbert (Waiter), Franklyn Farnum (Board Member), Lee Miller (Casino Guard), Basil Raish (Patient), Jeffrey Sayre (Auction Patron), Bess Flowers (Hotel Diner).

At Alcatraz penitentiary, Army Colonel Harris (Kenneth MacDonald) and Dr. J.P. Finley (Walter Kingsford) head a committee promising five prisoners that their sentences will be commuted if they take part in a scientific experiment. The five convicts, underworld tycoon Barry Morgan (Robert Shayne), his best friend Eddie Ganz (Sam Scar), Dan Stanley (Dick Cogan), Abner Smith (Kit Guard) and Paul Willewitz (Joe Ploski), agree to the terms and are taken by military police to a hospital where they are injected with metallic salt and given a high dose of radioactive isotopes in an effort to find a cure for a rare and fatal blood disease. The tests take place without the participation of Dr. Ross Williams (John Howard), the experiment's developer. All goes well but later Morgan finds scissors that have fallen from the pocket of Lieutenant Joan McKenna's (Joan Dixon) uniform and stabs Ganz through the heart, killing him. Ross arrives to find the publicity from the stabbing has caused the experiment to be abandoned. All five convicts are set free.

On the hospital grounds, Ross meets Joan's brother Dick (Harry Lauter), who suffers from the disease. Dick volunteers to help the doctor, who regains his enthusiasm about the project. Convincing the kindly Finley to delay destroying the isotopes, Ross feels Morgan's actions were not caused by the radiation. After assistant district attorney Walton (Lewis Martin) tells him the case is closed, Ross visits Morgan at his auction house and learns it is a front for a casino. When Ross informs Morgan he will not give up the quest to prove his theories correct, the crook lets him win at gambling and then has him mugged and robbed. Convinced that Morgan is hiding something, Ross takes Joan with him to Alcatraz where the warden (Raymond Largay) permits him to interrogate inmate Max Henry (Frank Cady), who was sent there with Morgan and Ganz after they were involved in an attempted escape from Leavenworth. Henry confirms that Morgan and Ganz were best friends and then shows his visitors his postcard collection, one being sent to Ganz from Lake Tahoe by a woman named Ethel. Learning that Ross and Joan have gone to Alcatraz, Morgan has his partner Duke Shaw (Kim Spaulding) trail them. When Ross arrives at the Ace High Club where Ethel is a cashier, he is knocked out and left in the woods. When he later meets with Joan, she tells Ross to stay at their hotel and she drives to the club and sees Ethel, convincing her to talk with the doctor after telling her that Ganz, her stepfather, was deliberately murdered. Ethel agrees to meet Ross at an abandoned house on a remote lake where Ganz secreted $250,000 from a robbery he committed with Morgan. Whey they get to the locale, Ethel informs Ross that Morgan had himself set to prison to find out about the money from Ganz. She then pulls a gun on Ross, saying she already found the money. Morgan and his henchmen arrive and he informs Ross that he and Ethel are married. When the doctor again refuses to give up his research, the gangster murders him. At a follow-up examination, Finley pretends to expose Morgan to more radioactive isotopes and tricks him into confessing to Ganz and Ross' murders. As Joan looks forward to a cure for her brother, the late Dr. Williams is commemorated on the cover of *Newsweek* magazine.

The sci-fi aspects of *Experiment Alcatraz* are relegated to the test in which the prisoners are subjected to high doses of radiation. The scenes are brief but effective. The film is one of the few from the period that has the hero killed off. Leading lady Joan Dixon was borrowed by Crystal

Productions from RKO, which subsequently issued the feature theatrically. A compact programmer, *Experiment Alcatraz* was producer-director Edward L. Cahn's first brush with science fiction; he would go on to helm *Creature with the Atom Brain* (1955), *Invasion of the Saucer Men* (1957), *It! The Terror from Beyond Space* (1958) and *Invisible Invaders* (1959).

Variety called the production a "lowercaser that will serve only to fill out the ordinary double bill.... Cahn's direction lacks pace but his production achieves okay values for the limited budget. Script was ineptly written and dialog unconvincing. Principals do what they can. Irving Gertz's music score is more successful than the story-telling."

Experiment Perilous (1944; 91 minutes)

PRODUCER-SCREENPLAY: Warren Duff. EXECUTIVE PRODUCER: Robert Fellows. DIRECTOR: Jacques Tourneur. From the novel by Margaret Carpenter. PHOTOGRAPHY: Tony Gaudio. EDITOR: Ralph Dawson. MUSIC: Roy Webb. MUSIC DIRECTOR: C. Bakaleinikoff. ART DIRECTORS: Albert S. D'Agostino & Jack Okey. SOUND: John E. Tribby & James G. Stewart. SPECIAL EFFECTS: Vernon L. Walker. COSTUMES: Edward Stevenson. GOWNS: Leah Rhodes. ASSISTANT DIRECTOR: Dewey Starkey.

CAST: Hedy Lamarr (Allida Bederaux), George Brent (Dr. Huntington Bailey), Paul Lukas (Nicholas Bederaux), Albert Dekker (Clag Claghorn), Carl Esmond (Dr. John Maitland), Olive Blakeney (Clarissa "Cissie" Bederaux), George N. Neise (Alexander Gregory), Margaret Wycherly (Maggie), Stephanie Bachelor (Elaine), Mary Servoss (Miss Wilson), Julia Dean (Deria), William Post, Jr. (Mr. MacDonald), Billy Ward (Alexander Bedereux), Alan Ward (Shoes), Nolan Leary (Bellhop), Larry Wheat (Caterer), Sam McDaniel (Train Porter), Edward Clark (Train Steward), Joel Friedkin (Brakeman), Broderick O'Farrell (Frank), Jack Deery, Eddie Hart (Doormen), Lillian West (Salesperson), Almeda Flower (Store Clerk), Terry Frost (Emergency Room Doctor), Mike Lally, Dick Bartell (Interns), Perc Launders, Bert LeBaron (Ambulance Attendants), Charles McMurphy (Policeman), Mitchell Ingraham (Bellhop), Janet Clark (Maid), Evelyn Falke (Clarissa Bederaux at Age 5), Peggy Miller (Clarissa Bederaux at Age 8), Michael Orr (Nicholas Bederaux at Age 3), Georges Renavent (Voice Teacher), Adrienne D'Ambricourt (French Teacher), Michael Visaroff (Ballet Master), John Mylong (Nicholas Bederaux, Sr.), John Elliott (Hotel Telephone Operator), Sherry Hall (Hotel Clerk George), Gino Corrado (Diner), Paul Kruger, Fred Hueston, Max Linder, Eric Mayne, James Carlisle, Field Norton (Night Club Patrons), Edward Biby, James Conaty (Art Exhibitions Patrons).

Based on Margaret Carpenter's 1943 novel, *Experiment Perilous* is a polished, posh but modest psychological horror melodrama that Richard B. Jewell and Vernon Harbin in *The RKO Story* (1982) concluded "was excessively verbose and unnecessarily complicated by multiple flashbacks, but the superlative acting of [Paul] Lukas and [Hedy] Lamarr and the supple, probing direction of Jacques Tourneur created a psychological thriller of absorbing quality." The feature was a fine recreation of early 20th century America with much of its story taking place in a sumptuous Gotham mansion, a redressing of a set built for *The Magnificent Ambersons* two years before. Art directors Albert S. D'Agostino and Jack Okey were nominated for an Academy Award. Cary Grant and Gregory Peck were originally considered for the male lead, Laraine Day and Maureen O'Hara for the role that went to Hedy Lamarr. In his career study of Lamarr in *Screen Facts* (Vol. 2, No. 5, 1965), Gene Ringgold said that *Experiment Perilous* was "career-wise, one of the best things to happen" to the actress. He adds, "And for a fabulous day's pay, Hedy did a good day's work and, under Jacques Tourneur's capable direction, she gave what is, in my opinion, easily her best performance...."

In 1903 New York City, psychiatrist Huntington "Hunt" Brailey (George Brent) is returning home on a train through a terrific thunderstorm. Another passenger, Clarissa "Cissie" Bedereaux (Olive Blakeney), a small, bird-like woman, is frightened by the storm and talks with the doctor. She tells him she is coming back after five years, having been away for health reasons. They have lunch on the train the next day and she informs him she is writing a biography of her younger brother Nick (Lukas) and his beautiful wife Allida (Lamarr). Saying she does not want to live with her brother, she asks Hunt to take her luggage to his hotel where she plans to rent rooms. After getting home, Hunt goes to a party to show off a new sculpture by his friend Clag Claghorn (Albert Dekker) and learns from artist John Maitland (Carl Esmond) that Cissie died that afternoon at the Bedereaux home. Clag says he was once in love with Allida; the artist's girlfriend Elaine (Stephanie Bachelor) calls Allida a very beautiful woman. At Hunt's hotel, the maid, Maggie (Margaret Wycherly), accidentally leaves Cissie's valise in his room. Clag takes Hunt to an art gallery to see a portrait of Allida done by Maitland and he becomes fascinated with her and agrees to accompany Clag to a tea that night at the Bedereaux family's Murray Hill mansion. There he meets the distant young

George Brent and Hedy Lamarr in *Experiment Perilous* (1944).

woman. In confidence, her husband informs Hunt that their small son (Billy Ward) suffers from night fears and he needs help, the fault lying with Allida. Nick makes an appointment to meet Hunt at his office and says he thinks his wife is insane because she sends herself daisies and tries to frighten their boy. Hunt agrees to observe Allida. When Nick informs him she is shopping at a nearby store, he goes there and tells her he wants to help her and she invites him to dinner the next day. That night Hunt finds Cissie's valise and begins reading her manuscript which details how her mother died when Nick was born; the next year their father (John Mylong) committed suicide. Years later the siblings meet a young Allida while on a New England vacation and they take her to Europe where she is given an education and presented to Parisian society. Nick proposes to Allida and she accepts but some time later when he gives her a birthday party he learns that his wife is in love with writer Alec Gregory (George N. Neise). Hunt's reading is interrupted by a phone call from Allida, who wants him to follow her husband when he visits their son at night. Disturbed, Hunt goes to Clag's studio and is trailed by a stranger. There he informs Clag that Cissie did not die from a heart attack as her brother alleged (she told him she did not have heart problems after spending five years in a sanitarium). Returning to his apartment, Hunt sees that Cissie's valise has been stolen. The next evening he goes the Bedereaux mansion for dinner and is surprised to learn their son is named Alec, after the writer. Hunt later overhears Nick trying to frighten the boy with tales of witches, intimating that Allida is a beautiful witch. Hunt has Allida meet him at a restaurant and tells her get out of the mansion—and that he loves her. He also asks her about Alec Gregory and she says he was run down and killed the night of her birthday after having left with Nick. Getting assurance from Clag that Nick is at their club, Hunt goes home and writes a letter saying he thinks Nick killed Cassie and Alec and plans to murder him. He leaves the missive in the hotel safe. The following day Allida arrives at Hunt's office with the news that Nick plans to sail to Boston and kill himself along the way. Going back to the Murray Hill mansion, the two hear Alec crying and Allida goes to comfort her son. Nick appears dressed as the butler and holds Hunt at bay with a gun. He admits to killing his sister and Alec and says he tried to drive his wife insane. He also announces he has rigged the gas stove outside his son's room to explode. The two men fight and Hunt manages to overpower Nick and rescue Allida and Alec, who are unconscious from the gas fumes. An explosion destroys the mansion. At a hospital, Clag learns that Allida, Hunt and Alec have survived unharmed. Later Hunt entertains Alec at his country house while a representative (William Post, Jr.) from the district attorney's office informs Allida that he believes her husband did not commit suicide and it was him and not the butler who was killed in the explosion. She begs the man to drop the investigation for her son's sake and he agrees to do so. After he leaves, she joins Hunt and Alec as they stroll through a field of daisies.

Boxoffice enthused, "On many counts, the film assays as a sure-fire top revenue producer. The inescapable magnetism of the topline trio should attract customers in SRO droves and the picture is well qualified to send them away thoroughly satisfied and spreading the right kind of word-of-mouth gospel." *The New York Herald Tribune* said "it belongs in the front rank of the year's mystery thrillers" and Wanda Hale in *The New York Daily News* termed it an "absorbing melodrama." *The New York Sun* wrote, "Topnotch murder mystery. Story unfolds quietly, logically. Slowly the mystery grows, the suspense tightens." *PM* determined *Experiment Perilous* to be "a cut above thrillers, in addition to its heavyweight cast." *Variety* thought it "one of those strange and weird dramas that occasionally get screen presentation. This one is well done, carrying interest at good, suspenseful pitch, and has the bright marquee dressing of Hedy Lamarr, George Brent and Paul Lukas." *The Film Daily* said, "The picture succeeds rather well in conveying a sense of fear and of establishing an air of doom. It is unfortunate that the story is not more convincing or more lucidly developed.... The film is most triumphant is recapturing the atmosphere of the period."

On September 10, 1945, George Brent and Virginia Bruce starred in "Experiment Perilous" on CBS's *Lux Radio Theatre.*

The Face at the Window (1932; 53 minutes)

PRODUCER: Julius Hagen. DIRECTOR: Leslie S. Hiscott. SCREENPLAY: H. Fowler Mear, from the play by F. Brooke Warren. PHOTOGRAPHY: Sydney Blythe. EDITOR: Lister Laurance. SOUND: Carlisle Mounteney.

CAST: Raymond Massey (Paul le Gros), Isla Bevan (Marie de Brisson), Claude Hulbert (Peter Pomeroy), Eric Maturin (Count Fournal), Henry Mollison (Lucien Courtier), A. Bromley Davenport (Gaston de Brisson), Harold Meade (Dr. Renard), Dennis Wyndham (Lafonde), Charles Groves (Jacques), Berneoff & Charlot (Dancers), David Miller.

F. Brooke Warren's 1897 play *The Face at the Window* was first filmed in Australia in 1919 by D.B. O'Connor Feature Films. The next year a five-reel version done in England by British Actors starred C. Aubrey Smith, Gladys Jennings and Jack Hobbs. In 1932 Julius Hagen produced the first sound rendition. The most noted edition of the melodrama was done by producer-director George King in 1939 for British Lion, starring Tod Slaughter, Marjorie Taylor and John Warwick. The 1932 film, now considered lost, was issued in England by Radio Pictures, which co-financed it with Hagen's Real Art Productions.

The Face at the Window was Raymond Massey's second starring film, the actor having made his official screen debut as Sherlock Holmes in *The Speckled Band* (1931). Before that he had a bit as a pacifist in the futuristic *High Treason* (1929). After the Real Art feature he went to Hollywood to appear in *The Old Dark House* (1932) and was also in *Things to Come* (1936) and *Arsenic and Old Lace* (1944).

In 1880 Paris, a madman who emits the howl of the wolf after committing bank robberies uses poison to murder night watchmen. The London police are baffled and call upon noted detective Paul le Gros (Massey) to assist them. The culprit is Count Fournal (Eric Maturin) who lusts after beautiful Marie de Brisson (Isla Bevan) and tries to blame his killing of her father (A. Bromley Davenport) on her lover, Lucien Courtier (Henry Mollison). Le Gros sets out to trap the fiend by using a device invented by Dr. Renard (Harold Meade) in which an electric current is applied to the body of Fournal's latest victim, supposedly causing him to write his killer's name.

David Quinlan in *British Sound Films: The Studio Years 1928–1959* (1984) said it was "dated, theatrical stuff."

The 1939 *Face in the Window* starring Tod Slaughter is the best known due mainly to its emphasis on horror. Slaughter delightfully chews up the scenery as the cunning, lustful, maniacal madman, who has a monstrous, deformed twin brother he uses to do his dirty work. Harry Terry played the title face. The feature was reissued in England in 1942 by Ambassador Films.

The Falcon and the Co-Eds (1943; 68 minutes)

PRODUCER: Maurice Geraghty. DIRECTOR: William Clemens. SCREENPLAY: Ardel Wray & Gerald Geraghty. STORY: Ardel Wray. PHOTOGRAPHY: J. Roy Hunt. EDITOR: Theron Warth. MUSIC DIRECTOR: C. Bakaleinikoff. ART DIRECTOR: Albert S. D'Agostino. SOUND: Terry Kellum & James G. Stewart. SET DECORATIONS: Darrell Silvera & William Stevens. COSTUME DESIGN: Renie. SPECIAL EFFECTS: Vernon L. Walker. DIALOGUE DIRECTOR: Leslie Urbach. ASSISTANT DIRECTOR: Harry Mancke.

CAST: Tom Conway (Tom Lawrence, the Falcon), Jean Brooks (Vicky Gaines), Rita Corday (Marguerita Serena), Amelita Ward (Jane Harris), Isabel Jewell (Mary Phoebus), George Givot (Dr. Anatole Graelich), Cliff Clark (Inspector Timothy Donovan), Edward Gargan (Detective Bates), Barbara Brown (Dean Keyes), Juanita Alvarez [Nita Hunter], Ruth Alvarez, Nancy McCollum (The Ughs), Patti Brill (Beanie Smith), Olin Howlin (Goodwillie), Ian Wolfe (Eustace L. Hartley), Margie Stewart (Pam), Margaret Landry (Sarey Ann), Carole Gallagher (Elsie), Barbara Lynn (Mildred), Mary Halsey (Switchboard Girl), Perc Launders (Mechanic), Elaine Riley (Ellen Lee), Dorothy Christy (Maya Harris), Anne O'Neal (Miss Hicks), Dorothy Maloney [Dorothy Malone], Rosemary LaPlanche, Dorothy Kelly, Daun Kelly, Julia Hopkins, Barbara Coleman (Co-eds), Mike Lally (Father), Ruth Cherrington, Vangie Beilby (Dowagers), Bess Flowers, James Conaty, Colin Kenny, William H. O'Brien (Audience Members).

Many fans of RKO's popular series "The Falcon" consider *The Falcon and the Co-eds* the best of the lot. Released in November 1943, it was the sixth of 13 entries and the third to feature Tom Conway in the title role as suave sleuth Tom Lawrence. Despite containing quite a bit of comedy and even a couple of musical numbers, the feature has a brooding atmosphere that includes murder, insanity, psychic premonition, obsession and a ghostly voice. Karl and Sue Thiede noted in "The Falcon Saga" in *Views & Reviews* (Winter, 1972) that producer Maurice Geraghty "reached the peak of the series with this film, as it is almost pure mystery with very light touch of comedy.... The mood of the film with Margarita [sic] (Rita Corday) seemingly talking with wind and sea, is eerie. The photography of the sea with its rolling waves pounding relentlessly on the rocks further contributes to the mood of death within the film. The nature sounds without music create the best effects.... All supporting cast members are excellent with the film's sixty-eight–minute running time being tightly edited. The same high quality established in this film is maintained throughout the remaining entries in the series which Geraghty produced."

Co-ed Jane Harris (Amelita Ward) sneaks out of the exclusive BlueCliff Seminary for Girls and phones police headquarters asking for Tom Lawrence, the Falcon (Conway). She tells Detective Bates (Edward Gargan) it involves a murder and he tells her that Tom lives at the Maren Apartments. Bates' superior, disgruntled Inspector Timothy Donovan (Cliff Clark), says they had better check out the story. When Tom arrives home, Jane greets him with a kiss and is disappointed that he does not remember having met her in her actress mother's stage dressing room seven years before. She informs Tom that one of her professors, Jamison, was murdered although the official verdict was heart failure. She says her roommate Marguerita Serena (Corday) prophesied the death. When Donovan and Bates show up, Jane drives off in Tom's car. The lawmen question him about the murder and he sends them on a wild goose chase to the Crown Hill Convent, telling them to check with the mother superior. Tom takes a bus to the town near the Blue-Cliff seminary and gets a ride in the school's bus driven by Goodwillie (Olin Howlin). Tom claims to be the father of one of the co-eds, and three little girl passengers dubbed the Ughs (Juanita Alvarez, Ruth Alvarez, Nancy McCollum), the caretaker's daughters, think he means Beanie Smith (Patti Brill). Along the way they see Marguerita walking along the road. When Tom tells the driver to stop, she disappears; the girls say she has gone down the Devil's Ladder, a path leading from the cliff to the sea. At the school, Tom locates Jane in Dr. Anatole Graelich's (George Givot) psychology class and she announces that Tom is a famous psychologist. The professor asks him to lecture the class on his latest theory and Tom spouts double talk about criminal impulses until he is interrupted by Beanie, who tells the school's dean, Miss Keyes (Barbara Brown), she is not his daughter. In the dean's office, Tom claims to be an insurance investigator looking into Jamison's murder, and Graelich says there was nothing odd about the professor's death. When asked about Marguerita's prediction, Graelich says the girl's father was a famous composer who committed suicide. Co-ed Elsie (Carole Gallagher) says there is a voice coming from Jamison's room. Tom goes with Miss Keyes and Graelich to investigate and they find music instructor Mary Phoebus (Isabel Jewell) there; she claims she wants to protect Jamison's poems. Graelich notes that the late professor was in ill health and that is why he signed the death certificate as heart failure. In the rehearsal hall, Tom meets the school's drama teacher Vicky Gaines (Jean Brooks), who is directing a student show. Vicky has a confrontation with Marguerita, who refuses to use a foil in the production. Tom reminds Jane about his car and she informs him it is at the village garage and says she only took it to lure him to the school. She also claims that Vicky knew Jamison better than anyone and that Marguerita has predicted another death. After seeing Vicky and Graelich huddled together in the hall, Tom follows the woman, who takes a bicycle and rides into town. Tom hitches a ride with the Ughs in their pony cart and enlists their aid in finding Vicky, who is talking with the town's undertaker, Hartley (Ian Wolfe). Vicky offers to show Tom around the town but he locks her out of the funeral parlor and confronts Hartley, who pulls a gun on him. Tom gets the weapon along with a paper saying that Jamison died of an overdose of codeine. Hartley admits that Graelich tried to cover up the cause of death. Later Tom drives Vicky back to school and they stop near the Devil's Ladder where he reads a Jamison poem that was dedicated to her. She admits the professor was in love with her and she rejected him, which she believes was the cause of his suicide. At the show that night, Tom asks Graelich why he falsified Jamison's death certificate and he denies doing so. Donovan and Bates show up and confront Tom, who claims to know the killer's identity. When the show's fencing exhibition is cancelled, Tom seeks out Vicky, who tells him Marguerita refused to take part in it. They hear a scream and see Marguerita standing over Miss Keyes' body as Vicky finds a foil nearby. Tom follows Marguerita to her father's home where he finds her listening to one of his concertos. She says her father was insane. Searching Graelich's room, Tom locates a picture taken on an ocean cruise. When Graelich arrives home, Tom tells him that he is the most likely murder suspect

Edward Gargan, Amelita Ward, Cliff Clark and Tom Conway in *The Falcon and the Co-eds* **(1943).**

since he and Jamison both were interested in Vicky. Graelich admits he married an American woman but kept it a secret since Miss Keyes did not allow wedded couples to teach at BlueCliff. Hearing a scream, Tom finds Jane being interrogated by Donovan and Bates. He forces her to turn over a letter Miss Keyes wrote to her mother saying she was being dismissed from the school. When the co-ed gets mouthy, Tom spanks her. A gunshot is fired at Tom, Donovan and Bates. Tom sees a woman running away and follows her to the school's dormitory. There he bumps into Mary, who becomes hysterical, and he also sees the same picture Graelich had in Vicky's room. Vicky informs Tom that she met Graelich in Europe while on a vacation and they fell in love. Tom then slips out of the dorm as Donovan and Bates are run off by the house mother (Anne O'Neal) for trying to interrogate the co-eds. In a meeting the next day in the dean's office, Donovan announces that Miss Keyes' will left the school to Vicky and he accuses her and Graelich of the murders. He orders them taken to jail but Tom cautions him not to arrest the duo without evidence. Bates arrives with Margerita who claims she may have committed the killings. When the girl runs away to the cliffs, Tom follows Vicky who gets a gun and goes after the hysterical girl. Along the way Vicky informs Tom she never married Graelich but Tom tells her the professor did marry someone and he believes it was Mary. He deduces that Mary committed the murders after becoming mentally unbalanced from always seeing Vicky and Graelich together. The Ughs inform them that Marguerita and Mary are at the Devil's Ladder. There Marguerita tells Mary she saw her standing over Miss Keyes' body but Mary says there is no hope for her since her father was insane. The co-ed begins to hear her dead father's voice telling her to jump into the sea as Tom arrives and calls to Mary, who is startled and tumbles backward over the cliff. Later, as Tom starts to leave the school, Jane's mother, actress Maya Harris (Dorothy Christy), arrives with her ingénue (Elaine Riley), who begs him to investigate trouble at their theater. Tom drives away with the young actress as the Ughs proclaim his greatness to Donovan and Bates.

The Falcon and the Co-eds cost $125,000 to produce and was lensed in the late summer of 1943. Tom Conway dominates the affair as the urbane detective who usually gets involved in various capers thanks to his fondness for the fair sex. In this case he is surrounded by a bevy of pretty co-eds plus an attractive drama teacher who, alas, loves a somewhat pudgy psychology instructor. The picture moves along quickly with most of its amusement provided by lunkhead Bates, the forever fainting co-ed Elsie and the Ughs, three brats who even do an Andrews Sisters impersonation. Plot-wise, the most memorable aspect of the picture is its melancholy, haunting atmosphere. Don Miller in *B Movies* (1973) called it the series' "best ... with William Clemens again displaying his unobtrusive directorial skill, heightened by some splendid photography by J. Roy Hunt."

Boxoffice opined, "Tom Conway's crime-solving this time is done against a background of a luxurious girls' school, with some magnificent views of the Pacific from a cliff, and a bevy of good-looking young women in nearly every scene. That's enough to intrigue the mystery fans." *Variety* called it a "lively and neatly concocted whodunit." Wanda Hale in *The New York Daily News* dubbed it "the most amusing and baffling of the series." *The Film Daily* was not so complimentary: "As far as suspense and excitement go, the latest of the Falcon series of melodramas is not quite up to the standard of its predecessors. Tom Conway plays the Falcon with his customary suaveness and man-of-the-world air." In *The Detective in Hollywood* (1978) Jon Tuska called *The Falcon and the Co-eds* "one of the best in the series."

In addition to starring as the Falcon and appearing in producer Val Lewton's horror classics *Cat People, The Seventh Victim* and *I Walked with a Zombie* (qq.v.), Russian-born Englishman Tom Conway, brother of George Sanders, also was in the genre efforts *Bride of the Gorilla* (1951), *The She-Creature* (1956), *Voodoo Woman* (1957) and *The Atomic Submarine* (1959), the last three for producer Alex Gordon. He co-starred in the Emmy-winning "The Glass Eye," a 1957 segment of TV's *Alfred Hitchcock Presents*. He also portrayed Bulldog Drummond in two 1948 features, *The Challenge* and *13 Lead Soldiers*, and on radio he starred as the Saint and Sherlock Holmes. From 1951 to 1954 he had the title role in the ABC-TV detective series *Mark Saber*.

The Falcon in Mexico (1944; 70 minutes)

PRODUCER: Maurice Geraghty. DIRECTOR: William Berke. SCREENPLAY: George Worthing Yates & Gerald Geraghty. PHOTOGRAPHY: Frank Redman. EDITOR: Joseph Noriega. MUSIC DIRECTOR: C. Bakaleinikoff. ART DIRECTOR: Albert S. D'Agostino. SOUND: Frank McWhorter & James G. Stewart. SET DECORATIONS: Claude Carpenter & Darrell Silvera. COSTUME DESIGN: Renie. SPECIAL EFFECTS: Vernon L. Walker. TECHNICAL ADVISOR: John Mari. ASSISTANT DIRECTOR: William Dorman.

CAST: Tom Conway (Tom Lawrence, the Falcon), Mona Maris (Raquel), Martha MacVicar [Martha Vickers] (Barbara Wade), Nestor Paiva (Manuel Romero), Mary Currier (Paula Dudley), Cecilia Callejo (Dolores Ybarra), Emory Parnell (Winthrop "Lucky Diamond" Hughes), Joseph Vitale (Anton), Pedro de Cordoba (Don Carlos Ybarra), Fernando Alvarado (Pancho Romero), Bryant Washburn (Humphrey Wade), George J. Lewis (Castro), Bob O'Connor (Martinez), Frank Mayo (Inspector O'Shea), Bert Moorhouse (Detective Marks), Julian Rivero (Mexican Doctor), Tony Roux, Leo Martin, Frank Henry (Taxi Cab Drivers), Wheaton Chambers (Jarvis), Alan Ward, Sherry Hall (Ajax Patrolmen), Greta Christensen (Isabel), Nina Campana (Landlady), Frank O'Connor (Officer O'Connor), Ruth Alvarez, Nita Hunter (Singers), Geneva Hall, Theodore Rand (Dancers), Iris Bynam (Maid), Chiche Baru (Senorita), John Eberts, Manuel Lopez (Fishermen), Roque Ybarra, Jr. (Chico), Lillian Nicholson (Indian Woman), Dorothy Olivero (Maid), Lorraine Rivero (Head Waitress), Chester Carlisle (Grenville).

The spectral presence of famous deceased artist Humphrey Wade (Bryant Washburn), and the theft of his valuable paintings, is the crux of *The Falcon in Mexico*, issued by RKO early in 1945. The ninth film in the "Falcon" series, it was the fifth to headline Tom Conway as the debonair sleuth. This solid adventure is best known for containing footage from Orson Welles' aborted *It's All True*, shot in 1942 in Brazil. Here the South American footage substituted for Mexico. *The Falcon in Mexico* is a fast-paced, exciting and highly satisfying affair with good doses of mystery and more than a tinge of the supernatural.

After telling pretty Isabel (Greta Christensen) he is now a respectable investment broker and she is the only woman in his life, Tom Lawrence (Conway), the Falcon, spies Dolores Ybarra (Cecilia Callejo) trying to break into an art gallery. After she begs him to help her, Tom uses a skeleton key to open the door. She says she wants a picture she painted but after seeing it Tom realizes she was the model. Dolores admits it was done by Humphrey Wade, an artist who died in 1929. After stumbling upon the dead body of the gallery owner, Tom notices that the woman has run off and he is captured by two security guards (Alan Ward, Sherry Hall) who do not believe him when he tells them about Dolores. Eluding the guards, Tom takes the painting to Winthrop Hughes (Emory Parnell), known as "Lucky Diamond" because of the huge ring he wears. Tom identifies the picture as a genuine Wade; he collects the artist's works. Hughes tells Tom to talk with Wade's daughter Barbara (Martha Vickers). At her hotel, Barbara says she thinks her father may be still alive because when she was recently ill, she thought he came to her. When two policemen (Frank Mayo, Bert Moorhouse) arrive at Barbara's apartment, she and Tom escape through a window and decide to fly to Mexico where her father is buried. In Mexico, Barbara leaves with a man and Tom hires taxi driver Manuel Romero (Nestor Paiva) and his young son Pancho (Fernando Alvarado) to follow them to Casa Dolardo, a country inn, where Barbara's father used to paint. Tom is introduced by Barbara to beautiful Raquel (Mona Maris) and her husband Anton (Joseph Vitale), the man who took her to the hostel. Raquel and Anton are dancers and the latter warns Tom to leave the country. Raquel later requests a rendezvous with him at the village park where she asks him to give up the search for Wade and then becomes angry when Tom says he might prove she is guilty of bigamy if the artist is still alive. At the inn, owner Paula Dudley (Mary Currier) shows Tom and Barbara the studio where Wade worked. When Barbara feels the presence of her father, she and Tom enter another room and find a freshly painted picture in a cabinet. Paula informs them it is her work since she studied under Wade. Tom suspects she might be creating forgeries to cash in on Wade's posthumous fame. Going to his room, Tom finds Dolores trying to find her portrait. She runs away and he follows but she escapes. Returning to the room, he is knocked out and the picture stolen. Tom asks Paula about Dolores and she tells him the young woman is the daughter of ranchero Don Carlos Ibarra (Pedro de Cordoba). Tom visits Don Carlos and tells him Dolores may be in danger; Don Carlos informs Tom that his daughter is in the United States helping to retrieve a picture. When Tom says Dolores is back home, the two men search for her. The villagers later bring in her body, saying she was drowned. Tom returns to the hotel and confronts Paula, again meets Raquel and Anton and then finds Manuel going through his luggage and dismisses him. Hughes arrives at the hotel, minus his signature ring, for a vacation and that night someone tries to poison Barbara's dinner. Tom deduces that the person who tried to kill Barbara also murdered Dolores and the art gallery proprietor since they suspected Wade was alive. Paula accuses Raquel of wanting to keep her first husband dead and Anton claims Paula also had a motive, having tried to pass off her work as Wade's. Barbara recovers and claims he father came to see her. Tom tries to chase the phantom but Paula stops him at gunpoint until Manuel gets the drop on her. Paula departs and Tom and Raquel search her room and find the missing picture. Tom goes in search of Paula and locates

Tom Conway and Mona Maris in *The Falcon in Mexico* (1945).

her body in a lakeside boat. Manuel informs Tom that he is a police officer who has two other policemen (George J. Lewis, Frank O'Connor) trailing him. A woman (Lillian Nicholson) takes Barbara to her father's crypt but Tom arrives proving it is empty with the woman admitting that Anton paid her to take Barbara there. During a village fiesta a masked man tells Barbara he is her father. Revealing himself, he tells her he has remained hidden since the value of his work has soared after his apparent suicide. Wade informs her that she is in danger, and then he is shot and killed. Tom believes Hughes is the killer because he is in financial trouble and with Wade alive the artists' work would be devalued. With the help of Manuel, Tom conceives the ruse that Wade survived the attack and wears the mask the artist wore when he was shot. Hughes attempts to kill him but is shot by Manuel. Since the case is closed, Tom says goodbye to Barbara and returns to the United States.

 	Boxoffice called *The Falcon in Mexico* "one of the best of the tried-and-true whodunit series." *Variety* called the movie "a most tangled murder mystery" and termed it "a strong entry in the Falcon series.... Drama is crisply displayed through compact script by George Worthing Yates and Gerald Geraghty, and paceful direction by William Berke." In a follow-up review the trade paper declared it the "most entertaining of the series.... Tom Conway again does a neat acting job as the elusive detective...." Both reviews played up the *It's All True* footage without crediting the source. *The Film Daily* declared, "Latest in the Falcon series is one of the best. Pictorial and musical appeal big asset."

The Falcon's Adventure (1946; 61 minutes)

PRODUCER: Herman Schlom. DIRECTOR: William Berke. SCREENPLAY: Aubrey Wisberg. PHOTOG-
RAPHY: Frank Redman & Harry Wild. EDITOR: Marvin Coil. MUSIC: Paul Sawtell. MUSIC DIRECTOR:
C. Bakaleinikoff. ART DIRECTORS: Albert D'Agostino & Walter E. Keller. SOUND: Earl B. Mounce &
Jean L. Speak. SET DECORATIONS: Michael Oren Bach & Darrell Silvera. SPECIAL EFFECTS: Russell A.
Cully.

CAST: Tom Conway (Tom Lawrence, the Falcon), Madge Meredith (Louisa Braganza),
Edward Brophy (Goldie Locke), Robert Warwick (Kenneth Sutton), Myrna Dell (Doris Bland-
ing), Steve Brodie (Benny), Ian Wolfe (Prof. J.D. Denison), Carol Forman (Helen Ray), Joseph
Crehan (Inspector Cavanaugh), Phil Warren (Mike Geary), Tony Barrett (Paolo Ray), Harry
Harvey (Detective Sergeant Duncan), Jason Robards (Lieutenant Evans), Andre Charlot (Enrico
Braganza), Doreen Tyrden (Night Club Singer), David Cota (Jimmy), Fred Graham (Police
Driver Joe), Dudley Dickerson (Dining Car Waiter), Effie Laird (Dowager), Norman Mayes
(Pullman Car Porter), Robert Bray (Doorman), William J. O'Brien (Night Club Waiter), Bill
Walker (Train Porter), Bud Wolfe (Police Driver), David Sharpe, Duke Taylor (Yacht Crewmen),
Drew Miller, Lee Frederick (Policemen), Jeffrey Sayre (Club Patron), Jack Chefe (Headwaiter),
Bonnie Blair (Hat Check Girl).

The final effort in RKO's highly successful Falcon series, *The Falcon's Adventure* was a remake
of *A Date with the Falcon* (q.v.). It was the thirteenth series entry and Tom Conway's tenth appearance as debonair detective Tom Lawrence. Released late in 1946, the feature got most of its playdates early the next year and proved to be a passable finale to the adventures of the suave sleuth,
wonderfully portrayed by Conway. Like its predecessor, the feature's tenuous sci-fi connection
dealt with a secret formula for manufacturing diamonds. Competently produced and well acted
by its pleasant cast, the feature contains enough action and comedy (most supplied by the delightful Edward Brophy's dimwitted Goldie Locke) to satisfy series followers.

As Tom Lawrence (Conway) and Goldie (Brophy) head for some fishing in the Adirondacks,
he spots a beautiful woman apparently being
kidnapped in a taxi cab and rescues her as the
driver escapes. She turns out to be Luisa Braganza (Madge Meredith), whose uncle, Enrico
Braganza (Andre Charlot), has developed a
formula for making synthetic diamonds for
industrial use. Police Inspector Cavanaugh
(Joseph Crehan) and Detective Sergeant Duncan (Harry Harvey) arrive on the scene after
Tom and Goldie depart with Luisa and find the
woman's purse, learning she is staying at the
Hotel Bradshaw. There Tom meets Enrico,
who says his formula is being sought by several
industrial groups and that he and his niece are
going to Miami to confer with Prof. J.D. Denison (Ian Wolfe), a Brazilian who got Enrico the
financing he needed to develop his formula.
After Tom and Luisa leave, the cab driver, really
hoodlum Mike Geary (Phil Warren), enters the
apartment and kills the old man. Tom returns
looking for his cigarette case and is knocked

Tom Conway in *The Falcon's Adventure* (1946).

Lobby card for *The Falcon's Adventure* (1946) picturing Myrna Dell, Tom Conway and Madge Meredith.

out. Cavanaugh and Duncan show up and arrest Tom for Enrico's murder but as they are taking him to police headquarters Goldie helps his boss escape. Returning to the hotel, Tom is given the formula by Luisa and he promises to meet her in Miami. On the train there, Tom and Goldie are tricked by Doris Blanding (Myrna Dell) and her boyfriend Benny (Steve Brodie) into exchanging compartments. The duo use gas pellets on Tom and Goldie, and Doris takes what she thinks is the formula she finds hidden under Tom's pillow. When they awake, Tom informs Goldie the formula stolen was a bogus one. In Miami, Tom has Goldie go to the Kennel Club where he spots Luisa's maid Helen Ray (Carol Forman) and her husband Paolo (Tony Barrett). Earlier Tom and Goldie has spied Helen and Paolo near Denison's home. Meeting with the ill Denison, Tom is confronted by Benny and Doris and during a fight the old man dies of a heart attack and Tom is knocked out near the body. Benny calls the police before he and Doris depart. Upon awakening, Tom finds the dead man and leaves with Goldie. The police arrive, find Tom's wallet and suspect him of killing Denison. Cavanaugh and Duncan fly to Miami on the same plane as Luisa and ask Police Lt. Evans (Jason Robards) to help them find Tom. That night Tom sees Cavanaugh and Duncan at the Patio Club and makes a call sending them on a wild goose chase with Goldie driving their cab, which he later abandons. Tom and Goldie confront Helen and Paolo and they say they want the formula to pay off gambling debts and get them out of the country; Tom agrees to stake them at the dog races in Havana. At her hotel, Luisa is approached by Kenneth Sutton (Robert Warwick) who tells her that Denison interested him in financing her uncle's formula, which he wants to buy, and he invites her to go with him on his yacht, the *Sea Star,* back to her home in Brazil, and she agrees. Luisa asks Tom to give her the formula and after doing so he sees her drive away with Sutton and Doris and follows them. Tom sends a telegram to Doris and Benny asking them to come to an alligator emporium where he has Goldie wear an alligator head and scare the two into admitting they work for Sutton, who wants the formula so it will not compete with his industrial diamond syndicate. On the yacht, Sutton tells Luisa to give him the formula. When she refuses, he calls Geary, but Tom and Goldie arrive and fight it out with the crooks as the police come and arrest the killers.

Variety reported, "A semblance of care seems to be all that's necessary to make a whodunit surefire program fare, and this latest in the 'Falcon' series has that. Swiftly paced and competently mounted, *The Falcon's Adventure* moves fast enough so that the few inconsistencies probably will never be noticed." *Boxoffice* complained, "In his swan song, the Falcon fails to fly very high. In fact, he barely gets off the ground—probably because he was suffering from malnutrition as a result of being restricted on a diet of thin cliches." *The Film Daily* said, "This compact thriller has good production, the action content is emphasized and the title character, 'The Falcon,' has a merry time through it all."

The Falcon's Alibi (1946; 67 minutes)

PRODUCER: William Berke. EXECUTIVE PRODUCER: Sid Rogell. DIRECTOR: Ray McCarey. PHOTOGRAPHY: Frank Redman. EDITOR: Philip Martin, Jr. MUSIC DIRECTOR: C. Bakaleinikoff. ART DIRECTORS: Lucius Croxton & Albert D'Agostino. SOUND: Terry Kellum & Francis M. Sarver. SET DECORATIONS: Darrell Silvera. ASSISTANT DIRECTOR: James Anderson.

CAST: Tom Conway (Tom Lawrence, the Falcon), Rita Corday (Joan Meredith), Vince Barnett (Goldie Locke), Jane Greer (Lola Carpenter), Elisha Cook, Jr. (Nick), Emory Parnell (Metcalf), Alan Bridge (Inspector Blake), Esther Howard (Gloria Peabody), Jean Brooks (Baroness Lena), Paul Brooks (Alex Olmsted), Jason Robards (Harry Beaumont), Morgan Wallace (Bender), Lucien Prival (Baron), Edmund Cobb (Detective Williams), Eddie Borden (Postman), Harry Harvey (Racing Bettor), Forbes Murray (Mr. Thompson), Larry Wheat (Burke), Alphonse Martell (Louie), Myrna Dell (Dancing Partner), Nan Leslie (Cashier), Edward Clark (Coroner), Mike Lally, Jack Stoney (Thugs), Frank Pershing (Police Guard), Alf Haugen (Club Doorman), Bob Alden (Bellhop), Betty Gillette (Elevator Operator), Jeffrey Sayre (Club Patron).

At the horse races, Tom Lawrence (Tom Conway), the Falcon, is attracted to beautiful Joan Meredith (Rita Corday), who is with her employer Mrs. Gloria Peabody (Esther Howard) and a coterie of friends, including Harvey Beaumont (Jason Robards). When burly Metcalf (Emory Parnell) annoys Joan, Tom stops him and is invited to Gloria's birthday party. This forces Tom to tell his pal Goldie Locke (Vince Barnett) they will have to cancel their reservations in Miami. At the party, Joan confides in Tom that pesky Metcalf is an insurance investigator looking into the theft of Gloria's expensive pearl necklace. She claims that when she had it copied, it turned out to be paste. Club singer Lola Carpenter (Jane Greer) tells hotel disc jockey Nick (Elisha Cook, Jr.) they must keep their marriage a secret and as they kiss they are surprised by the arrival of Gloria, Joan, Tom and Goldie. When waiter Louie (Alphonse Martell) is preparing food for the birthday party, he is shot. Tom and Joan find the body and realize that the pearls have been stolen. Police Inspector Blake (Alan Bridge) investigates the murder and learns of the theft. He says there have been five robberies in six months at the hotel and Joan hires Tom to find the necklace. That night a shot is fired at Tom and Goldie through their hotel window as Nick returns to his upstairs studio while a recording of his voice is playing. At poolside the next day, Tom comments to Lola about the expensive ring she is wearing. She claims it is an imitation but he knows its true value. Tom tells Goldie to start a trash can fire in Beaumont's room and Goldie,

Lobby card for *The Falcon's Alibi* (1946).

hiding in the closet, observes Beaumont rush in and check a large book before putting out the fire. Later Tom and Goldie search the room and Tom finds the pearls concealed in the hollowed-out book and takes them. Tom tries to bait a trap by having the hotel owner, Bender (Morgan Wallace), a known fence, buy the pearls, but he refuses. Tom then mails the necklace to his hotel room as Nick takes a similar set to Bender, who tells him they are phonies. When the pearls arrive at Tom's apartment, he and Goldie are surprised by Blake and they take him to Beaumont's room but find him murdered. Blake arrests Tom and Goldie for the crimes but later lets them go, giving them 24 hours to find the culprit. Tom, Joan and Goldie go back to the club and when Tom searches Lola's dressing room he finds an inscribed picture of Nick to his wife. He also over-hears Lola and her boss, bandleader Alex Olmsted (Paul Brooks), discuss their romance. Later Lola tries to tell Nick about Alex but he informs her he has committed the robberies in order to buy her expensive gifts and he begs her to leave with him. Out of fear she agrees. Lola tells Alex what has happened and after he departs, Nick confronts his unfaithful wife and shoots her. As Nick sneaks back into Station KGR's studios through an open window, he finds Joan. She is there searching for Tom, who has found Lola's body. Realizing Nick is the killer because of the transcription playing his voice, Joan tries to escape. As the disc jockey is about to kill her, Tom arrives. Nick attempts to get away via the fire escape but falls to his death. Blake later informs Tom and Joan that Gloria and Beaumont were trying to defraud Metcalf's insurance company.

The twelfth and penultimate outing in the series, *The Falcon's Alibi* has luscious co-star Jane Greer sing "Come Out, Come Out" and "It Just Happened to Happen." The film's horror aspect comes from Elisha Cook, Jr.'s, portrayal of a psychotic killer who uses radio recordings to cover his theft and murder operations. He also has an unhealthy obsession with his beautiful but two-timing spouse. As the "Owl's Nest" disc jockey, Cook plays records by Charlie Barnet, Les Brown, the King Cole Trio ("Heavenly"), Jimmy Dorsey, Skinnay Ennis and Gene Krupa. In a bit of self-promotion, Frances Langford is heard singing "Dreaming Out Loud" from RKO's *The Bamboo Blonde*, issued the same year.

Boxoffice enthused that as far as Falcon films went, this one was "among the more exciting and suspenseful adventures of the suave super-sleuth ... [Conway] is supported by a cast that is definitely above average. Such thespic alignment, aided by the fact the story—boasting no less than three murders—is cleverly contrived, are the main contributing factors to the film's appeal.... Ably directed by Ray McCarey." *Variety* called it a "neatly plotted whodunit ... better than average for 'The Falcon' series in all departments. William Berke's production achieves topnotch values for budget expenditure, and direction by Ray McCarey unfolds the intrigue at a brisk pace.... Script by Paul Yawitz gives good lines and characters to the standard situations. Conway does an interesting job of his Falcon interpretation."

Fantasia (1940; 106 minutes; Color)

PRODUCER: Walt Disney. DIRECTORS: Samuel Armstrong, James Algar, Bill Roberts, Paul Satterfield, Hamilton Luske, Jim Handley, Ford Beebe, Norm Ferguson, T. Hee & Wilfred Jackson. STORY DIRECTION: Joe Grant & Dick Hunter. STORY DEVELOPMENT: Lee Blair, Elmer Plummer, Phil Dike, Sylvia Moberly-Holland, Norman Wright, Albert Heath, Bianca Majolie, Graham Held, Perce Pearce, Carl Fallberg, William Martin, Leo Thiele, Robert Sterner, John Fraser McLeish, Otto Englander, Webb Smith, Erdman Penner, Joseph Sabo, Bill Peed, George Stallings, Campbell Grant & Arthur Heinemann. SPECIAL PHOTOGRAPHIC EFFECTS: Gail Papineau & Leonard Pickley. MUSIC: Johann Sebastian Bach, Ludwig van Beethoven, Paul Dukas, Rachel Field, Modest Mussorgsky, Amilcare Ponchielli, Franz Schubert, Igor Stravinsky & Pyotr Ilyich Tchaikovsky. MUSIC DIRECTOR: Edward H. Plumb. MUSIC EDITOR: Stephen Csillag. ART DIRECTORS: Robert Cormack, Bruce Bushman, Arthur Byram, Curtiss D. Perkins, Al Zinnen, Tod Codrick, Charles Phillipi, Zack Schwartz, John Hubley, Dick Kelsey, McLaren Stewart, Kenneth Anderson, Yale Gracey, Hugh Hennesy, J. Gordon Legg, Lance Nolley, Herbert Ryman, Zack Schwartz, Kay Nielsen, Charles Payzant, Thor Putnam, Terrell Stapp, Ernest Nordi & Kendall O'Connor. SOUND: William E. Garity, J.N.A. Hawkins & C.O. Slyfield. PRODUCTION SUPERVISOR: Ben Sharpsteen. LIVE ACTION ANIMATORS: Cy Young, Art Palmer, Daniel McManus, George Rowley, Edwin Aardal, Joseph Meador, Cornett Wood, Arthur Babbitt, Les Clark, Don Lusk, Robert Stokes, Riley Thompson, Marvin Woodward, Preston Blair, Edward Love, Ugo D'Orsi, Philip Duncan, John McManus, Paul Busch, Dan Tobin, Paul B. Kosloff, Berny Wolf, Jack Campbell, John Bradbury, John Moore, Milt Neil, Bill Justice, John Elliotte, Walt Kelly, Don Lusk, Lynn Karp, Murray McLennan, Robert W. Youngquist, Harry Hamsel, John Lounsbery, Howard Swift, Preston Blair, Hugh Fraser, Harvey Toombs, Norman Tate, Hicks Lokey, Art Elliott, Grant Simmons, Ray Patterson, Franklin Grundeen, John McManus, William N. Shull, Robert W. Carlson, Jr., Lester Novros & Don Patterson. ANIMATION SUPERVISORS: Fred Moore, Vladimir Tytla, Wolfgang Reitherman, Joshua Meador, Fred Moore, Ward Kimball, Eric Larson, Arthur Babbitt, Oliver M. Johnston, Jr., Don Towsley & Norman Ferguson. BACKGROUND PAINTINGS: Joe Stanley, John Hench, Nino Carbe, Ethel Kulsar, Claude Coats, Stan Spohn, Albert Dempster, Eric Hansen, Ed Starr, Brice Mack, Edward Levitt, Ray Huffine, W. Richard Anthony, Arthur Riley, Gerald Nevius, Roy Forkum, Charles Conner, Merle Cox, Ray Lockrem & Robert Storms. LIVE ACTION MODELS: Bela Lugosi, Nigel de Brulier, Marge Belcher [Marge Champion], Joyce Coles, Hattie Noel, Princess Omar, Irina Baronova, Roman Jasinsky, Tania Riabouchinska & Wilfred Jackson. CAST: Leopold Stokowski and the Philadelphia Orchestra (Themselves), Deems Taylor (Himself), Walt Disney (Voice of Mickey Mouse), Julietta Novis (Vocal Soloist), Charles Henderson (Chorus Conductor), James MacDonald (Percussionist), Paul J. Smith (Violinist).

First conceived in 1937 and given theatrical release early in 1940, *Fantasia* is one of Walt Disney's most spectacular and involved productions, mainly an animated feature version of several classical music pieces and one popular song in a colorful and fascinating conglomerate. The colossal production cost nearly $2.5 million, employed over 100 musicians and 750 artists, resulting in 600,000 celluloid drawings. The music was performed mainly by Leopold Stokowski and the Philadelphia Orchestra. The classical compositions used are "Toccata and Fugue in D Minor" by Johann Sebastian Bach, "The Nutcracker Suite" by Pyotr Ilyich Tchaikovsky, "The Sorcerer's Apprentice" by Paul Dukas, "The Rite of Spring" by Igor Stravinsky, "Pastoral Symphony" by Ludwig van Beethoven, "Dance of the Hours" by Amilcare Ponchielli and "Night on Bald Mountain" by Modest Mussorgsky. Walt Disney Productions distributed the feature until the spring of 1941 and during that period its running times ran between 120 and 135 minutes in the various venues where it was shown. RKO took over its release in 1942 and pared it to 81 minutes. Over the years *Fantasia* had a number of reissues and in 1982 Deems Taylor's narration was replaced by Hugh Douglas. The National Board of Review and *The New York Times* voted the feature one of the ten best of 1940 and it received an award from the New York Film Critics Circle. Leopold Stokowski and Walt Disney received special Academy Awards for the film in 1942. For its 50th anniversary in 1990, *Fantasia* was completely restored and a decade later seven new sequences were added and it was entitled *Fantasia 2000*, running 75 minutes.

After explaining the three different types of music to be animated in *Fantasia* (precise, non-specific, abstract images), Deems Taylor introduces Leopold Stokowski and the Philadelphia Orchestra, which leads off with "Toccata and Fugue in D Minor," dealing with abstract images. Non-specific but definite pictures are used in the ballet "The Nutcracker Suite" and Mickey Mouse plays the title role in "The Sorcerer's Apprentice." It has Mickey causing havoc by wearing his master's magic hat with a water-carrying broom multiplying into a veritable army that floods the sorcerer's castle. Evolution is presented in "Rite of Spring" centered on the coming and demise of dinosaurs. "The Pastoral Symphony" takes place on Mount Olympus with Zeus amusing himself by starting a bacchanal among its denizens. Various animals perform "Dance of the Hours" while "Night on Bald Mountain" has a demon celebrate Walpurgis Night by raising the dead; sunrise ends his frolic as villagers carol "Ave Maria."

For genre fans, "The Sorcerer's Apprentice," "The Rite of Spring" and "Night on Bald Mountain" hold the most fascination. All three segments are expertly animated and the musical pieces are highly entertaining. Mickey Mouse highlights "The Sorcerer's Apprentice" as a water carrier who tries to use his master's magic to save himself work only to create a catastrophe. The scenes with the hordes of water-carrying marching brooms are especially impressive. Equally absorbing are the dinosaur scenes in "The Rite of Spring" with the reptiles' demise as the planet gets hotter. "Night on Bald Mountain" is an intense horror piece with the demon Chernabog, a frightful creation, who resurrects the dead and tortures them with hellfire. Bela Lugosi served as a live-action model for Chernabog, although there is some debate as to whether or not any drawings of him were used to simulate the demon. Watching the film, however, one can readily spot certain movements by Chernabog that could easily have originated with Lugosi.

Two of *Fantasia*'s horror sequences had been filmed before. In 1930 Fritz Feld played the title role in *L'apprenti Sorcier* (The Sorcerer's Apprentice), one of the French Visual Tone Poem series designed by William Cameron Menzies. The French also did a version of *Une Nuit Sur le Mont Chauve* (A Night on Bald Mountain) in 1933, using the technique Pin-Screen Animation. Both of these well-done shorts are included in the excellent DVD compilation "Grotesqueries," released by Reel Curiosities in 2006.

Critical and audience reception to *Fantasia* was mixed. Leonard Maltin noted in *The Disney Films, 3rd Edition* (1995) that it "was Disney's most ambitious undertaking and in all respects his most controversial endeavor. Not much of a money-maker in its initial release, it has, in the past few years, become a phenomenal favorite of the younger generation...." Upon its initial release, *Boxoffice* said it "defies all precedent" and called it "a concert on film." While the trade publication said it was "unsuitable for children" the reviewer felt, "The whole, however, is done in magnificent color, in brilliant imagination, and in lasting recognition of Disney's enormous talents." *The Film Daily* determined, "Not merely one cinematic milestone, but several of them and just as certainly, it is box office for class audiences."

The Flying Deuces (1939; 69 minutes)

PRODUCER: Boris Morros. DIRECTOR: A. Edward Sutherland. STORY & SCREENPLAY: Ralph Spence, Harry Langdon, Charles Rogers & Alfred Schiller. PHOTOGRAPHY: Art Lloyd. EDITOR: Jack Dennis. MUSIC: John Leipold & Leo Shuken. MUSIC DIRECTOR: Edward Paul. SONG: Nora Bayes & Jack Norworth. ART DIRECTOR: Boris Leven. SOUND: William Wilmarth. PRODUCTION MANAGER: Joe Nadel. PRODUCTION ADVISOR: Rudolph Mate. SPECIAL EFFECTS: Howard A. Anderson. AERIAL PHOTOGRAPHER: Elmer Dyer. CHIEF PILOT & TECHNICAL ADVISOR: Frank Clarke. ASSISTANT DIRECTOR: Robert Stillman.

CAST: Stan Laurel (Stan), Oliver Hardy (Oliver), Jean Parker (Georgette), Reginald Gardiner (Francois), Charles Middleton (Commandant), Jean Del Val (Sergeant), Clem Wilenchick [Crane Whitley] (Corporal), James Finlayson (Jailor), Michael Visaroff (Innkeeper), Richard Cramer (Delivery Driver), Frank Clarke (Pilot), Kit Guard, Eddie Borden, Billy Engle, Sam Lufkin, Jack Chefe (Legionnaires), Christine Cabanne, Mary Jane Carey, Monica Bannister, Bonnie Bannon (Georgette's Friends).

Following the termination of their contracts with producer Hal Roach, Stan Laurel and Oliver Hardy appeared in *The Flying Deuces*, filmed as *The Aviator* and released by RKO in November 1939. The following year the comedy greats would reunite for two more features with Roach, *A Chump at Oxford* and *Saps at Sea*, before signing with 20th Century–Fox. *The Flying Deuces* is a reworking of their 1931 four-reeler *Beau Hunks* and both cast Charles Middleton as a fort commander. The picture was produced by Boris Morros, former Paramount music director, who later was identified as a longstanding agent for the Soviet Union. While often amusing, the film is hardly one of the comedy team's best although it did display Hardy's fine singing voice with a rendition of "Shine On Harvest Moon" during which he and Laurel also do a brief dance number. The fantasy elements come at the finale when Hardy is shown ascending to Heaven and then returning as a talking horse. A running gag has Hardy saying that if he is reincarnated, he wants to come back as a horse. *The Flying Deuces* was reissued theatrically by Astor Pictures in 1949.

Des Moines, Iowa, fishmongers Stan (Laurel) and Oliver (Hardy) are vacationing in Paris with Oliver falling in love with beautiful Georgette (Jean Parker), the daughter of the owner (Michael Visaroff) of the inn where they are staying. Unaware that Georgette and her friends are amused that he has given her flowers and candy, plus his picture, Oliver buys her a big diamond ring and plans to ask to her marry him. Her husband, Legionnaire Francois (Reginald Gardiner), shows up and informs Georgette he has made arrangements for her to join him at his post; Oliver, unaware that she is married, proposes to her and she turns him down. Disappointed, Oliver takes back the picture, flowers and candy and tells Stan he is going to end it all. Deciding to drown himself in the Seine River, Oliver expects Stan to join him. After several futile attempts, Francois comes along and, after hearing Oliver's story, suggests he join the Foreign Legion to forget. Thinking it will only take a few days for him to get over Georgette, Oliver, along with Stan, signs up but at their first muster the duo cause such havoc they are taken to the commandant (Middleton), who informs them they will be paid the equivalent of three cents a day for their services. Stan and Oliver refuse to work for such low wages but end up on the laundry detail. After much arduous work Oliver forgets Georgette and he and Stan plan to return home. Hearing that the two new recruits have deserted, the commandant orders them placed under arrest. Georgette arrives at the airport and is met by Francois, who leaves to get a car. When Oliver sees the young woman, he thinks she has returned to him and begins kissing her. Francois tells Oliver to keep away from his wife or he will leave him at the mercy of the desert vultures. The commandant arrives with his men and arrest Stan and Oliver for desertion. They are taken to the fort prison and locked in a cell by the jailer (Jimmy Finlayson). The commandant heads a military tribunal that finds Stan and Oliver guilty and sentences them to he hung at sunrise. Someone throws a message to the prisoners advising them of a tunnel under their cell floor that leads outside the walls of the fort. The two try to crawl to safety but Stan causes a landslide, forcing them to dig their way out, and they end up in Francois' cellar. The next morning the jailer sees his prisoners have escaped and the commandant orders a manhunt. Finding their way to Georgette's bedroom, Stan and Oliver hide in her portable clothes closet. She faints when Stan sneezes, causing the closet to fall over. Francois finds Oliver trying to revive his wife; Stan and Oliver escape through a window only to be hunted by the Legionnaires. Eventually they return to their cell, go back through the tunnel and back into Francois' cellar before making a getaway to the airport. There they hide in a plane while the soldiers hunt for them. Stan accidentally starts the plane's engine and it takes off. The plane bounces all over the fort, frightening the Legionnaires before it nose-dives and crashes. Stan is not hurt but Oliver's spirit ascends into the clouds. Later, while bumming around, Stan hears Oliver call him and he finds his pal has returned as a mustachioed horse wearing a derby.

The Hollywood Spectator called it "a frankly slapstick affair.... Portions are very funny." *Variety* said, "Picture is a hodgepodge of elemental horseplay and slapstick.... Overall, it's pretty dull, but may get by with the juvenile audiences for mild attention." Jess Zunser complained in *Cue,* "The picture [Laurel & Hardy are] trying to palm off as a movie is a confused, conglomerate mess of unfunny, broad humors and broader burlesque—bulging with whiskered gags, senile jokes, and decrepit slapstick lifted bodily from the infancy of the movies."

The Film Daily reported, "Laurel and Hardy's new picture is full of laughs and should be popular with lovers of comedy everywhere. It has much fresh material and some sequences that should score in any theater." *The Hollywood Reporter* declared, "There's not much to this new Laurel-Hardy comedy, mainly because of lack of story material, but [it's still] better than the average feature-length show with the pair of funsters." *Box Office Digest* thought it "takes rank as probably the best of the Laurel-Hardy feature efforts.... It has its laughs aplenty, a pretty steady stream of them, with two or three high spot sequences that really go to town." William K. Everson wrote in *The Films of Laurel and Hardy* (1967), "Despite a script concocted by their old cronies and the presence in the cast of such reliable comedy foils as [Jimmy] Finlayson and [Charles] Middleton, it just didn't jell and seemed to lack the old spontaneous camaraderie of the Roach films." He also complained, "The film was cheaply made, with the RKO sound stages themselves thinly disguised to serve as 'sets' for desert fort and plane hangar."

Forty Naughty Girls (1937; 63 minutes)

PRODUCER: William Sistrom. DIRECTOR: Edward Cline. SCREENPLAY: John Grey, from the story "The Riddle of the Forty Naughty Girls" by Stuart Palmer. PHOTOGRAPHY: Russell Metty. EDITOR: John Lockert. MUSIC DIRECTOR: Roy Webb. ART DIRECTORS: Van Nest Polglase & Feild M. Gray. SOUND: Earl A. Wolcott. COSTUME DESIGN: Renie.

CAST: James Gleason (Inspector Oscar Piper), ZaSu Pitts (Hildegarde Martha Withers), Marjorie Lord (June Preston), George Shelley (Bert), Joan Woodbury (Rita Marlowe), Frank M. Thomas (Jeff "Pop" Plummer), Tom Kennedy (Detective Casey), Alan Edwards (Ricky Rickman), Alden [Stephen] Chase (Tommy Washburn), Eddie Marr (Windy Bennett), Ada Leonard (Lil), Barbara Pepper (Alice), Edward

LeSaint (Coroner), Bob McKenzie (Backstage Doorman Max), Eddie Borden (Stage Board Man), Lynton Brent (Ticket Taker Joe), Frank O'Connor (Stage Manager), Bud Jamison (Theater Doorman), Donald Kerr (Call Boy), Elizabeth Russell, William Corson (Couple in Front of Theater).

Released in September 1937, *Forty Naughty Girls* was the last of RKO's six Hildegarde Withers mysteries, this one being based on Stuart Palmer's 1934 story "The Riddle of the Forty Naughty Girls." It was the second teaming of James Gleason as Inspector Oscar Piper and ZaSu Pitts as Miss Withers, following *The Plot Thickens* (1936) [q.v.]. Previously Gleason did the Piper role opposite Edna May Oliver as Miss Withers in *Penguin Pool Murder* (1932), *Murder on the Blackboard* (1934) and *Murder on a Honeymoon* (1935), and Helen Broderick in *Murder on a Bridle Path* (1936) [qq.v.]. The three Oliver features were vastly superior to this foray, by far the worst in the group. Although competently made and acted, *Forty Naughty Girls* is plagued with too many musical numbers but its worst fault is making Miss Withers a clumsy buffoon instead of the quick-witted schoolmarm-sleuth of yore. One unfunny bit has her going around sniffing people hoping to recognize the odor of a perfume she detected at the scene of the film's first murder. Although nicely attired in a gown by Renie, Pitts' Miss Withers, a fluttery, fussy, middle-aged snoop, is hardly in line with the intrepid schoolteacher created by Stuart Palmer, and played that way by Oliver, Broderick and even Pitts in the previous series entry. Although running slightly over one hour, the film badly drags and is a chore to sit through.

At the Broadway theater hosting the hit production *Forty Naughty Girls,* press agent Windy Bennett (Eddie Marr) meets with producer Ricky Rickman (Alan Edwards), who is engaged to the show's star Rita Marlowe (Joan Woodbury). Ricky has just closed the sale of the motion picture rights for the show for $100,000, half of which will go to its author, Tommy Washburn (Alden Chase). Windy makes a pass at ingénue June Preston (Marjorie Lord) and then kisses Rita in her dressing room. Prop manager Pop Plummer (Frank M. Thomas) later tells Rita that someone has taken one of his revolvers. Pop then hears Tommy arguing with Windy, who wants half of his take from the picture sale. Lead singer Bert (George Shelley) loves June; when he finds out that Windy made a pass at her, he threatens to kill him. Just as the show is about to start, Police Inspector Oscar Piper (Gleason) arrives with Hildegarde Martha Withers (Pitts), his longtime crime-solving rival. After a production number with Bert, June goes to her dressing room to change costumes and finds Windy's body. Ricky informs his friend Piper, who says that Windy was shot in the back of the head. Tommy tells Piper that Bert threatened to kill Windy over June. A nitrate test exonerates both June and Bert. When Piper goes to Windy's office, he is knocked out. After coming to, Piper searches Windy's desk and finds a secret bank book and evidence that Tommy stole his play from deceased author George Collins. Arriving at the murder scene, Miss Withers notices a strange scent on Windy's handkerchief and later locates the perfume in Rita's dressing room. Rita admits being with Windy earlier but denies killing him. Piper tells Miss Withers and Ricky that Tommy stole the play and was being blackmailed by Windy. During a scene in the play, Rita shoots Tommy, not realizing her prop gun is loaded. Piper questions Pop, who says he loaded the gun, but it is soon proved the weapon only contained blanks. The coroner (Edward LeSaint) tells Miss Withers that the bullet was fired from below the victim. She explores the theater's basement and finds a hole in the ceiling. Piper and his bumbling assistant Casey (Tom Kennedy) also search the basement and play and a cat-and-mouse game with Miss Withers before Casey pulls a lever that sends her on stage during a ballet number. Piper finds a gun and deduces it was timed to fire when the stage shot took place. When Piper arrests Pop for murdering Tommy, Rita informs him that Pop is her father. Ricky denies knowing about Rita and Windy. Miss Withers goes to Ricky's office and accidentally finds a letter addressed to him from the Globe Detective Bureau. When Piper again announces that Pop killed both Windy and Tommy,

Miss Withers informs him that Ricky is the murderer. She reveals the letter proves Ricky had Rita and Windy followed and she also matches a button missing on his shirt to one she found in the basement, where he lost it while shooting Tommy. When a nitrate test on his gloves proves positive, Ricky tries to escape with a gun Casey filled with blanks and is captured.

Boxoffice considered *Forty Naughty Girls* "a good enough murder mystery to garner satisfactory audience reception.... [It] is neither as baffling nor as amusing as its predecessors." *The New York Herald Tribune* said it "is not up to some of the earlier Stuart Palmer film stores in this series ... but it manages to be entertaining, nevertheless, and the backstage background is both authentic and exciting.... [It] will probably divert you, while not making many demands on you."

"[I]t is long on comedy and it is extremely short on ingenuity, suspense and excitement. However, it has good enough qualities in it to make it passable murder entertainment," wrote *The New York World-Telegram*. *The New York Times* decreed, "Rather enjoyable, and so long drawn out that you feel the author is having fun toying with the idea...." *Variety* pretty well summed it up by calling the picture "decidedly tame" and adding "[M]aterial is pretty weak and considerably dated."

From the Earth to the Moon (Warner Bros., 1958; 101 minutes; Color)

PRODUCER: Benedict Bogeaus. DIRECTOR: Byron Haskin. SCREENPLAY: Robert Blees & James Leicester. PHOTOGRAPHY: Edwin B. Du Par. EDITOR: James Leicester. MUSIC: Louis Forbes. SOUND: Weldon Coe. PRODUCTION DESIGN: Hal Wilson Cox. COSTUME DESIGN: Gwen Wakeling. SPECIAL EFFECTS: Lee Zavitz. VISUAL EFFECTS: Albert M. Simpson.

CAST: Joseph Cotten (Victor Barbicane), George Sanders (Stuyvesant Nicholl), Debra Paget (Virginia Nicholl), Don Dubbins (Ben Sharpe), Patric Knowles (Josef Cartier), Carl Esmond (Jules Verne), Henry Daniell (Morgana), Melville Cooper (Bancroft), Ludwig Stossel (Aldo Von Metz), Morris Ankrum (President Ulysses S. Grant), Robert Clarke (Narrator).

On May 18, 1868, munitions manufacturer Victor Barbicane (Joseph Cotten) arrives at his palatial estate, Victory, for a midnight meeting with members of the International Armaments Club, to discuss his new explosive, Power X. He tells the group, that includes banker Morgana (Henry Daniell), scientist Aldo Von Metz (Ludwig Stossel), businessman Josef Cartier (Patric Knowles) and writer Jules Verne (Carl Esmond), that he plans to use Power X to propel a projectile to the Moon where he will test its potential. Although they question his reason, the men agree to help him finance the project. Barbicane's arch-enemy Stuyvesant Nicholl (George Sanders), who worked for the Confederacy during the Civil War, challenges him to a duel. Barbicane refuses and asks Syndicated Press writer Bancroft (Melville Cooper) to publicize his invention. Nicholl then informs Congress that he has developed an impenetrable substance and calls for Barbicane to try and destroy it with Power X. A test site is set up and, using only a small cannon with a tiny amount of the explosive, Barbicane not only destroys Nicholl's metal shield but also the small mountain behind it. As a result, Barbicane and his crew start work on a rocket. The project comes to a halt after a clandestine meeting with President Ulysses S. Grant (Morris Ankrum) in which he is told that 22 nations fear that the cannon is being built for world conquest. As a result, Barbicane is pilloried in the press and threatened by mobs who have been put out of work because of his decision. Morgana and his cohorts offer to buy the formula for Power X for several million dollars but Barbicane refuses and they turn against him. While examining a piece of the metal from Nicholl's alloy with his assistant Ben Sharpe (Don Dubbins), Barbicane realizes it is now the hard substance he needs for his rocket. He then seeks an alliance with Nicholl on the moon trip project; metallurgist Nicholl's daughter Virginia (Debra Paget) urges her father not to trust him. During the construction of the rocket, Ben and Virginia find they are attracted

Spanish poster for *From the Earth to the Moon* (Warner Bros., 1958).

to each other and when the rocket is about to be launched, she hides in one of the spacesuits just before lift off. After surviving the launch in special pressurized chambers, Barbicane, Nicholl and Ben find the ship's gyroscope is askew. Barbicane levels it off and Nicholl announces that he has sabotaged the voyage in the name of God by cutting the propeller wires. Ben discovers Virginia on board and Nicholl realizes he has doomed his daughter as well as himself. When Barbicane tries to repair the damages, he is caught in an electric current. Nicholl causes him to be badly shocked, making Virginia doubt her father's integrity. She apologizes to Barbicane for her father's behavior. When the vessel is hit by huge meteors, Barbicane navigates it to safety, impressing Nicholl with his skill. On Earth, Bancroft announces that he believes the voyage is a fake and says that Barbicane has gone into hiding with his supporters' money. On the ship Barbicane reveals his intended plans of selling the formula for Power X to all nations in order to prevent future wars. The ship is caught between the pull of space and the moon and Barbicane and Ben realize their only hope is using its rockets to split the ship into four parts. Since the hull is the safest part of the vessel, Nicholl knocks out Ben and he and Barbicane carry him there, where he is locked in with Virginia. Barbicane fires the rockets, with Virginia and Ben cast back to Earth while he and Nicholl head for the far side of the moon. Just before their capsule leaves the moon's pull, the two lovers see a flare on the surface, signifying Barbicane and Nicholl have landed safely. Back on Earth, Von Metz theorizes that the rocket crashed on the moon but Verne declares that the voyage occurred in the realm of imagination.

Based on two Jules Verne novels, 1865's *De la Terre a la Lune* and 1870's *Autour de la Lune*, *From the Earth to the Moon* is not an unlikable film but its lack of a proper budget resulted in a basically slow, dull production. It gets a bit more exciting in his final third after the rocket launch. Spare, but somewhat effective, special effects add a bit to the proceedings but scenes like a slow (60 seconds–plus) countdown are liabilities. In one sequence Morgana compares Barbicane to Columbus. The pressurized cylinder prop that housed the astronauts during takeoff was later used in the Mexican horror comedy *La Casa del Terror* (Azteca, 1957) with that footage incorporated into the American version, *Face of the Screaming Werewolf* (ADP, 1964).

Variety reported, "It is handsome, well cast and timely. Unfortunately, it is a horse-and-buggy treatment of a rock-propelled theme and as confusing as a scientific formula for solid fuel." Bosley Crowther in *The New York Times* complained that the writers "seemed to base their script more on recent data about rocket launching than the fantasies of Mr. Verne [and] the director failed to correct their mistake"; he dubbed it "mixed-up science fiction decked out in fancy costumes." In *Horrors: From Screen to Scream* (1975), Ed Naha called *From the Earth to the Moon* an "elaborate but essentially empty interpretation of Jules Verne's tale of space travel. Talky and stiff.... Special effects somewhat less than spellbinding." Philip Strick in *Science Fiction Movies* (1976) said, "Byron Haskin brought style but stifling sobriety" to the feature, while C.J. Henderson in *The Encyclopedia of Science Fiction Movies* (2001) noted, "The special effects are adequate, and it's somewhat interesting to see this unusual cast in a science fiction film, but only somewhat." He also termed the film "slow-moving."

From the Earth to the Moon was not screened in Great Britain until March 1964, when it was released there by Rank.

Fun and Fancy Free (1947; 73 minutes; Color)

PRODUCER: Walt Disney. ANIMATION DIRECTORS: Jack Kinney, Hamilton Luske & Bill Roberts. LIVE ACTION DIRECTOR: William Morgan. STORY: Homer Brightman, Harry Reeves, Ted Sears, Lance Nolley, Eldon Dedini & Tom Oreb, from the stories "Bongo" by Sinclair Lewis & "Jack and the Beanstalk."

LIVE ACTION PHOTOGRAPHY: Charles P. Boyle. EDITOR: Jack Bachom. MUSIC: Eliot Daniel, Paul Smith & Oliver Wallace. MUSIC DIRECTOR: Charles Wolcott. SONGS: Ray Noble, Ned Washington, Leigh Harline, Bennie Benjamin, Luigi Denza, Buddy Kaye, Arthur Quenzer, George Weiss & Bobby Worth. SOUND: Robert Cook & Harold J. Steck. SOUND SUPERVISOR: C.O. Slyfield. EFFECTS ANIMATORS: Jack Boyd & George Rowley. DIRECTING ANIMATORS: Ward Kimball, Les Clark, John Lounsbery, Fred Moore & Wolfgang Reitherman. CHARACTER ANIMATORS: Hugh Frasher, Phil Duncan, Judge Whitaker, Arthur Babbitt, John Sibley, Marc Davis, Harvey Toombs, Hal King, Ken O'Brien & Jack Campbell. BACKGROUNDS: Ed Starr, Claude Coats, Art Riley, Brice Mack, Ray Huffine & Ralph Hulett. LAYOUT: Donald Da Gradi, Al Zinnen, Ken O'Connor, Hugh Hennesy, John Hench & Glen Scott. PROCESS EFFECTS: Up Iwerks. PRODUCTION SUPERVISOR: Ben Sharpsteen. TECHNICOLOR DIRECTOR: Natalie Kalmus. ASSOCIATE TECHNICOLOR DIRECTOR: Moran Padleford.

CAST: Edgar Bergen (Himself), Dinah Shore (Narrator/Singer), Charlie McCarthy (Himself), Mortimer Snerd (Himself), Luana Patten (Herself), Cliff Edwards (Voice of Jiminy Cricket), Anita Gordon (Voice of Singing Harp), Billy Gilbert (Voice of Willie the Giant), Clarence Nash (Voice of Donald Duck), The King's Men (Themselves), The Dinning Sisters (Themselves), The Starlighters (Themselves), Pinto Colvig (Voice of Goofy), James MacDonald (Voices of Mickey Mouse & Lumpjaw), Walt Disney (Voice of Mickey Mouse).

The two stories in *Fun and Fancy Free* were first slated for filming by the Walt Disney organization in 1941 but union problems and World War II prevented production. Late in 1945, work resumed on the project. The finished product tells the animated tales "Bongo" and "Mickey and the Beanstalk," with wraparound animated footage featuring Jiminy Cricket and live action sequences with Edgar Bergen and his dummies Charlie McCarthy and Mortimer Snerd, and child actress Luana Patten. The soundtrack includes popular vocalists Dinah Shore (who also narrates "Bongo"), Cliff Edwards (repeating his Jiminy Cricket role from *Pinocchio* [q.v.]), Anita Gordon, the King's Men, the Dinning Sisters and the Starlighters. While James MacDonald does most of the Mickey Mouse voice work, as well as that of the villainous bear Lumpjaw, Walt Disney can briefly be heard as Mickey in footage shot in 1941, the last time he did the mouse's voice. Beautifully animated in outstanding Technicolor, *Fun and Fancy Free* is one of Disney's lesser efforts. The "Bongo" sequence is uninteresting and "Mickey and the Beanstalk" is not much better although it comes to life near the finale when Willie the Giant (voice of Billy Gilbert) chases Mickey and his pals down a beanstalk as they run off with a Singing Harp (voice of Gordon). The significance of the feature in the Disney canon is nicely summed up by Leonard Maltin in *The Disney Films, 3rd Edition* (1995): "*Fun and Fancy Free* was one of the bread-and-butter movies Disney made after the war to get material into release as quickly as possible, and regain his studio's lost momentum. As such, it is a pleasant enough film, but hardly outstanding. Its greatest notoriety derives from the fact that it is one of the few Disney feature films to include his short-subject stars Mickey Mouse, Donald Duck, and Goofy."

Trying cheer up an unhappy doll and teddy bear, Jiminy Cricket sings "I'm a Happy-Go-Lucky Fellow" and plays a phonograph record telling the story of Bongo, the Wonder Bear, a circus performer who is kept caged when he is not working and who longs to be free. One day Bongo discovers the door to his train car unlocked and escapes on a unicycle, finding himself in a wonderful forest, but soon has trouble adapting to the wild. He meets a pretty bear named Lulubelle and immediately falls in love and she feels the same about him. Their happiness is interrupted by the arrival of the giant Lumpjaw, who wants Lulubelle for himself. When Lulubelle slaps him, Bongo thinks it is a rejection and rides away but soon sees other bears doing the same thing as a sign of affection. Bongo goes back for Lulubelle but is drawn into a fight with Lumpjaw, who he manages to outmaneuver. Eventually both bears are caught on a log and sent hurling over a waterfall, but Bongo gets caught on a tree branch while Lumpjaw is swept away. Bongo is happily reunited with Lulubelle.

Advertisement for *Fun and Fancy Free* (1947).

After cheering the doll and the teddy bear with the record, Jiminy Cricket finds a birthday invitation for Luana Patten (herself) from Edgar Bergen (himself) and his dummies Charlie McCarthy and Mortimer Snerd. He goes to the party as Bergen tells the story of Happy Valley, where a Singing Harp (voice of Gordon) keeps the area prosperous. When she disappears, the valley turns desolate and three farmers, Mickey Mouse, Donald Duck and Goofy, nearly starve before selling their cow. Donald and Goofy become angry when Mickey gets supposedly magic beans for the bovine but overnight they grow into a giant beanstalk that carries the trio's house into the heavens. The three awake to find they are near a castle. Exploring it, they see a feast and while eating they awaken the Singing Harp, who tells them she has been taken prisoner and locked in a jewelry box by an ogre, Willie the Giant (voice of Gilbert). Willie has the power to turn into anything and when Mickey tries to trick him he places Donald and Goofy in a box; Mickey manages to escape. While the giant sleeps, Mickey steals the key to the box and after several close calls frees his friends. The three take the harp and escape down the beanstalk with Willie following them. Mickey cuts down the beanstalk, killing Willie. This upsets Mortimer but when Bergen tries to tell him it was just a story, Willie pulls off the roof, causing Edgar to pass out. Willie then lumbers through Hollywood trying to find Mickey.

Nine songs are included in *Fun and Fancy Free* but only the title tune and "Lazy Countryside" are memorable. The latter was recorded at the time by Tony Martin on Victor Records (20–2396). The number sung by Cliff Edwards, "I'm a Happy-Go-Lucky Fellow," was done for *Pinocchio* (q.v.) in 1939 but not included in its final release.

The New York Herald Tribune wrote, "There are few flashes of brilliance in *Fun and Fancy Free*, but it offers the tried and true Disney spectacle, ideal for children and sufficiently diverting for adults." *The New York Sun* opined, "Not one of Disney's best. It is pleasant enough, just two children's tales told with plenty of slapstick in color cartoon." *The New York Journal American* thought it "delightful entertainment" while *The New York Post* felt it "has its ups and downs." *PM* declared, "Will delight millions and millions of children.... So much of it is first-rate and imaginative and original that one cannot be too disturbed about the lesser elements." On the down side, *Variety* called it "a dull and tiresome film that even the most rabid Disney addicts will not find to their taste. The whole combo is uninspired and belabored, completely unlike Disney." *The Film Daily* stated, "Walt Disney's latest contribution to the gaiety, delight, and entertainment of the nation is another film to be loved by children, provide mental stimulation to adults and produce box office figures as well-rounded as the animated characters that flutter, caper, parade, emote and glide through its various scenes.... The music is gay, lilting, smooth. Loaded with the best in imaginative animation, again Disney delivers up what is required."

Disney made two previous versions of "Jack and the Beanstalk." The first was in 1922 for his Laugh-O-Gram company and 11 years later he produced the animated cartoon "Giantland." "Bongo" and "Mickey and the Beanstalk" were later released theatrically by Disney as short subjects and in 1968 "Mickey and the Beanstalk" was seen on NBC-TV's *Walt Disney's Wonderful World of Color* with the animated character Ludwig Von Drake replacing Edgar Bergen and his dummies and Luana Patten in narrating the tale. In 1964 Disneyland Records issued the soundtrack of *Fun and Fancy Free* on a long-playing album (DQ-1248) and four years later the label released a studio cast album of "Mickey and the Beanstalk" (ST-3974) narrated by Robbie Lester with Jimmie Dodd and the Mouseketeers Chorus and Orchestra. It included a ten-page color booklet.

A Game of Death (1945; 72 minutes)

PRODUCER: Herman Schlom. EXECUTIVE PRODUCER: Sid Rogell. DIRECTOR: Robert Wise. SCREENPLAY: Norman Houston, from the story "The Most Dangerous Game" by Richard Connell. PHOTOGRAPHY: J. Roy Hunt. EDITOR: J.R. Whittredge. MUSIC: Paul Sawtell. MUSIC DIRECTOR: C. Bakaleinikoff. ART DIRECTORS: Lucius O. Croxton & Albert S. D'Agostino. SOUND: Philip Mitchell. SET DECORATIONS: James Altwies & Darrell Silvera. COSTUMES: Renie. SPECIAL EFFECTS: Vernon L. Walker. ASSISTANT DIRECTOR: Doran Cox.

CAST: John Loder (Don Rainsford), Audrey Long (Ellen Trowbridge), Edgar Barrier (Erich Kreiger),

Russell Wade (Robert Trowbridge), Russell Hicks (Mr. Whitney), Jason Robards (Captain), Gene Stutenroth [Gene Roth] (Pleshke), Noble Johnson (Carib), Robert Clarke (Helmsman), Bruce Edwards (Collins), Victor Romito (Mongol), Edmund Glover (Quartermaster), James Dime (Bulgar), Jimmy Jordan (Steward).

Released late in November 1945, this remake of *The Most Dangerous Game* (q.v.) utilized the hunting dogs footage from that production. Noble Johnson appears in both films, his role here as a mute is also augmented by stock footage of his part in *The Most Dangerous Game*. *A Game of Death* re-teams John Loder and Audrey Long who appeared in *The Brighton Strangler* (q.v.) while Edgar Barrier dominates the proceedings as the madman Erich Kreiger. Overall, *A Game of Death* is a more than acceptable redo of *The Most Dangerous Game* and stands on its own as a satisfying program feature. The art direction and sets are impressive as are Paul Sawtell's music score and Vernon L. Walker's special effects.

Author and big game hunter Don Rainsford (Loder) is the sole survivor when the yacht on which he is a passenger sinks after running into a coral reef. Managing to avoid sharks, Don swims to shore where he sees a castle. He is made welcome by its owner Erich Kreiger (Barrier), a hunter who knows of Don and invites him to join his dinner party that includes siblings Ellen (Long) and Robert Trowbridge (Russell Wade). Kreiger's servant Pleshke (Gene Roth) shows Don where he can change into dry clothes. While doing so Don notices the windows are barred. At dinner Kreiger informs his guests that he bought the island and made it a hunting preserve, stocked with many dangerous animals. When their host excuses himself, Ellen tells Don to be wary of Kreiger and that two other guests have disappeared. At the stroke of eleven, Kreiger orders his guests to bed and during the night Don hears the barking of hunting dogs and a man's scream. Soon Ellen enters Don's room and informs him her brother is missing. As they search the house, Don and Ellen enter Kreiger's trophy room and find human skulls on the walls. Robert appears and says he unlocked the trophy room door and the trio make their way to a boathouse where they watch Kreiger and his men return with a dead body. Don tells Ellen and Bob that Kreiger is a homicidal killer, the result of being gored in the head by a wild animal. Since the windows in Ellen's room have no bars, Don asks Ellen and Bob to cover for him. He makes his way into the jungle where he lays a series of booby traps. The following morning, Ellen gets Pleshke to delay breakfast long enough for Don to return to his room. Pleshke informs his boss, who goes to Don's room but finds him asleep. When Kreiger announces there will be a hunt that night, Don pretends to want to join him and Kreiger admits he intentionally lured boats to the reefs in order to have human prey to hunt. He also tells Don the hunted that night will be Robert. When Pleshke discovers soiled sheets on Don's bed, he informs Kreiger, who makes Don a prisoner, guarded by a killer dog. Kreiger hunts Robert in the jungle and kills him with an arrow. Don improvises a harness and fetters the dog and takes Ellen to the boathouse where they see Kreiger return with Robert's body. Don then challenges Kreiger to a hunt and the madman agrees to set him free if he can survive until sunrise. Ellen goes with Don into the jungle as Kreiger hunts them with a high-powered rifle. When the hunted elude him, Kreiger sends his dogs after them with Don attacked by one of the beasts at the edge of a cliff. Kreiger shoots at Don as he and the dog plunge over the edge. Returning to his castle with Ellen, Kreiger is confronted by Don, who survived the fall after Kreiger's bullet killed the dog. Kreiger informs Don he is free but Don confronts the madman and a fight ensues, joined by Pleshke. Kreiger is wounded by a bullet and Don kills Pleshke. Don and Ellen go to the boathouse to get a launch so they can escape from the island. Kreiger attempts to shoot them but dies from his wound.

Variety noted, "Despite the implausibility of yarn, it has expert direction and some good acting to make it a juicy horror cantata.... Robert Wise has directed in a tempo that sustains suspense and accentuates the chillerdiller motif." *The Film Daily* called *A Game of Death* an "absorbing, weird and exciting story.... J. Roy Hunt's photography captures the mood to give action mystery fans some unexpected thrills." *Boxoffice* enthused, "Frankenstein, Dracula, the Ape Man and other assorted dispensers of horror might as well move over and make room for this spine-tingler which will have the chill devotees clutching at their seats, the juvenile customers moaning in their sleep and disciples of story consistencies pulling their hair. For horrification-at-any-price technique the film ranks with the best and there is sufficient action and suspense to further qualify it as a prime booking project." In his one paragraph putdown of *A Game of Death*, Bosley Crowther (*New York Times*) asserted, "The stuff that some people pay to see!" *The Anniston* (Alabama) *Star* called it an "exciting adventure story."

Other cinematic variations of Richard Connell's story include *Run for the Sun* (1956), *Bloodlust* (1961) and *Hard Target* (1993).

Genius at Work (1945; 65 minutes)

PRODUCER: Herman Schlom. EXECUTIVE PRODUCER: Sid Rogell. DIRECTOR: Leslie Goodwins. SCREENPLAY: Monte Brice & Robert E. Kent. PHOTOGRAPHY: Robert de Grasse. EDITOR: Marvin Coll. MUSIC DIRECTOR: C. Bakaleinikoff. ART DIRECTORS: Ralph Berger & Albert S. D'Agostino. SOUND: Roy Granville & Richard Van Hessen. SET DECORATIONS: Darrell Silvera. GOWNS: Renie. SPECIAL EFFECTS: Vernon Walker. ASSISTANT DIRECTOR: Harry D'Arcy.

CAST: Wally Brown (Jerry Miles), Alan Carney (Mike Strager), Anne Jeffreys (Ellen Brent), Lionel Atwill (Latimer Marsh/The Cobra), Bela Lugosi (Stone), Marc Cramer (Lieutenant Rick Campbell), Ralph Dunn (Lieutenant Gilley), Forbes Murray (John T. Saunders), Robert Clarke (Radio Host Ralph), Phil Warren (Radio Announcer Tom Jennings), Harry Harvey (Elevator Captain), Kanza Omar (Exotic Dancer), Warren Jackson, Eddie Hart, Al Choals (Detectives), Brick Sullivan (Policeman), Eddie Borden, Irene Mack (Autograph Seekers), George Holmes (Newsman), Larry Wheat (Butler), Jimmy Jordan (Page Boy), Peter Potter (Radio Announcer), Bob O'Connor (Headwaiter), Muriel Kearney (Cigarette Girl), Bonnie Blair (Hat Check Girl), Billy White (Newsboy), Katherine Lytle (Café Patron), William J. O'Brien (Audience Member).

In an apparent attempt to cash in on the popularity of Universal's Bud Abbott and Lou Costello, RKO teamed vaudevillians Alan Carney and Wally Brown for several features, the last two being horror comedies, *Zombies on Broadway* (q.v.) and *Genius at Work*, both with Bela Lugosi. The latter films gave momentum to the Carney-Brown tandem but the studio dropped them just as they were beginning to come into their own as celluloid comedy stars. While often belittled, *Genius at Work*, a remake of the studio's *Super-Sleuth* (q.v.), is a fast-paced, amusing comedy that not only spotlights the two stars, but also comely heroine Anne Jeffreys and villains Lionel Atwill and Lugosi. Atwill and Lugosi make a good team and they share practically every scene together; Lugosi does quite well with the role of the homicidal Stone. The film was Atwill's final feature, he died in 1946 while making the Universal serial *Lost City of the Jungle*. His *Lost City* scenes were finished by George Sorel. Filmed between August and November 1945, *Genius at Work* was not issued theatrically by RKO until late in October 1946.

A mysterious man enters the estate of industrial tycoon John T. Saunders (Forbes Murray) and knocks him out. The next day newspapers announce that the abduction of the wealthy man is the work of a fiend known as the Cobra. None-too-bright radio actors Jerry Miles (Brown) and Mike Strager (Carney) headline the popular *Crime of the Week Program* on the Spartan Broadcasting System and, following scripts written by pretty Ellen Brent (Jeffreys), they chastise the police, particularly Homicide Lieutenant Rick Campbell (Marc Cramer), for failing to capture the master criminal. Ellen is able to foretell the actions of the Cobra thanks to noted criminologist

Lionel Atwill and Bela Lugosi in *Genius at Work* (1946).

Latimer Marsh (Atwill). Rick and his partner, Lieutenant Gilley (Ralph Dunn), visit the next broadcast as Jerry and Mike predict that the ransom note left for Saunders is only an excuse by the Cobra to kill his victim. Following the show, Rick asks to escort Ellen home and warns Jerry and Mike that the Cobra might kill them too. The man who abducted Saunders is Stone (Lugosi), the henchman of Marsh, who is the Cobra. Stone warns his boss that Ellen is becoming too accurate in her predictions and Marsh decides to get her to drop the case. He calls Jerry and Mike and suggests they have dinner with him at a café, where Stone throws a knife at his boss during a floor show. This scares the radio stars and, after the mayor threatens to ban them from the air, they tell Ellen they want to stop the Cobra broadcasts. She says they must catch the fiend themselves. Ellen informs Jerry and Mike they will apologize to Rick and the police force during their next broadcast and she invites Rick and Gilley to a studio dinner where they will disclose important information about the case. Becoming concerned about Ellen's actions, Stone suggests to Marsh that he lure her to his estate, Marsh Manor, to see his files on the Cobra. When she arrives with Jerry and Mike, Marsh shows them his gallery of torture devices. As Ellen consults with Marsh on the case, Stone nearly decapitates Mike when he gets too near a guillotine. Later that night, Ellen, Jerry and Mike go back to Marsh Manor to open a filing cabinet that Marsh always keeps locked. As Ellen and Jerry try to open the cabinet, Mike stumbles onto Marsh's workroom where he finds a pair of muddied shoes. Marsh and Stone catch Ellen and Jerry trying to open the cabinet, which Marsh reveals contains liquor bottles. As they drive away from Marsh Manor, Ellen reveals to Jerry and Mike that she thinks Marsh is the Cobra. The night of the banquet, Marsh and Stone sneak into the radio building and lure Ellen away from the broadcast with a fake phone call. Stone uses chloroform to knock out Ellen as Marsh tries to murder Mike with a blowgun dart fired from a place of concealment; he misses and kills the announcer (Phil Warren). Marsh and Stone make a getaway after leaving the blowgun in Ellen's hand. Jerry and Mike run into another studio and tell a show's host (Robert Clarke) that the police are to blame for letting the killing happen, but they are silenced by Gilley. Rick takes Ellen to headquarters since she is a suspect, not only for having the blowgun, but because a woman's footprints were found near

Lobby card for *Genius at Work* (1946) picturing Wally Brown, Alan Carney, Marc Cramer and Anne Jeffreys.

Saunders' dead body. She is cleared when the footprints do not match hers and since lipstick, which she always wears, was not found on the murder weapon. Ellen gets a message from Jerry and Mike saying they are going to Marsh Manor to capture the Cobra and she tells Rick about her theory that Marsh is the fiend. Jerry and Mike get the drop on Marsh and Stone but when Jerry goes to get rope to tie them up, Marsh is able to fool Mike into shooting all the bullets in his gun. The two radio stars are placed in a torture device. Ellen arrives with Rick and Gilley, and they set Jerry and Mike free. Rick suggests that Jerry and Mike be used as bait to catch the Cobra, saying his identity will revealed at a special broadcast. The night of the show, Marsh and Stone arrive at the broadcast building disguised as an old couple and when the elevator captain (Harry Harvey) will not admit them to the broadcast, Jerry and Mike, who feel sorry for the elderly folks, show them how to get in the back way. During the broadcast, Marsh again attempts to use a blowgun to kill the radio stars but Rick has put wax dummies in their place. When he fails to kill Jerry and Mike, the angry Marsh begins shooting at the studio, thus revealing his hiding place. As the police look for the killers, Jerry and Mike hide in a prop room, not knowing Marsh is on a widow ledge outside. When Stone shoots his way into to the room, Jerry and Mike also get on the ledge, followed by Stone. During a shootout, Rick kills Marsh. Stone gets a police bullet as he tries to follow Jerry and Mike up a ladder to the roof. Jerry accidentally knocks Mike off the roof but he is saved by grabbing onto a flagpole.

Variety declared, "Lightweight slapstick comedy.... [I]t's flimsy film fare with about equal mixture of chuckles and dullness.... Screenplay development is more hysterical than hilarious and every type of sight gag and situation is rung in to force the laughs." *Boxoffice* stated, "Reminiscent of the ice age are the chills which dominate the proceedings in this comedy approach to the horror play. Whether the carnival of cliches will please spectators will depend upon individual tastes." "Uninspired and ordinary" is how *The Film Daily* felt about the production, adding, "As comedy the film falls flat due primarily to the poverty of material that has gone into the screenplay of Robert E. Kent and Monte Brice. The picture tries hard to be humorous but succeeds only in being for the most part embarrassingly unfunny, both lines and situations being productive of little in the way of genuine laughter.... It's evident there was no genius at work here." *The Hollywood Reporter* also dubbed it "ordinary."

A longtime writer and director of shorts for RKO, director Leslie Goodwins previously helmed Alan Carney and Wally Brown in *The Adventures of a Rookie* and *Rookies in Burma* (both 1943).

The Ghost Camera (Olympic Pictures, 1933; 66 minutes)

PRODUCER: Julius Hagen. DIRECTOR: Bernard Vorhaus. SCREENPLAY: H. Fowler Mear, from the story "A Mystery Narrative" by Jefferson Farjeon. PHOTOGRAPHY: Ernest Palmer. EDITOR: David Lean. ART DIRECTOR: James A. Carter. SOUND: Carlisle Mounteney. COIFFEUR: Charles. ASSISTANT DIRECTOR: Arthur Barnes.

CAST: Henry Kendall (John Gray), Ida Lupino (Mary Elton), John Mills (Ernest Elton), S. Victor Stanley (Albert Sims), George Merritt (Detective), Felix Aylmer (Coroner), Davina Craig (Amelia Wilkinson), Fred Groves (Barnaby Rudd), Charles Paton (Pig Farmer).

The Ghost Camera was one of several quota features RKO co-financed with producer Julius Hagen's Real Art Products. Filmed in under two weeks at the Twickenham Studios, this speedy little affair is more of a Hitchcock-type romantic thriller than a horror film although it does contain genre elements: the spectral image of a murder plus the dark, spooky locales of an actual Roman ruin in Surrey. Radio Pictures released the feature in Great Britain where it was reissued in 1948 by H & S Film Service, minus a minute of running time. It was first shown in the U.S. in the late summer of 1933 by Olympic Pictures. Favorite Films reissued it stateside in 1947.

Druggist John Gray (Henry Kendall) returns from an unexciting holiday and finds a camera that does not belong to him among his luggage. His assistant, Albert Sims (S. Victor Stanley), suggests he develop the film to ascertain its owner. After making one exposure he is called out of his laboratory. When he returns he finds the camera and the photograph have been stolen. John thinks the negative depicted a murder so he develops the four remaining exposures, one picturing a young woman at the address 17 Mill Street. After several false tries he locates the place and meets Mary Elton (Ida Lupino), the girl in the picture. He tells her about the camera and she thinks it belongs to her brother Ernest (John Mills), who has been missing for several days since setting out on a hike in the country to take pictures to enter in a contest at his club. A police detective (George Merritt) questions Mary about Ernest's whereabouts and informs her he may be implicated in a diamond robbery at the jewelers where he is employed. John deduces from the photos the locale where Ernest may have gone and he and Mary drive there, followed by the detective. After talking to a farmer (Charles Paton) who cannot identify the pictures, John speculates they were taken from a train and he and Mary drive to the line's next stop which turns out to be an inn shown in one of the photos. After Mary interrogates the landlord (Fred Groves), she convinces John they should stay the night, although he insists on separate rooms. As she is sleeping, a man sneaks into Mary's room and tries to strangle her but is frightened away by her screams. She runs into John's arms and begs him to stay with her. The next morning John asks about the nearby Norman Arches, a ruin, and he and Mary walk there; along the way she tells him about Ernest being implicated in the diamond robbery. At the eerie site, John finds bloodstains and Mary stumbles over a man's corpse. The police are called and find the victim was involved in the robbery. A manhunt is begun for Ernest who is arrested and taken before a coroner's (Felix Aylmer) court where he first denies any knowledge of the crime. After the evidence against him is summarized by the coroner, he admits he gave two robbers the combination to the safe housing the diamond and wanted to return it. He knew the two men were to meet at the ruin and followed them there, placing a camera which took a picture of the killing. Escaping, he hid until he was found by the law. The jury finds Ernest guilty. John later tries to reconstruct how the camera was stolen. The detective arrives with a search warrant and when they find the camera, John becomes suspicious. The two men fight with John taking away the man's gun. The bogus policeman turns out to be the killer and Ernest is exonerated as John and Mary try to quietly elope but are enveloped by a large crowd. Ernest takes their picture as the lovers kiss.

While top-billed Henry Kendall is a bit stodgy as the bespectacled, stiff-upper-lip leading man, comely teenager Ida Lupino takes the acting honors. It was Lupino's fourth feature, released a year before she began working in Hollywood, and John Mills' second. The film's main interest is in editor David Lean's visually innovate quick cuts to expand the narrative. Geoff Brown in *The Unknown 1930s: An Alternative History of the British Cinema, 1929–1939* (1998) attributes the film's success to Lean and director Bernard Vorhaus, who he said "strives to add tension and visual interest to the piffling mystery plots.... In *The Ghost Camera* he does everything to avoid the commonplace courtroom shots of judge, defendant, accused and jury. John Mills staggers down the aisle into court to the lurching of a subjective camera. The judge, Felix Aylmer, lays out the incriminating evidence in forcefully intercut close-ups that grow progressively closer. We hear the jury's verdict indirectly, only gauging it from the sight of the clerk covering his pencil drawing of Mills with prison bars." When released in the U.S. in the summer of 1933, *Variety* termed it "an unusual mystery thriller with a good story.... Palpably designed for quota purposes, the picture goes considerably beyond that category...."

The Ghost Ship (1943; 69 minutes)

PRODUCER: Val Lewton. DIRECTOR: Mark Robson. SCREENPLAY: Donald Henderson Clarke. STORY: Leo Mittler. PHOTOGRAPHY: Nicholas Musuraca. EDITOR: John Lockert. MUSIC: Roy Webb. MUSIC DIRECTOR: C. Bakaleinikoff. ART DIRECTORS: Albert S. D'Agostino & Walter E. Keller. SOUND: Francis M. Sarver. SET DECORATIONS: Claude Carpenter & Darrell Silvera. GOWNS: Edward Stevenson. SPECIAL EFFECTS: Vernon L. Walker. ASSISTANT DIRECTOR: Ruby Rosenberg. TECHNICAL CONSULTANT: Dr. Jeron Criswell.

CAST: Richard Dix (Captain Will Stone), Russell Wade (Tom Merriam), Edith Barrett (Ellen Roberts), Ben Bard (Bowns), Edmund Glover (Edmund "Sparks" Winslow), Lawrence Tierney (Louie Parker), Skelton Knaggs (Finn), Herb Vigran (Chief Engineer Mac), Dewey Robinson (Boats), Sir Lancelot (Billy Radd), Paul Marion (Pete the Greek), Boyd Davis (Charlie Roberts), Robert Bice (Raphael), Tom Burton (William Benson), Alec Craig (Blind Beggar), Harry Clay (Tom McCall), George DeNormand (John), Charles Lung (Long John), Steve Winston (Ausman), Nolan Leary (Stenographer), Norman Mayes (Carriage Driver), Jack Gardner (Joe Snitz), Eddie Borden (Leonard), Charles Regan, Russell Owen, John Burford, Mike Lally (Crewmen), Steve Forrest (Sailor), Bob Stevenson, Charles Norton (German Sailors), Shirley O'Hara (Ellen's Sister).

Producer Val Lewton's fifth foray for RKO Radio was *The Ghost Ship* which deals with a decent man going mad through no fault of his own. The title comes not from a haunted vessel but instead invokes the image of what happens to a sea captain whose years at the authoritarian helm leave him a murderous madman, unable to trust himself or anyone else. Richard Dix gives a bravura performance as Captain Stone, one of the best in his long, distinguished career. Dix dominates the proceedings and deftly portrays Stone's descent into self-doubt and murder. Although obviously low-budget, the feature is compact and well acted with a fine supporting cast (although Russell Wade is rather plain as the third officer who eventually brings about the captain's downfall). This was Mark Robson's second directorial effort for Lewton, Robson having previously done *The Seventh Victim* (q.v.). He would follow it with *Youth Run Wild* (1944) and two more horror offerings, *Isle of the Dead* and *Bedlam* (qq.v.). A rather impressive "B" effort, *The Ghost Ship* did not have much of an opportunity to entertain wartime audiences. RKO released it in the summer of 1943 but soon after Samuel R. Golding and Norbert Faulkner sued the studio, saying it plagiarized their 1942 play *A Man and His Shadow*. *The Ghost Ship* was withdrawn from circulation and after a lengthy court battle RKO lost the lawsuit and the film was not seen again until it was released to TV in the mid–1950s. It is interesting that the narration in the film comes from the character of Finn (Skelton Knaggs), a mute. The cast boasts two future stars, Lawrence Tierney, who has a substantial role, and Steve Forrest in a bit as a sailor.

The new third officer on the ship *Altair,* Tom Merriam (Wade) is about to board the vessel when a blind beggar (Alec Craig) cautions him about the ship. Paying the man no heed, he goes aboard, passes mute crewman Finn (Knaggs), and meets Captain Will Stone (Dix), a veteran seaman. At first Stone is very friendly but soon admonishes Merriam for unnecessarily killing a moth. As the crewmen are being recognized by First Officer Bowns (Ben Bard), the body of one of them is found on deck and Stone says he probably died of a heart attack. As they set sail, Stone tells Merriam it will be a long voyage and they will have lots of time to talk. Merriam also learns that his predecessor died of convulsions. He meets radio operator Sparks (Edmund Glover), who tells Merriam he avoids officers, but the two become friendly and the radio man nicknames the new third officer Tertius. When Merriam notices a large hook has not been secured, he mentions it to Stone, who says he does not want to mar the fresh coat of paint on it. As the wind rises, the hook swings wildly and destroys a lifeboat before being secured. At breakfast the next day, Stone tells Merriam the incident was his fault. One of the crewmen, Pete (Paul Marion), comes down with appendicitis, forcing Stone to perform an operation with instructions via radio. Seeing Stone is not up to the ordeal, Merriam takes over and saves the man's life. Merriam gives Stone credit for the surgery. Since the crew is short-handed, sailor Louie (Tierney) suggests to Stone they stop at the next port and sign on a new hand. Later when Louie is working in the chain locker, Stone shuts the hatch door. Not realizing Louie is still in the locker, the crewmen slide the heavy chain back into it, crushing Louie. When Merriam finds out what happened, he accuses Stone of murdering Louie. Bowns and Sparks refuse to heed Merriam's warnings about Stone, and when the ship anchors at San Sebastian, Merriam files a complaint against Stone with the Dunham Shipping Line. Company agent Charlie Roberts (Boyd Davis), an old friend of Stone, conducts the investigation. After hearing the testimony of several crew members, including Bowns, Boats (Dewey Robinson) and Billy Radd (Sir Lancelot), he dismisses the charges. Merriam resigns his commission and later meets Roberts' daughter Ellen (Edith Barrett), who says she has known Stone for 15 years. She also claims Merriam needs feminine companionship and offers to introduce him to her younger sister (Shirley O'Hara). Stone relates to Roberts that he feels some people are turning against him. That night Ellen informs Stone she is legally free to marry him but he replies he feels like he is on the verge of losing control and asks for time to get over it. She says he can have all the time in the world. While on shore leave, some sailors harass Jamaican Billy. Merriam comes to his rescue and is knocked out. Unaware that Merriam has resigned his commission, the ship's crewmen take him back to the vessel and he does not wake up until the next morning after it sails. Merriam confronts Stone, saying he will pay for his passage back to San Pedro, but Stone replies he will be a guest on the voyage without any responsibilities. Merriam discovers the door and porthole locks in his cabin have been removed and he is snubbed by the crew. After someone tries to sneak into his cabin that night, Merriam goes to Stone's cabin looking for a weapon and is surprised by the captain, who raves that his authority over the crew cannot be questioned. Sparks gets a communication from Roberts inquiring if Merriam is on the ship and Stone sends a reply that he is not. Showing Stone's response to Merriam, Sparks says he is beginning to believe Merriam's story and will take the matter up with Bowns in the morning. Leaving Merriam's cabin, Sparks is met by Stone and drops the reply, which is found by Finn, who cannot read. The following day Stone says Sparks was lost in heavy seas and Merriam accuses him of killing the radio operator. Stone says Merriam is losing his mind and orders Bowns to restrain him with ropes and a hypo. Later Finn gives the missive to Bowns who consults with chief engineer Mac (Herb Vigran) about taking action against Stone. The captain overhears their conversation. Going to his cabin, he gets a dagger and is about to stab Merriam when he is attacked by Finn. The two fight with Finn stabbing Stone to death. Merriam takes command of the vessel and upon arrival in San Pedro he sees the blind beggar and then is greeted by Roberts' younger daughter.

Boxoffice called *The Ghost Ship* "eerie and exciting," adding "Chiller addicts should find their sought-after shivers in abundant quantity, while the casual customers who catch it on the underside of dualers will find it, at the least, novel entertainment." Bosley Crowther in *The New York Times* deemed it "a nice little package of morbidity all wrapped around in gloom.... Blood is let rather gratuitously and there is a lot of B-grade big-talk in this film." *Variety* complained, "Script, which evidently aimed for a Joseph Conrad groove, fails to put over temperamental conflict idea in understandable fashion, and direction does not overcome this handicap." *The Film Daily* stated, "Very much befogged, *The Ghost Ship* will have no easy time of it making port. Persons who are not hopelessly addicted to melodrama will find the proceedings on the dull side, with no more than fair suspense and a script built along routine lines.... The best thing about the production is the sense of mystery that hangs over the freighter on which the story is laid." In *TV Movie Almanac & Ratings 1958 & 1959* (1958), Steven H. Scheuer called it "Brutally violent, but extremely well done film; fine performances."

According to a 1943 article in *The Hollywood Reporter,* RKO hired psychic phenomena and extra-sensory perception expert Dr. Jeron Criswell as technical consultant for *The Ghost Ship.* Criswell, a close friend and spiritual advisor to Mae West, later starred in the popular West Coast TV show *Criswell Predicts* and authored a book with the same title in 1968. A native of Princeton, Indiana, he appeared in the Edward D. Wood, Jr., features, *Plan 9 from Outer Space* (1958) and the theatrically unreleased *Night of the Ghouls* (1959), plus *Orgy of the Dead* (1965), which Wood wrote.

Ghost Valley (1932; 54 minutes)

DIRECTOR: Fred Allen. STORY & SCREENPLAY: Adele Buffington. PHOTOGRAPHY: Ted McCord. EDITOR: William Clemens. MUSIC: Max Steiner. ART DIRECTOR: Carroll Clark. SOUND: Earl A. Wolcott.

CAST: Tom Keene (Jerry Long), Merna Kennedy (Jane Worth), Kate Campbell (Aunt Susan Trumpett), Mitchell Harris (Judge Drake), Ted Adams (Gordon), Harry Bowen (Marty), Harry Semels (Pawnee), Billy Franey (Scrubby Watson), Tom London (Red), George "Gabby" Hayes (Dave), Jack Kirk (Blacksmith), Slim Whitaker, Al Taylor (Gang Members), Buck Moulton (Deputy Sheriff Buck), Ernie Adams (Diner).

In the fall of 1931, RKO Pathé purchased Adele Buffington's story "Ghost City" and hired her to write a screenplay to star Tom Keene, the studio's cowboy star. Keene first appeared on screen late in the silent era under his own name, George Duryea, and with the coming of sound he starred in RKO's *Beau Bandit* and *Pardon My Gun* (both 1930) as well as World Wide's *The Dude Wrangler* the same year. As a result, RKO changed his name to Tom Keene and signed him to star in a series of well produced "B" Westerns beginning with *The Sundown Trail* (1931). He headlined a dozen oaters for the company and as *The* (Huntington, Pennsylvania) *Daily News* noted of *Ghost Valley*, the fifth in the series, released in May 1932, "Keene's westerns are rated by the critics a step ahead of all other outdoor pictures for they are produced at great expense— not just thrown together." The same reviewer noted that the feature "is just packed with novelties—action, comedy, thrills and the most beautiful photography ever seen on the screen." Keene starred in a trio of Zane Grey Westerns for Paramount, *Sunset Pass* (1933), *Drift Fence* and *Desert Gold* (both 1936), as well as headlining eight historical dramas for E.B. Derr's Crescent Pictures in 1936 and '37. In 1934 he starred in King Vidor's social drama *Our Daily Bread* for Viking Pictures. Between 1937 and 1942 he was in a dozen sagebrush yarns for Monogram before changing his name to Richard Powers in the mid–1940s. Under that moniker he was featured in the genre outings *The Great Alaskan Mystery* and *Jungle Woman* (both 1944), *Dick Tracy's Dilemma, Seven Keys to Baldpate* and *Dick Tracy Meets Gruesome* (all 1947) [qq.v.] and *Red Planet Mars* (1952). In the 1950s he became associated with writer-producer-director Edward D. Wood, Jr., and headlined a half-dozen TV shows for him, including the unsold pilot *The Crossroads Avenger*, as well as starring in the Wood-produced and -directed stage show *The Tom Keene Revue*. Billed as Tom Keene, his final film was Wood's *Plan 9 from Outer Space* (1958).

Ghost Valley was filmed as both *Ghost City* and *Ghost Town* but Monogram Pictures grabbed the first title for its January release *The Ghost City* starring Bill Cody and Andy Shuford. Buffington slightly revamped the plot and sold another screenplay to Warner Bros. that became *Haunted Gold,* released late in 1932 and starring John Wayne. That production utilized footage from the Ken Maynard silent *The Phantom City* (First National, 1928), also written by Buffington. Fred

Poster for *Ghost Valley* (1932).

Allen, who directed *Ghost Valley*, did the silent film's titles, and both features were supervised by Harry Joe Brown and photographed by Ted McCord. Slim Whitaker played an outlaw gang member in both *Ghost Valley* and *Haunted Gold*.

In the windswept, deserted mining town of Ghost City, called Boom City thirty years before, Judge Drake (Mitchell Harris) receives a wire from a Chicago detective saying he cannot locate Jerry Long (Keene), an heir to the property. Jerry is the adopted son of the late owner whose niece, Jane Worth (Merna Kennedy), is also an heir. Drake and his cohort Gordon (Ted Adams) are in cahoots to cheat the heirs out of the property since they have discovered a lost gold vein in the area's mine. Jerry arrives in Kona Lake, 30 miles north of Ghost City, and tells a blacksmith (Jack Kirk) he wants to find horse peddler Scrubby Watson (Billy Franey), the only inhabitant of the once prosperous mining town. Jerry befriends clothes salesman Marty (Harry Bowen), who is broke and hungry. Jane and her Aunt Susan Trumpett (Kate Cambell) arrive in town on a motorized stage and are met by Drake and Gordon. Jerry is attracted to Jane and to impress her he asks Marty to lend him one of his dress suits in return for a free dinner. When Marty orders more food than Jerry can pay for, he is thrown in jail. Drake offers Jerry one thousand dollars to impersonate himself, since the judge does not know his true identity. Drake tells him he wants Jerry to convince Jane to sell her interest in Ghost City since an investor wants to use the site to establish a divorce city. Drake asks Jerry to bring Marty along as his valet. When Scrubby arrives, Jerry lets him in on the ruse. At Ghost City, Gordon tells his gang members to scare the newcomers. Red (Tom London) pretends to be a phantom rider and plays the organ at the town church and warns them to leave. While Scrubby and Jerry chase the phantom, Drake informs Jane and her aunt that the rider is the head of a gang of desert outlaws wanting the town for a hideout. Jerry chases the rider to the abandoned mine and finds his black cloak. Aunt Susan is abducted at the church but Jerry, as the phantom, saves her. Returning to the house where they are staying, Jane, Aunt Susan, Drake and Gordon find Jerry in his room, and Jane thinks he is a coward. The next day Marty sees a stranger going into the town's hotel; Jane and Aunt Susan go with him there. As the phantom, Jerry locks the women in a closet and gets the drop on Drake, Gordon and their men and escapes. He eludes them as Marty explores a mine shaft and is captured. Jerry feigns a fear of horses and does not accompany Jane, Aunt Susan, Drake and Gordon to the mine in search of Marty. Drake's servant, Pawnee (Harry Semels), warns the gang of their approach. In trying to scare the women, the outlaws cause Jane's horse to bolt and run away but she is saved by Jerry in the guise of the phantom. Thinking she is unconscious, Jerry kisses Jane and she pulls the cape away from his face, revealing his true identity. Upset at Jerry for kissing her and thinking he is the leader of the desert outlaws, she tells Drake she will sell and return to Boston. When Jerry goes to the mine to find Marty, who has been tied up by the gang, he is captured. Jerry breaks free of his bonds and eludes the gang by getting onto a cable car, jumping onto a roof and sliding down a tall chimney before mounting his horse. He follows the judge's car carrying the women and along the way runs into a posse that rounds up Drake's gang. Jerry rides into Kona Lake in time to stop Jane from selling her property and fights with Drake and Gordon. The law arrives and arrests the crooks. Jerry and Jane go to rescue Marty but drive off the road as they kiss.

Ghost Valley is a highly atmospheric horror-mystery-Western with its windy, spooky deserted town and dark mine sequences. It was filmed at the ghost town of Hornitos, California, and also utilized brief Bronson Canyon shots. According to RKO's publicity, a secret tunnel Joaquin Murietta used a half-century before to elude pursuers was utilized in the feature. The passage connected a dance hall and saloon in Hornitos and was frequently the secret headquarters of the famed bandit, "California's Robin Hood."

The Film Daily opined, "There is a mass of plot and counterplot in this western, with plenty of mystery to keep the customers coming.... It is fast action, fights and hard riding all the way, and should go strong." *The Mason City* (Iowa) *Gazette* called it "a new western that deals with a new theme entirely, it is a mystery film of unusual merit," and the Ukiah, California, *Dispatch-Democrat* concurred: "Here is one [western] that is entirely different in theme which involves many ideas not found in other plays of this type." *The Monitor-Index* (Moberly, Missouri) stated, "In this picture you'll get all the horses and gun fighting that the average 'drama of the wide open spaces' offers, and on top of that you'll get a big, extra ration of mystery-thrills and horrors!" It also called the film "fast-moving" with "a weird plot."

Made for approximately $40,000, *Ghost Valley* grossed over $100,000 at the box office. It was released in France as *La Vallee des Fantomes* (The Valley of the Phantoms).

Gildersleeve's Ghost (1944; 63 minutes)

PRODUCER: Herman Schlom. DIRECTOR: Gordon Douglas. STORY & SCREENPLAY: Robert E. Kent. PHOTOGRAPHY: Jack Mackenzie. EDITOR: Les Millbrook. MUSIC: Paul Sawtell. MUSIC DIRECTOR: C. Bakaleinikoff. ART DIRECTORS: Albert S. D'Agostino & Carroll Clark. SOUND: Francis Sarver. SET DECORATIONS: Darrell Silvera & William Stevens. GOWNS: Renie. MAKEUP: Mel Berns. SPECIAL EFFECTS: Vernon L. Walker. ASSISTANT DIRECTOR: Harry Mancke.

CAST: Harold Peary (Throckmorton P. Gildersleeve/Spirits of Randolph Q. Gildersleeve & Jonathan Q. Gildersleeve), Marion Martin (Terry Vance), Richard LeGrand (Peavey), Amelita Ward (Marie), Freddie Mercer (Leroy Forrester), Margie Stewart (Marjorie Forrester), Marie Blake (Harriet Morgan), Emory Parnell (Police Commissioner Haley), Nicodemus Stewart (Chauncey), Frank Reicher (Dr. John Wells), Joseph Vitale (Henry Lennox), Lillian Randolph (Birdie), Charles Gemora (Gorilla), Jack Norton (Drunk), Earle Ross (Judge Hooker), Chris Drake, Tom Burton, Steve Winston, Harry Clay (Newsmen), Mary Halsey (Blonde).

Gildersleeve's Ghost, released in June 1944, was the last of a quartet of features RKO made based on the popular NBC radio series *The Great Gildersleeve* (1941–57). It was preceded by *The Great Gildersleeve*, *Gildersleeve's Bad Day* and *Gildersleeve on Broadway* (all 1943). Harold Peary starred as Gildersleeve, having originated the role on the radio series *Fibber McGee and Molly* (NBC, 1935–56), and he played the part in three previous RKO features, *Look Who's Laughing* (1941), *Here We Go Again* (1942), both with Jim and Marian Jordan as Fibber McGee and Molly, and *Seven Days Leave* (1942). Peary was Gildersleeve on radio until 1950 when he left the series to star in another radio program, *Honest Harold* (CBS, 1950–51), also called *The Hal Peary Show*. Willard Waterman took over the part of Gildersleeve and continued in it until the series left the airwaves in 1957. Waterman also starred in an NBC-TV version of *The Great Gildersleeve* (1955–56) that featured Lillian Randolph as Gildy's housekeeper Birdie, a part she played on radio and in the quartet of RKO *Gildersleeve* features.

Filmed as *Gildersleeve, Detective*, *Gildersleeve's Ghost* is a modest comedy thriller built around the antics of portly star Peary with Gildersleeve a somewhat conniving windbag who chases women and loves his family. The film is fast-paced and fairly amusing and not only includes a menacing gorilla but also real ghosts, something not common in spook comedies. The film's weakest aspect is its rather abrupt ending, which leaves Gildersleeve's possible romance with a beautiful blonde and his running for police commissioner unresolved. *Boxoffice* thought it "a very funny hour of entertainment [which] will steal the show from many a ponderous top-o'-bill feature." On the other hand, *Variety* called it "a minor league affair, filled with elemental nonsense and broad attempts at comedy that seldom get beyond the sophomoric stage." *The Film Daily* stated, "The latest of the Gildersleeve series of comedies is better than most of its predecessors if not the best of the lot.... The situations are funny though at no time believable."

On their nightly prowl, the spirits of Randolph Q. Gildersleeve (Peary) and his nephew Jonathan Q. Gildersleeve (Peary) read a newspaper story about their descendant, Throckmorton P. Gildersleeve (Peary), Summerfield's water commissioner, running for police commissioner against the incumbent Haley (Emory Parnell), who has been in office for a dozen years. The two specters decide to aid their relative by creating a situation where he can bring to light the invisibility experiments of Dr. John Wells (Frank Reicher) and his cohort Henry Lennox (Joseph Vitale) at spooky Wagstaff Manor. They spy on the two scientists and see them make a gorilla (Charles Gemora) invisible and then re-materialize him. The madmen attempt to do the same with kidnapped showgirl Terry Vance (Marion Martin) but Wells' new formula is not successful with her. Wells informs Lennox that once his formula is perfected, he can control the world. The ghosts set the gorilla free and it arrives in Summerfield just as Gildersleeve is leading a campaign parade that includes his niece Marjorie (Margie Stewart) and nephew Leroy (Freddie Mercer), who live with him; his campaign manager, druggist Peavey (Richard LeGrand); and journalist Harriet Morgan (Marie Blake), who wants to get Gildersleeve to the altar. When they arrive back home, Leroy dresses in a gorilla costume, telling his uncle it will appeal to animal lovers. Scoffing at his nephew's idea, Gildersleeve goes to the kitchen to get a snack for Peavey and himself, and finds the gorilla sitting at the table. Thinking it is Leroy, he threatens to take a strap to him, but when he goes to get one he runs into his nephew. When he goes back to the kitchen with Leroy, Marjorie, Peavey and his housekeeper Birdie (Randolph), the gorilla is gone and none of them believe his story. Wanting to protect his family and the community, Gildersleeve calls the police. Haley and Judge Hooker (Earle Ross) come to hear his story, which Haley claims is a campaign ploy. The judge is also skeptical but orders Haley to investigate. Gildersleeve has Peavey put on the gorilla costume and the two follow the animal's tracks to Wagstaff Manor where the real gorilla shows up, with Gildersleeve thinking it is Peavey. When Gildersleeve spots the real Peavey, he believes he is the gorilla and knocks him out with a wrench. Wells and Lennox see what has happened and when Gildersleeve tells them he has knocked out a gorilla, Wells removes the phony head revealing Peavey. Gildersleeve insists Wells treat Peavey in his office and Marie (Amelita Ward), the maid, tries to tell Gildersleeve what is going on in the house but is ushered away by Lennox. Wells informs Peavey that he thinks Gildersleeve is suffering from dementia. The gorilla shows up and Gildersleeve hides in a bathroom and sees the animal disappear through a sliding wall. Terry arrives to take a shower but becomes invisible and Gildersleeve thinks she is a ghost. Re-materializing, the young woman spies Gildersleeve and demands he kiss her. Pinning Gildersleeve under her bed, Terry becomes invisible as he calls for Peavey, who arrives in the room with Wilson, who suggests Gildersleeve get a good night's rest and then see a psychiatrist. As Gildersleeve and Peavey are about to leave Wagstaff Manor, his niece and nephew arrive with Birdie and Haley in a car driven by Haley's chauffeur, Chauncey (Nicodemus Stewart), Birdie's boyfriend. A thunderstorm ensues and Haley suggests they all stay the night. After he has placed his guests in their rooms, Wells tells Terry to torment Gildersleeve in

Harold Peary, the star of *Gildersleeve's Ghost* (1944).

front of Peavey and Haley. Gildersleeve takes refuge in a bedroom shared by Terry and Marie, who kisses him and then yells for help. A frustrated Haley puts Gildersleeve under technical arrest and places him in Chauncey's custody. Gildersleeve convinces Chauncey to help him locate the gorilla and they check the sliding wall in the bathroom and it leads to a wine cellar. There they are confronted by the gorilla but Gildersleeve manages to lock the animal in a cage and leaves Chauncey to guard him. Terry, who pretends to be dead, tells Chauncey she will haunt him if he does not deny seeing the gorilla, who she sets free. When Gildersleeve returns to the wine cellar with Peavey and Haley, he finds the gorilla gone and Chauncey saying he never was there. Peavey tells Gildersleeve he should withdraw from the election. After being locked in a bedroom, Gildersleeve is visited by Leroy, who tells him to put on the gorilla outfit in order to capture the real simian. He does so as Chauncey informs Haley, who unknowingly handcuffs his chauffeur to the real gorilla. Wells tries a new formula on Terry, who becomes visible for good, but he then tells her she is of no more use to him. Realizing the madman plans to kill her, Terry escapes just as the gorilla breaks the handcuffs and carries her into the woods. When Gildersleeve learns what has happened, he takes a bunch of bananas and goes after the gorilla in an attempt to rescue Terry. Marie informs Haley about Wells and Lennox and their experiments. After the two are arrested, everyone goes in search of Gildersleeve, who has becomes the gorilla's best friend.

The Great Jasper (1933; 85 minutes)

PRODUCER: David O. Selznick. ASSOCIATE PRODUCER: Kenneth Macgowan. DIRECTOR: J. Walter Ruben. SCREENPLAY: H.W. Haneman & Samuel Ornitz, from the novel by Fulton Oursler. PHOTOGRAPHY: Leo Tover. EDITOR: George Hively. MUSIC: Max Steiner. ART DIRECTORS: Carroll Clark & Van Nest Polglase. SOUND: John E. Tribby. SPECIAL EFFECTS: Harry Redmond, Sr.

CAST: Richard Dix (Jasper Horn/Jasper the Great), Edna May Oliver (Madame Talma), Florence Eldridge (Jenny Horn), Wera Engels (Norma McGowd), Walter Walker (Daniel McGowd), David Durand (Andrew Horn as a Child), Bruce Cabot (Roger McGowd), Betty Furness (Sylvia Bradfield), James Bush (Andrew Horn), Herman Bing (Herman Beaumgartner), Robert Emmett O'Connor (Kelly), John Larkin (Chippy), Dorothy Gray (Sylvia Bradfield as a Child), Bruce Line (Bruce McGowd as a Child); Gwen Lee, Shirley Chambers, Gretchen Wilson, Jackie Bjorkland, Eleanor Wesselheoff, Jean Barry, Edith Hallor.

RKO released a number of movies dealing with fake spiritualists including *The Great Jasper*, which came to theaters in March 1933. The feature offers star Richard Dix a sturdy role as a womanizer who finally finds success bilking unsuspecting customers as a phony fortune teller. It also gives Edna May Oliver a delightful, albeit brief, part as the astrologist who introduces him to the racket. Based on Fulton Oursler's 1930 novel, *The Great Jasper* is not an overly convincing melodrama, but its fortune-telling sequences are interesting and Dix, Oliver and the rest of the cast manage to put it over thanks to J. Walter Ruben's steady direction. Dix was one of RKO's top draws, having previously headlined the genre efforts *Seven Keys to Baldpate* (1929) and *The Public Defender* (1931) [qq.v.], as well as *Cimarron* (1930), which won the Academy Award for Best Picture. Florence Eldridge replaced Julie Haydon in the role of Jasper's puritanical wife Jenny.

Jasper Horn (Dix) drives a horse-drawn car for Daniel McGowd (Walter Walker), who plans to replace his fleet with electric trolleys. When the other drivers go on strike, Jasper volunteers to drive the new trolley, despite threats of bodily harm from an angry mob. When his run proves a success, Jasper and his morally stern wife Jenny (Eldridge) are invited for a weekend at McGowd's country home. There the woman chasing Jasper romances his boss' wife Norma (Were Engels), a beautiful European. The two have a secret affair and she becomes pregnant, giving birth to a son nine months later. After working as a motorman for McGowd for a decade,

WHAT DID
SOLOMON SAY?

Consult Jasper . he sees all—knows
all—tells all—about love . that's why
they called him THE GREAT JASPER .
He had a WAY with ALL women
. and JUST COULDN'T HELP IT!

Richard
DIX
IN JASPER'
The GREAT JASPER
with
WERA ENGELS
EDNA MAY OLIVER
•
Directed by
J. WALTER RUBEN
•
Produced by
DAVID O. SELZNICK

Advertisement for *The Great Jasper* (1933).

Jasper is accused by the man of being the father of his son Roger (Bruce Line) and fires him. The ever-optimistic Jasper tells Jenny of his plans for a new life for them and their feeble son Andrew (David Durand), but she refuses to leave with him. Jasper takes the boy to Atlantic City where he meets middle-aged fortune teller Madame Talma (Oliver), who takes a liking to him. Since both like to imbibe, Madame Talma takes Jasper under her wing and teaches him the fake spiritualist racket, dubbing him the Great Jasper. Success in his new field comes quickly for Jasper, and Andrew's health greatly improves. Jenny comes to see her husband and son and becomes upset by Jasper's trade. Rejecting his pleas for reconciliation, Jenny starts a boardwalk hot dog stand business and has Andrew come to live with her. Due to her drinking, Madame Talma's health begins to fail and she makes a will leaving her business to Jasper, who inherits it when she dies. Jasper's success continues and several years later he is visited by the now grown Roger McGowd (Bruce Cabot), a bandleader, and his still very attractive mother. When Jenny sees Jasper with Roger and his mother, she realizes the true relationship between the trio and decides to leave Atlantic City. The now grown Andrew (James Bush) is engaged to marry pretty Sylvia Bradfield (Betty Furness), whom he has known since they were children. Roger meets Sylvia and, being a ladies man like his real father, seduces her and sends Jasper a telegram saying they are planning to elope. His health failing and wanting forgiveness from his wife and son for his past, Jasper tries to stop Roger but fails. As he is dying, Jasper is forgiven by Jenny.

Hollywood Filmograph called *The Great Jasper* "excellent entertainment. Dix put everything he had into his portrayal of Jasper Horn and turns in a performance that is top notch." *Picture Play* felt "on the whole it does not satisfy.... The acting is good," while *The New Movie Magazine* called it "one of the funniest sex-shows of the season." Mordaunt Hall in *The New York Times* stated, "Notwithstanding the capable performances of several in the cast, the incidents are not a little tiresome. Mr. Dix tries hard to cope with the peculiarities of his role." *The Film Daily* declared that it contained "plenty of amusement and a sufficient portion of dramatic entertainment." *Photoplay* stated that it was "chiefly noteworthy for a grand performance by Richard Dix.... Inevitably reminiscent of *Cimarron*—but it isn't a *Cimarron*, though." *Motion Picture* enthused, "Richard Dix in one of the best performances of his career as a fortune-telling yogi who has a wink that is irresistible and who is unrepentant right to the end. Clever—nay, brilliant—fun." *Variety* was less enthralled: "Okay as a critics' film but looks like an in-and-outer. Should strike in the met spots where sophisticated will like, but whether there's actually that femme appeal in this story of a promiscuous Irish lover is questionable.... Strictly a chatty picture that must depend mostly on what it suggests rather than what it actually projects." *The New York Mirror* declared, "Don't miss *The Great Jasper*. It is an exhilarating screen play," and *The New York News* wrote, "It is decidedly worth seeing and hearing." *The New York Post* noted that it "builds up into a rousing and perverse comedy" while *The New York Herald-Tribune* dubbed it "better than average." "For the discriminating adult audience, this one is a rare treat," announced *The Hollywood Reporter*. The reviewer added, "Far removed from the beaten paths of orthodox formula, it is more than conventional drama, a finely drawn character sketch, acting with great feeling and fine shadings by Richard Dix, and splendidly directed with sympathy and sincerity by J. Walter Ruben, who deserves a rousing kudo for approaching his subject in exactly the proper psychology.... This will be one of the unforgettable roles of Dix's career." Leonard Maltin in *Film Fan Monthly* (October 1973) said that Edna May Oliver's "scenes almost make the film worth watching, but tired soap-opera plotting and dialogue weigh down a potentially colorful story." *Harrison's Reports* rated the film's box office performance as "poor."

Guns of Hate (1948; 61 minutes)

PRODUCER: Herman Schlom. DIRECTOR: Lesley Selander. SCREENPLAY: Ed Earl Repp & Norman Houston. STORY: Ed Earl Repp. PHOTOGRAPHY: George E. Diskant. EDITOR: Desmond Marquette. MUSIC: Paul Sawtell. MUSIC DIRECTOR: C. Bakaleinikoff. ART DIRECTORS: Albert S. D'Agostino & Feild Gray. SOUND: John L. Cass & Terry Kellum. SET DECORATIONS: Darrell Silvera & William Stevens. SPECIAL EFFECTS: Russell A. Cully.

CAST: Tim Holt (Bob Banning), Nan Leslie (Judy Jason), Richard Martin (Chito Rafferty), Steve Brodie (Anse Morgan), Myrna Dell (Dixie Merritt), Tony Barrett (Matt Wyatt), Jim Nolan (Sheriff Bradley), Jason

Robards (Ben Jason), Robert Bray (Rocky Morgan), Marilyn Mercer (Mabel), Herman Howlin (Deputy Sheriff Fred), Ralph Bucko (Saloon Customer).

Between 1940 and 1952, Tim Holt headlined over 40 B Westerns at RKO. His films were profitable and helped keep the studio afloat during some hard financial times. *Guns of Hate* was one of five Holt vehicles released by the company in 1948, the year he placed seventh in the *Motion Picture Herald*'s annual poll of top moneymaking Western stars. *Guns of Hate* is not a horror film nor does it contain genre plot elements. It does, however, deal with the discovery of the Lost Dutchman Mine, about which Wikipedia states, "According to many versions of the tale, the mine is either cursed, or protected by enigmatic guardians who wish to keep the mine's location a secret."

The Lost Dutchman Mine is purported to contain a fortune in gold and is supposedly located in the Superstition Mountains east of Phoenix, Arizona. It was discovered in the 1800s by Jacob Waltz, a German immigrant, who refused to divulge its location. Since the early 1890s thousands of people have searched for the Lost Dutchman and it is considered to be the country's most famous vanished mine.

While job-seeking, Arizona wranglers Bob Banning (Tim Holt) and Chito Rafferty (Richard Martin) come across Ben Jason (Jason Robards), whose wagon has lost a wheel. They help him fix it and he offers them jobs working for him as well as payment in gold he claims is from the Lost Dutchman Gold Mine, which he has discovered. They decline his offer but since they are going to get to the town of Rimrock before him, Ben asks Bob to meet his niece, Judy Jason (Nan Leslie), who is set to arrive on the stage. When they get to Rimrock, Bob and Chito take the nugget to the assayer's office and there Matt Wyatt (Tony Barrett) offers them fifty dollars for it and they sell. Matt recognizes the nugget as being from the Lost Dutchman mine. Bob meets Judy when she gets off the stage and her uncle soon arrives and tells her about finding the legendary lost mine. As they prepare to drive to the town of Trinity to register the claim in Judy's name, Matt overhears their conversation and takes the nugget to saloon owner Anse Morgan (Steve Brodie). He proposes that Morgan have his men waylay the Jasons, take the old man's money belt and map to the claim and register it in their names. Anse decides to get the map for himself and takes along his henchman, Rocky Morgan (Robert Bray). They find Jason and Judy in the desert on the way to the old man's ranch and shoot at them. Jason tells Judy to take the buckboard and find the sheriff (Jim Nolan) while he holds off the marauders. Anse kills Jason, taking his money belt and the map. Bob and Chito hear the shooting and run off the attackers. Judy arrives with the sheriff and his deputy (Herman Howlin) and the two cowboys are arrested for the murder. When they are taken back to town and put in jail, Bob and Chito are spotted by Dixie Merritt (Myrna Dell), an old flame of Chito's who works at Anse's saloon. She protests to the sheriff that the two cowboys are innocent. Anse and Rocky come back to Rimrock and Anse informs Matt they were sent on a wild goose chase. Bob and Chito use the ruse of starting a fire in their jail cell to get the drop on the sheriff and escape. Bob and Chito ride to the site of the ambush, looking for clues. Judy gets the drop on Bob but is disarmed by Chito. At first she thinks the cowboys murdered her uncle and stole his map but Bob tries to convince her they are innocent and tells her about Matt knowing about her uncle's strike. Bob and Chito return to Rimrock where Bob slugs Matt to make him tell the truth. Bob has to leave when the sheriff arrives. Bob follows Matt, who goes to confront Anse, as Chito leads the sheriff and his deputy out of town. Dixie tells Bob she saw a money belt in her boss' office and when he looks for it he finds Wyatt forcing Anse to open his safe. Wyatt runs away with the map as Bob is confronted by Anse, whom he knocks out in a fight. Bob takes the money belt, eludes Rocky and gives the belt to Dixie to take to Judy at the Jason ranch. Anse and Morgan see Dixie leave town and follow her to the ranch where Judy reveals that the mine is located at the dead end of Latigo Canyon. Anse leaves Rocky to guard the women and heads to the mine with his gang. There he spies Matt carrying out bags of gold. He confronts the assayer and shoots him and orders his henchmen to load the rest of the gold onto a wagon. Bob and Chito arrive at the Jason ranch and scare off Morgan, who heads to the mine to warn Anse. Bob and Chito follow Morgan after telling Judy and Dixie to find the sheriff and his posse and bring them to the mine. Bob and Chito pin down the crooks at the mine; Morgan jumps onto the wagon and makes a getaway but Bob follows. During a brutal fight, Bob knocks out Anse and returns to the mine where Chito and the lawmen have captured the rest of the gang. Judy tries to get Bob to stay on at her ranch but Chito rides off in a frenzy after Dixie asks him when they are going to get married.

Guns of Hate contains all the prerequisites needed for an entertaining B Western: a stalwart hero and humorous sidekick, a beautiful leading leady, dastardly villains, an acceptable plot with lots of fighting, riding and shooting sequences, all blended into a speedy hour's viewing. The feature's main highlight, however, it is beautiful desert locales, nicely photographed by George E. Diskant. The Annapolis, Maryland, *Evening Capital* called it an "action-packed Western adventure" and *The Amarillo* (Texas) *Globe* stated, "Plenty of gun play, hard riding and narrow escapes enliven the exciting story.... Lesley Selander directed ... in a style that keeps the action moving swiftly." *Independent Exhibitors Film Bulletin* noted, "*Guns of Hate* continues the Tim Holt series reputation for satisfactory Western fare." *Variety* reported "its many good points are neutralized to some extent by lack of spectacular stunts and some of the worst shooting yet demonstrated by a western hero...." Reviewing the film as *Guns of Wrath*, *The Film Daily* stated, "Good buy in Westerns. Plentifully loaded with action, good performances.... Picture has an energetic production. Lesley Selander's direction keeps things happening all the time with proper action punctuations in the right places."

The Lost Dutchman Mine has been the subject of several films and television programs. It was used as part of the plot of the low-grade exploitation feature *The Irish Gringo* (1935), starring Pat Carlyle, William Farnum and Bryant Washburn. The best known movie about the subject is *Lust for Gold*, a 1949 Columbia release starring Glenn Ford and Ida Lupino. Its plot was reworked by the studio for the 1956 release *Secret of Treasure Mountain*; both films featured William Prince. A 1954 documentary feature, *Lost Dutchman Mine*, was made available on tape as *The Lost Dutchman Mine: The True Story of Death Mountain*. A sci-fi angle regarding the lode was used in the obscure *The Sagittarius Mine* (1972), a Gold Key release. The mine was the subject of an episode of NBC-TV's *Laramie* in 1961 and it has been featured on the documentary series *In Search of ...* (1977), *Unsolved Mysteries* (1989), *World of Treasure* (1995) and *Treasure: The Lost Dutchman Mine* (1998).

Hansel and Gretel (1954; 72 minutes; Color)

PRODUCER: Michael Myerberg. DIRECTORS: Michael Myerberg & John Paul. SCREENPLAY: Padraic Colum, from the opera by Engelbert Humperdinck with German libretto by Adelheid Wette. PHOTOGRAPHY: Martin Munkacsi. EDITOR: James F. Barclay. MUSIC CONDUCTOR: Franz Allers. SET DECORATIONS: Evalds Dajevskis. COSTUMES: Ida Vendicktow. ANIMATORS: Sky Highchief, Joe Horstman, Inez Horstman, Kermit Love, Hobart Rosen, Don Sahlin & Teddy Shepard. CHARACTER DESIGNS: James Summers. PRODUCTION MANAGER: William F. Rogers, Jr.

VOICE CAST: Anna Russell (Rosina Rubylips, the Witch), Mildred Dunnock (Mother), Frank Rogier (Father), Constance Brigham (Hansel/Gretel), Helen Boatwright (Dew Fairy), Delbert Anderson (Sandman), Apollo Boys Choir (Angels/Children).

"Hansel and Gretel" was first published as part of "Grimm's Fairy Tales" in the 1810s in Germany and in 1893 it became a noted opera with music by Engelbert Humperdinck and libretto by his sister, Adelheid Wette. Edison first filmed the story in 1909 and there have been many film variations since, including this animated version that RKO distributed beginning late in 1954. Made in New York City by producer Michael Myerberg at his studio, it took two years to complete. The puppets used were called "kinemins" and they had very flexible facial expressions. They were electronically operated on a magnet stage setting and for the most part were quite realistic. Highly entertaining for both children and adults, *Hansel and Gretel* had a box office return of $1.3 million and was reissued in 1965 by New Trends Associates.

Hansel (voice of Constance Brigham) and Gretel (voice of Brigham) are the children of a poor broom maker (voice of Frank Rogier) and his wife (voice of Mildred Dunnock). They live in a forest, eating only stale bread. A neighbor brings the starving family a pitcher of milk but the children decide not to drink it until their mother returns. Instead they try to forget their hunger by playing with two animals, Little Bear and Susan, a goose, neglecting their chores. When their mother returns she is very angry with them for not completing their work and swings a broom, accidentally causing the milk to spill. She sends them into the forest to find strawberries but her husband soon arrives with food he purchased from selling his wares. As their parents search for them, Hansel and Gretel are lured further away by a witch, Rosina Rubylips (voice of Anna Russell), who plans to turn them into gingerbread. Hansel finds strawberries with Little Bear while Gretel and Susan pick wild flowers. The children eat the strawberries and search for more. As night arrives, the frightened children are lulled to sleep by the Sandman (voice of Delbert Anderson) and protected by singing angels (Apollo Boys Choir). The next day the children find a gingerbread house and begin eating it as Little Bear implores them to leave. Rosina ties up Hansel and plans to bake him in her outdoor oven but Gretel helps him to escape and they run away. Using her hat's crystal eye ornament spell, Rosina brings them back and puts Hansel in a cage and orders Gretel to get food to fatten him. When Rosina rides on her broomstick, Gretel manages to get the chain off Hansel's cage and breaks the witch's spell over him. Ready to eat the children after turning them to gingerbread, Rosina tells Gretel to help her but the little girl acts confused. When the witch gets too close to the oven, the children push her inside and slam the door. The oven and the witches' house vanish and the gingerbread statues along its path become children who were under Rosina's spell. Hansel and Gretel's parents find them and a gingerbread witch appears in the space formerly occupied by the oven. The family happily returns home, followed by Little Bear and Susan.

Bosley Crowther in *The New York Times* enthused, "[T]he work is a charming entertainment in both the musical and novelty line.... With very good color photography and against cunning cut-out sets, this picture has the quality of a truly visualized fairy tale. The very aspect of delicate fabrication complements the creation of make-believe. In the simplicity of the performance and the presentation of the music, too, Mr. Myerberg's ambitious production merits appreciative praise.... And the music, under Franz Allers' direction, has real operatic class." *Variety* reported, "Done in exquisite Technicolor that underscores the great craftsmanship that has gone into this film, *Hansel and Gretel* is unusual not only for the tasteful and imaginative way in which it tackled its subject but also for the 'actors' themselves.... [They] are a triumph in themselves.... It has visual beauty, but it also has movement.... In bringing it to the screen with such a fine sense for the demands of the medium, Myerberg deserves a vote of thanks from millions of youngsters who can't get to an opera house." *Boxoffice* noted, "The kinemins, which walk, talk and use dozens of facial expressions, are a remarkable novelty which will draw squeals of delight from the little kiddies.... For adults, the biggest selling points are the novelty angle, the fine operatic score by Humperdinck and the voice of Anna Russell."

Having Wonderful Crime (1945; 70 minutes)

PRODUCER: Robert Fellows. ASSOCIATE PRODUCER: Theron Warth. DIRECTOR: A. Edward Sutherland. SCREENPLAY: Howard J. Green, Parke Levy & Stewart Sterling, from the novel *Having a Wonderful Crime* by Craig Rice. PHOTOGRAPHY: Frank Redman. EDITOR: Gene Milford. MUSIC: Leigh Harline. MUSIC DIRECTOR: C. Bakaleinikoff. ART DIRECTORS: Albert S. D'Agostino & Al Herman. SOUND: Jean L. Speak & James G. Stewart. SET DECORATIONS: Claude Carpenter & Darrell Silvera. GOWNS: Edward Stevenson. SPECIAL EFFECTS: Vernon L. Walker. ASSISTANT DIRECTOR: Clem Beauchamp.

CAST: Pat O'Brien (Michael J. Malone), George Murphy (Jake Justus), Carole Landis (Helene Justus), Lenore Aubert (Gilda Mayfair), George Zucco (The Great Movel/Mr. King), Anje Berens [Gloria Holden] (Phyllis Gray), Richard Martin (Lance Richards), Charles D. Brown (Mr. Winslow), Wee Willie Davis (Zacharias), Blanche Ring (Elizabeth Lenhart), Chili Williams (Polka Dot Blonde), Josephine Whittell (Myra Lenhart), Edward Fielding (Dr. Newcomb), Don Barclay (Bartender), Chester Conklin (Motor Court Owner), Cyril Ring (Hotel Desk Clerk), Frank Mayo, Eddie Dunn (State Policemen), Emory Parnell (Desk Sergeant), Dewey Robinson (Huntington Murder Suspect), Vernon Dent (Fat Guest), Larry Wheat (Butler), Marc Cramer (Announcer), Jimmy Jordan (Usher), Margaret Landry (Secretary), Frances Morris (Irritated Theater Patron), Walter Soderling (Gatekeeper), George McKay (Stage Manager), Edith Hallor (Maid), Alexander Pollard (Room Service Waiter), Claire McDowell, Mildred Harris, Elaine Riley, Rosemary La Planche, Joan Dix, Eddie Borden, Virginia Belmont, Lee Trent, Tom Burton, Steve Winston, Harry Clay, John Shaw, Chris Drake, Margie Stewart, Nancy Marlow (Guests), Sherry Hall (Truck), Elmer Jerome (Window Washer), Marilyn Gladstone, Ellen Hall, Evalene Bankston, Lorraine Clark, Virginia Cruzon, Mary Jane Dolan, Karen Haven, Shirley Johnson, Shelby Payne, Mary Starr, Sheryle Starr, Kerry Vaughn (Bathing Beauties), Brooks Benedict, Jack Gargan, Kenner G. Kemp, Larry Steers (Bar Customers).

Craig Rice's (pen name of Georgiana Ann Randolph Craig) hard-drinking fictional lawyer-sleuth Michael J. Malone first came to the screen in the spring of 1945 when RKO released *Having Wonderful Crime*, based on the author's 1943 novel *Having a Wonderful Crime*. It was mostly filmed at Carmel, California's Del Monte Lodge. While mainly a fast-paced and somewhat forced mystery-comedy, the feature did have some horror overtones, specifically the character of stage illusionist The Great Movel, played by genre favorite George Zucco. Also in the cast is Gloria Holden, billed as Anje Berens, who had the title role in Universal's *Dracula's Daughter* (1936), and was a mystic in *Miracles for Sale* (1939), the last feature directed by Tod Browning. Here, however, the actress basically does a Miriam Hopkins takeoff. The supporting cast also includes Lenore Aubert, who later appeared in *Abbott and Costello Meet Frankenstein* (1948); Richard Martin, usually Tim Holt's sidekick in his B Western series for the studio; and Wee Willie Davis, a professional wrestler whose ring career spanned the 1930s into the 1960s before he became a wrestling promoter in Louisville, Kentucky. Like fellow grapplers Mike Mazurki, Tor Johnson and Karl "Killer" Davis, he appeared in a number of feature films, including the Sherlock Holmes drama *Pursuit to Algiers* (1945). Davis was the co-inventor of Glowmeter, a display that projected an automobile's speed on its windshield. Also featured is Blanche Ring, famed Broadway musical star of the 1910s who introduced such popular songs as "Rings on My Fingers," "In the Good Old Summertime" and "Come Josephine in My Flying Machine."

Pat O'Brien, top billed as Michael J. Malone, made *Man Alive* (q.v.) the same year for producers Robert Fellows and Theron Warth; *Having Wonderful Crime* greatly toned down Malone's heavy drinking. George Murphy and Carole Landis enacted the roles of Malone's zany pals, newlyweds Jake and Helene Justus, but neither seemed comfortable in the parts or with the quick repartee. Landis' hairstyle is not becoming and nearly negates her innate physical charms. Finally, the unmasking of the killer is a big disappointment since the character had little involvement in the proceedings until the denouement. Like *Man Alive*, *Having Wonderful Crime* was not a popular box office item.

At the Chicago law office of her friend, attorney Michael J. Malone (O'Brien), dizzy blonde

Helene Justus (Landis) holds a murder suspect (Dewey Robinson) at bay with a gun but accidentally wings Malone when the bad guy rushes her. Helene's new husband, Jake Justus (Murphy), knocks out the suspect and all three take a powder to avoid involvement with the police. They take refuge in a theater where master illusionist The Great Movel (Zucco) is performing. While doing his vanishing act, Movel disappears as Malone, Jake and Helene flee the theater to again elude the law. Since Jake and Helene are going to Loonheart Lodge for their honeymoon, Malone insists on coming along. While driving there, Helene accidentally forces a car off the road. The driver is Gilda Mayfair (Aubert), a member of Movel's troupe, who is worried about her trunk. The trio take her and the trunk to the lodge, unaware they are being followed by a mysterious man. Upon arrival, the lodge's porter, Zacharias (Davis), takes their luggage while Jake and Helene register and tells the clerk (Cyril Ring) that Malone and Gilda are married, to conceal Gilda's identity. The mysterious man tries to get Zacharias to give him Gilda's trunk but Malone arrives on the scene and the man says he made a mistake and leaves. Malone has the trunk taken to his room. When Gilda sees the mystery man in the lobby, she faints. Movel's other assistant, Lane Richards (Martin), arrives at the hotel and hides outside Malone's room. When Gilda sees him, she waves to him to leave. The hotel doctor (Edward Fielding) leaves a sedative for Gilda; Malone, Jake and Helene each give her a dose of it, causing the young woman to pass out. When Malone and Jake open the trunk they find the props for Movel's act but also a false bottom containing a hollow cane concealing a check for $50,000 written to the illusionist by Elizabeth Lenhart (Ring), who co-owns the lodge with her sister Myra (Josephine Whittell). Going to the lobby, Malone is attracted to diver Phyllis Gray (Holden) who has arrived to take part in a water carnival. The mystery man goes to Gilda's room and asks her who tried to kill him and demands the check. When she says she does not know to both questions, he seeks out the trunk while she calls Lance. The mystery man, who is Movel, finds the check is missing from the hollow cane where he put it just as someone stabs him with a sword. Jake and Helene find Movel's body in the trunk and go to get Malone, who has taken Phyllis to the lake for a moonlight boat ride. The newlyweds take Malone back to the lodge, leaving Phyllis to drift alone on the lake. Back in their suite, the trio see the trunk is missing and Jake reports the theft to the hotel management. Malone finds a poster for Movel's act in the trunk and realizes the magician was the mysterious man. Winslow (Charles D. Brown), the manager, arrives and wants to call the police but Malone and Jake convince him to let them have 12 hours to solve the case in order to avoid any adverse publicity for the lodge. As Malone, Jake and Helene search for the trunk, Malone sees it on the lawn but is forced to help Jake get Helene out of a laundry chute where she has become lodged. When they finally get to the grounds, the trunk is missing and they are nearly killed when someone pushes a large cement block off the roof. After searching Lance's room and not finding him there, Malone remembers Phyllis is still in the boat and goes to apologize to her. As he arrives at the pier, she is climbing out of the water and angrily goes back to the lodge. Gilda shows up wanting Malone's help: She explains that Lance is her fiancé and that he was jealous of Movel and the two had an argument the day the illusionist disappeared. She was afraid Lance had killed Movel and put his body in the trunk so she took it out of town to protect him. Gilda informs Malone that Lance has moved into a motor court and they go there looking for him but the owner (Chester Conklin) does not know his whereabouts. Joined by Jake, Helene and Zacharias, Malone and Gilda comb the woods looking for Lance. Gilda finds him unconscious. When he comes to, they take Lance to Malone's room and the next day Malone and Jake go to see Elizabeth Lenhart, leaving Helene to watch Lance. When the gatekeeper (Walter Soderling) denies them entrance, Malone and Jake hitch a ride on a window washer's (Elmer Jerome) truck. After climbing a ladder, they spy Helene talking with Elizabeth. Helene informs the old lady, an ex-actress, that Gilda and Lance are suspected of killing Movel and gets her to write Malone a check for $50,000 so he can defend the couple. Back at the lodge, Helene gives Malone the check but it is blank. The following day at the Water Carnival, Elizabeth writes another check to Malone. Not long after, a flag pole falls, nearly killing the old lady and her sister. When Malone tries to re-win Phyllis by showing her the check, the ink fades away, making him suspect Myra substituted invisible ink. Malone gets a note from Zacharias telling him to go to the boathouse and there he finds the body of the porter. Winslow arrives and admits he was short on funds at the lodge due to betting on horses and bad tips. He says Myra paid him to get back the check her sister wrote to Movel, who he killed along with Zacharias, because he suspected him of the crime. Winslow manages to knock out Malone and places him in Movel's trunk, which he drops into the lake. When Jake and Helene arrive looking for Malone, Winslow ties them up and leaves them to die of asphyxiation when he leaves the motor boat's engine running. A drenched Malone climbs onto the pier and saves his friends, telling them he escaped from the trunk through the hollow bottom. Returning to the lodge, the trio watch as the surprised Winslow is arrested and taken to jail.

Bosley Crowther in *The New York Times* wrote off *Having Wonderful Crime*, stating, "It rambles through elaborate confusions and a great deal of unfunny talk, all of which very thinly disguises the fact that it has nothing to tell.... This picture may safely be forgotten as a pitiful but harmless offense." More on the mark was *Variety* which dubbed it "a razzle-dazzle murder mystery developed in nonsensical style. Strictly broad escapist fare.... Loosely knit tale never pauses long enough to establish credulity, but continually races along with accentuated slapstick." *The Motion Picture Herald* complained, "[T]he film as a whole suffers from a confused story line." *The Film Daily* termed *Having Wonderful Crime* "a mystery comedy that doesn't come off, although it tries awfully hard to make something of itself. The film presents synthetic entertainment that strikes a false note in its attempts to be smart and nonchalant."

The Hunchback of Notre Dame (1939; 116 minutes)

PRODUCER: Pandro S. Berman. DIRECTOR: William Dieterle. SCREENPLAY: Sonya Levien. ADAPTATION: Bruno Frank, from the novel by Victor Hugo. PHOTOGRAPHY: Joseph H. August. EDITORS: William Hamilton & Robert Wise. MUSIC: Alfred Newman. ART DIRECTORS: Van Nest Polglase & Al Herman. SOUND: John E. Tribby. SET DECORATIONS: Darrell Silvera. COSTUMES: Walter Plunkett. SPECIAL EFFECTS: Vernon L. Walker. DANCE DIRECTOR: Ernst Matray. TECHNICAL ADVISOR: Louis Vandenecker. ASSISTANT DIRECTORS: Edward Killy & Argyle Nelson.

CAST: Charles Laughton (Quasimodo), Sir Cedric Hardwicke (Frollo), Thomas Mitchell (Clopin), Maureen O'Hara (Esmeralda), Edmond O'Brien (Gringoire), Alan Marshal (Captain Phoebus), Walter Hampden (Archdeacon of Paris), Harry Davenport (King Louis XI), Katharine Alexander (Madame le Lys), George Zucco (Procurator), Fritz Leiber (Old Nobleman), Etienne Girardot (Doctor), Helene Whitney (Fleur de Lys), Minna Gombell (Queen of Beggars), Arthur Hohl (Olivier), Curt Bois (Student), George Tobias (Hangman Beggar), Rod La Rocque (Phillippe), Spencer Charters (Court Clerk), Kathryn Adams, Dianne Hunter (Fleur de Lys' Companions), Sig Arno (Tailor), Barlowe Borland (Dubois), Victor Kilian (Hangman), Charles Halton (Printer), Tempe Pigott (Madeleine), Ferdinand Munier (Defense Counsel), Angela Mulinos (Helene), Gretl Dupont (Lissy), Hector Sarno (Knight), Dewey Robinson (Butcher), Arthur Millet (Count Graville), Gisela Werbisek (Grandmother), Margaret McWade (Young Sister), Paul Newlan (Whip Man), Eddie Abdo (Singer), Lionel Belmore (Trial Judge), Rondo Hatton, Russ Powell (Ugly Contestants), Charlie Hall (Mercury), Louis Adlon (Venus), Edward Groag (Moon), Arthur Dulac (Mars), Norbert Schiller (Saturn), Cy Kendall, Harry V. Vejar, J.C. Fowler (Noblemen), Dick Dickinson (Man with Wooden Leg), Vangie Beilby, Elsie Prescott (Contestants), Otto Hoffman (Deaf Judge), Edmund Cobb, Elmo Lincoln, Ralph Dunn, Alexander Granach (Soldiers), Al Herman (Fat Soldier), Alan Copeland (Choir Boy), Harry Cording (Guard), Harold DeGarro (Man on Stilts), Charles Drake (Young Priest), Vallejo Gantner (Merchant), Nestor Paiva (Citizen in Street), Peter Godfrey (Monk),

Frank Mills, Mike Lally (Beggars), Ray Long (Skeleton Dancer), Rudolf Steinboeck, Joseph P. Mack (Actors), Antonio Pina (Ladder Man), Ward Shattuck, Earl Clyde (Jugglers), Alan Spear (Contortionist), James Fawcett (Ball Walker), Lillian Nicholson (Fleur de Lys' Servant).

RKO spent over $1.8 million to make *The Hunchback of Notre Dame*, based on Victor Hugo's 1831 novel. Publicity at the time claimed the production cost between $2.5 and $3 million, with the film eventually bringing in over $3.1 million at the box office. Released at the end of 1939, the movie was a spectacular recreation of fifteenth century Paris, replete with a 190-foot replica of the Notre Dame Cathedral, with impressive interior design and detail. It was Oscar-nominated for Best Musical Score and Best Sound Recording. Charles Laughton gave a stunning performance as the deformed title character and he was supported by a wonderful cast, especially Sir Cedric Hardwicke as the evil Frollo, Thomas Mitchell as the beggar's king, Harry Davenport as the jovial King Louis XI, and Walter Hampden, in his screen debut, as the Archdeacon of Paris. Also debuting in the feature was Edmond O'Brien as the poet Gringoire. Making her U.S. film debut was Maureen O'Hara as the ravishing beauty Esmeralda. The scenes in which her looks contrast with Quasimodo's grotesqueness are among the many highlights of the movie. The film was especially impressive in recreating the filth, squalor and superstition of the period. Its main drawback was a happy ending in contrast to the Hugo novel. It was reissued by RKO theatrically in 1946 and 1957.

In fifteenth century Paris, King Louis XI (Davenport) comes to see a printer (Charles Halton) who is operating a press, which the king hopes will help to enlighten the people. His chief justice, Frollo (Hardwicke), calls it horrifying and warns that the land is being overridden by witches, sorcerers and gypsies. When a band of gypsies are denied entrance to the city, one of them, the beautiful Esmeralda (O'Hara), manages to sneak by the guards on Fool's Day. The king and his entourage watch a play by poet Gringoire (O'Brien) that calls for enlightenment, which is shouted down by the crowd. Esmeralda dances for the merrymakers and gets the attention of Gringoire as well as Frollo. Quasimodo (Laughton), a hideous deaf hunchback who is the bell ringer at the cathedral of Notre Dame, is discovered by the crowd watching the proceedings and he is made King of Fools. Frollo, who is Quasimodo's protector, puts a stop to the show and leads the hunchback away as Esmeralda is nearly arrested. She runs to the cathedral and is given sanctuary by the Archdeacon of Paris (Hampden), Frollo's brother. When he finds her in the church, Frollo orders Esmeralda to leave and she says his hand has the mark of the devil. She prays to the Virgin Mary to help her people and is overheard by the king, who says he will consider her request. Fascinated by Esmeralda, Frollo takes her to Quasimodo for protection but she runs away; Frollo tells the hunchback to bring her back. Gringoire is awakened by Esmeralda's screams and calls for help. Captain Phoebus (Alan Marshal), a nobleman, comes to the girl's rescue and orders Quasimodo arrested. Esmeralda is taken in by the Queen of Beggars (Minna Gombell) while Gringoire ends up in the beggars' court where he is nearly hanged on the orders of Clopin (Mitchell), the king of beggars, until Esmeralda saves him by agreeing to become his wife. While Gringoire has fallen in love with her, Esmeralda tells him she loves Phoebus. Quasimodo is sentenced to endure 50 lashes and an hour of public disgrace on the pillory. Gringoire asks the archdeacon to stop the whipping but he is unable to comply. After the sentence is carried out, the hunchback is tormented by the crowd, who laugh when he cries out for water. Esmeralda gives Quasimodo water and after he is set free he staggers back to Notre Dame, telling Frollo what the girl did for him.

Frollo arranges for Esmeralda and Gringoire to entertain at an outdoor party for the nobility. Phoebus sees Esmeralda and ushers her away but while he is making love to her, he is murdered and she is blamed. Frollo confesses to his brother that he killed a man because a woman bewitched

Poster for *The Hunchback of Notre Dame* (1939).

him. The archdeacon says Frollo is mad and renounces him. When Gringoire comes to see Esmeralda in jail, she says she realizes Phoebus did not love her. Frollo orders the destruction of the printing press while at Esmeralda's trial Gringoire argues she is innocent but the procurator (George Zucco) calls her a witch. Quasimodo comes to the trial and confesses to murdering Phoebus but is laughed out of court. Frollo secretly watches while Esmeralda is tortured into a confession but the king orders her to undergo a trial by ordeal, which she fails. Frollo sentences Esmeralda to be hanged. The day of the execution, Quasimodo observes from the cathedral as the archdeacon refuses to give Esmeralda public penance because he believes her innocent. Frollo orders the hanging to proceed but Quasimodo swings on a rope from the cathedral and carries away Esmeralda, taking her to the sanctuary of the church. As Frollo gets the nobles to sign a petition to the king ending the right of sanctuary, Quasimodo falls in love with Esmeralda and tells her she must never leave the church or she will be hanged. When the people gather to protest the suspension, Frollo admits to the king that he killed Phoebus. The archdeacon tells the king that Frollo committed the crime because of his love for the gypsy girl and the king orders Frollo's arrest. Clopin leads an army of beggars to the cathedral demanding Esmeralda; Quasimodo thinks they have come to hang her. He drops heavy boulders and stones on them, killing Clopin. When some men use one of the boulders as a battering ram, he pours molten metal on the crowd, which disperses as the king's soldiers arrive. When Frollo tries to attack Esmeralda, Quasimodo protects her and throws Frollo off the bell tower to his death. Gringoire informs the people that the king has pardoned Esmeralda and that gypsies can live anywhere in France. Quasimodo watches as Esmeralda leaves with Gringoire and tells a gargoyle he wishes that he too were made of stone.

Frank S. Nugent in *The New York Times* compared this 1939 RKO production to the 1923 Universal film starring Lon Chaney as the hunchback and claimed the remake was "even more horrendous. It is to Mr. Laughton's credit that he is able to act at all under his makeup, to suggest exultation, hatred and evoke pity.... Yet we cannot truthfully say we enjoyed him or his picture. The film is almost unrelievedly brutal and without the saving grace of unreality which makes Frankenstein's horrors a little comic.... It is handsome enough of production and its cast is expert.... [It is] a bit too coarse for our tastes now." *The Film Daily* declared, "Compelling dynamic entertainment should register sensationally at the box-office and add immeasurably to screen's dignity as well as fine art.... Seldom has costume drama been so infused with suspenseful dramatic action; seldom has spectacle been so enriched with adventure, so fascinatingly aglow with the essence of romance; seldom, importantly, has a sense of the climactic been so timely manifested; seldom, finally, has music been more adroitly used as cinematic embroidery." *The Hollywood Reporter* wrote, "The sheer immensity of this production ... and the majestic manner in which it has been handled mark it as a motion picture of distinction.... Entirely aside from its story value, this is a production, directorial and photographic masterpiece.... Much of it belongs in the definite horror bracket, much of it is tense, suspensive melodrama, much of it is medieval pageantry, but the horror angle has the definite edge." *Variety* called it a "mighty horror tale," adding, "The elaborate sets and wide production sweep overshadows to a great extent the detailed dramatic motivation of the Victor Hugo tale. While the background is impressive and eye-filling, it detracts many times from the story being unfolded, especially in the first half. Charles Laughton's grotesque makeup as the deformed and imbecilic bell ringer of Notre Dame Cathedral is not exactly palatable for patrons sensitively inclined." David J. Hanna in *Film Bulletin* stated, "From start to finish it is absorbing, fascinating entertainment—spectacular, vivid and breathtaking. It is obvious that no effort was spared to assure its box office potentialities. Interest is centered largely on Charles Laughton whose interpretation of Quasimodo is thrillingly effective." Howard Barnes in *The New York Herald Tribune* proclaimed, "Whether you judge the new offering on grounds of Grand Guignol horror, fidelity to the original book or exciting and sustained action, it is every inch as good as its predecessor. Charles Laughton gives a terrifying and only occasionally hammy portrayal. William Dieterle has staged the show brilliantly, keeping it swift-paced, significant and savage."

Starting at the time of the film's release, and continuing even today, there have been comparisons between the way Lon Chaney, in the 1923 *Hunchback*, and Laughton interpreted the role of Quasimodo. While Chaney did not have the advantage of sound, he was a master of pantomime and his self-created makeup was definitely horrific. On the other hand, Laughton brought pathos to the part with Quasimodo being one of the most memorable of his screen portrayals. The Victor Hugo work has been filmed many times, starting in 1905 with *Esmeralda*, a title also used for a 1922 British production starring Sybil Thorndike and Booth Conway. Sandwiched between them was Fox's 1917 release *The Darling of Paris*, starring Theda Bara and Glen White. Anthony Quinn and Gina Lollobrigida were Quasimodo and Esmeralda in the 1956 French feature *Notre-Dame de Paris*, which was released in the U.S. the next year by Allied Artists as *The Hunchback of Notre Dame*. There was a BBC-TV production of the Hugo work in 1965 with Peter Woodthorpe and Gay Hamilton and in 1977 NBC-TV filmed it with Warren Clarke and Michelle Newell. Anthony Hopkins was Quasimodo and Lesley-Anne Down played Esmeralda in a 1982 CBS-TV feature, Disney Studios did an animated version of the work in 1996 and the next year Mandy Patinkin portrayed Quasimodo in a TNT-TV outing. The 1939 version was also released on video in a computer colorized version.

I Walked with a Zombie (1943; 69 minutes)

PRODUCER: Val Lewton. DIRECTOR: Jacques Tourneur. SCREENPLAY: Curt Siodmak & Ardel Wray. STORY: Inez Wallace. PHOTOGRAPHY: J. Roy Hunt. EDITOR: Mark Robson. MUSIC DIRECTOR: C. Bakaleinikoff. ART DIRECTORS: Albert S. D'Agostino & Walter Keller. SOUND: John C. Grubb. SET DECORATIONS: Al Fields & Darrell Silvera. ASSISTANT DIRECTOR: William Dorfmann.

CAST: James Ellison (Wesley Rand), Frances Dee (Betsy Connell), Tom Conway (Paul Holland), Edith Barrett (Mrs. Rand), James Bell (Dr. Maxwell), Christine Gordon (Jessica Holland), Theresa Harris (Alma), Sir Lancelot (Calypso Singer), Darby Jones (Carre Four), Jeni LeGon, Kathleen Hartsfield (Dancers), Richard Abrams (Clement), Alan Edmiston (Mr. Wilkins), Norman Mayes (Bayard), Clinton Rosemond (Coach Driver), Martin Wilkins (Houngan), Jieno Moxzer (Native with Saber), Vivian Dandridge (Melisse), Rita Christiani, Doris Ake (Melisse's Friends), Arthur Walker (Ti-Joseph), Melvin Williams (Infant).

Filmed during a three-week period in October–November 1942 and issued theatrically at the end of April 1943, *I Walked with a Zombie* is loosely based on Charlotte Bronte's 1847 novel *Jane Eyre* which 20th Century–Fox filmed the next year. It was the second of three horror thrillers Jacques Tourneur directed for producer Val Lewton, preceded by *Cat People* and followed by *The Leopard Man* (qq.v.). The film's chief assets are J. Roy Hunt's brooding, shadowy cinematography, the eerie sets by Al Fields and Darrell Silvera, and locales flavorfully dressed by art directors Albert S. D'Agostino and Walter E. Keller. These are accentuated by the soft, subdued music score composed by the uncredited Roy Webb. The small ensemble cast also does much to contribute to the mood of the proceedings, especially Tom Conway as the dour plantation owner whose life is changed by his feelings for Frances Dee as the nurse he hires to care for his catatonic wife (Christine Gordon). Dee, who replaced Anna Lee, exudes just the right amount of innocence, strength and looks to make the role work. James Ellison, who has sometimes been criticized for mediocre performances, is quite good as the hard-drinking brother. The makeup for Edith Barrett as the matriarch of the family is excellent; it is hard to believe she was only 36 at the time of the film's release and married to Vincent Price, who was four years her junior; they were the parents

Lobby card for *I Walked with a Zombie* (1943) picturing Christine Gordon, Tom Conway and Frances Dee.

of a two-year-old son. The calypso song used in the film to tell the tragedy of the love triangle between the two brothers and the now catatonic woman was written and performed by Sir Lancelot. The most gruesome character in the movie is the bug-eyed zombie Carre Four, terrifically portrayed by Darby Jones, who essentially repeated the part in *Zombies on Broadway* (q.v.) two years later. *I Walked with a Zombie* is one of the very best of the psychological horror features produced by Val Lewton for RKO and beautifully exemplifies his theory that the unseen is more frightening than a multitude of visual scares. RKO reissued the feature twice, in 1952 and again in 1957.

In snowy Ottawa, Canada, novice nurse Jessica Connell (Dee) is hired for $200 a month by a jobber (Alan Edmiston) to tend a plantation owner's wife on the Caribbean island of St. Sebastian. Her new employer, Paul Holland (Conway), who runs the family sugar plantation, meets her at Antigua with a boat and they sail to his home at Fort Holland. During the voyage he tells her the area is not beautiful like she thinks but here everything dies, including the stars. She is driven to the Holland compound by a driver (Clinton Rosemond) who informs her of the island's history, saying the Hollands imported slaves there. A slave ship's masthead, the arrow-ridden T-Misery, stands in the estate's front yard. That evening Jessica meets Paul's half-brother, Wesley Rand (Ellison), who explains they had different fathers with Paul attending school in England while he was educated in Buffalo. He also informs her that their mother, Mrs. Rand (Barrett), does not live with them but instead operates a dispensary in the local village. At night, Betsy hears a woman crying and follows the sounds to a tower where she is accosted by a blonde woman on the stone stairs. When the woman corners her, Jessica screams. Paul and the servants arrive; Paul tells Betsy the woman is his catatonic wife Jessica (Gordon), and has her maid Alma (Theresa Harris) take her back to her room. Betsy informs Paul she was not aware her patient was a mental case. The next day Paul takes Betsy to task for her actions the night before and says she should not take to heart the native superstitions. He says that generations of slavery have made the locals superstitious, causing them to cry at the birth of a child and celebrate death. Dr. Maxwell (James Bell) arrives to see Jessica and relates how his patient became catatonic due to a tropical fever that burned out part of her spinal cord. Calling her a beautiful zombie, Maxwell says Jessica is a sleepwalker who will never awaken and there is no cure. The following day Betsy walks to the village where she meets Wesley, who drinks heavily and becomes upset when a calypso singer (Sir Lancelot) performs a song about the Holland family history. By evening Wesley has passed out and Mrs. Rand arrives, introduces herself to Betsy, and has her son sent back to the estate. Mrs. Rand accompanies Betsy home and asks her to use her influence with Paul to remove whiskey from the dinner table so Wesley will not be tempted. Later Betsy makes the request but Paul refuses. At dinner that evening, Paul tells Betsy about voodoo and changes his mind regarding the whiskey, causing a row between him and his brother. Later that evening Betsy hears him playing Rubenstein's "Romance" on the piano with him telling her he regrets bringing her to St. Sebastian and that he drove his wife to madness. Betsy admits to herself that she loves Paul and must try to make Jessica well for his sake. She suggests to Dr. Maxwell that Jessica might be cured by insulin shock and Paul hesitantly agrees. The procedure fails. When Paul tries to soothe the disappointed Betsy, Wesley torments his brother by saying that Paul has fallen in love with the nurse. Alma tells Betsy that Jessica can be cured by voodoo but when she brings up the subject with Mrs. Rand, Betsy is told to forget the notion. That night Betsy gets directions to the Home Fort, a voodoo hamlet, from Alma and leads Jessica through the wind-blown cane fields where they see a sacrificed animal and a human skull, with the path protected by Carre Four (Darby Jones), a fearsome zombie. He lets them pass and they arrive at the Home Fort but when Betsy attempts to communicate through a door with the voodoo priest she is whisked inside and sees Mrs. Rand. The older woman informs her that she uses voodoo to try and help the natives but nothing can be done for Jessica. The natives are unnerved by the presence of Jessica and one of them (Jieno Moxzer) drives a saber in her arm but she does not bleed. Mrs. Rand urges Betsy to quickly take Jessica home. Paul tells Betsy he does not love Jessica and does not want her brought back to normalcy. The natives want to bring Jessica back to the Home Fort to finish a ritual. During the frenzy of their drum-beating, Paul tells Betsy he fears for her and wants her to return home. While sleeping in Jessica's room, Betsy sees a looming shadow and runs to Paul for help. The two find Carre Four coming toward them but Mrs. Rand orders him back to the Home Fort and he complies. The following morning Paul tells his mother that Betsy is leaving. Dr. Maxwell arrives to say the native unrest has caused the initiation of a legal investigation into Jessica's mental state. Mrs. Rand informs him that will not be necessary because when she saw the evil Jessica try to tear her family apart by attempting to run away with Wesley, she put her under a voodoo spell and turned her into a zombie. Both her sons and the physician scoff at her declaration with the doctor saying she was tricked by her own imagination. As the natives work to draw her to the Home Fort, that night Jessica tries to leave Fort Holland but is stopped and Paul and Betsy. Later Wesley tells Betsy he wants her to set Jessica free; Betsy admits she loves Paul. When Jessica again tries to leave, Wesley opens the gates and follows her after pulling an arrow out of T-Misery's statue. Wesley kills Jessica with the arrow and carries her to the seashore, followed by Carre Four. Native fishermen later find Paul and Jessica's bodies and return them to Fort Holland.

At the time of their release, most of Val Lewton's psychological horror films met with some

Lobby card for *I Walked with a Zombie* (1943).

critical deprecation although they enjoyed public acceptance. While definitely scary, their contents hardly compared with world events. *Boxoffice* was skeptical of the feature: "Walking with a zombie in a voodoo atmosphere is supposed to make the hair stand on end, or, if not that, to stir up nervous palpitations. There may be audiences where this film will have this effect. There are probably many more where the adult customers will go out to the smoking room to await the start of the main feature."

Variety reported, "Film contains some terrifying passages, but is overcrowded with trite dialog and ponderous acting.... With few exceptions, cast walks through the picture almost as dazed as the zombies." *The New York Times* wrote, "With its voodoo rites and perambulating zombie, *I Walked with a Zombie* probably will please a lot of people. But to this spectator, at least, it proved to be a dull, disgusting exaggeration of an unhealthy, abnormal concept of life." *The Film Daily* said, "Even devotees of horror films will find it tough to extract more than a passing amount of entertainment from *I Walked with a Zombie*[,] an utterly fantastic affair in which not very much happens, nor much that is of any great interest. There is plenty of gabbing but not much action to speak of.... Jacques Tourneur's direction is a bit too static for this kind of thing. The director does, however, help to build up the eeriness of the film and to create a certain feeling of suspense." According to *Photoplay*, "It creeps along with an eerie dread, a slow devastating dark thing that holds and fascinates. And while one is well aware it's so much hooey, the story is told with such conviction it can't be taken lightly.... Frances Dee is beautiful, dignified and charming as the nurse, which, come to think of it, may account in part for the plausibility of the tale." Rose London in *Zombie: The Living Dead* (1976) called it an "extraordinary movie about voodoo," adding, "The pacing of the film is full of exquisite terror.... If not quite as haunting as Lewton's *Cat People*, his zombie film is another of his superb exercises in suggesting terror without slapping the audience in the face with it like a wet rag in a fairground Haunted House." In *The Encyclopedia of Horror Movies* (1986), Phil Hardy enthused, "This is a haunting nightmarishly beautiful tone poem of voodoo drums, dark moonlight and somnambulist ladies in floating white, brought to perfection by Tourneur's direction, [J. Roy] Hunt's camerawork and [Ardel] Wray's dialogue.... Tourneur's best film, *I Walked with a Zombie* is a small masterpiece."

I Walked with a Zombie was reworked in 2001 by RKO Productions as *Ritual*, also called *Tales from the Crypt Presents: Ritual*.

India Speaks (1933; 78 minutes)

PRODUCER: Walter Futter. DIRECTORS: Walter Futter & Richard Halliburton. DIALOGUE: Norman Houston. PHOTOGRAPHY: J. Peverell Marley, Robert Connell & H.T. Cowling. MUSIC DIRECTOR: Samuel Wineland. TECHNICAL DIRECTOR: David Miller.

CAST: Richard Halliburton (Narrator), Rose Schulze (White Goddess).

Walter Futter Productions made *Africa Speaks*, which proved to be a moneymaking documentary for Columbia Pictures in 1930. Three years later RKO released Futter's similar outing *India Speaks*. Basically a travelogue peering into the hidden secrets of the Far East, the feature contained a prologue stating that on-location footage in India was interpolated with scenes filmed in Hollywood. The feature was narrated by noted adventurer Richard Halliburton, who did not appear in any of the India scenes although his narration was in the first person. With advertising catchlines like "Heathen gods unashamed, look down on human orgies!," "Below Zero and stark naked!" and "A virgin chosen to wed a living God!," *India Speaks* proved to be a successful exploitation item which was novelized by Will C. Murphey in the year of its release. Despite being in theaters as late as 1949, *India Speaks* today is considered a lost film.

In India, a world traveler (voice of Halliburton) hears strange tales of a White Goddess, a Russian girl whose parents were murdered. She was taken to the Himalayan mountains where Tibetan Lamas raised her to be the bride of the living Buddha. Determined to find her, the traveler first is exposed to the worship of the Goddess of Kali, a ten-armed deity, in the Hindu temples, and then is discouraged by the sight of street beggars and others living in hunger and poverty while animals such as cows are peacocks are considered sacred. He is also exposed to India's caste system, including Untouchables, whose shadows are considered debased. Finding guidance from a noted Guru, the traveler views the Ceremony of Treemiri in which pilgrims apply self-torture on spike beds and have objects pounded into their bodies with no visible effects or pain. The Guru then takes the adventurer to the jungles of East India where they see dangerous pythons and vampire bats, the latter thought to have the souls of lowly reincarnated humans. When they arrive in the Kashmir town of Srinigar, the Guru departs but says he will return in two weeks. The traveler visits the lovely Shalimar Gardens and then travels to the Ganges River where he sees more Hindu rites such as cremation. Finding the Guru has died, the traveler observes as Crow People, a sect whose members believe in theft, capture a lion caught in a fierce fight with a tiger. Arriving in Delhi, the traveler disguises himself to partake in a Moslem prayer service but is almost captured when he is declared to be an intruder. Going with a caravan of snow camels, the traveler reaches the Himalayas but is ambushed by Robber Monks in a mountain pass and rescued by a lama who turns out to be the benefactor of the White Goddess. Believing the traveler has been ordained by Buddha to return the young woman to her people, the lama takes him to the Forbidden Valley. There at Ram Gelong, the lama tries to get his comrades to set her free but they refuse. During a ceremony which will sacrifice the White Goddess to the living Buddha, an earthquake strikes, causing a mountainslide. The traveler and his benefactor manage to escape but the White Goddess refuses to go with them, preferring to meet her destiny.

One of the more sensational topics proffered in *India Speaks* is polyandry, which allows a woman to have multiple husbands. The film claimed Tibet was the only place in the world where a woman could legally have a dozen or more spouses, the practice being accepted for the protection of women since the majority of men were shepherds who were away from home most of the time. With the country being wild and lawless, women would be unprotected without plural husbands. Halliburton first wrote about this practice in the book *The Royal Road to Romance*.

"As wonder after wonder, thrill after thrill, revelation after revelation unfolds, the audience comes to look upon *India Speaks* as a magic carpet that has transported them to a world they never knew existed for many of the scenes in *India Speaks* throw a spotlight on Mother India's secrets that have been kept in impenetrable darkness for thousands of years," declared the *Lowell* (Massachusetts) *Sun*. The *Mason City* (Iowa) *Globe-Gazette* called it "a daring and outstanding spectacle" while *The Corona* (California) *Daily Independent* dubbed the film "one of the most dramatic and thrilling stories ever photographed in an exotic locale." Mordaunt Hall in *The New York Times* termed the feature "a curious concoction of fact and fiction.... Although there is no denying the interest of the authentic scenes of 'the land of drama and romance,' it is somewhat disconcerting to be called upon to believe what the screen voice is saying at one moment and then appreciate that in the next breath one is listening to a fanciful escapade." *The New Movie Magazine* reported that the film contained "some of the strangest scenes that have ever come to the screen.... If there is a shred of romance in your soul you'll like this picture.... [It] is packed with thrills." According to *Variety*, "It turns out to be just a wearisome ... travelog, irritatingly interrupted by indifferent acting on phony dramatic scenes." *The Film Daily* raved, "Exciting, interesting and thrilling adventure film with unusually fine narrative. Adventure fans will find complete satisfaction in this excellent compilation of scenes from all parts of India and the mysterious Tibet." *The New York American* termed it a "fascinating film record" while *The New York Herald-Tribune* felt it was "a commendably filmed but poorly edited travelogue." *The New York News* said it "is packed with hair-raising jungle scenes, majestic architectural settings, and landscapes that typify the great beauty of India. The picture holds your interest and is thrilling." *The New York Mirror* wrote that it "says little that hasn't been said in less ambitious travelogues" while *The New York Sun* opined, "Compared to the average commented-upon travelogue, it has its share of interest. It is better photographed than most of them, and several scenes of Indian religious fanatics are quite repellently effective."

India Speaks was reissued theatrically in the spring of 1941 as *The Bride of Buddha* by Record Pictures in a truncated 63-minute version that deleted the original prologue, thus eliminating the fact it contained simulated scenes. In reviewing this version, *Variety* said it was "largely a glorified travelog" and complained, "The festival of horror, shown as part of the India native's idea of annual pilgrimages, is too gruesome for the screen. Also the burning of human bodies." Film Classics brought the feature back to theaters in 1949 as *Captive Bride of Shangri La* and in Great Britain it was released as *Bride of the East*. Due to its controversial nature, *India Speaks* was withdrawn from release in India.

Ingagi (1930; 75 minutes)

PRODUCER: William Alexander. EXECUTIVE PRODUCER: Nat H. Spitzer. DIRECTOR: William Campbell. SCREENPLAY: Adam Hull Shirk. PHOTOGRAPHY: Harold Williams, L. Gillingham, Ed Joyce, Fred Webster & George Summerton. EDITOR: Grace McKee. MUSIC: Edward Gage.

CAST: Sir Hubert Winstead, Captain Daniel Swayne, Arthur Clayton (Explorers), Charles Gemora (Gorilla), Louis Nizor (Narrator).

One of the all-time great con games of the motion pictures business was *Ingagi*, which claimed to be a factual photographed documentary of Darkest Africa that not only recorded the flora, fauna and customs of the region but also delved into the legend of women cohabiting with gorillas. In addition, its explorers claim to have discovered a terrible new species, the Tortadillo. Produced by Congo Pictures, owned by Nat Spitzer, the film was quickly debunked as a hoax that used 16-year-old documentary footage from *Heart of Africa* interpolated with new scenes featuring Charles Gemora as a fearsome gorilla. In addition, the monstrous Tortadillo proved to be a leopard turtle enhanced with attached scales, wings and tail. The more adverse publicity the film received, the more the public flocked to see it, with box office receipts eventually pushing past $4 million.

RKO involvement with the feature was twofold: The studio owned several of the theaters where it was first screened in the spring of 1930 and RKO gave it an official release in March 1931, although the bulk of its later showings came via Road Show Pictures. The feature's success was the determining factor in RKO's deciding to make *King Kong* (1933) [q.v.]. The screenplay for *Ignagi* is credited to Adam Hull Shirk, the author of the 1927 play *The Ape* which was filmed in 1934 as *The House of Mystery*. The play's title, but not its plot, was used in 1940 for the Boris Karloff vehicle *The Ape*. Both films were made by Monogram.

The storyline of *Ingagi* has noted British explorers Sir Hubert Winstead and Captain Daniel Swayne leading an expedition into Central Africa in 1926. They are constantly being stalked by dangerous animals like lions, leopards and hippopotamuses, along with a huge python. Their worst encounter is with a poisonous reptile which they dub the Tortadillo. Eventually they reach the area they are seeking in order to study the legend of gorilla worship and see a virgin sacrificed to a giant simian. They find a tribe of such creatures with their human female mates and their offspring. During a battle with the gorillas, one of the beasts is killed. Its female human mate mourns the loss of her "husband."

Following the film's initial release, the American Society of Mammalogists did a background check on Winstead and Swayne and found they did not exist. The Federal Trade Commission investigated *Ingagi* and divulged the truth that tribal scenes, including some with female nudity, were filmed at the Los Angeles Zoo. It was proved that some of the native women were extras from Central Casting and the film's "pygmies" were Los Angeles area black children made up to look like adults. The Hays Office eventually banned *Ingagi* after sculptor Charles Gemora admitted to them that he played the monster in the film and that the gorillas-abducting-women subplot was faked. In 1938 *Ingagi* was reissued as *The Love Life of a Gorilla* and at the time Gemora told the *Hollywood Citizen News* he devised and built the suit for $1,000 with each hair of the costume attached to a cloth foundation like a wig. He noted, "I designed the head myself. My own eyes show through holes in the mask, while there is a lever which attaches the ape's mouth to my chin. When I open my own mouth, the ape shows his teeth and curls his lips."

At the time of *Ingagi*'s release, the *Motion Picture Times* noted, "African picture of the sensational type that will bring in the curiosity addicts with standout business.... Up to the parts showing a gorilla carrying off a black woman, the shots may be legitimate Africa scenes. But the tale about women living with the beasts and the scene showing the black awaiting the arrival of the gorilla is too much for a person with average intelligence to swallow." *The Film Daily* called it "thrilling" and added, "For those who like picture of big game hunting in Africa, this production should provide some choice moments of entertainment.... A 500-pound gorilla dragging a native woman through the jungle is particularly startling." *The New Movie Magazine* stated, "A much

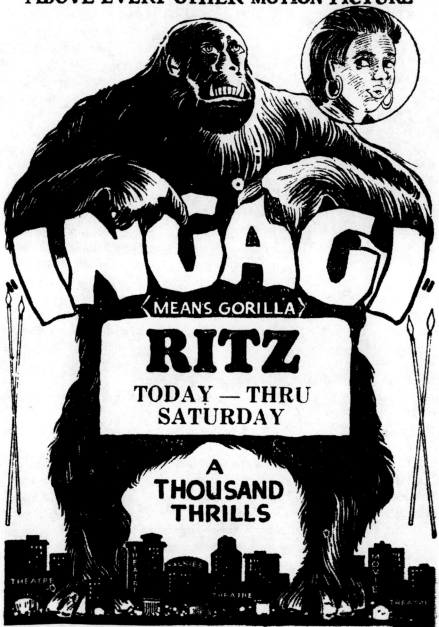

Advertisement for *Ingagi* (1930).

discussed picture owing to the disagreement concerning the antecedents of the gorilla (Ingagi). Some say he is human, others insist that he was not born and bred in Hollywood, but after seeing the picture it doesn't seem to matter a great deal."

When *Ingagi* opened in San Diego, California, in February 1930, *The San Diego Sun* reported, "One of the highlights of the film is the discovery of a native tribe that yearly gives one of their women to the gorillas. Actual photographs of the ceremonies attending the sacrifice have been secured. Further on in the jungle, the explorers found children, apparently the result of mating of the apes and the native women. These children, it is claimed, give rise to further discussion of the Darwinian theory, over which a long battle has raged recently." The same source called it "a weird, sensational film, comparable to nothing that has gone before." The movie broke all previous box office records at the San Diego theater showing it and was held over for a second week.

When *Ingagi* was back in theaters in the fall of 1932, its publicists declared: "Never before, probably, in a single motion picture film, has there been a greater variety of animals shown, than in *Ingagi*, the celebrated jungle film.... Among the beasts and birds and reptiles shown are: Kongoni, zebra, wildebeest, roebuck, impalla, giraffe, hippos, rhinos, lions, leopards, monkeys, elephants, hyenas, pythons, crocodiles, vultures, cow heron, buffalo, etc. A monkey and giraffe convention is shown where the beasts assemble and are finally thrown into confusion by the loud trumpeting of a herd of elephants. The final portrayal of an unbelievable tribal legend of the Congo brings to a climax one of the greatest game films that has ever been made and one that will never be forgotten."

There is some animal footage in *Ingagi* from *Chang* (1928), a box office flop from producers Merian C. Cooper and Ernest Schoedsack, the duo that later made *King Kong* (q.v.). Just as *Ingagi* used scenes from other films, sequences from it were later interpolated into *Angkor* (1937), reissued as *Forbidden Adventure*, *Forbidden Adventure in Angkor*, *Gorilla Woman*, *Jungle Gorillas* and *The Private Life of Ingagi*. Outside of its title, *Son of Ingagi* (Sack Amusements, 1940) bears no relationship to the 1930 feature.

Isle of the Dead (1945; 72 minutes)

PRODUCER: Val Lewton. EXECUTIVE PRODUCER: Jack J. Gross. DIRECTOR: Mark Robson. SCREENPLAY: Ardel Wray. PHOTOGRAPHY: Jack MacKenzie. EDITOR: Lyle Boyer. MUSIC: Leigh Harline. MUSIC DIRECTOR: C. Bakaleinikoff. ART DIRECTORS: Albert S. D'Agostino & Walter E. Keller. SOUND: Jean L. Speak & James G. Stewart. SET DECORATIONS: Darrell Silvera & Al Greenwood. GOWNS: Edward Stevenson. ASSISTANT DIRECTOR: Harry Scott.

CAST: Boris Karloff (General Nikolas Pherides), Ellen Drew (Thea), Marc Cramer (Oliver Davis), Katherine Emery (Mary St. Aubyn), Helene Thimig (Kyra), Alan Napier (Mr. St. Aubyn), Jason Robards (Albrecht), Ernst Dorian (Dr. Drossos), Skelton Knaggs (Andrew Robbins), Sherry Hall (Colonel Kobestes), Erik Hanson (Officer).

Arnold Bocklin's 1880 painting *Isle of the Dead* was the inspiration for producer Val Lewton's initial film with Boris Karloff, *Isle of the Dead*, which ended up being filmed in two parts. (The painting also inspired a 1913 Danish film of the same title.)

The RKO production began in July 1944, but after a week's filming Karloff had spinal surgery and when he returned to work a month later it was in Lewton's *The Body Snatcher* (q.v.). Filming on *Isle of the Dead* resumed early in December 1944 and it wrapped after 12 days of shooting. RKO did not release it until the following September, often in tandem with *Zombies on Broadway* (q.v.). Lewton, who worked uncredited on the script (as did Josef Mischel), imbued the feature with his typical atmospheric aura but the rather drab, slow-moving plot tended to negate much of its fright factor. Karloff does not look well and Ellen Drew is too old for the part of the young girl accused of being the Greek equivalent of a vampire. Katherine Emery replaced Rose Hobart in the role of the British counsel's wife who goes into trances, while Marc Cramer is a typically bland Lewton romantic lead. Helene Thimig as the superstitious Kyra, Jason Robards as an archaeologist and Ernst Dorian as a doctor give the best performances. The film does have

Lobby card for *Isle of the Dead* (1945) picturing Boris Karloff and Marc Cramer.

some spooky moments which are accentuated by Jack MacKenzie's camerawork; the most frightening scene involves Emery trying to claw her way out of a coffin after being buried alive. Karloff would work for Lewton a third time in *Bedlam* (q.v.).

In 1912 Greece, following the rout of enemy forces, General Nikolas Pherides (Karloff) orders his friend Colonel Kobestes (Sherry Hall) to commit suicide after the men under the colonel's command fail in battle. Called "The Watchdog" because of his obsession with Greece and its laws, Pherides admits to *Boston Star* correspondent Oliver Davis (Cramer) that he is not without feelings. Since they are near the island where his wife is buried, Pherides asks Davis to go with him to her tomb. As they cross the battlefield strewn with dead soldiers, they are informed by Dr. Drossos (Dorian) that the casualties must be buried quickly because of plague and typhus. On the island, Pherides finds his wife's tomb has been vandalized and her body is missing. The two men hear a woman singing and follow the sound to a house where they are greeted by the owner, archaeologist Albrecht (Robards). He says he bought the place from native woman Kyra (Thimig) who stayed on as his housekeeper. When asked about the vandalism, Albrecht explains it happened 15 years before when the locals were looking for Greek artifacts to sell. Kyra says the people burned the dead because one of them was evil. Having dinner with Albrecht are British counsel Mr. St. Aubyn (Alan Napier) and his wife Mary (Emery), her nurse, native girl Thea (Drew), and tin salesman Avery Robbins (Skelton Knaggs), a heavy drinker who cannot wait to get back to England. Not feeling well, Robbins leaves the group. Thea is asked to pour wine for the newcomers; when she see Pherides, she refuses to serve him. Albrecht asks Pherides and Davis to stay the night and they agree. During the night, Thea goes to Van Aubyn's room to get

GAPING GRAVES!...WALKING DEAD!
UNSEEN VAMPIRES!

Nameless terror
stalks six people
...a beautiful girl is
BURIED ALIVE!

BORIS KARLOFF IN
ISLE OF THE DEAD

with ELLEN DREW • MARC CRAMER

Produced by VAL LEWTON • Directed by MARK ROBSON • Written by Ardel Wray

RKO RADIO

Advertisement for *Isle of the Dead* **(1945).**

his wife's medicine and on the way back she meets Pherides, who says Kyra sent him because the girl was doing evil. He asks her why she refused to serve him and she says it was because he killed her people for not paying taxes. When Robbins is found dead the next day, Pherides fears it may be the plague and sends for Dr. Drossos. The doctor confirms his opinion and orders the island quarantined. Kyra says a blood-sucking demon, the varvoloka, is on the island and she claims Thea is the evil one. Dr. Drossos explains that the plague is carried by fleas and the imminent hot south winds will kill them. St. Aubyn is stricken and soon dies with Pherides finding Thea near his body. Mary refuses to believe her husband is dead but the next day she tells the doctor she has a fear of being buried alive because she has fainting spells and trances. He promises to make every known test if she is stricken. Albrecht prays to the Greek god Hermes for protection as Dr. Drossos falls victim to the plague. Following his death, Kyra says Thea is the cause of the deaths. Coming from a primitive village, Pherides believes Kyra's declarations and tells Davis to stay away from Thea. When Thea goes to meet Davis, Pherides orders her back to her room and tells her to keep away from the others as she might be a varvoloka, although he says he hopes he is wrong. Thea is told by Mary that she is a good person and then goes to meet Davis, but as they kiss Pherides appears, saying he will kill Thea if she is a varvoloka. Davis promises to take Thea away the next day but Pherides wrecks the island's only boat. When Mary finds out, she berates Pherides but soon falls to the floor of her bedroom as Thea tends to her. During the night, Thea hears Kyra torment her outside Mary's bedroom with accusations of being a varvoloka. The next morning Kyra informs Pherides that Mary's room is like a tomb. When he breaks down the door,

Lobby card for *Isle of the Dead* (1945).

he finds Thea near the woman's dead body. Pherides accuses Thea of killing her mistress and Davis tells the girl to go to the island's ruins to avoid the general. Pherides, Davis and Albrecht bury Mary in the island's crypt, unaware she is in a trance and still alive. The south hot winds arrive but Pherides comes down with the plague and during the night Kyra sits by his bedside as they hear screaming, knocking and clawing from the crypt. Kyra says one who dies by a varvoloka will become one. Keeping away from Pherides, Thea wanders around the island and glimpses the figure of a woman in white. Mary, now insane, steals Poseidon's spear from the sleeping Albrecht's desk and stabs Kyra. She hides in the woman's room as Thea comes to bed. Pherides later drags himself into the room and finds Kyra. Thinking Thea killed her, he attacks the girl but is stabbed by Mary, who goes outside, pursued by Davis and Albrecht. She runs to a wall and falls over it into the sea. The dying Pherides tells Albrecht he saw the varvoloka and he is told that the evil spirit has been destroyed. The next day, Davis and Thea leave together.

Variety reported, "*Isle of the Dead* is a slow conversation piece about plagues and vampires on an eerie Greek island.... Some good sets, acting and moody atmosphere give the yarn a better backing than it deserves." "It will take an audience of horror habitués to appreciate to the full the elements of witchcraft embodied in the film. There are numerous deaths under terrifying circumstances, guaranteed to convulse the kiddies," noted *Boxoffice*. *The New York Times* termed it "more horrible than horrific.... [P]oor Boris Karloff, who must be pretty tired of this sort of monkey business by now, stumbles through the picture with a vacant, tired stare." *The Film Daily* stated, "*Isle of the Dead* will send chills running up and down the spine of the person with sensitiveness of that portion of the anatomy. The shocker fans will be pleased to the depths, while those who have little taste for this sort of entertainment will find cause for amusement in the melodramatic hocus-pocus that is strictly a pipe dream." The British *Kinematograph Weekly* stated, "The picture is a vague as well as ugly essay in the supernatural, and the attempt to link its grisly title to Greek mythology only adds to the confusion. Boris Karloff has no idea whether he is coming or going as the general, and the same applies to the rest." The feature did not pass the British Censor until 1955. Rose London noted in *Zombie: The Living Dead* (1976), "[T]he atmosphere is stronger than the action. It is all mood and little moment. It was nearly the end of Lewton's career as a major master of horror films."

It's a Wonderful Life (1947; 130 minutes)

PRODUCER-DIRECTOR: Frank Capra. SCREENPLAY: Frances Goodrich, Albert Hackett & Frank Capra, from the story "The Greatest Gift" by Philip Van Doren Stern. ADDITIONAL SCENES: Jo Swerling. PHOTOGRAPHY: Joseph Walker & Joseph F. Biroc. EDITOR: William Hornbecks. MUSIC: Dimitri Tiomkin. ART DIRECTOR: Jack Okey. SOUND: Richard Van Hessen & Clem Portman. SET DECORATIONS: Emile Kuri. COSTUMES: Edward Stevenson. MAKEUP: Gordon Bau. SPECIAL PHOTOGRAPHIC EFFECTS: Russell A. Cully. ASSISTANT DIRECTOR: Arthur S. Black.

CAST: James Stewart (George Bailey), Donna Reed (Mary Hatch Bailey), Lionel Barrymore (Henry F. Potter), Thomas Mitchell (Uncle Billy Bailey), Henry Travers (Clarence Oddbody), Beulah Bondi (Mrs. Bailey), Frank Faylen (Ernie Bishop), Ward Bond (Officer Bert), Gloria Grahame (Violet Bick), H.B. Warner (Mr. Gower), Frank Albertson (Sam Wainwright), Todd Karns (Harry Bailey), Samuel S. Hinds (Peter "Pa" Bailey), Mary Treen (Tilly Bailey), Virginia Patton (Ruth Dakin Bailey), Charles Williams (Eustace Bailey), Sarah Edwards (Mrs. Hatch), William Edmunds (Martini), Lillian Randolph (Annie), Argentina Brunetti (Mrs. Martini), Bobbie Anderson (Little George Bailey), Ronnie Ralph (Little Sam Wainwright), Jean Gale (Little Mary Hatch), Jeanine Ann Roose (Little Violet Bick), Danny Mummert (Little Marty Hatch), Georgie Nokes (Little Harry Bailey), Sheldon Leonard (Bartender Nick), Frank Hagney (Potter's Servant), Ray Walker (Luggage Shop Owner Joe), Charles Lane (Lester Reineman), Edward Keane (Tom), Carol Coomes [Carol Combs] (Janie Bailey), Karolyn Grimes (Zuzu Bailey), Larry Simms (Pete Bailey), Jimmy Hawkins (Tommy Bailey), Carl "Alfalfa" Switzer (Freddie Othello), J. Farrell MacDonald (Tree Owner), Charles Halton (Bank Examiner Carter), Stanley Andrews (Mr. Welch), Marian Carr (Jane Wainwright), Alan Bridge (Sheriff), Ernie Adams (Ed), Harry V. Cheshire (Dr. Campbell), Harry Holman (Mr. Partridge), Tom Fadden (Tollhouse Keeper), Ellen Corby (Miss Davis), Harry Landon (Marty Hatch), Mark Roberts (Mickey), Charles C. Wilson (Charlie), Garry Owen (Bill Poster), Eddie Fetherston (Bank Teller Horace), Arthur Stuart Hall (Mr. Randall), Effie Laird (Mrs. Johnson), Dick Elliott (Neighbor), Frank Fenton, Jack Bailey (Violet's Boyfriends), Lane Chandler (Bar Customer), Adriana Caselotti (Singer), Meade "Lux" Lewis (Piano Player), Sam Ash, Sam Flint (Bankers), Edward Clark (Board Member), Tom Coleman, Mike Lally, Wilbur Mack, Philip Morris (Customers), Michael Chapin (Little George's Friend), Eddie Kane, Herbert Heywood (Depositors), Milton Kibbee (Photographer), Priscilla Montgomery (Student), Bert Moorhouse, Dick Gordon (Deputies), Lew Davis (Teacher), Helen Dickson, George Noisom (Dance Attendees), Frank O'Connor, Brooks Benedict (Military Men), Franklin Parker (Newsman), Cy Schindell (Bouncer), Almira Sessions (Secretary), Max Wagner (Cashier), Charles Sullivan (Bartender), Brick Sullivan, John Indrisano (Citizens), Moroni Olsen, Joseph Granby (Angels' Voices), Jimmy the Crow (Himself).

A heartwarming affirmation of the worth of the individual, *It's a Wonderful Life* has remained an audience favorite since it was first distributed by RKO Radio Pictures early in 1947. Based on a story that Philip Van Doren Stern originally placed in his 1943 Christmas cards, the film was the initial production of Liberty Films, founded by Samuel J. Briskin, Frank Capra, George Stevens and William Wyler. Made for slightly over $1.5 million, it marked the return to the big screen of producer-director Frank Capra and star James Stewart following World War II military service. It earned Capra the Golden Globe Award for Best Director and Academy Award nominations for Best Director, Best Actor (Stewart), Best Editor (William Hornbeck) and Best Sound Recording. While its fantasy sequence takes up only a short part of the feature near the end, it is well conceived, nicely orchestrating Angel Clarence's (Henry Travers) words "Each

Advertisement for *It's a Wonderful Life* (1947).

man's life touches so many other lives." Capra does a masterful job of bringing together all the elements with Stewart giving one of his best performances as George Bailey. He is matched by Donna Reed's underplayed work as the woman who loves him, while Lionel Barrymore basically repeats his annual radio role of Scrooge from "A Christmas Carol" in the role of the skinflint, grasping banker. Thomas Mitchell and Beulah Bondi are seen all too briefly. The picture is loaded with outstanding cameo performances, such as H.B. Warner as the druggist, Samuel S. Hinds as Stewart's father, Lillian Randolph as maid Annie, Charles Lane as a rent collector, J. Farrell Mac-Donald as a disgruntled property owner, Charles Halton as a bank examiner, Stanley Andrews as an angry husband, Dick Elliott as an irritated neighbor and Harry Holman as the high school principal.

On Christmas Eve 1945, two celestial voices (Moroni Olsen, Joseph Granby) hear prayers for George Bailey (Stewart) from the small town of Bedford Falls. Since George is scheduled to commit suicide at 10:45 p.m. they call in second class angel Clarence Oddbody (Travers) to save him. If he carries out the mission, Clarence is promised his wings. To make him familiar with George's situation, Clarence is shown his life, starting in 1919 when as a boy (Bobbie Anderson) George saves his younger brother Harry (Georgie Nokes) from drowning in a frozen lake. George loses hearing in one of his ears after catching a cold in the rescue. Once recovered, he returns to work at Mr. Gower's (Warner) drugstore and covers for his employer when he mistakenly gives a diphtheria patient poison pills. Gower rectifies the mistake after George does not deliver the medicine and promises never again to mention the error. When the town's richest man, miser Henry F. Potter (Barrymore), tries to take over the Bailey Building and Loan Association, which is run by George's father Peter Bailey (Hinds) and his heavy-drinking brother Billy (Mitchell), George comes to his father's defense as Potter insults him in an effort to destroy the family business. Nine years later, after having saved for a world trip he plans to take before entering college, George attends Harry's (Todd Karns) high school graduation and sees Mary Hatch (Reed), who has been in love with him since she was a little girl. During a Charleston dance contest, a rival (Carl "Alfalfa" Switzer) for Mary's affections opens the movable floor, causing George and Mary to fall into the swimming pool below. The rest of the dancers, including the school's principal (Holman), jump in too. George walks Mary home but before he can kiss her, Uncle Billy arrives saying Peter has suffered a stroke. When his father dies, George delays his world trip and does not attend college but instead takes over the family business in order to keep it out of Potter's hands. Four years pass and Harry graduates from college after having become a football star. George learns that Harry has married Ruth Dakin (Virginia Patton) and her father has offered him a job doing research in a glass factory. Realizing that Harry will not stay in town to run the Building and Loan Association and that his plans for getting away from Bedford Falls have again been thwarted, George is told by his mother that Mary is home from school. Instead of going to see her, he wanders around the town and runs into Violet Bick (Gloria Grahame), who has always liked him. When she spurns his plans for them to spend the night in the outdoors, he ends up at Mary's home. The disgruntled George tells her he will never get married, then realizes how much he loves her. On a rainy day they are married. Just as they are leaving town for an extended honeymoon, there is a run on the local bank and George has to use the money he saved for the honeymoon to save the family business. George and Mary spend their wedding night in a vacant hotel which she has always wanted to own, serenaded by their friends, cab driver Ernie Bishop (Frank Faylen) and policeman Bert (Ward Bond).

As time goes by, George and Mary have four children; she spends her spare time in fixing up the home and George begins Bailey Park, a housing development for people who cannot get loans from Potter's bank. When one of his rent collectors (Lane) warns Potter that George is encroaching on his business, Potter offers George $20,000 a year to manage his affairs. Although tempted, George turns down Potter and vows to never let him get full control of Bedford Falls. Although he did not fight in World War II, being 4-F because of his hearing loss, George is very proud that Harry is a hero, winning the Medal of Honor. On Christmas Eve, Uncle Billy plans to deposit $8,000 in Potter's bank, but Potter accidentally gets hold of the money. Violet comes to George for a loan since she plans to leave town and go to New York City. After searching everywhere but still unable to find the money, Uncle Billy tells George about losing it and George realizes he could be jailed for embezzlement of company funds. Going home, George takes his frustrations out on Mary and the children, then apologizes to them before leaving. He goes to Potter for a loan but is told that since his only collateral is an insurance policy, he is worth more dead than alive. Potter cajoles him to go to the riffraff he has helped for so long and promises to swear out a warrant for his arrest. Running his car into a tree, George goes to a bar. After getting into a fight, he plans to jump off a bridge but ends up helping Clarence, who has fallen into the icy waters. As they get warm in a tollhouse and talk with its keeper (Tom Fadden), George says he wishes he had never been born and Clarence, his guardian angel, complies. George and Clarence then got back to town but nobody there knows George and he finds it now called Pottersville, a vile place filled with dance halls, night clubs, bars, gambling and burlesque. He runs into Violet, a good time girl who does not recognize him. George visits his mother, an embittered woman who runs a boarding house, and she tells him Uncle Billy is in an insane asylum where he belongs. He finds Mary a lonely librarian and when he tries to talk to her she runs from him. Going back to the bridge, George says he wants to live again, Clarence grants his wish and Bert takes him home. There he is reunited with his children and Mary arrives saying his friends are contributing the money needed to cover his losses. As George stands with his family, surrounded by their friends, he hears a bell ring, meaning that Clarence has been given his wings.

Critical reaction to *It's a Wonderful Life* was somewhat mixed. *The New York Herald Tribune* said, "Has moments that are trying but they are easily forgotten in the fluency and realism of a forthright and deeply felt motion picture. Loaded with artistry and sincerity ... it is engrossing and universally pertinent." According to *The New York Post*, "Capra seems to have lost his touch. He is trying for the big meaningful sentiments and as often as not falling into embarrassing theatrics. His sense of comedy seems to have rusted during the years away from Hollywood.... A picture built along noble lines." *The New York World Telegram* stated, "Like many another Capra masterpiece, this is a humorous fantasy." Bosley Crowther in *The New York Times* called it a "quaint and engaging modern parable on virtue being its own reward." *Variety* reported, "Capra brought back to *Life* all his oldtime craft, delicate devotion to detail and character delineation as well as his sure-footed feeling for true dramatic impact, as well as his deft method of leavening humor into right spots at right times. He again proves he can fashion what ordinarily would be homilizing hokum into gleaming, engaging, entertainment for all brows—high, low or beetle." *The Film Daily* summed it up best by stating, "This is one of the great ones. A stirring, profound, intensely human story of exceptional merit."

Stewart and Reed repeated their roles in a March 10, 1947, *Lux Radio Theatre* broadcast of "It's a Wonderful Life" on CBS and Stewart did the part again on radio's *Hallmark Playhouse* on May 8, 1949, for the same network. The feature was colorized in 1988 and in 2002 George H.W. Bush, 41st president of the United States, did a narration of the film for its NBC-TV broadcasts. *It's a Wonderful Life* was reworked as the 1977 ABC-TV telefeature *It Happened One Christmas*, starring Marlo Thomas.

Jungle Headhunters (1951; 66 minutes; Color)

PRODUCER: Julian Lesser. ASSOCIATE PRODUCER: Lewis Cotlow. SCREENPLAY: Joseph Ansen & Larry Lansburgh. PHOTOGRAPHY: Jules Bucher, W. Baker, J. Welo & Bodo Wuth. EDITOR: Robert Leo. MUSIC DIRECTOR: Paul Sawtell. SOUND: Joel F. Moss. PRODUCTION SUPERVISOR: Larry Lansburgh.
CAST: Lewis Cotlow (Narrator).

In 1949 RKO Radio enjoyed one of its few financial successes of the year with the African documentary *Savage Splendor*, which dealt with the animals and plants of the Dark Continent as well as emphasizing the habits of several native tribes. It was a filmed report of the Armand Denis-Lewis Cotlow expedition. Two years later the studio tried to duplicate its box office success with a similar affair, this time about the Amazon Basin, in *Jungle Headhunters*, a Thalia Productions effort. Here Lewis Cotlow, who also narrated, leads a solo quest and, unlike the previous feature which had no horror elements, this outing addresses in detail the Jivaro tribe's practice of shrinking their enemies' heads. The latter sequence was staged specifically for the production although based on actual tribal practices.

Beginning off the Panama coast, an expedition lead by Cotlow (himself) calls upon the San Blas Indian tribe, noted for their colorful attire and coconut production. Arriving at the Port of Belem in Brazil, the expedition members go up the Amazon River by boat and see a variety of birds and other wildlife. They stop to visit the Bororos tribe and observe their fishing skills before taking canoes into Peru to see the Yagua tribe, with whom they hunt leopards using blowguns. Going to the Guano Islands near the Peruvian coast, the explorers observe guanyos and seals, and then return to the mainland to join the Colorados Indians in body painting. Then the expedition travels to the western part of the Andes Mountains in search of the Jivaro tribe, who are headhunters. Locating the Indians, Cotlow and his men observe the capture and beheading of an enemy tribesman and the steps taken to shrink his head, which the Jivaros consider a trophy. As the expedition ends, Cotlow concludes that the only way to survive in the Amazon Basin is through cruelty.

Boxoffice called *Jungle Headhunters* "a spellbinder," adding that the head-shrinking sequences were "in sufficiently good taste so as not to offend even the most squeamish, while other assets include some remarkably beautiful photography...." *The New York Times* dubbed it "a high-class Amazon travelogue" although feeling that Cotlow "has fallen short of the standard he set in his previous effort. This should not be construed to mean that he has failed to capture the highly interesting way of life the Brazilian rain forest imposes on man and beast." *Variety* declared the feature "an appealing adventure film," noting, "Bare-bosomed native girls, colorful costumes, extreme ruggedness of the mileage traveled by dugout, mule back and on foot, and the flora and fauna of the jungle are ably lensed under trying conditions and have been processed in Technicolor to show off the multitude of hues."

Killers from Space (1954; 71 minutes)

PRODUCER-DIRECTOR: W. Lee Wilder. ASSOCIATE PRODUCER: Fred M. Muller. SCREENPLAY: William Raynor. STORY: Myles Wilder. PHOTOGRAPHY: William H. Clothier. EDITOR: William Faris. MUSIC: Manuel Compinsky. MUSIC SUPERVISOR: Alec Compinsky. SOUND: George E.H. Hanson. MAKEUP: Harry Thomas. LIGHTING: Jim James. PRODUCTION SUPERVISOR: Mack V. Wright. OPTICAL EFFECTS: Consolidated Film Industries.
CAST: Peter Graves (Dr. Doug Martin), James Seay (Colonel Banks), Steve Pendleton (FBI Agent Briggs), Frank Gerstle (Dr. Kurt Kruger), John Merrick (Deneb Tala/The Leader), Barbara Bestar (Ellen Martin), Shep Menken (Major Clift), Jack Daly (Power House Guard), Ron Kennedy (Sergeant Powers), Ben Welden (Tar Baby 2 Pilot), Burt Wenland (Sergeant Bandero), Lester Dorr (Gas Station Attendant),

Robert Roark (Guard), Ruth Bennett (Miss Vincent), Mark Scott (Narrator), Roy Engel (Police Dispatcher), Coleman Francis (Power Plant Employee).

Producer-director W. Lee Wilder, older brother of Billy Wilder, made two genre features released by United Artists, *Phantom from Space* (1953) and *The Snow Creature* (1954). Sandwiched between them was the RKO film *Killers from Space*, issued early in 1954. Although the UA features are no gems, they are superior to *Killers from Space*, a tacky, talky, static production with silly-looking aliens and a plethora of grainy stock footage. It was star Peter Graves' second sci-fi outing, Graves having previously appeared in *Red Planet Mars* (1952). Made as *The Man Who Saved the Earth*, it was based on a story by Wilder's son Myles. It was filmed at Bronson Canyon in Griffith Park. The credits for *Killers from Space* are shown at the end of the feature. Scenes from the 1930 Fox production *Just Imagine* are briefly seen to illustrate a planet in the Astron Solar System, the home of the aliens in *Killers from Space*.

During an A-bomb test at Soledad Flats, Nevada, Dr. Doug Martin (Graves) is flying in an observation plane, the Tar Baby 2, when the pilot (Ben Welden) sees a large flashing light on the ground just after the detonation. Descending to get a better look at the object, the pilot loses control and the plane crashes. The pilot's body is found but there is no trace of Doug. Colonel Banks (James Seay), the chief of the military base, tells Doug's wife Ellen (Barbara Bestar) he has probably been killed but not long after he shows up in a dazed condition. Upon examination by Major Clift (Shep Menken), the base doctor, it is discovered Doug has a large scar on his chest, one he did not have before the crash. Clift is puzzled since it is obviously a healed surgical

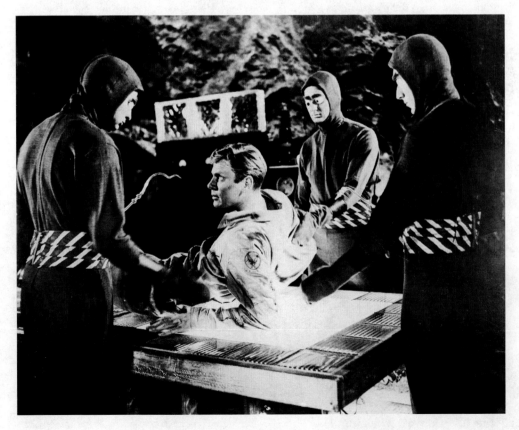

Peter Graves (center) in *Killers from Space* (1954).

scar. FBI Agent Briggs (Steve Pendleton) suspects that Doug may be an imposter and wants him to account for every minute following the crash. Information from Washington, D.C., proves Doug's identity and Ellen is allowed to take him home. Clift cautions her to make sure he keeps quiet and gets plenty of rest.

At 3 a.m. Doug is awakened by two large eyes at his bedroom window and calls the base to find out when the next atomic test will take place. Refused the information, he plans to go to the base until he is calmed by Ellen. The next day he reads that the blast took place the night before and drives to the base where Clift and Briggs tell him he cannot go back to work because he is not considered a good security risk. Doug stays in his office until evening and then opens a safe in the office of his project partner Dr. Kurt Kruger (Frank Gerstle) and examines top secret documents. Briggs questions Kruger about Doug and then goes to Doug's home where he interrogates Ellen before putting out an all points bulletin for Doug. Briggs finds Doug at the test site placing a paper under a rock. Doug knocks out the FBI agent and drives away. He crashes his car while trying to escape the police and wakes up at the base hospital yelling, "They're here, they're going to destroy us." Given a shot of sodium pentothal, Doug reveals to Banks, Briggs, Kruger and Clift that he woke up in a cavern after the plane crash, surrounded by three beings dressed in black with large eyes. He sees his heart placed back in his chest and after the procedure he meets Deneb Tala (John Merrick), the chief of the aliens. He is told he died in the crash and was brought back to life and that he is in a subterranean cavern. The alien says he is a scientist and that his race travels by an electron bridge. Through video images Doug is shown how the aliens, who originated in the Astron Solar System on the planet Astron Delta, had to conquer nearby planets when their sun began to die. They now surround the Earth, planning to take over the planet and destroy all humans. Since they accumulate energy from atomic bomb tests, Deneb Tala orders Doug to get the information they need as to the scheduling of the tests. Doug tries to escape but finds himself lost in a maze where he sees giant mutated insects and lizards. The alien tells him the creatures are being bred to depopulate the planet and then will be destroyed to fertilize it for his race when they take over. Realizing that Doug will not willingly help the aliens, Deneb Tala mesmerizes him and orders Doug to provide the atomic test dates. Back in the hospital, Doug knows Banks, Briggs and Clift do not believe him although Briggs and Kruger investigate the bomb site. Resisting the alien faces he sees, Doug begins working with a slide ruler and comes up with a way to destroy the aliens by cutting off their power source, which he believes is the local electric plant. He shows his findings to Kruger but when he realizes his partner will not help, Doug escapes from the hospital and heads to the electric plant, followed by Ellen, Briggs and Kruger. Finding the control room, Doug is able to turn off the power for ten seconds, causing a gigantic explosion that destroys the aliens.

Killers from Space got little respect from the critics. *Boxoffice* complained, "No success whatsoever met this obvious attempt to parlay some stock footage, a collection of pseudo-scientific props and touches of trick photography into a suspenseful space-opera that might capitalize on the current popularity of pictures of its category." *Variety* called it "a routine affair where more adroit handling might have upped it to a true chiller. Film's major premise is imaginative enough.... Simply hasn't been developed enough to matter." Donald C. Willis in *Horror and Science Fiction Films: A Checklist* (1972) declared, "Graves at his worst in silly film," while Phil Hardy in *Science Fiction* (1984) stated, "A cheaply made, cheap film." Welch Everman in *Cult Science Fiction Films* (1995) enthused, "This is what low-budget filmmaking is all about.... [It] is 30 percent footage from other sources—stock atomic bomb tests, military and police scenes, nature documentaries, even segments lifted from William Cameron Menzies' classic *Things to Come* of 1936. It also repeats its own footage endlessly—you'll love watching star Peter Graves run through the same

Lobby card for *Killers from Space* (1954).

cave again and again and again." In *The Encyclopedia of Science Fiction Movies* (2001), C.J. Henderson wrote, "This is a spectacularly bad movie.... Everything about this one is terrible. The sets are so underdressed that it's hard to tell when the characters are on the army base or in a private home. Every wall looks exactly the same.... [T]he music is melodramatic drivel pulled from piles of stock background music, and not too good stuff, either. Could there be anything funnier than second-rate animation used via monitor to show Graves the wonders of the alien's home world.... [T]here actually was a good story buried underneath all the bad direction, terrible effects, and exploitative producing."

King Kong (1933; 100 minutes)

PRODUCERS-DIRECTORS: Merian C. Cooper & Ernest B. Schoedsack. EXECUTIVE PRODUCER: David O. Selznick. SCREENPLAY: James Creelman & Ruth Rose, from an idea by Edgar Wallace & Merian C. Cooper. PHOTOGRAPHY: Eddie Linden, J.O. Taylor & Vernon L. Walker. EDITOR: Ted Cheesman. MUSIC: Max Steiner. SOUND: Earl A. Wolcott. SOUND EFFECTS: Murray Spivack. SETTINGS: Carroll Clark & Al Herman. COSTUMES: Walter Plunkett. CHIEF TECHNICIAN: Willis H. O'Brien. TECHNICAL STAFF: Marcel Delgado, E.B. Gibson, Orville Goldner & Fred Reese. ART TECHNICIANS: Byron L. Crabbe & Mario Larrinaga. PRODUCTION ASSISTANTS: Archie F. Marshek & Walter Daniels.

CAST: Fay Wray (Ann Darrow), Robert Armstrong (Carl Denham), Bruce Cabot (Jack Driscoll), Frank Reicher (Captain Englehorn), Sam Hardy (Charles Weston), Noble Johnson (Native Chief), Steve Clemento (Witch Doctor), James Flavin (Second Mate Briggs), Victor Wong (Charlie), Ethan Laidlaw (First Mate Adams), Paul Porcasi (Fruit Vendor), Reginald Barlow (Ship's Engineer), G. Raymond Nye (Police Captain), Roscoe Ates (Press Photographer), LeRoy Mason, Vera Lewis, Dorothy Gulliver, Earl

Dwire, Jim Thorpe, Florence Dudley, Larry Steers, Carlotta Monti, Gay Sheridan, Lillian Young (Theater Patrons), Harry Strang (Police Headquarters Officer), Dick Curtis, Roy Brent, Charlie Hall, George Magrill, Sam Levine, Sailor Vincent, Blackie Whiteford, Charles Sullivan, Duke Green, Buddy Mason (Crewmen), Roy Stewart, Syd Saylor, Lynton Brent, Eddie Boland, Harry Bowen, Jack Chapin, Frank O'Connor, Frank Mills, Charles O'Malley, Edward Stevens, Paddy O'Flynn, Ed Rochelle, Eddie Hart (Newsmen), Lee Phelps (Cameraman), Everett Brown, Madame Sul-Te-Wan, Etta McDaniel, Ruby Dandridge, Floyd Shackelford, Edgar "Blue" Washington, Ivory Williams, Nathan Curry (Natives), Merian C. Cooper, Russ Powell, Dusty Mitchell, Eric Wood (Pilots), Ernest B. Schoedsack (Plane Machine Gunner), Allen Pomeroy (Motorcycle Policeman), Gil Perkins, Harry Tenbrook (Sailors), Sandra Shaw (Woman Dropped from Hotel Window), Frank Fanning, Monte Vandergrift (Policemen), Pat Harmon, Lew Harvey (Gunmen), Larry McGrath, Harry Keaton, Mae Marrin, King Mojave (Ballyhooers), Joe Smith Marba (Train Motorman), Jack Pratt (Radio Announcer), Ivan Thomas (Conductor).

The apex of RKO's genre efforts, and one of the greatest horror films of all time, *King Kong* came to theaters in March 1933, after many months of filming. Metro-Goldwyn-Mayer offered to buy the feature from the studio for over $1 million, or a $400,000 profit for RKO, but the offer was declined. The film made a $1.1 million profit for RKO in its first release and greatly helped the studio to stay afloat financially in a year in which it lost nearly $4.4 million from 49 releases. *King Kong* would be reissued to healthy profits in 1938, 1942, 1946, 1952 and 1956. Each time RKO found itself in financial turmoil, which was often, it re-released the movie, garnering grosses sufficient to help keep it going.

Regarding the meticulous methods used in the film's production, *The International Photographer* (March 1933), noted, "The picture was actually 55 weeks in production with two to ten cameras on the set. The negative used amounted to 238,000 feet, although there are only 10,000 feet in the finished picture. Some astonishing camera tricks were employed which in many cases required weeks before the desired results were obtained. The old method of using 'matte' shots was almost entirely eliminated and various new methods in advance of anything done heretofore were introduced. In one sequence 65 electricians were at work and 350 lamps were throwing their powerful beams over the set." The article also stated that it took two weeks in New York at the Empire State Building to film the exciting finale.

Merian C. Cooper and Ernest B. Schoedsack co-produced and co-directed *King Kong*. Their association began in 1923 when they formed Cooper-Schoedsack Productions which made the documentaries *Grass* (1925) and *Chang* (1927). In 1931 RKO producer David O. Selznick assigned Cooper to complete a project called *Creation* with animated work by Willis O'Brien and Marcel Delgado. The idea of a giant gorilla soon became part of the mix with Edgar Wallace, who had signed a three-month contract with RKO, writing a script called *The Beast*, which he changed to *Kong*. It has been claimed that Wallace had nearly nothing to do with the creation of *King Kong* and that his name was associated with the film in order to take advantage of his massive popularity. In reality, the basic storyline of *King Kong* has its origins in the author's 1927 novel *The Hairy Arm,* which tells of a movie company working in rural England and fighting the machinations of an evil nobleman who uses a huge simian creature to carry out his orders. The final screenplay draft was by James Creelman and Ruth Rose, the wife of Ernest B. Schoedsack. The novelization of *King Kong* by Delos W. Lovelace has continuously been reprinted since it was first published in 1933.

The highlight of *King Kong* is its special effects which were created by O'Brien and his technical staff, Marcel Delgado, E.B. Gibson, Orville Goldner and Fred Reese. Not only did their stop motion photography beautifully create Kong but also the various other prehistoric denizens of Skull Island. Just as impressive are the island settings done by Carroll Clark and Al Herman, with the assistance of Thomas Little and Ray Moyer. Uncredited Clark was the film's production

Poster for *King Kong* (1933).

designer and he and Herman also served as its art directors. The photography of Eddie Linden, J.O. Taylor and Vernon L. Walker visually brought to life the production and Max Steiner's vibrant score gave it movement. *King Kong* is the fastest-moving 100 minutes in movie history.

For Fay Wray and Robert Armstrong, *King Kong* provided the roles that made them cinema immortals. Wray became the first "Scream Queen" in interpreting Ann Darrow, the luscious blonde desired by Kong in this reworking of the fairy tale "Beauty and the Beast." When Wray died in 2004, the lights of the Empire Statue Building were dimmed the next night in her memory.

The role of Carl Denham was the part of a lifetime for Robert Armstrong, who repeated it in *The Son of Kong* (q.v.), and enacted the character again, under another name, in *Mighty Joe Young* (q.v.) 16 years later. Wray and Armstrong also appeared in *The Most Dangerous Game* (q.v.) which was filmed by *King Kong*'s production team during the same period. Some sets were used in both features.

Theatrical agent Weston (Sam Hardy) arrives at the steamer *Venture,* docked in Gotham harbor, to see Carl Denham (Armstrong), a world-famous maker of documentary movies. Denham tells the ship's captain, Englehorn (Frank Reicher), that he wants to start on their voyage soon, before the monsoon season begins. When Weston informs Denham he will not provide an actress for him because of his recklessness, the moviemaker vows to find one himself and heads for downtown New York. There he sees a starving young woman, Ann Darrow (Wray), try to steal an apple from a fruit vendor (Paul Porcasi). Denham saves her from arrest and buys her dinner. He learns that Ann once worked as an extra in a Long Island film studio and since she is very attractive, he offers her a part in his new film. At first she demurs until he convinces her the proposition is strictly business. Jack Driscoll (Bruce Cabot), second in command on the ship, resents having a woman on board but after six weeks becomes attached to Ann as they voyage to the South Seas. Denham reveals to Englehorn and Jack their final destination, an unknown island due west of Sumatra. As Denham takes camera tests of Ann wearing a Beauty and the Beast costume, he orders her to scream as she envisions something very tall and frightening. Nearing their destination, the ship is enshrouded in thick fog and is forced to drop anchor. The next morning the skies clear and the crew sees the island, with a mountain in the shape of a skull. A huge wall separates a peninsula from the rest of the island. Denham, Ann, Englehorn, Jack and several crewmen row to the island where they see the natives engaging in an elaborate ceremony. Denham starts to film the event but the native chief (Noble Johnson) spies him and halts the ritual. Englehorn is able to converse with the chief, who tells him a young woman is being prepared to become the bride of Kong. Seeing blonde Ann, the chief wants to trade her for six of his women and give *her* to the deity. Refusing the offer, Denham and the others return to the ship but Denham plans to return the next day to see what is on the other side of the giant wall. That night natives board the *Venture* and abduct Ann. Charlie (Victor Wong), the ship's cook, sounds an alarm and Denham, Englehorn, Jack and a dozen men head to the island, carrying two boxes of gas bombs. Ann is taken by the natives and tied to an altar as a huge gong is rung, calling for Kong. A giant simian appears and carries off Ann but they are pursued by the men from the ship. Following Kong's trail, the men come upon a stegosaurus which they knock out with one of the bombs and kill with bullets. Finding that Kong has waded across a fog-shrouded lake, the men build a raft and go after him but are upset and thrown into the water by a gigantic brontosaurus. The beast chases the men as they get to shore, killing two of them. Running through the jungle, they are spotted by Kong, who has carried Ann across a ravine with a fallen log as a bridge. Kong shakes the crewmen off the log, sending them to their deaths in the ravine below. Jack manages to take shelter in a crevice. Kong plays a game of cat and mouse with Jack who slashes at the beast's finger with his knife. A huge allosaurus tries to get Ann; Kong fights with the thunder lizard, eventually breaking its jaws. After Kong carries Ann away, Jack follows the giant while Denham heads back toward the native village. Kong takes Ann to his cave lair where she is attacked by a giant snake which Kong kills after a ferocious fight. Kong toys with Ann, infatuated with his new possession. When a pteradodon tries to carry off Ann, Kong hears her screams and saves her, crushing the flying lizard. Jack manages to get to Ann and carries her to the edge of a cliff and they begin to climb down it on a long vine. Kong begins pulling up the vein and the two jump into the river below. Jack and Ann run through the jungle back to the wall where they

Lobby card for *King Kong* (1933) picturing Fay Wray, Robert Armstrong and Bruce Cabot.

are greeted by Denham and Englehorn. Denham still wants to go after Kong but is soon told the giant creature is approaching. The crewmen close and bolt the wall's huge doors and the natives join them in trying to reinforce them as Kong tries to retrieve Ann. He breaks through the doorway and ransacks the village, killing many natives. He follows the outsiders to the shore where Denham brings him down with a gas bomb. Denham then orders chains and other materials be brought from the ship so a raft can be made to take Kong back to civilization where he plans to display him for all the world to see.

Several months later, Kong, now called "The Eighth Wonder of the World," is heavily manacled and showcased on the stage of a Broadway theater. Denham tells the sellout audience about Ann and Jack's harrowing Skull Island adventure and how they will be married the next day. When photographers begin taking pictures of them, Kong thinks they are hurting Ann and breaks free. He runs rampant, destroying everything in his path, before finding Ann in a hotel room and again abducting her. After wrecking an elevated passenger train, he takes Ann to the highest locale in the city, the Empire State Building. Jack suggests to the police they use airplanes to shoot at Kong and he is attacked by four gunners. Although he destroys one of the planes, Kong is hit repeatedly by bullets. Kong caresses Ann for the last time and falls to his death in the street below. When a policeman tells Denham the planes got Kong, he replies that it was Beauty who killed the Beast.

The critics heaped nearly unanimous praise on *King Kong*. *The International Photographer* stated, "It is something really new and intriguing for the jaded appetite of the screen play fan. That overworked word 'colossal' is entirely applicable in this case. The story is fantastic.... Merian

C. Cooper and Ernest Schoedsack ... made this tremendous undertaking a reality. A bow is also due to technician Willis O'Brien for some of the fantastic effects achieved. The photography of the picture is one of the outstanding features of the season...." *Photoplay* opined, "It is too bad that 'colossal' and 'super-colossal' have been bandied about so freely—for here is a real hair-raiser to which those terms are appropriate.... [Y]ou'll get thrills such as the screen rarely affords." *The New Movie Magazine* called *King Kong* "the outstanding novelty of the year. Thrills to the nth degree ... but a swell show in the bargain." *Motion Picture* termed it "the mechanical marvel of the Technocratic age.... [It] beggars description. All that can be said is 'You will never know the extent of what the movies can do till you've seen this tale.'" *The Hollywood Reporter* declared, "It is a great piece of imagination, hatched in the brain of a showman for showmen, produced in grand style and good taste, and most capably acted and directed.... Fay Wray has never been more beautiful before on the screen, nor acted so well as she does in this production. Robert Armstrong, out of the villain class for the time being, is more than capable in the role of the director. Bruce Cabot, while not astonishing in his histrionic ability, does ably by the hero." *The New York American* wrote, "An amazing, madly imaginative, furiously fantastic film. *King Kong*, a truly colossal achievement, crashes to a unique height in the annals of motion picture entertainment. Probability, possibility are tossed aside and the screen given over to as wildly thrilling an adventure as has ever been conceived in fiction or in fact. Its sweep and speed are such that its implausibilities are forgotten." *The New York Herald-Tribune* termed it "an interesting and effective stunt, produced with considerable imagination," while *The New York Journal* felt it was "spectacular, utterly fantastic and satisfyingly implausible." *The New York Mirror* enthused, "*King Kong* is a unique picture, fantastic and exciting. It is mad, deranged and vastly entertaining. Don't miss it." A "spectacular bolt of celluloid" is how *The New York News* described the picture, adding, "You don't for one minute have the feeling that there's anything real about *King Kong*, but you're being constantly entertained while the picture's on view." *The New York World-Telegram* stated, "This *King Kong* is one of the very best of all the screen thrillers, done with all the cinema's slickest camera tricks...." According to *The New York Times*: "Through multiple exposures, processed 'shots' and a variety of angles of camera wizardry, the producers set forth an adequate story and furnish enough thrills for any devotee of such tales." *The New York Sun* dubbed it "a consistently chilling movie spectacle," adding, "[G]o to laugh at *King Kong* and you will find yourself really chilled by most of it." Less enthusiastic was *The New York Post*: "*King Kong* is not as effective as it should have been. Its fantasy element has moments of humor, but its thrills are weakened by their evident effort to be thrilling." *Picture Play Magazine* concurred, "Easily the most unusual and imaginative picture of many months, this nevertheless fails of its purpose. Entertaining, yes, but it does not inspire awe or terror nearly as much as laughter. Not ridicule, you understand, but pleased giggles. This is because the subject is too utterly fantastic for credibility." Donald F. Glut summed it up nicely when he wrote in *Classic Movie Monsters* (1978), "*King Kong* is not only one of the best fantasy pictures of all time but simply one of the greatest movies of any genre. The story is perfectly paced, the special effects superb. Only the acting and dialogue are dated by today's standards, but those supposed faults actually contribute to the picture's charm." Chris Steinbrunner and Burt Goldblatt concurred in *Cinema of the Fantastic* (1972): "*King Kong* was an instant smash and has remained so. Even television has not sapped its vigor; indeed, it has been one of the medium's greatest audience-getters. And rightly so; *Kong* is an authentic masterpiece and has all the appeal and reach one would expect from a great work of art."

Thanks to *King Kong*'s immediate and overwhelming box office success, RKO rushed the sequel *The Son of Kong* (q.v.) into production and issued it at the end of 1933. Over the years there have been many imitation–Kong movies plus two box office bust remakes, in 1976 and 2005.

The Last Days of Pompeii (1935; 96 minutes)

PRODUCER: Merian C. Cooper. DIRECTOR: Ernest B. Schoedsack. SCREENPLAY: Ruth Rose. ADAP-
TATION COLLABORATOR: Boris Ingster. STORY: James Creelman & Melville Baker. PHOTOGRAPHY: J.
Roy Hunt. EDITOR: Archie F. Marshek. MUSIC: Roy Webb. MUSIC RECORDIST: P.J. Faulkner, Jr. ART
DIRECTORS: Van Nest Polglase & Al Herman. SOUND: Clem Portman. SOUND EFFECTS: Walter Elliott.
SET DECORATIONS: Thomas Little. COSTUMES: Aline Bernstein. PHOTOGRAPHIC EFFECTS: Vernon L.
Walker. CHIEF TECHNICIAN: Willis O'Brien. PRODUCTION ASSOCIATE: John Speaks. ART TECHNICIAN:
Byron Crabbe. SPECIAL EFFECTS: Harry Redmond, Sr. PHOTOGRAPHIC TECHNICIAN: Eddie Linden.
CAST: Preston Foster (Marcus), Basil Rathbone (Pontius Pilate), Alan Hale (Burbix), John Wood (Flav-
ius), Louis Calhern (Prefect), David Holt (Young Flavius), Dorothy Wilson (Clodia), Wyrley Birch
(Leaster), Gloria Shea (Julia), Frank Conroy (Galus Tenno), William V. Mong (Cleon), Murray Kinnell
(Simon), Henry Kolker (Warder), Edward Van Sloan (Calvus), Zeffie Tilbury (Wise Woman), John David-
son (Phoebus), Ward Bond (Murmex of Carthage), Jason Robards (Tax Collector), Helen Freeman
(Martha), Edwin Maxwell (The Augur), Margaret McWade (Calvus' Wife), Winston Hibler (Marcellus),
Marc Loebell (Lucius), Curley Dresden (Gladiator Cato), Maurice Black (Gladiators' Attendant), Theodore
Lorch (Slaver), Ole M. Ness (Drusus), Thomas E. Jackson (The Lanista), Jack Mulhall (Games Spectator),
John T. Murray (Pontius Pilate's Servant), Bruce King (Scythian Prisoner), Reginald Barlow (Slave Market
Janitor), Michael Mark (Nobleman), Jim Thorpe (Coin Thrower), Tom Brower (Runaway Slave).

Since 1900 there have been more than a half-dozen screen adaptations of Lord Edward
George Bulwer-Lytton's novel *The Last Days of Pompeii,* published in 1843. The 1935 Radio Pictures release *The Last Days of Pompeii* carries a disclaimer saying it was not based on the novel
other than its description of the ancient Italian city that was buried by Mt. Vesuvius' eruption
in 79 AD. The feature was producer Merian C. Cooper and director Ernest B. Schoedsack's
intended spectacular follow-up to their box office blockbuster *King Kong* but despite posh production values and top-notch special effects, the film failed to recoup its $800,000-plus budget;
not until RKO re-issued it on a double bill with *Kong* in 1938 did it break even. It also saw re-
release theatrically by RKO in 1946 and 1949. Released in the fall of 1935, the feature is not
especially interesting plot-wise but its climactic destruction scenes are outstanding, thanks to
the work of chief technician Willis O'Brien and his crew, with especially fine visual effects miniatures by the uncredited Marcel Delgado. While the acting is more than acceptable, the only real
standout performance is from Basil Rathbone in a well-etched portrayal of Pontius Pilate. The
figure of Jesus Christ is presented twice in the feature, first unseen as he heals protagonist Marcus'
(Preston Foster) adopted son Flavius (David Holt), and then at the finale as a nebulous figure
accepting Marcus into Heaven. For horror fans, only the aftermath of Vesuvius' eruption gives
cause for much interest but as noted these scenes are the highlight of an otherwise disappointing
effort from the Cooper-Schoedsack team. Schoedsack's wife, Ruth Rose, did the screenplay in
collaboration with Boris Ingster. James Creelman, who co-adapted *King Kong* with Rose, was
given story credit with Melville Baker.

In ancient Pompeii, blacksmith Marcus (Foster) fixes the chain on a slave intended for the
gladiators' arena for slave dealer Cleon (William V. Mong). Nobleman Galus Tanno (Frank Conroy) notices Marcus and suggests he would make a successful gladiator. Marcus informs him he
is a man of peace who is content with his wife Julia (Gloria Shea) and their baby son. Galus gives
Marcus a silver piece and he takes his family to the market to spend it. Julia and the baby are run
down by a chariot. Marcus' neighbor Clavus (Edward Van Sloan) tells him the doctor will not
come because he has spent all his money trying to save his wife; the tax collector (Jason Robards)
threatens to evict him. To get the needed funds, Marcus goes to the arena and defeats his opponent, whom he is then forced to kill. Returning home, Marcus learns that both his wife and son
are dead and he vows never again to be poor. He soon becomes the star gladiator in the Pompeii

Poster for *The Last Days of Pompeii* (1935).

arena. After killing one opponent he adopts the man's orphan son, Flavius (Holt). He buys Leaster (Wyrley Birch), a slave Greek scholar, to tutor Flavius and soon loses his will to kill and devotes himself to caring for the boy. After being defeated by Murmex of Carthage (Ward Bond) in battle, Marcus sustains a serious injury that ends his gladiator career. Although he despises Cleon, Marcus goes to work for him in the slave trade. He meets an old woman (Zeffie Tilbury) who foresees the future and she tells Marcus to take Flavius to meet a great man. Thinking she means the governor of Judea, Pontius Pilate (Rathbone), Marcus and Flavius travel there and in Jerusalem they are presented to Pilate. Marcus is offered a chance to lead an expedition of prisoners against Pilate's enemies the Amenites and share whatever treasure he can capture. Agreeing, Marcus is assisted by Burbix (Alan Hale), who soon becomes his trusted friend. They route the Amenites and return laden with wealth. Upon his return to Jerusalem, Marcus learns from Leaster that Flavius is near death after being thrown from his horse; the slave suggests that Marcus take Flavius to a man known as "Master and Lord." When he does so, the boy is healed. For two days Marcus waits for Pilate, who is conducting a trial in which he agrees to crucify a man he believes innocent. Pilate tells Marcus to leave the city, fearing an unruly mob may steal his treasure. As he is departing, Marcus is met by Simon (Murray Kinnell), who begs him to help the condemned man who is about to be crucified. Marcus learns that the man is the one who healed Flavius but, not wanting to lose his gold, he turns his back on Simon and flees the city with his adopted son and Burbix. Returning to Pompeii, Marcus becomes the richest man in the city and the head of its arena. Now grown to manhood, Flavius (John Wood) opposes Marcus' use of slaves in the arena and plots to lead a group of them to freedom in Britain. He loves slave girl Clodia (Dorothy Wilson) and is haunted by the memory of the man who healed him although Marcus says the event is only a dream. The city's prefect (Louis Calhern) informs Marcus that someone is helping slaves to escape as Pilate arrives to see Marcus on his way to Rome. Pilate has agreed to take Flavius with him to Rome, where his fortune will be made, but Flavius refuses to go. Pilate confirms to Flavius that his memories of the healer are factual. The prefect's soldiers later capture the runaway slaves and bring them to Pompeii to take part in the latest games. Flavius is one the prisoners; Marcus is informed of this by Leaster. Marcus tries to free Flavius but the prefect orders the slaves sent to the arena. When the prefect refuses to stop the games, Marcus goes to the dungeon and orders the gatekeeper (Henry Kolker) to free his adopted son. The gatekeeper declines. As the battle between the slaves and the gladiators begins, Mt. Vesuvius erupts and the arena collapses. An injured Flavius frees Clodia and other women slaves while Pompeii burns. Marcus helps the warder's son, who has been injured, and tells Burix to leave behind his wealth as he aids the wounded in escaping to his wharf. Holding the prefect and his men at bay, Marcus orders his boat, which carries Flavius and Clodia, to sail away from the dying city. Marcus is killed by one of the soldiers. As Pompeii lies totally destroyed, Marcus sees a bright light and is blessed by the Master.

Harrison's Reports called *The Last Days of Pompeii* "a great spectacle with considerable drama. From excellent to very good." Andre Sennwald in *The New York Times* declared it "a shade too long for complete comfort," adding, "Although it is persuasively staged ... the work is rather more absorbing in its straightforward melodrama than in the later phases when the defiant gladiator is getting religion." *Boxoffice* enthused, "Magnificent production that will undoubtedly go down in the motion picture industry as an artistic achievement." *Variety* said, "As a document of the times this production is just routine. It's as a melodrama against the background of harsh laws and customs and the premonition of a town doomed to extinction that the picture stands up as film fare."

The Last Days of Pompeii was novelized, with stills from the film, in the November 1935 issue of *Movie Action* magazine. As might be expected, that periodical gave it a rave review: "A spectacle beyond your wildest dreams! A gripping, chilling masterpiece!" Drawings from archaeological remains were used to recreate Pompeii, including the Temple of Jupiter which occupied 30,000 square feet on three RKO-Pathé sound stages. The gladiators' arena filled one acre of ground with thousands of extras employed. The armor worn by Preston Foster weighed 70 pounds and his helmet an additional nine pounds. During the three months of production on the feature, Foster received multiple injuries.

As noted, there are several screen versions of Bulwer-Lytton's novel. The first was in 1900, an 80-foot British adaptation, and in 1908 it was done in Italy as *Gli Ultimi Giorni di Pompei* (The Last Days of Pompeii). Three years later, two more Italian versions appeared and one of them, a nine-reel feature directed by Mario Caserini, is extant. In 1948 Micheline Presle, George Marchal and Marcel Harrand starred in the French *Les Derniers Jours de Pompei* (The Last Days of Pompeii). Steve Reeves, Christine Kaufmann and Fernando Rey starred in the 1959 Italian feature *Gi Ultimi di Pompei* (The Last Days of Pompeii), directed by Marion Bonnard and co-scripted by future Spaghetti Western helmsmen Sergio Leone, Duccio Tessari and Sergio Corbucci. United Artists released it in the U.S. in 1960.

The Leopard Man (1943; 66 minutes)

PRODUCER: Val Lewton. DIRECTOR: Jacques Tourneur. SCREENPLAY: Ardel Wray, from the novel *The Black Alibi* by Cornell Woolrich. ADDITIONAL DIALOGUE: Edward Dein. PHOTOGRAPHY: Robert de Grasse. EDITOR: Mark Robson. MUSIC: Roy Webb. MUSIC DIRECTOR: C. Bakaleinikoff. ART DIRECTORS: Albert S. D'Agostino & Walter E. Keller. SOUND: J.C. Grubb. SET DECORATIONS: Darrell Silvera & Al Fields. ASSISTANT DIRECTOR: William Dorfman.

CAST: Dennis O'Keefe (Jerry Manning), Margo (Clo-Clo aka Gabriella), Jean Brooks (Kiki Walker), Isabel Jewell (Maria), James Best (Dr. Galbraith), Margaret Landry (Teresa Delgado), Abner Biberman (Charlie How-Come), Tula Parma (Consuelo Contreras), Ben Bard (Chief Roblos), Ariel Heath (Eloise), Richard Martin (Raoul Belmonte), Brandon Hurst (Cemetery Caretaker), William Halligan (Mr. Brunton), Ottola Nesmith (Senora Contreras), Robert Anderson (Dwight Brunton), Jacqueline deWit (Helene Brunton), Fely Franquelli (Rosita), Elias Gamboa (Senor Delgado), Kate Lawson (Senora Delgado), Robert Spindola (Pedro Delgado), Sidney D'Albrook, Jack Chefe, John Eberts, Rene Pedrini (Waiters), David Cota (Boy Singer), Jacques Lory (Phillippe), Marguerita Sylva (Marta), Belle Mitchell (Senora Calderon), Charlie Lung (Grocer Manuel), John Dilson (Coroner), Mary MacLaren (Nun), Tom Orosco (Window Cleaner), Joe Dominguez, Bob O'Connor, Ed Agresti (Policemen), George Sherwood (Police Lieutenant), Betty Roadman (Clo-Clo's Mother), Rosa Rita Varella (Clo-Clo's Little Sister), John Piffle (Flower Vendor), Rosita Delva, Jose Portugal (Lovers), Manuel Paris (Smoker), Juan Ortiz (Plainclothes Policeman), John Tetterner (Minister), Russell Wade (Gringo in Car), Dora Leyva, Colin Kenny, Robert Karnes (Club Patrons), William H. O'Brien (Bartender), Rose Higgins (Weaver), Dynamite (Leopard).

The Leopard Man was the third and final film Jacques Tourneur directed for producer Val Lewton; it is also the weakest. Preceded by *Cat People* (1942) and *I Walked with a Zombie* (1943) [qq.v.], it failed to properly exude a fear of the unknown which made the first two features so rewarding. Outside of a rather posh nightclub set and an interesting museum, *The Leopard Man* has a tatty look about it, lacking the visual polish associated with the RKO product. In fact, the feature has more of the aura of a Monogram production than one from RKO despite exterior filming in Santa Fe, New Mexico. Even the title is somewhat of a misnomer. The cat in the proceedings is actually the black leopard who appeared in *Cat People*; also, noting the killer's gender eliminates several female suspects. In an effort to boast its box office appeal, RKO tried to borrow Lon Chaney, Jr., from Universal for the part played by Dennis O'Keefe, and Rita Corday was originally cast in the role eventually given to Jean Brooks.

Despite its somewhat worn look and overall lack of chills, *The Leopard Man* is not without its moments. Particularly memorable are the scenes with young Teresa (Margaret Landry) being stalked by the leopard from an arroyo to her house, with its attack on her only being heard as her mother (Kate Lawson) and younger brother (Robert Spindola) try in vain to unlock the door of the family home to let her in. Even spookier are the scenes in the graveyard where Consuelo (Tula Parma) tries to find a way out after being locked in when her lover (Richard Martin) failed to keep a date with her. The murder of dancer Clo-Clo (Margo) is not nearly as suspenseful. The killer, a former zoology professor now running a desert community museum, is nicely played by James Bell, but the character's underlying motivations are hazy at best, no doubt a stricture of then prevailing industry censorship. The feature was based on Cornell Woolrich's 1942 novel *The Black Alibi*. RKO reissued the chiller theatrically in 1952 and 1957.

Upon the insistence of her publicity agent Jerry Manning (O'Keefe), dancer Kiki Walker (Brooks) enters a New Mexico night spot leading a black leopard on a leash, in order to rattle her local competition, castanet dancer Clo-Clo (Margo). To get even, Clo-Clo lunges at the cat with her castanets, causing it to break away from Kiki and run from the club. As Clo-Clo walks home after the performance, she hears Senora Delgado (Kate Lawson) tell her young daughter Teresa (Landry) to get corn meal from a nearby store for her father's (Elias Gamboa) dinner. When the child says she is afraid, her mother locks her out of the house and tells her not to return without the corn meal. Finding the store closed, Teresa goes to another store where the owner (Charlie Lung) gives her the corn meal on credit. On the way back Teresa is frightened by the big cat and runs screaming to her house and begs to be let in. The lock on the door jams as Teresa's mother hears her screams and sees blood flowing into the room from under the door. The next day the coroner (John Dilson) declares that Teresa died accidentally as Kiki gives money to the Delgado family to help with the funeral. Attending the inquest is Dr. Galbraith (Bell), the curator of a local museum displaying Indian arts and crafts. He tells the guilt-ridden Jerry that the girl's death was not his fault. Police Chief Roblos (Ben Bard) recruits a posse to search for the big cat and Jerry at first refuses to join but later goes along, as does Dr. Galbraith. At the club that evening, fortune teller Maria (Isabel Jewell) does a reading for Clo-Clo and says she will receive money from a rich man but is disturbed by turning up a death card. The following day Clo-Clo tries to get a free flower from a vendor (John Piffle) and receives one from Rosita (Fely Franquelli), a maid in the wealthy Contreras household. She is buying flowers for the birthday of Consuelo (Tula Parma), the daughter of Senora Contreras (Ottola Nesmith). Consuelo gets a message from her boyfriend, Raoul Belmonte (Richard Martin), to meet him at the local cemetery. Although apprehensive, Consuelo's mother lets her keep the rendezvous. The young man does not appear and, forgetting the time, Consuelo finds she has been locked in the graveyard by its caretaker (Brandon Hurst). Frightened by the night sounds and almost falling into a newly dug grave, Consuelo manages to get the attention of a man outside the cemetery walls who promises to go for help. Her badly clawed body is later found and suspicion falls on the leopard but Jerry has doubts. He consults the owner of the cat, Charlie How-Come (Abner Biberman), who says the animal is not dangerous and is probably hiding in the desert under some brush starving to death. Since both Dr. Galbraith and Roblos think the leopard is the killer, Jerry goes with Charlie to the museum to talk with the curator, who suggests to Charlie that he may have committed the crimes while drunk. Thinking himself guilty, Charlie asks Roblos to put him in jail and the lawman complies. That evening Clo-Clo meets a wealthy older man (William Halligan) at the club and he gives her one hundred dollars, fulfilling part of Maria's prophecy. Clo-Clo consults Maria, who says she lied about the money although she again turns up a card of death. When she gets home, Clo-Clo cannot find the money and goes outside to look for it, rejecting

Advertisement for *The Leopard Man* (1943).

the attentions of a gringo (Russell Wade) driving a new convertible. Sensing danger, Clo-Clo attempts to run but is attacked and fatally mauled. Roblos announces he is sending for state hunters and lets Charlie out of jail. Jerry questions Dr. Galbraith as to what kind of man would kill in such a fashion and is told there is no specific answer. Jerry and Kiki plan to return to Chicago but find they are broke, both having given their money to Clo-Clo's family and the Delgados. They decide to stay and track down the killer. Charlie informs Jerry he found his panther dead by an arroyo. Jerry tells Roblos he saw Dr. Galbraith in that area but the lawman refuses to question him. Jerry then goes to Raoul and talks him into catching Consuelo's murderer, informing him it was a man and not an animal. That night the people of the town gather for an annual religious procession. Eloise (Ariel Heath), the club's cigarette girl, asks Dr. Galbraith the origins of the ceremony and he tells her it is a reminder of how, centuries ago, the village of peaceful Indians was wiped out by Spanish Conquistadors. As the ceremony begins, Dr. Galbraith returns to the museum to work but is interrupted by Kiki, who says she wants to watch the procession from there. She urges him to turn off the lights and when he does, she drops a set of castanets. Dr. Galbraith lunges at Kiki but is frightened away by Jerry and Raoul and joins the procession. Jerry and Raoul manage to take Dr. Galbraith aside and he confesses to killing both Consuelo and Clo-Clo, having become tormented by the sight of Teresa's mangled body. He says he did not want to kill them but had to. Raoul shoots and kills Dr. Galbraith. Later Jerry and Kiki confirm they are in love.

Boxoffice thought *The Leopard Man* only "average supporting fare" while Bosley Crowther in *The New York Times* claimed, "The most horrifying thing about it is that it actually gets on a screen.... [It] is nothing but a feeble and obvious attempt to frighten and shock the audience with a few exercises in mayhem." *Photoplay* was concise: "We weren't scared." *Variety* was a bit kinder, saying the feature carried a "regulation formula for generating audience suspense, and succeeding partially in attaining that premise." Still the reviewer complained, "Story and script both lack the clear-cut and direct line treatment accorded *Cat People* and follows too many confusing paths to make it more than passable fare for the general audiences." *The Film Daily* stated, "Lovers of melodrama should take *The Leopard Man* very much to their hearts. The film has been well put together, its story being told with powerful suspense that is sustained effectively nearly all the way. The film breaks down at the end when it fails to give a satisfactory explanation of the reasons that drove the villain to murder.... The film gains much from its atmospheric treatment." In his essay "The American B Film: A Fond Appreciation" in *Focus on Film* (Nov.–Dec. 1970), Don Miller wrote that *The Leopard Man* is "in many ways the most impressive of this unique producer's [Lewton] RKO gems.... There hasn't been another film within memory, B or otherwise, where the sound track has been used as intelligently, or as effectively.... After many viewings, *The Leopard Man* maintains its original impression of high artistry on a low budget, as did all Lewton's RKO films."

Lord Edgware Dies (1934; 82 minutes)

PRODUCER: Julius Hagen. DIRECTOR: Henry Edwards. SCREENPLAY: H. Fowler Mear, from the novel by Agatha Christie. PHOTOGRAPHY: Sydney Blythe. EDITOR: Lister Laurence. ART DIRECTOR: James A. Carter. SOUND: Carlisle Mounteney. COSTUMES: Louis Brooks.

CAST: Austin Trevor (Hercule Poirot), Jane Carr (Lady Jane Edgware), Richard Cooper (Captain Hastings), John Turnbull (Inspector Japp), Michael Shepley (Captain Roland Marsh), Leslie Perrins (Bryan Martin), C.V. France (Lord Edgware), Esme Percy (Duke of Merton), Kynaston Reeves, Ellen Pollock, Brenda Harvey, Quinton McPherson, Phyllis Morris.

Based on Agatha Christie's 1933 novel *Thirteen at Dinner, Lord Edgware Dies* was the third and final Hercule Poirot feature made by producer Julius Hagen in England. It was preceded by *Alibi* and *Black Coffee*, both done by Twickenham Films and released in 1931. In all three outings, the Belgian detective was portrayed by Austin Trevor. Richard Cooper was Poirot's associate Captain Hastings in *Black Coffee* and *Lord Edgware Dies*. The latter production was distributed in Great Britain by Radio Pictures but got no U.S. release. While still extant, *Lord Edgware Dies* is rarely screened; when it *is*, the feature usually riles Christie purists in that Austin does not look or sound like the Poirot of Dame Agatha's novels and stories. One should remember, however, that Hollywood was just as guilty in its presentation of fictional sleuths, i.e., Warner Bros.' Perry Mason productions.

Detective Hercule Poirot (Trevor) and his friend Captain Hastings (Cooper) are invited to the country estate of Lord Edgware (C.V. France) and his beautiful American actress wife, Jane (Jane Carr). She wants Poirot to help her get a divorce from her older, wealthy husband so she can marry the Duke of Merton (Esme Percy), who is richer. Consulting with Edgware, Poirot finds out that he plans to agree to the divorce but the next day he is murdered. Since Lady Edgware was seen entering the study where her husband was killed, she is arrested by Inspector Japp (John Turnbull). Poirot sets out to prove her innocence. He becomes involved in a convoluted brew of dual identities and look-alikes before finally trapping the killer.

Scott Palmer reported in *The Films of Agatha Christie* (1993) that "Trevor again made an interesting, if not ideal, Poirot; Richard Cooper was a competent Hastings, and the excellent John Turnbull gave a good performance as Inspector Japp...." In *British Sound Films: The Studio Years 1928–1959* (1984), David Quinlan called *Lord Edgware Dies* a "workmanlike if wordy whodunit."

The Christie novel was filmed a second time by CBS-TV in 1985 as *Thirteen at Dinner* starring Peter Ustinov as Poirot with Jonathan Cecil as Hastings and David Suchet as Inspector Japp. Suchet was the perfect Poirot in the London Weekend Television series *Agatha Christie's Poirot*, in which he portrayed the Belgian sleuth in more than 40 episodes beginning in 1989. They were shown in the U.S. on PBS. Later he resumed the role in a third version of Agatha Christie's work, the 1999 Carnival Films production *Lord Edgware Dies*, a small-screen feature broadcast by A&E Television.

The Lost Patrol (1934; 73 minutes)

Executive Producer: Merian C. Cooper. Associate Producer: Cliff Reid. Director: John Ford. Screenplay: Dudley Nichols, from the story "Patrol" by Philip MacDonald. Adaptation: Garrett Fort. Photography: Harold Wenstrom. Editor: Paul Weatherwax. Music: Max Steiner. Art Directors: Van Nest Polglase & Sidney Ullman. Sound: Philip J. Faulkner & Clem Portman. Music Recording: Murray Spivack.

Cast: Victor McLaglen (The Sergeant), Boris Karloff (Sanders), Wallace Ford (Morelli), Reginald Denny (George Brown), J.M. Kerrigan (Quincannon), Billy Bevan (Hale), Alan Hale (Matlow Cook), Brandon Hurst (Corporal Bell), Douglas Walton (Pearson), Sammy Stein (Abelson), Howard Wilson (Aviator), Paul Hanson (Jock MacKay), Neville Clark (Lieutenant Hawkins), Frank Baker (Rescue Patrol Colonel/Arab), Francis Ford, Abdullah Abbas (Arabs).

In regards to horror, RKO is probably best known for its Val Lewton productions in the 1940s which emphasized fear of the unknown. Almost a decade before those films, however, the studio made *The Lost Patrol*, which is not a horror film although its main theme was fear of the unseen. In this case, members of a British patrol, trapped in a desert oasis, are being picked off one by one by an enemy which only makes itself known by deadly sniper fire. As a result, each of the survivors slowly descends into madness, except for the character portrayed by Boris Karloff, a religious fanatic already in the throes of insanity. Filmed in the desert near Yuma, Arizona, *The Lost Patrol* was made under difficult conditions: Temperatures neared the 130-degree mark during the day. As a result, numerous scenes were shot silent with sound added during the editing process. Its small cast, all male, provide well-etched performances, particularly Victor McLaglen as patrol leader Sergeant, Karloff as the mad Sanders, Wallace Ford as ex-showman Morelli and J.M. Kerrigan as veteran soldier Quincannon. Harold Wenstrom's desert photography is especially appealing and Max Steiner's music score, which was nominated for an Academy Award, greatly helps in keeping up the feature's pace. The film proved to be a modest moneymaker for RKO and set the stage for director John Ford and McLaglen re-teaming in *The Informer* (1935) which netted McLaglen an Oscar for Best Actor.

The source story by Philip MacDonald was filmed as a silent in 1929 by British International Films and issued in the United Kingdom by Fox and in the U.S. by Pro Patria. In that production, Victor McLaglen's younger brother Cyril McLaglen played the role of sergeant. In 1939 RKO re-filmed it as a western, *Bad Lands* (q.v.); Douglas Walton appeared in both RKO features but in different roles. *The Lost Patrol* was re-issued theatrically by RKO in 1949 and 1954, the latter issuance an edited version.

During the Arab insurrection in Mesopotamia in 1917, a British patrol finds itself stranded in the desert when its commissioned officer is killed by a sniper. The sergeant (McLaglen) assumes command and one of the men, Sanders (Karloff), objects when only a brief service is performed at the fallen man's burial. The sergeant orders the men to keep marching and soon they come across an oasis with a deserted mosque. The sergeant tells soldier Quincannon (Kerrigan) that they must depend on their horses to get back to the brigade. The patrol spends the night at the oasis and in order to impart courage to a raw recruit, Pearson (Walton), the sergeant gives him the responsibility of guard duty. That night a strong wind develops and the next morning Pearson is found shot and the horses missing. Another soldier, Corporal Bell (Brandon Hurst), has been badly wounded. The men argue about the loss of the horses and Sanders becomes upset when George Brown (Reginald Denny) tells about his amorous adventures with pretty maidens in Malaya. The sergeant informs the patrolmen they must stay in the oasis and wait for the brigade. Hale (Billy Bevan), who regales the men with stories about his young wife, climbs to the top of a palm tree to observe the terrain and is shot down. The sergeant then has the men draw to see who will make a run for help. MacKay (Paul Hanson) is chosen and he takes Matlow Cook (Alan Hale) along with him. They leave when the moon is down. The next day Abelson (Sammy Stein), affected by the intense heat, walks toward a mirage and is shot. Morelli (Ford) brings him back but, wanting to take part in the fight, the injured Bell goes for his gun and is killed. That evening Morelli sees something moving and it turns out to be two horses carrying the mutilated bodies of MacKay and Cook. Quincannon goes mad, runs into the sand shooting at the enemy and is killed. Sanders tells Morelli to repent his sins and that he is going to save him. When Morelli informs the sergeant he is going to shut up Sanders for good, the religious fanatic tells the sergeant that Brown has left to avenge the others. As they watch the desert, Morelli says he is a "Jonas" who brings bad luck to everyone he meets. He tells the sergeant about loving a girl who was his partner in a high wire act and how after a major success a rope broke and she was killed. The sergeant says his wife died when their son was born and all he lives for is the good of the boy. When a small plane lands near the oasis, the sergeant and Morelli try to warn the pilot (Howard Wilson) away but he pays no attention and is shot by a sniper. Sanders accuses the sergeant of killing the pilot and is tied up by Morelli. The sergeant and Morelli run to the plane and gets its gun and then set the plane on fire, hoping the light of the blaze will attract another patrol. Sanders breaks

Lobby card for *The Lost Patrol* (1934) insert picturing Billy Bevan and Boris Karloff.

free, carries a cross into the sand dunes and is shot and killed. Morelli tries to stop him and he too is shot. The sergeant buries them both and prepares to fight his unseen enemy. Five Arabs invade the oasis and he shoots them with the plane's gun. The patrol arrives to rescue the now deranged sergeant.

The New York News commented, "The realism of *The Lost Patrol* makes it the most effective horror film I've ever seen. There is nothing artificial about it. It is easy to believe the strange adventures pictured here might have happened. The picture is masterfully directed by John Ford." *Harrison's Reports* stated that *The Lost Patrol* did "Excellent to Fair" at the box office, adding, "It is an excellent production, but its drawing powers seem to be different in different localities." Mordaunt Hall in *The New York Times* felt the picture "is highly effective from a photographic standpoint, but the incidents are often strained ... Mr. McLaglen gives a praiseworthy account of himself." *The Hollywood Reporter* opined, "Everything in Radio's *The Lost Patrol* is good with the exception of the story and there is less story than could be told in a single reel of telling; as a consequence the dragging-out of the yarn to six or more reels causes the picture to become quite boresome before half the length is reached." The reviewer commended Steiner's musical score, Wenstrom's photography and the acting "topped by the work of Victor McLaglen, Reginald Denny, Wallace Ford and Billy Bevan." *The New York American* termed it "stark, vivid, gripping, fairly dripping with drama, an excellent picture of men without women.... [I]t is as tense an offering as the season may boast." *The New York Herald-Tribune* called the film "a grim, romantic and genuinely stirring military melodrama.... Certainly it is the finest of the recent crop of motion pictures. Admirably directed by John Ford." *The New York Journal* enthused, "It's one of the most stirring war pictures to have come out of Hollywood.... John Ford's direction is brilliant as he develops the absorbing document with chokingly mounting suspense. It's grim and disturbing. But you'll find it absorbingly impressive." *The New York Sun* declared, "It is a powerful picture, splendidly directed, acted and photographed; and it offers about as gruesome an hour as you can find...." *The New York World Telegram* called it "almost a great film and certainly one of the finest that have come out of Hollywood. It has depth, remarkably complete characterizations, moments of strong animal excitement, picturesque figures of enlisted men, banded but helpless against death, and excitement that will cause you to hold your breath. A vigorous, gripping, heart-tearing film." *Motion Picture* opined, "Strong drama never stopping to compromise in its relentless, merciless telling, *The Lost Patrol* may be considered by many too heavy; by others, courageous ... [McLaglen] ... achieves the very finest performance he has ever given. Wallace Ford, Reginald Denny, J.M. Kerrigan and Douglas Walton are, likewise, particularly outstanding in a perfect cast. Boris Karloff does a remarkable piece of work as a Biblically mad trooper." *Photoplay* concurred: "There's not much story, but the dramatic performance of the entire male cast is the finest seen in many a day." "If you like your pictures grim, uncompromisingly honest, and intensely dramatic, here is exactly what you've been hoping for," wrote *Picture Play Magazine*. The British *Picture Show* heralded, "A great film, but a grim one. It has one big thing to recommend it. It does not introduce a love interest." A negative review came from *The New Movie Magazine*: "*The Lost Patrol*, while different, isn't so very good. Neither director nor cast has been competent for the job at hand. The acting is routine and Mr. Ford, apart from his gift for shooting sand dunes impressively, is pretty routine too."

On February 15, 1934, to tie in with the national release of *The Lost Patrol*, a one-hour version of its soundtrack was broadcast by Los Angeles radio station KNX. This was the first time in motion picture history that a film's soundtrack was broadcast throughout the country.

Make Mine Music (1946; 74 minutes; Color)

PRODUCTION SUPERVISOR: Joe Grant. DIRECTORS: Bob Comack, Clyde Geronimi, Jack Kinney, Hamilton Luske & Josh Meador. WRITERS: Homer Brightman, Dick Hunter, Dick Kinney, John Walbridge, Tom Oreb, Dick Shaw, Eric Gurney, Sylvia Holland, T. Hee, Ed Penner, Dick Kelsey, Jim Bodrero, Roy Williams, Cap Palmer, Jesse March & Erwin Graham. MUSIC DIRECTOR: Charles Wolcott. MUSIC ASSOCIATES: Ken Darby, Oliver Wallace & Edward H. Plumb. SONGS: Ken Darby, Eliot Daniel, Al Cameron, Ted Weems, Ray Gilbert, Bobby Worth, Eddie Sauter, Alec Wilder, Osvaldo Farres, Charles Wolcott, Allie Wrubel, Henry Creamer & Turner Layton. ART SUPERVISORS: Mary Blair, John Hench & Elmer Plummer. SOUND: Robert O. Cook & C.O. Slyfield. ANIMATORS: Les Clark, Ward Kimball, Milt Kahl, John Sibley, Hal King, Eric Larson, John Lounsbery, Oliver M. Johnston, Jr., Fred Moore, Hugh Fraser, Judge Whitaker, Harvey Toombs, Tom Massey, Phil Duncan, Hal Ambro, Jack Campbell, Cliff Nordberg, Bill Justice, Al Bertino, John McManus & Ken O'Brien. EFFECTS ANIMATORS: George Rowley, Jack Boyd, Brad Case, Andy Engman & Don Patterson. PROCESS EFFECTS: Ub Iwerks. BACKGROUNDS: Claude Coats, Art Riley, Ralph Hulett, Merle Cox, Ray Huffine, Albert Dempster, Thelma Witmer & Jim Trout. LAYOUT: A. Kendall O'Connor, Hugh Hennesy, Al Zinnen, Ed Benedict, Charles Philippi, Donald Da Gradi, Lance Nolley, Charles Payzant & John Niendorf. COLOR CONSULTANT: Mique Nelson.

CAST: Nelson Eddy (Narrator/Character Voices), Dinah Shore (Singer), The Goodman Quartet [Benny Goodman, Cozy Cole, Sid Weiss, Teddy Wilson] (Themselves), The Andrews Sisters [LaVerne, Maxene, Patty] (Themselves), Jerry Colonna (Narrator), Andy Russell, Thurl Ravenscroft (Singers), Sterling Holloway (Narrator), Tania Riabouchinskaya, David Lichine (Dancers), The Pied Pipers, the Ken Darby Chorus, the King's Men (Themselves).

Walt Disney Studios' initial post–World War II release, *Make Mine Music*, was also its first "package feature," an amalgam of short, and often unrelated, segments combined in one production. Released in August 1946, it used mainly musical stars to relate ten animated stories. For horror fans there is a rather stolid retelling of "Peter and the Wolf" with a very fierce title creature, but the feature's highlight is the finale sequence, "The Whale Who Wanted to Sing at the Met." This delightful fantasy wonderfully showcases the vocal talents of Nelson Eddy, one of America's greatest singers. Eddy not only narrates the segment but also supplies all of its many voices and sings a variety of songs, from operatic arias and to his radio theme, "Shortnin' Bread." In one sequence he sings the tenor, baritone and bass parts.

Filmed as *Swing Time*, the feature was successful enough for Disney to continue the format with *Melody Time* (q.v.). *Make Mine Music* is one of the studio's lesser efforts, aside from the "Whale" finale, which was re-released separately in 1954 by RKO Radio as the short subject *Willie the Operatic Whale*. Two sequences featuring Benny Goodman and his quartet were sewn together and released as the 1954 short *Two for the Record*, and four other segments, "After You've Gone," "All the Cats Join In," "Casey at the Bat" and "Johnny Fedora and Alice Bluebonnet," were combined with five parts from *Melody Time* into the 1955 feature *Music Land*. In 1954 *Johnny Fedora and Alice Bluebonnet*, *The Martins and the Coys* and *Casey at the Bat* were also issued as short subjects by RKO. The next year the studio did the same with *Peter and the Wolf*.

Make Mine Music opens with the King's Men doing an exuberant "Rustic Ballad" about the feuding of "The Martins and the Coys." A "Tone Poem," "Blue Bayou," performed by the Ken Darby Chorus, is followed by the rousing "All the Cats Join In," a "Jazz Interlude." In "Ballad in Blue," Andy Russell sings "Without You"; next Jerry Colonna narrates the baseball tale "Casey at the Bat," from the 1888 poem by Ernest Lawrence Thayer. A "Ballade Ballet" has the figures of Tania Riabouchinskaya and David Lichine dancing as "Two Silhouettes," followed by Sterling Holloway narrating Sergei Prokofiev's "Peter and the Wolf." The surrealistic "After You've Gone" is performed by the Benny Goodman Quartet, and the Andrews Sisters sing about the romance between two hats in the "Love Story" song "Johnny Fedora and Alice Bluebonnet." The tenth segment is an "Opera Pathetique" headlining Nelson Eddy as "The Whale Who Wanted to Sing at the Met," the ultimately tragic tale of a ghostly voice at sea and a sea monster who turned out to be the title character.

Boxoffice opined, "Modestly, [Disney] designates it a musical fantasy in ten parts, which description doesn't begin to reflect the inspired artistry, the consummate technical skill, the breathtaking beauty and new heights of imagination which went into the film's making." Bosley Crowther was less enthusiastic in *The New York Times*: "For this latest feature-length picture from the Disney atelier is peculiarly like a basket of assorted Easter eggs—vivid, motley, ornamental and just-a-bit questionable in spots." *Variety* termed *Make Mine Music* a "Walt Disney treat," adding, "Disney's blend of cartoonic color, is almost celluloid portraiture. And the blending of broad cartoon comedy with ballads and ballets, live and opera, whimsy and whamsy, are surefire entertainment." In *The Disney Films, 3rd Edition* (1995), Leonard Maltin called *Make Mine Music* "a film of ups and downs, the ups being most of the popular material and the downs the attempts to work with classical music, and/or become 'artistic.'" He also stated that it was "a sharp disappointment to the millions who had eagerly awaited another Disney classic." In *The Animated Movie Guide* (2005), Martin Goodman noted, "With the exception of some of the animated segments there is little for today's younger viewers to relate to. *Make Mine Music* is a relic of Disney's America, a film more suited for cultural historians than audiences." He adds that the high point is "The Whale Who Wanted to Sing at the Met," "the only segment that holds up credibly today.... [I]t is the saving grace of an otherwise mediocre film."

For the record, the songs sung in the "Whale" sequence by Eddy are "Shortnin' Bread," "Largo al Factotum" from "The Barber of Seville," "Chi Me Frena?" from "Lucia Di Lammermoor," "I Pagliacci," "Tristan and Isolde," "Devil's Song" from "Mefistofele," "Mag Der Himmel Euh Verbegen" from "Martha" and "The Whale Who Wanted to Sing at the Met." He recorded most of the numbers for Columbia Records and they were released on a trio of 78 rpm disks (nos. 4342–4344) in the fall of 1946.

Man Alive (1945; 70 minutes)

EXECUTIVE PRODUCER: Robert Fellows. ASSOCIATE PRODUCER: Theron Warth. DIRECTOR: Ray Enright. SCREENPLAY: Edwin Harvey Blum. STORY: John Tucker Battle & Jerry Cady. PHOTOGRAPHY: Frank Redman. EDITOR: Marvin Coil. MUSIC: Leigh Harline. MUSIC DIRECTOR: C. Bakaleinikoff. ART DIRECTORS: Albert S. D'Agostino & Al Herman. SOUND: Francis M. Sarver. SET DECORATIONS: Victor Gangelin & Darrell Silvera. SPECIAL EFFECTS: Vernon L. Walker. ASSISTANT DIRECTOR: James Casey.

CAST: Pat O'Brien (Michael O'Flaherty "Speed" McBride), Adolphe Menjou (Kismet), Ellen Drew (Constance "Connie" Sanders McBride), Rudy Vallee (Gordon Tolliver), Fortunio Bonanova (Professor Zorada), Joseph Crehan (Dr. James P. Whitney), Jonathan Hale (Osborne), Minna Gombell (Aunt Sophie Bennett), Jason Robards (Henry Fletcher), Jack Norton (William T. "Willie the Wino" Lafferty), Robert Homans (Uncle Barney McBride), Carl "Alfalfa" Switzer (Ignatius Lafferty), Gertrude Astor (Madame Zorada), Tom Kennedy (Bartender), Vivienne Oakland (Ma Fogarty), George McKay (Captain Fogarty), Myrna Dell, Donna Lee (Fogarty Sisters), Robert Clarke (Taxi Driver), Fred "Snowflake" Toones (Piano Player), Johnny Strong (Legal Clerk), Donn Gift (Messenger Boy), Gertrude Short (Floozie), Larry Wheat (Clerk), Larry McGrath, Fred Howard, Frank Shannon, Harry Brown (Show Boat Men), Jack Kenny, Bill Beauman, Fred Houston (Beards), Eilene Janssen, Carol Coombs, Marjean Neville, Jean Vanderwitt (Angels).

Service station magnate "Speed" McBride (Pat O'Brien) comes home with a bowling trophy he won but forgets his wife Connie's (Ellen Drew) birthday. She gets flowers from a former beau, Gordy Tolliver (Rudy Vallee), who arrives announcing he has been divorced for two years. Connie and her Aunt Sophie (Minna Gombell) are delighted to see Gordy, who spends the evening reminiscing with Connie as the two ignore "Speed." When Connie and Aunt Sophie invite Gordy to spend the night, "Speed" accuses his wife of still having feelings for her school chum and claims she married him on the rebound. Going to a bar, "Speed" gets drunk and meets Willie the Wino (Jack Norton); the two exchange clothes after being thrown out of the establishment. Willie drives "Speed"'s car and runs off a pier. "Speed" wakes up hearing angels singing and sees Kismet (Adolphe Menjou) dressed in a devil's costume and stoking a furnace aboard the showboat *Natchez Belle,* which Kismet ran onto a sandbar. "Speed" thinks he has died until Kismet shows him his obituary in the newspaper and he realizes it was Willie who was drowned. He finds a letter in Willie's coat from the man's long-abandoned son Ignatius (Carl "Alfalfa" Switzer). When "Speed" recovers, he and Kismet go to town and he calls Connie but she hangs up thinking he is a ghost. The two men arrive at "Speed"'s house where they overhear attorney Osborne (Jonathan Hale) read the "deceased's" will, which urges Connie to forget him and start a new life. Realizing Gordy is after Connie, Kismet convinces "Speed" to pretend to be a ghost and scare him away. After "Speed" and Kismet replace mementoes she has packed, Connie asks Aunt Sophie to bring in psychic Dr. Zorda (Fortunio Bonanova) and his wife (Gertrude Astor) for a séance. At the session, "Speed" answers the mystic's questions, scaring away the fakers. That night during a thunderstorm, "Speed" tells Connie to reject Gordy. When she does so the next day, her suitor calls in the family doctor (Joseph Crehan) to examine her. The physician tells Connie she is imagining things and suggest she re-marry. Gordy proposes to Connie and she accepts. "Speed" demands to talk to his wife and, thinking he is a hallucination, she fires a gun at him. As Connie and Gordy are about to begin planning their wedding, "Speed" masquerades as his Uncle Barney (Robert Homans) from Ireland while Kismet pretends to be his pal Finnegan. When Connie announces that she plans to wed Gordy that day, the two men inform her that "Speed" is alive but suffering from amnesia. As the trio head to the showboat to find "Speed," Gordy calls the preacher to postpone the wedding and accidentally gets his fingers stuck in a bowling ball. The real Uncle Barney arrives and Gordy informs him that Connie has gone to the showboat. There, for Connie's benefit, "Speed" pretends to have lost his memory but Ignatius shows up thinking "Speed" is his long-lost father. Uncle Barney gets on the showboat and Kismet tries to keep both him and Ignatius under wraps by locking them in separate cabins. Pretending to be his uncle, "Speed" tells Connie to be loyal to her husband and when he returns as himself the two nearly reconcile until the real uncle and Ignatius both confront them. "Speed" tells his uncle he is trying to win back his wife, Connie overhears and they are reunited. As they leave for home, Gordy drives up and Kismet helps him get rid of the bowling ball by causing him to fall in the river.

Rudy Vallee in *Man Alive* (1945).

Man Alive is a fast-paced screwball comedy that kids ghosts and séances. Ellen Drew, surprisingly unattractive, is fine as the none-too-bright wife with Pat O'Brien, Adolphe Menjou and Rudy Vallee taking the acting honors. Fortunio Bonanova and Gertrude Astor make the most of their brief screen time as the fake seers. Bosley Crowther in *The New York Times* called the film "a modest little farce of no mentionable merit or consequence." More on the mark was *Boxoffice* which opined, "As every showman knows, a screwball comedy is much like a watermelon—it's either very good or it's not fit for human consumption. Because of a lightning-paced screenplay boasting several original slants, a cast of seasoned and enthusiastic troupers and good direction, this easily qualifies for the former classification.... [I]t's a pretty safe bet to please rank and file spectators, to keep them laughing." *Variety* declared, "Sheer frenzy of its broad, slapstickish plot will force a number of chuckles and give it some chance in lesser runs before neighborhood audiences.... Ray Enright's direction isn't helped much by the flimsy script.... Characters are slimly drawn, and puckish quality that could have given it a lift fails to come through in the development." *The Film Daily* noted, "Aided by a novel, fast-moving screenplay, Pat O'Brien, Ellen Drew, Adolphe Menjou and Rudy Vallee give spirited performances to point up this screwball comedy."

The film's working titles were *The Amorous Ghost* and *The Passionate Ghost.*

Melody Time (1948; 75 minutes; Color)

PRODUCTION SUPERVISOR: Ben Sharpsteen. CARTOON DIRECTORS: Clyde Geronimi, Wilfred Jackson, Hamilton Luske & Jack Kinney. WRITERS: Winston Hibler, Erdman Penner, Harry Reeves, Homer Brightman, Ken Anderson, Ted Sears, Joe Rinaldi, Bill Cottrell, Art Scott, Jesse Marsh, Bob Moore & John Walbridge. LIVE ACTION PHOTOGRAPHY: Winton C. Hoch. EDITORS: Donald Halliday & Thomas

Scott. MUSIC DIRECTORS: Eliot Daniel & Ken Darby. ASSOCIATE MUSIC DIRECTOR: Paul J. Smith. SPECIAL MUSIC ARRANGEMENTS: Vic Schoen & Al Sack. SONGS: Benny Benjamin, George Weiss, Bobby Worth, Ray Gilbert, Kim Gannon, Walter Kent, Allie Wrubel, Joyce Kilmer, Oscar Rasbach, Ernesto Nazareth, Johnny Lange & Eliot Daniel. SOUND: Robert O. Cook & Harold J. Steck. SOUND DIRECTOR: C.O. Slyfield. EFFECTS ANIMATORS: Jack Boyd, Dan MacManus, Josh Meador & George Rowley. SPECIAL PROCESSES: Ub Iwerks. CHARACTER ANIMATORS: Harvey Toombs, Ed Aardal, Cliff Nordberg, John Sibley, Ken O'Brien, Judge Whitaker, Marvin Woodward, Hal King, Don Lusk, Rudy Larriva, Bob Cannon & Hal Ambro. BACKGROUNDS: Art Riley, Brice Mack, Ralph Hulett, Ray Huffine, Merle Cox & Dick Anthony. LAYOUT: Hugh Hennesy, A. Kendall O'Connor, Al Zinnen, Don Griffith, McLaren Stewart, Lance Nolley, Robert Cormack, Thor Putnam & Donald Da Gradi. COLOR-STYLING: Mary Blair, Claude Coats & Dick Kelsey. TECHNICOLOR COLOR DIRECTOR: Natalie Kalmus. ASSOCIATE TECHNICOLOR COLOR DIRECTOR: Morgan Padleford. FOLKLORE CONSULTANT: Carl Carmer.

CAST: Roy Rogers (Himself), Dennis Day (Voices of the Old Settler/Johnny Appleseed/Angel), The Andrews Sisters [LaVerne, Maxene, Patty], Fred Waring & His Pennsylvanians, Freddy Martin & His Orchestra, Ethel Smith, Frances Langford (Themselves), Buddy Clark (Narrator/Singer), Bob Nolan & the Sons of the Pioneers [Tim Spencer, Pat Brady, Hugh Farr, Karl Farr], The Dinning Sisters [Ginger, Jean, Lou] (Themselves), Bobby Driscoll (Bobby), Luana Patten (Luana), Pinto Colvig (Voice of Aracuan Bird), Trigger, the Smartest Horse in the Movies (Himself).

Following the release of *Song of the South* (1946) and *Fun and Fancy Free* (1947) [qq.v.], Walt Disney Studios returned to its "package features" format began with *Make Mine Music* (1946) [q.v.], releasing *Melody Time* in the spring of 1948. Here seven segments, an admixture of animation and live action, are combined into a film that features popular music stars (Roy Rogers, Dennis Day, the Andrews Sisters, Fred Waring, Freddy Martin, Buddy Clark, the Sons of the Pioneers, the Dinning Sisters) in telling its varied stories, all of which rely heavily on fantasy elements. More entertaining than *Make Mine Music*, the feature can hardly be called top-notch Disney although it did produce the classic western ballad "Blue Shadows on the Trail," written by Eliot Daniel and Johnny Lange. As far as horror is concerned, the feature is lacking unless one counts the tall tales in the "Pecos Bill" finale that has Bill's fiancée, Slue Foot Sue, propelled into outer space and ending up on the Moon. Otherwise, the movie is only mild entertainment, highlighted by the segments "The Legend of Johnny Appleseed" and "Pecos Bill." When *Melody Time* was released on home video in 1998, the "Pecos Bill" segment was altered to greatly downplay the title character's nicotine addiction.

An animated ice skating tale with Frances Langford singing "Once Upon a Winter Time" opens the feature, followed by Freddy Martin and His Orchestra, with Jack Fina on the piano, doing "Bumble Boogie," a modernized version of Nikolay Rimsky-Korsakov's "Flight of the Bumble Bee." Dennis Day supplies three voices, including the title character, in "The Legend of Johnny Appleseed," about how a Pennsylvania farmer doing his part to tame the frontier by spending 40 years planting apple trees along the westward migration trails. Its finale has Johnny being taken to Heaven to continue his work. The Andrews Sisters sing the story of "Little Toot," from the 1939 story by Hardie Gramatky, about a mischievous tugboat who manages to exonerate himself after embarrassing his father. Joyce Kilmer's 1918 poem "Trees" is sung by the choral group Fred Waring and His Pennsylvanians, and "Blame It on the Samba" features pianist Ethel Smith and the vocalizing of the Dinning Sisters. It details the misadventures of Donald Duck and Joe Carioca at the Café de Samba and their run-in with Aracuan Bird (voice of Pinto Colvig). The final segment has Roy Rogers, along with Bob Nolan and the Sons of the Pioneers, narrating "Pecos Bill" to youngsters Bobby Driscoll and Luana Patten. It tells of Bill, accidentally left behind by his pioneer family and raised by Ma Coyote, saving a colt from vultures and naming it Widowmaker. The two become the wildest varmints in the West until Bill falls for Slue Foot Sue. When she attempts to ride the horse, their ill-fated romance ends in tragedy for Bill, who returns to the coyotes.

Made as *Something to Sing About, Melody Time* became one of the first motion pictures to have a television tie-in when clips of the film were shown on the DuMont Network's "Small Fry Club" on May 24, 1948, with Luana Patten also appearing on the show. Victor Records recorded two segments of the film: Dennis Day narrated "The Legend of Johnny Appleseed" (4–370), which Disneyland Records reissued on LP (DQ-1260) in 1964; and Roy Rogers along with Bob Nolan and the Sons of the Pioneers waxed "Pecos Bill," which Victor Records released on three 78 rpm records (4–375). The two segments were also issued on a long-playing album by Camden Records(CAL/CAS-1054) in 1964.

The *Melody Time* segments "Trees," "Bumble Boogie," "Once Upon a Winter Time," "Blame It on the Samba" and "Pecos Bill" were combined with four episodes from *Make Mine Music* to become the 1955 feature *Music Land*. "Trees" and "Bumble Boogie" were in the 1955 theatrical short *Contrast in Rhythm. Little Toot* and *Once Upon a Wintertime* were released as individual shorts by RKO in 1954 while *Blame It on the Samba* and *Johnny Appleseed* were issued in the same format the next year by the studio.

Regarding the various stories in *Melody Time, Harrison's Reports* wrote, "Several are more entertaining than others, but all have been executed with an imagery, artistry, and dexterity, that is nothing short of magnificent." Regarding the "Pecos Bill" episode, the reviewer said, "This segment is extremely well done and should provoke many laughs." The same trade paper rated the film's box office performance as "Good."

Boxoffice stated that the film "probably is the best [Disney has] made in that category [animated].... [The] assembly leaves one overall impression of breathtaking beauty, infectious merriment, and haunting music...." *Variety* noted, "As to be expected, the technicians on the Disney staff have given this one a flawless stamp, technically perfect and artistically stimulating. Beautifully photographed in Technicolor, it's a show that rates all connected with its making a top credit." *The Film Daily* enthused, "You can call out all the old laudatory adjectives and round up a new collection for Walt Disney's latest contribution to the gaiety of the nation." Leonard Maltin wrote in *The Disney Films, 3rd Edition* (1995), "*Melody Time* was the last of Disney's musical mélanges, and certainly one of the best. In its choice of material, presentation, and artistic style it managed to avoid most of the pitfalls of its predecessors and emerge as a solidly enjoyable outing." Martin Goldman opined in *The Animated Movie Guide* (2005), "*Melody Time* was the last of Disney's postwar anthology features, and by this time the formula was tired. Less than half the shorts are of any interest, and one can almost feel the animators pushing for something more creative to do.... While *Melody Time* has a few good visual moments, it must be considered a vast underachievement by the Disney studio."

Mexican Spitfire Sees a Ghost (1942; 70 minutes)

PRODUCER: Cliff Reid. DIRECTOR: Leslie Goodwins. SCREENPLAY: Charles E. Roberts & Monte Brice. PHOTOGRAPHY: Russell Metty. EDITOR: Theron Warth. MUSIC DIRECTOR: C. Bakaleinikoff. ART DIRECTORS: Albert S. D'Agostino & Carroll Clark. SOUND: John E. Tribby. GOWNS: Renie.

CAST: Lupe Velez (Carmelita Lindsay/Maria), Leon Errol (Matt Lindsay/Lord Basil Epping/Hubble), Charles "Buddy" Rogers (Dennis Lindsay), Elisabeth Risdon (Della Lindsay), Donald MacBride (Percy Fitzbadden), Minna Gombell (Edith Fitzbadden), Don Barclay (Fingers O'Toole), John McGuire (Luders), Lillian Randolph (Hyacinth), Mantan Moreland (Lightnin'), Harry Tyler (Bascombe), Marten Lamont (Harcourt), Jane Woodworth, Julie Warren (Secretaries), Richard Martin (Chauffeur), Barbara Moffett (Woman in Waiting Room).

Between 1939 and 1943, RKO made eight "Mexican Spitfire" features starring Lupe Velez and Leon Errol. *Mexican Spitfire Sees a Ghost*, released in the summer of 1942, was the sixth entry. Although first-billed Velez plays the title role, she has little to do in this affair, which is dominated by Errol who plays three different parts. The cheaply made feature is a confusing, dull, forced "comedy" that only picks up steam at the finale. Its trio of villains are vague, although they appear to be enemy saboteurs. The "ghost" of the title is one of the bad guys in a clanking suit of armor trying to scare off house guests. Made as *Mexican Spitfire and the Ghost*, the film, when first released, was usually the main feature on a double bill with Orson Welles' *The Magnificent Ambersons* (1942). Leslie Goodwins directed all of the "Mexican Spirtfire" movies. He also helmed *Crime Ring* (1938) and *Genius at Work* (1946) [qq.v.] for RKO as well as Universal's *Murder in the Blue Room* and *The Mummy's Curse* (both 1944).

Bumbling Lord Basil Epping (Errol), distributor of Parliament Scotch Whiskey, gets a telegram from Edith Fitzbadden (Minna Gombell), his former girlfriend, saying that she and her high-strung brother Percy (Donald MacBride) are coming from Canada to visit him at his country estate. Since the business is having financial problems, Dennis Lindsay (Charles "Buddy" Rogers), Basil's partner, hopes the wealthy Percy will invest in the company. Not wanting to see the Fitzbaddens, Basil goes moose hunting and tells Dennis to take care of the visitors. Dennis consults his uncle Matt Lindsay (Errol) and his wife Della (Elisabeth Risdon) about the matter and Della warns him to keep his hot-headed wife Carmelita (Velez) home. Matt tells Dennis to take Della to meet the Fitzbaddens and he will take Carmelita to the fights. Dennis and his aunt drive to the Epping estate and are met by real estate agent Bascombe (Harry Tyler), who says the house has not been lived in for a year and it has a bad reputation. Bascombe is in cahoots with Luders (John McGuire) and Fingers O'Toole (Don Barclay), who have been staying in the house while they make nitroglycerin in the cellar. Della calls Matt and tells him to meet the visitors since she and Dennis have to clean up the place. The Fitzbaddens arrive with Matt and Carmelita, who pretend to be Basil's butler Hubble and maid Maria. Finding out Basil is not there, the Fitzbaddens decide to leave, so Carmelita gets Matt to pretend to be their host. Matt is made to resemble Basil via a wig made from dog hair. Having gotten his hunting dates mixed up, Basil decides to go to his country estate. There Edith thinks Matt is Basil and flirts with him while Percy tries to take him in a card game. Needing money, Matt pretends to be Basil and gets it from Edith, saying Matt borrowed it from him and did not pay it back. Basil shows up and joins the card game, causing confusion since his behavior is the opposite displayed to the Fitzbaddens just minutes before. Basil leaves as Matt returns, Percy wants his winnings only to find the money missing. Edith tries to search the servants and Fingers, who stole the money, has it taken away from him by Luders, who returns it. Fingers again filches the money as Edith searches Hubble, who is surprised to find the money gone. Matt's wig, hidden in a clock, is taken by the dog. They locate the animal under a sofa with the wig and try to entice him out by sounding like cats. The Fitzbaddens observe their antics and want to see Basil, so Matt again puts on the disguise with Della observing him. When Basil comes upstairs, Della thinks he is her husband and castigates him as Fingers again returns the money. Called by Edith, Bascombe, who also claims to be the local constable, arrives to investigate the theft and says the house is haunted. Percy and Edith start to leave but find out they missed the last train and will have to stay the night. Dressed in his night shirt, Basil is confronted by Della, who thinks he is Matt. She tries to get him into her bedroom, with Basil and Edith witnessing the scene. Fingers puts on a suit of armor and pretends to be a ghost. When Carmelita and Della run to their spouses for help, Basil and Edith are upset as Carmelita, Matt and Della see the spirit. Basil and Percy get into a fight and Basil orders Percy out of the house. Dennis tells Matt about the argument, saying he has lost the contract with Percy. Matt once more disguises himself as Basil and gets Percy to sign the contract. The real Basil then runs into Percy and again orders him off the property. Fingers falls into the cellar, frightening Luders and Bascombe, who think he is the police, and the two go upstairs with the nitro, running into Percy. The collision causes the nitro to explode, leaving the place in a shambles.

In its two-paragraph review, *The New York Times* observed of Leon Errol that "without his varied talents [this film] might easily have been a more boresome offering. As it is, Mr. Errol, stumbling through a maze of no less than three identities, is the comedy's sole saving grace...." *Boxoffice* noted that the title character "is becoming more and more unimportant while the bulk of the Thespic burdens fall on the capable shoulders of Leon Errol.... The results are fantastically farcical and funny most of the way." *Photoplay* found it "loud, noisy and sometimes funny." *Variety* noted, "Leon Errol's corking, if repetitious dual comedy impersonation should carry this B programmer through as a supporting feature for satisfactory returns...."

Midnight Mystery (1930; 68 minutes)

PRODUCER: William LeBaron. ASSOCIATE PRODUCER: Bertram Millhauser. DIRECTOR: George B. Seitz. SCREENPLAY: Beulah Marie Dix, from the play *Hawk Island* by Howard Irving Young. PHOTOGRAPHY: Joseph Walker. EDITOR: Otto Ludwig. ART DIRECTOR: Max Ree. SOUND: Clem Portman. PHOTOGRAPHIC EFFECTS: Lloyd Knechtel.

CAST: Betty Compson (Sally Wayne), Lowell Sherman (Tom Austen), Raymond Hatton (Paul Cooper), Hugh Trevor (Greg Sloane), Ivan Lebedeff (Mischa Kawelin), Rita LaRoy (Madeline Austen), Marcelle Corday (Harriet Cooper), June Clyde (Louise Hollister), Sidney D'Albrook (Barker), William P. Burt (Rogers).

Midnight Mystery is an effective, flavorful mystery thriller somewhat hampered by stilted dialogue and too much of it. On the other hand, its compact cast gives good performances and for horror fans it provides an atmospheric romp in an isolated, spooky old castle during a wild storm. Joseph Walker's fluid camerawork is especially effective and is enhanced by lighting effects that highlight the shadowy environs of the castle, where all of the action takes place. Interestingly, none of the people involved are particularly likable except mystery writer Sally Wayne (Betty Compson). The rest are from "the cream of society" and include her rich, obtuse fiancé (Hugh Trevor), a bickering married couple (Raymond Hatton, Marcelle Corday), a dizzy blonde (June Clyde) and an oily lawyer (Lowell Sherman), who wants Sally, and whose wife (Rita LaRoy) is having an affair with a Russian pianist (Ivan Lebedeff). Only Hatton's character provides much in the way of levity with his continual talk of gruesome murders. Director George B. Seitz keeps the action moving at a fairly good clip. The title is somewhat of a misnomer in that there is never a mystery as to the killer's identity. Issued by Radio Pictures early in the summer of 1930, it was based on the 1929 play *Hawk Island* which had a modest Broadway run.

At a house party in a remote Florida coast island castle belonging to wealthy Greg Sloane (Trevor), his fiancée, mystery writer Sally Wayne (Compson), reads the last chapter from her new book to guests Paul Cooper (Hatton) and his wife Harriet (Corday), Russian pianist Mischa Kawelin (Lebedeff), Louise Hollister (Clyde) and criminal lawyer Tom Austen (Sherman) and his wife Madeline (LaRoy). Greg chides Sally for writing such trash and she informs him she has contracts for two more books. As a storm rises, Sally proclaims the location and atmosphere of the castle the right place for a murder. While the others have dinner, Mischa plays the piano. When Madeline comes into the music room he puts in a piano roll and makes love to her, not knowing Tom is seated in a high back chair facing away from them. Fearing they will be caught, Madeline goes outside while Mischa joins the others. When his employee Rogers (William P. Burt) brings the mail, he also gives Greg the key to the boat house so no one can get off the island. After Madeline comes in out of the storm, Greg and Sally argue over her books. She informs him she must work for a living and calls off their engagement. Tom gives Sally a résumé

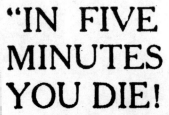

"IN FIVE MINUTES YOU DIE!

Start Praying Now!"

Just one of 1,000 thrills in Radio's

MIDNIGHT

MYSTERY

A female Philo Vance solves it—just for Love!

BETTY COMPSON
LOWELL SHERMAN

**June Clyde—Hugh Trevor
Ivan Lebedeff—Raymond Hatton**

Advertisement for *Midnight Mystery* (1930).

of actual murder cases while Greg reads a letter and then seeks out Mischa. The two men argue, Greg orders Mischa out of the house and he leaves in anger. Greg loads a revolver and is seen by his butler, Barker (Sidney D'Albrook). The lights go out, and a scream and a shot are heard. Greg stumbles into the living room and tells the others he just shot Mischa. They look out a window and see a body floating in the water. The lights come back on and Greg informs his guests that he shot Mischa because he was not fit to live. Holding them at bay with his gun, Greg goes upstairs. Tom tells Sally that Greg is not worth her love and says he cares for her. Mischa later sneaks into the dark house, quickly followed by Sally who goes to Greg's room and tells him to leave with her before the police arrives. Sally tells Greg she still loves him. He laughs and informs her that he and his best friend Mischa faked the shooting, and Sally angrily calls him cruel. In the living room, Greg informs Mischa that he must show himself to prove he was not shot and they agree to do so the next morning at breakfast.

Mischa tells Greg he overheard Tom disparage him to Sally. Greg goes to bed and Tom returns, finding Mischa. He says he found the dummy Greg and Mischa used in their trick and then spots the revolver Greg left behind when he went to bed. When Mischa tells Tom that no one but he and Greg know that he is alive, Tom tells him he was in the music room when the pianist and his wife were making love. Tom shoots Mischa, drags his body to a window and drops it into the sea. The next morning the storm has passed with Greg arriving at breakfast and informing his aghast guests that Mischa will soon make an appearance. Just then Barker and Rogers bring in Mischa's body. Seeing his friend dead, Greg tells the group the shooting was a gag they pulled because everyone was so thrilled with murders. While Greg looks for his revolver, Sally finds a button clutched in Mischa's hand. Tom accuses Greg of murdering Mischa and tells Sally they must get in touch with the police. A distraught Sally goes to her room but is followed by Tom. As he waits for her, he swallows a drink she left on the table beside her bed thinking it is whiskey. Tom tells Sally he loves her but she says she plans to kill herself because of Greg. When she finds the glass empty, Sally informs Tom she put poison in the drink and then calls for the others to come to her bedroom. Thinking he is dying, Tom confesses to the murder of Mischa. Sally says the drink contained only a sedative as she suspected Tom of killing Mischa (the button she found in his hand was from the living room couch). She said she used the ploy to get Tom to confess in order to save Greg. As Tom is led away by the others, Sally and Greg reconcile.

Motion Picture Times called *Midnight Mystery*, "Good entertainment and produced in such a manner that it gets away from the usual run of mystery thrillers. The audience knows the true conditions of the mystery but some of the players do not and that makes it all the funnier...." *The New York Times* called it "an ingenious and interesting plot ... but a somewhat disappointing solution to a clever crime prevents the film from being entirely satisfactory." *Variety* complained, "The fact is that the thrills do not deliver punch in the film-fan sense; the comedy doesn't inspire laughs, and it's a disappointment all around." *Hollywood Filmograph* said director Seitz "has scored another good one for RKO. With a well-balanced cast, [he] brings out several exceptionally tense scenes.... Betty Compson will certainly set masculine hearts to fluttering in this role. She is gorgeously beautiful throughout the picture. Her voice is lovely and everything she says is interesting.... A clean, thrilling mystery drama; a brilliant job of directing by George B. Seitz." RKO publicity for the film also highlighted Seitz's work as noted in the *Charles City* (Iowa) *Daily News and Evening Intelligencer*: "Full credit for the smooth-flowing reality of *Midnight Mystery* should undoubtedly go to George B. Seitz, the director, who has had a finger in many a mystery film drama. This time he has topped his success with a fine flourish, bringing to the talking screen a plausible and well-turned-out thrill melodrama that holds interest from the first electrifying flash to the final fade-out." In *Film Fan Monthly* (March 1974), Leonard Maltin wrote, "A talky mystery whose plot is constructed in such as way as to virtually eliminate any vestige of suspense.... Director Seitz's attempt to make sophisticated use of sound in opening scenes doesn't work out either; in a party sequence the camera moves about, with many characters talking at once, and a piano playing in the background. The mixing, however, destroys this ambitious idea, since the voices are not kept distinct, and the piano is playing so loudly that one can hardly hear the dialogue at all."

Top-billed Betty Compson was enjoying a screen resurgence with the coming of talkies and *Midnight Mystery* was the apex of her career after scoring a huge success in her first RKO effort, *Street Girl* (1929). Appearing in nearly 200 films, she became a star with *The Miracle Man* (1919); her other genre efforts include *The Great Gabbo* (1929), *Destination Unknown* (1933) and the similar *Strange Cargo* (1940), *Killer at Large* (1936), *The Mystic Circle Murder* (1939) and the title role in *Invisible Ghost* (1941). As noted in the film's reviews, director Seitz was a veteran thriller director going back to a trio of Pearl White serials, *The Exploits of Elaine* (1914), *The Romance of Elaine* and *The New Exploits of Elaine* (both 1915). He went on to helm *Drums of Jeopardy* (1931) and *The Thirteenth Chair* (1937). Associate producer Bertram Millhauser later wrote the Universal "Sherlock Holmes" features *The Spider Woman* (1943), *The Pearl of Death* (1944) and *The Woman in Green* (1945) as well as *The Invisible Man's Revenge* (1944).

Mighty Joe Young (1949; 94 minutes)

PRODUCER-STORY: Merian C. Cooper. EXECUTIVE PRODUCER–SECOND UNIT DIRECTOR: John Ford. DIRECTOR: Ernest B. Schoedsack. SCREENPLAY: Ruth Rose. PHOTOGRAPHY: J. Roy Hunt. EDITOR: Ted Cheesman. MUSIC: Roy Webb. PRODUCTION DESIGN: James Basevi. SET DRESSER: George Atwills. ASSISTANT ART DIRECTOR: Howard Richmond. SOUND: John L. Cass & Clem Portman. SOUND EDITOR: Walter Elliott. COSTUME DESIGN: Adele Balkan. MAKEUP: Mel Berns. PRODUCTION MANAGER: Lloyd Richards. TECHNICAL CREATOR: Willis H. O'Brien. FIRST TECHNICIAN: Ray Harryhausen. SECOND TECHNICIAN: Pete Peterson. TECHNICAL STAFF: George Lofgren & Fitch Fulton. SPECIAL PHOTOGRAPHIC EFFECTS: Bert Willis. OPTICAL EFFECTS-OPTICAL PHOTOGRAPHY: Linwood Dunn. PHOTOGRAPHIC EFFECTS: Harold Stine & Herb Willis. ASSISTANT DIRECTOR: Sam Ruman.

CAST: Terry Moore (Jill Young), Ben Johnson (Gregg), Robert Armstrong (Max O'Hara), Frank McHugh (Windy), Douglas Fowley (Jones), Denis Green (Crawford), Paul Guilfoyle (Smith), Nestor Paiva (Brown), Regis Toomey (John Young), Lora Lee Michel (Little Jill Young), James Flavin (Officer Shultz), Primo Carnera, Man Mountain Dean, Wee Willie Davis, Karl "Killer" Davis, Bomber [Henry] Kulky, Sammy Menacker, The Swedish Angel, Ivan Rasputin, Sammy Stein, Max the Iron Man (Themselves), Richard Lane (City Attorney), Byron Foulger (Mr. Jones), Mary Field (Secretary), Chester Clute (Doctor), Wilbur Mack (Mr. McTavish), Charles Lane, James Burke (Producers at Bar), Ellen Corby (Orphanage Matron), Joyce Compton (Alice), Iris Adrian (Gloria), Frank Scannell (Pierson), Tom Kennedy, Eddie Parker, Tom Steele (Policemen), Joe Ploski (Bindlestiff), Jack Pennick (Truck Driver Sam), Charles Flynn, Russ Clark, Mike Lally, Ray Hyke, Carey Loftin, Duke Green, Bud Wolfe (Deputy Sheriffs), Paul Maxey (Bascomb), Madame Sul-Te-Wan (Young's Housekeeper), Cliff Clark (Police Guard Moran), Joel Fluellen, Mansfield Collins (Tall Natives), Kermit Maynard (Cowboy Red), Fred Kennedy, Frank McGrail, Richard Farnsworth, Bryan "Slim" Hightower (Cowboys), Robert Johnson (Ali), Milton Shockley (Native), Edward Short (Ahmed), Janet Warren (Receptionist), Kay Christopher, Ann Archer, Luella Bickmore (Nurses), Hal Meltone (Bank Messenger), David McKim (Soda Jerk), Cerrita Camargo, Leonard Bluett (Specialty Dancers), Jack Gargan, Joe Gray, Dick Ryan (Waiters), Pat Barton (Cigarette Girl), Mary Gordon (Old Woman), Eddie Dunn, Garry Owen, Rory Mallinson, Charles Regan (Bartenders), Bobby Barber (Diner), Frank Conroy, John Gallaudet, Joey Ray, Archie Twitchell, Joe Devlin, Ray Walker, Joey Ray, Al Murphy, Michael Brandon (Reporters), Anne Nagel, Edward Gargan, James Craven, Norman Willis, William Newell (Bar Customers), Irene Ryan (Southern Bar Customer), Tom Daly (Greeter), Bess Flowers (Night Club Patron), William Schallert (Gas Station Attendant), Lewis Martin (Officer O'Brinsky), Harry Strang, Charles Sherlock (Policemen), Donald Kerr (Diner Owner), Selmer Jackson (Judge), Robert Tafur (Head Waiter), Lee Tung Foo (Waiter), Max Willenz (Sketch Artist), Bill Wallace (Player), Billy Wayne (Stage Manager), Juan Varro (Gigolo), Anne O'Neal, Netta Packer (Autograph Seekers), Max Wagner, Jack Perry (Tough Guys), Franklin Parker (Photographer), Marc Krah (Desk Sergeant), Norman Nesbitt (Police Announcer), Lew H. Snowden (Orchestra Leader), Sharon Bell, Katherine Brennan, Marilyn Brennan, Carol Coombs, June Hedin, Peggy Miller, Gloria Moore, Marsha Northrup, Pamela Payton (Girls), Dwayne Hickman, Wally Koford, Gregory Marshall, George McDonald (Boys).

An offshoot of *King Kong* (q.v.), *Mighty Joe Young* was produced by Arko, Inc., a combination of RKO and Argosy Pictures, the latter belonging to John Ford and Merian C. Cooper. Ernest B. Schoedsack directed *Mighty Joe Young* and co-directed *King Kong*; his wife, Ruth Rose, did the screenplay for both features. Willis O'Brien won an Academy Award for Best Special Effects for *Mighty Joe Young* and he too worked on *King Kong* as did Ted Cheesman, who edited both movies. Perhaps the strongest attachment between the two films is Robert Armstrong, whose bombastic stage impresario Max O'Hara in *Mighty Joe Young* is a broad comic version of *King Kong*'s Carl Denham. Ray Harryhausen first came to public attention with *Mighty Joe Young* due to his excellent stop-action animation, which he greatly enhanced since the technique was first used in *Kong*. A former horse wrangler and stuntman who had been in films since the early 1940s, Ben Johnson got his first taste of stardom in *Mighty Joe Young* while former child actress Terry Moore was nicely cast as the young woman who raised and loved Mr. Joseph Young. The film is littered with numerous delightful cameos but Frank McHugh is wasted as O'Hara's press agent as are Douglas Fowley, Paul Guilfoyle and Nestor Paiva as the drunks who send Joe on a destructive rampage. James Flavin, a member of the ship's crew in *King Kong*, is seen to advantage as the police officer assigned to execute Joe Young. Filmed as *The Great Joe Young* and *Mr. Joseph Young of Africa*, *Mighty Joe Young* was made on a $1.8 million budget and failed to recoup its cost.

Mighty Joe Young is fairly entertaining although not in the same vein as *King Kong*. The title character is much too likable to be feared and much of the proceedings is on the comedic side, although several sequences with Joe are highly exciting and very well done. This is particularly true of the scenes in which cowboys try to lasso Joe, his drunken rampage through the Golden Safari Club and the finale in which he saves orphans stranded in a burning building. The latter sequence was tinted a garish red which was restored for home video release. Overall, though, *Mighty Joe Young* is average, much more of a family film than a horror feature. *Mighty Joe Young*, except for fine production values, comes off as a poor relation to *Kong*.

In Africa, lonely little Jill Young (Lora Lee Michel) purchases a baby gorilla from two natives (Joel Fluellen, Mansfield Collins) and names him Joe. Her farmer father (Regis Toomey) warns her that when Joe grows up, he will become dangerous. A dozen years pass and in New York City show business producer Max O'Hara (Armstrong) makes plans with his press agent, Windy (McHugh), for an African safari in which he will capture animals to feature in a new Hollywood night spot, the Golden Safari. Oklahoma champion roper Gregg (Johnson), who just finished working a rodeo at Madison Square Garden, asks Max for a job and the impresario decides to use cowboys to capture lions, thinking it will make good publicity. Six months later Max is about to wrap up the safari when Crawford (Denis Green), its leader, sees Joe, now ten feet tall, approach their camp. Havoc ensues as Joe wrecks the camp and the cowboys try unsuccessfully to rope him. Gregg is about to shoot Joe when Max stops him, saying he wants the gorilla alive. Joe grabs the frightened Max and is about to throw him over a cliff when a now grown-up Jill (Moore) arrives and calms the simian. The angry Jill orders Max and his troupe off her land, saying Joe is her friend. Max later apologizes to Jill and offers her and Joe the starring spot in his new nightclub. Since her father died six months before and she wants to see the world, Jill signs a contract with the fast-talking Max. Joe shows up and becomes agitated when he sees Max and Gregg but Jill placates him with bananas.

At his club's opening Max tells the press very little about his new attraction, who he bills as "Mr. Joseph Young of Africa." During the show, Max introduces Jill who plays "Beautiful Dreamer" on a piano as Joe comes up through the stage floor supporting the rotating platform with Jill and the piano on it. The capacity crowd is enthralled. Next Max has Joe engage in a tug of war with ten strongmen (Primo Carnera, Man Mountain Dean, Wee Willie Davis, the Swedish Angel, Karl "Killer" Davis, Sammy Menacker, Ivan Rasputin, Bomber Kulky, Max the Iron Man, Sammy Stein), whom he dumps into a pool. Then Joe boxes with former heavyweight boxing champion Carnera, whom he throws into the audience. While the act is successful, Joe has to be locked in a cage when not performing and this upsets both Jill and Gregg, who also has become Joe's friend. Jill informs Max that she and Joe are returning to Africa since they have worked for him for ten weeks and he agrees but asks for more time. Seven weeks later he has Joe do an act in which the customers throw huge fake coins at him. When a drunk (Paiva) hits Joe with a bottle, he becomes angry and Gregg has the curtain brought down. Later Jill dines with Gregg and the two realize they are in love. The drunk and his pals (Fowley, Guilfoyle) are told to behave by Max and to get even they seek out Joe's cage and give him liquor. When one of them burns Joe while lighting a cigarette, the gorilla goes berserk, tears off the door of his cage and rampages through the nightclub, destroying it. Jill arrives with Max and Gregg and she gets Joe back into his cage. At a hearing the prosecuting attorney (Richard Lane) demands that Joe be killed and the judge (Selmer Jackson) concurs. On the night Joe is to be shot by a police officer (Flavin),

Max stages a fake heart attack that lures Joe's guard (Cliff Clark) away from his cage. Jill and Gregg sneak the gorilla into a van, planning to drive him to a freighter Max has hired to take them back to Africa. Along the way they commandeer a truck to keep the police off their trail. When Gregg takes a detour, they get stuck in mud and Joe pushes the truck free. With the police closing in on them, Jill, Gregg and Joe drive past an orphanage that is on fire. They stop to help and Jill goes upstairs to save stranded children as Gregg uses a rope to climb the side of the building. He finds Jill and the children but they are trapped by the fire. Joe climbs a tree and rescues Jill. Gregg is able to lower the children to the ground with his rope and jumps to safety only to see a little girl still stranded on the top floor. Joe climbs back up the tree and saves the child, but the tree catches fire and eventually falls, injuring Joe although the little girl is unharmed. Max informs Jill that now no one will shoot Joe. Two months later as Max is planning a new aquatic act, Windy shows him recently arrived home movies from Africa of Jill, Gregg and Joe on their farm.

Variety reported that *Mighty Joe Young* "is fun to laugh at and with, loaded with incredible corn, plenty of humor, and a robot gorilla who becomes a genuine hero. The technical skill of the large staff of experts gives the robot life, both for audience thrills and sympathy, and helps to tie together the ten-twent'-thirt elements of the story...." *Boxoffice* concurred: "Hokum in unlimited quantities and of unabashed quality ignites this pinwheel of adventure, fantasy, action and humor.... Cooper apparently approached his chore with tongue in cheek, which resulted in the offering being sufficiently flexible so that spectators can look at it for laughs or for thrills, depending upon the individual." *The New York Times* opined, "The emphasis is on comedy and the huge Mr. Joseph Young of Africa, to give the star of the film full credit rating, can be screamingly funny and appealing at times, it must be admitted. But the mighty Mr. Young also has a streak of ferociousness that is every bit as awesomely terrifying as was the fury of his first cousin, Mr. Kong.... [It] is not nearly as consistently funny as the producers hoped it would be, but it certainly is a most unusual show.... The wonder of *Mighty Joe Young* is the mobility of the mechanical star, but even that novelty wears thin after a while." More terse was Donald C. Willis in *Horror and Science Fiction Films: A Checklist* (1972): "More like *Son of Kong* than *King Kong*: cute ape, ridiculous, uninvolving story." Donald F. Glut pointed out in *Classic Movie Monsters* (1978), "*Mighty Joe Young* never garnered the critical acclaim or popularity of its 1933 inspiration. Though a more realistic gorilla than Kong, Joe Young was more lovable than monstrous and his screen adventure lacked the spectacle of its two predecessors."

A colorized *Mighty Joe Young* has been released on video. In 1998 Disney remade the movie with a plot focused more on animal rights; it starred Bill Paxton, Charlize Theron, David Paymer, Regina King, Peter Firth, Linda Purl and Lawrence Pressman. Terry Moore, star of the 1949 version, and its special effects guru Ray Harryhausen had cameo roles.

The Miracle of the Bells (1948; 120 minutes)

PRODUCERS: Jesse L. Lasky & Walter MacEwen. DIRECTOR: Irving Pichel. SCREENPLAY: Ben Hecht & Quentin Reynolds, from the novel by Russell Janney. PHOTOGRAPHY: Robert de Grasse. EDITOR: Elmo Williams. MUSIC: Leigh Harline. MUSIC DIRECTOR: C. Bakaleinikoff. SONGS: Jule Styne, Sammy Cahn, Pierre Norman & Russell Janney. ART DIRECTORS: Albert S. D'Agostino & Ralph Berger. SOUND: Philip N. Mitchell & Clem Portman. SET DECORATIONS: Darrell Silvera & Harley Miller. MAKEUP: Gordon Bau. SPECIAL EFFECTS: Russell A. Cully & Clifford Stine. WARDROBE: Renie. SCRIPT SUPERVISOR: J. Davies. ASSISTANT DIRECTOR: Harry D'Arcy.

CAST: Fred MacMurray (Bill Dunnigan), Valli (Olga Treskovna), Frank Sinatra (Father Paul), Lee J. Cobb (Marcus Harris), Harold Vermilyea (Nick Orloff), Charles Meredith (Father Spinsky), Jim Nolan

(Tod Jones), Veronica Pataky (Anna Klovna), Philip Ahn (Ming Gow), Frank Ferguson (Mike Dolan), Frank Wilcox (Dr. Jennings), George Chandler (Telegrapher Max), Ray Teal (Koslick), Dorothy Sebastian (Kate Orwin), Billy Wayne (Tommy Elmore), Syd Saylor (Freddy Evans), Thayer Roberts (Movie Earl of Warwick), Franz Roehn (Movie Cauchon), Herbert Evans (Movie Nobleman), Pat Davis, Jack Gargan (Assistant Directors), Ned Davenport, Charles Miller (Movie Priests), Jim Pierce, Robert Bacon, Duncan MacDonnell, Roger Creed (Movie Soldiers), George Cathrey, Roy Darmour, Bill Wallace, Mel Wixon, Hamilton Warren, Mike Sandler, Bob Thorn, Peter Erickson (Reporters), Tom Stevenson (Milton Wild), Michael Raffetto (Harold Tanby), Regina Wallace (Martha), Ian Wolfe (Grave Digger), Dorothy Neumann (Miss Millhouser), Al Eben, Kenneth Terrell, Jerry Jerome, Al Murphy, David Perry, Jack Stoney, Alonzo Price, David McMahon (Miners), Maxwell Hamilton (Ray Tanner), Charles Wagenheim (Mr. Kummer), Bert Davidson (Bob Briggs), Oliver Blake (Slenka), Max Wagner (Baggage Man), Perry Ivins (Druggist), Jack Lindquist (Boy), Richard Mickelson, Bill Clauson (Bell Ringer's Sons), Frank Pharr (Bell Ringer), Snub Pollard, Franklyn Farnum, Beth Taylor (Worshippers), Brooks Benedict, Maxine Johnston (Drunks), Mabel Colcord (Miracle Witness), Sidney D'Albrook, Ed Peil, Sr., Art Dupuis, Budd Fine, Sam Lufkin, Donald Kerr, Fred Graham, Lyle Tayo, Bobby Barber (Citizens), Quentin Reynolds (Voice of Radio Announcer).

The Miracle of the Bells was released in March 1948 by RKO to considerable publicity and a barrage of favorable reviews. Based on Russell Janney's 1946 bestselling novel, the film was heralded as a multi-million dollar production and considered one of the most important features of the year. The studio even went to the expense of constructing a Pennsylvania mining community on its Culver City ranch. Unfortunately, the result was an overlong, stodgy melodrama that failed to hold audience interest. Despite all the publicity, it quickly faded from view. Very little about the feature, or its production, seemed to jell. Ben Hecht's adaptation of Janney's book leaves out several important plot aspects, including the reformation of an atheist union boss, while Irving Pichel's direction remains pedestrian throughout its monotonous two hours. While Fred MacMurray is passable in the lead role (a part better suited to William Holden); Alida Valli, billed as Valli and on loan from producer David O. Selznick, fails to breathe any warmth into the pivotal role of a dying actress; and Frank Sinatra gives a weak, almost passive portrayal of a parish priest. On the other hand, the film's smaller parts are expertly enacted, especially Harold Vermilyea as an oily undertaker, Philip Ahn as a restaurant owner, and George Chandler as a telegrapher. Ahn's makeup, which turned the 37-year-old actor into an aged man, is particularly well-done.

Bill Dunnigan (MacMurray), press agent for Excelsior Studios in Hollywood, arrives in Coaltown, Pennsylvania, known as Little Poland, to bury the woman he loves, Olga Treskovna (Valli), an actress. He is met at the railroad station by undertaker Nick Orloff (Vermilyea), who wants one hundred dollars up front for the funeral since four years before he got stuck burying the dead woman's lush father. As they drive through town Bill recalls the first time he met Olga several years before, when she was a member of the chorus of a burlesque show directed by his pal Tommy Elmore (Billy Wayne). Olga is about to be fired but Bill convinces Tommy to give her a second try. Orloff ups the price of Olga's funeral to $150 since the pallbearers all want to be paid. Bill remembers that a year after their first meeting, he ran into Olga in a small town where she was starring in a play, *Girl of the Ozarks*. Having been attracted to her since the first time they met, Bill goes to her dressing room and since it is Christmas Eve they go out to dinner. They dine at a Chinese restaurant where the proprietor, Ming Gow (Ahn), prepares their meal himself, giving it to them as a holiday gift. Olga tells Bill about growing up in Coaltown and says it killed her Polish parents and vows to make good in Hollywood. On the way to their hotels, Olga looks at the stars and tells Bill one of them was given to her by her father the day she was born and she makes him a present of half of it. Orloff makes arrangements for Olga's funeral at Coaltown's biggest church, St. Leo's Catholic Church, thus further inflating the price of her

Poster for *The Miracle of the Bells* (1948).

funeral. Bill informs him that Olga wanted her funeral at St. Michael's Church, which is in a poor parish. Bill goes to see the priest at St. Michael's, Father Paul (Sinatra), who says he wants no money for the funeral and Bill tells him he is nearly broke. Father Paul listens as Bill talks about going to work for Hollywood producer Marcus Harris (Lee J. Cobb) at Excelsior Studios where his former client, actress Anna Klovna (Veronica Pataky), is starring in *Joan of Arc*. The temperamental star fights with Harris and director Mike Dolan (Frank Ferguson) and when she disparages the United States, Harris fires her and decides to shelve the picture. Bill sees Olga, who says she has just lost her job as Anna's stand-in, and she invites him to her apartment that night for dinner. There she tells him about her failure to break into the movies and he suddenly realizes she would be right for the part of Joan. After testing with Harris for the role, Joan is given the lead in the three million dollar epic. During filming, Olga is plagued with a hacking cough and as the production nears its end she is sent to a doctor (Frank Wilcox) who informs Bill that she is suffering from tuberculosis brought on by breathing coal dust as a child. The doctor says immediate surgery and rest might save her but Olga insists on finishing the movie. The next day Olga dies in a hospital but not before telling Bill she has fulfilled her destiny in bringing hope to the people of Coaltown. Harris decides not to release the film although Bill begs him to; Bill quits his job. Telling Olga's story to Father Paul gives Bill the inspiration to have all five churches in the town ring their bells for three days and nights in her memory. After writing bogus checks to cover the cost, Bill wires Harris for $10,000 and then remembers how Olga, on her death bed, said she wanted to be buried next to her parents and have the church bells at St. Michael's rung as six angels with wings stand by her coffin. The ringing of the bells generates nationwide publicity but Father Spinsky (Charles Meredith) of St. Leo's threatens to put Bill in jail for writing bad checks if Olga's funeral is not held at his church. Harris wires the money but tells Bill him he is going to re-film *Joan of Arc* with Genevieve James. Pennsylvania's governor proclaims a day of mourning for Olga to be observed by all denominations. The next morning a dejected Bill follows the huge crowds to St. Michael's Church and just before Olga's funeral two religious statues turn and face her coffin. The congregation is sure a miracle has taken place and Bill runs to tell Father Paul, who says the event was caused by ground breaking under the church pillars from the pressure of the crowd on its floor. Bill insists the event could still be divine intervention. When the news is broadcast across the country, Harris finds out. He comes to Coaltown and asks Bill to return to his job, saying he will immediately release *Joan of Arc* in Olga's memory. In her honor he plans to use the profits to build a Coaltown hospital.

Nearly all the critics lauded *The Miracle of the Bells*. *Harrison's Reports* deemed it "excellent mass entertainment ... [a] powerful human interest drama, of a quality rarely achieved in motion picture production," while the *Independent Exhibitors Film Bulletin* declared it "a wonderful, entertaining motion picture...." *Boxoffice* called it "a solid hit ... adroitly combining fact and fancy, realism and spiritual overtones, in a manner that can hardly fail to strike a responsive chord in the hearts of all but the most cynical audiences." *Variety* considered the film "a tremendously moving drama. Told with compelling simplicity and great heart, it will rate audience acclaim that counts for heavy grosses. As a goodwill messenger for Hollywood, film also is potent." *The Film Daily* tagged it "a strange, rare and strongly affecting drama. In its content it has a profoundly different theme that engrosses one and unfailingly maintains a strong grip on imagination. Dramatically it is an infrequent and rare good thing. [Co-producer] Lasky, always noted for extreme good taste in productions that bear his name, lives up to his fine standard...." *Motion Picture Daily* noted, "Immense audience satisfaction seems destined to be the happy fate of this sterling attraction.... Valli is excellent, MacMurray never better. Sinatra a pleasant surprise." *Motion Picture Herald* reported, "So freighted with entertainment values as to guarantee a tip-top box office experience," and *The Exhibitor* predicted, "A picture certain to land among the higher successes everywhere." *Independent Film Journal* called it "big box office" and *Film Bulletin* opined, "A wonderful, enthralling picture destined to rank with the outstanding successes of recent years." *Showmen's Trade Review* thought it "outstanding entertainment...." Dissenting in *The New York Times,* Bosley Crowther declared, "[T]he picture is pompous and funeral, both in image and in tone, as though the whole thing were in the nature of a two-hour-long death bed scene."

Miracle of the Bells director Pichel had considerable genre association, both in front of and behind the camera. As an actor he appeared in *Murder by the Clock* (1931), *The Return of the Terror* (1934), *Topper Takes a Trip* (1938), *Dick Tracy's G-Men* and *Torture Ship* (both 1939), but is probably best remembered as Sandor, the human consort of the title character in *Dracula's Daughter* (1936). He also co-directed *The Most Dangerous Game* (1932) [q.v.] and solo-helmed *Before Dawn* (1933) [q.v.], *She* (1935) [q.v.], *Earthbound* (1940), *Mr. Peabody and the Mermaid* (1948), *The Great Rupert* (1949) and *Destination Moon* (1950).

On May 31, 1948, MacMurray and Sinatra repeated their roles in "The Miracle of the Bells," an episode of the CBS series *Lux Radio Theatre.* A computer colorized version of *The Miracle of the Bells* has been released on home video.

The Monkey's Paw (1933; 58 minutes)

PRODUCERS: Pandro S. Berman & Merian C. Cooper. DIRECTORS: Wesley Ruggles & Ernest B. Schoedsack. SCREENPLAY: Graham John, from the story by W.W. Jacobs and the play by Louis N. Parker. PHOTOGRAPHY: Edward Cronjager, Jack MacKenzie, J.O. Taylor & Leo Tover. EDITOR: Charles L. Kimball. MUSIC: Max Steiner. ART DIRECTOR: Carroll Clark. SET DECORATIONS: Thomas Little. MAKEUP: J. Baker, Sam Kaufman & Mae Mark. SPECIAL EFFECTS: Vernon L. Walker, Lloyd Knechtel, Linwood G. Dunn & Harry Redmond, Sr.

CAST: C. Aubrey Smith (Sergeant Major Tom Morris), Ivan Simpson (John White), Louise Carter (Jenny White), Bramwell Fletcher (Herbert White), Betty Lawford (Rose), Winter Hall (Mr. Hartigan), Herbert Bunston (Sampson), Nina Quartero (Nura), J.M. Kerrigan (Corporal O'Leary), Le Roy Mason (Afghan), Gordon Jones (Soldier), Harry Strang, Harold Hughes, Angus Darrock (Sergeants), Nigel De Brulier (Prologue Hindu Fakir), Nick Shaid (Hindu Fakir), Sidney Bracey (Pensioner), James Bell (Flute Player), Lal Chand Mehra (Hindu Lover), Harry Allen (Commissioner), George Edwards (Juggler), Joey Ray (Merchant), Agnes Steele (Barmaid), Will Stanton (Bookmaker), Eddie Miller (Mule Driver), Leo Britt (Lance Corporal), Scott McKee (Electrician), Gordon Magee (Police Sergeant), John George (Hindu), C. Monsoor (Orchestra Leader).

On a windblown, snowy night in rural England, Tom Morris (C. Aubrey Smith), a retired sergeant major in the British army, recounts many tall tales of his adventures in India, including the loss of an arm. He details battles and Hindu customs and then brings up a monkey's paw he acquired from a Hindu fakir (Nigel de Brulier). Morris is a guest in the home of John (Ivan Simpson) and Jenny (Louise Carter) White and he tells them a person may have three wishes come true by rubbing the monkey's paw, although the results will be surprising and frightful. He then shows them the object. As he is leaving, John takes it from Morris' coat pocket. John informs Jenny that he stole the object jokingly and then relates the story to their son Herbert (Bramwell Fletcher), who is about to leave for his job at an electric plant. When Jenny goes to bed, John makes a wish on the monkey's paw: £200, so that Herbert and his fiancée Rose (Betty Lawford) can purchase a house. The following day an attorney (Winter Hall) for the plant comes to the White home to tell them their son is dead. He explains that Herbert, while laughing to his co-workers about the legend of the monkey's paw, was mangled when he accidentally fell into some machines. He then presents John and Jenny with an insurance check for £200. After Herbert's funeral, Jenny and Rose torment John about what he did and he becomes remorseful. Jenny takes the monkey's paw and wishes her son back to life. They soon hear a loud pounding at their door. As Jenny tries to open it, John realizes the awful physical state Herbert will be in and makes a third and final wish on the monkey's paw that their son return to his tomb. When the door is opened, there is no one there. John awakens to find it was all a dream and learns that Herbert has received a promotion giving him the money needed for him and Rose to get married.

In 1932 former actor Wesley Ruggles, brother of Charles Ruggles, ended his directorial contract with RKO by filming a 31-minute version of W.W. Jacobs' 1902 story "The Monkey's Paw." Studio executives expected a feature-length rendition of the creepy tale so co-producer Merian C. Cooper assigned Ernest B. Schoedsack to film filler sequences, including battle scenes, to bring the production up to six reels. Cooper and Schoedsack were working on *King Kong* (q.v.) during this time and two other alumni of that production, Marcel Delgado and Orville Goldner, made the title talisman. *The Monkey's Paw* is now considered a lost film. Surviving pictorial material show the production to be quite atmospheric. In an interesting bit of casting, the prologue sequence features Lal Chand Mehra, the Indian attaché for the East Olympic Games, playing the small role of a Hindu lover.

Contemporary reviews of *The Monkey's Paw* were mixed. *The International Photographer* said it "is greatly handicapped by its unrelenting somber mood. Even the inevitable happy ending that wags its tail at the end is hardly sufficient to dispel the gloom. The cast is uniformly capable, but the lack of a dominate screen personality is keenly felt.... The photography is an example of what can be done with the new supersensitive emulsions using very little light." The *Rushton*

Lobby card for *The Monkey's Paw* (1933).

(Louisiana) *Daily Leader* deemed it "a thrilling action drama," adding, "[It's] an authentic picture of English home life ... one of the most absorbing pictures of the year...." The *Muscatine* (Iowa) *Journal and News-Tribune* thought it "spellbinding.... *The Monkey's Paw* is an audacious blasting of our belief that we have risen above superstition. It proves that the civilized man is savage in his belief of the power of good luck pieces.... [I]t is not a mystery tale. It contains no dark dungeons, clanking chains, specters or groans. There is nothing to solve—but decidedly there is something to think about in this story laid in a pretty English cottage." "Take out several reels of this mystery picture and you would have an excellent and substantial thriller short. In its present form as a full-length feature it is pretty thin stuff," wrote *Motion Picture,* adding, "Still it has its suspense and this should satisfy." *Photoplay* opined, "This film has little entertainment value although the British cast is a capable one. Wesley Ruggles' direction too is good but seems wasted on such a dull story." *Variety* reported, "Too late to ride along with the goose-pimple cycle of last year and too morbid to be regarded with great favor in its own right." Harry Burns in *Hollywood Filmograph* complained, "The public is fed up with this sort of stuff.... It lacks names and actors who can hold interest. Everybody seems to be overacting, instead of forgetting that they eye of the camera is on them.... [It] fails miserably as screen fodder. The dialogue is uninteresting and boresome.... Photographic work of Leo Tover is not up to his high standard.... Radio Picture have made worse films and spent more money, which is about the only consolation stockholders will find." *The Film Daily* stated, "Although made in Hollywood, this production has a dominant British flavor, especially notable in the cast, and therefore is best suited for those audiences. For the general run of American fans it is not likely to register, although the very efficient cast and excellence of staging, direction and photography would be appreciated by the class patrons." *Harrison's Reports* noted the feature had a "fair" box office performance.

Monkey's Paw publicity claimed that the film's property boy, Ted Burton, who was in charge of the title talisman, handled it only wearing gloves because he did not want to touch the charm with his bare hands. Allegedly the film's cast took this as a compliment: "It proved they had been able to make the story real to at least one member of their first-hand audience."

"The Monkey's Paw" was initially staged as a one-act play in London in 1903 (a year after the Jacobs story was published), with Cyril Maude and Lena Ashwell. Louis N. Parker's play based on the story was produced in 1922. Between those years, in 1915, the first of a trio of British films entitled *The Monkey's Paw*, a three-reel production starring John Lawson, was released by Magnet. In 1923 a six-reel British feature of the story starred Moore Marriott and Marie Ault. Twenty-five years later (1948) a third British version was issued by Butchers headlining Milton Rosmer and Meg Jenkins. The tale was reworked as *Espiritismo* for a 1961 Mexican film that was shown on U.S. TV in a dubbed version called *Spiritism*. The Jacobs story was also the basis for the segment "Are You Afraid of the Dark?" in the 1973 anthology *Tales That Witness Madness*, a British production issued in the U.S. by Paramount. Short films of *The Monkey's Paw* came out in 1978, starring Herb Graham and Evelyn Coffman; in 2003 from Tribal Film Entertainment with Chris Perrons and Sylvia Mains; and in 2012 from Lewisworks Studios starring Josh Burns and Rosemary Gearheart. A 2013 feature from TMP films headlined Stephen Lang and C.J. Thomson.

There have been a number of radio adaptations of "The Monkey's Paw," including episodes of *Favorite Story*, broadcast September 18, 1948; two CBC Radio productions, *Mystery Theatre* (1966) and *Nightfall* (July 11, 1980); *Fear on Four* (September 22, 2007); *New Radio Theatre* (February 6, 2011); and *Christopher Lee's Fireside Tales* on BBC (December 30, 2011).

"The Monkey's Paw" was an early broadcast on British television, first in 1938 with Olive Walters and Nigel Stock. On U.S. television, CBS-TV's *Suspense* telecast a version on May 17,

1949, starring Boris Karloff and Mildred Natwick and again on October 3, 1950, headlining again Natwick with Stanley Ridges. A version of the story was telecast April 7, 1953, on *Your Jeweler's Showcase* with Rhys Williams, Una Merkel and Walter Kingsford. NBC-TV's *Great Ghost Stories*, broadcast July 20, 1961, presented it as a segment starring R.G. Armstrong and Mildred Dunnock. It was reworked as "The Monkey's Paw—A Retelling" on *The Alfred Hitchcock Hour* on CBS-TV, telecast April 19, 1965, starring Leif Erickson, Jane Wyatt and Lee Majors. England's Anglia Television did it as part of *Great Mysteries* with Cyril Cusack, Meg Jenkins (star of the 1948 film) and Patrick Magee, on November 10, 1973.

The Most Dangerous Game (1932; 63 minutes)

EXECUTIVE PRODUCER: David O. Selznick. ASSOCIATE PRODUCER: Merian C. Cooper. DIRECTORS: Ernest B. Schoedsack & Irving Pichel. SCREENPLAY: James Creelman, from the story by Richard Connell. PHOTOGRAPHY: Harry Gerrard. EDITOR: Archie Marshek. MUSIC: Max Steiner. ART DIRECTOR: Carroll Clark. SOUND: Murray Spivack & Clem Portman.

CAST: Joel McCrea (Robert Rainsford), Fay Wray (Eve Trowbridge), Robert Armstrong (Martin Trowbridge), Leslie Banks (Count Zaroff), Noble Johnson (Ivan), Steve Clemento, Dutch Hendrian (Tartars), William B. Davidson (Captain), Hale Hamilton (Bill), James Flavin (First Mate), Landers Stevens (Doc), Arnold Gray, Phil Tead (Passengers), Buster Crabbe (Sailor).

When RKO began production on *The Most Dangerous Game*, based on Richard Connell's 1924 same-name short story, *Harrison's Reports* forecast, "[I]t is horrible and it is hardly con-

Lobby card for *The Most Dangerous Game* (1932) picturing Joel McCrea and Fay Wray.

ceivable that any one can make an acceptable picture out of it." With regards to subject matter, the trade journal was accurate but the film proved to be popular, grossing $443,000 on a $219,000 budget. Among its most horrific scenes are those in Count Zaroff's (Leslie Banks) "trophy room" where human heads are mounted on the wall and one is shown being pickled in a large vat. The story takes place almost solely at night on a remote island with an impressive old fortress and foggy swamps. Max Steiner's rousing music score adds much to the proceedings as does Carroll Clark's art direction and uncredited Thomas Little's impressive sets. When it was previewed, the picture ran 78 minutes, but 15 minutes were shorn from it for general release and in the process scenes with Creighton Chaney (later Lon Chaney, Jr.), Ray Milland, Walter McGrail, Cornelius Keefe and Leon Waycoff (later Leon Ames) ended up on the cutting room floor. Overall, *The Most Dangerous Game* is a repellent but exciting and fast-paced affair dominated by the evil Zaroff, wonderfully portrayed by Banks, and Henry Gerrard's splendid photography.

The film was made by the production team of Merian C. Cooper and Ernest B. Schoedsack, who was filming *King Kong* (q.v.) at the same time. Both films share some of the same sets, especially the jungle locales, as well as cast and crew. James Creelman was involved in the scripts for both features, Schoedsack co-directed *The Most Dangerous Game* while he and Cooper, *Game's* associate producer, co-directed *King Kong*. For both movies, Carroll Clark and Thomas Little worked on art direction and settings, Max Steiner composed music scores, Walter Plunkett did uncredited costume designs and Murray Spivack worked on the sound. David O. Selznick executive-produced both. Fay Wray, Robert Armstrong, Noble Johnson, Steve Clemento, James Flavin and Arnold Gray appeared in the two features.

In *The Most Dangerous Game* Joel McCrea makes a more than adequate stalwart hero and Fay Wray is a decorative leading lady, but Robert Armstrong is woefully miscast as her weak-willed, drunken brother. Acting honors go to Banks as the crazed Count Zaroff, in a role that would have been well-suited to Bela Lugosi or Lionel Atwill. It marked Banks' film debut as well as his only Hollywood production; he later appeared in the genre outings *The Tunnel (Transatlantic Tunnel)* (1935), *Jamaica Inn* (1939) and *The Door with Seven Locks (Chamber of Horrors)* (1940). Olympic gold medal winner, and future star, Buster Crabbe doubled for Joel McCrea on *The Most Dangerous Game* and can be spotted as a sailor who falls off a sinking yacht.

While in dangerous waters, the captain (William B. Davidson) of a yacht belonging to Bill (Hale Hamilton) wants to turn back but is told to go ahead by his boss although the channel lights in front of them are not in the correct chart position. Two of Bill's guests, big game hunter Bob Rainsford (McCrea) and Doc (Landers Stevens), are discussing the ethics and irony of hunters and hunting when the yacht strikes a coral reef and begins to sink. The vessel explodes and only Bob and the captain survive but the latter soon falls victim to a shark. Bob makes it to shore and in a short time comes upon an old fortress where he is admitted by a mute servant, Ivan (Johnson), who works for the owner, ex-patriot Cossack Count Zaroff (Banks). He soon meets siblings Eve (Wray) and Martin Trowbridge (Armstrong), the survivors of an earlier shipwreck near the island. Zaroff informs the trio that hunting is his life, how he escaped the Russian Revolution with most of his fortune and bought the island, his suffering sometimes from severe headaches, and his use of the long bow to hunt "the most dangerous game." He tells them the joys of first killing and then loving. As Zaroff plays the piano, Eve shows Bob a group of vicious hunting dogs in the courtyard below and informs him that the two sailors who escaped with her and Martin have disappeared. As Zaroff sends Eve to bed, Bob announces that he too is tired but Zaroff and the drunk Martin plan to make an evening of it with Zaroff leading Martin into his trophy room. During the night Bob is awakened by Eve, who says she is frightened because her brother is missing and asks Bob to help her search for him. Going downstairs they find the

Joel McCrea and Fay Wray in *The Most Dangerous Game* (1932).

trophy room unlocked and its walls lined with human heads. As they hide, Zaroff and his two Tartar servants (Clemento, Dutch Hendrian) bring Martin's body in on a stretcher. Eve accuses Zaroff of killing her brother and she is taken away and Bob is shackled. Bob realizes that Zaroff's "most dangerous game" is humans. Zaroff informs Bob he shifts the channel lights in order to get prey for his hunts and if the victims can survive until dawn they will be set free. He says that to date, no one has won but himself. Zaroff wants Bob to hunt with him but he refuses and is given a hunting knife as Zaroff informs him they will play "outdoor chess." A distraught Eve goes with Bob as they head into the jungle and after three hours reach the sea. They build a Malay death trap to stop Zaroff but he manages to avoid it and goes to get a high-powered rifle. Bob and Eve set another trap by covering an opening over a deep ravine but again Zaroff manages to escape. He calls for his hunting dogs while Bob and Eve head into a foggy swamp. Leading the dogs, Ivan is impaled on a sharp-ended pole left by Bob as he and Eve take refuge in a huge tree, only to be surrounded by the dogs. They escape through the top of the tree onto a plateau that takes them to a grotto under a waterfall and there Bob fights with one of the dogs and is shot at by Zaroff, falling into the water below. Eve is taken back to the fortress and later Zaroff orders her to come to him as he plays the piano. Bob returns and informs Zaroff that his bullet hit the dog and that he fell with the animal into the water. Zaroff pulls a gun and the two men fight with Zaroff being stabbed in the back by one of his arrows. Bob fights with one of the servants (Clemento), breaking his back, and he and Eve run to the boat house in order to escape the island. After shooting a second servant (Hendrian), Bob starts the boat and he and Eve leave the island just as the fatally injured Zaroff tries to kill them with his bow and arrow. He collapses and falls into the courtyard below, where he is devoured by the dogs.

Picture Play wrote of *The Most Dangerous Game*, "Like many horror pictures, this is too determined. Consequently it falls short of its mark and merely becomes fantastic, holding interest on the score of what the players will be up to next rather than any cumulative suspense or mounting thrill." *Photoplay* felt, "It's originality with capital letters. Joel McCrea almost out–Weissmullers Johnny Weissmuller, while Leslie Banks is a refined and therefore twice-as-fascinating edition of *Frankenstein*. Acting honors go to Banks.... Don't pass this one by." *Motion Picture* concurred, "For sustained thrills, for suspense that steadily mounts to the very last scene, this picture of the ghastly sport of a madman on a lost and lonely island will be hard indeed to top.... Don't miss sixty of the most exciting minutes of your life." Mordaunt Hall in *The New York Times* called it "a highly satisfactory melodrama. It has the much-desired virtues of originality, which, in no small measure, compensates for some of its gruesome ideas and its weird plot." In a follow-up review, Hall praised Banks' portrayal of Zaroff, "which in less talented hands might easily have been stereotyped. His poise is impressive and likewise the clarity of his enunciation. He never caricatures the part, always lending rationality to the madness, if one can say so, by keeping both feet on the ground." Wood Soanes stated in the *Oakland* (California) *Tribune* that the film "is not a contender for the ten best honors of the year. It is useful only to introduce [Leslie] Banks who is one of the stage's most proficient comedians and who, of course, is cast as the sinister madman without a grain of humor in his make-up." Bryan Senn summed things up in *Golden Horrors: An Illustrated Critical Filmography of Terror Cinema, 1931–1939* (1996): "James Ashmore Creelman's screenplay adapts Richard Connell's short story into a taut, intelligent, literary work of cinematic art. The characters are well drawn, the dialogue is excellent, and the screenplay's structure draws the viewer into this nightmare situation and holds him fast until the final reel. Of course, credit must be given to directors Ernest B. Schoedsack and Irving Pichel for their masterful pacing and camerawork, which find a base in the literate screenplay and leaps forward to create a roller coaster ride of excitement."

In England, *The Most Dangerous Game* was released as *The Hounds of Zaroff*. RKO remade the story in 1945 as *A Game of Death* (q.v.), using footage from the 1932 version. In 1956 the plot was filmed for a third time as *Run for the Sun*, a United Artists release with Richard Widmark, Jane Greer, Trevor Howard and Peter Van Eyck. The storyline has been reworked for numerous other big screen and television outings. *The Most Dangerous Game* was colorized by Legend Films in 2006 under the supervision of Ray Harryhausen.

Mummy's Boys (1936; 68 minutes)

PRODUCER: Lee Marcus. DIRECTOR: Fred Guiol. SCREENPLAY: Jack Townley, Philip G. Epstein & Charles Roberts. STORY: Jack Townley & Lew Lipton. PHOTOGRAPHY: Jack MacKenzie. EDITOR: John Lockert. MUSIC DIRECTOR: Roy Webb. ART DIRECTORS: Van Nest Polglase & Feild M. Gray. SOUND: James G. Stewart.

CAST: Bert Wheeler (Stanley Wright), Robert Woolsey (Aloysius C. Whittaker), Barbara Pepper (Mary Browning), Moroni Olsen (Dr. Edward Sterling), Frank M. Thomas (Philip Browning), Willie Best (Catfish), Frank McDonald (Rasheed Bey), Frank Lackteen (Egyptian Informant), Charles Coleman (Kendall the Butler), Mitchell Lewis (Haroun Pasha), Frederick Burton (Professor Edwards), Dewey Robinson (Hotel Manager), Tiny Sandford (Foreman), Edward Keane (Captain), Noble Johnson (Tattoo Artist), John Davidson (Café Manager), Frank Moran (Larson), Ethan Laidlaw (Peters), Pedro Regas, Nick Shaid (Fakirs), Ritz Rozelle (Telephone Operator), Pat Somerset, Jack Rice, George Lollier (English Officers), Al Haskell, Gil Perkins (Egyptian Officers), Gerald Rogers (Cockney Sailor), Edith Craig (Harem Girl).

Bert Wheeler, Robert Woolsey and unidentified actresses in *Mummy's Boys* (1936).

While *Mummy's Boys* is not looked upon favorably by either contemporary critics or film historians, the feature is a fairly pleasing affair, especially for fans of Wheeler and Woolsey's silly shenanigans. It does not take itself seriously and contains the humorous running gag of Wheeler's character needing to sleep in order to remember anything important. Despite the title, the only mummy in the film is in a sequence where the villain dresses like one and tries to get rid of the members of an Egyptian expedition so he can keep a pharaoh's treasure for himself. The tomb set and its treasure room are visually impressive.

During a thunderstorm, a mysterious man wearing a turban lurks outside the home of Philip Browning (Frank M. Thomas). Browning is visited by Professor Edwards (Frederick Burton), who tells Browning and his daughter Mary (Barbara Pepper) that he wants to return the artifacts they took from the tomb of Egyptian Pharaoh Pharatime, since nine of the expedition members have died from what he believes is a curse. Edwards dies while talking to them. Incompetent ditch diggers Stanley Wright (Wheeler) and Aloysius C. Whittaker (Woolsey) answer a newspaper advertisement placed by Browning wanting men to go with him to Egypt since he plans to carry out Edwards' wishes. Arriving at the Browning mansion they learn the man in the turban, Rasheed Bey (Francis McDonald), is the only other applicant. Stanley, who can only remember things after he has slept, and Aloysius are hired by Browning and another member of the original expedition, Dr. Edward Sterling (Moroni Olsen). Stanley sees Mary and the two are attracted to each other. On the sea voyage to Egypt, the steamer runs into a derelict boat, causing a panic, and Stanley tries to save Mary by giving her Aloysius' life jacket. As the captain (Edward Keane) declares the voyage is a jinx, two crewmen (Frank Moran, Ethan Laidlaw) find a stowaway, Catfish (Willie Best), who wants to return to Cairo. Stanley and Aloysius hire him as their guide, not realizing he means his birthplace, Cairo, Illinois. Arriving in Egypt, the expedition members stay at the Hotel D'Orient where Stanley and Aloysius flirt with sheik Haroun Pasha's (Mitchell Lewis) four wives. When Pasha leaves the harem girls in a café while he searches for two missing wives, Stanley and Aloysius again try to romance them, only to have the sheik return and go after them with a knife. To escape him, Stanley and Aloysius put on harem outfits and Pasha thinks they are his missing wives until Aloysius' veil falls off and they run away from him. The two men come across a fakir (Pedro Regas) who places Stanley in a basket and then rams a sword through it. When the basket lid is removed, it is shown to be empty. Aloysius runs back to the hotel to tell Browning and Sterling that Stanley is missing only to find him there reading a newspaper. When Sterling disappears, Browning asks Stanley and Aloysius to complete the mission and take care of Mary if anything happens to him. He gives them a map revealing the location of Phara-time's tomb. To prevent the forgetful Stanley from losing it, Aloysius has a tattoo artist (Noble Johnson) draw it on his back. The expedition crosses the desert in a camel caravan and stops at an oasis before finding the tomb. The next day someone tries to kill Aloysius with a boulder, Catfish is found tied up and the expedition's camels are stolen. When Browning disappears, Aloy-sius reads the letter of instructions which tells where to dig in order to find the entrance to the tomb. When they open the tomb, Stanley, Aloysius, Barbara and Catfish find it full of bats but they manage to return the artifacts. In a secret room Sterling shows a bound Browning the treasure he found on the first expedition and admits killing all the others in order to keep it all for himself. A cave-in blocks the entrance to the tomb and as Stanley, Aloysius, Barbara and Catfish search for another way out, Stanley finds a diary dropped by Sterling detailing the murders. Catfish comes across Sterling and runs away, saying he saw a ghost. Appearing before the others, Sterling tells them he cannot remember what happened after being in Cairo and that it must be the curse. Stanley says the diary mentions a secret entrance to the tomb but he cannot remember where he hid the book. As Sterling tries to give Stanley a poison shot, he runs away. Aloysius locates the diary, and discovers that it belongs to Sterling. Browning frees himself as the authorities arrive and start digging into the tomb. To scare the others, Sterling dresses as a mummy and hides in a sarcophagus and then chases them around the tomb's treasure room, trying to dispatch them with the poison shot. Aloysius knocks him out with a vase and he and Stanley tie up Sterling as Browning finds them. The authorities open the tomb and Rasheed Bey reveals he is a member of the Egyptian secret police. Stanley tries to ask Mary to be his wife but forgets what he wants to say to her.

Mummy's Boys met with mixed notices. According to *The Hollywood Reporter*, "This pro-vides a better-than-average frame for their [Wheeler & Woolsey] mad capers, which seldom leave the well beaten track," while *Motion Picture Daily* declared that it "is no better than their last few offerings and will appeal only to fans whose loyalty cannot be shaken." *The Film Daily* reported, "That there are all degrees of humor is proved by this comedy. Audiences whose taste for fun lies along path of the obvious and slapstick may find this palatable; but those patrons who like laughs served with some semblance of the spice of cleverness and the salt of subtlety will be disappointed.... Fred Guiol, comedy's director, does as well as could be expected with the material—as does the cast." Much more damning was *Variety* which complained, "Net result of the dialog is about four snickers." The reviewer concluded, "Poorly acted, raggedly written and indifferent treatment all around, film as entertainment misses."

Murder on a Bridle Path (1936; 66 minutes)

ASSOCIATE PRODUCER: William Sistrom. DIRECTORS: Edward Killy & William Hamilton. SCREEN-PLAY: Dorothy Yost, Thomas Lennon, Edmund H. North & James Gow, from the novel *The Puzzle of the Red Stallion* by Stuart Palmer. PHOTOGRAPHY: Nicholas Musuraca. EDITOR: Jack Hively. MUSIC DIREC-TOR: Roy Webb. ART DIRECTORS: Van Nest Polglase & Feild Gray. SOUND: Clem Portman.

CAST: James Gleason (Inspector Oscar Piper), Helen Broderick (Hildegarde Martha Withers), Louise Latimer (Barbara Foley), Owen Davis, Jr. (Eddie Fry), John Arledge (Joey Thomas), John Carroll (Latigo Wells), Leslie Fenton (Don Gregg), Christian Rub (Chris Thomas), Sheila Terry (Violet Feverel), Willie Best (High Pockets), John Miltern (Pat Gregg), Spencer Charters (Warden Sylvester Mahoney), James Donlan (Detective Kane), Gustav von Seyffertitz (Dr. Max Bloom), Frank Reicher (Dr. Peters), Maurice Cass (Schultz), Barlowe Borland (Pipe Shop Proprietor), Al Morris [Tony Martin] (Violet's Escort), Harry Jans, Mike Lally (Newsmen), Monte Vandergrift (Detective Bart), Dewey Robinson (Turkish Bath Masseur), Frank Mills, Frank Marlowe (Bridle Path Riders), Murray Alper, Harry Bowen (Taxi Drivers), Jack Rice (Hotel Manager), Maxine Jennings (Partygoer).

Following Edna May Oliver's move from RKO to MGM, RKO cast Helen Broderick as Miss Hildegarde Martha Withers, the crime-solving school teacher, in *Murder on a Bridle Path*, issued in the spring of 1936. It was based on the novel *The Puzzle of the Red Stallion* by Stuart Palmer, published the same year. James Gleason, who had appeared opposite Oliver as Inspector Oscar Piper in the Miss Withers adventures *Penguin Pool Murder* (1932), *Murder on the Black-board* (1934) and *Murder on a Honeymoon* (1935) [qq.v.], was elevated to top billing in this effort. Unfortunately *Murder on a Bridle Path* is not in the same league as its predecessors. It qualifies as a horror thriller for a well-designed, spooky mansion and for its killer, a homicidal maniac driven insane over the treatment of his son by his employer. The madman not only commits two murders but he also tries to bring about the death of an old man by hanging him upside down and swinging him like a pendulum. Critics have complained that Helen Broderick did not handle the Miss Withers part well but in truth she is fine but too attractive for the role. Future singing superstar Tony Martin can be spotted early in the proceedings as the first victim's date.

Following a party, divorcee Violet Feverel (Sheila Terry) has an altercation with her sister Barbara Foley (Louise Lorimer) and the latter's boyfriend, Eddie Fry (Owen Davis, Jr.). She heads to a local stable and rejects the attentions of its owner, Latigo Wells (John Carroll), a former suitor, and goes for a ride, but is followed by a stranger, who she earlier slapped, riding a bicycle. Violet is thrown from her horse while riding on a bridle path and killed. The medical examiner, Dr. Max Bloom (Gustav von Seyffertitz), says it was an accident when questioned by Police Inspector Oscar Piper (Gleason). Also on the scene is schoolteacher Miss Withers (Broderick), leading a horse with blood on it. Dr. Bloom concludes that the horse was shot with an air rifle. Piper and Miss Withers go to the stable where they question the attendant, High Pockets (Willie Best). Wells tells Piper that Violet slapped a man at the stable that morning, and he is taken to jail for not admitting that he also argued with the murdered woman. Miss Withers and Piper go to Violet's apartment and confront Barbara and Eddie, who say they are going away to get married. Eddie declares that Violet made trouble for everyone while Barbara reveals that her sister's ex-husband, Don Gregg (Leslie Fenton), had reason to hate her. Left alone, Barbara hides Violet's diary and a gun. Eddie informs Piper that Don is in jail for not paying alimony. Chris Thomas (Christian Rub), a servant of Violet's former father-in-law Pat Gregg (John Miltern), comes to the apartment to ask her to see the old man, who is in bad health. He is told of Violet's murder and Piper and Miss Withers accompany him to the Greggs' Long Island home. They meet Chris' crippled son Joey (John Arledge) and discover Pat Gregg unconscious. Miss Withers finds a receipt for Don's alimony. The family doctor (Frank Reicher) announces the old man had a stroke and that Violet was an evil woman. Miss Withers questions Pat, who is pleased to hear that Violet is dead; Chris says the murdered woman was a troublemaker. Piper learns from the jail warden, Mahoney (Spencer Charters), that Don was released the night before and later in his office shows Mahoney that the court order for his release is a forgery. Unaware that he is being hunted by the police, Don goes to Violet's apartment and learns from Barbara that his ex-wife has been murdered. Miss Withers arrives to talk with Barbara and convinces Don to see Piper. On the way, both Miss Withers and Don are arrested by dimwitted Police Detective Kane (James Donlan) and taken to headquarters. Don tells Piper he did not know about the phony writ and that he spent the night at the Central Baths with his story confirmed by an attendant (Dewey Robinson). Don and his father argue over the murder and Don gets a call saying that Barbara wants to see him. The police department's handwriting expert (Maurice Cass) informs Piper that Don did not forge the writ. High Pockets telephones Miss Withers saying there is trouble at the stables. When she and Piper arrive there, Eddie informs them that Violet gave Wells $900. Wells claims Don tried to rent a horse the morning Violet was killed and that he followed her on a bicycle. The handwriting expert confirms the signature on the fake writ belongs to Pat Gregg. Piper orders Kane to take all the suspects to the Gregg home and he and Miss Withers precede them there. After finding Gregg dead at his desk, Miss Withers deduces that someone tried to kill him the day before by hanging him upside down and returned to finish the job. Piper and Miss Withers talk with Chris, who says the old man and his son quarreled. When Kane arrives with the suspects, Eddie says Violet hated Pat Gregg and would have liked to have killed him. While searching the house, Miss Withers finds incriminating evidence in Chris' room; he appears and admits killing Violet. He says Pat Gregg's horse crippled his son Joey years before and he saved $900 and gave it to Pat to bet on a horse so he could have money for an operation for the young man. Instead Pat gave the money to Violet to cover Don's back alimony and then laughed at Chris when he demanded the return of the money. He said he killed Violet and her ex–father-in-law because he hated them. He then tries to bludgeon Miss Withers but misses and falls down the stairs and dies.

  The Christian Science Monitor commented, "Too much dull talk in this one." On the other hand, *The Film Daily* opined, "Good melodrama that should find favor with mystery fans. Excellently acted and well directed." *Variety* wrote, "It's a murder mystery that pulls its punches, showing how the fine comedy abilities of Helen Broderick and James Gleason can be thoroughly submerged by a poor script." *Boxoffice* noted, "This one falls short of its predecessors in the department of wisecracking dialogue, but the finished troupers like Gleason and Helen Broderick ... could make even the Congressional Record funny and they get the utmost out of their opportunities." *Motion Picture Daily* felt it contained "a large portion of enjoyable comedy." The *New York World-Telegram* found it "pretty disappointing in plot, action and sleuthing, all of which are definitely second-rate." The *Motion Picture Herald* concluded, "Plot construction successfully sustains suspense until the crime solution, which is not indicated in advance." The *New York Herald-Tribune* declared, "The interest of the piece lies in the adroit performances of both Mr. Gleason and Miss Broderick and the humor which underlies it." *Harrison's Reports* rated the picture's box office performance as "Fair to Poor."

  James Gleason went on to appear as Piper in two more Miss Withers features with ZaSu Pitts, *The Plot Thickens* (1936) and *Forty Naughty Girls* (1937) [qq.v.].

Murder on a Honeymoon (1935; 74 minutes)

  PRODUCER: Kenneth Macgowan. ASSOCIATE PRODUCER: Kenneth Hempstead. DIRECTOR: Lloyd Corrigan. SCREENPLAY: Seton I. Miller & Robert Benchley, from the novel *The Puzzle of the Pepper Tree* by Stuart Palmer. Photography: Nicholas Musuraca. Editor: William Morgan. Music Director: Alberto Columbo. Art Directors: Perry Ferguson & Van Nest Polglase. Sound: John L. Cass. Special Photographic Effects: Vernon L. Walker.

Cast: Edna May Oliver (Hildegarde Martha Withers), James Gleason (Inspector Oscar Piper), Lola Lane (Phyllis La Font), George Meeker (Roswell T. Forrest, alias Tom Kelsey), Dorothy Libaire (Kay Deving), Harry Ellerbe (Marvin Deving), Chick Chandler (Dick French), Sleep 'n' East [Willie Best] (Willie), Leo G. Carroll (Joseph B. Tate), DeWitt Jennings (Captain Beegle), Spencer Charters (Police Chief Britt), Arthur Hoyt (Dr. O'Rourke), Matt McHugh (Madden), Morgan Wallace (McArthur/Arthur J. Mack), Brooks Benedict (Tom Kelsey, alias Roswell T. Forrest), Rollo Lloyd (Hotel Clerk), Irving Bacon (Pelican Carrier), James P. Burtis (Sergeant Mike), Robert Homans (Police Stenographer), Lynne Carver (Blonde Actress), Pietro Sosso (Casino Watchman), Harry Allen (Gardener), Billy Dooley (Seaplane Porter).

Edna May Oliver appeared as amateur sleuth–schoolteacher Miss Withers for the third and final time in *Murder on a Honeymoon*, issued by Radio Pictures in February 1935. It was preceded by *Penguin Pool Murder* (1932) and *Murder on the Blackboard* (1934) [qq.v.], both co-starring James Gleason as her police inspector cohort, Oscar Piper. Gleason repeated the role for the third time in *Murder on a Honeymoon*, the weakest of the trio of mystery features he made with Oliver. Based on Stuart Palmer's 1933 novel *The Puzzle of the Pepper Tree,* the script was co-authored by Robert Benchley but it lacks the pep and overall humor of its predecessors. Its main asset is location shooting on Santa Catalina Island. Besides three murders, the only horrific aspect of the proceedings has Miss Withers and Piper searching for clues in a supposedly empty, dark and creepy casino at night. *Harrison's Reports* stated the film's box office performance was "Fair to Poor."

On a 20-minute seaplane flight from the California coast to Santa Catalina Island, vacationing schoolteacher Miss Withers (Oliver) sees another passenger, Roswell T. Forrest (Brooks Benedict), become ill and offers him smelling salts. Famed film director Joseph B. Tate (Leo G. Carroll) gives the man a drink from his flask. Also on the plane are newlyweds Marvin (Harry Ellerbe) and Kay (Dorothy Libaire) Deving, actress Phyllis La Font (Lola Lane), and Captain Beegle (DeWitt Jennings), a former rum runner, plus the pilot, Dick French (Chick Chandler), and co-pilot Madden (Matt McHugh). Upon landing, it is discovered that the man is dead and Miss Withers goes to Police Chief Britt (Spencer Charters) claiming there is evidence of poison and murder although the coroner, Dr. O'Rourke (Arthur Hoyt), says Forrest died from heart failure. Britt opens a letter addressed to the deceased claiming that a gang is out to get him. Tom Kelsey (George Meeker) arrives to identify Forrest, saying the man was his employer. After Britt announces he will investigate the matter, Miss Withers wires New York City Police Inspector Oscar Piper (Gleason), asking for information on the dead man. Piper is informed that the deceased was being sought by the state attorney since he was scheduled to testify against the Graves mobster gang. Piper gets permission from the police commissioner to handle the case and heads to Santa Catalina Island, fearing for Miss Withers' life. As Britt interrogates the people on the seaplane, he gets a wire from Piper saying the Graves gang offered $10,000 for Forrest's demise. The next day Miss Withers overhears Phyllis tell Tate to give her a part in his movie or she will go to the police. Piper arrives to see Miss Withers snooping and the two go to the police station and see that Forrest's body is missing. Miss Withers goes to question Phyllis, who is crying and admits she knows something about the case. Piper learns from the Devings that they saw the pilots takes a body out of the hotel and leave with it in a car. The pilots deny they removed Forrest's body and say it was Tate, who asked them to take him to the location where his company is filming. Miss Withers then has Phyllis inform Piper that Tate's flask has two separate compartments and he did not drink the same liquor as Forrest. At the filming location, Tate admits that the flask has two compartments but says his liquor was not poisoned. Back at the hotel, Piper sees Phyllis and Tom together and suspects them of getting rid of Forrest. Miss Withers observes hotel guest Arthur Mack (Morgan Wallace) get an envelope from the clerk (Rollo Lloyd) and overhears him give the combination to a post office box. Later she sees him put an envelope in the box; retrieving it, she finds it contains $10,000. Miss Withers pays porter Willie (Willie Best) to watch the box and report back to her when someone opens it. That evening Piper calls Miss Withers and tells her to come to the casino where he has found the wheelbarrow used to carry away Forrest's body. There he find a drunk Captain Beegle and the newlyweds, who have been to a dance. When Marvin Deving starts to tell Piper something about the case, he is shot and killed. Piper suspects Beegle of the crime until he finds out the captain was dining with Britt when the murder took place. The next day Miss Withers notices a tree outside her room has changed positions and when Piper and Britt dig it up they find Forrest's body. Piper arrests Tom for the crime but the man says he is Forrest and that he and the real Kesley, his bodyguard, switched identities to throw off the Graves gang. Willie informs Miss Withers that the pilots opened the post office box only to reveal he was guarding the wrong one. When Miss Withers finds a pack of Rialto cigarettes in a pool with dead fish, she goes to the hotel and searches Mack's room, not knowing he has seen her. When she returns to her own room, Mack gets the drop on her, ties her up and leaves her in a closet. She awakens to find Piper and Britt have rescued her and goes with them to Mack's room where they find him murdered. Miss Withers says the case

can be solved if Kay can answer one question. When Miss Withers offers the young widow a cigarette, she refuses it and the schoolteacher tells her she knew it contained poison. Kay pulls a gun on Piper and Miss Withers, admitting she and her husband were hired to kill Forrest and she shot Mack for double crossing them. Piper manages to knock out Kay. Later Piper finds out that Miss Withers has arranged for lovers Phyllis and Tom to go to Mexico on Beegle's new schooner and then hands him a sworn statement from Tom he can present to the grand jury. Phyllis has given Miss Withers her dog and when she and Piper open her closet they find out she has had pups.

Motion Picture reported, "Logic, plausibility, reason have been sacrificed to action and entertainment and the result is a fast-moving, hilarious picture with plenty of laughs mixed up with three murders." Andre Sen-

Edna May Oliver, James Gleason and Morgan Wallace in *Murder on a Honeymoon* (1935).

nwald in *The New York Times* thought *Murder on a Honeymoon* was the best of the Oliver-Gleason collaborations: "Briskly paced and endearingly funny, it tears along through a succession of intermediary problems which are quite as exciting as the final unveiling of the killer.... [It] unravels the case with fascinating skill, without losing its admirable sense of humor." *Boxoffice* declared it "splendid," with "plenty of suspense and hilarious comedy. The dialogue is clean and clever. Should register big with Edna May Oliver fans." *The New Movie Magazine* dubbed it "one of the real good mysteries of the year" and *Variety* termed the feature "better than average.... Plot is just a once over lightly proposition, but jammed with laughs and with the one important element—a surprise finish."

Murder on a Honeymoon* was directed by Lloyd Corrigan, who was better known as a jovial character actor; he played art dealer Arthur Manleder in Columbia's Boston Blackie series. When Oliver left RKO to work at MGM, Helen Broderick took over the role of Miss Withers in the next outing, *Murder on a Bridle Path* (q.v.).

Murder on Approval (1956; 70 minutes)

PRODUCERS: Robert S. Baker & Monty Berman. DIRECTOR: Bernard Knowles. SCREENPLAY: Kenneth R. Hayles. PHOTOGRAPHY: Monty Berman. EDITOR: Jack Slade. ART DIRECTOR: Wilfred Arnold. SOUND: Leo Wilkins. PRODUCTION MANAGER: Charles Permane. PRODUCTION CONTROLLER: Ronald C. Liles. MAKEUP: John O'Gorman. HAIR STYLIST: Helen Penfold. CONTINUITY: Ann Forsyth. ASSISTANT DIRECTOR: John Goodman.

CAST: Tom Conway (Tom "Duke" Martin), Delphi Lawrence (Jean Larson), Brian Worth (Geoffrey Blake), Michael Balfour (Barney Wilson), Campbell Cotts (Robert Coburn), John Horsley (Detective Inspector Taylor), Ronan O'Casey (Stefan Gordoni), Launce Maraschal (J.D. Everleigh), Colin Tapley (Lord Valchrist), Alan Gifford (Henry Warburg), Grace Arnold (Lady Hawksley), John Colicos, Reg Morris (Thugs), Mayura (Yasmina), John Watson (Detective Sergeant Grant), Marianne Stone (Mrs. Wilson), Derrick Whittingham (Print Shop Manager), Frank Pemberton (Garage Attendant), Neil Wilson (Fingerprint Expert), Olive Kirby (Lady Hawksley's Maid), Rosamund Waring (Receptionist), Margaret Rowe (Stewardess), Maureen Connell (Beautiful Girl at Airport).

A British production company, CIPA, owned by Robert S. Baker and cinematographer Monty Berman, attempted to recreate the aura of the popular Falcon series of the previous decade by starring Tom Conway in a new group of detective adventures set in England. The first, *Barbados Quest*, was issued in its homeland in the summer of 1955 by RKO Radio. A year later RKO released it stateside as *Murder on Approval*. While not in a league with the Falcon films, *Murder on Approval* is a speedy, somewhat complicated and fairly entertaining "B" mystery involving a cursed stamp. Conway still exuded the sophisticated charm of a woman chaser who keeps one step ahead of the law and he is abetted by a comedy sidekick, Barney (Michael Balfour), an ex-convict like the character of Goldy Locke in the Falcon series. Berman's photography is a plus, the film being made during the winter with its gray atmosphere adding a gritty look to London locales and rural environs. The feature was successful enough in its homeland to warrant a sequel, *Breakaway* (q.v.), but it did not result in the hoped-for series.

Wealthy American J.D. Everleigh (Launce Maraschal), arriving in London by plane, is greeted by Lord Valchrist (Colin Tapley), a rare stamp expert. They drive to see stamp dealer Robert Coburn (Campbell Cotts), who agreed to sell Everleigh the rare Barbados Overprint stamp for £10,000. Geoffrey Blake (Brian Worth), who identifies himself as Coburn's manager, hands the stamp over to Everleigh on the condition the terms of the sale are not published for six months. Returning to New York City, Everleigh visits fellow collector Henry Warburg (Alan Gifford) and sees that he too has a Barbados Overprint although there are only supposed to be

Lobby card for *Murder on Approval* (1956) picturing Delphi Lawrence and Tom Conway.

four in the world and three of them are in private collections. Everleigh offers his friend, private detective Tom "Duke" Martin (Conway), $20,000 to get back his payment if his stamp is counterfeit. Tom questions Everleigh about the sale and realizes that Blake manipulated the stamps. Flying to London, Tom is met at the airport by his ex-convict pal Barney Wilson (Balfour), who takes him to a swank apartment he rented from a friend doing time. When Tom interviews Coburn, the dealer denies any knowledge of the stamp deal with Everleigh and also says he does not know Blake. Tom and Barney drive to the estate of Lady Hawksley (Grace Arnold), whose late husband was the owner of the Barbados stamp offered for sale. Blake, Lady Hawksley's nephew by marriage, sees the two men arrive and Tom mistakes Lady Hawksley's lovely secretary Jean Larson (Delphi Lawrence) for Lady Hawksley. Lady Hawksley tells Tom that she still owns the stamp and it was Coburn who made its valuation. Everleigh sends Tom a cable saying two more Barbados Overprint stamps have surfaced, both from Coburn's agency. That night Tom and Barney break into Coburn's office and surprise a man robbing the safe. The man escapes but Tom finds a hat with the initials S.G. When Tom and Barney return to their apartment, they find Jean waiting there. She tells Tom it was Blake who took the stamp to Coburn for valuation. Police Inspector Taylor (John Horsley) investigates the robbery of Coburn's safe and the stamp dealer tells him about Tom's visit. Taylor tells Tom not to get involved in police business. After Jean returns, she, Tom and Barney drive to the Ajax Printing Works in Lambeth and learn that the hat Tom found at the robbery scene belongs to engraver Stefan Gordoni (Ronan O'Casey); Tom tells Barney to shadow him. Tom and Jean go back to Lady Hawksley's estate to look at her Barbados stamp and they find that it is missing. Bake informs them he made a deal with Coburn to sell the stamp. Tom returns to his apartment only to be knocked out by two thugs (John Colicos, Reg Morris). Barney awakens him and says Gordoni has quit his job. Tom and Jean go to see Gordoni's friend, exotic dancer Yasmina (Mayura), with Tom finding a clue in her dressing room that leads them to Gordoni's residence. Meanwhile Gordoni confronts Coburn saying he wants more money for having engraved plates of the Bardabos Overprint. Tom waits for Gordoni in his flat, and when he arrives the engraver is shot before he can reveal the identity of the swindler. Tom and Jean chase the getaway car which leads them to the garage of an apartment building where Coburn resides. Tom informs Coburn that Gordoni has been murdered, and when Taylor arrives Tom tells him about the murder. The getaway car and Gordoni's body cannot be found. When Coburn packs to leave the city, Blake says they must get the plates and destroy them. Barney reports to Tom that Everleigh's stamp is genuine after having it examined by another expert. Tom gets a telephone call warning him to leave the country and Jean also urges him to do so. The next day Gordoni's body is fished out of the Thames River and Taylor goes to see Tom, saying he is going to ask for a deportation order. Changing his mind about leaving, Tom locates Yasmina at a café and she says she posted a package for Gordoni the night before. Tom goes back to see Coburn but finds him murdered and is seen by a housekeeper (Marianne Stone). Blake and his thugs abduct Jean and Barney; Barney is told to have Tom bring the stamp and the plates to a rendezvous in the country. Taylor investigates Coburn's murder and puts out a wanted order for Tom after the housekeeper identifies his picture. Barney is abducted by Blake's two henchmen. Tom gets the drop on them and locks them up when they arrive at Lady Hawksley's estate. Tom finds Blake cleaning out the safe but as he starts to call the police, Jean stops him at gunpoint. Tom informs Jean that Blake, not Coburn, shot Gordoni as he claimed and he also informs her that Blake murdered Coburn. When Blake attempts to kill Tom, Jean shoots him as Taylor and his men arrive. The lawmen call for an ambulance for the injured Blake. Tom informs Jean he will do everything he can to help her. The case closed, Tom flies home with a beautiful girl (Maureen Connell) he met at the airport.

Boxoffice called *Murder on Approval* "a minor, mildly entertaining British-made murder mystery.... Pictures of this type do nothing to increase the popularity of British films in the U.S." In *British Sound Films: The Studio Years 1928–1959* (1984), David Quinlan dubbed it a "tired thriller, not very well acted."

Murder on the Blackboard (1934; 71 minutes)

EXECUTIVE PRODUCER: Pandro S. Berman. ASSOCIATE PRODUCER: Kenneth Macgowan. DIRECTOR: George Archainbaud. SCREENPLAY: Willis Goldbeck, from the novel by Stuart Palmer. PHOTOGRAPHY: Nicholas Musuraca. EDITOR: Archie Marshek. MUSIC DIRECTOR: Max Steiner. ART DIRECTORS: Van Nest Polglase & Albert S. D'Agostino. SOUND: John L. Cass. COSTUMES: Walter Plunkett.

CAST: Edna May Oliver (Hildegarde Martha Withers), James Gleason (Inspector Oscar Piper), Bruce Cabot (Addison Stevens), Gertrude Michael (Jane Davis), Regis Toomey (Detective Smiley North), Tully Marshall (Mr. McFarland), Frederick Vogeding (Otto Schweitzer), Edgar Kennedy (Detective Donahue), Jackie Searl (Leland Stanford Jones), Barbara Fritchie (Louise Halloran), Gustav von Seyffertitz (Dr. Max Von Immen), Tom Herbert (Detective McTeague), Jed Prouty (Dr. Levine), Wade Boteler (Diner Customer), Frank Mills (Diner Worker), Milton Vandergrift (Policeman), Tommy Bupp (Student).

The teaming of Edna May Oliver and James Gleason as Miss Withers and Inspector Piper in *Penguin Pool Murder* (q.v.) clicked with the moviegoing public and the two were reunited in *Murder on the Blackboard*, which Radio Pictures released in the summer of 1934, eighteen months after the initial outing. It was based on Stuart Palmer's 1932 novel, the third to feature the murder-solving old maid schoolteacher. At the finale of *Penguin Pool Murder* Miss Withers and Piper

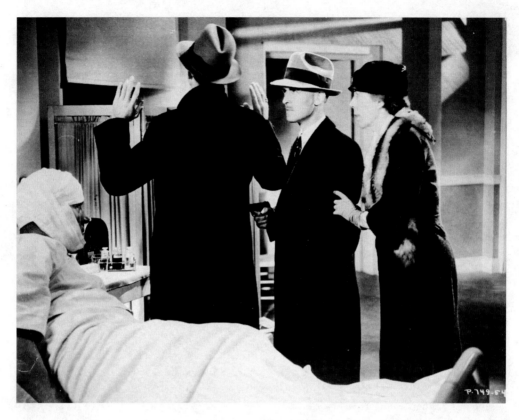

Edgar Kennedy, James Gleason and Edna May Oliver corner the killer in *Murder on the Black-board* (1934).

are headed to the marriage license bureau but the nuptials were called off in the second book, *Murder on Wheels* (1932), and not included in *Murder on the Blackboard*, a faithful adaptation of the Palmer work with one exception: In the book, Oscar Piper is knocked out while investigating the murder and remains comatose for most of the adventure, with Miss Withers handling the case with Detective Donahue. The film version had Donahue (Edgar Kennedy) in the hospital and Piper sharing the screen time with Miss Withers. The best of RKO's half-dozen Hildegarde Withers features, *Murder on the Blackboard* is an entertaining blend of mystery and comedy interspersed with such horror trappings as the murder victim beaten to death after being slowly poisoned and her body nearly incinerated, along with the hunt for the killer in the dark, spooky basement of an elementary school. In said basement is a half-dug grave, a partially false ceiling leading to a bootleg liquor consignment and a hatchet flying through the darkness, nearly decapitating Miss Withers.

At almost 3:30 p.m. slovenly elementary school janitor Otto Schweitzer (Frederick Vogeding) rouses himself from a drunken stupor to open the doors for the students to leave at the end of the school day. The principal, Mr. McFarland (Tully Marshall), visits comely teacher Janey Davis (Gertrude Michael) and asks her to dine with him that night but a call from his wife changes his plans. He sees Janey has a gun in her purse and she tells him it belongs to her roommate and colleague, Louise Halloran (Barbara Fritchie), who is sick and afraid. Science and shop teacher, Addison "Ad" Stevens (Bruce Cabot), who is also the assistant principal, tries to avoid Louise and goes to see Janey after McFarland leaves. After the two kiss, Ad admits having a brief flirtation with Louise the previous summer at McFarland's camp. In her classroom, Louise draws a series of musical notes on the blackboard. Otto shows up demanding money and she threatens him with jail. Another teacher, Miss Withers (Oliver), keeps a pupil, Leland (Jackie Searl), after school for spreading the rumor that Louise has a crush on McFarland. An hour later Miss Withers finds Louise murdered in the school's cloakroom and sends Leland to telephone Inspector Piper (Gleason). By the time he arrives with detectives Smiley North (Regis Toomey) and Donahue (Kennedy), the body has disappeared. As Miss Withers, Piper and Smiley search for the corpse, Donahue hears noises from the school basement and goes to investigate, only to be knocked unconscious. He is diagnosed with a concussion and taken to the hospital while Smiley finds someone has been digging a grave in the cellar. As Piper investigates, Miss Withers goes through Louise's desk and finds a bottle of liquor and in Ad's science room she discovers a dead ant in a benzine bottle The fire alarm goes off and the murderer escapes with Miss Withers realizing the school furnace is still operating so late in the day. Returning to the cellar, Miss Withers, Piper and North find Louise's body in the furnace. A drunk Otto shows up claiming to be a rich man and Piper has him held as a murder suspect. That night, as McFarland slips out of Janey's apartment building and hides under the steps, Miss Withers arrives by taxi, closely followed by Ad and Janey. Miss Withers informs the couple of Louise's murder and they tell her they are planning to be married. Miss Withers discovers Janey and Louise held a lottery ticket worth $300,000, which was sold to them by Otto. Janey searches for Louise's love letters but cannot find them. McFarland telephones and asks Miss Withers to come to his home. There he asks her to investigate the case. While he is getting her a drink, she finds part of a letter he wrote to Louise in the fireplace. The next day Piper questions Janey and Ad, accusing Janey of murdering her roommate for the lottery winnings. Miss Withers shows Piper the letter she found at McFarland's house and he admits having an affair with Louise, who threw him over for Ad. He also says Louise threatened to give the letters he wrote her to his wife. After the questioning is finished, Dr. Levine (Jed Prouty) announces to Miss Withers and Piper that Louise was dying of pernicious anemia of the bones. Miss Withers, Piper and North return to the school's cellar to hunt for evidence when someone turns out the lights and a hatchet is thrown at Miss Withers. She finds a secret opening in the ceiling that leads to a room containing boxes of liquor and deduces this is where Otto got the whiskey he sold Louise. Back on the street, Miss Withers and Piper learn that Otto has broken jail and they suspect him of being the hatchet thrower. Piper goes to see Donahue in the hospital and finds he has regained consciousness but cannot remember who hit him. The coroner (Gustav von Seyffertitz) confirms that Louise died of pernicious anemia of the bones and upon being questioned by Miss Withers admits that small doses of benzine in liquor could have led to her demise. Saying she knows the killer's identity, Miss Withers has Piper place a story in the newspapers saying Donahue has recovered his memory. That evening the suspects are told by Piper that Donahue has had a relapse and they can go home. Miss Withers and Piper then hide near Donahue and await for the killer to arrive. After four hours a figure appears and pours a liquid in Donahue's medicine. Miss Withers turns on the lights and Piper gets the drop on Ad, who drinks the poison. Before dying, he says he and Louise were secretly married the previous summer and that he killed her to have Janey and the lottery money.

An amusing coda to the story has Miss Withers and Piper in a diner going over the case with her telling him the musical notes Louise drew on the blackboard repeated the letters "AD," thus naming her killer. Becoming worried about Janey, Miss Withers calls and is indignant to find she is having breakfast in her apartment with Smiley North. Before leaving, Piper asks Miss Withers if he can "come up and see her some time" and when she complains about being "insulted at my age," a scruffy diner (Wade Boteler) announces, "Better late than never, sister."

Photoplay declared that *Murder on the Blackboard* had "plenty of action, suspense and thrills," while *Hollywood Filmograph* complained about "big gaps that left us wondering what the whole thing was all about. Here's a murder and comedy, hand in hand.... All in all, the story is good but it needs more brushing up and smoothing out." *The Marion* (Iowa) *Sentinel* termed it "ace high entertainment" and Mordaunt Hall in *The New York Times* wrote, "In some respects the story is quite ingenious, and when most such yarns depend large on spine-chilling effects and screams this *Murder on the Blackboard* has the saving grace of a sense of humor." *The Hollywood Reporter* opined, "Miss Oliver is priceless as Snoopy. Her indignant sniffs, her important adjusting of her tatty little fur piece, and her knowing glances at dead ants and lighter fluid, make grand comedy. Gleason is clever and amusing as the inspector.... [Director] George Archainbaud imbued the piece with real eeriness.... The photography of Nicholas Musucara is just what a mystery needs." *The New York Herald-Tribune* claimed, "The film, as a story, has no great significance, but it's deftly handled by Mr. Archainbaud," while *The New York Journal* enthused, "Miss Oliver turns the film into diverting entertainment that is further enhanced by some really amusing dialogue. You'll find the piece fun." *The New York Post* felt the film was "thoroughly interesting and entertaining" and *The New York Sun* agreed: "It's right at the top of its class as a bright and lively farce-mystery drama." *The New York World-Telegram* noted, "A nicely devised little problem, with clues that are neither too closely guarded nor too openly revealed, and that lends itself to a solution that is not too far-fetched. All of which makes for an excitingly eventful, smooth, colorful thriller." *Picture Play Magazine* said, "Ingeniously plotted, well acted, and amusingly written, this is a novelty among murder mysteries and is one of the best.... Again Edna May Oliver plays the role briskly, nervously, and with consummate skill, all making for a brilliant performance with the light touch accented."

The Detroit Council of Catholic Organizations graded the feature as being unsuitable for children or adolescents.

Oliver and Gleason teamed for a third time as Miss Withers and Oscar Piper in *Murder on a Honeymoon* (q.v.).

The Mysterians (Metro-Goldwyn-Mayer, 1959; 85 minutes; Color)

PRODUCER: Tomoyuki Tanaka. DIRECTOR: Ishiro Honda. SCREENPLAY: Takeshi Kimura. STORY: Sigeru Kayama & Jojiro Okami. PHOTOGRAPHY: Haijime Koizumi. EDITOR: Koichi Iwashita. MUSIC: Akira Ifukube. PRODUCTION DESIGN: Teruaki Abe. PRODUCTION MANAGER: Yasuaki Sakamoto. SOUND: Masanobu Miyazaki. SOUND EFFECTS: Ichiro Minawa. SPECIAL EFFECTS DIRECTOR: Eiji Tsuburaya. SPECIAL EFFECTS PHOTOGRAPHERS: Hidesaburo Araki & Sadamasa Arikawa. SPECIAL EFFECTS ART DIRECTOR: Akira Watanabe. ENGLISH DUBBING DIALOGUE: Peter Riethof & Carlos Montalban. ENGLISH DUBBING SUPERVISOR: Jay Bonafield. ASSISTANT DIRECTOR: Koji Kajita.

CAST: Kenji Sahara (Joji Atsumi), Yumi Shirakawa (Etsuko Shiraishi), Momoko Kochi (Hiroko Iwamoto), Akihiko Hirata (Ryoichi Shiraishi), Takashi Shimura (Dr. Tanjiro Adachi), Susumu Fujita (General Morita), Hisaya Ito (Captain Seki), Yoshio Kosugi (Commander Sugimoto), Fuyuki Murakami (Dr. Nobu Kawanami), Tetsu Nakamura (Dr. Koda), Yoshio Tsuchiya (Mysterians' Leader), Yutaka Sada (Captain Miyamoto), Ren Imaizumi (Hayami), Takeo Oikawa (Television Announcer), Tadao Nakamaru (First Lieutenant Yamamoto), George Furness (Dr. Svenson), Harold Conway (Dr. DeGracia), Byron Morrow (General), Soji Ubukata (Dr. Noda), Shin Otomo (Officer Kawada), Akio Kusama (Chief Togawa), Rinsaku Ogata (Officer Oata), Jiro Kumaai (Colonel Ito), Hideo Mihara (General Emoto), Haru Nakajima (Moguera), Minosuke Yamada (Secretary of Defense Hamamoto), Mitsuo Matsumoto (Reporter), Shoichi Hirose, Eisuke Nakanishi (Detectives), Rikji Sanjo (Mrs. Shiraishi), Katsumi Tezuka, Hideo Unagami (Mysterians), Mitsuo Tsuda, Kamayuki Tsubono (Defense Meeting Members), Heihachiro Okawa (Board Member), Yasuhiro Shigenobu, Haruya Kato, Senkichi Omura (Villagers).

In 1958 RKO purchased the distribution rights to Toho Films' *Chikyu Boeigun* (Earth Defense Force) which had been released in its homeland of Japan in December 1957. Re-titling it *The Mysterians* and proclaiming it "The Greatest Science-Fiction Picture Ever Conceived by the Mind of Man," the studio developed an elaborate advertising campaign hoping to cash in on the burgeoning popularity of Japanese sci-fi films that began with *Godzilla, King of the Monsters!* (1956). Unfortunately RKO ceased distributing films before its release but *The Mysterians* was eventually picked up by Metro-Goldwyn-Mayer which issued it in May 1959. Three minutes of footage was clipped from the original version for its dubbed U.S. showings.

Ishiro Honda, who directed *Godzilla*, helmed *The Mysterians* and the thrust of the film, lensed in magnificent Toho Scope and Eastman Color, was its special effects and miniatures. Especially impressive is the sequence where a fissure swallows a village followed by the appearance of a giant metal, rodent-looking robot. A smaller version of the monster briefly appears near the end of the feature as it bores its way from under the ground and upsets one of the military's death ray deflectors. Even more spectacular are the seemingly endless battles between the aliens and the military, a harbinger of such conflicts in a multitude of future Japanese sci-fi efforts. On the minus side, the film's plot, excluding the battles, is hollow and the Mysterians are hardly menacing as they run around in costumes more compatible with Hollywood movie serials. In one scene the aliens inform Japanese scientists they are pacifists while holding them at bay with ray guns! Even more ridiculous is some of the English dubbing. In the scene where some men are trapped in the fire surrounding a small village, they sound like Dixie rubes, as does the military commander who orders and then calls off one of the strikes against the aliens. The subplot of having aliens wanting to breed with Earth women was not as frayed in the late 1950s as it is today but does little to advance the proceedings. An amusing scene has one of the leading ladies showing complete revulsion at the thought of marrying an alien. Overall *The Mysterians* is a visually attractive affair with top-notch special effects but a vapid plot.

At a village festival, astronomer Ryoichi Shiraishi (Akihiko Hirata) suddenly breaks off his engagement to Hiroko Iwamoto (Momoko Kochi), much to the consternation of his sister Etsuko (Yumi Shirakawa) and her scientist boyfriend, Joji Atsumi (Kenji Sahara), Ryoichi's best friend. Ryoichi disappears after a forest fire develops nearby with the conflagration mysteriously burning from the roots up. Dr. Tanjiro Adachi (Takashi Shimura), Ryoichi's superior, does not agree with his Mysteroid Report concerning a mythical star but he gets word of a village on Mount Fuji being destroyed in an instant after a fissure develops. As they investigate the incident, Joji and several policemen see a giant silver robot, Moguera, emerge from the side of a hill and march toward a nearby town. The local authorities tell the citizens to cross the Koyama Bridge and the military fights the robot, which shoots death rays from its eyes. As the robot crosses the bridge, it is exploded, destroying the invader. After an examination of the robot, Dr. Adachi announces it was made of an alloy not present on Earth and was radio-controlled. He is not sure if it comes from outer space. Dr. Adachi observes activity coming from the dark side of the Moon and Joji informs him that he and Etsuko saw UFOs near the destroyed Fuji village. Newspaper headlines declare that Dr. Adachi has announced an invasion from the Moon. As Dr. Adachi, Joji and a group of scientist and military people observe a lake near Fuji where UFO activity has been sighted, a huge dome emerges from the ground. A voice from the dome invites Dr. Adachi, Joji and three others to come inside for a conference and promises they will not be harmed. Inside the sphere they are met by the Mysterian leader (Yoshio Tsuchiya) and his minions, who inform them that their planet had the H-bomb one hundred thousand years ago. Just before it was destroyed in an atomic war, their ancestors settled on Mars. They demand two miles of land and want to marry Earth women in order to continue their race. The leaders says they have abducted three women and also want Etsuko and Hiroko. When government leaders are informed of the demands, war is declared on the invaders. As the military mobilizes around the dome, Ryoichi appears on television before his sister, Hiroko and Joji and says he has joined forces with the Mysterians since they mean no harm and can advance the cause of science by thousands of years. Joji informs Dr. Adachi of Ryoichi's actions but the attack on the dome is ordered and easily repulsed by the Mysterians despite the use of artillery and flame throwers. Dr. Adachi calls for the nations of the world to unite against the invaders and after Ryoichi again appears on television demanding 75 acres of land, world leaders agree to join the fight. After a second attack fails, Dr. Adachi vetoes the idea of using H-bombs but agrees on a new weapon, the Markalite Cannon, a huge lens that will deflect the invaders' death rays. The Mysterians abduct Etsuko and Hiroko and take them to the dome. Joji discovers a cave that leads to a tunnel entrance to the dome as the third attack on the Mysterians begins to show some effect. The aliens request the attack be stopped and then cause a gigantic flood that devastates the area. As Joji tries to disable the dome's control room, he is captured. Ryoichi, who has discovered the duplicity of the aliens, helps him and the women escape. Before saying goodbye to Joji, Ryoichi gives him his completed Mysteroid research and says the Mysterians tricked him. He goes back into the dome and destroys its control center as the Markalite Cannon causes the dome to explode. When the aliens' craft leaves the Earth, some of them are destroyed. Dr. Adachi proclaims that the human race must learn from the Mysterians' errors.

"By far the best and most explosive of the rash of science fiction–monster pictures, this Japanese-made film has CinemaScope and Eastman Color to add to the startling effects which will thrill the youngsters, teenagers, and all devotees of modern action fare," wrote *Boxoffice*. According to *The New York Times*, "The Mysterians, cool cats who had their own hydrogen bomb during our Stone Age, speak perfect English. In a visored get-up not unlike Jack Haley's Tin Woodman costume in *The Wizard of Oz*, they manage to make a heck of a racket before slithering back to Planet Five.... This Metro release is crammed with routine footage of death rays and scrambling civilians, not one of whom can act." *Variety* was more middle of the road: "As corny as it is furious, *The Mysterians* is red-blooded phantasmagoria—made in Japan and dedicated to those undiscerning enough to be taken in by its hokum...." In *Horrors: From Screen to Scream* (1975), Ed Naha opined, "Imaginative Japanese special effects lift this invasion from space theme from the 'B' film doldrums," while Welch Everman in *Cult Science Fiction Films* (1995) took a philosophical approach: "*The Mysterians* is a very conservative and isolationist film, and though its politics don't hold up very well in our time, it spoke eloquently to audiences of the late fifties in Japan and in the United States, because it said what people needed it to say." C.J. Henderson wrote in *The Encyclopedia of Science Fiction Movies* (2001), "This is one of the best science fiction movies ever produced in Japan. Although still nothing more than pulp fiction, it moves in a linear, understandable progression without the inanity inherent in most Toho productions. The special effects are highly respectable, and the miniature work is the usual stunning display."

The Mysterious Desperado (1949; 61 minutes)

PRODUCER: Herman Schlom. DIRECTOR: Lesley Selander. SCREENPLAY: Norman Houston. SCRIPT SUPERVISOR: Daniel B. Ullman. PHOTOGRAPHY: Nicholas Musuraca. EDITOR: Les Millbrook. MUSIC: Paul Sawtell. MUSIC DIRECTOR: C. Bakaleinikoff. ART DIRECTORS: Albert S. D'Agostino & Feild Gray. SET DECORATIONS: Darrell Silvera & Jack Mills. SOUND: Phil Brigandi & Clem Portman. ASSISTANT DIRECTOR: John E. Pommer.

CAST: Tim Holt (Tim Holt), Richard Martin (Chito Rafferty), Edward Norris (Ramon Bustamante), Movita Castaneda (Luisa), Frank Wilcox (Elias P. Stevens), William Tannen (Bart Barton), Robert Livingston (Honest John Jordan), Robert B. Williams (Whitaker), Kenneth MacDonald (Sheriff Anders), Frank Lackteen (Pedro), Leander De Cordova (Padre), Leo J. McMahon (Deputy Sheriff), Kermit Maynard (Saloon Customer).

Filmed as *In Old Capistrano* and *Renegade of the Rancho, The Mysterious Desperado* was the 30th of 47 RKO B Westerns that Tim Holt starred in between 1940 and 1952. During that time he was also in *The Magnificent Ambersons* (1942), *Hitler's Children* (1943), both for RKO, *My Darling Clementine* (1946) and *The Treasure of the Sierra Madre* (1948). Like his earlier *Guns of Hate* (q.v.), *The Mysterious Desperado* was produced by Herman Schlom, directed by Lesley Selander and scripted by Norman Houston, who co-wrote the earlier feature. *The Mysterious Desperado* had such genre trappings as a dark, spooky, cobwebbed hacienda, a cloaked figure and sidekick Chito's (Richard Martin) fear that their arrival there might "wake the dead." Like *Guns of Hate*, the feature was also blessed with lovely desert scenery. On-location shooting was done at the San Fernando Mission.

Arizona rancher Tim Holt (Holt) and his pal Chito Rafferty (Martin) are digging post holes when Chito gets a letter saying his uncle has died intestate, with Chito being an heir. The two depart for Santo Domingo, California, where they come upon Bart Barton (William Tannen) and Honest John Jordan (Robert Livingston) selling acreage. Chito has a verbal confrontation with the two men before he and Tim go to see land administrator Elias Stevens (Frank Wilcox). Since he is out of town on business, they talk with his clerk, Whitaker (Robert B. Williams), who sends Barton and Jordan to get rid of Chito as he and Tim dine in the local saloon. The two real estate men are badly beaten in the fight; when it is over, Tim tells Chito he believes they were hired to kill him (Chito). Tim and Chito go to the Bustamante ranch where Chito spent his childhood, and find it rundown. Once they get inside, Chito is attacked by a man. Tim overpowers Chito's attacker and he turns out to be Ramon Bustamante (Edward Norris), the deceased's son. When Ramon finds out that his cousin Chito is the heir to the rancho, he accuses him of trying to cheat him out of his inheritance. Ramon runs away when informant Pedro (Frank Lackteen) brings Stevens and Sheriff Anders (Kenneth MacDonald). They tell Tim and Chito that Ramon is wanted for the murder of his father and cannot inherit the property. Chito wants to go home and Tim agrees but that night a mysterious cloaked figure enters the hacienda. Tim gets the drop on the intruder, who turns out to be half-breed Luisa (Movita Castaneda), Ramon's fiancée. She informs them that Ramon and his father fought bitterly over their romance and on the day of their intended wedding the old man was murdered but not by Ramon. A masked man fires at them and Tim believes Chito was the intended victim. Tim and Chito visit Stevens the next morning and he says the estate will make Chito very wealthy but he will need to prove his identity. Tim says Chito has papers showing he was once a member of the Arizona Rangers. When the two leave town, Stevens signals Barton and Jordan to follow them. During a shootout in the desert, Chito receives a leg wound and Barton is shot by Tim. Jordan takes Barton to his ranch while Tim goes with Chito to the San Gabriel Mission where he is doctored by Luisa and the local priest (Leander De Cordova). Tim gets Luisa to signal Ramon, who is hiding in the nearby mountains, and he meets him at the hacienda where Ramon proclaims his innocence. Pedro sees Ramon arrive at the ranch and leads the sheriff and his men there. Ramon is arrested and blames Tim for his capture. When Sheriff Anders gets Ramon to town, Whitaker wants him hung immediately but the lawman locks him in jail. Stevens organizes a citizens' committee to quickly try and convict Ramon and tells Jordan to keep Barton out of sight, fearing he will confess. As Tim prepares to leave the mission with Chito, Luisa tells him she will not forgive him for betraying Ramon; the padre says he believes him to be innocent. Tim and Chito wait for Jordan in the desert and follow him to his ranch where they get the drop on him and the badly wounded Barton. Chito takes Barton to the hacienda while Jordan manages to elude Tim and ride to town. After Tim sees Jordan with Stevens, he stops Ramon from being hung and the two men go back to the Bustamante home where Chito threatens to use a knife to make Barton confess. Barton says Stevens killed Manuel's father in order to get control of the property and he and Jordan were hired to get Chito out of the way. Stevens and his henchman attack the ranch but Tim escapes on a horse, followed by Jordan, and locates the sheriff and his posse. Jordan rides back to warn Stevens as Ramon is wounded in a shootout with the bad men. Just as the crooks are about to break into the hacienda, Tim arrives with the sheriff and his posse and subdues Stevens. Later, after the marriage of Ramon and Luisa, Chito kisses the bride and he and Tim return to their ranch.

The *Annapolis* (Maryland) *Capitol* called *The Mysterious Desperado* "an out-of-the-ordinary Western drama." *Variety* reported, "Oater fans and Saturday matinee trade will find this one likable.... Herman Schlom's production gets the most value from story and scenic background, and the Paul Sawtell score contributes neatly to thriller-suspense mood developed by [Lesley] Selander's direction." *Boxoffice* noted, "From a commercial approach this can be considered a standard entry in the series of low-budget westerns starring Tim Holt and it doubtlessly will serve its function just as well as the average predecessor. If one wishes to be critical, however, it can be recorded that the film lacks the action and speed which marked some earlier Holt giddyappers."

The Nitwits (1935; 81 minutes)

ASSOCIATE PRODUCER: Lee Marcus. DIRECTOR: George Stevens. SCREENPLAY: Fred Guiol & Al Boasberg. STORY: Stuart Palmer. PHOTOGRAPHY: Edward Cronjager. EDITOR: John Lockert. MUSIC DIRECTOR: Roy Webb. SONGS: Dorothy Fields, Jimmy McHugh, L. Wolfe Gilbert & Felix Bernard. ART DIRECTORS: Van Nest Polglase & Perry Ferguson. SOUND: Philip J. Faulkner, Jr.

CAST: Bert Wheeler (Johnny), Robert Woolsey (Newton), Fred Keating (William Darrell), Betty Grable (Mary Roberts), Evelyn Brent (Alice Lake), Erik Rhodes (George Clark), Hale Hamilton (Winfield Lake), Charles Wilson (Captain Jennings), Arthur Aylesworth (Lurch), Willie Best (Sleepy), Lew Kelly (Hazel), Edgar Dearing (Officer Riley), William Gould (Police Sergeant), Joey Ray (Himself), Arthur Treacher (Tennis Equipment Carrier), Ed Peil, Jr. (Detective Eddie), Billy Wayne (Martin), Donald Haines (Office Boy Hal), Joan Andrews (Singer), Frances Grant, Jack Ellis (Dancers), Pat Harmon, Constantine Romanoff (Singing Inmates), Dick Curtis, Bob Reeves (Stakeout Policemen), Donald Kerr, Dick Gilbert, Ham Kinsey, Pat West (Henchmen), Floyd Shackelford (Gambler), Martin Cichy (Policeman).

The Nitwits, released by RKO Radio Pictures early in the summer of 1935, was the 13th feature to star the comedy team of Bert Wheeler and Robert Woolsey, who launched their Hollywood careers in two big musicals for the studio, *Rio Rita* (1929) and *Dixiana* (1930). After that they headlined a series of features for RKO that displayed their broad brand of humor along with doing one for Columbia, *So This Is Africa* (1933). George Stevens, who directed the duo in their previous effort, *Kentucky Kernels* (1934), helmed this fast-paced but sometimes convoluted affair that not only featured a murderous maniac called "The Black Widow" but also a device invented by Woolsey that makes people tell the truth. Also incorporated into the comedy murder mystery plot are two pleasing songs, "Music in My Heart," nicely sung by Wheeler and Betty Grable, and "You Opened My Eyes," plus a dance number by Wheeler and Grable, who previously appeared with the comedy team in *Hold 'Em Jail* (1932). In addition to the usual Wheeler and Woolsey admixture of slapstick and one-liners, plus a plethora of goofy situations, a funny running gag has Woolsey continuously knocking down a dignified man (Arthur Treacher) carrying tennis equipment. There is also an extended, somewhat amusing sequence involving the boys trying to get away from a dumb flatfoot, nicely portrayed by Edgar Dearing. Willie Best, who did a trio of films with Wheeler and Woolsey, has a few good moments as a gambling janitor. The mystery plot is only a framework on which to hang the script, which some sources claim was augmented by director Stevens, along with future director Leslie Goodwins and Grant Garrett, since the killer is revealed long before the wrap-up. The story was written by Stuart Palmer, author of the "Hildegarde Withers" mysteries, several of which were filmed by RKO. At 81 minutes, *The Nitwits*, which was filmed as *Murder Song* and *Nitwits*, was the longest of Wheeler and Woolsey's starring vehicles and even then it was cut before release, deleting parts played by Dorothy Granger, Etienne Girardot and Robert Middlemass. Despite its length, *The Nitwits* is a pretty fair effort that provides quite a bit of humor but hardly any chills. It was co-scripted by Fred Guiol, who would direct the team's next three features, including the genre outings *The Rainmakers* (1935) and *Mummy's Boys* (1936) [qq.v.].

As crooner Joey Ray (himself) sings "You Opened My Eyes" for music publisher Winfield Lake (Hale Hamilton), cigar store operator Johnny (Wheeler) pines for his girlfriend, Mary Roberts (Grable), Lake's secretary. Johnny's partner, Newton (Woolsey), has invented a machine which makes people tell the truth. Lake's wife Alice (Evelyn Brent) catches Lake making a pass at Mary and then informs him she has received another extortion letter from "The Black Widow." She demands that her husband hire ace detective William Darrell (Fred Keating) to protect him. Mary informs Johnny that Lake needs a murder song and she wants him to write it so they can get the money they need to get married. As Johnny and Newton collaborate on a tune about the Black Widow, Darrell agrees to guard Lake. Johnny and Mary play a punch board, hoping to get a wedding ring, but instead she wins a revolver. Johnny writes the song, entitled "The Black Widow Will Get You If You Don't Watch Out," and the next day Newton tries to audition it for the frightened Lake, who rebuffs his efforts. In his office, Lake is confronted by disgruntled song-writer George Clark (Erik Rhodes), who claims he is being cheated on the royalties from his song "You Opened My Eyes." Lake calls in his auditor, Lurch (Arthur Aylesworth), who cannot account for the monetary disparity and Lake says he may call in an outside auditor. Mary has office boy Hal (Donald Haines) deliver a note to Johnny telling him to get his song to Lake. When Johnny does, he finds the music publisher making a pass at Mary and slugs him. Lake tries to placate Johnny by offering to publish his song but Johnny orders Mary to quit her job and they both leave. As Lake sits, a rubber black widow spider slides onto his desk and he is shot through a hole in the ceiling. Going after Johnny, Newton finds Lake's body and runs out only to knock down a man (Treacher) carrying tennis equipment. Lurch finds the corpse and calls the police, but not before trying to pry open Lake's desk. Newton thinks Johnny killed Lake. Mary returns to the dead man's office for her things, picks up the revolver on his desk and hides on the terrace as the police, led by Captain Jennings (Charles Wilson), arrive. Darrell finds the fake spider on Lake's desk while Lurch informs Jennings that Clark had an argument with the mur-dered man that morning. Jennings orders Clark brought in for questioning, along with Johnny and Hazel (Lew Kelly), an addled songwriter who also saw Lake that day. Lurch also informs Jenning that the gun on Lake's desk is missing. When Jennings finds Mary with the revolver, she is held her for Lake's killing. To save Mary, Johnny confesses to the crime and to save Johnny, Newton confesses. Jennings orders both men off the premises. In order to visit Mary in jail, Johnny and Newton use stilts. Mary informs Johnny she saw Lurch trying to break into Lake's desk. When Alice announces to Darrell she has received another extortion letter from the Black Widow, he advises her, and all his other clients being blackmailed by the mystery crook, to pay.

Robert Woolsey and Bert Wheeler in *The Nitwits* (1935).

At midnight during a thunderstorm, Johnny and Newton go to the Lake Building to use Newton's invention on Lurch. Jennings and his men, who are there to capture the Black Widow since the payoffs are to take place that night, order them out of the building. They find another entrance, as do two mysterious strangers and a group of black gamblers whose crap game has been raided by the police. On the third floor of the building, janitor Sleepy (Willie Best) lets his gambler pals finish their game in the Imperial Costume Company. Newton installs his invention on Lurch's chair and then tries to open Lake's desk. Hazel shows up and Johnny and Newton chase him, thinking he is the Black Widow, but capture Darrell by mistake. The detective tells the boys he has his reputation to protect and he must solve the case and free Mary. Darrell has Johnny and Newton help him re-enact Lake's murder and, sitting in Lurch's chair, he confesses to being the Black Widow. Newton believes his machine has made a mistake for the first time. As Newton sits at Lake's desk, he is nearly shot from above and he and Johnny are held at gunpoint by one of the strangers who followed them into the building. When the stranger, who turns out to be Lurch, tries to open the desk, he is shot. Darrell then takes Johnny and Newton upstairs to capture the murderer. Jennings has Mary brought to Lake's office and proves her gun did not kill Lake. Darrell knocks out Johnny and Newton but is thwarted in getting the money when he finds the gamblers and Sleepy have found it. Donning a skeleton outfit, Darrell tries to scare off the gamblers as Mary informs Jennings about Lurch trying to open Lake's desk. They discover Lurch murdered and the other stranger, who turns out to be Clark, tied up. Johnny and Newton revive and think the Black Widow has killed Darrell. While Darrell chases the gamblers, Johnny and Newton find the money. Darrell is soon after them with a large sword. Darrell calls in his henchmen (Billy Wayne, Donald Kerr, Dick Gilbert, Ham Kinsey, Pat West) to help him retrieve the money and a melee ensues between them, the gamblers, Sleepy, Johnny and Newton. Newton manages to knock out most of the gang members and Darrell is apprehended by the police. Newton gives Mary and Johnny a wedding ring he got from the punch board.

Photoplay enthused, "Wheeler and Woolsey mixed up in a murder case are at their funniest. The gags and giggles and roars are so fast you have to hang on or roll in the aisle. They use every device for laughs known to man…. It is rowdy, hilarious, and not a dull moment."

"This time it's a full-grown whodunit, with the director sticking to the plot and weaving the comedy into the fabric," reported *Variety*. The reviewer added, "Not a bad job, but the combination runs too long for best results in spite of some undeniably funny business and a finish that moves with the speed of the oldtime pantomime slapstick…. Nicely directed, but the script would have profited by editing before production." In *Movie Comedy Teams* (1985), Leonard Maltin called *The Nitwits* one of Wheeler and Woolsey's best: "The film's hilarious chase climax borrows liberally from several 'Boy Friends' comedies directed by [George] Stevens when he was with Hal Roach."

Pearl of the South Pacific (1955; 83 minutes; Color)

PRODUCER: Benedict Bogeaus. DIRECTOR: Allan Dwan. SCREENPLAY: Jesse Lasky, Jr. ADDITIONAL DIALOGUE: Talbot Jennings. STORY: Anne Hunger. PHOTOGRAPHY: John Alton. EDITORS: Carlo Lodato & James Leicester. MUSIC: Louis Forbes. PRODUCTION DESIGN: Van Nest Polglase. SET DECORATIONS: Bertram Granger. SOUND: Jean L. Speak. COSTUMES: Gwen Wakeling. MAKEUP: Emile LaVigne & Mel Berns. HAIR STYLIST: Myrl Stoltz. PRODUCTION SUPERVISOR: John E. Burch. ASSISTANT DIRECTOR: Lew Borzage.

CAST: Virginia Mayo (Rita Delaine), Dennis Morgan (Dan Merrill), David Farrar (Bully Hague), Basil Ruysdael (Tuan Michael), Lance Fuller (George), Murvyn Vye (Halemano), Lisa Montell (Momu), Carol Thurston (Native Mother).

In *Allan Dwan: The Last Pioneer* (1971), director Dwan told Peter Bogdanovich that *Pearl of the South Seas* was "a terrible picture. It should never have been done. We tried to talk [producer Benedict] Bogeaus out of that one—I don't know how he got involved. And everything went wrong on that. It was a mess. But a comedy to me. I was laughing all the way through it, and Bogeaus couldn't understand why I was amused since it was tragedy." It was the fifth of ten features Dwan directed for Bogeaus, seven of them for RKO release. Their penultimate collaboration, *Enchanted Island* (1958), also a South Seas melodrama, was scheduled to be issued by RKO but the studio closed and it was picked up by Warner Bros.

Dwan is too harsh on *Pearl of the South Pacific* which is a fairly effective adventure yarn that interpolates genre subplots such as a hidden temple, a native god and a giant octopus guarding a sacred grotto containing priceless black pearls. With exterior filming in Tahiti and at Malibu Beach, the production is delightfully lensed in Technicolor and Superscope, with John Alton's cinematography a highlight. Also a plus is beautiful Virginia Mayo wearing a form-fitting sarong for most of the footage as she masquerades as a missionary. Handling the stalwart leading man chore is Dennis Morgan, who two decades before made his screen debut as Stanley Morner in another aquatic affair, *I Conquer the Sea!* (1936). The villainy is nicely done by British actor David Farrar while Lance Fuller is bland as a native lad in love with an equally dull Lisa Montell. Murvyn Vye looks a bit too well fed as the island's chief. Top acting honors go to Basil Ruysdael portraying a benevolent Caucasian high priest who tries to protect his people and their way of life.

Waking from a drunken binge, Dan Merrill (Morgan) finds his schooner afloat in the South Seas and his former girlfriend, blonde Rita Delaine (Mayo), now the love of his partner, Bully Haig (Farrar), a passenger. Rita informs Dan she picked up native Te Kop in Fort Good, planning

Poster for *Pearl of the South Pacific* (1955).

to have him show her and Bully the island where he came from with a priceless black pearl. She offers to cut Dan in on the deal only to find that Te Kop has died. With over a million dollars at stake, Dan agrees to take Rita and Bully to the island but he and Rita argue over their lost romance which she claims was destroyed by his greed for money. Dan kisses Rita, starting a fight with Bully which is halted when the island is sighted. A wedding festivity is taking place there with the island's high priest, aged white man Tuan Michael (Ruysdael), declaring that native god Tagaloa approves of the marriage between his son George (Fuller) and Chief Halemano's (Vye) daughter Momu (Montell). George admits to his father that he is unsure of the marriage because of his desire to see the outside world, but Tuan Michael tells him their island is tranquil and the people are happy and he wants to keep it that way. As the ceremony is about to be completed, word comes of the arrival of strangers and Tuan Michael postpones the wedding to join the natives in meeting the newcomers in their kayaks. Tuan Michael warns Dan and Bully not to set foot on the island as Rita comes on deck dressed as a missionary. George is immediately attracted to her and begs his father to let her come to the island or he will stay with her. Rita boards a kayak and is taken to the island and Tuan Michael takes her to a temple and tells her he will protect the island as long as he can. He also says that, for her own protection, she must stay within the confines of the edifice and not roam the island. That night Rita cannot sleep because of the heat and she goes to the shore where she meets George and they walk in the water. Jealous Momu steals and burns Rita's clothes. When Dan swims to the island to check on her, he finds Rita wrapped in a blanket. The natives spot him and Dan runs back to the shore. Halemano informs Rita that if she wants to live, she should return to the ship and go away. Later Tuan Michael warns his son about Rita but she plays music for the island children and comes to the rescue of a small boy who falls from a tree, breaking his ankle. Rita helps Tuan Michael, who tends to the boy's fracture. When Dan's boat becomes lodged on a reef, Tuan Michael warns him and Bully not to come ashore while repairs are being made. That night a native informs Halemano that the boat is able to sail and he wants to force the invaders to leave but Tuan Michael tells him to wait. Tuan Michael has doubts about Rita's sincerity. She later brings George aboard the boat and as Bully shows him the vessel, she confesses to Dan that she thinks Tuan Michael is on to their scheme. Wanting the pearls, Dan rebuffs her plea to drop the plan and then kisses her again and gets slapped. Back on the island, George gives Rita flowers. When they go into the forest, Momu informs her father, who tells her not to spy on them. Rita and George sit by a large pool and he tells her the pearls are located in it but that it is taboo to dive there. She scoffs at his story and jumps into the water only to be confronted by a giant octopus. George saves Rita and they swim to a grotto. There they find a burial ground for high priests, with a canister brimming with black pearls. They swim back to shore and Rita kisses George and tells him to let Dan and Bully come to the island for fresh water. Later Dan and Bully arrive on the island but they bring jugs of liquor and get George and some of the other natives drunk. Dan shows George the black pearl Te Kop stole from the island and Rita asks him to dive for more but he refuses. When the other natives refuse to dive for the pearls, Bully starts beating them. Rita tries to stop him just as Tuan Michael arrives and then has a stroke after a confrontation with Bully. Rita goes back to the temple to look after Tuan Michael and again asks Dan to give up the quest for the pearls but he refuses. After he and Dan uses their knives to kill the sea devil, George agrees to dive for the gems but brings back worthless seed pearls. Halemano accuses Rita of bringing a curse to the island and gives her two moons to cure Tuan Michael or leave. As Tuan Michael starts to recover, he begs Rita to leave with Dan and forget about the island, telling her an Indian prince brought the black pearls to the island so they would no longer be a power for evil. George brings Rita several black pearls and tries to kiss her but she rebuffs him and Dan snatches the gems away from him. An angry Rita tells George she will be his woman and will stay on the island with him. Momu begs Tuan Michael to reunite her with George. Bully gets George to dive for the pearls one last time and after he does, Bully stabs him. Dan finds George's body but runs away as two natives approach and call for help. Dan gives a luau for the natives but when Halemano learns that George has been stabbed he orders his warriors to attack the invaders' boat. Bully and his crew try to fight off the natives but a fire-bearing lance falls into the boat's cabin where gunpowder is stored. Dan arrives on the boat and fights with Bully, who is killed by a native spear. Dan jumps from the craft just before it explodes. The natives return to the island and Halemano orders Rita to be killed by spears. When Tuan Michael learns his son will live, he goes to stop Halemano, who is held at gunpoint by Dan, who has arrived to rescue Rita. Tuan Michael convinces Halemano to set Rita and Dan free and the two ask to remain on the island. After their request is granted, Tuan Michael leads the natives in finishing the wedding ceremony between George and Momu.

The New York Times declared, "*Pearl of the South Pacific* would shame an oyster." *Boxoffice* reported, "Here's a brimming measure of undiluted hokum that will have critics unsheathing their most biting sarcasm, but which will probably go out and play to profitable business.... The process [Superscope] and color, because of an excellent job of photography, are the feature's best assets, with the former showing up to what is its possible best to date." *Variety* termed it a "routine South Seas adventure ... just mildly diverting," adding, "Footage has a few thrills.... John Alton's lensing and tints are good...."

Penguin Pool Murder (1932; 70 minutes)

EXECUTIVE PRODUCER: David O. Selznick. ASSOCIATE PRODUCER: Kenneth Macgowan. DIRECTOR: George Archainbaud. SCREENPLAY: Willis Goldbeck. STORY: Lowell Bretano, from the novel *The Penguin Pool Murder* by Stuart Palmer. PHOTOGRAPHY: Henry Gerrard. EDITOR: Jack Kitchin. MUSIC DIRECTOR: Max Steiner. SOUND: Hugh McDowell, Jr.

CAST: Edna May Oliver (Hildegarde Martha Withers), Robert Armstrong (Barry Costello), James Gleason (Inspector Oscar Piper), Mae Clarke (Gwen Parker), Donald Cook (Phil Seymour), Edgar Kennedy (Officer Donovan), Clarence H. Wilson (Bertrand B. Hemingway), James Donlan (Security Guard Fink), Gustav von Seyffertitz (Dr. Max Bloom), Guy Usher (Gerald "Gerry" Parker), Mary Mason (Secretary), Rochelle Hudson (Telephone Operator), Joe Hermano (Chicago Lew), William LeMaire (Guard Mac-Donald), Wilfred North (Judge), Sidney Miller (Isadore Marx), Dorothy Vernon (Robbery Victim), Chuck Hamilton (Officer Jack), A.S. "Pop" Byron (Strauss), Edith Fellows (Student).

Often described as a comedy-mystery, *Penguin Pool Murder* has its share of horrific displays, including a hatpin shoved into the brain of a murder victim and the dark, creepy catwalks behind the various tanks of the Gotham aquarium where two homicides are perpetrated by a fiend who not only tries to frame two innocent people for the crimes, but also accuses the film's heroine Miss Withers (Edna May Oliver), a spinster schoolteacher with a penchant for solving murders. Based on Stuart Palmer's 1931 novel *The Penguin Pool Murder,* the feature was issued by Radio Pictures late in 1932. It was shown in Great Britain as *The Penguin Pool Mystery.* Perfectly cast as Miss Withers and her police inspector adversary, Oscar Piper, Edna May Oliver and James Gleason went on to play the roles in two follow-ups, *Murder on the Blackboard* and *Murder on a Honeymoon* (qq.v.), before Oliver left RKO and signed with MGM. Gleason continued as Piper opposite Helen Broderick as Miss Withers in *Murder on a Bridle Path* (q.v.) and finished the series with ZaSu Pitts as the schoolmarm in *The Plot Thickens* and *Forty Naughty Girls* (qq.v.).

When her lover hangs up on her when she needs money, socialite Gwen Parker (Mae Clarke) calls former boyfriend Philip Seymour (Donald Cook) and asks him to meet her at the New

York Aquarium. Her husband, Wall Street stockbroker Gerald Parker (Guy Usher), overheard the conversation with Philip and accuses her of being unfaithful, and she threatens to divorce him. Parker has made a series of bad investments that has left him and several other investors broke. One of his clients, Bertrand B. Hemingway (Clarence H. Wilson), the aquarium director, accuses Parker of deliberately defrauding him. Hemingway sees Gwen arrive at the aquarium and, after spotting her with Philip, anonymously phones Parker and tells him the whereabouts of his wife. The angry Parker rushes to the aquarium and confronts Gwen and Philip, accusing the latter of trying to break up his home. Philip hits Parker, knocking him out, and moves him behind the penguin tank. Gwen and Philip try to exit the building but are confronted by Hemingway, who insists they come to his office to see an exotic fish. Elementary school teacher Miss Withers (Oliver) arrives with her pupils

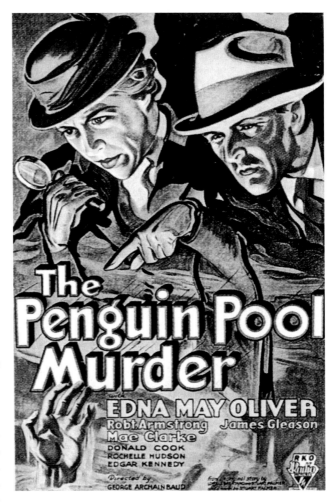

Poster for *Penguin Pool Murder* (1932).

and when deaf mute thief Chicago Lew (Joe Hermano) steals a woman's (Dorothy Vernon) purse and tries to flee, Miss Withers trips him with her umbrella. Lew is arrested by Officer Donovan (Edgar Kennedy), who gets into an argument with security guard Fink (James Donlan) over who will get the reward for the crook's capture. Miss Withers screams when she sees a body fall into the penguin tank. It is Gerald Parker. Commotion from the patrons brings Hemingway, Gwen and Philip to the scene; Gwen faints when she sees her husband's body and she is aided by lawyer Barry Costello (Robert Armstrong), a penguin fancier, who offers her his professional services. Police Inspector Oscar Piper (Gleason) arrives and declares it a clear case of homicide. Donovan finds Lew hiding behind a fish tank and he and several others, including Gwen, Philip and Hemingway, are questioned by Piper as Miss Withers takes notes. To protect Gwen, Philip confesses to killing Parker but Miss Withers doubts he is guilty. Philip is arrested but Piper gets a telephone call from Dr. Max Bloom (Gustav von Seyffertitz), the medical examiner, saying Parker was stabbed by a sharp instrument in his right ear. Piper, along with Miss Withers and Hemingway, search the catwalks behind the aquarium tanks for a gray fedora hat which Miss Withers saw in the tank. While they are searching, Donovan is knocked out and dragged into the men's room

Edna May Oliver, James Donlan and James Gleason in *Penguin Pool Murder* (1932).

where he is found by Piper. The next morning Piper goes to Miss Withers' apartment for her notes on the interrogations and she makes him breakfast. While there, he gets word from Bloom that Parker was probably killed with a hatpin and Miss Withers, who lost a hatpin at the aquarium, realizes that hers was the murder weapon. She goes to Parker's office and talks with his telephone operator (Rochelle Hudson) who says her boss got a call the afternoon before saying his wife was in trouble. Miss Withers suggests to Piper that since only the two of them and Dr. Bloom know Parker was stabbed in the right ear, a statement should be given to the newspapers saying the victim was stabbed in the left ear. When Gwen makes a declaration through Costello, saying she thinks Philip murdered her husband, Philip is convinced she has betrayed him. That night Miss Withers and Costello go to the aquarium to find the fedora and see Hemingway remove a hat band from the throat of a penguin. Miss Withers calls Piper to say she has found the hat band but the lights go out; by the time they come back on, it has disappeared. Piper arrives and Miss Withers finds the hat band in Hemingway's pipe, partially burned. The district attorney takes the case away from Piper and indicts both Gwen and Philip for the murder of Gerald Parker. Costello comes to Piper with a note from Lew, saying he knows the killer's identity. Miss Withers joins Piper and Costello when they go to the Tombs to see Lew, but find him hanged in his cell. Costello admits he smuggled steel wire into the jail in hopes of making Philip admit his guilt and that it was Philip who managed to get out of his cell and hang Lew. During Gwen and Philip's trial, Costello accuses Miss Withers of being Parker's jilted lover and of stabbing him in the right ear. Since the killer was only one of four people who knew the correct ear, Miss Withers declares Costello is the murderer. Gwen tells the court that Costello was her lover and wanted to get rid of Gerald, blaming Philip for the crime. When Costello tries to shoot Gwen with a gun concealed in his briefcase, Piper stops him as Miss Withers faints. After she revives, Piper informs Miss Withers that Costello confessed to killing both Parker and Lew, the latter having seen him commit the first murder. Piper and Miss Withers watch from a window to see Gwen and Philip reunited, but when they are, Philip slaps Gwen and walks away. Piper then suggests he and Miss Withers join forces, she agrees, and they run off to the marriage license bureau.

Photoplay called *Penguin Pool Murder* a "mystery with a laugh.... Edna May Oliver is a scream as the teacher." Helen Boyce wrote in *The International Photographer*, "[D]espite the seriousness of the situation, excellent entertainment and not a little comedy.... Miss Oliver has a part that will please many of her admirers." *The New York Times* stated, "It is a humorous murder story which stirs up quite a good deal of interest, but scarcely comes up to expectations in its denouement. However, it is one of those comicalities that possess a good share of fun and therefore the murder mystery is, to the audience, not of great consequence." *Motion Picture* said, "Better than the unraveling of the plot, which holds very little surprise or suspense, are the eccentric gyrations of Edna May Oliver, who deserts her schoolroom to become an amateur detective, and the delightful dumbness of James Gleason as the man from headquarters. These two, to a large degree, and with adroitness, lift what would otherwise be a rather tame murder mystery into the realm of first-class entertainment." *The New Movie Magazine* declared the film a "better than average mystery yarn and Edna May Oliver as the school 'marm' who refuses to believe in anything until she has proved it herself, makes the show well worth seeing." The *Hollywood Filmograph* noted, "For thrills, mystery, splendid acting and fine direction [this film] is quite out of the usual and should find favor with any audience." "Forced comedy and obvious situations hurt fair mystery story," penned *The Film Daily*. *Harrison's Reports* predicted, "There is plentiful interesting and laugh-exciting material in this story.... A good bet." The same publication stated the feature's box office performance was "fair."

Although Miss Withers and Oscar Piper were marriage-bound at the end of *Penguin Pool Murder*, they remained single for the other films in the series.

The Perfect Alibi (1931; 76 minutes)

PRODUCER-DIRECTOR: Basil Dean. SCREENPLAY: A.A. Milne & Basil Dean, from the play *The Fourth Wall* by A.A. Milne. PHOTOGRAPHY: Jack Mackenzie & I.C. Martin. EDITOR: Jack Kitchin. MUSIC DIRECTOR: Ernest Irving. ART DIRECTOR: Clifford Pembe. SOUND: Richard Willmar. PRODUCTION MANAGER: James B. Sloan. ASSISTANT DIRECTOR: John E. Burch.

CAST: Robert Loraine (Carter), Warwick Ward (Laverick), Frank Lawton (Jimmy Hilton), C. Aubrey Smith (Arthur Hilton), Dorothy Boyd (Mollie Cunningham), Ellis Jeffreys (Mrs. Green), Nigel Bruce (Manager), Jack Hawkins (Alfred), Tom Reynolds (Inspector Mallet), David Hawthorne (Sergeant Joe Mallet), Audrey Carten (Jane).

Basil Dean, following a successful career as a theatrical producer and director, formed Associated Talking Pictures (A.T.P.) in 1930 and signed with Radio Pictures, which was to distribute his company's product. Following the 1930 release of *Escape* came *Birds of Prey* the same year. Dean produced, directed and co-wrote *Birds of Prey* with A.A. Milne, the work based on the latter's 1928 play *The Fourth Wall*. When the feature was issued in the U.S. in 1930 by RKO as *The Perfect Alibi*, it was shorn of 12 minutes but still seemed interminably long due to incessant talk. The slight horror angle involves a revenge motif and the workmanlike manner in which the killers try to give themselves an alibi. For today's audiences, about the only interest this curio holds is seeing later screen stalwarts Frank Lawton, C. Aubrey Smith, Nigel Bruce and Jack Hawkins (in his film debut) working at the start of the sound era. Dean went on to start Ealing

Studios in 1931 but soon left the RKO fold when the company wanted him to make low-budget productions for quick playoffs in the British market.

A dinner party is in progress at Heron Court, the remote English estate of rich Arthur Hilton (Smith), the guardian of Mollie Cunningham (Dorothy Boyd). The guests are enthralled by their host's tales of his adventures in Colonial Africa and how he was involved in the capture of a murderous gang. He relates that the killers swore to get revenge on him and were let go on a technicality. Both Mollie and Jimmy Hilton (Lawton), Arthur's nephew, dislike one of the guests, Laverick (Warwick Ward). When the rest of the guests attend a flower show the next day, another caller, Carter (Robert Loraine), tells Arthur he believes Laverick is one of the killers. Seeing Laverick approach, Carter hides behind a curtain. When Arthur confronts Laverick with the accusation, the man draws a gun. Arthur attempts to call the police and is shot by Carter. Scotland Yard Sergeant Joe Mallet (David Hawthorne) gets the call but becomes suspicious when it is cut off and goes to get his father, Inspector Mallet (Tom Reynolds), who is at the flower show. Carter makes several changes at the murder scene to make it look like suicide. Mallet and his son investigate as Laverick and Carter provide alibis for each other. After the police leave and most of the houseguests have retired for the night, Mollie and Jimmy agree that his uncle did not kill himself. Mollie notices a blotter on the dead man's desk has been changed; this makes the two young people doubt Laverick and Carter's alibis. Mrs. Green (Ellis Jeffreys), who is engaged to Carter, comes looking for a pen and informs Mollie and Jimmy that she saw her fiancé burning papers. Realizing that Mollie and Jimmy suspect him of killing Arthur, Carter tells Laverick they should leave Heron Court. The next day Mollie lets Carter know she believes Laverick is the murderer while the latter is being driven to the train station by Jimmy. Laverick is unaware that Mollie and Jimmy have put her jewelry in his luggage; Jimmy stops and asks Joe Mallet to search them for the missing jewels. Joe finds the gems and takes Laverick and Jimmy back to Heron Court. Realizing Mollie has the evidence she needs to prove he murdered her guardian, Carter threatens to shoot her unless she gives him the blotting paper he changed on Arthur's desk. He does not realize Mollie has locked them in the room or that her friend Jane (Audrey Carten) is hiding behind a curtain and has heard his confession. Mollie tells Carter the gun is not loaded as Inspector Mallet and his men break in and arrest the killer.

Mordaunt Hall in *The New York Times* noted that the production "may not be endowed with imaginative direction, but because of the author's intriguing story and C. Aubrey Smith's excellent performance, it succeeds in being an entertaining study of a cool, calculating murderer." *Variety* was less kind: "It's a common kind of a detective story.... That A.A. Milne wrote the story for the stage doesn't make it any better through Basil Dean's adaptation for the screen. Nor did the same Dean help it any through his direction." The reviewer also complained about "poor recording" and "the English manner of speaking when in huddles not easily caught by Americans," concluding it "should have been left on English soil." *The Film Daily* opined that it "holds attention and interest except in a few spots when the action retards. It is the type of story that carries considerable appeal due to its suspense, mystery and romance.... The entire cast is satisfactory and the direction forceful except is sequences when excessive dialogue becomes tiresome." A "disaster, a slow-moving thriller" is how David Quinlan termed it in *British Sound Films: The Studio Years, 1928–1959* (1984).

Peter Pan (1953; 77 minutes; Color)

DIRECTORS: Clyde Geronimi, Hamilton Luske & Wilfred Jackson. STORY: Ted Sears, Erdman Penner, Bill Peet, Winston Hibler, Joe Rinaldi, Milt Banta, Ralph Wright & Bill Cottrell, from the play by Sir

James M. Barrie. EDITOR: Donald Halliday. MUSIC: Oliver Wallace. MUSIC EDITOR: Al Teeter. VOCAL ARRANGER: Jud Conlon. MUSIC ORCHESTRATOR: Edward H. Plumb. SONGS: Sammy Cahn, Sammy Fain, Oliver Wallace, Erdman Penner, Ted Sears, Winston Hibler, Frank Churchill & Jack Lawrence. SOUND: Robert O. Cook & Harold J. Steck. SOUND DIRECTOR: C.O. Slyfield. EFFECTS ANIMATORS: George Rowley, Blaine Gibson, Dan MacManus, Joshua Meador. CHARACTER ANIMATORS: Hal King, Cliff Nordberg, Hal Ambro, Don Lusk, Ken O'Brien, Marvin Woodward, Art Stevens, Eric Cleworth, Fred Moore, Bob Carlson, Harvey Toombs, Judge Whitaker, Bill Justice, Hugh Fraser, Jerry Hathcock & Clair Weeks. SPECIAL PROCESSES: Ub Iwerks. DIRECTING ANIMATORS: Milt Kahl, Franklin Thomas, Wolfgang Reitherman, Ward Kimball, Eric Larson, Oliver Johnston, Jr., Marc Davis, John Lounsbery, Les Clark & Norman Ferguson. COLOR & STYLING: Mary Blair, Claude Coats, John Hench & Donald Da Gradi. BACKGROUNDS: Ray Huffine, Art Riley, Albert Dempster, Eyvind Earle, Ralph Hulett, Thelma Witter, Dick Anthony & Brice Mack. LAYOUT: Mac Stewart, Tom Codrick, A. Kendall O'Connor, Charles Philippi, Hugh Hennesy, Ken Anderson, Al Zinnen, Lance Nolley, Thor Putnam & Don Griffith.

VOICE CAST: Tom Conway (Narrator), Bobby Driscoll (Peter Pan), Kathryn Beaumont (Wendy Darling), Hans Conried (Captain Hook/George Darling), Bill Thompson (Mr. Smee/Pirates), Heather Angel (Mary Darling), Paul Collins (John Darling), Tommy Luske (Michael Darling), Candy Candido (Indian Chief), June Foray (Mermaid/Squaw), Connie Hilton, Margaret Kerry (Mermaids), Johnny McGovern, Robert Ellis, Tony Butala, Stuffy Singer, Jeffrey Silver (Lost Boys), Thurl Ravenscroft (Chorus Singer), Don Barclay (Mr. Starkey), Roland Dupree, Carol Coombs, Karen Kester, Norman Jean Nilsson, Anne Whitfield (Voices).

Walt Disney first planned to film Sir James M. Barrie's 1904 play *Peter Pan* in 1935, and was ready to go into production in 1940 after having acquired the rights to the work from the copyright holders, the Hospital for Sick Children in London. The coming of World War II nixed these plans and it was not until 1949 that Disney actually began work on *Peter Pan*. To help his animators, Disney filmed a working model, live-action version with Roland Dupree as Peter Pan, Henry Brandon as Captain Hook and Margaret Kerry as Tinker Bell. In the various stage productions of the play, Peter was played by an actress and Tinker Bell had only been a light beam. *Peter Pan* was first filmed in 1925 by Paramount with Betty Bronson in the title role, directed by Herbert Brenon. The Disney version took two years to complete and in the meantime a stage production *Peter Pan* had a 321-performance run on Broadway during the 1950–51 season, starring Jean Arthur as Peter and Boris Karloff as Captain Hook, followed by a three-month tour. The Disney film cost nearly $4 million and required 500,000 separate drawings. RKO released it in February 1953 and continued to distribute it until Buena Vista, Disney's distributing company, took it over in the fall of 1955. During that time *Peter Pan* showed a profit of over three million dollars.

Peter Pan, a very entertaining and colorful production, nicely captures the feel of the Barrie work while modernizing it for contemporary audiences. Its animation is particularly impressive, as is its use of Technicolor. The voice cast does well by the various roles, especially Hans Conried, who followed stage tradition of having the same actor play both Captain Hook and George Darling. The animated fantasy's only real letdown is its ten non-memorable tunes which for the most part do nothing to further its storyline. Victor Records issued the songs on an extended play 45 rpm set (EPA-407) and as a long-playing album (LPM-3101) in 1953 and in 1960 paired them with "Alice in Wonderland" on its budget label Camden Records (CAL-1009). Bobby Driscoll and Kathryn Beaumont repeated their film roles as Peter and Wendy on the disk. Driscoll and Beaumont also did the parts on the Disneyland Records' soundtrack of the film in 1962 (ST-3910), issued with an eleven-page booklet, and reissued in 1963 (DQ-1206). It was issued a third time as a picture disc on the same label in 1982 (3110). In addition to the records, Driscoll and Beaumont were Peter and Wendy on the December 21, 1953, CBS radio broadcast of "Peter Pan" with John Carradine as Captain Hook. Buena Vista theatrically reissued *Peter Plan* a half dozen times before releasing it to home video in 1990.

In a house on a quiet street in Bloomsbury, London, lives George Darling (voice of Conried), his wife Mary (voice of Heather Angel), and their children Wendy (voice of Beaumont), John (voice of Paul Collins) and Michael (voice of Tommy Luske). George becomes disgruntled after being unable to find his gold cufflinks since he and his wife are attending a swank party. He puts Nana, the family's beloved Saint Bernard nanny, outside and announces it is time for the nearly grown Wendy to have a room of her own. After George and Mary leave for the party, the pixie Peter Pan (voice of Driscoll) appears with his fairy cohort Tinker Bell, who loves him. Since the Darling children believe in him, Peter returns to their house to get back his shadow which Wendy has procured. As Wendy sews Peter's shadow back on him, Tinker Bell grows jealous and is accidentally locked in a clothes drawer. When Wendy tells Peter this is her last night in the nursery, he asks her to come home with him to Neverland and tell bedtime stories to his gang of Lost Boys, who have never had a mother. When Wendy attempts to kiss Peter, the angry Tinker Bell gets out of the drawer and stops her. Wendy's brothers awaken and see Peter and he offers to teach the three siblings to fly with the aid of pixie dust and they go to Neverland. There Peter's enemy, Captain Hook (voice of Conried), plots ways to get even with Peter, who cut off the pirate's hand and gave it to a crocodile who follows Hook in search of the rest of him. As jovial Mr. Smee (voice of Bill Thompson) tries to shave Hook, they hear the crocodile approach (he has swallowed a clock) and avoid the hungry reptile. Hook kidnaps pretty Indian maiden Tiger Lily, daughter of the tribal chief (voice of Candy Candido), hoping to force her to tell him where Peter lives with the Lost Boys. Hook spies Peter and the Darling children and attacks them with cannon balls. Peter has Tinker Bell take the Darlings to his lair but instead she tells the Lost Boys that Wendy is an enemy and they shoot at her. Peter comes to Wendy's rescue and angrily banishes Tinker Bell. While Peter introduces Wendy to Neverland's beautiful mermaids, who quickly become jealous of her, the Lost Boys take John and Michael to battle the local Indians. They are soon surrounded and captured. The chief informs his captives they will be burned at the stake unless Tiger Lily is set free. Hook and Smee take Tiger Lily by boat to Skull Rock but Peter imitates Hook's voice and tells Smee to set her free. Hook and Peter engage in a swordfight with Hook falling from a cliff into the crocodile's mouth. Smee saves Hook as Peter takes Tiger Lily back to her tribe. During a celebration that night in the Indian village, Wendy becomes jealous when Tiger Lily makes advances to Peter. When Smee informs Hook about Tinker Bell's banishment, Hook lures the fairy to his ship and tells her he is leaving Neverland forever and wants to apologize to Peter. Using this ploy, Hook learns from Tinker Bell the location of Peter's lair in the trunk of Hangman's Tree and then imprisons her in a lamp. Back at his den, Peter is informed by Wendy that she and her brothers are returning home the next morning and the Lost Boys want to go with them. As they leave the tree, the group is captured by Hook's men and Peter receives a supposed present from Wendy which is really a bomb. On the ship, Wendy, her brothers and the Lost Boys refuse to join the pirates and are sentenced to walk the plank. Tinker Bell escapes and goes back to the tree to warn Peter but the bomb explodes and injures her. Finding the hurt Tinker Bell, Peter tells her she means more to him than anything in the world. Once he is sure Tinker Bell has recovered, Peter goes to the pirate ship to rescue Wendy and the boys. He engages in a tremendous swordfight with Hook, who eventually loses and is chased from Neverland by the crocodile. Peter and Tinker Bell take the pirate ship back to London and say goodbye to Wendy and her brothers. The Lost Boys return with Peter and Tinker Bell since they are not ready to grow up. Returning home with Mary, George brings Nana back into the house and informs Wendy that she can remain in the nursery. Wendy says she is ready to become an adult and tells them about the adventures she and her brothers had with Peter in Neverland. The Darlings do not believe her story until they see a pirate ship sailing in front of the Moon. George says he has a strange feeling that he saw the ship long ago when he was very young.

Peter Pan met with great critical success. *Boxoffice* wrote, "All of the consummate artistry that characterizes the work of Walt Disney and his gifted staff is apparent in every frame of this thoroughly delightful feature-length animated cartoon.... Audiences are sure to applaud the gallery of its endearingly whimsical characters." *Variety* called it "a feature cartoon of enchanting quality for those old enough to look upon the original as a venerable classic, and for the youngsters who will be getting their first glimpse of it." In *The Disney Films, 3rd Edition* (1995), Leonard Maltin opined, "It is difficult to find fault with *Peter Pan*; it is one of Disney's brightest, most straightforward animated features, a film in which everything clicks. One is tempted to say that it lacks the innovative brilliance of a *Pinocchio* [q.v.] (which is perfectly true), but it seems unfair to criticize the film for what it isn't, when it *is* such an unpretentious, delightful endeavor."

In 2002 Buena Vista released a *Peter Pan* sequel called *Return to Never Land*, which was originally planned for home video but was shown first in theaters. This animated outing updated the characters with Peter Pan coming to the rescue of Wendy Darling's daughter, who has been abducted by Captain Hook.

The Phantom of Crestwood (1932; 77 minutes)

EXECUTIVE PRODUCER: David O. Selznick. ASSOCIATE PRODUCER: Merian C. Cooper. DIRECTOR: J. Walter Ruben. SCREENPLAY: Bartlett Cormack. STORY: Bartlett Cormack & J. Walter Ruben. PHOTOGRAPHY: Henry Gerrard. EDITOR: Archie F. Marshek. MUSIC DIRECTOR: Max Steiner. ART DIRECTOR: Carroll Clark. SOUND: D.A. Cutler.

CAST: Ricardo Cortez (Gary Curtis), Karen Morley (Jenny Wren), Anita Louise (Esther Wren), Pauline Frederick (Faith Andes), H.B. Warner (Priam Andes), Mary Duncan (Dorothy Mears), Sam Hardy (Pete Harris), Tom Douglas (Allen Herrick), Richard "Skeets" Gallagher (Eddie Mack), Aileen Pringle (Mrs. Walcott), Ivan Simpson (Henry T. Herrick/Mr. Vayne), George E. Stone (The Cat), Robert McWade (Herbert Walcott), Hilda Vaughn (Carter), Gavin Gordon (Will Jones), Matty Kemp (Frank Andes), Eddie Sturgis (Bright Eyes), Clarence Wilson (Apartment House Manager), Robert Elliott (Police Detective), Allan Cavan (Highway Patrol Officer), Bess Flowers (Bank Secretary), Mike Lally (Bank Customer), Graham McNamee (Himself).

As radio began to cut into Hollywood profits with the coming of sound, RKO became a pioneer in having the two mediums work in tandem for their mutual benefit. The studio had successfully used Amos 'n' Andy in *Check and Double Check* (1930) [q.v.] and Phillips H. Lord's homespun character Seth Parker in *Way Back Home* (1931), but *The Phantom of Crestwood* combined radio and the movies in what RKO claimed to be "the most famous mystery story of all time." From August 26 to September 30, 1932, Eunice Howard and Ned Weaver starred in six installments of the broadcast "The Phantom of Crestwood" over 58 stations on the NBC Red network. The culmination of the mystery, however, was not revealed on the radio show but instead in the motion picture *The Phantom of Crestwood* which Radio Pictures premiered on October 14, 1932. To promote both the radio program and the film, NBC and RKO sponsored a contest in which participants could write a 500-word ending to the story with 100 prizes totaling $6,000 in cash to be awarded. The famous authors and editors acting as judges on the several thousand entries submitted were Peter B. Kyne, Albert Payson Terhune, O.O. McIntyre, Hugh Weir, Julia Peterkin and Montague Glass. In addition, an extensive advertising campaign was waged to promote the project, including display ads in the country's leading newspapers and magazines, radio announcements, window displays in 1900 Woolworth stores and the publication of the story in *Mystery Magazine*. On screen *The Phantom of Crestwood* was billed as "The Radio Pictures Broadcast Special."

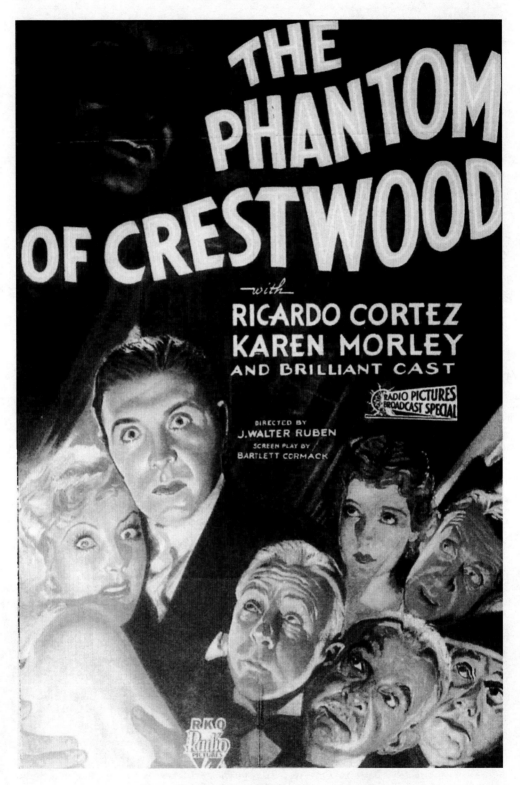

Poster for *The Phantom of Crestwood* (1932).

All the ballyhoo paid off as *The Phantom of Crestwood*, budgeted at $188,000, grossed $436,000. The film opens with a nearly two-minute introduction by famed radio announcer Graham McNamee, who noted that the picture's ending did not necessarily correspond with any of the essays received in the promotional contest. The movie is a slick, polished production well-directed by J. Walter Ruben, who co-wrote the story with Bartlett Cormack, the author of its screenplay. Especially effective is Henry Gerrard's photography which highlights the somewhat spooky La Casa de Andes, the remote house with secret passageways where two murders take place. Carroll Clark's art direction adds flavor to the story as does Max Steiner's background music. Set during a stormy night, the story is highlighted by a floating ghostly face and a house full of suspects, all of whom had the motive to commit murder. The film is populated with an excellent cast, with top acting honors going to Ricardo Cortez as a dapper hoodlum turned sleuth, Karen Morley as the world-weary call girl victim, and Pauline Frederick as a woman who prizes her family's heritage above all else.

In Los Angeles, Gary Curtis (Cortez) follows Jenny Wren (Morley) and is questioned by a police detective (Robert Elliott) who recognizes him from New York City. Gary trails Jenny to the Harbor National Bank where he sees her remove papers from a safety deposit box. She goes to see the bank's president, Priam Andes (H.B. Warner), and tells him she is leaving the country but before she does he is to give a farewell party for her at his remote ranch at Crestwood, inviting Senatorial candidate Herbert Walcott (Robert McWade) and his wife (Aileen Pringle), Will Jones (Gavin Gordon) and his fiancée Dorothy Mears (Mary Duncan), and Eddie Mack (Richard "Skeets" Gallagher). She also informs him that her younger sister Esther (Anita Louise) is returning home from finishing school and has fallen in love with his nephew, Frank Andes (Matty Kemp). Gary goes to Jenny's apartment, pretending to be a prospective renter, and after he leaves, Esther arrives with Frank, who tells Jenny they must convince his stern aunt, Priam's sister Faith Andes (Frederick), to permit them to wed. That night at the Crestwood party, Frank, while playing darts, informs the guests that the house was built in 1804 and contains secret passageways. Priam introduces another guest, Mr. Vayne (Ivan Simpson), who earlier saw Jenny at the bank. Herbert, Will and Eddie are not happy to see Jenny when she arrives, since they all had affairs with her, as did Priam. Faith also shows up and expresses unhappiness at Frank planning to marry Esther. A severe storm erupts as Jenny meets with Priam, Herbert, Will and Eddie in the library. She demands $50,000 from Will, $100,000 from Priam, $25,000 from Eddie and $250,000 from Herbert. They accuse her of blackmail since she threatens to expose their past relationships with her. Priam tells Jenny that Vayne is attracted to her and will give her anything she wants. Jenny's maid, Carter (Hilda Vaughn), arrives with a package for her containing a fraternity pin. She tells the men it belonged to a young man, Allen Herrick (Tom Douglas), who committed suicide when she refused his marriage proposal because he would not inherit his family's fortune if he married her. Jenny goes onto a patio where she sees Allen's face. When Vayne comes to her aid, she tells him she saw a ghost. At 3 a.m., after everyone has retired, Gary breaks into the house just as Jenny falls down the stairs with a dart in her back. He leaves Jenny on the sofa and goes back outside as the others in the house find her body. A landslide, caused by heavy rain, cuts Crestwood off from the outside world. Faith calls the Highway Patrol and as the phone goes dead Gary returns, bringing with him gangster Pete Harris (Sam Hardy) and his henchmen, The Cat (George E. Stone) and Bright Eyes (Eddie Sturgis). Gary informs the group that he has come for letters that Jenny had; they are wanted by his employer in New York. Gary suggests to Pete that they had better catch Jenny's killer or they might be blamed for the crime. Since Esther is the only one in the house not present, Gary and Frank go to her bedroom which they find empty. They locate the unconscious Esther in Jenny's room. Reviving, Esther tells the two men she was

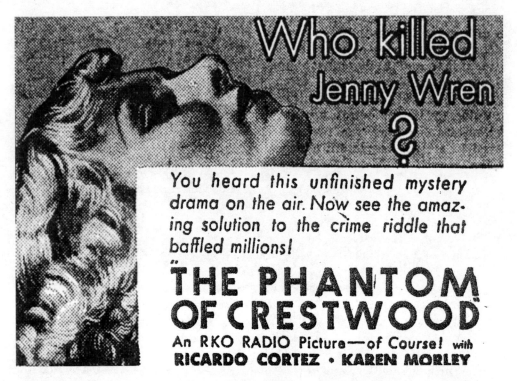

Advertisement for *The Phantom of Crestwood* **(1932).**

told by Faith she could not marry Frank and when she went to Jenny for solace, her sister screamed after seeing something at the window. Gary finds a candle holder which he deduces was used to try and kill Esther. Will confesses that he used to know Jenny, and Carter claims that Herbert came to see Jenny in her bedroom. Esther becomes distraught after seeing her sister's dead body. Gary questions Herbert, who admits he pleaded with Jenny to wait to be paid until his Senatorial campaign was over. He says Vayne interrupted them and he left. When questioned by Gary, Vayne says he was infatuated with Jenny but left her room when she asked him to. Going to his room, he says he saw Frank knock on Jenny's door. Frank admits to Gary he talked with Jenny at two a.m. about Esther and he asked her not to blackmail his uncle. The lights go out and Pete drags in Vayne, who says he is really Henry T. Herrick, whose son Tom died because of Jenny. Herrick says he made a death mask of his son and used it to torment Jenny, whom he planned to kill. He admits using the candle holder to knock out Esther and then saw Jenny hit by the dart. Herrick says he wishes he had killed Jenny and then dies of a heart attack. A dart strikes Esther but it does not kill her and she is carried to her room. The Cat informs Gary and Pete that Carter left the room before the attack and they search for her. Pete and Gary search near the cliffs for Carter, and Gary finds a passageway that leads to the house. In it they find Carter's body (with a dart in her neck) and the death mask. A door in the tunnel leads into the living room and Gary informs Pete he found the letters belonging to his client. Realizing the murderer threw the dart that killed Jenny from behind her, he uncovers a cracked jewel from a ring in the hallway outside her bedroom. Going to Esther's room, Gary finds it empty and he says Faith killed Jenny and plans to kill Esther. Faith takes Esther through the passageway to the cliff as Gary informs Frank his aunt plans to murder his fiancée. Frank shows Gary and Pete a trap door in the floor of Esther's room that goes into the passageway. As Faith is about to push Esther off the cliff to keep her from marrying Frank, Gary confronts her with the broken jewel. A police airplane flies overhead as Faith purposely drops off the cliff and into the ocean.

The New York Times' Mordaunt Hall called *The Phantom of Crestwood* "[a]nother of those mechanically contrived murder mysteries, in which the authors revel in having half a dozen persons suspected of the crime before the real slayer is revealed…. Actually the story is quite interesting up to the time Jenny Wren passes out of the picture, but after that it is nothing more than one of the familiar tales of its type." The *New England Film News* stated, "This film is a neatly conceived murder mystery with the usual finger of suspicion pointed at numerous people. Ricardo Cortez, enactor of a dozen detective roles, turns in an excellent performance, as does Karen Morley as the unfortunate victim." *Motion Picture* called it "a smooth, well-oiled mystery drama," and *Motion Picture Magazine* related, "It is presented in agreeable, though undistinguished form and emerges as a melodrama somewhat above the average usually found in pieces of this kind…. Really, the story creaks with conventionality, but as it has pleased radio listeners it may also interest film fans. It boasts a long and impressive cast, especially Pauline Frederick, who is outstanding." *Photoplay* thought it "a diverting picture, but one that doesn't get you excited as its chilling screams and eerie goings-on promised." *Variety* reported that the film "has been given a handsome production, offers a plot with ample motivating, carefully avoids clutching hands and enlists the services of an exceptional cast." *The Film Daily* said, "Plenty of suspense, action and spook stuff make this okay for heavy murder mysteries addicts…. And anyone who enjoys involved murder mysteries that keep the audience guessing who did the killing, will find plenty to occupy them." According to *The Galveston* (Texas) *Daily News*, "If this is not the perfect mystery drama, we do not know what could be. The skill of its construction is such that any of a dozen characters might have killed the luscious and unscrupulous gold-digger…. Story, acting, direction, photography, all are uncannily good…. The settings are quietly, disturbingly realistic."

Pinocchio (1940; 87 minutes; Color)

SUPERVISING DIRECTORS: Ben Sharpsteen & Hamilton Luske. STORY ADAPTATION: Ted Sears, Otto Englander, Webb Smith, Bill Cottrell, Joseph Sabo, Erdman Penner & Aurelius Battaglia, from the novel *L'avventure di Pinocchio* by Carlo Collodi. MUSIC: Leigh Harline & Paul J. Smith. SONGS: Ned Washington, Leigh Harline & Paul J. Smith. ART DIRECTORS: Charles Philippi, Hugh Hennesy, Kenneth Anderson, Dick Kelsey, A. Kendall O'Connor, Terrell Stapp, Thor Putnam, John Hubley, McLaren Stewart & Al Zinnen. SEQUENCE DIRECTORS: Bill Roberts, Norman Ferguson, Jack Kenney, Wilfred Jackson & T. Hee. ANIMATION DIRECTORS: Fred Moore, Franklin Thomas, Milt Kahl, Vladimir Tytla, Ward Kimball, Arthur Babbitt, Eric Larson & Wolfgang Reitherman. CHARACTER DESIGNERS: Albert Hurter, Joe Grant, John P. Miller, Campbell Grant, Martin Provensen & John Walbridge. ANIMATORS: Jack Campbell, Berny Wolf, Don Towsley, George Rowley, Oliver M. Johnston, Jr., Don Lusk, John Lounsbery, Norman Tate, John Bradbury, Lynn Karp, Charles Nichols, Art Palmer, Joshua Meador, Don Tobin, Robert Martsch, John McManus, Don Patterson, Preston Blair, Les Clark, Marvin Woodward, Hugh Fraser & John Elliotte. BACKGROUNDS: Ray Huffine, Claude Coats, Merle Cox & Ed Starr. LIVE ACTION MODELS: Marjorie Bell [Marge Champion], T. Hee.

VOICE CAST: Dickie Jones (Pinocchio), Cliff Edwards (Jiminy Crickett), Christian Rub (Geppetto), Walter Catlett (J. Worthington Foulfellow), Evelyn Venable (The Blue Fairy), Frankie Darro (Lapwick), Charles Judels (The Great Stromboli/ Coachman), Don Brodie (Carnival Barker), Mel Blanc (Gideon), Patricia Page (Marionettes), Marion Darlington (Birds), Jack Mercer (Rough House Statue).

As a pre-release advertising ploy, on December 25, 1939, John Garfield starred on CBS' *Lux Radio Theatre* in an adaptation of Walt Disney's "Pinocchio," which RKO released theatrically two months later. On the one-hour presentation, Cliff Edwards narrated the story and also appeared in the role of Jiminy Crickett. Walt Disney and some of the other actors in the film also were on the program. Based on the 1882 novel by Carlo Collodi, the animated feature *Pinocchio* earned Academy Awards for Best Original Score and the song "When You Wish Upon a Star," which became Disney's signature tune. In the film it was sung by Edwards, who also provided the voice of Jiminy Crickett. In production for three years, *Pinocchio* used 300,000 drawings and cost $2.5 million. RKO lost nearly $100,000 during its initial release but they made a profit on the feature following re-release in 1945. *Pinocchio* had six more theatrical re-issues through 1992. The feature is an entertaining, heartwarming fantasy highlighted by the usual excellence of the Disney Studios' animation, camerawork and color. It not only produced "When You Wish Upon a Star" but also a half-dozen other tunes, including "Give a Little Whistle" and "Hi Diddle Dee Dee, an Actor's Life for Me." Edwards recorded "When You Wish Upon a Star" and "Give a Little Whistle" for Victor Records (26477) in 1940. Disneyland Records released the film's soundtrack on long-playing albums in 1956 (WDL-4002), 1959 (DQ-1202) and 1963 (ST-4905) and as a picture disc in 1981 (3102). In 1949, Edwards recorded the *Pinocchio* songs on a 78 rpm album for Victor Records (Y-385), which was also issued on extended play 45 rpm discs (45–5353) and on a long-playing album on the Camden label (CAL/CAS-1967) in 1965; and in 1950 he did a ten-inch album, "Song Hits from *Pinocchio*" for Decca Records (DL-5151), which was reissued on that label as an LP (DL-8387). In 1957 Edwards did another "Pinocchio" album for Disneyland Records (3905) and in 1961 he recorded "Pinocchio" on the Golden Records (LP-77) label.

Jiminy Crickett (voice of Edwards) sings "When You Wish Upon a Star" and tells the story of a woodcarver, Geppetto (voice of Christian Rub), who lives in a quiet little village and makes clocks and toys. He also carves a life-sized puppet he calls Pinocchio (voice of Dickie Jones) and wishes on a star for him to become real. Jiminy takes up residence in the old man's workshop for the night and sees the arrival of the Blue Fairy (voice of Evelyn Venable) who grants the sleeping woodcarver's wish and gives life to Pinocchio. She makes Jiminy the conscience of Pinocchio. Geppetto wakes up thinking there is a prowler in his home only to be overcome with joy when he finds Pinocchio is alive. He introduces his new son to his best friends, the cat Figaro and fish Cleo, who he calls his "water baby." The next day as he is off to school, Pinocchio is told by Jiminy that the world is full of temptation. Along the way Pinocchio comes under the influence of a fast-talking fox, J. Worthington Foulfellow (voice of Walter Catlett), who convinces him to become an actor. Foulfellow takes Pinocchio to see a puppeteer, the Great Stromboli (voice of Charles Judels), who is so impressed with him that he stars Pinocchio in his puppet show. Pinocchio is a sensation and makes a lot of money for Stromboli, who decides to exhibit him all over Europe. As Geppetto and his pets await Pinocchio's return with a feast, Pinocchio attempts to go home but Stromboli locks him in a cage. Jimmy, who gave up on Pinocchio after he failed to attend school, goes back to check on him and finds his friend caged. Jiminy is unable to open the lock but the Blue Fairy arrives and asks Pinocchio why he failed to go to school; with each succeeding lie, his nose gets longer. When he promises to be good, Pinocchio is freed by the Blue Fairy but as he leaves with Jiminy for school he runs into Foulfellow, who entices him to take a vacation on Pleasure Island. Again ignoring Jiminy's warnings, Pinocchio takes a stagecoach and then a boat to the island along with lots of other boys. He becomes friends with Lampwick (voice of Frankie Darro) and the two smoke cigars, drink beer and play pool. A disgusted Jiminy plans to leave the island but finds out the coachman (voice of Charles Judels) who brought the boys there turns them into donkeys and sells them. Jiminy attempts to save Pinocchio, who sees Lampwick become a donkey while Pinocchio partially transforms by growing long ears and a tail. Jiminy leads Pinocchio to a rocky cliff and they jump into the ocean. They eventually swim to shore but, returning home, Pinocchio finds Geppetto and his pets are gone. A white bird brings a message saying Geppetto went looking for Pinocchio and was swallowed by a mean whale called

Monstro. Pinocchio, followed by Jiminy, leaps into the sea and swims to the ocean floor in search of Geppetto. Eventually they locate Monstro and are drawn into the whale when it swallows a school of salmon, which are caught by the starving Geppetto, who is living on a derelict ship in the whale's belly with Figaro and Cleo. Geppetto and his pets are overjoyed to see Pinocchio, who comes up with a plan for their escape. He builds a huge fire on the ship and then they use a raft to escape. The furious whale disgorges Pinocchio, Geppetto, Figaro, Cleo and Jiminy and then tries to catch them. As Geppetto is about to drown, Pinocchio saves him and Monstro crashes into a huge rock. Geppetto is left alive on the beach but Pinocchio does not survive. Back home, Geppetto mourns over the body of his son and the Blue Fairy appears and makes Pinocchio a real boy because of his heroism in saving Geppetto. Jiminy is given a gold badge for his service to Pinocchio. Everyone celebrates with all the happy clocks.

Photoplay enthused, "Certainly this is the best example of [an] animated cartoon feature ever made; it may even be one of the best motion pictures of any type ever produced. The performances of the various characters are equal to those of the finest human talent.... You'll love every moment and every sequence. Seeing it will be the nicest present you can give yourself this year." *Hollywood* declared it "another film touched with sheer enchantment in the conception and the telling of the story and also above reproach in its animation.... Though there are not so many songs hits in *Pinocchio* as in *Snow White*, it is far more the real fairy tale, and Disney will be hard-pressed to top himself in his next film." *The Film Daily* stated, "*Pinocchio* is a tribute to the skill and ingenuity of Walt Disney and his small army of adaptors, animators, and lyric and music writers who made the characters of a famous story so captivating and enchanting that the picture is certain to charm children of all ages from 6 to 60." Leonard Maltin wrote in *The Disney Films, 3rd Edition* (1995), "In *Pinocchio*, Disney reached not only the height of his powers, but the apex of what many of his (later) critics considered to be the *realm* of the animal cartoon. The wonder, the brilliance of *Pinocchio*, is in the depicting the wondrous fantasy of the story ... things that could not be shown with equal effectiveness by a live-action movie."

Besides the enduring popularity of the title character, *Pinocchio* also introduced Jimmy Crickett, as voiced by Cliff Edwards, who reprised him in *Fun and Fancy Free* (q.v.) and continued to do the role into the 1960s in Disney short subjects, television programs and recordings. During the 1920s Cliff Edwards, also known as "Ukulele Ike," sold over 70 million records with numerous song hits like "June Night," "Ja Da" and "Sunday."

The Plot Thickens (1936; 69 minutes)

ASSOCIATE PRODUCER: William Sistrom. DIRECTOR: Ben Holmes. SCREENPLAY: Clarence Upson Young & Jack Townley, from the story "The Riddle of the Dangling Pearl" by Stuart Palmer. PHOTOGRAPHY: Nicholas Musuraca. EDITOR: John Lockert. ART DIRECTORS: Van Nest Polglase & Feild Gray. SET DECORATIONS: Darrell Silvera. SOUND: George D. Ellis. GOWNS: Edward Stevenson.

CAST: James Gleason (Inspector Oscar Piper), ZaSu Pitts (Hildegarde Martha Withers), Owen Davis, Jr. (Bob Wilkins), Louise Latimer (Alice Stevens), Arthur Aylesworth (Kendall), Paul Fix (Joe), Richard Tucker (John Carter), Barbara Barondess (Marie), James Donlan (Detective Jim), Agnes Anderson (Dagmar), Oscar Apfel (H.G. Robbins), Lew Kelly (Officer Cassidy), John Miltern (Museum Guard Gordon), Frank Fanning (Officer Bowman), Alyce Ardell (Josephine), John T. Bambury (Midget), Bodil Rosing (Theresa), George Sorel (Threatening Man), Billy Dooley (Gas Station Worker), Reed Howes (Museum Guard), Mary Gordon (Museum Patron with Goldfish), Tom Quinn (Suspect), John Indrisano (Museum Patron).

Edna May Oliver was perfectly cast as eccentric schoolmarm Miss Hildegarde Withers in *Penguin Pool Murder* (1932), *Murder on the Blackboard* (1934) and *Murder on a Honeymoon*

James Gleason, ZaSu Pitts and Oscar Apfel in *The Plot Thickens* (1936).

(1935) [qq.v.}, with James Gleason playing thick-headed Police Inspector Oscar Piper in all three. Gleason continued in the Piper role when Oliver left RKO for MGM and was replaced by Helen Broderick in *Murder on a Bridle Path* (1936) [q.v.] and he did the part for the fifth time opposite ZaSu Pitts as Miss Withers in *The Plot Thickens*, issued by Radio Pictures at the end of 1936. For the first time a Miss Withers film was not based on a Stuart Palmer novel but instead on a short story by the author, "The Puzzle of the Dangling Pearl," published in 1933. While the film was a slight improvement over *Murder on a Bridle Path* plot-wise, Pitts was miscast as Miss Withers. She would play the part again in 1937's *Forty Naughty Girls* (q.v.). Outside of the scene at the Cosmopolitan Museum where Miss Withers is nearly knocked down by a mummy falling out of its sarcophagus, there is little of the horrific in this entry other than the character of a young boy who turns out to be a hideous-looking midget (John T. Bambury), a member of a gang of jewel thieves.

In New York City's Courtland Park, astrology-following Officer Cassidy (Lew Kelly) comes across Bob Wilkins (Owen Davis, Jr.) and Alice Stevens (Louise Lorimer) arguing over the attentions given to her by an older man, wealthy John Carter (Richard Tucker). When the angry Bob leaves, Alice calls Carter to come get her. The man's butler, Kendall (Arthur Aylesworth), finds him being threatened by a stranger (George Sorel). After Carter leaves, his maid Marie (Barbara Barondess) slips out with the chauffeur, Joe (Paul Fix), and they are followed by Kendall, who is jealous of Joe. As Carter picks up Alice, Bob returns and the two men have a fight which is broken up by Cassidy. Carter refuses to press charges. He drives Alice to a lonely spot and tries to make love to her but as she gets out of the car, Carter is shot and killed. Alice goes to a service station but Bob arrives and she informs him of what happened and he tells her to drive home in his car. The next morning Inspector Piper (Gleason) and his assistant, Detective Jim (James Donlan), arrive at the Carter mansion, where Kendall has found his employer's body in the library. Having stood up his nemesis, crime-solving schoolteacher Miss Withers (Pitts), at a golf game, Piper informs her he is working a grocery store robbery. A short time later Miss Withers arrives as Piper questions Theresa (Bodil Rosing), Carter's cook, who says he saw a man resembling Joe bring Carter into the house the night before. As Joe denies the accusation, Miss Withers finds a large emerald in a case on Carter's desk. Cassidy informs Piper about Bob and Alice arguing over the dead man in the park. Kendall tells Miss Withers about Carter's argument with the threatening stranger. A jeweler apprises Miss Withers that the gem she found is the Louvre Museum's Sultan emerald, stolen 12 years before. Officer Bowman (Frank Fanning) sees her with the stolen emerald and arrests her but lets her go after she shows him her police courtesy badge. Back at headquarters, Miss Withers finds Piper questioning Bob and Alice and she says she has known them since they were in kindergarten. When Bob is confronted with the fact that his fingerprints were found in Carter's car, he admits putting the man's body in his garage. Miss Withers tells Piper about the emerald and suggests it is tied in with the murder since Carter was obviously associated with jewel thieves. When Piper and Miss Withers try to question Joe, Kendall informs them he has resigned and Marie says Kendall threatened Joe after he found out she was with the chauffeur the night before. Miss Withers again searches Carter's library and is knocked out by Joe, who steals the priceless Cellini Cup. Kendall admits to Piper that he found Carter in the garage and brought his body into the library. Miss Withers goes to the Cosmopolitan Museum to see the Cellini Cup, which is housed there; she talks with the cup's guard, Gordon (John Miltern), who soon dies after falling down a flight of stone stairs. Piper gets a telegram from Paris saying the emerald thieves got out of prison two years before and then receives a call from Miss Withers asking him to come to the museum. Soon after he arrives, an alarm goes off in the Egyptian Room where nothing is disturbed. Miss Withers discovers that the Cellini Cup has been stolen. Piper locates it in a package in the museum's cloak room, but Miss Withers thinks it is a fake since only Carter's prints are found on it. While all the museum patrons are being searched, Piper becomes suspicious of a young boy who turns out to be a midget member (Bambury) of the jewel theft gang. He also becomes suspicious of a clay model being taken out of the museum by sculptor Dagmar (Agnes Anderson) and find the Cellini Cup inside it. Miss Withers motions to Piper to let the young woman go and they follow her to the escape car driven by Joe. Later Piper brings all the suspects to his office along with a hobo, really Jim in disguise, who he says saw Carter's murder take place. Joe grabs a gun and tries to escape but it is filled with blanks.

Photoplay reported, "As if this bang-up mystery weren't entertaining enough, they've given us ZaSu Pitts with her fluttery hands and cocksure James Gleason to dress it up in fine style!" *The New York Herald-Tribune* wrote, "What makes it a bit more entertaining than many other screen murder-mysteries is the lightness of Mr. Gleason and Miss Pitts and the unique setting of the story.... [It] is confusing at times, nor does it seem so spritely as some of the earlier ones in the series." *The New York Times* termed it "a reasonably entertaining baffler" and *The New York World Telegram* opined, "The finished result is a series of lethal hijinks that has a certain amount of nimble-plot complication and some slick sleuthing but which is singularly lacking in physical action, suspense and excitement." *Variety* noted, "The Gleason-Pitts combination is a good one for stories of this trim, Miss Pitts' dumb-as-a-fox approach as a lady dick matching well with the slightly comical flavor Gleason applies to Piper.... [It's] sufficiently interesting in its line to satisfy the fans it will attract." *The Hollywood Reporter* enthused, "This is easily among the top comedy crime puzzlers of the year." The *Cleveland* (Ohio) *Press* called it a "fairly well-told little mystery yarn, not new but passably entertaining" and *The Boston Herald* felt it an "acceptable combination of comedy and mystery.... Contains its full share of humor." The reviewer, however, declared, "Previously, Edna May Oliver and Helen Broderick had appeared in the role, both of them making a better job of it than Miss Pitts." *The Boston Post* thought, "The hard-boiled Mr. Gleason and the fluttery Miss Pitts get a nice quota of laughs."

The Pointing Finger (1934; 67 minutes)

PRODUCER: Julius Hagen. DIRECTOR: George Pearson. SCREENPLAY: H. Fowler Mear, from the novel by Rita [Eliza Margaret Humphries]. PHOTOGRAPHY: Ernest Palmer. EDITOR: Lister Laurence. MUSIC-COMPOSER-DIRECTOR: W.L. Trytel. ART DIRECTOR: James A. Carter. SOUND: Carlisle Montgomery. ASSISTANT DIRECTOR: Arthur Barnes.

CAST: John Stuart (Lord Ronnie Rollestone/Ronald Rollestone), Violet Keats (Lady Mary Stuart), Leslie Perrins (Captain James Mallory), Michael Hogan (Pat Lafone), A. Bromley Davenport (Lord Arthur Edensore), Henrietta Watson (Lady Anne Rollestone), D.J. Williams (Grimes), Clare Greet (Landlady).

The Pointing Finger is one of 35 feature films RKO made with producer Julius Hagen's Real Art Productions between 1932 and 1935, which Radio Pictures released in Great Britain. Based on the 1907 novel by Rita (Eliza Margaret Humphries), the film was never shown in the United States. Although it promises to be a horror film about a terrible curse connected with the picture of a pointing, hooded figure, it is mostly a convoluted melodrama with lots of talk but little action or atmosphere. In addition, its budget limitations are obvious in that it takes place on only three sets: an old English manor house, a dingy London flat and some stagebound scenes supposedly set in Africa. Top-billed John Stuart does what he can with dual roles while the best performance in the movie is delivered by Michael Hogan as a crook who sees the error of his ways. Second-billed Viola Keats is a particularly wooden leading lady. About the only horror offered in the feature is talk of the curse and a quick scene at the finale when the villain dons a black cowl and pretends to be a ghost. The film was re-issued in England by Ambassador Film Productions.

Since he will become the next Earl of Edensore, Ronnie Rollestone (Stuart) is told by his father, Lord Edensore (A. Bromley Davenport), the history of the centuries-old painting of a hooded figure with a pointing finger. He says it's a portrait of the monk who was executed when the manor house, then an abbey, was given to the Edensore family by King Henry VIII during the Reformation. The monk put a curse on the family, which is to end with the eighth Earl, Ronnie. Lord Edensore gives his son a book which contains the secret of the pointing finger and says his grandfather died staring at the picture. While Ronnie plans to make his third and last expedition to Africa, his father wants him to stay and marry his cousin, Mary Stuart (Keats), the daughter of his sister, Lady Anne (Henrietta Watson). In London, crook Pat Lafone (Hogan) tells a cohort, Grimes (D.J. Williams) that he will soon come into a lot of money. Ronnie and Mary's cousin, Major James Mallory (Leslie Perrins), arrives at Pat's cheap flat and offers him a large sum to get rid of Ronnie while he is in Africa so James can be next in line as the Earl of Edensore. Pat gleefully agrees but while on the expedition he becomes friends with Ronnie, who tells him he loves Africa and does not want to return home to his responsibilities. When a hostile tribe attacks, Pat runs into the jungle, leaving Ronnie to the natives. Ronnie returns to Edensore Abbey many months later to find his father is dying. Just before he dies, the old man denies that Ronnie is his son. Mary soon notes that Ronnie is reading without glasses and that he has changed. Mallory arrives home from Egypt and is surprised to find Ronnie at the abbey and asks to stay the weekend. Mallory then goes to London and accuses Pat of double-crossing him. Pat reminds him he was never paid. Pat tells Mallory that Ronnie was captured and murdered by savages and demands to see the man who calls himself Ronnie. Mallory says he will take Pat to the abbey. After Mallory leaves, Pat writes a letter to Mary saying he has information about Ronnie. Mary later goes to see Pat as Grimes listens to their conversation. Pat informs Mary that Ronnie is dead, having been killed in Africa and when she offers to pay him to keep quiet he tells her he will find out what happened to Ronnie in order to earn his money. That weekend at the abbey, Mallory introduces Pat to Mary and he takes her aside and says he is working in her interest. When Ronnie is introduced to Pat by Mallory, he immediately recognizes his old friend and they spend the rest of the evening reminiscing about the African expedition, although Ronnie says his memory is clouded by a bout with malaria. Pat tells Mary that he is sure Ronnie is an imposter. Pat returns to his flat to find the police there with Grimes along with a nearly dead man whom Pat recognizes as Ronnie. Grimes is rebuffed by Pat when he suggests they bump off Ronnie and instead Pat wires Mary about Ronnie's appearance while Grimes telephones Mallory. While Pat and Mary go for a car, Mallory shows up and he and Grimes try to abduct Ronnie, but Pat returns and stops them. Mary drives Ronnie to the abbey while Pat holds Mallory and Grimes at gunpoint. At the abbey, Lady Anne recognizes Ronnie. The imposter (Stuart) comes into the room and informs her and Mary that he and Ronnie are half-brothers. He says he rescued Ronnie from the savages and the two agreed to exchange identities since Ronnie wanted to remain in Africa. While being held a prisoner by Pat, Mallory uses the time to translate the secret of the pointing finger. When he is let go, he returns to the abbey and locates a hidden passage and a cowl. He puts it on and enters Ronnie's bedroom through a secret door. Mallory tries to scare Ronnie to death but Pat arrives and stops him, ordering him out of the house. Pat asks Ronnie's forgiveness for deserting him in Africa. Ronnie calls for his half-brother Ronald and dying, he asks him to look out for Mary.

The novel *The Pointing Finger* was first filmed in England in 1922 by Stoll and was directed by George Ridgwell. It starred Milton Rosmer, Madge Stuart, J.R. Tozer, Teddy Arundell and Gibb McLaughlin as the Monk.

Port Sinister (1953; 65 minutes)

PRODUCERS-SCREENPLAY: Aubrey Wisberg & Jack Pollexfen. ASSOCIATE PRODUCER: Albert Zugsmith. DIRECTOR: Harold Daniels. PHOTOGRAPHY: William Bradford. EDITOR: Fred R. Feitshans, Jr. MUSIC: Albert Glasser. SOUND: Roy Meadows. PRODUCTION MANAGER: Carl Hiecke. SET DECORATIONS: Clarence Steensen. PRODUCTION DESIGN: Theobold Holsopple. MAKEUP: Harry Thomas. SPECIAL PHOTOGRAPHIC EFFECTS: Jack Rabin. MECHANICAL EFFECTS: Rocky Cline. WARDROBE: Einar H. Bourman.

CAST: James Warren (Tony Ferris), Lynne Roberts (Dr. Joan Hunter), Paul Cavanagh (John Kolvac), William Schallert (Collins), House Peters, Jr. (Jim Garry), Marjorie Stapp (Coast Guard Technician), Helen Winston (Florence), Eric Colmar (Christie), Norman Budd (Akers), Anne Kimbell (Nurse), Robert Bice (George Burt), Merritt Stone (Nick), Ken Terrell (Hollis), Dayton Lummis (Mr. Lennox), Charles Victor (Coat Guard Lieutenant), E. Guy Hearn (Captain Crawley).

An explorer, Tony Ferris (James Warren), believes that the sunken Caribbean city of Port Royal is about to rise again and he tries to get a grant from a Miami marine foundation run by Lennox (Dayton Lummis) to lead an expedition to the spot. An organization scientist, Dr. Joan Hunter (Lynne Roberts), disagrees with Tony's theory and argues against giving him the funds. Loving adventure, Lennox grants Tony's request and assigns the disgruntled Joan to be the expedition's scientific historian. That night, John Kolvac (Paul Cavanagh) rummages through Tony's

Lynne Roberts menaced by a giant crab in *Port Sinister* (1953).

belongings and steals his plans as well as a map of Port Royal, showing the possible location of hidden treasure. When Tony returns, Kolvac knocks him out. The next day Kolvac and his cohorts George Burt (Robert Bice) and Nick (Merritt Stone) sign on as the sailing ship *Neptune*'s boatswain, first mate and radio operator, respectively. While loading the vessel, George stages an accident that injures the captain (E. Guy Hearn), and Kolvac takes over his position. An old enemy of Kolvac, Collins (William Schallert), threatens to expose his past unless he is added to the crew. After Joan arrives on board, they set sail although Tony has disappeared. He wakes up in a South Carolina hospital and manages to get away but fails to reach the *Neptune* before it sails. He cannot contact the ship because Kolvac has dismantled the radio and thrown away tubes needed to operate it. The vessel is caught in a hurricane and the Coast Guard will not fly Tony to the craft. Upon the advice of a pretty technician (Marjorie Stapp), Tony seeks the services of heavy-drinking pilot Jim Garry (House Peters, Jr.), who agrees to fly him to the place he believes Port Royal will surface. After 36 hours both vessels survive the hurricane, but the airplane runs out of gas and is forced to coast, before using parachutes to move it along. The *Neptune* arrives near the spot Tony predicted and Port Royal rises above the ocean's surface. After the waters calm, Kolvac locks Joan in her cabin and he and George and the crew row to the island. Splitting the men into two groups, Kolvac takes Collins and Christie (Eric Colmar) in search of the treasure and they find it in the cellar of the governor's palace. Christie is devoured by a giant crab. Tony and Jim arrive at the island as Joan breaks out of her cabin and swims to shore. Wanting to keep the treasure for themselves, Kolvac and Collins get the other crewmen drunk and go back for it.

They run into Joan and tie her up so she will be eaten by the monster. Tony and Jim hear her scream and save her from the creature, which they kill with bullets. The trio then tries to get gas from the ship for the plane, which Kolvac and Collins decide to commandeer to escape from Port Royal with the treasure. Joan uses herself as a decoy to lead George, Nick and two other crewmen, Akers (Norman Budd) and Hollis (Ken Terrell), away from Tony and Jim as they go for the gasoline. Getting the fuel, Tony and Jim return to the ship and Jim fixes it so only he can pilot it. Joan becomes trapped in a crevice as Tony and Jim get cornered by the sailors. Pretending to be wounded, Jim helps Tony lure their attackers and defeat them in a fight and then set Joan free. As they are collecting the treasure, Collins turns on Kolvac and is about to kill him when he is surprised by George, who shoots him. A tremor causes George to drop his gun and he shot by Kolvac. In order to reach the plane, Tony, Joan and Jim must cross a stretch of lava crust with quicksand beneath while being pursued by Nick, Akers and Hollis. They manage to get across but Akers and Nick fall through and are killed. The island is about to submerge again as Tony, Joan and Jim reach the plane. Kolvac appears with a chest filled with jewels. Unable to get the chest aboard the plane, Kolvac is swallowed by a lava flow, as is Nick. Tony and Joan start a budding romance as they fly away to safety with Jim.

Released theatrically in the spring of 1953, *Port Sinister* was the third and last film RKO did with producers Aubrey Wisberg and Jack Pollexfen's American Pictures Company. Filmed on the RKO lot with location shooting at Palos Verdes, California, it was the most inert of the trio, preceded by *Captive Women* (q.v.) and *Sword of Venus* (1953), a swashbuckler. The latter feature was directed by Harold Daniels, who also did *Port Sinister*; the producers wrote both features. Having scored a mild success with *The Man from Planet X* (1951), Wisberg and Pollexfen seemed to lose ground artistically with each subsequent picture. *Port Sinister* is a tatty production that promises much but delivers mostly boredom. The brief scenes of the rising and re-submerging of Port Royal are tepid at best and the inclusion of a clunky-looking giant crab provides unintentional humor. The feature is darkly photographed and the Port Royal setting is obscured by heavy mist and fires. Apparently some standing sets from *Captive Women* were used to simulate the sunken city. James Warren makes a wooden hero while the usually reliable Lynne Roberts is a bland heroine. Only villains Paul Cavanagh, William Schallert and Robert Bice add interest to the proceedings. The *Neptune* is briefly shown in some ragged stock footage with the loading dock scene obviously a cramped set.

Dubbed "a very mediocre melodrama" by *Variety*, *Port Sinister* was also condemned by the reviewer as "nothing to be recommended as entertainment, other than the doubtful angle of its thrills cues laughs instead of the intended chills...." More damning was *Boxoffice*: "Unbelievably amateurish in conception and execution is this independently made opus, which purports to be action drama that fails utterly on all counts."

Port Sinister was reissued theatrically in 1956 by Mutual Productions of the West as *Beast of Paradise Isle*.

Once the abode of privateers, both Dutch and English, in the 16th and 17th centuries, the Jamaican city of Port Royal, founded in 1518, was a thriving seaport until it was devastated by an earthquake in 1692. It never regained its former glory, especially after being hit by several damaging hurricanes and another earthquake in 1907.

The Public Defender (1931; 69 minutes)

PRODUCER: William LeBaron. ASSOCIATE PRODUCER: Louis Sarecky. DIRECTOR: J. Walter Ruben. SCREENPLAY: Bernard Schubert, from the novel *The Splendid Crime* by George Goodchild. PHOTOGRAPHY:

Edward Cronjager. EDITOR: Archie F. Marshek. COSTUME DESIGN–SCENERY: Max Ree. SOUND: John E. Tribby.

CAST: Richard Dix (Pike Winslow aka The Reckoner), Shirley Grey (Barbara Gerry), Purnell Pratt (John Kirk), Ruth Weston (Rose Harmer), Edmund Breese (Frank Wells), Frank Sheridan (Charles Harmer), Alan Roscoe (Inspector Malcolm O'Neill), Boris Karloff (The Professor), Nella Walker (Aunt Matilda), Paul Hurst (Doc), Carl Gerard (Cyrus Pringle), Robert Emmett O'Connor (Detective Brady), Phillips Smalley (Thomas Drake), Emmett King (Eugene Gerry), Walter James (Police Captain Anderson), William Halligan (Auctioneer Lynn Austin), Frank Darien (Waiter), Broderick O'Farrell (Board of Directors' Investigator), Rochelle Hudson, Roberta Gale (Telephone Operators), Gordon [Bill] Elliott, Florence Wix, Ronald R. Rondell (Country Club Guests), Symona Boniface (Auction Patron).

A precursor of cinema superheroes such as Batman, the Spider and Superman, the Reckoner is the mysterious crime-fighter hero of *The Public Defender*, who routs villains while hiding behind the identity of wealthy playboy Pike Winslow, portrayed by Richard Dix. Dix, whose screen career at RKO was on a roll following *Seven Keys to Baldpate* (q.v.) in 1929 and the 1930 Academy Award–winning Best Picture *Cimarron*, is nicely cast as the granite-jawed crusader who brings in the villains, rectifies bank fraud and saves the woman (Shirley Grey) he loves. While not a costume-wearing masked hero, the Reckoner is a larger-than-life one. Appearing in the supporting cast is Boris Karloff as "The Professor." The busy Karloff would appear in nine more features from the time *The Public Defender* was released in August 1931, until he gained screen immortality at the end of the year in *Frankenstein*.

Four members of the Central Realty Trust Company's board of directors, John Kirk (Purnell Pratt), Charles Harmer (Frank Sheridan), Cyrus Pringle (Carl Gerard) and Thomas Drake (Phillips Smalley), accuse the company's treasurer, Eugene Gerry (Emmett King), of being remiss in his duties when their business goes bankrupt. The four men call for Gerry's arrest. Drake's personal papers are stolen and a calling card marked with the scales of justice is left behind by the thief, a mystery man known only as the Reckoner (Dix). That evening while at dinner, Barbara Gerry (Grey), daughter of the accused treasurer, tells rich stockbroker Pike Winslow (Dix) about her father being accused of fraud while another club diner, Charles Harmer, finds one of the Reckoner's cards under his plate. Later that night, Winslow, who is really the Reckoner, talks with his cohorts Doc (Paul Hurst) and the Professor (Karloff) about Gerry's situation, since he wants not only to help him but because he also is attracted to Barbara. To aid Barbara and her

Aunt Matilda (Nella Walker) financially, Winslow clandestinely obtains Gerry's estate at auction and then has Doc and the Professor help him purloin Harmer's business records. Following the theft, Kirk hurries to Harmer's well-guarded home, which is being watched by Winslow, Doc and the Professor. The frightened Harmer wants Kirk to take their business papers with him and hide them but he refuses and quickly departs. Winslow and his men storm the house, over-

Shirley Grey and Richard Dix in *The Public Defender* (1931).   power Harmer and his staff

Richard Dix will go on to still greater triumphs under the Titan banner..

"Cimarron" lifted him to the starry heights!...

"Frontier" and "Marcheta" will entrench him snugly in the affections of millions the world over.

RICHARD DIX IN
PUBLIC DEFENDER

Trade advertisement for *The Public Defender* (1931).

and take the documents. When Pringle gets one of the Reckoner's cards, he goes to see Kirk and tells him he plans to go to the police. Kirk threatens Pringle and then tries to calm him. Pringle is later murdered. The Reckoner is accused of the killing and Doc and the Professor tell him to stay undercover but Winslow plans to get the evidence needed to trap the killer. During a conversation with his pal Inspector Malcolm O'Neal (Alan Roscoe), Winslow learns that there were fingerprints on the card left beside Pringle's body. When Roscoe is ordered to go to Kirk's home in hopes of preventing the Reckoner from killing Kirk, Winslow asks to go along with the police. As the Reckoner is about to appear, the lights fail and Winslow uses the cover to obtain the papers he needs. During the confusion, Kirk finds Winslow with the documents and tries to stop him but is thwarted by an explosion. Winslow makes a getaway and Kirk informs O'Neal of the Reckoner's identity. They trail Winslow to Barbara's home and just before he is arrested, Winslow gets Kirk to grab a lipstick-coated paper, thus getting his fingerprints. Winslow compares them to the prints on the documents, proving Kirk is the murderer.

The Film Daily called *The Public Defender* "a fresh, snappy piece of work.... The cast is well chosen and understands what it is all about. Dix will make new friends with this one." While *Photoplay* though the feature "disappointing," *International Photographer* differed: "There are plenty of thrills.... A great majority of the sequences are stern in character, stern rather than tender, with a mild leavening of mirthful moments.... [It is] a fast and fascinating melodrama." *The New York Times* reported, "*The Public Defender* is reminiscent of that school—never to be graduated, fortunately—which deal in a sort of socialistic thievery.... And like most members of an age and character of *The Public Defender*, this one has its moments of excitement. Not many, of course, but some." *Variety* felt most viewers would find "the picture good entertainment of the fast-moving kind that has laughs in some of the dialog, thrills in some of the action, and the kind of star they have always figured Richard Dix should be." *Exhibitors' Forum* called it a "somewhat different but interesting story," adding, "A new director, J. Walter Ruben, deserves credit for his fine work. Dix fans should like this one and it rates better than average entertainment value."

Quest for the Lost City (1954; 64 minutes; Color)

PRODUCERS: Sol Lesser & Dorothy Howell. ASSOCIATE PRODUCER: Bill Park. DIRECTOR-PHOTOGRAPHY: Dana Lamb. SPECIAL PHOTOGRAPHY: Nelson S. Knaggs. EDITOR: Robert Leo. MUSIC: Paul Sawtell.

CAST: Dana Lamb, Ginger Lamb, Tom Harmon (Themselves), Hal Gibney (Narrator).

Football great and broadcaster Tom Harmon (himself) introduces Dana and Ginger Lamb (themselves) and they discuss their various survival techniques in hostile environments. Harmon details how he survived as an Army air pilot during World War II thanks to a kit the couple helped create. The Lambs then present the story of their trek to Central America in search of a lost Mayan city. They filmed the expedition with a time-delayed movie camera. The couple leave the United States and travel through Mexico to the Chiapas rain forest on the border with Guatemala. The lost city is supposedly in this locale and they obtain a small airplane so they can map the area. For the next three months they fly over the rain forest in search of the lost city, eventually spotting some ruins. They trek on foot to the spot, killing local game for food and living off the forest. They photograph the area's flora and fauna and nearly run out of fresh water but then discover a large lake. They continue their search only to be impeded by huge barrier cliffs but eventually find an underground cavern that takes them to the other side where they meet a Mayan tribe with whom they reside for three months. Winning the confidence of the Mayans, the Lambs are told that the local gods will allow them to see the ruins, known as the city of the dead. The Mayans lead them to the lost city where they find an array of archaeological treasures, including beautiful carvings, huge stone walls and large altars. They also begin to explore a nearby cave but a storm causes the area to flood. Dana builds a canoe while Ginger battles malaria. At last they manage to escape the rising waters and head home but vow to return to further explore the lost city.

Quest for the Lost City, despite its premise of trying to locate a forgotten city of the dead, is geared more for the armchair adventurer than horror fans. *Boxoffice* noted, "In its obvious amateurishness lies much of the charm and conviction of this thoroughly fascinating subject, that will have the average spectator gaping with wonderment at the hardships and ingenuity that entered into its filming." Regarding the Lambs' adventure, *Variety* declared, "Their search for a lost Maya city, a trek made under the most primitive of conditions, is heady enough vicarious adventure for those comfortably seated away from the steamy, buggy jungle."

The Rainmakers (1935; 78 minutes)

ASSOCIATE PRODUCER: Lee Marcus. DIRECTOR: Fred Guiol. SCREENPLAY: Leslie Goodwins & Grant Garett. STORY: Fred Guiol & Albert Treynor. PHOTOGRAPHY: Ted McCord. EDITOR: John Lockert. MUSIC DIRECTOR: Roy Webb. SONG: Louis Alter & Jack Scholl. ART DIRECTORS: Van Nest Polglase & Feild M. Gray. SOUND: George D. Ellis. SOUND EFFECTS: Walter Elliott. COSTUMES: Walter Plunkett. PHOTOGRAPHIC EFFECTS: Vernon L. Walker.

CAST: Bert Wheeler (Billy), Robert Woolsey (Roscoe), Dorothy Lee (Margie Spencer), Berton Churchill (Simon Parker), George Meeker (Orville Parker), Frederic Roland (Henry Spencer), Edgar Dearing (Kelly), Clarence Wilson (Hogan), Eddie Borden, George Magrill (Hobos), Edward LeSaint, Jack Richardson (Engineers), Don Brodie, Nelson McDowell, Bob McKenzie, Warren Jackson, Billy Bletcher, Donald Kerr, John Ince, Pat Harmon, Billy Engle, Joe Smith Marba, Lon Poff, Bill Wolfe, Frank Hammond, Robert Graves, Robert Milasch (Citizens), Edward Hearn, Frank Moran, Ed Brady, Eddie Sturgis (Farmers), Peggy Walters (Secretary), Eddie Dunn (Dispatcher), Harry Bowen, Billy Dooley (Switchmen), Harry Bernard, Leo Sulky (Firemen), Jack Curtis (Railroader).

Released in the fall of 1935, *The Rainmakers* was the sixteenth of twenty feature films the comedy team of Bert Wheeler and Robert Woolsey made for RKO Pictures. Like its immediate predecessor *The Nitwits* (q.v.) and a successor, *Mummy's Boys* (q.v.), it had genre overtones but it proved to be one of the weakest of the duo's efforts. It was leading lady Dorothy Lee's tenth feature with Wheeler and Woolsey; *The Rainmakers* did not show her to good advantage other than singing a duet with Wheeler on "Isn't Love the Sweetest Thing." The feature's very minor claim to a genre element is Woolsey as a confidence artist who by accident manages to concoct a rainmaking machine. Fred Guiol, who co-wrote the original story for *The Rainmakers*, would direct Wheeler and Woolsey in *Mummy's Boys* (q.v.).

Con man Roscoe the Rainmaker (Woolsey) is run out of Goober County, a Midwest locale, by drought-ridden farmers after he tries to demonstrate his rainmaking apparatus, the magno-magnetizer, which only brings a dust storm. He retreats to the farm house of drought-ruined farmer Billy (Wheeler) where he tries to end it all. Billy calms the depressed Roscoe and agrees to go with him to Lima Junction, California, his next scheduled demonstration stop. There a crooked, rich landowner, Simon Parker (Berton Churchill), wants banker Henry Spencer (Frederic Roland) to certify a $50,000 check so he and his son, Orville (George Meeker), can hoodwink area farmers into investing in a bogus irrigation project. Orville is romancing Spencer's pretty daughter Margie (Lee). When Spencer is unable to certify the check because of excessive loans he has made to the locals, Simon threatens him with a bank audit. Roscoe and Billy arrive in town and Spencer sees a way out of his troubles while Billy is attracted to Margie. Roscoe plans to demonstrate his machine at the local fairgrounds where he claims it will make rain out of electricity it draws from the crowd. To halt the demonstration, Simon calls a meeting to discuss the area's drought, using his advertisement to block out Roscoe's. Since no one shows up at the fairgrounds, Billy comes up with a scheme to fake a train wreck to draw a crowd. They obtain the right to use two trains only to later learn the rain machine has disappeared. When the men hired to run the trains find out dynamite will be used to create a crash, they back out; Roscoe and Billy, who do not know about the explosive, agree to drive them. The two almost lose control of their expresses before eventually getting them to the fairgrounds, where Margie finds that Orville has stolen the rainmaking machine. Roscoe demonstrates his invention and it miraculously brings rain, saving the area. Margie discards Orville in favor of Billy.

The Film Daily called *The Rainmakers* a "fairly entertaining farce in typical Wheeler and Woolsey style...." *Boxoffice* noted that the stars "have been saddled with an even more illogical story than usual and it is to their credit that they garner a fair share of laughs." *The New York Times* dubbed it "considerably less than hilarious.... The picture's chief fault is that it promises

Bert Wheeler and Robert Woolsey in *The Rainmakers* (1935).

too much.... [It] will please the youngsters; beyond that, deponent sayeth not." *Motion Picture Daily* declared, "Juvenile entertainment tastes will probably enjoy the picture most" while the *Christian Science Monitor* said it was "a poor example of slapstick melodrama." *Variety* complained, "In briefer length this might have stood more chance of success, but the first 50 minutes are too slow, too talky and too lacking in inventiveness to save 20 minutes of runaway train stuff which forms the climax."

The Rainmakers was novelized with pictures from the film in the December 1935 issue of *Movie Action* magazine. *Harrison's Reports* declared its box office performance "poor."

The Reluctant Dragon (1941; 73 minutes; Color and Black-and-White)

DIRECTOR: Alfred L. Werker. CARTOON DIRECTOR: Hamilton Luske. SCREENPLAY: Ted Sears, Al Perkins, Larry Clemmons, Bill Cottrell & Harry Clark. STORY: Erdman Penner, T. Hee, Joe Grant, Dick Hunter & John P. Miller. PHOTOGRAPHY: Bert Glennon. EDITOR: Paul Weatherwax. MUSIC: Frank Churchill & Larry Morey. SONGS: Frank Churchill, Larry Morey & Charles Wolcott. ART DIRECTOR: Gordon Wiles. CARTOON ART DIRECTORS: Ken Anderson, Hugh Hennesy & Charles Philippi. SOUND: Frank Maher. SET DECORATIONS: Earl Wooden. PRODUCTION MANAGER: Earl Rettig. SPECIAL EFFECTS: Ub Iwerks & Joshua Meador. ANIMATORS: Ward Kimball, Fred Moore, Milt Neil, Wolfgang Reitherman, Bud Swift, Walt Kelly, Jack Campbell, Claude Smith & Harvey Toombs. ASSISTANT DIRECTOR: Jasper Blystone. CARTOON ASSISTANT DIRECTORS: Ford Beebe, Jim Handley & Erwin Verity.

CAST: Robert Benchley (Himself), Frances Gifford (Doris), Buddy Pepper (Humphrey), Nana Bryant (Mrs. Benchley), Claud Allister (Voice of Sir Giles), Barnett Parker (Voice of the Dragon), Billy Lee (Voice of the Boy), Florence Gill (Herself), Clarence Nash (Himself/Voice of Donald Duck), Jimmy Luske (Jimmy), Alan Ladd (Al), Frank Faylen (Orchestra Leader Frank), Walt Disney, Hamilton MacFadden, Louise Currie, Norm Ferguson, Ward Kimball, Truman Woodworth, Maurice Murphy, Frank Churchill, Jack Kinney, Ken Anderson, Hamilton Luske, Ted Sears, Fred Moore, John Dehner, Wolfgang Reitherman, James MacDonald (Themselves), Verna Hillie (Sculptor), J. Donald Wilson, John McLeish (Narrators), Gerald Mohr (Studio Guard/Narrator), Raymond Severn, Leone De Doux (Voices of Baby Weems), Linda Warwood (Voice of Baby Weems' Mother), Paul Colvig (Voice of Goofy), Steve Pendleton (Security Chief), Henry Hall (Guard), Lester Dorr (Slim), Art Gilmore (Voice of Franklin D. Roosevelt), Eddie Marr (Voice of Walter Winchell), Val Stanton (Voice of Courier), The Rhythmaires (Singers).

Sandwiched between *Fantasia* and *Dumbo* (qq.v.), *The Reluctant Dragon* was almost a throwaway feature produced by Walt Disney and released by RKO in the summer of 1941. Designed to show off the Disney studio and its method of operations, the feature does include two sequences of interest to genre fans although both of them are decidedly comedic and not horrifying. While the bulk of the movie has Robert Benchley observing the workings of the Disney organization, it does include the cartoons "Baby Weems" and "The Reluctant Dragon." The former is about a two-day-old baby who talks and becomes a national celebrity, even composing symphonies. A fever reverts the baby to normalcy and he is dismissed by the public but loved by his parents. "The Reluctant Dragon," although the title of the movie, runs only 12 minutes and is about a benign dragon (voice of Barnett Parker) who loves to drink tea and recite poetry. He becomes friends with a boy (voice of Billy Lee) as well as the knight, Sir Giles (voice of Claud Allister), who is supposed to kill him. Dragon and knight engage in a fake fight with the former pretending to be vanquished only to become a beloved village pet. The last segments of the film are in Technicolor. Overall *The Reluctant Dragon* is a pleasant affair but for the most part its interest is historical rather than as mass entertainment. It is one of the few Disney films never to be reissued theatrically. In 1950 RKO released a segment of the movie featuring Goofy (voice of Pinto Colvig), "How to Ride a Horse," as a short subject.

Robert Benchley (himself) is told by his wife (Nana Bryant) to try and convince Walt Disney to film the 1898 story "The Reluctant Dragon" by Kenneth Grahame. She drives her husband to the Disney Studios at Burbank and there he is taken on a tour by an annoying but exuberant guide, Humphrey (Buddy Pepper). Finally getting away from Humphrey, Benchley finds himself in a drawing class where the subject is an elephant. Next he goes to a music soundstage and sees Clarence Nash and Florence Gill (themselves) singing opera as Donald and Clara Duck. Nash teaches Benchley to talk like Donald Duck until Humphrey arrives. Benchley ditches the guide again and enters the sound department where he observes a scene from *Dumbo* being dubbed with sound effects and music. In the camera department he is shown how Donald Duck is animated and then observes the model and paint shops. Next a storyboard artist (Alan Ladd) shows off his latest work, "Baby Weems," and then Benchley watches animators at work. After viewing a recently finished cartoon, "How to Ride a Horse," Benchley is accosted again by Humphrey and meets Walt Disney (himself) in a screening room and is shown "The Reluctant Dragon," which the studio just completed. When his wife takes him home, she scolds her husband for being too late in bringing Disney the story and he gets even by replying to her in Donald Duck's voice.

Photoplay deemed *The Reluctant Dragon* "one of the cleverest ideas ever to pop into that fertile mind of Walt Disney and results in this rare combination of a Cook's tour of the Disney studio, a behind-the-scenes glimpse of Mickey Mousedom and two of Disney's latest cartoon features.... Cleverly thought out and executed." *Boxoffice* wrote, "Different from any previous

Disney effort, *The Reluctant Dragon* combines human and cartoons with a highly variable result. It is pretty lightweight for feature length." "A bold and nervy stroke" is how *Variety* termed the movie, adding, "It's an out-and-out trailer for the Disney studios—a trailer which Disney and RKO hope to sell at feature picture prices." The reviewer felt that the picture "has plenty of entertaining qualities [but it's] a lot less than sensational." *The Film Daily* declared, "As entertainment for general audiences, this offering is first rate, as an educational feature on the 'inside' of cartoon production, it is a fascinating film, and as a feature attraction exploiting Disney, his studio and product, it is tops...." Leonard Maltin noted in *The Disney Films, 3rd Edition* (1995), "*The Reluctant Dragon* is an extremely pleasant film, but little more. In its attempt to tell a mass audience how cartoons are made, it whitewashes much of the technique and omits most of the detail. It gives the erroneous impression that the soundtrack is matched to the cartoon, instead of vice versa. It uses actors in the roles of animators, musicians, cameramen, and never lets up in on the real creative process that produces Disney's cartoons. It's certainly a far cry *from the cinema*-verite technique that has more recently been used to show filmmakers at work." Martin Goodman in *The Animated Movie Guide* (2005) called *The Reluctant Dragon* "possibly Disney's most forgettable film," adding that the Dragon's segment "is an exercise in pure silliness."

The Return of Peter Grimm (1935; 84 minutes)

PRODUCER: Kenneth Macgowan. DIRECTOR: George Nichols, Jr. SCREENPLAY: Francis Edward Faragoh, from the play by David Belasco. PHOTOGRAPHY: Lucien Andriot. EDITOR: Arthur Schmidt. MUSIC DIRECTOR: Alberto Colombo. ART DIRECTORS: Van Nest Polglase & Sturges Carne. SOUND: George D. Ellis. COSTUMES: Walter Plunkett.

CAST: Lionel Barrymore (Peter Grimm), Helen Mack (Catherine), Edward Ellis (Dr. Andrew Macpherson), Donald Meek (Mayor Everett Bartholomew), George Breakston (William Van Dam), Allen Vincent (Frederik), James Bush (James), Ethel Griffies (Martha Bartholomew), Lucien Littlefield (Colonel Tom Lawton), Ray Mayer (Clown), Greta Meyer (Marta), Lois Verner (Freckled Girl).

David Belasco's play *The Return of Peter Grimm* first appeared on Broadway in the 1911–12 season, running 231 performances. It starred David Warfield and Thomas Meighan. Warfield also did a two-year tour with the play and appeared in its 1921 Broadway revival. Fox filmed *The Return of Peter Grimm* in 1926; directed by Victor Schertzinger, it starred Alec B. Francis, John Roche and Janet Gaynor. As his final production at RKO, Kenneth Macgowan made a sound version which was released in the fall of 1935. Although a ghost story, *The Return of Peter Grimm* is hardly a horror effort but is instead a melodrama about spiritual transformation and redemption. Genre fans expecting the kind of chills associated with *Dracula* (1931) and *Frankenstein* (1931) must have been sorely disappointed with this talky, somewhat stagebound effort highlighted by well-etched performances, especially Lionel Barrymore in the title role and Edward Ellis as his physician friend. Helen Mack and James Bush are adequate as lovers while Allen Vincent supplied another of his offbeat characterizations. Donald Meek and Ethel Griffies are well cast as a grasping married couple and George Breakston provides good work as a dying boy. He was also in *Great Expectations* (1934), as the young Pip, and *Life Returns* (1935) and in adulthood he produced and directed several films, including *The Manster* (1962).

Although he scoffs at spiritualism, wealthy nursery owner Peter Grimm (Barrymore) conducts a séance at his home. Attending are his close friend, Dr. Andrew Macpherson (Ellis), his ward Catherine (Mack), his secretary James (Bush), and Mayor Bartholomew (Meek) and his wife Martha (Griffies). When the séance proves to be half-hearted, the Bartholomews leave and Dr. Macpherson agrees to stay for dinner. Grimm's nephew Frederik (Vincent) arrives by train and is offered a lift to the Grimm home by young William Van Dam (Breakston), who hands out flowers to newcomers thanks to the generosity of Grimm. The orphaned William is being raised by Grimm. As they wait for Frederik, Grimm tells Catherine he is content with her living in his home and thanks Dr. Macpherson for her being there. Grimm tells Dr. Macpherson that Frederik is coming home from Europe and he wants Catherine to marry him. As Catherine picks flowers, William questions her about marrying James since he has seen them kissing. Dr. Macpherson cautions Grimm about his health and says whoever dies first should return and communicate with the other. Grimm ridicules the notion. As Grimm sprays his roses, music is heard and William says a circus is in town. A clown (Ray Mayer), who knows Grimm, invites him and his friends to the show. Grimm has James write a nasty letter to a man who wants to buy his business. Seeing Frederik and Catherine together, he informs James that they will soon be engaged. When Frederik proposes marriages to Catherine, she turns him down. Dr. Macpherson tells the ailing William to get more rest. The Bartholomews arrive and Martha thanks Grimm for helping the poor and William suggests that she thinks Grimm is about to die. Rejecting the notion, Grimm has William gets circus tickets. After the Bartholomews leave, Grimm asks Catherine to sing to him and he writes in his Bible. He tells Catherine and Frederik he wants them to get married and he gives Catherine his mother's wedding ring. After smoking his pipe, Grimm dies. At his funeral the minister talks of life in the hereafter. Later William becomes very ill and is attended by Dr. Macpherson, who informs Catherine that she can break off her engagement to Frederik if she wants but she says she promised Grimm. Catherine informs Frederik they must remain in the house after their marriage and take care of William. Martha finds Grimm's will and that evening Frederik reads it while the old family dog, Toby, barks outside. Grimm's ghost comes into the house as Frederik complains that he would have been named in the will had Grimm not given so much to charity. This upsets the Bartholomews, who leave. Frederik asks Colonel Lawton (Lucien Littlefield) to help him sell the property. Although she cannot hear him, Grimm tells Catherine not to marry Frederik so she will be happy and he can find peace. Dr. Macpherson arrives and tells Catherine they may get a sign from Grimm, who tells the doctor to help her. Catherine informs James that she does not want to marry Frederik and they kiss. When she says she will not break the promise she made to Grimm, James tells Catherine he will take her away with him. Grimm begs to be heard and asks Catherine to burn her wedding dress as he is setting her free. Grimm goes to William's room and as the doctor sleeps he talks with the dying boy. He asks him to remember his mother and the man who was with her. William awakens Dr. Macpherson and tells him that Grimm is with them as Frederik comes into the room. Frederik is questioned about the boy's mother and claims he does not know what happened to her. Upon prompting from Grimm, Frederik says William's mother followed him to Holland and committed suicide. A telegram arrives for Frederik saying the man who wanted to buy Grimm's business is dead. When the lock falls from Grimm's Bible, Dr. Macpherson finds that Grimm left his property to Catherine, her husband and children. The wedding is cancelled, and Catherine and James wonder if Grimm realizes they will be wed. William asks Peter to go with him. After he takes a brief nap, they leave together, along with Toby.

Picture Play wrote, "Don't think that this is a spook subject or that it has to do with the usual spiritualistic manifestations.... It is tender, touching and very human, serious but gloomy.... This picture is notable for restraint, taste and acting that is sound and true." *Photoplay* reported, "Lionel Barrymore in top form, a fine supporting cast and intelligent artistic treatment make this old favorite well worth its screen revival.... Eerie at times, but leavened by humor and perfect in taste throughout." "Excellent entertainment" stated *Boxoffice,* adding, "Photography is excellent and direction by George Nichols, Jr., is commendable." *Christian Science Monitor* proclaimed,

"Peter Grimm alive is one of the most meandering characters to inch about the screen and returning from the great beyond, he picks up his pace very little. The picture, from the familiar turn-of-the-century play, is a curious mixture of leisureliness and fatalism." *Stage* declared, "It is one of the least spectacular offerings of the current output. It is fireside, homey, family stuff, with a lot of talk about books and flowers, and a minimum of story." Andre Sennwald stated in *The New York Times,* "It looks mighty like a phony drama under the searching scrutiny of this year of gracelessness. Despite the care with which RKO Radio Pictures sets its ancient bones in motion again, it seldom is able to rescue the spectator from a mood of overpowering ennui." *Variety* declared, "*The Return of Peter Grimm* is somber fantasy. It's deathbed and spiritualism vein is superimposed upon old-fashioned reading-of-the-will mechanics. As a theme its appeal is limited to those who believe in spooks and as drama it's pretty dull and boresome...." *Harrison Reports* rated its box office performance as "Fair to Poor."

Lionel Barrymore again enacted the title role in "The Return of Peter Grimm" on CBS' *Lux Radio Theatre* on February 13, 1939. Hosted by Cecil B. DeMille, the cast also included Maureen O'Sullivan, Edward Arnold, Alan Ladd, Gavin Muir, Lou Merrill and Frank Nelson.

Riding on Air (1937; 70 minutes)

PRODUCER: David L. Loew. ASSOCIATE PRODUCER–DIRECTOR: Edward Sedgwick. SCREENPLAY: Richard Flournoy & Richard Macaulay, from the story "All Is Confusion" by Richard Macaulay. PHOTOGRAPHY: Alfred Gilks. EDITOR: Jack Oglivie. MUSIC: Arthur Morton. SONG: Henry Cohen. ART DIRECTOR: John DuCasse Schulze. SOUND: T.A. Carman. SPECIAL EFFECTS: Fred Jackman. ASSISTANT DIRECTOR: Bill Ryan.

CAST: Joe E. Brown (Elmer Lane), Guy Kibbee (J. Rutherford "Doc" Waddington), Florence Rice (Betty Harrison), Vinton Haworth (Harvey Schuman), Anthony Nace (Bill Hilton), Harlan Briggs (Mr. Harrison), Andrew Tombes (Eddie Byrd), Clem Bevans (Sheriff), Harry C. Bradley (Mayor), Joseph Crehan (*Daily Blade* Editor), Monte Collins (Dick the Barber), Don Brodie (Charlie), Robert Emmett O'Connor (Detective Flynn), Tom Dugan (Detective Brad), Frank Sully (Harrison's Employee), Kernan Cripps (*Daily Star* Editor), Lester Dorr (*Daily Star* Reporter), Jack Norton (*Daily Blade* Reporter), Emmett Vogan, Bud Flanagan [Dennis O'Keefe] (Cargo Plane Pilots), George Lloyd (Detective), Si Jenks (Hard of Hearing Man), George Chandler (Barbershop Customer), Charlie Hall (Second Barber/Crooner), Budd Buster (Angry Townsman), Benny Burt, Murray Alper (Smugglers), Henry Roquemore (Air Patrol Official).

Wide-mouthed Joe E. Brown was a popular film comedian from the late 1920s into the mid–1940s, starring in a long line of medium-budget efforts which parlayed his screen image of a likable, bumbling hick who always came out on top following all types of adversity. In 1937 he teamed with director Edward Sedgwick for two features, *Riding on Air* and *Fit for a King*, which were made by Edward Sedgwick Productions and distributed by RKO Radio. Later Brown and Sedgwick made a trio of features for Columbia, *The Gladiator* (1938), *Beware Spooks!* (1939) and *So You Won't Talk?* (1940). *Riding on Air*, released in June 1937, presents Brown in his usual breezy format of a well-meaning, optimistic fumbler who is invention-crazy. The sci-fi aspect of the movie is a radio beam which can remotely control an airplane. Co-starred is Guy Kibbee as a bunco artist who tries to fleece the naïve Brown out of a $5,000 radio contest prize as well as getting citizens to invest in a bogus corporation formed to promote the futuristic invention. The film is based on Richard Macaulay's short story "All Is Confusion," which was the film's working title and its British release title. Macaulay also co-wrote the screenplay for the movie, which also had the working title *Sky High*.

The only employee of the *Claremont Chronicle,* Elmer Lane (Brown), bungles an advertisement placed in his newspaper by store owner Harrison (Harlan Briggs). The angry Harrison threatens to get Elmer fired but his girlfriend Betty (Florence Rice), Harrison's daughter, tries to protect him. Harvey Schuman (Vinton Haworth), correspondent for the *Chicago Daily Blade,* informs Betty that he plans to buy the *Chronicle* when his inheritance comes through. Betty tells Elmer, who says he wants to purchase the *Chronicle* for $5,000 and enters a radio contest to win the money. Betty complains about Elmer wasting his time on silly inventions. Elmer goes to Chicago and asks *Daily Star* editor Byrd (Andrew Tombes) to hire him as its Claremont correspondent. After getting the job, he promises to help the newspaperman capture a gang of perfume smugglers. While he is driving home, the top of his car is demolished when an airplane crashes on the road in front of him; Elmer rescues the pilot, his friend Bill Hilton (Anthony Nace). The next day Elmer demonstrates for Betty a new invention of Bill's, a model plane that travels on a radio beam. Elmer hears on the radio that he won the contest. In Chicago, crook Doc Waddington (Kibbee) is told to leave town and buys a ticket to Claremont after learning of Elmer's prize. When Elmer finds out that a rich financier is in town, he goes to interview Doc and tells him about Bill's invention. Doc convinces Elmer to invest his winnings in a corporation they will form to market the radio beam. That evening Elmer goes to see Betty and they realize that airplanes fly over the area every night at 10 p.m. and midnight. The following day, Betty learns from Elmer about his investment. She becomes angry and goes off with Harvey, but ends up crying in a telephone booth. Doc sells shares in the Radio Beam Airplane Company to local investors, including Harrison. That night Harvey finds the bullet-riddled body of wanted gangster Bugs Fuller and telephones the *Blade*'s editor, who tells him to get photographs and fly them to Chicago. Since Bill is unable to fly due to injuries from his crash, Harvey finagles novice pilot Elmer into flying him to Chicago to save the life of his wounded dog. After a perilous flight Elmer is met at the airport by *Blade* reporters who take pictures of him, resulting in such bad publicity that Byrd throws him out of the *Star*'s office. After returning home, Elmer is razzed by Harvey in the barbershop about his mistake and the two nearly fight when Harvey says he is going to get his inheritance and marry Betty. Elmer challenges Harvey to solve Fuller's murder and claims the victim was shot and then dropped from an airplane. After Elmer leaves, Doc informs Harvey that he will not be allowed to buy stock in the air beam company. Betty, hoping to make up with Elmer, brings Bill fruit and says Fuller may have been pushed out of one of the planes that fly over Claremont each night. Hoping to publicize their company, Elmer sends a picture of Doc and a story to the *Star* where he is recognized as a con artist. Finding out what Elmer did, Doc makes plans to skip town and sells Harvey, who is apologetic for his actions, 200 shares of stock for $5,000. The *Star*'s editor calls Harvey and tells him Doc is a swindler, and Doc ends up in jail. The sheriff (Clem Bevans) refuses to hand Doc over to an angry mob as Harvey blames Elmer for being in cahoots with the crook. As Elmer is about to fly away to look for the smuggler's airplane, the mob arrives at the airfield. After he leaves, Betty calms the crowd by convincing her father to back their air beam company stock. Elmer follows the wrong plane, which is carrying $100,000 worth of radium, and nearly shoots it down with a shotgun before being told to land by the air police. When Elmer is being interrogated by Chicago Detective Brad (Tom Dugan), Byrd refuses to identify him. After he is let go, Elmer flies home but spots a plane with a missing wheel. It belongs to the smugglers, who fire at him. Elmer radios Bill that he has located the crooks but they shoot away one of his struts. Bill tells Elmer to use the radio beam to fly the plane and then he climbs onto the wing and fix the strut. After the repair, Elmer radios the Chicago Air Police who think he is trying to fool them. The radio man (Henry Roquemore) tells him to shoot back at the smugglers with his gun. Elmer causes the smuggler's plane to crashland after he shoots the propeller; upon landing they are arrested by the police. Elmer lands safely and later flies home only to be told by Bill not to land because of a large crowd on the airfield. Betty radios Elmer to use his parachute while Bill has the radio beam land the plane. Eventually finding his parachute's ripcord, Elmer lands in a field and is greeted by Betty. The mayor (Harry C. Bradley) is about to give Elmer, who has sold the air beam company for $10,000, a new watch when a bus goes by, causing the parachute to carry Elmer and Betty into a tree. Elmer tries to kiss Betty when the limb breaks and they fall to the ground.

The Evening Huronite (Huron, South Dakota) declared that *Riding on Air* "is full of strenuous action, much of it exciting aerial stuff, and is generously supplied with romance as well." *Boxoffice* called it "a standard Joe E. Brown laugh-provoking performance.... It will be a riot with the juveniles and has enough of the gaggy situations, which have come to be expected in a Brown vehicle, to satisfy the humor desires of every type patron." *The New York Herald Tribune* stated, "Thanks to some clever aerial photography, the film is a comparatively amusing summer weight offering," while *The New York Times* felt it a "modest contribution to mirth and laughter." *The Film Daily* opined, "This one will please all the Joe E. Brown fans without a struggle, and especially the youngsters.... The plot is a pretty rambling affair without much logic, but then it gives Joe opportunity to do his amiable antics and garner the laughs, and that's all it was intended to do." *Variety* declared it "is out of the bottom of the basket. Will satisfy Joe E. Brown addicts but otherwise no dice. Yarn is so typical of the Joe E. Brown pictures it might have been a remake of several forerunners." *Independent Film Bulletin* said, "This is up to par for Joe E. Brown comedies.... The yarn, which is patently unoriginal, has been handled with an aim at speedy tempo, and average as fair fun for the unsophisticates." *The New York World-Telegram* proclaimed *Riding on Air* "a new high (or low if you are over six) in the serialized idiocies of Mr. Brown."

Rodan (1956; 72 minutes; Color)

PRODUCER: Tomoyuki Tanaka. U.S. VERSION PRODUCERS: Frank King & Maurice King. DIRECTOR: Ishiro Honda. SCREENPLAY: Takeshi Kimura, Ken Curium & Takeo Murata. U.S. VERSION SCREENPLAY: David Duncan. PHOTOGRAPHY: Isamu Ashida. EDITORS: Koichi Iwashita. U.S. VERSION EDITOR: Robert S. Eisen. MUSIC: Akira Ifukube. PRODUCTION DESIGN: Tatsuo Kita. SOUND: Masanobu Miyazaki. SPECIAL EFFECTS ART DIRECTOR: Akira Watanabe. SPECIAL EFFECTS DIRECTOR: Eiji Tsuburaya. SPECIAL EFFECTS OPTICALS: Hiroshi Mukoyama. FIRST ASSISTANT DIRECTOR: Jun Fukuda.

CAST: Kenji Sahara (Shigeru Kawamura), Yumi Shirakawa (Kiyo), Akihiko Hirata (Professor Kyuichiro Kashiwagi), Akio Kobori (Chief Nishimura), Kiyoharu Onaka, Yasuko Nakata (Newlyweds), Minosuke Yamada (Chief Osaki), Yoshifumi Tajima (Izeki), Mitsuo Matsumoto (Professor Isokawa), Kiyoshi Takagi (Dr. Minakami), Ichiro Chiba (Police Station Chief), Tazue Ichimanji (Haru), Jiro Kumara (Tashiro), Tsuruko Mano (Osumi), Junnosuke Suda (Coroner), Mitsuo Tsuda (Officer Takeuchi), Hideo Mihara (JASDF Commander), Ren Imaizumi (Sunagawa), Fuyuki Murakami (Professor Minami), Toshiko Nakano (Neighbor), Kiyomi Mizunoya (Otami), Rinsaku Ogata (Goro), Ichiro Nakatani, Yashiro Shigenobu, Jiro Suzukawa, Keiji Sakakida, Kanta Kisaragi, Tateo Kawasaki (Miners), Saburo Iketani (News Reader), Mike Daneen (Typing Soldier), Saeko Kuroiwa (Nurse), Jun'ichiro Mukai (Military Officer), Shigemi Sunagawa, Shoichi Hirose, Yasuhisa Tsutsumi, Yutaka Oka (F-86F Pilots), Masaki Machibana (Policeman), Kamayuki Tsubono (Crime Laboratory Officer), Bontaro Taira (Worker).

U.S. VERSION VOICE CAST: Keye Luke (Shigeru Kawamura), Paul Frees (Chief Nishimura), George Takei (Professor Kyuichiro Kashiwagi), Art Gilmore (Narrator).

The huge financial success in the U.S. of *Godzilla, King of the Monsters!*, released in 1956 by Trans-World, prompted Hollywood companies to obtain similar Japanese productions in the following years. Originally shown in its homeland in 1954 as *Gojira, Godzilla, King of the Monsters!* was a reworking of that Toho production with quite a bit of footage deleted to make way for American scenes directed by Terry O. Morse and starring Raymond Burr. The second such

Toho film to see stateside issuance was *Rodan* which was initially acquired by RKO but got official release in the summer of 1957 by Distributors Corporation of America (DCA). Made as *Sora no daikaiju Radon*, it was first shown in Japan a year earlier, running 82 minutes. The U.S. version runs ten minutes less even with the addition of stock military footage at the beginning showing bomb blasts. A number of changes were made to the American version to make it more streamlined and to emphasize the *two* Rodans in the film while in the Japanese version the second monster does not materialize until later in the proceedings. The U.S. version was produced by the brothers Frank and Maurice King. Keye Luke, best known as Charlie Chan's number one son Lee in films for Fox, 20th Century–Fox and Monogram, dubbed the voice of the lead character while George Takei from TV's *Star Trek* did the voice of his biology professor cohort. The first Technicolor Japanese monster movie to be released in the United States, *Rodan* proved to be strong at the box office but it was not until the end of 1958 that *Half Human*, another DCA release, made it stateside. Like most Japanese monster movies, *Rodan*'s highlights involve its special and visual effects. It's a fast-paced, entertaining sci-fi movie, one of the better of its genre. Although it's not stated in the U.S. version, the giant insects in *Rodan* were called the Meganulon (they also later appeared in 2000's *Godzilla vs. Megaguirus*).

As various points in the Pacific Ocean are used to test atomic and hydrogen bombs, a coal mining community in Southern Japan experiences abnormal seismic activity. When water floods a deep mine shaft, safety engineer Shigeru (Kenji Sahara; voice of Luke) investigates and finds the mutilated body of a miner. Another missing miner, Goro (Rinsaku Ogata), is blamed for his death but Shigeru, who is engaged to marry Goro's sister Kiyo (Yumi Shirakawa), believes him innocent. While searching for Goro in the mine, three more men are killed. Shigeru urges Kiyo to leave the area and as they talk they are attacked by a giant insect that causes a panic in the village. The local police call in the military and the monster kills two soldiers. As Shigeru and several soldiers look for Goro, they are attacked by the creature but bury it under a coal car. They manage to retrieve Goro's body before a cave-in kills the insect and cuts Shigeru off from the others. Biology Professor Kashiwagi (Akihiko Hirata; voice of Takei) goes to inspect the area and finds Shigeru wandering around in a state of shock. Kashiwagi reports that the insect was a prehistoric creature that roamed the Earth millions of years ago. A pilot reports seeing a large flying object before it destroys his plane. The object attacks numerous places over the Pacific Ocean and the authorities think there might be more than one UFO. Two newlyweds (Yasuko Nakata, Kiyoharu Onaka) go to a volcano near Mt. Toya and are carried away by a gigantic flying monster. Film from their camera reveals the wing of a giant bird. Shigeru's memory returns and he recalls being trapped in the mine shaft and seeing a gigantic egg and several of the prehistoric insects. The egg hatches and a huge bird emerges and feeds on the insects. Shigeru identifies a drawing of a Pteranodon as the thing he saw hatch in the mine and he returns there with Kashiwagi and some soldiers and find the piece of a shell before a landslide sends them back to the surface. Kashiwagi reports that the shell is over 20 million years old and reptilian. He also relates that the thing that hatched from it is a flying reptile weighing 100 tons with a 500-foot wing spread and all the destructive force of a typhoon. The professor says it belongs to a species called Rodan. He theorizes that the egg was hermitically sealed and buried by a landslide and that warm water from atomic explosions caused it to hatch. Rodan is located near the north rim of the Mt. Toya volcano and planes bomb the area but the creature emerges and flies away. A second Rodan also rises from the volcano and as planes track the two monsters, one drops into the sea and then emerges to destroy a bridge and cause widespread damage. Tanks prove useless against the creature as the second Rodan reappears, causing more chaos and destruction. The Rodans fly away together, leaving two cities in flames as officials declare they must be killed before they destroy the world. A week goes by and Kashiwagi believes the monsters have gone back underground. The military plans to bomb the crater at Mt. Toya, sealing the Rodans inside. The countryside around the volcano is ordered evacuated but Koyi tells Shigeru she wants to stay with him. The military bombards the crater and close off the cavern. As the volcano erupts, the two monsters emerge but one falls into the flaming lava and the other joins its mate and also dies. Shigeru wonders what other prehistoric creatures await to attack mankind.

Boxoffice called *Rodan* "truly terrifying and one of the most impressive visually to date." The reviewer praised the photographic effects of Eiji Tsuburaya as "amazingly realistic, probably because of the Japanese facility for creating miniatures." Danny Perry in *Guide for the Film Fanatic* (1986) wrote, "Ranks just below *Godzilla, King of the Monsters!* on the Japanese best monster-movie list. Kids in particular will enjoy this sci-fi fantasy.... Directed by Inoshiro Honda, who collaborated with his Godzilla special-effects expert, Eija Tsuburaya, to again create some extremely impressive scenes of destruction." In *Science Fiction* (1984) Phil Hardy noted, "The special effects are impressive, especially the volcanic eruption and the death of the monsters in the gushing lava." James O'Neill in *Terror on Tape* (1994) called *Rodan* "one of the best Japanese creature features" and C.J. Henderson said in *The Encyclopedia of Science Fiction Movies* (2001), "Better than a number of the Godzilla team's films, *Rodan* has a more interesting back story than most of the Toho fare and some very interesting takes on the main monster as well."

Rodan was shown in some locales as *Rodan, the Flying Monster*. The giant flying reptile was featured in five other Toho productions: *Ghidrah, the Three-Headed Monster* (1964), *Monster Zero* (1965), *Destroy All Monsters* (1968), *Godzilla vs. MechaGodzilla* (1993) and *Godzilla: Final Wars* (2004).

The Saint's Double Trouble (1940; 67 minutes)

PRODUCER: Cliff Reid. DIRECTOR: Jack Hively. SCREENPLAY: Ben Holmes, from the character by Leslie Charteris. PHOTOGRAPHY: J. Roy Hunt. EDITOR: Theron Warth. MUSIC DIRECTOR: Roy Webb. ART DIRECTORS: Van Nest Polglase & Albert S. D'Agostino. SOUND: Hugh McDowell, Jr. GOWNS: Renie. SPECIAL EFFECTS: Vernon L. Walker. PRODUCTION EXECUTIVE: Lee Marcus.

CAST: George Sanders (Simon Templar aka "The Saint"/Duke "Boss" Bates), Helene Whitney (Anne Bitts), Jonathan Hale (Inspector Henry Fernack), Bela Lugosi (Partner), Donald MacBride (Inspector John H. Bohlen), John F. Hamilton (Limpy), Thomas W. Ross (Professor Horatio T. Bitts), Elliott Sullivan (Monk Warren), Byron Foulger (Ephraim Byrd), Walter Miller (Bartender Mack), Edward Gargan (Turnkey Mike), William Haade (Helm "The Dutchman" Van Roon), Stanley Blystone (Detective Sadler), Ralph Dunn, Lee Phelps (Police Sergeants), Pat O'Malley (Delivery Man), Lal Chand Mehra (Express Office Clerk), Pat McKee, Donald Kerr (Card Players), Billy Franey (Shooting Witness), Sammy Stein (Police Officer), Jack O'Shea (Man on Street).

After Louis Hayward first portrayed Leslie Charteris' suave Simon Templar, alias The Saint, in *The Saint in New York* in 1938 for RKO, George Sanders took over the role in five more such adventures, the third being *The Saint's Double Trouble*, released early in 1940. Its 67 minutes contains a convoluted and rather hard-to-follow plot, further complicated by Sanders playing both the hero and his villainous doppelganger. For horror fans there is Bela Lugosi fourth-billed as a diamond smuggler and the plot ploy of having the gems transported in an Egyptian mummy. A similar scenario was used in the 1934 Reliable three-reeler *Arizona Nights*, only then it was Chinese being smuggled into the country via mummy cases. Overall, *The Saint's Double Trouble* is a fast-paced affair that is often too confusing to be entertaining. Sanders did not like the "Saint" series and he was succeeded in the part by Hugh Sinclair in the British-made *The Saint's Vacation*

(1941) and *The Saint Meets the Tiger* (1943), the latter issued by Republic. Louis Hayward did the Templar role again for RKO in *The Saint's Girl Friday* (1954).

In Cairo, Partner (Lugosi) sends a large box to Professor Horatio T. Bitts (Thomas W. Ross) in Philadelphia, with the return address listing Simon Templar (Sanders), who is also known as "The Saint." When the parcel arrives, Bitts and his daughter Ann (Helene Whitney) open it to find it contains the mummy of Pharaoh Amhed III, who died four thousand years ago. Bitts tells Ann, who does not approve of Templar although she had a girlhood crush on him, that Templar had promised years before to send him such an artifact. Inspector Henry Fernack (Jonathan Hale), in the city on a vacation, visits Inspector John H. Bohlen (Donald MacBride), who invites him to dinner with some of his former co-workers that night. As Bitts is about to go to a faculty meeting, Templar arrives and asks to see the mummy. Bitts gives him the key to the vault where he placed the mummy and leaves. Templar removes a package from inside the mummy. Ann finds Templar in the vault and returns a ring he once gave her, saying his reputation as a thief has cooled her feelings for him. As the two police inspectors are about to go to dinner, Bohlen gets a call saying there is a dead man in Bitts' yard. On the scene Fernack finds a calling card from the Saint. Templar tells Fernack he did not commit the murder and takes him to see Bitts, who confirms Templar's story about sending him the mummy. As Templar and Ann look at the mummy, she says she found the ring she returned to him near the dead man. After secretly removing a diamond from the mummy, Templar asks Fernack for 48 hours to solve the case. Crook Limpy (John F. Hamilton) goes to see jeweler Ephraim Byrd (Byron Foulger) with the diamonds entrusted to him by smuggling ring leader Boss (Sanders). Byrd refuses to take them unless they are cut and

Donald MacBride, Bela Lugosi, George Sanders, Elliott Sullivan, Jonathan Hale, J. Frank Hamilton and Ralph Dunn in *The Saint's Double Trouble* (1940).

refers him to the Dutchman (William Haade). Templar reads about the smugglers in the newspaper and connects them to the diamond he took from the mummy. Limpy returns to the gang's headquarters below the Four Bells Café and informs Boss that Byrd will not take the gems. Boss is a dead ringer for Templar. Taking the diamond he found to Byrd, Templar finds the man murdered with the Saint's card by the body. Bohlen gets a wire from Cairo asking him to hold the Dutchman if he is captured. At the gang's headquarters, Templar pretends to be Boss and learns that Partner is arriving that afternoon by plane. Dismissing Limpy and another gang member, Monk Warren (Elliott Sullivan), Templar searches the hideout and then goes to meet Partner. Later Boss is upset at Limpy and Monk for not telling him that Partner is in town and orders them outside. There they meet Partner, who goes to see Boss. When Boss hears that Partner thought he had met him at the airport, he realizes Templar is in town. When Templar goes to the headquarters, he is captured by the gang. Boss tells Partner he wants Templar out of the way but Partner cautions him that Templar might be worth more alive. Boss also informs Partner he had to kill the Dutchman, who jumped him when he was leaving Bitts' home. When Partner tells Boss he got only half the diamonds, Boss returns to Bitts' vault and finds the professor has just found the gems and shoots him. As he leaves with the diamonds, Ann arrives and thinks he is Templar, just as she did when Boss was there the first time. Templar manages to escape but learns he is wanted for Bitts' murder. Lifting a gun from a beat cop, Templar calls Ann and tells her to meet him across from the café. There she mistakes Boss for Templar. Boss has Monk drive Ann home and as they leave Templar jumps onto the back of the car. Boss learns that Templar has escaped. Monk attempts to kill Ann by running her car into a river but Templar saves Ann and sends her home. Templar confronts Monk and they return to the headquarters with Templar getting the drop on the gang. Bartender Mack (Walter Miller) arrives with a message for Boss, causing Templar to be captured again. He is tied up and left in a speedboat. Fernack and Bohlen go to the café and they arrest Boss, thinking he is Templar, along with Partner and Monk. Limpy makes a getaway in the boat. Fernack kills Limpy as Templar struggles to get free, finally swimming to safety. Templar sends another note to Fernack, this time saying he will escape from jail wearing a black dress and hat. In such attire, Templar goes to Boss' cell and demands the diamonds, but purposely leaves his revolver in plain sight and is knocked out. Boss puts on the black clothes and walks out of the jail only to be shot and killed by Fernack. Ann arrives and thinks Templar is dead. Fernack goes to Templar's jail cell and lets himself be handcuffed as his friendly rival escapes. Templar goes to Ann, letting her know he is still alive, and returns the ring to her. Behlan and Fernack arrive at the Bitts home looking for Templar, but he has escaped again.

Photoplay wrote of *The Saint's Double Trouble*, "It's all a bit confusing since [George] Sanders looks so much like Sanders you sometimes forget which man he's supposed to be, but there's plenty of suspense and the pace holds throughout." *Boxoffice* enthused, "Jammed with hairbreadth escapes, thrilling rescues and a coterie of diamond thieves, this latest intrigue of that devil-may-care adventurer, the Saint, is up to par for the series and should satisfy action fans." Frank S. Nugent in *The New York Times* judged the film to be "fair fun" but *Variety* called it "one of the slowest and most absurd of the recent ones...." *The Film Daily* felt it "a good mystery meller for general consumption." In *The Detective in Hollywood* (1978), Jon Tuska wrote, "It was a bit difficult for the viewer to tell the two Sanders portrayals apart, since he was obviously bored with both characters. The lookalike aspect did bring about some amusing routines."

For the record, Simon Templar and his nemesis the Boss can be identified separately since the Saint has a scar on his right wrist.

Saludos Amigos (1943; 45 minutes; Color)

PRESENTER: Walt Disney. SEQUENCE DIRECTORS: Bill Roberts, Jack Kinney, Hamilton Luske & Wilfred Jackson. STORY: Homer Brightman, Ralph Wright, Roy Williams, Harry Reeves, Dick Huemer & Joe Grant. STORY RESEARCH: Ted Sears, Bill Cottrell & Webb Smith. PHOTOGRAPHY: Walt Disney, Lee Blair & Larry Lansburgh. MUSIC: Ed Plumb & Paul Smith. MUSIC DIRECTOR: Charles Wolcott. SONGS: Charles Wolcott, Ned Washington, Ary Barroso, S.K. Russell, Zequinta Abreu, Aloysio Oliveira & Ervin Drake. ART SUPERVISORS: Herb Ryman, Jim Bodrero, Lee Blair, Mary Blair & Jack Miller. ANIMATORS: Fred Moore, Ward Kimball, Milt Kahl, Milt Neil, Wolfgang Reitherman, Les Clark, Bill Justice, Vladimir Tytla, John Sibley, Hugh Fraser, Paul Allen, John McManus, John Engman, Dan MacManus & Joshua Meador. BACKGROUNDS: Hugh Hennesy, Albert Dempster, Claude Coats, Ken Anderson, Yale Gracey, Al Zinnen, McLaren Stewart, Art Riley, Dick Anthony & Merle Cox. FOREIGN SUPERVISOR: Jack Cutting. TECHNICAL ADVISORS: Carmen Miranda & Gilberto Souto.

CAST: Fred Shields, Aloysio Oliveira (Narrators), Jose Oliveira (Voice of Joe Carioca), Clarence Nash (Voice of Donald Duck), Pinto Colvig (Voice of Goofy), Walt Disney, Lillian Disney, F. Molina Campos (Themselves), Frank Thomas (Artist).

With the loss of much of its European revenue due to World War II, Hollywood was more than glad to join forces with the United States government in promoting goodwill with Latin American countries which were seen as good areas to help recoup part of their financial losses. In that vein, Walt Disney and several members of his staff made a goodwill tour of South America in 1942 under the auspices of the State Department. Along the way they did sketches and paintings and 16mm color movies of their stops in Brazil, Argentina, Peru, Chile and Bolivia. At first planning to produce one-reel cartoons from the trip, Disney instead made a four-reel feature film originally titled *Greetings* and *Greetings Friends*. Like the earlier *The Reluctant Dragon* (q.v.), the feature, which was released in *Saludos Amigos* in the U.S., was a combination of live action and animation. Here the fantasy elements are evident in the film's four cartoons, one each with Disney regulars Donald Duck and Goofy, plus two new characters, mail plane Pedro and parrot Joe Carioca. As a result of the film's popularity, Joe soon joined Donald Duck and Goofy as one of Disney's recurring animated characters. Apparently in a further effort to promote inter-hemisphere relations, *Saludos Amigos* was premiered in Rio de Janeiro in August 1942 as *Alo Amigos* in the Portuguese language. Six weeks later it was shown in Buenos Aires in Spanish. RKO did not release it in the U.S. until February 1943.

Saludos Amigos produced three popular songs: the title tune which was nominated for a Best Song Academy Award, "Brazil" and "Tico Tico." "Brazil" was successfully recorded by Xavier Cugat and His Orchestra on Columbia Records (36651), Jimmy Dorsey and His Orchestra with vocals by Bob Eberly and Helen O'Connell on Decca Records (18460) and Eddy Duchin and His Orchestra, vocal by Tony Leonard, on Columbia Records (36400). It was revived by the Ritchie Family for a top ten hit in 1975 on the 2OC label (2201). Popular with orchestras, "Tico Tico" was prominently featured by Xavier Cugat. In 1959 Disneyland Records released the soundtrack to *Saludos Amigos* (WDL-3039) as an LP and reissued it the next year (WDL-1039).

Walt Disney and his wife Lillian (themselves) lead a group of studio employees on a tour of South America, collecting material for future film projects. In Argentina they meet artist F. Molina Campos (himself) and see the Pampas Gauchos in action. As a result, four cartoons are made. First Donald Duck (voice of Clarence Nash), a tourist in "Lake Titicaca," has a good time seeing the sights until he tangles with an ill-tempered llama who ends up throwing him off a bridge. At first he lands in a pottery market and then in the lake. "Pedro" is a novice mail plane who is assigned to fly over the Andes Mountains, after his father comes down with a cold; he must not collide with Aconcaqua, the highest peak in the Western Hemisphere. He foolishly wastes time playing and then runs into bad weather and runs out of fuel before finally arriving at his destination with only a postcard. In "El Gaucho Goofy," cowboy Goofy (voice of Pinto Colvig) is transposed to Argentina and pretends to be a gaucho, showing off with his supposed skills and dancing. The sights and sounds of Rio de Janeiro are featured in "Aquarela do Brasil" with Donald Duck developing from a tropical flower and meeting Joe Carioca (voice of Jose Oliveira), a parrot who teaches him to samba. The entire city ends up doing the dance.

Boxoffice thought *Saludos Amigos* contained "three typical Disney shorts, of top notch caliber, and reflecting the best of his mastery and artistry.... [T]he whole business is done in a gorgeous riot of Technicolor." The reviewer felt the brief feature was "top entertainment but, unfortunately, too short to carry a single-bill program or, even, topside of the dualers." *Hollywood* called the movie "a gay and brilliant salute to our Latin American neighbors. *Saludos Amigos* ranks tops in entertainment." Reviewing the movie as *Saludos*, *Variety* noted, "[I]t is a quick-moving, constantly varied, excellently produced job that, ending in a sock finale, made most of the customers protest principally that it ran only 45 minutes."

Leonard Maltin opined in *The Disney Films, 3rd Edition* (1995), "*Saludos Amigos* is a very disjointed film, but each of the four sequences is so enjoyable that it seems pointless to carp about construction, especially noting the way the film was put together 'on order.' Oddly enough, it is the cartoons that seem like interruptions to the live-action footage, instead of the other way around."

Animation intended originally for *Saludos Amigos* later appeared in two other Disney features, *The Three Caballeros* and *Melody Time* (qq.v.). The feature was reissued theatrically in 1949. In 1955 RKO released the four *Saludos Amigos* cartoons as individual short subjects.

Scattergood Survives a Murder (1942; 66 minutes)

PRODUCER: Jerrold T. Brandt. ASSOCIATE PRODUCER: Frank Melford. DIRECTOR: Christy Cabanne. SCREENPLAY: Michael L. Simmons, from the characters by Clarence Budington Kelland. PHOTOGRAPHY: Jack MacKenzie. EDITOR: Richard Cahoon. MUSIC: Paul Sawtell. SOUND: Richard Van Hessen. ART DIRECTOR: Bernard Herzbrun. ASSISTANT DIRECTOR: Ridgeway Callow.

CAST: Guy Kibbee (Scattergood Baines), John Archer (Dunker Gilson), Margaret Hayes (Gail Barclay), Wallace Ford (Wally Collins), Spencer Charters (Sheriff Joe Budington Tompkins), Eily Malyon (Mrs. Grimes), John Miljan (Rolfe Quentin), George Chandler (Sam Caldwell), Dick Elliott (Mathew Quentin), Florence Lake (Phoebe Quentin), Sarah Edwards (Selma Quentin), Willie Best (Hipp Jackson), George Guhl (Deputy Sheriff Newt), Eddy Waller (Lafe Allen), Margaret Seddon (Cynthia Quentin), Margaret McWade (Lydia Quentin), Frank Reicher (Thaddeus Quentin), Earle Hodgins (Coroner), Alfred Hall (Surrogate John Kingsley).

Clarence Budington Kelland's short stories about small town New England solon Scattergood Baines ran from 1920 to 1940 in *American Magazine*. In 1937 CBS brought the character to radio in the "Scattergood Baines" series starring Wendell Holmes. It ran until 1942 with Jess Pugh taking over the lead in the early 1940s. Mutual revived the series in 1949 starring Parker Fennelly. In 1941 RKO contracted with Pyramid Pictures for a series of six "Scattergood Baines" feature films starring Guy Kibbee. Preceded by *Scattergood Baines*, *Scattergood Pulls the Strings*, *Scattergood Meets Broadway* and *Scattergood Rides High* (all 1941), *Scattergood Survives a Murder* was the fifth in the series. The sixth and final feature was *Scattergood Swings It*; the box office returns had become so disappointing the title was changed to *Cinderella Swings It* (1943). All of them were directed by Christy Cabanne.

Released in October 1942, *Scattergood Survives a Murder* is a pretty effective mystery-comedy with a number of horror overtones, including a cat's claw murder weapon, a spooky old house with hidden panels, greedy heirs and a possibly murderous feline. It is all held together by the homespun philosophy of Scattergood Baines, nicely underplayed by Kibbee. He is supported by a fine cast with hero John Archer getting about as much screen time as Scattergood. John Miljan, Florence Lake, Frank Reicher, Dick Elliott and Sarah Edwards contribute their usual good work as the heirs and Eily Malyon is properly mysterious as the housekeeper dressed in black. Margaret Hayes is the newspaper reporter heroine and Wallace Ford and George Chandler contribute fast-talking characterizations as fellow newshounds. Comedy relief is nicely provided by George Guhl as a bumbling deputy sheriff, Willie Best as Scattergood's none-too-brave employee Hipp and Eddy Waller as a grumbling newspaper jack-of-all-trades. Spencer Charters nearly steals the show as the befuddled sheriff. Given decent production values (the Quentin manor was a redressing of the mansion set from the same year's *The Magnificent Ambersons*), the feature moves at a steady pace and never loses interest. The unmasking of the killer by Scattergood is nicely staged and the identity of the villain is kept well-hidden. Trans-America Films later re-issued *Scattergood Survives a Murder* as *Cat's Claw Murder Mystery*.

While dozing on the front porch of his store in Coldriver, a New England town, Scattergood Baines (Kibbee) is awakened by a car's backfire and his employee, Hipp Jackson (Best), is frightened by the noise. The car belongs to Dunker Gilson (Archer) who informs Scattergood that he has just purchased the *Coldriver Weekly Citizen* and asks for directions to get there. Dunker finds the office a mess and typesetter-pressman Lafe Allen (Waller) unimpressed by his new boss. Scattergood tells Dunker about the Quentin sisters, Cynthia (Margaret Seddon) and Lydia (Margaret McWade), millionaires who have not left their mansion in two decades. He suggests Dunker interview them. When he tries to do so, the old ladies' housekeeper, Mrs. Grimes (Malyon), informs him that they never see anyone. He tries to talk to Cynthia and Lydia through an open window but they close it, refusing to converse because it is Thursday. When the sisters go to see their pet cat Matilda, Mrs. Grimes informs them that the feline is sick and that she has arranged to take it to a veterinarian and insists they go along with her. Although they do not want to break their tradition of never leaving the house, the sisters agree to go but as they sit in their buggy when Mrs. Grimes locks the house, someone scares the horses by throwing pebbles at them. The two women are thrown from the runaway vehicle and killed. Boston News Service reporter Gale Barclay (Hayes) arrives to cover the reading of the sisters' will, along with two journalists Wally Collins (Ford) and Sam Caldwell (Chandler). Deputy Sheriff Newt (Guhl) is under orders not to let anyone but relatives into the house but Scattergood convinces him to let Dunker cover the story which he will share with the other reporters. Sheriff Tompkins (Charters) arrives with the Surrogate (Alfred Hall), who will read the will to the heirs: Thaddeus Quentin (Reicher), schoolteacher Phoebe Quentin (Lake), Rolfe Quentin (John Miljan), Selma Quentin (Edwards) and druggist Matthew Quentin (Elliott). Not present, and thought lost at sea, is Lloyd Quentin. Written in rhyme, the will leaves the sisters' estate to Matilda, with Mrs. Grimes getting $50 a day for the cat's care. A second will provides that if the cat dies, the estate will go, in order, to Thaddeus, Phoebe, Lloyd, Rolfe, Selma and Matthew. During the night a terrible noise is heard and Thaddeus is found dead with claw marks. Mrs. Grimes hides Matilda in a secret panel in her bedroom. The sheriff arrives with the coroner (Earle Hodgins), who says the death was caused by poisoning. Suspicion falls on Mrs. Grimes, who says Matilda has disappeared, until it is revealed that Phoebe will inherit the estate if the cat dies. Back in town, Scattergood sends Gail to Dunker's office trying to promote a romance but they are interrupted by Wally. The sheriff shows up and says he is going to arrest Mrs. Grimes, so Gail and Dunker go with him to the Quentin house only to be informed by Newt that the housekeeper has been clawed and murdered. Later Scattergood sends Hipp with Dunker to search the Quentin mansion. Meeting at midnight, the two men check the cellar where Dunker finds a family album and takes one of its photographs. He also uncovers a lynx skin with a missing paw. Gail shows up and locates something which she hides. While searching Mrs. Grimes' room, Dunker and Hipp find the dead cat behind a hidden panel and take it to Scattergood, who suggests they try to convince the murderer that the cat is alive. Dunker and Hipp paint another cat to look like Matilda. Gail comes to Dunker's office and shows him what she found, a cat's paw, hoping it will help him solve the case. The next day Dunker makes sure everyone in the mansion thinks the cat is still alive and that evening Scattergood gathers together the heirs and the journalists. Dunker shows them the picture he found which is of Lloyd and his small son. Scattergood brings out the cat's paw and tries to demonstrate on Wally how it was the murder weapon. The reporter refuses to be touched by the paw, saying it is poisoned. Scattergood then accuses Wally of being Lloyd's son and the murderer, who planned to claim the estate for himself. When Wally pulls a gun and tries to escape, Scattergood slows him up by blowing snuff in his face. The sheriff shoots and wounds Wally. The solving of the murders brings success to Dunker's newspaper; Gail, who has gotten her wish to write a column, agrees to marry him. When the sheriff tries to get Dunker to give him publicity, Scattergood suggests they leave the young people alone.

Variety dubbed *Scattergood Survives a Murder* "okay supporting fodder for the duals," adding "Kibbee dominates major portions of the footage, and juvenile leads, John Archer and Margaret Hayes, fill the bill nicely in the light romantic assignment."

Boxoffice complained, "The dialogue is puerile, the acting insincere and the direction wooden. If any honors were to be ladled out they should go to the black cat. It is not a picture for family trade because of the murders and screeching. Detective fans most likely will scoff at the potpourri." *Photoplay* summed it up: "It's Scatter-bad for our money." The same reviewer mistakenly claimed the John Archer character is accused of murdering the sisters and that RKO "better get back to their original theme in a hurry or they'll hear from us, by golly." *The Film Daily* thought it "run-of-the-mill stuff, although a few of the details have comparative freshness.... Christy Cabanne's direction does a great deal to enliven the proceedings."

The Secret Life of Walter Mitty (1947; 100 minutes; Color)

PRODUCER: Samuel Goldwyn. DIRECTOR: Norman Z. McLeod. SCREENPLAY: Ken England & Everett Freeman, from the story by James Thurber. PHOTOGRAPHY: Lee Garmes. EDITOR: Monica Collingwood. MUSIC: David Raksin. MUSIC DIRECTOR: Emil Newman. ART DIRECTORS: Perry Ferguson & George Jenkins. SOUND: Fred Lau. SET DECORATIONS: Casey Roberts. COSTUMES: Sharaff. MAKEUP: Robert Stephanoff. HAIR STYLIST: Marie Clark. SPECIAL PHOTOGRAPHIC EFFECTS: John P. Fulton.

CAST: Danny Kaye (Walter Mitty), Virginia Mayo (Rosalind van Hoorn), Boris Karloff (Dr. Hugo Hollinghead), Fay Bainter (Mrs. Eunice Mitty), Ann Rutherford (Gertrude Griswald), Thurston Hall (Bruce Pierce), Gordon Jones (Tubby Wadsworth), Florence Bates (Mrs. Emma Griswald), Konstantin Shayne (Peter van Hoorn), Reginald Denny (Colonel), Henry Corden (Hendrick), Doris Lloyd (Mrs. Letitia Follinsbee), Fritz Feld (Anatole of Paris), Frank Reicher (Karl Maasdam), Milton Parsons (Butler), The Goldwyn Girls [Mary Brewer, Sue Casey, Martha Montgomery, Lynn Walker, Patricia Patrick, Irene Vernon, Betty Cargyle, Karen X. Gaylord, Lorraine DeRome, Michael Mauree, Mary Ellen Gleason, Jackie Jordan, Georgia Lange] (Themselves), George Magrill (Wolf Man), Mary Forbes (Mrs. Pierce), Henry Kolker (Dr. Benbow), Lumsden Hare (Dr. Pritchard-Milford), John Hamilton (Dr. Remington), Charles Trowbridge (Dr. Renshaw), Joel Friedkin (Mr. Grimsby), Christine McIntyre (Miss Blair), Harry Harvey, Jr. (Office Boy), Mary Anne Baird (Model with Wolf Man), Jack Gargan (Photographer), Donna Dax (Stenographer), Warren Jackson (Business Manager), John Tyrrell, Raoul Freeman (Department Heads), Bess Flowers (Illustrator), Sam Ash (Art Editor), Phil Dunham (Composing Room Foreman), Harry Depp, Broderick O'Ferrell, Harold Miller, Wilbur Mack, Dick Earle, Edward Bilby, Frank McClure (Directors), Patsy O'Bryne (Charwoman), Ralph Dunn, Brick Sullivan, Frank Meredith (Policemen), Jack Cheatham (Baggage Man), Moy Wing (Elderly Chinese), Beal Wong (Chinese Restaurant Headwaiter), Weaver Levy (Chinese

Restaurant Waiter), Barbara Combs (Nurse), Pierre Watkin, Neal Dodd (Ministers), Netta Packer (Organist), Ernie Adams (Flower Truck Driver), Audrey Betz (Dowager), Frances Morris (Head Saleswoman), Helen Jerome Eddy (Lingerie Saleswoman), Syd Saylor (Henchman), Frank Ellis, Hank Worden, Billy Bletcher (Westerners), Dick Rush (Customs Official), George Lloyd, Eddie Acuff (Wells Fargo Cowboys), Lane Chandler (Billboard Cowboy), Vernon Dent (Bartender), Wade Crosby (Blacksmith), Dorothy Granger (Wrong Mrs. Follinsbee), Harry Woods (Wrong Mr. Follinsbee), Cy Schindell, Frank Marlowe (Taxi Drivers), Jack Overman (Taxi Driver Vincent), Ruth Lee (Commentator), Dorothy Christy, Margaret Wells (Store Officials), Kernan Cripps (Porter), Charles Wilson (Police Desk Sergeant), Frank LaRue, William Haade (Conductors), Minerva Urecal (Woman with Hat), Nolan Leary, Ted Billings, Tommy Hughes (Hucksters), Tom McGuire (Dublin Policeman), Mary Gordon (Mother Machree), Otto Reichow (German Pilot), William Newell (Taxi Cab Traffic Manager), Paul Newlan (Truck Driver), Anthony Marsh, Leslie Denison, Peter Gowland, Harold Temple Hensen, John Meredith, Leslie Vincent, Robert Altman (R.A.F. Pilots), Chris-Pin Martin (Waiter), Sam McDaniel (Doorman), Betty Blythe (Floor Manager), Maude Eburne (Fitter), Al Eben (Elevator Starter), Ethan Laidlaw (Helmsman), Don Garner (Young Seaman), Eddy Waller (Old Mariner), George Chandler (Second Mate), Sam Harris (Man on Sidewalk), Vincent Pelletier (Dream Sequence Narrator).

Based on James Thurber's short story and filmed as *I Wake Up Dreaming*, *The Secret Life of Walter Mitty* was made by producer Samuel Goldwyn on a $3 million budget and issued by RKO Radio in the fall of 1947, more than two and one-half years after work commenced on its script. Made to fit the talents of Danny Kaye, this fantasy-comedy is a must for fans of the actor but only so-so entertainment for other viewers. For horror fans, Boris Karloff appears as one of the villains although his screen time is limited. The fantasy aspects are the main drawing card for the film, which includes a large cast populated by well-delineated cameo roles. Virginia Mayo is a knockout as the mysterious Rosalind. Danny Kaye's wife, Sylvia Fine, composed the film's two musical numbers, "Anatole of Paris" and "Symphony of Unstrung Heroes," both already established Kaye routines. The feature proved to be one of the more popular Kaye screen vehicles and *Harrison's Reports* stated that it did "Good" box office business.

Meek, timid pulp fiction publishing house proofreader Walter Mitty (Kaye) spends his time daydreaming that he is a daring swashbuckler. His dishonest and overbearing boss, Bruce Pierce (Thurston Hall), takes advantage of Walter by stealing his work and then scolding him for daydreaming. After work Walter goes home to the home he shares with is mother Eunice (Fay Bainter) and has dinner with his fiancée, grasping and none-too-bright Gertrude Griswald (Ann Rutherford) and her overbearing mother Emma (Florence Bates). Tuning out the harping of the women, Walter dreams about being a heroic R.A.F. pilot who fights the Nazis and wins a beautiful French barmaid (Mayo). The next day he sees the same woman on a train ride to work and she pretends to be his girlfriend to get away from a strange man, Hendrick (Henry Corden). She introduces herself as Rosalind Van Hoorn and asks Walter to go with her to the waterfront to meet a friend. Walter takes a cab with Rosalind but soon jumps out to get to work, leaving behind his briefcase. Realizing what he has done, Walter goes back to the docks for the briefcase while Karl Maasdam (Frank Reicher), Rosalind's friend, puts a notebook in the briefcase before giving it back to Walter. The three agree to share a taxi. Karl dies and Walter and Rosalind go to the police. Rosalind disappears while Walter is talking to the law. That night Rosalind shows up at Walter's office and takes him to meet her uncle, Peter Van Hoorn (Konstantin Shayne), onetime curator of the Royal Netherlands Museum. Peter informs Walter that when the Nazis invaded his country he hid all the national treasure and made an inventory in a notebook which a criminal known as The Boot is trying to obtain. A frightened Walter departs but soon finds the notebook in his briefcase and sees Hendrick trailing him. Hiding the notebook in a corset in a department store's model salon, Walter does not realize the item is going to be sent to wealthy Mrs. Follinsbee (Doris Lloyd). The next day at work, Walter is threatened by Dr. Hugo Hollingshead (Karloff),

Virginia Mayo, Gordon Jones and Danny Kaye in *The Secret Life of Walter Mitty* **(1947).**

an accomplice of The Boot, and the scared Walter crawls onto a window ledge outside Pierce's office, causing his boss to again berate him. That night Walter goes home only to be humiliated by Tubby Wadsworth (Gordon Jones), a rival for Gertrude's affections. Walter fantasizes that he is a riverboat gambler who wins Rosalind away from Tubby. Rosalind returns the next day and convinces Walter to help her find the notebook, which they eventually locate in the corset at a fashion show. When Walter forgets to give the notebook to Peter, Rosalind comes to his house where Gertrude and her mother are staying the night. He manages to keep them from seeing Rosalind and Walter goes with her to Peter's apartment. There Rosalind finds that Peter has Karl's passport and puts the notebook in his desk without telling him. When Rosalind notices Peter's big shoes, she realizes he is The Boot, so he kidnaps her and gives Walter a sleeping draught. Upon awaking, Walter finds Peter informing his mother and Pierce that he is not mentally sound and that Rosalind is a figment of his imagination. Peter suggests they take Walter to see a psychiatrist, who turns out to be Dr. Hollingshead. The psychiatrist is able to convince Walter that everything that happened was a dream. When Walter is about to wed Gertrude the next day, he finds a charm that Rosalind gave him and rescues her from Peter. Just as the crooks are about to capture the fleeing couple, Mrs. Mitty, Gertrude, Pierce and Tubby show up with the police and all of them castigate Walter. Unable to stand it any longer, the worm turns and Walter tells them off, winning the respect of his boss and the love of Rosalind.

Independent Exhibitors Film Bulletin reported, "Here's a sure-fire attraction crammed with a vast variety of entertaining features.... Production quality is up to Goldwyn's high level." According to *The New York Times*, "*The Secret Life of Walter Mitty* is a big, colorful show and a good one. Perhaps it is just a little too big, for it is difficult to sustain a comedy for close to two hours without a letdown every so often. Much of the flavor of Thurber's character is lost because of the lack of contrast between Walter Mitty's dream world and actual experiences." *The New York Daily Mirror* declared it a "delightful funnybone tickler which will make you weak with laughter" while *The New York Herald-Tribune* complained, "The film should and could have been far better.... [This] fragile fantasy has been blown out of all proportions in its screen translation." *The New York World-Telegram* opined, "Not up to the extraordinary level of Danny's earlier ones, but with all its shortcomings it still manages to raise more hilarity in an audience than any but the best comedies we have had this season." More enthusiastic was *The New York Daily News:* "Danny Kaye's best comedy.... In spite of the fact that it runs over long, Danny manage to keep its audience laughing with and at him almost all the way through." *The New York Journal American* declared it a "sheer delight for customers" and *The New York Sun* concurred: "Rip-roaring funny film.... Laughs come fast and loud." *Time* thought it "Danny Kaye's funniest movie" while *Newsweek* lamented, "It is a depressing thought, but the followers of Danny Kaye will probably be entranced by *The Secret Life of Walter Mitty* in spite of the fact that the picture is a complete bastardization of the original, and great, short story by James Thurber." *The Chicago Daily Tribune* felt it was "very, very funny from beginning to end!" while *PM* declared it "packed with laughs."

Secrets of the French Police (1932; 57 minutes)

EXECUTIVE PRODUCER: David O. Selznick. ASSOCIATE PRODUCER: Willis Goldbeck. DIRECTOR: Edward Sutherland. SCREENPLAY: Samuel Ornitz & Robert Tasker. STORY: H. Ashton Wolfe. PHOTOGRAPHY: Alfred Gilks. EDITOR: Arthur Roberts. MUSIC DIRECTOR: Max Steiner. ART DIRECTOR: Carroll Clark. SOUND: George D. Ellis. SPECIAL EFFECTS: Vernon L. Walker. MAKEUP: Sam Kaufman.

CAST: Gwili Andre (Eugenie Dorain), Gregory Ratoff (General Hans Moloff), Frank Morgan (Inspector Francois St. Cyr), John Warburton (Leon Renault), Rochelle Hudson (Agent K-31), Christian Rub (Anton Dorian), Murray Kinnell (Surete Chief Bertillon), Arnold Korff (Grand Duke Maxim), Kendell Lee (Rena Harka), Lucien Prival (Baron Lomzoi), Guido Trento (Count de Marsay), Julia Swayne Gordon (Madame Danton), Kate Drain Lawson (Cecile Roudin/Madame La France), Evelyn Carter Carrington (Madame La Prop), Reginald Barlow (Perfect), Elinor Vanderveer (Moloff's Assistant), Cyril Ring (Police Official), Chester Gan (Servant), Harry Cording (Lounging Job Seeker), Michael Visaroff (Pickpocket), Sam Appel, Arthur Thalasso, Malcolm White (Detectives), Dina Smirnova (Russian), Virginia Thomas (Model).

At the funeral of his friend, French secret police agent Danton, Inspector St. Cyr (Frank Morgan) of the Paris Surete promises the man's widow (Julia Swayne Gordon) that his murderer will be sent to the guillotine. Beautiful Eugenie Dorain (Gwili Andre) meets her lover, pickpocket Leon Renault (John Warburton), at a café where she is spotted by Baron Lomzoi (Lucien Prival), a cohort of General Hans Moloff (Gregory Ratoff). When Eugenie's father, Anton Dorain (Christian Rub), objects to her seeing Leon, the two part company. Lomzoi, dressed as a chauffeur, helps Moloff's associate, Rena Harka (Kendell Lee), abduct the girl. That night Moloff questions Anton and learns that Eugenie, a Russian orphan, was given to him as a child by Danton. Moloff murders Anton. After investigating the crime, St. Cyr arrests Leon, although he suspects the man is innocent. St. Cyr offers the pickpocket his freedom in return for combing the city's underworld in search of the real killer. At his remote and heavily guarded chateau, Moloff uses hypnotism to convince Eugenie she is Princess Anastasia, the only surviving child of Russian Czar Nicholas II. He plans to present her to Nicholas' brother, Grand Duke Maxim (Arnold Korff), in return for a hefty reward. Maxim flies to Paris to identify his niece and is accompanied by Count de Marsay (Guido Trento). The war office, acting on Agent K-31's (Rochelle Hudson) information, reports to St. Cyr that Moloff is the son of a Chinese Mandarin princess and a Russian nobleman with a trace of insanity on his father's side. Rena becomes jealous of Eugenie and demands that Moloff let her impersonate the princess. While Maxim talks with Eugenie, Leon makes his way into the chateau's catacombs and finds a basement laboratory filled with stuffed and preserved animals, as well as the body of a naked woman. As Maxim rejects Eugenie being his niece and leaves with the count, Leon is nearly captured before making a hasty retreat from the chateau. On their way back to Paris, Maxim and his friend are killed when their car runs off the road, the accident caused by Moloff and his henchmen using a giant screen and projection equipment to make it look like a vehicle was about to hit them head-on. Investigating the crash with his chief (Murray Kinnell), St. Cyr finds a letter signed by Maxim acknowledging Eugenie as Anastasia. St. Cyr takes the missive, which Moloff planted on Maxim before he left the chateau, to the Russian and while there notices the life-sized statue of a naked woman. When Moloff leaves the room, St. Cyr scrapes porcelain from the statue and finds it covers a dead body, that of Rena, who Moloff murdered to keep quiet. After St. Cyr departs, Moloff makes plans to escape by motorboat through a secret passage while Leon arrives and tries to rescue Eugenie. They are captured by the madman and his minions as St. Cyr and his men use an underground waterway to get into the chateau. Moloff plans to turn Eugenie into a beautiful statue and torture Leon to death. St. Cyr has his men use a torch to break through a bolted door just as Moloff begins to drain off Eugenie's blood. The police swarm into the underground laboratory with St. Cyr saving Eugenie and Leon. In trying to escape, Moloff falls into his own equipment and is electrocuted. Later St. Cyr gives Leon and Eugenie one hour to catch a boat out of France. After they leave, he realizes his watch has been stolen.

Mystery writer Rufus King was originally signed by RKO to do the screenplay for *Secrets of the French Police*. It was to be based on a story by H. Ashton Wolfe, who turned out to be wanted by the police in England and France for swindles. The film is a cogent, fast-paced police story tinged with sci-fi and sadism. Gwili Andre is very beautiful as Eugenie but has little to do other than look decorative; she appears to be the studio's answer to Greta Garbo and Marlene Dietrich. Frank Morgan handles the police hero role in fine style and has an amusing scene in which he pretends to be drunk while actually gathering evidence. John Warburton's English accent offsets his supposed character of a French pickpocket, who only robs non-countrymen. The movie is stylishly made; its chief detriment is Gregory Ratoff, who mugs the part of the madman. Often quite verbose on screen, Ratoff is wooden in the Moloff part, one far better suited for Bela Lugosi or Lionel Atwill. The subplot of a beautiful woman's corpse being used for a statue (also an excuse for exhibiting a naked stone woman on screen) was also in Atwill's *Mystery of the Wax Museum* (Warner Bros., 1933). The chateau set was from another RKO release, *The Most Dangerous Game* (q.v.). Publicity for the feature claimed that "thousands of dollars of advanced scientific equipment was used in the laboratory scenes."

Issued late in 1932, this Radio Pictures release was made as *Mysteries of the French Police*. Mordaunt Hall in *The New York Times* wrote that so long as the film "confines itself to the scientific methods of tracing criminals, it is extremely interesting, but, unfortunately, a fantastic melodrama is involved in the proceedings and this is disappointing, even though, like so many poor film stories, it is well acted.... If the producers had use a more plausible story to detail the methods of the Paris police, this feature might have been quite engrossing." *Harrison's Reports* said, "The picture turned out poor." The Jefferson City, Missouri, *Daily Capitol News and Post-Tribune* declared, "This is an amazing, albeit, thrilling, series of murders, abductions, thievings, plotting and counter-plotting, ably acted out, well written, nicely photographed and beautifully directed." *The Beatrice* (Nebraska) *Daily Sun* opined, "*Secrets of the French Police* is believable, fast, full of suspense and is excellently directed by Edward Sutherland."

Photoplay announced, "This picture is thrilling, if not convincing.... [T]he trail taken by the French police is interesting to watch, though sometimes unbelievable." *Motion Picture* thought it "a detective thriller that is not only suspenseful, but unusual."

"A mixture between a horror picture and a mystery, this film, with the former controlled to the point where it is unobtrusive, will hold interest for numerous people. Bizarre and intriguing, it is vastly different from anything recent.... The acting is uniformly good throughout, despite absence of any well-known 'names' in the cast," reported *New England Film News*. Arthur Forde pronounced in *Hollywood Filmograph*, "[T]he great cast of players were hampered with a poor story and mediocre direction. We hardly think that *Secrets of the French Police* will rebound to the credit of Radio Pictures who produced it."

Director Edward Sutherland is mainly remembered for his comedy efforts like *International House* (1932), *Poppy* (1936), *Every Day's a Holiday* (1937) and *Abie's Irish Rose* (1946), but he also helmed other RKO genre features *The Flying Deuces*, *Beyond Tomorrow* and *Having Wonderful Crime* (qq.v.), as well as Paramount's *Murders in the Zoo* (1932) and Universal's *The Invisible Woman* (1940).

Seven Keys to Baldpate (1929; 72 minutes)

PRODUCER: William LeBaron. ASSOCIATE PRODUCER: Louis Sarecky. DIRECTOR: Reginald Barker. SCREENPLAY: Jane Murfin, from the novel by Earl Derr Biggers and the play by George M. Cohan. PHOTOGRAPHY: Edward Cronjager. EDITOR: Jack Kitchin. ART DIRECTOR: Max Ree. SOUND: Lambert E. Day. DIALOGUE DIRECTOR: Reginald Mack.

CAST: Richard Dix (William Halliwell Magee), Miriam Seegar (Mary Norton), Crauford Kent (Hal Bentley), Margaret Livingston (Myra Thornhill/Miss Brown), Joseph Allen (Peters), Lucien Littlefield (Thomas Hayden), DeWitt Jennings (Jim Cargan), Carleton Macy (Police Chief Kennedy), Nella Walker (Irene Rhodes), Joseph Herbert (Max), Alan Roscoe (Bland), Harvey Clark (Elijah Quimby), Edith Yorke (Mrs. Quimby).

Earl Derr Biggers' exciting mystery novel *The Seven Keys to Baldpate* was published in 1913 and the same year George M. Cohan adapted it to the stage. Wallace Eddinger starred in the Broadway production, with a run of 320 performances, and it proved so popular that a second company presented the play in Chicago. Cohan headlined the initial U.S. screen version of the work for Artcraft Pictures in 1917 with Anna Q. Nilsson. (It had already been filmed in 1916 in Australia by J.C. Williamson.) In 1925 Douglas McLean and Edith Roberts did a Paramount version directed by Fred Newmeyer. Radio Pictures released the first sound version of the story late in 1929 with Richard Dix essaying the role of the writer who accepts a bet that he can compose a mystery novel in a 24-hour period while staying at the remote, and supposedly deserted, Baldpate Inn. Having purchased the rights to the work, RKO remade it in 1935 and 1947 (qq.v.). All three RKO productions capture the comedy mystery flavor of the story although each have plot changes. The 1929 version is fast-paced and showed how quickly motion pictures adapted to the medium of sound.

Mystery writer William Hallowell Magee (Dix) is offered $5,000 by his friend Hal Bentley (Crauford Kent) to write a 10,000-word story in a 24-hour period while holed up at Bentley's summer resort, the Baldpate Inn, located six hours from New York City and closed for the winter. Magee accepts the wager but tries to back out after meeting Bentley's friend, Mary Norton (Miriam Seegar), a newspaper syndicate writer staying a week with Mrs. Irene Rhodes (Nella Walker), who is about to marry politician Jim Cargan (DeWitt Jennings). Bentley makes Magee keep his word and the writer takes the train to the inn, which is located on top of a high hill, during a snowstorm. Arriving at Baldpate, Magee is met by the caretaker, Elijah Quimby (Harvey

Radio Pictures Presents
RICHARD
DIX
in "SEVEN KEYS
TO BALDPATE"

Advertisement for *Seven Keys to Baldpate* (1929).

Clark), and his wife (Edith Yorke), who claims ghosts have been seen in the area. Elijah says it is just hermit Peters (Joseph Allen), who is trying to scare the locals. He tells Magee that he has the only key to the inn. After getting settled, Magee hears someone enter and overhears Bland (Alan Roscoe) making a call to Cargan saying he will hide money in the inn's safe for him. When Magee confronts Bland, the intruder pulls a gun on him but the writer manages to lock him in his room. When Magee starts to call the police, a third person enters the inn: Mary, who is followed by a frightened Irene, who has just seen Bland leave the building via the window in Magee's room. Magee retains Bland's gun as Mary tells him a man sent her to the inn with a key to get a story on the writer's wager with Bentley. The two women think they see a ghost but it turns out to be misogynist Peter, who departs when gunshots are heard. Another woman, Myra (Margaret Livingston), arrives and goes to the safe but is surprised by Magee when he turns on the lights. She tells him she is after the money in the safe since it belongs to her husband, railroad president Thomas Hayden (Lucien Littlefield), who is about to be cheated out of it by Cargan and his henchmen. Mary tells Magee the woman is an imposter and they need to get the money to save Irene from Cargan. As Magee, Mary and Irene watch, Cargan and his pal Max (Joseph Herbert) arrive to get the money and Cargan accuses Max of being in cahoots with Myra. Magee takes the money at gunpoint and tells Mary and Irene to return to New York City. The next to arrive is Hayden. When Magee tells him that his wife is there, he says she is at home. Magee brings Cargan and

Myra to see Hayden as Peter returns, followed by Bland, who works with Hayden. Hayden says Myra is not his wife and she claims Cargan tried to double cross both Bland and Hayden. Mary calls to say the money is missing and a scuffle ensues with Magee being captured by Cargan, who orders Mary not to notify the police and to return to the inn. Max kills Myra and wings Bland. Cargan has the woman's body taken upstairs. Magee breaks out of a locked room in time to see Myra's body being carried away and Max tells him he killed her. Cargan decides to blame the murder on Magee as Peters escapes and the sheriff (Carleton Macy) arrives. Magee tells him about the shooting but the victim's body cannot be found since Peters hid it in the cellar and then returned it upstairs after the police searched the area. Mary returns and says the money has been lost but Irene soon follows, announcing it is in the hotel safe in town (she stole it to protect Cargan). The sheriff calls and orders the parcel containing the money sent to the inn. When it arrives, he contacts his wife and tells her to take their children and go to Canada. He informs the group that he plans to take the money for himself but they jump him and Peter throws the package in the fireplace. Myra walks down the stairs as Bentley arrives with the seventh key to Baldpate. He tells an upset Magee that everyone involved is part of a local stock company and the evening's events were a hoax staged to show him that his novels are unrealistic. After everyone leaves, Magee returns to his writing and just before midnight he finishes his work, winning the bet with Bentley, who returns with Mary. Magee asks Mary to be his wife.

Richard Dix has a field day playing the part of Magee, combining just the right amount of comedy and dramatics needed to make the role believable. Mordaunt Hall in *The New York Times* said Dix "gives an agile and pleasing performance," adding, "It is one of those fanciful flights that compels one to withhold criticism until the denouement. In fact, it is an adventure which virtually defies derogatory comments." *Photoplay* declared it to be "a fine phonoplay version of the old laughter-and-thrill–provoking favorite. Richard Dix again battles the microphone to a knockout finish." "[A] most entertaining mystery story with an abundance of good comedy" is how the film was described by the *Berkeley* (California) *Daily Gazette*. *The Motion Picture Times* summarized the film's appeal, saying it contained "clever acting, keen suspense and an unusual climax to make it click nicely." The *British Weekly Kinema Guide* opined, "A good mystery thriller. Very well worked out and played by Richard Dix and Miriam Seegar." *Picture Play Magazine* decreed, "[In] his first picture for RKO, Richard Dix gives generously of himself to make it a success.... Mr. Dix's simulation of bewilderment is nicely acted, but it scarcely saves the picture from being middle class." Regarding the star, *Motion Picture* stated, "His voice is really splendid and he knows how to use it.... The illusion of suspense and mystery is maintained up to the final explanation of the strange events which leaves one with the feeling of having been slightly 'sold.'" *Variety* termed it "light, mechanical film fare.... This is supposed to be a comedy with a meller flush. It's a hybrid because of the hack way in which it unfolds in spots, and thus burlesque gets the laughs." In retrospect, Leonard Maltin wrote in *Film Fan Monthly* (July–August 1973), "This is the kind of film that proves that talkies did not have to move at a snail's pace; while hardly cinematically inventive, it moves briskly through its delightfully serpentine plot. Dix was never more buoyant."

Seven Keys to Baldpate (1935; 80 minutes)

ASSOCIATE PRODUCER: William Sistrom. DIRECTORS: William Hamilton & Edward Killy. SCREENPLAY: Anthony Veiller & Wallace Smith, from the novel by Earl Derr Biggers and the play by George M. Cohan. PHOTOGRAPHY: Robert De Grasse. EDITOR: Desmond Marquette. MUSIC: Alberto Colombo. ART DIRECTORS: Van Nest Polglase & Charles Kirk. SOUND: John E. Tribby.

CAST: Gene Raymond (William Magee), Margaret Callahan (Mary Norton/ Mary Johnson), Eric Blore (Professor Harrison Boulton/Detective Harrison), Grant Mitchell (Thomas Hayden), Moroni Olsen (Jim Cargan), Erin O'Brien-Moore (Myra Thornhill/Mrs. Hayden), Henry Travers (Lem Peters), Walter Brennan (Station Agent), Ray Mayer (Bland), Erville Alderson (Chief Roberts), Murray Alper (Max), Harry Beresford (Elijah "Lige" Quimby), Emma Dunn (Mrs. Quimby), Monte Vandergrift (Deputy Sheriff Jim), Philip Morris (Second Deputy Sheriff).

In June 1935, George M. Cohan staged a successful revival of his 1913 play *Seven Keys to Baldpate* with the Players Club in New York City and as a result RKO filmed its second screen version of the old chestnut with uncredited Glenn Tryon and Dorothy Yost providing additional dialogue to Anthony Veiller and Wallace Smith's screenplay, which "brought story up to date without sacrificing any of the laughs and chilling suspense that characterize the original" (*Provo* [Utah] *Evening Herald*). Unfortunately the main plotline of the proceedings, Magee's bet he can write an entire novel in a 24-hour period, is only vaguely revealed. Although buoyed by an able supporting cast and fine production values, the second RKO version of the work is weakened by the casting of bland Gene Raymond in the role of Magee. He has none of the screen magnetism or physical prowess that Richard Dix displayed in the 1929 version, leaving a limp impression and undermining the character's heroics. In addition, the film goes at a slower pace than the Dix version but runs eight minutes longer. Reissue prints at 69 minutes make this version more streamlined.

During a snowstorm, writer William Magee (Raymond) arrives at the remote Baldpate Inn and is admitted by the caretakers (Harry Beresford, Emma Dunn). He wants to write a novel within 24 hours in order to win a bet but is interrupted by the arrival of Bland (Ray Mayer), who places money in a safe after making a telephone call. When Magee reveals himself, Bland pulls a gun but the writer manages to lock the gangster in his room. Mary Norton (Margaret Callahan), a woman whom Magee had spotted earlier crying at the town's train depot, shows up saying she is an actress in hiding for a publicity stunt. A meek man Magee dubs Professor Boulton (Eric Blore) arrives, quickly followed by woman-hater Peters the Hermit (Henry Travers), who wears a sheet and tries to scare off strangers by pretending to be a ghost. They are followed by a beautiful woman calling herself Mrs. Hayden (Erin O'Brien-Moore), who claims she is trying to retrieve $200,000 (the proceeds from a diamond robbery) from private eye Cargan (Moroni Olsen), Bland's boss, who plans to wring it out of her husband, Thomas Hayden (Grant Mitchell). Later Boulton attempts to open the safe but is stopped by Magee, who then sees Mary try to open it. She tells him it contains the $200,000 and reveals to him the location of a secret passage at the inn. Bland, who escaped from Magee's room, returns with Cargan and Hayden and the trio open the safe as Cargan takes the money and leaves, assisted by his gunman Max (Murray Alper). Boulton knocks out Cargan and gets the money but is disabled by Magee who takes it and hides the loot in a vase. Bland knocks out Magee with the vase and places the money in an unlit wood stove. Peters starts to light a fire in the stove, finds the package with the currency, and places it under a chair cushion. Bland, who is in cahoots with Mrs. Hayden, makes a deal with Cargan and Hayden to split the money but when he goes to retrieve it from the stove he finds a fire going and thinks it has been burned. Since the crooks wanted the money from the reward for the stolen diamonds, thus cheating Hayden's insurance company, Cargan decides to take the gems for himself. Magee tries to stall the crooks while Mary gets the money. Mrs. Hayden reveals herself to be Myra Thornhill, Max's girlfriend. She accuses Max of stealing the diamonds at Cargan's behest and he shoots her. The police, led by Chief Roberts (Erville Alderson), arrive and Magee informs them of the killing. The policeman takes the money as Myra appears, saying the nearsighted Max missed her and she only pretended to be dead. Boulton announces he is an insurance investigator and the crooks are arrested and hauled away. Mary confesses she is a New York City news reporter and the smitten Magee, who failed to write his novel, proposes to her.

The 1935 release follows the basic premise of the 1929 outing but there are a number of variations, mainly among the denizens of the Baldpate Inn, which is identified as being near Asquewan Junction. Walter Brennan plays a small role as the town's train station agent. The Mary Norton (Callahan) character is first spied by Magee (Raymond) crying for no apparent reason at the train station when he arrives to write a novel at the deserted summer resort. When

Gene Raymond and Margaret Callahan in *Seven Keys to Baldpate* (1935).

the young woman shows up there, she claims to be an actress who has disappeared for publicity purposes but at the finale confesses to being *New York Blade* reporter Mary Johnson. The Jim Cargan (Olsen) character is now a private detective and owner of the Atlas Agency who is trying to get $200,000 from wealthy Thomas Hayden (Mitchell) who got that sum in insurance money because diamonds were stolen from him. Cargan's agent Bland (Mayer) is in league with Myrna (O'Brien-Moore), who claims to be Mrs. Hayden but who is the moll of Cargan's gunman Max (Alper). Peters the Hermit (Travers) is a local woman-hater who tries to scare people away from Baldpate by pretending to be a ghost. The third visitor to arrive with a key to the inn is dubbed Professor Harrison Boulton (Blore) by Magee and he claims to be a Rutgers University political economy instructor there to go over mid-term exams and get peace and quiet; in reality he is Detective Harrison of the London Indemnity Company investigating Hayden's attempt to falsely get insurance money from the diamonds. This version also pretty much keeps the viewer in the dark as Baldpate has no electric power and it also introduces a secret panel and a game of hiding the $200,000.

Thus the plot of the 1935 version switches from political graft and corruption to insurance embezzlement. While all the action at the inn in the 1929 film was staged, the events here are real, even the shooting of Myra, which is explained by Max having poor eyesight and simply missing his target. The one physical improvement the remake had over the first talkie is the inn itself is more elaborate and atmospheric with flavorful muted photography by Robert de Grasse.

Critics were divided over this version of the Biggers-Cohan work. *Boxoffice* called it a "good offering for the family audience, packed with thrills, laughs and melodrama without horror." *The Salt Lake* (Utah) *Tribune* proclaimed it "a high-speed romance carried on in a spooky atmosphere under the everpresent threat of desperate gangsters and blazing guns, and leavened with comedy situations." *The Film Daily* said, "This mystery comedy makes good entertaining program fare. Everyone connected with the production has caught the spirit of the piece, and the result is enjoyable material." *Movie Action* enthused, "A rollicking mystery farce, with mystery panels, mysterious hands, and all the rest." *Variety* opined, "Too much conversation and too little action makes this mystery comedy, old stage success, only fairly amusing.... Real dramatic suspense is

lacking and this screen transposition of Earl Derr Biggers' old novel and the Cohan play is ordinary." "The picture, following the script of the story, moves fast and is well acted.... Characterizations are convincing.... The suspense that threaded the original still functions," claimed the
Motion Picture Herald. *Motion Picture Daily* termed it "a pleasant, intermingling of mild mystery
and comedy" while the *Canadian Moving Picture Digest* dubbed it "an entertaining and exciting
picture." As far as box office performance, *Harrison's Reports* said it was only "fair."

Seven Keys to Baldpate (1947; 67 minutes)

PRODUCER: Herman Schlom. DIRECTOR: Lew Landers. SCREENPLAY: Lee Loeb, from the novel by
Earl Derr Biggers and the play by George M. Cohan. PHOTOGRAPHY: Jack MacKenzie. EDITOR: J.R.
Whittredge. MUSIC: Paul Sawtell. MUSIC DIRECTOR: C. Bakaleinikoff. ART DIRECTORS: Lucius O.
Croxton & Albert S. D'Agostino. SOUND: John C. Grubb & Terry Kellum. ASSISTANT DIRECTOR: James
Casey.

CAST: Phillip Terry (Kenneth Magee), Jacqueline White (Mary Jordan), Eduardo Ciannelli (Cargan),
Margaret Lindsay (Connie Lane), Arthur Shields (Professor Boulton), Jimmy Conlin (Pete the Hermit),
Tony Barrett (Max Rogers), Richard Powers [Tom Keene] (Steve Bland), Jason Robards (Hayden), Pierre
Watkin (Mr. Bentley), Erville Alderson (Station Master), Harry Harvey, Robert Bray (Policemen), Sam
McDaniel (Train Porter).

On a train headed to Asquewan Junction, mystery writer–criminologist Kenneth Magee
(Phillip Terry) notices that the manuscript for his new novel has been stolen. Disembarking at
the train station, he is directed to the Baldpate Inn by the station master (Erville Alderson). A
beautiful blonde, Mary Jordan (Jacqueline White), tells him he will be killed if he goes to the
inn. Walking through a snowstorm, Magee arrives at Baldpate only to find it inhabited by the
mysterious Cargan (Eduardo Ciannelli), who claims to be the caretaker. Magee tells him he has
a bet with businessman Bentley (Pierre Watkin), the inn's owner, that he can write a mystery
novel there in 24 hours, the prize being $5,000. Thinking he has the only key to the place, Magee
is surprised when Mary arrives with a key she says she found on the porch. The woman is near
hysterics, claiming something ghost-like touched her on the way there. As he tries to start work
in his room, Magee is accosted by "the hermit of Baldpate," Pete (Jimmy Conlin), a woman-hater
who says the place does not have a caretaker. Connie Lane (Margaret Lindsay) appears with
another key and Cargan claims she is his niece, staying with him for a few days. Magee overhears
Connie tell Cargan she wants her share and he then spies Mary slipping into a secret panel. From
the stairs Magee overhears Mary phone Bentley, telling him she has been successful in keeping
the writer from working on his novel. When she learns from her boss that the inn has no caretaker,
Mary tries to call the police but the line is cut. As Mary accuses Cargan of cutting the line, Professor Boulton (Arthur Shields) arrives with still another key, saying he has come to catch up on
some work. Mary confesses to Magee that she is Bentley's secretary. Another visitor, Steve Bland
(Richard Powers), comes to Baldpate and confronts Cargan. He carries stolen jewels which he
locks in the safe and then tries to extort more money from Cargan, who shoots him and drags
away his body. Mary tells Magee she plans to leave but they see Connie try to open the safe only
to be surprised by Boulton, who also tries to open it after she leaves. Mary opens the safe but
quickly closes it when Cargan shows up. Mary has Magee go with her through the secret passage
where they find Bland's body. As Magee and Mary try to escape from the inn by making a rope
of sheets, two more men, gangster Max Rogers (Tony Barrett) and jeweler Hayden (Jason
Robards), arrive. Cargan and Max want Hayden to give them $200,000 for the jewels which
they stole from him as part of an insurance swindle. Hayden reluctantly gives them the cash and
the two crooks leave the inn only to be captured by Boulton. Magee, who has escaped by the

sheet rope, finds the money. Max shoots Hayden while Magee and Mary return to the secret passage only to be confronted by Connie, who takes the money and hides it in a stove. Cargan and Max try to find the cash and Connie offers them a share of it with Max, her former lover. When Max overhears her plotting with Cargan, he kills her. Pete lights a fire in the stove, supposedly burning the money, and an angry Cargan knocks Magee out of a window and demands that Mary open the safe so he can get the jewels. Boulton arrives, announces he is an insurance detective and holds the crooks at bay. Magee runs into Pete, sends him for the police and returns to the inn. He knocks out Boulton, thinking he is one of the crooks. Cargan and Max decide to kill Magee and Mary but Pete returns with two policemen (Harry Harvey, Robert Bray) as Magee opens a closet containing Connie's body. Max tries to kill Magee but is shot by Boulton. The officers arrest the crooks and Magee returns to his novel, but quits, realizing he loves Mary.

Jack Haley and Boris Karloff were announced for the roles of Magee and Cargan when RKO prepared this third edition of *Seven Keys to Baldpate*. Released in the summer of 1947, the picture was pictorially pleasing and fairly fast-paced but its plot strayed still further from its original source. Phillip Terry portrays the writer in his best Fred MacMurray manner and Jacqueline White is bland as Mary. Ciannelli is credibly sinister as Cargan, who has gone from crooked politician in the 1929 film to a shady detective in the 1935 version to a gangster in this outing. Erville Alderson appears in both the 1935 and 1947 films; he is an energetic police chief in the former and the dour station master in the latter. This third RKO version is nicely atmospheric in its shadowy, remote hotel setting with sets from the studio's *The Magnificent Ambersons* (1942) belying its modest budget.

According to *Boxoffice*, "The picture adroitly blends the standard quota of chills and thrills with an alleviating dosage of comedy and romance to earn appraisal as above-average supporting fare. While the cast is none too heavy in marquee magnetism, it still boasts sufficient established names to add appeal to programs on which the film appears. Performances are entirely acceptable and the story is unfolded at a steady clip to attentive audiences." *Independent Exhibitors Film Bulletin* complained, "It is lacking in suspense and thrills, failing to open any doors to zestful action or original situations. Each overworked sequence labors clumsily into the following with little accomplished.... Performances, along with the direction and general production, are mediocre." *Variety* reported, "This one shapes up only as supporting comedy-mystery, plot having lost much of its thrill over the years. Production and direction don't give it much freshness or zip to overcome age.... Standard sliding panels, dead bodies, black cats and mysterious characters clutter up the scene without generating too much suspense or excitement." *The Film Daily* felt that this new version "measures up favorably with past performances and should again do its stuff providing the audience with whodunit entertainment in the light vein.... Lew Landers' direction is effective." *Harrison's Reports* called the film's box office receipts "Fair to Poor."

In 1983 a seventh filming of *Seven Keys to Baldpate* was released by Cannon as *House of the Long Shadows*. The locale was switched from upper New York to Wales where a writer (Desi Arnaz, Jr.) tries to complete a mystery novel in a remote castle belonging to a family of eccentrics portrayed by Vincent Price, Peter Cushing, Christopher Lee and John Carradine. The result was tepid at best. There have also been three television productions of the Cohan play. WNBT-TV in New York City presented a live version of the mystery comedy on July 7, 1946, starring Vinton Haworth, Eva Condon, Vaughn Taylor, George Mathews and Helen Jerome. On November 10, 1952, the syndicated series *Broadway Television Theatre* starred Buddy Ebsen as Magee in a presentation produced by WOR-TV. A decade later, on June 24, 1962, Fred Gwynne was Magee in a version done on NBC-TV's *DuPont Show of the Week*. The color production also featured Pat Stanley, Jayne Meadows, Joe E. Ross and Howard St. John. There were at least two radio adaptations of the work. Jack Benny and Mary Livingston starred in a version broadcast September 26, 1938, on CBS' *Lux Radio Theatre*, and on April 14, 1946, Walter Pidgeon and Martha Scott did "Seven Keys to Baldpate" on the ABC program *Theatre Guild of the Air*.

The Seventh Victim (1943; 71 minutes)

PRODUCER: Val Lewton. DIRECTOR: Mark Robson. SCREENPLAY: Charles O'Neal & DeWitt Bodeen. PHOTOGRAPHY: Nicholas Musuraca. EDITOR: John Lockert. MUSIC: Roy Webb. MUSIC DIRECTOR: C. Bakaleinikoff. ART DIRECTORS: Albert S. D'Agostino & Walter E. Keller. SOUND: John C. Grubb. SET DECORATIONS: Darrell Silvera & Harley Miller. ASSISTANT DIRECTOR: William Dorfman.

CAST: Tom Conway (Dr. Louis Judd), Kim Hunter (Mary Gibson), Jean Brooks (Jacqueline Gibson Ward), Isabel Jewell (Frances Fallon), Evelyn Brent (Natalie Cortez), Erford Gage (Jason Hoag), Ben Bard (Mr. Brun), Hugh Beaumont (Gregory Ward), Chef Milani (Jacob Romari), Marguerita Sylva (Bella Romari), Mary Newton (Esther Redi), Lou Lubin (Irving August), Wally Brown (Durk), Feodor Chaliapin, Jr. (Leo), Joan Barclay (Gladys), Elizabeth Russell (Mimi), Dewey Robinson (Subway Conductor), Jameson Shade (Swenson), Eve March (Mildred Gilchrist), Ottola Nesmith (Mrs. Lowood), Sarah Selby (Miss Gottschalk), Edythe Elliott (Mrs. Swift), Ann Summers (Miss Summers), Milton Kibbee (Joseph), Marianne Mosner (Miss Rowan), William Halligan (Paul Radeaux), Richard Davies (Radeaux's Partner), Betty Roadman (Mrs. Wheeler), Charles Phillips, Howard Mitchell (Policemen), Bud Geary, Kernan Cripps (Missing Persons Bureau Clerks), Wheaton Chambers (Father of Missing Girl), Barbara Hale (Subway Passenger), Cyril Ring, Henry Herbert (Palladists), Lloyd Ingraham (Night Watchman), Patty Nash (Nancy), Lorna Dunn, Eileen O'Malley (Mothers), Tiny Jones (Newspaper Vendor), Adia Kuznetzoff (Ballet Dancer), Edward Thomas, Patti Brill, Mary Halsey, Edith Conrad, Norma Nilsson (Performers).

Producer Val Lewton fourth feature for RKO Radio, *The Seventh Victim*, released at the end of August 1943, was originally intended to be Lewton's second one for the studio, following his initial success *Cat People* (q.v.) the previous year. Instead it was preceded by *I Walked with a Zombie* and *The Leopard Man* (both 1943) [qq.v.], after Lewton decided to alter the approach in DeWitt Bodeen's original story and brought in Charles O'Neal (father of Ryan O'Neal) to collaborate on what became one of the producer's most enigmatic productions. Bodeen's initial draft had a young woman about to become the seventh victim of a murderer, making it necessary for her to learn the killer's identity to save her life. The finished script retained the vulnerable heroine but instead it had her in a web of mystery and deceit as she tries to find her older sister, a beautiful but morbid character at odds with a coven of devil worshippers. The film introduced Kim Hunter to the screen as the young protagonist and it also marked the directorial debut of Mark Robson, who had edited Lewton's initial trio of RKO releases, all directed by Jacques Tourneur. Tourneur had originally been assigned to *The Seventh Victim* but was switched to *Days of Glory* (1944). Tom Conway got top billing in *The Seventh Victim* as psychiatrist Dr. Louis Judd, the same character he played in *Cat People* although his character was killed off in that outing. In its tightly edited 71 minutes, *The Seventh Victim* manages to emit an aura of dread that is exemplified by Nicholas Musuraca's beautifully executed photography capturing the horror of the unknown in a large city at night. Thanks to its slick production values, the feature belies its low budget. In the opening scenes, the mansion from *The Magnificent Ambersons* (1942) is used for the locale of a girls' school, Highcliff.

The acting in *The Seventh Victim* is finely nuanced and adds greatly to the film's overall sense of doom and underlying evil. The suave Conway carries off the Judd role quite effectively, giving the character more of a human touch than was evidenced in *Cat People*. Hunter scores as the beleaguered young heroine and Erford Gage is fine as a disillusioned poet. Hugh Beaumont nicely handles the difficult role of a man in love with both his wife and her sister. Evelyn Brent, Mary Newton and Ben Bard give coldly chilling performances as the lead Satanists, while Isabel

Lobby card for *The Seventh Victim* (1943).

Jewell contributes a well-edged portrayal of a mentally (and probably sexually) confused hairdresser. Also effective in brief roles are Wally Brown (who would later team with Alan Carney to star in the RKO genre efforts *Zombies on Broadway* and *Genius at Work* [qq.v.]) and Feodor Chaliapin, Jr., as the devil cult's hired killers. Topping them all, however, is the breathtakingly beautiful Jean Brooks as the intended seventh victim. While not on screen for very long, she manages to leave a deep impression in her portrayal of a young woman obsessed with dying and fleeing from evil. From 1943 to 1947 Brooks appeared in 11 features for RKO, eight of them with Tom Conway, including *The Falcon and the Co-eds* and *The Falcon's Alibi* (q.q.v.). *The Seventh Victim* is one of the outstanding horror and *film noir* features of the 1940s.

A student at Highcliff Seminary, Mary Gibson (Hunter), is called in by the headmistress (Ottola Nesmith) and told that her tuition has not been paid by her sister Jacqueline (Brooks) for six months. Mary is offered a teaching position but decides to leave to find Jacqueline, whom she had not heard from for some time. A young assistant (Eve March) tells Mary not to come back and instead make a life for herself outside Highcliff. Going to New York City, Mary seeks out Jacqueline at the business she operates, La Sagasse, a cosmetics store and factory. There Mrs. Redi (Newton) informs Mary that Jacqueline sold her the store six months before. A hair stylist, Frances Fallon (Jewell), who is friends with Jacqueline, tells Mary she saw her sister recently at a Greenwich Village Italian restaurant, Romari's. Mary goes there and inquires about her sister and Mrs. Romari (Marguerita Silva) informs her that Jacqueline rented one of the rooms above the restaurant and had the lock changed but never moved in. When Mary asks to see the room,

Mr. Romari (Chef Milani) breaks the apartment door's lock, revealing a chair with a noose hanging above it. A tubercular young woman, Mimi (Elizabeth Russell), lives in another apartment. When a policeman (Howard Mitchell) suggests Mary go to the Bureau of Missing Persons, restaurant customer Jason Hoag (Gage), a washed-up poet and book store clerk, takes an interest in Mary. At the bureau, Mary is accosted by private detective Irving August (Lou Lubin), who wants fifty dollars to find Jacqueline within 48 hours. Mary says she does not have the money but he decides to pursue the matter after being warned away by another gumshoe, Paul Radeaux (William Halligan). When Mary checks at the morgue, she is told to see attorney Gregory Ward (Beaumont) who tells her he loves Jacqueline. He says Jacqueline lives in a world of her own fantasy, thus explaining the noose and her enchantment with dying. Gregory takes Mary to dinner and says he wants to help her. Mary goes back to her lodgings, the Hotel Chatsworth, where August is waiting for her. August says Jacqueline did not sell her business to Mrs. Redi and that she is locked in a room at La Sagasse. August and Mary go there. As August enters the room, Mary hides from the night watchman (Lloyd Ingraham) and sees the detective emerge from the shadows. He falls to the floor, having been stabbed. Mary runs out of the building and gets on a subway where she observes three drunken revelers, two of them (Brown, Chaliapin, Jr.) supporting the third, who turns out to be the dead August. Finding the conductor (Dewey Robinson), Mary tells him about the three men but they have disappeared. Mary tells Gregory what happened and he tries to find a logical explanation. He also informs her that he has found her a teaching job at a Greenwich Village settlement house where she will be working with small children. Leaving the Hotel Chatsworth, Mary takes a room over the Romaris' restaurant. Psychiatrist Dr. Louis Judd (Conway) tells Gregory he needs $100 to continue Jacqueline's support and the lawyer informs him about Mary searching for her sister. Gregory also asks to see Jacqueline but Judd warns him she is on the verge of insanity. When Mary learns from Gregory about Judd's request, she goes to him, demanding to see Jacqueline. He takes her to a converted mansion but they find Jacqueline's room empty and he quickly leaves. As Mary remains in the room, Jacqueline makes a fleeting appearance and disappears. Back at her lodgings, Mary finds Radeaux and his partner (Richard Davies) who inform her they have been hired by Jacqueline's husband, Gregory, to locate her. As they dine that evening at the Romaris' restaurant, Gregory tells Mary he kept his marriage to Jacqueline a secret for her protection. Mrs. Romari suggests Jason try to make them laugh. Instead he promises Mary he will find Jacqueline for her. Jason escorts Mary and Gregory to a party at the home of one-armed Natalie Cortez (Brent) and there talks to Judd regarding Jacqueline. Going to the library the next day, Jason charms the librarian (Sarah Selby) into telling him that Judd and Mrs. Redi checked out a book on devil worship. Jason has Mary return to La Sagasse to learn more about Mrs. Redi and while Frances does her hair she finds out that the store's new logo is a devil worship diagram. Mrs. Redi later chides Frances for telling Mary about the trademark. While taking a shower, Mary realizes she is not alone and finds out her visitor is Mrs. Redi, who informs her that Jacqueline murdered August out of fright and that she had to help get rid of the body. She also suggests Mary return to Highcliff. Going to see Jason at his skylight apartment, Mary tells him she is leaving. Because he loves her, he suggests she contact Gregory, who wants his wife to go to the police. Jason asks Judd to find Jacqueline and also to take his new volume of poems, his first in ten years since losing the girl he loved after she started seeing Judd, to his publisher. He admits his love for Mary has renewed his interest in writing. Judd brings Jacqueline to Jason's apartment and she tells Mary and Gregory that she tried to quit the devil worshippers and they locked her in a room at La Sagasse where they wanted her to commit suicide with a pair of scissors. When August came into the room, she thought he was one of them and struck out at him. Gregory tells his wife to rest before they go to the police and

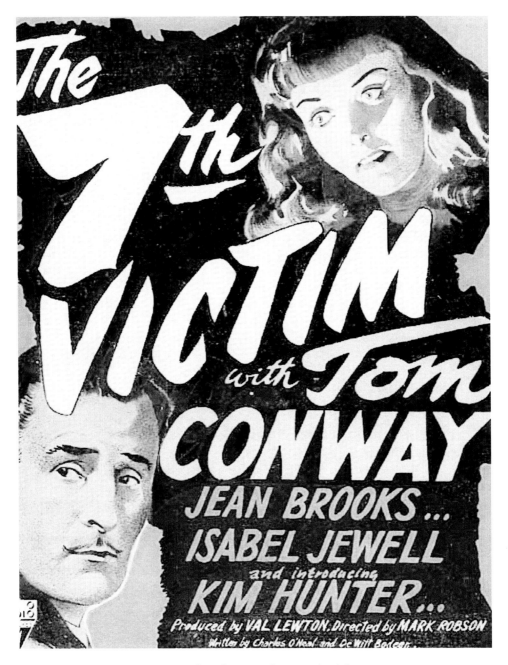

Poster for *The Seventh Victim* (1943).

he suggests she stay with Mary. The next day Mary gets a call at school saying that Jacqueline left with two men. When she later informs Judd and Gregory, they decide to go to Natalie's apartment. There the devil worship cult, led by Natalie and Brun (Bard), try to get Jacqueline to drink poison. When she is about to take the poison, Frances knocks it out of her hand, saying she was only happy when she was with Jacqueline, the only person to ever show her kindness. Brun tells Jacquline to go, sending one of the cult members (Chaliapin) to kill her, but she manages to elude him by taking up with a troupe of theatrical revelers. Judd informs Jason that the girl he loved did not die, but has been in an asylum for the last ten years. At Natalie's apartment they learn that Jacqueline has gone. Jason calls the cult a poor, wretched group of people who have taken the wrong turn and Judd recites part of "The Lord's Prayer." After Judd informs them that Jacqueline has not been harmed, Mary and Gregory wait for her to return and they admit they are in love but Mary declares she can never betray her sister. Jacqueline returns to her room at the Romaris and meets Mimi, who says she is dying but plans to enjoy what life she has left. Later Mimi leaves for a night on the town and hears a snapping sound in Jacqueline's room.

Contemporary reviewers were not kind to *The Seventh Victim*. *Variety* complained, "A particularly poor script is the basis for the ills besetting this mystery melodrama.... Tom Conway has the lead, and while he's generally a satisfactory performer, he, too, can't extricate himself from the maze of circumstances that abound in this totally unbelievable hocus-pocus...." Bosley Crowther in *The New York Times* stated, "[W]e have no more notion of what *The Seventh Victim* ... is about than if we had watched the same picture run backward and upside down.... Apparently the people at [RKO] just had a collective nightmare, and this is the horrible result." *Boxoffice* agreed, "Something went wrong with this one. It may have been a story with continuity and understandable motivation when it went before the cameras, but the way it emerges on the screen it leaves the impression a number of essential links are missing...." *The Film Daily* wrote, "Although this melodrama leaves much to be desired, it should manage to get by with the type of audience for which it has been designed. Chiefly in the film's favor is its mood, which creates a feeling of doom.... The story has been told with a fair amount of suspense and one or two exciting moments. Its chief fault is that it lacks clarity."

Since the late 1950s the standing of *The Seventh Victim* has greatly improved. "Suspenseful, eerie, but overly complicated thriller" is how Steven H. Scheuer felt about it in *TV Movie Almanac & Ratings 1958 & 1959* (1958). In *An Illustrated History of the Horror Film* (1967), Carlos Clarens wrote, "Lewton's masterpiece may well be *The Seventh Victim*. Rarely has a film succeeded so well in capturing the nocturnal menace of a large city, the terror underneath the everyday, the suggestion of hidden evil." In an article on the movie in *Filmgraph* (Vol. 2, No. 1, 1971), Doug McClelland termed it "one of the most absorbing, creative chillers of any day." Donald C. Willis wrote in *Horror and Science Fiction: A Checklist* (1972) that it "almost successfully unites the separate strains of horror and melodrama in the Lewton series, and the last chilling, numbing scene does unite them, briefly in what is perhaps the most effective instance of suggested horror in any Lewton movie. There is the usual quota of lines to make you flinch, and the leads are dull, but for once the moodiness (here mainly talk about failure and unhappiness) is integral to the horror. Jean Brooks is *not* one of the dull leads, and her attractively melancholic 'presence' dominates." In *Val Lewton: The Reality of Terror* (1973), Joel E. Siegel opined, "*The Seventh Victim* is so rich and so compact that only after a second viewing can most audiences begin to apprehend its beauties." Ed Naha in *Horrors: From Screen to Scream* (1975) declared it "a viable piece of paranoia.... Some of the Satanic elements [are] genuinely eerie, making later films like *Rosemary's Baby* look like *Bambi*." Phil Hardy in *The Encyclopedia of Horror Movies* (1986) said, "Though competently directed by Robson (his first film), the strong suit of this wonderfully eerie thriller ... is its evocative script. So much so, it almost matches *I Walked with a Zombie* as a film haunted by death and despair.... *The Seventh Victim* isn't quite well directed enough to be called a masterpiece. But almost."

She (1935; 94 minutes)

PRODUCER: Merian C. Cooper. DIRECTORS: Irving Pichel & Lansing C. Holden. SCREENPLAY: Ruth Rose, from the novel by H. Rider Haggard. ADDITIONAL DIALOGUE: Dudley Nichols. PHOTOGRAPHY:

J. Roy Hunt. Editor: Ted Cheesman. Music: Max Steiner. Art Directors: Van Nest Polglase & Al Herman. Sound: John L. Cass. Set Decorations: Thomas Little. Costume Design: Aline Bernstein & Harold Miles. Dance Director: Benjamin Zemach. Production Associate: Shirley Burden.

Cast: Helen Gahagan (She/Hash-A-Mo-Tep), Randolph Scott (Leo Vincey), Helen Mack (Tanya Dugmore), Nigel Bruce (Horace Holly), Gustav von Seyffertitz (Prince Minister Billali), Samuel S. Hinds (John Vincey), Noble Johnson (Amahaggar Chief), Lumsden Hare (Dugmore), Jim Thorpe (Guard Captain), Julius Alder (High Priest), Arnold Gray, Bill Wolfe (Priests), Ray Corrigan, Jerry Frank (Guards).

Hoping for a spectacular follow-up to *King Kong* (q.v.), producer Merian C. Cooper made *She*, based on H. Rider Haggard's 1887 novel. Ruth Rose did the screen adaptation with additional dialogue by Dudley Nichols. The locale of the mythical kingdom of Kor was changed from Africa in the book to the outer reaches of the Arctic. Other holdovers from *Kong* included editor Ted Cheesman and Max Steiner, who did the less than memorable music score. Helen Mack, who co-starred in *The Son of Kong* (q.v.) for producers Cooper and Ernest B. Schoedsack, was also in *She* as was Noble Johnson, who played the native chief in both *King Kong* and *The Son of Kong*. Here he was cast in a similar role as the leader of a group of prehistoric cave dwellers. *She* was released theatrically by Radio Pictures in the summer of 1935, three months ahead of Cooper and Schoedsack's other effort at a film spectacular to follow *King Kong*, *The Last Days of Pompeii* (q.v.). Both films lost money at the box office, with *She* coming up $180,000 short of its production costs.

She is pictorially satisfying but often arid plot-wise. It contains a spectacular avalanche sequence and impressive cave scenes, and the kingdom of Kor is shown to be a Shangri-La–like Asgard with a colossal palace, the Hall of Kings, that includes the re-dressed doors and wall from *King Kong*. Unfortunately the action is badly slowed by two boring ceremonial dances, the second being the elaborate but too long Festival of the Sacred Wall. *She* was made on the largest set ever constructed up to that time on the RKO lot. The first part of the movie is quite entertaining, exciting and fast-paced. When the title character emerges, however, the film, while more visually impressive, slows considerably. Another drawback is the leads. While Nigel Bruce is his usual good-natured character as a scientist in quest of the flame of life, Randolph Scott is passable as the hero and Helen Mack is only slightly better as the young woman he learns to love. RKO had wanted Joel McCrea and Frances Dee, who were married, for the two roles. While stage actress Helen Gahagan, in her only film, handles the title character in a satisfactory manner, she hardly has the looks or feeling of an alluring 500-year-old siren. The best acting in the movie comes from Gustav von Seyffertitz as She's loyal prime minister and Lumsden Hare as a brutish trader. Originally running 102 minutes, *She* was released theatrically at 94 minutes.

As he awaits the arrival of his nephew Leo Vincey (Scott), scientist John Vincey (Samuel S. Hinds) talks with his associate Horace Holy (Bruce) about his impending death from radiation poisoning. John wants to turn over to Leo his work on finding a way to overcome time. Leo arrives and John tells him of his theories, and he and Horace show Leo a 500-year-old letter written by the wife of their ancestor, also named John Vincey. She managed to escape with a servant, who was killed by a huge beast, from an unknown realm north of Siberia and make it to Poland. According to the letter, Vincey saw the flame that brings eternal life and was murdered because he refused to abandon her. Before she died in Poland, Vincey's wife left their son a small gold statue of a woman surrounded by flames. John gives the figure to Leo and shows him a portrait of their ancestor with the two men being lookalikes. John tells Leo that after 17 years he and Horace have failed to recreate the flame but their experiments prove it does exist. Just before he dies, John asks Leo to continue his work with Horace and locate the flame. Months later Leo and Horace stop at a trading post in the Arctic and are invited to spend the night by the owner, Dugmore (Hare), who resides there with his daughter Tanya (Mack). When Dugmore sees the

Lobby card for *She* (1935).

statuette he thinks the two men are gold hunters and tells them if they do not let him guide them across the Sugel Barrier, he will make sure they cannot hire local guides, since they are superstitious about the area. Tanya tells Leo and Horace about a native legend of a white woman who returned from the Sugel Barrier with terrifying stories. Leo objects when Dugmore plans to take Tanya with them but he says she is needed to cook and he does not want her left alone at the trading post to be at the mercy of the locals. After several days the expedition reaches the glacier and the natives discover the frozen bodies of a man (wearing a gold chain) and a giant beast. Horace deduces that the man must have been Mrs. Vincey's servant and the creature is a long-extinct saber-toothed tiger. Dugmore tries to break the ice around the gold chain and is warned he will could cause an avalanche. When the others head back, Dugmore again strikes at the ice and a huge mountain of snow kills him and covers up the camp. Leo, Horace and Tanya are saved by taking refuge under a rocky overhang and they quickly spy a cave opening exposed by the avalanche. Entering the cavern, the trio finds volcanic formations and are soon surrounded by a tribe of primitive men who lead them to a large cavern. Horace thinks they are friendly but Leo is not so sure and tries to make a getaway with Tonya. When Leo sees the chief (Johnson) order a red hot metal mask placed on Horace, he fires his gun and a fight ensues. Leo is wounded but the natives draw back when a group of spear-carrying soldiers arrive on the scene. Their leader, Prime Minister Billali (von Seyffertitz), speaks English and he takes Leo, Horace and Tanya through the cavern to the kingdom of Kor. There Billali confers with his queen, Hash-A-Mo-Tep, or She (Gahagan), who demands to see Leo. Emerging from a mist, She thinks Leo is the reincarnation of her long-dead lover, John Vincey. She orders Leo taken to her chambers beyond the forbidden door and when he revives she tells him he is the man for whom she has been waiting. Later She sits on her thrown with Leo at her side and orders his attackers put to death with the native chief thrown into flames. When Leo objects, She tells him that she rules by terror but he asks her to spare the other natives. She agrees to do so but after he leaves she tells Billali to have them killed. Horace wants Leo to learn from She the location of the sacred flame and in a pool She shows Leo the past and takes him to John Vincey's body. She sets the corpse on fire and tells Leo that John has been reborn and that her mourning is over. She informs Leo that the flame has kept her young for over 500 years. When Leo tells Horace and Tayna that She plans to show him the flame and that he will stay with her and send them back home, Horace tells him he is a fool and will die from his folly like his ancestor. Tanya tries to reason with Leo, saying that She is not normal. Tanya later begs She to let Leo go back with her and Horace. When She refuses, Tanya asks to stay but it is denied. The angry Tanya informs She that she fears her because she is young and human and that She is old and it is too late for Leo to love her. After Tanya leaves, Billali tells She he saw Tanya come from Leo's arms and suggests that Tanya be used as the veiled sacrifice in the Festival of the Secret Well. During the elaborate ceremony, Leo recognizes Tanya as the sacrifice and attempts to save her, starting a fire and locking the court doors as he escapes with Tanya and Horace. The trio runs through the cave pursued by She's guards and eludes them by jumping a precipice. Searching for an escape route, the trio come across She and Billali at the site of the sacred flame. When Leo rejects She for Tanya, She says she will wait for the young woman to grow old. To save Tanya, Leo agrees to go through the flame if She precedes him. She calls to the flame four times and each eruption of fire makes her grow older until she is an aged crone. When she dies, Billali, who has served her for 40 years, mourns. As he leaves with Leo and Tanya, Horace says they are turning their backs on the greatest secret in the world. Months later, back in London, Horace finishes reading his report on their adventures with Leo and Tanya and says while he thinks She may have overexposed herself to the radiation, it still may have been some greater power that reached out to destroy her.

Photoplay called *She* "a spectacle of magnificent proportions…. There are human sacrifices, gorgeous 'Dance of Death,' and a macabre atmosphere throughout…. Entire supporting cast is excellently convincing." *The New York Times* wrote the Haggard novel "has been converted by RKO Radio into a gaudy, spectacular and generally fantastic photoplay which is likely to find its greatest favor with the younger generation. The adult reaction, we fear, will be decidedly luke-warm." "Artistic version of Sir Rider Haggard's novel that will appeal to followers of the spectac-ular," is how *Boxoffice* viewed the production. The reviewer added, "It has been given massive fantastic settings which with a talented cast and weird dances lavishly executed, partially com-pensate for lack of intense drama the original possessed." Regarding the two leads, the trade mag-azine wrote, "Miss Gahagan gives reality and glamour" to the title role while Scott "shows great restraint and marked histrionic ability." *The New Movie Magazine* opined, "If you go for the bizarre in pictures, then this is the one to check for future reference." *Variety* wrote, "Lovers of the weird and incredible may stamp *She* as a thrill but in the main it's not [box office]. Those not addicted to Welsh rarebit delirium in their literature will perhaps find the picture not only unable to lull the critical faculty, but slow and heavy in movement." The reviewer noted, "Cam-erawork of J. Roy Hunt is standout. So, too, is the art direction…. It's a cameraman's triumph, an art director's picnic and a dancing master's joy." *Picture Play Magazine* stated, "Strange, unearthly fantasy is seldom seen on the screen. When it is, it rarely done with the technical brilliance of this. Marvelous feats of the camera are performed in imaginative settings that suggest nothing one has seen before…. [It's] interesting as spectacle, not as drama." The fan publication felt that Helen Gahagan enacted the title role "with taste, dignity and fine distinction. She is truly regal." *Hollywood* enthused, "Spectacle-loving Merian C. Cooper outdoes all previous efforts in pro-ducing this fantastic adventure-mystery-spectacle…. [T]he picture is one of the most elaborate since *The Lost World*…. If you liked *King Kong*, don't miss this one." *The Film Daily* stated, "This is a gorgeous mammoth spectacle—a success no doubt from an artistic, mechanical, musical and photographic point of view. However, success from a box office standpoint is problematical. In gaining its hugeness and pretentiousness, the story has not been given equal consideration and becomes uninteresting, little happens that is exciting and the piece is overtalk active."

An opera singer and stage actress, Helen Gahagan was the wife of actor Melvyn Douglas. Later in the 1930s she gave up acting, became politically involved and in 1944 was elected to Congress from California as Helen Gahagan Douglas. In 1950 she ran for the U.S. Senate but lost to another California member of Congress, Richard M. Nixon. Her Democratic primary opponent that year dubbed her the "Pink Lady" because of her left-wing views and it is claimed that during the campaign she tried to buy up and destroy all prints of *She* in order to avoid political embarrassment.

There have been at least ten other movie versions of the Haggard novel. The initial filming was a short 1899 production by Georges Méliès in France called *La Danse du Feu* (The Dance of Fire) and *La Colonne de Feu*; it was shown in the U.S. as *Haggard's "She"—The Pillar of Fire* and *The Pillar of Fire*. In 1908 Edison produced a 1000-foot version and three years later Thanhouser did a two-reel edition starring James Cruze and Marguerite Snow. Alice Delysia and Henry Victor headlined a five-reel British version in 1916 and the next year Valeska Suratt had the title role in a Fox five-reeler. The best known silent version of *She* was made by the British company Artlee in 1925. Directed by Leander De Cordova and scripted by Walter Summers, it starred Betty Blythe and Carlyle Blackwell. In 1953 *Malika Salomi*, an Indian production, redid the Haggard story, and thirty years after the RKO feature, Hammer Films–7 Arts made a color version with Ursula Andress, Peter Cushing, Christopher Lee and Andre Morell. In 1967 the same studio reworked the Haggard tale as *The Vengeance of She* featuring Olinka Berova, John Richardson, Edward

Judd, Andre Morell and a bevy of scantily clad starlets. The 1982 Italian feature *She* was a sci-fi adventure that bore only a slight resemblance to Haggard's work.

The 1935 *She* was reissued theatrically by RKO in 1949 on a double bill with *The Last Days of Pompeii* (q.v.) and in 2006 Legend Films released a DVD that included both the original theatrical release and a colorization done under the direction of special effects wizard Ray Harryhausen. Among the bonus material on the disc is eight minutes of footage deleted from the 1935 release. These scenes involve Tanya going to She's chambers to see the unconscious Leo, with a confrontation between the two women, and Billali being shown the gold statuette by Horace.

A Shot in the Dark (1933; 53 minutes)

PRODUCER: Julius Hagen. DIRECTOR: George Pearson. SCREENPLAY: George Pearson & Terence Eagan, from the novel by Gerald Fairlie. PHOTOGRAPHY: Ernest Palmer. EDITOR: Lister Laurence. ART DIRECTOR: James A. Carter. COIFFEUR: Charlie. ASSISTANT DIRECTOR: Arthur Barnes.

CAST: Dorothy Boyd (Alaris Browne), O.B. Clarence (the Rev. John Malcolm), Jack Hawkins (Norman Paul), Michael Shepley (Vivien Waugh), Davy Burnaby (Col. Michael Browne), A. Bromley Davenport (Peter Browne), Russell Thorndike (Dr. Stuart), Hugh E. Wright (George Yarrow), Henrietta Watson (Angela Browne), Margaret Yarde (Kate Browne), John Vyvian (Police Inspector).

During a terrible thunderstorm, bedridden miser Peter Browne (A. Bromley Davenport) orders his niece Alaris (Dorothy Boyd) to turn out the lights in his bedroom because he fears being murdered. For protection he has electric wires strung around the outside of the house. Peter raves to his niece that his doctor thinks he is a neurotic and mad and he chastises her for loving Norman Paul (Jack Hawkins), whom he says is an idle loafer after his money. Alaris tells her uncle that if she did not know how ill he was, she could hate him. Going downstairs, Alaris turns off the electric current to the outside wires and admits Norman, who wants her to go away with him. She refuses, saying she owes everything to her uncle and any sudden shock might kill him. Finding a loaded revolver in a desk drawer, Norman puts it in a safer location. Norman goes back into the storm as she returns upstairs to give her uncle medicine. Since he refuses to have the bedroom lights on, she mistakenly takes a bottle labeled "poison" from the medicine cabinet. She leaves and someone shoots at Peter but misses and he hears a maniacal laugh. The next day at his inquest, Dr. Stuart (Russell Thorndike) rules that Peter's death was a suicide. The local police inspector (John Vyvian) is not satisfied with the verdict. Before lawyer George Yarrow (Hugh E. Wright) arrives to read Peter's will, Norman again asks Alaris to leave with him and she refuses. Also at the estate for the reading are Peter's pompous brother Colonel Michael Browne (Davy Burnaby) and his wife Angela (Henrietta Watson), his nephew Vivien Waugh (Michael Shepley) and his sister Katie Browne (Margaret Yarde). The relatives are surprised when the lawyer tells them the will is in the form of a photograph record. When he plays it, the voice of Peter announces he was murdered. Just then a golf ball sails through a window and the local vicar, the Rev. John Malcolm (O.B. Clarence), arrives, apologizing for the accident. Yarrow discovers the recording is missing and everyone looks for it in vain. Malcolm is told by Yarrow that Peter claimed on the record that he was murdered and the vicar suggests they call the police. Instead Alaris insists Malcolm stay and help investigate with Vivien quipping that the vicar has a reputation of being "a bit of a Sherlock Holmes." Malcolm and Norman look in Peter's room and discover a secret passage to an old dungeon. Alaris is accused of killing her uncle due to the mix-up with the poison bottle but it is soon revealed that all the other relatives have motives for wanting the old man dead. After considerable deduction Malcolm proves that it was the destitute Vivien who murdered his uncle, hoping to obtain Peter's estate.

Another is the series of program features British producer Julius Hagen's Real Art Productions made with RKO in the early 1930s, *A Shot in the Dark* was released in Great Britain by Radio Pictures. It got no stateside play dates. Made at Twickenham Film Studios, it has a very atmospheric opening involving a thunderstorm and a spooky old house with a cadaverous old man (Davenport) claiming he is going to be murdered. Ernest Palmer's photography is especially effective in these early scenes. Following the man's death, the film basically becomes a talky whodunit that is somewhat helped by a crime-solving vicar (Clarence), sort of a male counterpart to Agatha Christie's Miss Jane Marple. Also effective is an eerie underground dungeon and a stirring music score by uncredited W.L. Trytel. Even at less than one hour, *A Shot in the Dark* is a tedious crime-solving exercise with the villain all too apparent.

Of more interest than the film are some of its participants. *A Shot in the Dark* is based on the 1932 novel by Gerard Fairlie, the model for H.C. McNeile's famous character Hugh "Bulldog" Drummond. Following McNeile's death in 1937, Fairlie took over the Drummond series and wrote seven more adventures with the character between 1938 and 1954. Portraying Dr. Stuart in the film is Russell Thorndike, brother of actress Dame Sybil Thorndike. Although he appeared in nearly two dozen feature films between 1922 and 1955, including *Scrooge* (1923), Thorndike is best known for creating the literary character Dr. Syn. *A Shot in the Dark* was one of actor Jack Hawkins' first films as a leading man; he also appeared in the genre efforts *The Perfect Alibi* (*Birds of Prey*) (1930) [q.v.], *The Lodger* (1932), *Death at Broadcasting House* (1934), *The Frog* (1937), *Tales That Witness Madness* and *Theater of Blood* (both 1973).

The Sign of Four (World Wide, 1932; 73 minutes)

PRODUCER: Basil Dean. DIRECTOR: Graham Cutts. SCREENPLAY: W.P. Lipscomb, from the novel by Sir Arthur Conan Doyle. PHOTOGRAPHY: Robert G. Martin & Robert de Grasse. EDITOR: Otto Ludwig. MUSIC DIRECTOR: K. Ernest Irving. ART DIRECTOR: Clifford Pember. SOUND: A.D. Valentine. PRODUCTION SUPERVISOR: Rowland V. Lee. ASSISTANT DIRECTOR: James G. Kelly.

CAST: Arthur Wontner (Sherlock Holmes), Isla Bevan (Mary Morstan), Ian Hunter (Dr. John H. Watson), Graham Soutten (Jonathan Small), Miles Malleson (Thaddeus Sholto), Herbert Lomas (Major John Sholto), Gilbert Davis (Inspector Atherly Jones), Margaret Yarde (Mrs. Smith), Roy Emerton (Bailey Meade), Clare Greet (Mrs. Hudson), Edgar Norfolk (Captain Morstan), Moore Marriott (Mordecai Smith), Kynaston Reeves (Bartholomew Sholto), Togo (Tonga), Ernest Sefton (Barrett), Mr. Burnhett (Tattoo Artist), Charles Farrell (Carnival Attendee).

Arthur Wontner made the third of his five screen appearances as Sherlock Holmes in *The Sign of Four*, done by Associated Talking Pictures at England's Ealing Studios. It was released by Radio Pictures in Great Britain where it was also called *The Sign of Four: Sherlock Holmes' Greatest Case*. In the United States it was advertised as *The Sign of 4* and was issued in August 1932 by World Wide Pictures. Wontner previously played Holmes for producer Julius Hagen in *Sherlock Holmes' Fatal Hour* (1931) and *The Missing Rembrandt* (1932) and would return to work for Hagen in *The Triumph of Sherlock Holmes* (1935) and *Silver Blaze* (1937), which was released in the U.S. in 1941 by Astor Pictures as *Murder at the Baskervilles*. A number of Sherlock Holmes enthusiasts consider Arthur Wontner the finest portrayer of the immortal sleuth.

Based on Conan Doyle's 1890 novel, *The Sign of Four* is a fine adaptation and one of the best Sherlock Holmes features of the 1930s. Its only drawback is the difficulty in understanding some of the dialogue when delivered quickly and with heavy British accents. Particularly hard to follow is the scene in a smoky waterfront pub with Holmes (Wontner), in disguise as an old seaman, trying to extract information from a bartender (Margaret Yarde) with the dialogue being almost incomprehensible. Otherwise the feature is top-notch, flavorful, nicely paced and full of

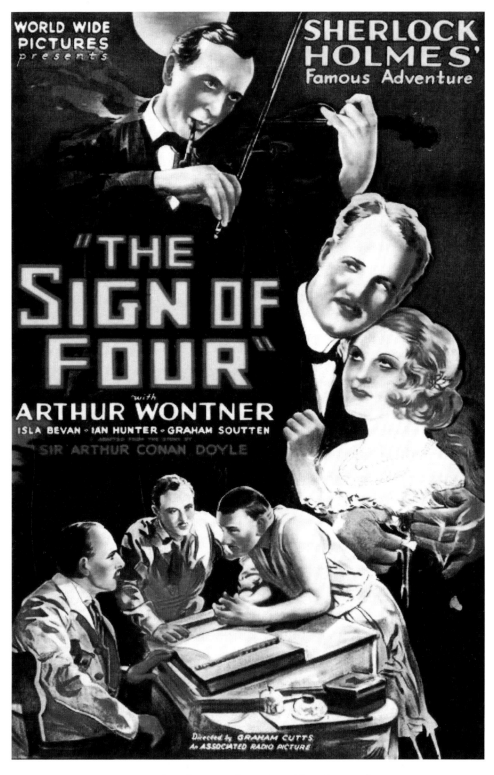

Poster for *The Sign of Four* (World Wide, 1932).

action and interesting characters, including the bizarre Tonga (Togo), who bites the heads off snakes as part of a fun fair attraction. There is also the dim-witted, tattooed giant Bailey Meade (Roy Emerton), who with Tonga is in cahoots with the murderous one-legged gorilla man Jonathan Small (Graham Soutten) in trying to obtain a cursed treasure. Ian Hunter makes an energetic Dr. Watson while Isla Bevan is the attractive heroine with whom he falls in love. Miles Malleson as Thaddeus Sholto is very similar to Aubrey Mather's elfin character in a later Universal Sherlock Holmes feature, *The House of Fear* (1945). The film's production supervisor, Rowland V. Lee, directed the genre efforts *The Mysterious Dr. Fu Manchu* (1929), *The Return of Dr. Fu Manchu* (1930), *Love from a Stranger* (1937), *Son of Frankenstein* and *Tower of London* (both 1939). *Sign of Four* producer Basil Dean earlier directed *The Return of Sherlock Holmes* (1929). *The Sign of Four* was one of eight features RKO co-produced in England in 1932 with Dean's Associated Talking Pictures.

At a prison located in the Andaman Islands, Major John Sholto (Herbert Lomas) connives with an associate, Captain Morstan (Edgar Norfolk), to locate precious stones worth $250,000 stolen from an Indian rajah. The only man who knows the location of the treasure of Agra is one-legged prisoner Jonathan Small (Soutten), who agrees to share it with them for his freedom. Small warns Sholto and Morstan he will extract a terrible revenge if they double cross him. Finding the gems in an abandoned fortress, Sholto and Morstan fight over them with Sholto killing Morstan. In London many years later, wheelchair-bound Sholto reads in the newspaper that Small has escaped from prison along with Bailey Meade (Emerton). Sholto summons his sons Thaddeus (Malleson) and Bartholomew (Kynaston Reeves) and begs them not to let Small kill him. He tells them about finding the treasure and murdering Morstan and then shows them a priceless string of pearls which he wants them to give to Morstan's daughter Mary (Bevan). Hearing the sound of a wooden leg, the old man sees Small's face at the window and dies. Small later uses his trade as a tattoo artist to disguise Meade so he can work incognito at a fun fair sideshow. Mary receives an anonymous note along with a package containing the pearls. Thaddeus returns home to find Small and Meade have ransacked it looking for the treasure and he tells them he does not know where it is hidden but does admit the pearls were sent to Mary. That night Small and Meade break into Mary's shop but do not find the pearls. The next day she gets another note, this time telling her to come that evening with two friends to a house on Acacia Road. Mary next receives a missive saying not to call the police or she will be killed. Going to see Sherlock Holmes (Wontner), Mary faints and is cared for by Dr. Watson (Hunter), who is attracted to her. Recovering, she tells them her father disappeared years before in the Orient, shows them a drawing with four crosses and discusses the break-in at her shop. Holmes suggests she stay with him and Watson at Baker Street until the time of the rendezvous when they will accompany her to Acacia Street. Holmes informs Watson this is the most intricate case he has ever come across. At the rendezvous site, the Sholto house, the trio is met by Thaddeus who takes them to Bartholomew. He says they found the treasure. They find Bartholomew has been murdered and the gems stolen. Holmes sends Thaddeus for the police and investigates the scene, finding in the dead man's head a poison dart used by the natives of the Andaman Islands. Holmes also finds small footprints on the window sill and the impression of a stump on the floor. Exploring the attic where the treasure was hidden, Holmes realizes the killers came into the house by a window opening onto the roof. Scotland Yard Inspector Atherly Jones (Gilbert Davis) arrives with his men and immediately theorizes that Thaddeus murdered his brother and stole the treasure. When Jones has Thaddeus taken in for questioning, Holmes tells the accused man he can clear him. Examining a rope used to enter the Sholto house, Holmes recognizes it was made by Mordecai Smith (Moore Marriott) and deduces that he helped Small and Meade escape from prison.

He also believes Small plans to leave the country on a steamer. Going to find Smith, Holmes tells Watson to guard Mary. Disguised as an old seaman, Holmes locates the waterfront pub owned by Smith and flirts with his bartender wife (Yarde). He learns from her that her husband is on board his ship, along with Small and Meade. On the vessel, Small gives a bag containing the diamonds to a third accomplice, the grotesque Andaman Islands native Tonga (Togo), who keeps warm by sleeping with snakes. Although Meade informs Small the law is after them because he saw policemen at Mary's florist shop, Small says he will not leave the country until he gets the pearls. Still dressed as the old seaman, Holmes barges into his Baker Street rooms and tells his landlady Mrs. Hudson (Clare Greet) and Jones that he has come for the reward since he can identify the killer. Quickly removing his disguise, Holmes scares the pair and then asks Jones to assist him the next day. Watson asks Mary to go with him to a fun fair to see if she can recognize the tattooed man, since Meade earlier bought flowers at her shop. At the fun fair Mary spies Meade as he gives his spiel to the crowd but he also sees her. Meade informs Small about Mary and as Watson tries to telephone Holmes she is abducted by Meade and Small. Along with Tonga, the crooks take Mary with them as they hire a cab to get to Smith's boat. As he searches for Mary, Watson runs into Holmes, who is disguised as a workman, and they follow the crooks in a police boat. When Smith realizes he cannot outrun the law, he docks at a warehouse where Small takes the pearls away from Mary, who has kept them on her person since the robbery attempt. In a showdown, Holmes shoots Tonga and wounds Small. Holmes scuffles with Small as Watson fights with Meade. Holmes pushes Small into the Thames River, where his wooden leg pulls him under the water. Watson knocks out Meade and he and Holmes rescue Mary. When Jones and his men arrive, Holmes gives him the gems and Smith, and then produces the pearls, which he took from Small, and hands them to Mary. The amused Holmes then watches as Watson proposes to Mary.

The Hollywood Reporter called *The Sign of Four* "one of the more log-

Sherlock Holmes' Greatest, Most Thrilling Adventure!

THE SIGN OF 4

—Plus—
TIM McCOY
—in—
"Fighting For Justice"

Advertisement for *The Sign of Four* (World Wide, 1932).

ical of the Holmes adventures tales," adding, "It has pace, suspense and excitement.... The photography ... has caught the eerie atmosphere to perfection.... And the acting in every role is swell
with more especial tribute due to Arthur Wontner as the immortal Sherlock Holmes and Graham
Soutten as the vindictive Jonathan Small.... This is good, clean, entertainment all the way through,
and what's even better, it's entertainment for the whole family." *The New York Times* praised
Wontner as Holmes ("an excellent interpretation") but added, "The film unfortunately has several
serious defects. The lighting is frequently poor and the photography lacks the clarity and depth
of the Hollywood product. Perhaps more disconcerting is the fact that the dialogue, as spoken
by the all–British cast, is often unintelligible to American ears.... [It] should have been a better
than average piece of detective melodrama except for its technical lapses." *Photoplay* declared,
"You'll enjoy every minute of this famous story played excellently by an all–English cast. Arthur
Wontner makes a perfect Holmes." *Variety* panned its "conspicuously poor lighting" and "spotty
recording," adding, "There is also faulty direction, permitting principals in several situations to
garble and literally gargle their diction by too rapid recitation of lines." On the other hand the
reviewer felt it "is still the best of the Doyle series produced overseas." *The Film Daily* called *The
Sign of Four* "one of the finest detective mysteries we have ever seen screened ... with Wontner
giving a brilliant performance." *The Motion Picture Herald* declared, "A Sherlock Holmes splendidly portrayed. Arthur Wontner is the Sherlock of Arthur Conan Doyle to the life, and the
audience cannot help but be impressed by the characterization." *The Salt Lake* (Utah) *Tribune*
said the feature "is crammed with suspense and thrilling action." *The Kingsport* (Tennessee) *Times*
termed it "an elaborate picturization."

Harry Benham portrayed Sherlock Holmes in the first screen adaptation of *The Sign of
Four*, also called *Sherlock Holmes Solves the Sign of Four* (1913), a two-reeler for Thanhouser, and
Eille Norwood tackled the role in a 1923 feature for the British company Stoll. It was one of 45
shorts and two features in which Norwood played Holmes between 1921 and 1923. Ian Richardson was a very fine Holmes in the excellent 1983 production of the story made in Great Britain
by Mapleton Films. The same year the Soviet Union's Lenfilm Studio produced a version of the
tale, *Sokrovischa Agry* (The Treasure of Agra), with Vasili Livanov as Holmes. Peter O'Toole did
the voice of Holmes in the Pacific Arts animated short feature *Sherlock Holmes and The Sign of
Four* in 1984. In 1987, England's Granada Television/ITV telecast a version starring Jeremy Brett,
and in 1991 Charlton Heston was Holmes in *The Crucifer of Blood*, a re-working of the story
which turned the most innocent person from the original work into a murderous fiend. Matt
Frewer portrayed Holmes in the 2001 television feature *The Sign of Four* for Hallmark Entertainment.

Sinbad the Sailor (1947; 116 minutes; Color)

PRODUCER: Stephen Ames. DIRECTOR: Richard Wallace. SCREENPLAY: John Twist. STORY: John Twist
& George Worthing Yates. PHOTOGRAPHY: George Barnes. EDITOR: Frank Doyle. MUSIC: Roy Webb.
MUSIC DIRECTOR: C. Bakaleinikoff. MUSIC ORCHESTRATOR: Gil Grau. ART DIRECTORS: Albert
D'Agostino & Carroll Clark. SOUND: Clem Portman & John E. Tribby. SET DECORATIONS: Darrell Silvera
& Claude Carpenter. SPECIAL EFFECTS: Vernon L. Walker & Harold E. Wellman. MAKEUP: Gordon Bau.
MEN'S COSTUMES: Dwight Franklin. GOWNS: Edward Stevenson. PRODUCTION ASSISTANT: Edward
Killy. EDITORIAL SUPERVISOR: Sherman Todd. MARINE TECHNICAL ADVISOR: Capt. Fred E. Ellis.
TECHNICOLOR COLOR DIRECTOR: Natalie Kalmus. ASSOCIATE TECHNICOLOR COLOR DIRECTOR:
Morgan Padelford. ASSISTANT DIRECTOR: Lloyd Richards.
CAST: Douglas Fairbanks, Jr. (Sinbad/Prince Ahmed), Maureen O'Hara (Shireen), Walter Slezak
(Melik/Jamal), Anthony Quinn (Emir of Daibul), George Tobias (Abbu), Jane Greer (Pirouze), Mike
Mazurki (Yusuf), Sheldon Leonard (Auctioneer), Alan Napier (Aga), John Miljan (Moga), Barry Mitchell

[Brad Dexter] (Muallin), Cy Kendall (Hassan-Ben-Hassan), Charles Stevens (Ruri), Nick Thompson (Street Beggar), Charles Soldani, Chuck Hamilton, Mikandor Doraff, Joe Garcia (Merchants), Billy Bletcher (Auction Crier), Hugh Prosser (Guard Captain), Louis Jean Heydt (Mercenary), Paul Guilfoyle (Camel Drover), Harry Harvey (Execution Crier), George Lloyd (Lancer Guard), Phil Warren, George Chandler, Ben Welden (Commoners), Lida Durova (Slave), Dolores Castelli, Milly Reauclaire, Teri Toy, Joan Webster, Leslie Charles, Norma Brown, Ann Cameron, Geraldine Sutter, Angela Gregg, Amy Cordoni Leialoha, Florita Romero, Helen Tracy, Ona Chavers, Barbara McLean, Patty McLean, Coletta Holmgren, Anna Marie Walters, Bea Narvey, Nancy Monegan (Wives), Vonne Lester, Jean Lind, Mary Bradley, Norma Creiger (Dancing Girls), Ira Buch Woods (Eunuch), Lee Elson, Dennis Waters, Bill Shannon (Officers), Bruce Brewster, Joe Dixon, Eddy Hart, Wade Crosby, Gordon Clark (Soldiers), Al Murphy (Tiller Man), Dave Kashner (Overseer), Max Wagner (Overseer's Assistant), Glenn Strange (Galley Overseer), Norbert Schiller (Timekeeper), Bill Sunholm (Oarsman), Eddie Abdo (Chanter), Stanley Doering (Archer), Don Avalier (Ship Officer).

In an effort to emulate the swashbuckling success of his famous father, Douglas Fairbanks, Jr., starred in the title role of *Sinbad the Sailor*, which RKO Radio issued theatrically early in 1947. Filmed in beautiful Technicolor, this overlong adventure fantasy nicely showcases its stars, including the gorgeous Maureen O'Hara and villains Walter Slezak and Anthony Quinn. Moving along at a fair clip, the film is pictorially satisfying but its plot is mundane and it certainly cannot be compared to the top-notch silent-era Fairbanks Sr. vehicles *The Mark of Zorro* (1920), *Robin Hood* (1922), *The Thief of Bagdad* (1924) and *The Black Pirate* (1926). For fantasy films fans, *Sinbad the Sailor* has little to offer other than a baggala, or ship, and a medallion, both of which are supposed to be cursed. The cast, settings, photography, music and Technicolor are all excellent. At various times called *The Adventures of Sinbad the Sailor*, *Strange Adventures of Sinbad the Sailor* and *The Strange Adventures of Sinbad* during production, the film cost nearly $2.5 million and ended up making a slight profit.

In ancient Persia, adventurer Sinbad (Fairbanks) tells the story of finding a vessel near the port of Basra, with all the crew dead after being poisoned. He locates a map on the ship that appears to show the island of Deryabar, where Alexander the Great supposedly kept his fabulous treasure. He also finds a stained glass window that pictures an island scene, the same as on a medallion he received when he was small. Sinbad thinks he might be the vanished ruler of the island, Prince Ahmed. While Sinbad is planning to sail to Deryabar, the map is stolen and the law says the ship he found must be auctioned. Hoping to discourage other bidders, Sinbad spreads the rumor that the vessel is cursed but a veiled woman bids anyway. Winning the ship, Sinbad pays for it with coin taken from the auctioneer (Sheldon Leonard) by his sidekick Abbu (George Tobias). The woman invites Sinbad to her home and he goes not knowing she is Shireen (O'Hara), consort of the Emir of Daibul (Quinn). Shireen assumes Sinbad is Prince Ahmed and he thinks her interest in the ship means she knows the route to Deryabar. Sinbad uses his charms to melt the heart of Shireen and she tells him not to pursue the treasure. When someone tries to stab Sinbad, he is able to thwart the effort; the attacker's scimitar has the name of criminal Jamal engraved on it. The next day Sinbad and his crew sail for Deryabar and he becomes aware that Shireen is ahead of him on a ship, powered by slaves. Although Mongol Melik (Slezak), his barber, warns Sinbad not to follow Shireen, Sinbad continues on a course that leads to the palace of the Emir of Daibul. Sinbad locates Shireen's quarters and after an argument, she calls the guards. Captured and brought to the emir, who also thinks Sinbad is Prince Ahmed, Sinbad conjures a trick with a lamp to abduct Shireen and return to his ship. Both Sinbad and Shireen realize that neither knows the way to Deryabar and he reveals to her his real identity. As Shireen resents Sinbad's condescending attitude toward her, Melik says he will guide the ship to Deryabar, since he memorized part of the map when he saw it in Daibul. The emir follows with his men. While

Douglas Fairbanks, Jr., Maureen O'Hara and Anthony Quinn in *Sinbad the Sailor* (1947).

Sinbad's ship is lost in a fog, a traitor sets fire to it. In a fight, Sinbad is knocked out and Shireen steals his medallion, which she believes is cursed, and hands it over to the emir. When the emir learns that Melik knows the way to Deryabar, he tries to beat the information out of him and plans to make Shireen watch Sinbad suffer a slow death. Sinbad saves himself with the scimitar and tells the emir to return his medallion. Melik announces he is really Jamal, with Sinbad again being captured as the ship nears Deryabar. On the island, Sinbad, Shireen, Melik and the emir find an old man, Aga (Alan Napier), who says he is the father of Prince Ahmed. When Sinbad reveals the medallion to Aga, the old man says that years before he left his young son with sailors so that he wouldn't be captured by looters. Aga claims the ship belonged to a pretender and that Alexander's treasure is only imagined. Melik says he will kill Sinbad unless Aga reveals the treasure's location. Sinbad claims he found the medallion in a bazaar and he and the emir make Melik drink from a vial they believe houses the poison that killed the first crewmen. The drink does not faze Melik so Aga tells him the location of the treasure and proclaims Sinbad to be his son. The emir and Melik enjoy their newfound wealth as Sinbad and Shireen, who have fallen in love, escape from the island. The delayed poison kills Melik, and the emir dies when the slaves on his boat shoot off a fire bomb. After revealing some of the treasure from Deryabar, Sinbad leaves with Shireen for a new adventure.

    The New York World-Telegram said *Sinbad the Sailor* was "told with a relish for excitement and laughter." *The New York Daily News* declared, "Artistically done up to delight the eyes, if little else.... Should appeal to the young folk." *The New York Herald Tribune* called the feature a "fanciful hodgepodge of costumed panoply which has less genuine excitement than a horse opera.... Escapist nonsense embellished with lively incidents galore." "To audiences in a mood for a fairy tale, told in lavish, Technicolorful detail, the acrobatics, adventures and amours of the seagoing gent out of Arabian Nights can supply two hours of diverting entertainment," opined *Boxoffice*. Bosley Crowther in *The New York Times* complained, "The plot is too thick for us— and we rather suspect that it will baffle even more analytic minds. As a consequence, the usually desirable element of dramatic suspense is virtually zero in this powwow, and the film's fascination depends on the occasional exhibitions of Mr. Fairbanks or the splashy costumes and sets." *PM* wrote, "The Hollywood Sinbad is completely earthbound.... It is full of highflown, overstuffed language.... The action also flops.... The adventures RKO have given Sinbad are pretty common- place." *The Film Daily* wrote, "Douglas Fairbanks Jr. has a fine romp in this pleasant fantasy.... Embroidered into the story is a garish, colorful, mystic, gay and slightly overplayed fantasy derived from legend and fashioned into a pleasantry."

Eight years after *Sinbad the Sailor*, RKO released a semi-sequel, *Son of Sinbad* (q.v.).

Snow White and the Seven Dwarfs (1938; 83 minutes; Color)

PRODUCER: Walt Disney. SUPERVISING DIRECTOR: David Hand. SEQUENCE DIRECTORS: Perce Pearce, Larry Morey, Bill Cottrell, Wilfred Jackson & Ben Sharpsteen. SCREENPLAY: Ted Sears, Richard Creedon, Otto Englander, Dick Rickard, Earl Hurd, Merrill De Maris, Dorothy Ann Blank & Webb Smith, from *Grimm's Fairy Tales* by Jacob Grimm & Wilhelm Grimm. MUSIC: Frank Churchill, Paul Smith & Leigh Harline. SONGS: Frank Churchill, Larry Morey & Paul Smith. ART DIRECTORS: Kenneth Anderson, Charles Philippi, Hugh Hennesy, Terrell Stapp, McLaren Stewart, Harold Miles, Tom Codrick, Gustaf Tenggren, Kendall O'Connor & Hazel Sewell. CHARACTER DESIGNERS: Albert Hurter & Joe Grant. SUPERVISING ANIMATORS: Norman Ferguson, Fred Moore, Hamilton Luske & Vladimir Tytla. ANIMA- TORS: Frank Thomas, Dick Lundy, Arthur Babbitt, Eric Larson, Milton Kahl, Robert Stokes, James Algar, Al Eugster, Cy Young, Joshua Meador, Ugo D'Orsi, George Rowely, Les Clark, Fred Spencer, Bill Roberts, Bernard Garbutt, Grim Natwick, Jack Campbell, Marvin Woodward, James Culhane, Stan Quackenbush, Ward Kimball, Wolfgang Reitherman, Robert Martsch. BACKGROUNDS: Samuel Armstrong, Migue Nel- son, Merle Cox, Claude Coats, Phil Dike, Ray Lockrem & Maurice Noble. LIVE ACTION MODELS: Eddie Collins, Marge [Champion] Belcher & Louis Hightower.

VOICE CAST: Adriana Caselotti (Snow White), Lucille La Verne (Queen/Witch), Billy Gilbert (Sneezy), Otis Harlan (Happy), Eddie Collins (Dopey), Pinto Colvig (Grumpy/Sleepy), Harry Stockwell (Prince), Moroni Olsen (Magic Mirror), Zeke Clements (Bashful), Roy Atwell (Doc), Stuart Buchanan (Huntsman Humbert), James MacDonald, The Fraunfelder Family (Yodelers), Marion Darlington, Pury Pullen (Birds).

Walt Disney's first feature film and the first animated feature-length movie, *Snow White and the Seven Dwarfs* was in production from 1934 to late in 1937 with an eventual cost of nearly $1.5 million. Over 30 animators plus 269 associates worked on the production, which also required 65 effects animators, 20 layout artists and 25 water color background artists. For the first time Disney used live action performers in full costume who were filmed for the animators to study. Some of the dwarfs' mannerisms and personalities were patterned after the performers who did their voices. Sneezy was voiced by Billy Gilbert, famous for his elongated comedy sneeze, while squat Dopey was modeled after his voice actor, Eddie Collins, as was the jolly, round Happy, modeled after Otis Harlan who provided his voice. Bashful's voice was done by country music singer-songwriter Zeke Clements, who got the job after Jay C. Flippen withdrew to appear on Broadway. The Witch was voiced by Lucille La Verne and her characteristics were based on the actress' performance in *A Tale of Two Cities* (1935). Its very scary horrific aspects include the evil queen (voice of La Verne), her Magic Mirror (voice of Moroni Olsen) and her transformation into the Witch. Especially well done are the visually exciting scenes when the dwarfs give chase to the Witch through a terrifying thunderstorm and her demise after being shadowed by two vultures. Some of the film's scenes were considered so horrifying that the British Board of Film Censors gave it a rating which required that children could only view it with adult accompaniment.

Snow White and the Seven Dwarfs premiered late in 1937 and was nationally distributed early the next year by RKO. The feature proved to be very successful, netting RKO $8.5 million on its first release. The studio reissued it in 1944 and 1952. It got five more theatrical re-releases by Disney's Buena Vista Pictures between 1958 and 1987. The Academy of Motion Picture Arts and Sciences gave Walt Disney a special award for the feature and *The Film Daily* named it one of the ten best movies of 1938. An article in the *Hollywood* (California) *Citizen News* (January 31, 1938) stated that foreign-language editions were being made in Dutch, French, German, Italian, Norwegian and Swedish. A radio version of "Snow White and the Seven Dwarfs," done by Walt Disney Productions, aired on CBS' *Lux Radio Theatre* on December 26, 1938. Eight songs were performed in the film, the most popular being "Some Day My Prince Will Come," "Heigh Ho, Heigh Ho, It's Off to Work We Go" and "Whistle While You Work." The film's soundtrack was issued on long-playing albums by Disneyland Records in 1957 (WDL-4005), 1962 (DQ-1201) and 1980 (3101) and on Disney's Buena Vista Records (102) in 1975.

A groundbreaking movie, *Snow White and the Seven Dwarfs* set the stage for the multitude of feature-length animated movies that have followed, including many Disney productions released by RKO into 1955. Filled with excellent animation and beautiful color, the movie is rightfully considered a classic. Martin Goodman summed up the movie's appeal in *The Animated Movie Guide* (2005): "[It] contains countless laughs, joys, and tears and its impact remains just as powerful nearly 70 years after it was made. The movie is an emotional and artistic experience rarely equaled in animation's history, and its many accolades are well deserved."

A haughty, evil Queen (voice of La Verne) daily asks her Magic Mirror (voice of Olsen) who is fairest one of all and she is always told it is herself. One day the Mirror says Snow White (voice of Adriana Caselotti) is the most fair. Snow White is the Queen's stepdaughter and is kept as a drudge, although she dreams of meeting a prince and being taken away from her life of hard work. A handsome prince (voice of Harry Stockwell) makes himself known to Snow White and says he will return for her. Enraged because she has been bested by Snow White, the Queen orders her huntsman Humbert (voice of Stuart Buchanan) to take the girl into the forest and kill her; to prove he carried out her orders, he is to bring back the her heart. Once they are in the forest, Humbert cannot bring himself to kill Snow White and tells her to run away. He returns to the Queen with a pig's heart, claiming he carried out her command. Snow White becomes frightened in the deep forest by all its eyes and shadows in the night. She falls asleep from exhaustion and awakens the next morning to find herself surrounded by a legion of friendly animals and birds. They take her to a cottage which she finds filthy and rundown. Since it appears that seven children reside in the abode, she has the birds and animals help her clean the place and begin making dinner. Exhausted again, Snow White falls asleep in the large bedroom. The owners of the cottage are seven dwarfs who are away working in their diamond mine. At quitting time they return home and, seeing the place clean, they think someone has come to harm them. When they see a figure sleeping under a sheet on a bed, they think it is a monster and plan to kill it but Snow White suddenly wakes up. Realizing that the cottage is inhabited by dwarfs and not children, she guesses their names: Doc (voice of Roy Atwell), Bashful (voice of Clements), Dopey (voice of Collins), Sneezy (voice of Gilbert), Happy (voice of Harlan), Sleepy (voice of Pinto Colvig) and Grumpy (voice of Colvig). She soon wins them over—all except Grumpy, who does not like females. Snow White offers to stay in the cottage and cook and clean for the dwarfs and they accept. Before going off to work the next day the dwarfs warn Snow White to beware the evil Queen. They do not know the Queen has used her magic powers to transform herself into the Witch. The Witch concocts a poisoned apple which she plans to give Snow White in order to kill her (the Magic Mirror has told her that Snow White still lives). The only antidote for the poison is a first kiss from a prince. The Witch takes the apple to the cottage and convinces Snow White to make a wish on it and then take a bite. The birds and animals sense that something is not right and go for the dwarfs, who realize the Witch has come to harm Snow White. As they run to their cottage to save the girl, Snow White dies. Seeing the dwarfs are after her, the Witch runs away as a terrible thunderstorm commences. After a long chase up a rocky cliff, the Witch

Advertisement for *Snow White and the Seven Dwarfs* (1938).

tries to kill the dwarfs by rolling a boulder down on them but the ledge on which she is standing gives way and she falls into a gorge with the boulder crushing her. The dwarfs mourn Snow White but cannot bring themselves to bury her. They build a coffin of gold and glass and keep a constant vigil. One day the prince hears about Snow White, opens the coffin and kisses her. Snow White returns to life and, after kissing the dwarfs farewell, she rides away with the prince to live happily ever after.

Critical appraisal of *Snow White and the Seven Dwarfs* was ecstatic. *Photoplay* stated, "Here, truly, is something absolutely new in the amusement world. That Walt Disney is a genius in fantasy and drawing needs no restatement here, but in *Snow White and the Seven Dwarfs* he has attempted his most ambitious achievement and succeeds marvelously as he has in the past with *Mickey Mouse* and *Donald Duck* and all the Silly Symphonies.... He is still greatest when he deals with animals and dwarfs, yet never once does the happy make-believe mood of this seven-reel production fail to beguile you." *Stage* wrote, "Mr. Disney's dream has come true. With an incredible amount of labor, money and artistry, he has produced a ninety-minute respite from all reality." "The tale is entrancing," announced *The New Yorker,* while *Cue* wrote, "Disney reaches new heights in imaginative, pictorial, dramatic, color cartoons." *The Film Daily* enthused, "Here is a picture so masterfully produced and of much unusual entertainment value that it will make motion picture history. A sure-fire sensation.... It has such clever and human touches that it never lags through its 80 minutes." *Variety* reported, "There has never been anything in theaters quite like Walt Disney's *Snow White and the Seven Dwarfs* ... an absorbingly interesting and, at times, thrilling entertainment. So perfect is the illusion, so tender the romance and fantasy, so emotional are certain portions when the acting of the characters strikes a depth comparable to the sincerity of human players, that the film approaches real greatness." *Scholastic* termed it "a movie masterpiece."

At the time of its release, there was some speculation that animation might take over the feature film field. W.E. Oliver wrote in the *Los Angeles Evening Herald and Examiner* (December 18, 1937), "If this first full-length Disney production plants a new milestone in the history of the screen industry, as many anticipate, the complete monarchy of flesh and blood stars may be invaded by animated characters made up of paint and imagination. The high salaries and fan monopoly enjoyed by the Gables, Henies, Garbos, Taylors, Lombards, Temples and Withers may even be alarmingly infringed on."

So This Is Washington (1943; 64 minutes)

PRODUCERS: Ben Hersh & Jack William Votion. DIRECTOR: Ray McCarey. SCREENPLAY: Leonard Praskins & Roswell Rogers. STORY: Roswell Rogers & Edward James. PHOTOGRAPHY: Harry Wild. EDITOR: Duncan Mansfield. MUSIC DIRECTOR: Lud Gluskin. ART DIRECTOR: Hans Peters. SOUND: Percy Townsend. SET DECORATIONS: Ben Berk. ASSISTANT DIRECTOR: Ruby Rosenberg.

CAST: Chester Lauck (Lum Edwards), Norris Goff (Abner Peabody), Alan Mowbray (Chester W. Marshall), Mildred Coles (Jane Nestor), Roger Clark (Robert Blevins), Sarah Padden (Aunt Charity Speers), Matt McHugh (Department Store Night Watchman), Minerva Urecal (Mrs. Pomeroy), Jimmie Dodd (Earl), Heinie Conklin (Steve Reynolds), Dan Duncan (Grandpappy Speers), Barbara Pepper (Taxi Driver Betty), Chester Conklin (Pocket Machine Gun Inventor), Lloyd Ingraham (Parachute Inventor), Wilbur Mack (Memory Tablets Inventor), Ben Taggart (Senator Vickers), Boyd Irwin, Ben Erway (Congressmen), Eddie Kane (Department Store Manager), Cyril Ring, Brooks Benedict (Hotel Desk Clerks), Jack Rice (Golf Hotel Desk Clerk), Jack Gargan (Newsman).

So This Is Washington, released in the late summer of 1943, was the fourth of six feature films RKO did with Jack William Votion Productions based on the rural characters "Lum 'n Abner," stars of a popular radio series broadcast from 1931 to 1954 and starring Chester Lauck and Norris Goff. It was topical in its presentation of the boys' patriot spirit, in this case their supposed inventing of a type of synthetic rubber for the Allied cause. While most of the action takes place in the nation's capital, the first and last parts of the feature are set in Pine Ridge, Arkansas, where Lum and Abner are proprietors of the Jot-Em-Down Store and the proceedings include a number of rustic characters, including a lovable aunt (Sarah Padden), a lazy hick (Jimmie Dodd), a dotty old man (Dan Duncan) and an uppity neighbor (Minerva Urecal). The half-dozen Lum 'n Abner features proved profitable with the studio continuing on the bandwagon of comedy radio characters in movies, including the Great Gildersleeve and Scattergood Baines.

In the small Arkansas town of Pine Ridge, longtime friends Lum Edwards (Lauck) and Abner Peabody (Goff) run the Jot-Em-Down Store with the international conflict also making it Section Headquarters with the boys operating as the area's air raid wardens, tire inspectors, draft board and ration board. After listening to Chester W. Marshall (Alan Mowbray), the head of the nation's Civilian Aid in War Effort Board, begging the common man to contribute to the war effort, Abner works in the store's backroom trying to develop synthetic licorice. Lum scoffs at his efforts until he realizes the result is actually synthetic rubber and the boys head to Washington to give Marshall the formula. Once there, they find there is no place to stay and end up on a park bench. A stranger (Matt McHugh) offers to rent them a room for eight dollars a night. The next day they wake up in a department store display window and are nearly thrown out by the manager (Eddie Kane) when they meet Robert Blevins (Roger Clark), a young man from Pine Ridge who writes a column for the *Washington Whirligig* that is critical of Marshall, although he is in love with the bureaucrat's pretty secretary, Jane Nestor (Mildred Coles). Robert offers to let Lum and Abner stay at his place. After viewing such sites as the Capitol building and the Lincoln and Washington monuments, the boys are back on the park bench since Robert is unable to finagle them an appointment with Marshall. There they overhear a Senator (Ben Taggart) discussing a local problem to which Lum gives him the answer. Soon members of Congress are asking the boys for advice and they become a sensation. When Marshall shows up to see them, they do not know his identity and give him the brush as they head to his office for an appointment. Once they realize they are talking to Marshall, Lum and Abner present the synthetic rubber invention and he calls a press conference to show off the discovery and as well as getting even with the newspapers for ridiculing him. During the demonstration Abner bumps his head, loses his memory and thinks he is a hep cat named Buster V. Davenport. The press mocks Marshall even further as a result and his superiors give him one week to get the formula or be fired. Lum and Abner, accompanied by Marshall, take the train back to Pine Ridge in hopes that Abner will regain his memory but he fails to recognize old friends like Aunt Charity Speers (Padden) and her father, Grandpappy (Duncan), who ran the store in their absence, and station master Steve Reynolds (Heinie Conklin). As a final resort Lum agrees to hit Abner with a mallet in hopes of bringing back his memory but instead he strikes Marshall. Abner bumps his head on a shelf and returns to his senses just as Jane shows up saying that scientists have analyzed Abner's formula and proved it is a synthetic asphalt that can be used for airplane landing fields. Lum and Abner are rewarded with government jobs, Lum as a dollar-a-year advisor on farm problems and Abner his assistant with a $10,000 annual salary. As Robert and Jane find romance, Marshall is convinced he is Buster V. Davenport.

The slight sci-fi angle of *So This Is Washington* is Abner's invention of a supposed synthetic rubber compound. Otherwise the production is a pleasant comedy, one sure to please fans of the radio comedians. It also takes a deft jab at the nation's capital, including its housing shortage and protocol. The latter apparently got RKO in some hot water with the government, according to Michael H. Price and John Wooley in *Forgotten Horrors 3!* (2003): "[T]he War Department's Office of Censorship socked RKO with a Do Not Export order—complaining that the picture poked fun at rationing, depicted members of Congress as buffoons and razzed a prominent Army physician."

While the censors may not have been happy, the public took to the production as noted in the February 11, 1944, issue of the *Big Spring* (Texas) *Herald*: "Lum and Abner's latest picture ... has done something none of their three others did. It hit first-run theaters, it clicked in the cities as well as in the villages and small towns. In Hollywood that's success." According to the *Burlington* (North Carolina) *Daily Times* (December 11, 1943), "[T]he new film deals with comedy, avoids any serious vein at all. The result is a laugh fest of homespun humor and riotous situation gags played against the contrasting hectic, cosmopolitan atmosphere of Washington D.C." *Boxoffice* stated, "On the air these men seem real, but in films the gag men straining for laughs make caricatures of them at times. This is one of those times." *Photoplay* disagreed: "Lum and Abner have finally hit their movie stride in this satiric comedy of current life in Washington. The gags are timely and hilarious." *The Film Daily* considered it "an improvement over other Lum and Abner pictures" and "less exasperating" than the team's earlier offerings. The reviewer concluded, "*So This Is Washington* is still corn but it's a superior grade of corn. Some of the stuff in fact is really good."

So This Is Washington premiered in the Arkansas town of Walters, which changed its name to Pine Ridge in honor of the radio program. Since no building in the area was large enough to house the influx of visitors, the event was held in a Chautauqua tent.

The Son of Kong (1933; 69 minutes)

EXECUTIVE PRODUCER: Merian C. Cooper. ASSOCIATE PRODUCER: Archie Marshek. DIRECTOR: Ernest B. Schoedsack. STORY & SCREENPLAY: Ruth Rose. PHOTOGRAPHY: Eddie Linden, J.O. Taylor & Vernon L. Walker. EDITOR: Ted Cheesman. MUSIC: Max Steiner. ART TECHNICIANS: Byron L. Crabbe & Mario Larrinaga. SOUND: Earl A. Wolcott. SOUND EFFECTS: Murray Spivack. SETTINGS: Van Nest Polglase & Al Herman. CHIEF TECHNICIAN: Willis H. O'Brien. TECHNICIANS: Marcel Delgado, E.B. Gibson, Fred Reese, Carroll Shepphird & W.G. White.

CAST: Robert Armstrong (Carl Denham), Helen Mack (Helene Peterson), Frank Reicher (Captain Englehorn), John Marston (Nils Helstrom), Victor Wong (Charlie), Ed Brady (Red), Lee Kohlmar (Process Server Mickey), Clarence Wilson (Peterson), Katherine Clare Ward (Mrs. Hudson), Gertrude Short (Reporter), Gertrude Sutton (Scrubwoman), James B. Leong (Chinese Trader), Noble Johnson (Native Chief), Steve Clemento (Witch Doctor), Frank O'Connor (Process Server), Harry Tenbrook, Constantine Romanoff, Oscar "Dutch" Hendrian, Clayde Peyton, Jack Richardson, Frank Mills, Homer Watson, Tex Higginson, Gene Rossi, Cy Clegg, Ken Kuntz, J. Goff, F. Garrety, Harry Cornbleth (Crewmen), Ed Lenegan (Messenger), Ed Rochelle (Newsboy), Sam Levine (Fruit Peddler), Jimmy Leon (Bartender), Nathan Curry (Native).

Realizing the box office potential of *King Kong* (q.v.) even before its March 1933 release, RKO executives assigned producers Merian C. Cooper and Ernest B. Schoedsack to make a sequel tentatively titled *Jamboree*. Production was halted in the spring so Schoedsack could direct Robert Armstrong in *A Blind Adventure* (1933), and resumed once that feature was completed. Schoedsack's wife Ruth Rose, who co-scripted *King Kong*, wrote the story and screenplay for the sequel which recast Armstrong as Carl Denham, along with Frank Reicher as Captain Englehorn and Victor Wong as Charlie the ship's cook, from the original. Noble Johnson and Steve Clemento, as Skull Island's native chief and witch doctor, are also back briefly in the sequel. The new offering is a much lighter effort than the original, with the return to Skull Island not taking place until nearly 40 minutes into the proceedings. An ancient temple and the earthquake destruction of the island are its photographic highlights; a quartet of prehistoric animal scenes are well done. Willis H. O'Brien animated Marcel Delgado's new creations, a giant bear, a large walking reptile and a sea serpent, while reusing a stegosaurus model originally used from *King Kong* (the footage was cut from *Kong*). Max Steiner again did the music score, although it in no way compares with his fantastic work on the original. The picturesque exteriors were filmed on Santa Catalina Island. The title character is a serio-comic creature, fierce in battle but benign toward humans. In fact, the script makes it appear that Little Kong adopts Carl Denham to replace the father the showman wrested away from Skull Island.

Radio Pictures released *The Son of Kong* late in 1933 and today it is not highly regarded. Had *King Kong* never been made, the production would stand as one of the better monster movies of the 1930s but in comparison to his dad, Little Kong comes off second best by far. Still the feature was a financial success, grossing over $600,000 on a $269,000 investment.

Following the destruction wrought by the giant ape Kong in New York City, filmmaker Carl Denham (Armstrong) is beset by reporters, lawsuits and process servers. Staying in a seedy boarding house, Denham says he wishes he had left Kong on Skull Island. Charlie (Wong), the cook on the ship that brought Kong to Gotham, arrives with a message for Denham from the its captain, Englehorn (Reicher). With the help of friendly process server Mickey (Lee Kohlmar), Denham manages to sneak away to the ship, the *Venture*, but Mickey soon returns with the news that the grand jury is going to indict Denham. Englehorn suggests to Denham they partner in

John Marston, Robert Armstrong and Helen Mack in *The Son of Kong* **(1933).**

hauling freight in the East Indies and they soon set sail. After finding little business in several ports they stop at Dakang where they attend a tatty animal act called Peterson's Famous International Show. When pretty Helene Peterson (Helen Mack) sings "Runaway Blues," Denham is attracted to her and tells Englehorn she has personality. That night Helene's alcoholic father, Peterson (Clarence Wilson), drinks with outcast sea captain Nils Helstrom (John Marston), who is being investigated over the loss of his last ship. The two get into a fight with Helstrom hitting Peterson with a bottle. In falling, Peterson knocks over a lantern, setting his show tent on fire. Helstrom runs away as Helene sets the animals free, pulls her father from the fire and saves a few possessions before the tent is consumed. Peterson dies from his injuries and the next day Helene unsuccessfully tries to recapture their act's monkeys. Denham meets Helene, who tells him about the fire. When Helene finds Helstrom, she accuses him of killing her father and says she is going to the magistrate. Helstrom sees Denham in a bar and Denham informs Englehorn it was Helstrom who gave him the map to Kong's island. Helstrom tells them he lost his last ship on a reef bank and cannot get work. He also asks Denham if he found the treasure on Kong's island. The three men agree to search for it but before he leaves, Denham gives Helene money to get passage back to the States. During the trip, Englehorn tells Denham he thinks Helstrom is getting too friendly with the crew, unaware that Helstrom is trying to incite them to mutiny so he can take over the ship. Charlie finds stowaway Helene and she and Helstrom are unhappy to see each other. Helstrom warns Helene to keep quiet about her father's death. When they reach Skull Island, the crew led by Red (Ed Brady), take over the ship and force Denham, Helene and Englehorn into a life boat. Charlie goes with them, clandestinely bringing two rifles. When Helstrom tries to take command, the mutineers throw him in the water and the outcasts reluctantly take him aboard their lifeboat. Reaching shore, Denham, Helene, Englehorn and Helstrom are ordered off the island by the chief (Johnson) and witch doctor (Clemento) who are angry over the destruction and loss of life caused by Kong. They search for another landing place and locate a small inlet. Denham searches a narrow passageway, followed by Helene. They find a Little Kong, stuck in quicksand, and Denham pushes down a tree which the ape uses to get free. Finding an ancient temple, Denham and Helene decide to search for the treasure while a stegosaurus chases Englehorn, Helstrom and Charlie into a cave. When a giant bear attacks Denham and Helene, Little Kong comes to their rescue and defeats it in a fight. During the fracas, Little Kong's paw is injured and Denham bandages it for him. The next morning, Englehorn, Helstrom and Charlie are able to get away from the cave as Denham and Helene knock down part of a wall that leads to a gigantic stone idol topped by an enormous jewel. Little Kong retrieves the gem for them but a giant lizard enters the grotto and Little Kong kills it. Englehorn, Helstrom and Charlie find the temple and Helstrom is surprised to learn about the treasure since he had lied about its existence. When he sees Little Kong, the frightened Helstrom runs to the lifeboat but is killed by a sea serpent. An earthquake strikes the island as Denham returns to the temple for the treasure. Helene, Englehorn and Charlie make it to the boat and row away as the island begins to sink beneath the sea. On the last bit of land, Little Kong holds up Denham who manages to get into the lifeboat before Little Kong sinks beneath the waves. The four survivors drift for days before being found by a ship. As they return home, Denham and Helene agree to

A giant lizard and King Kong's offspring do battle as Robert Armstrong and Helen Mack watch in *The Son of Kong* (1933).

give one-third of the treasure each to Englehorn and Charlie, and the other third for themselves, since they have fallen in love.

Boxoffice called *The Son of Kong* "a mere splinter off the old block.... The film has a few mechanical thrills, and is spiced with hokum." *Motion Picture Daily* wrote, "The story lags up to the last two reels. It is mildly entertaining and probably will find better results with children than adults. The mechanics in operating the colossal creatures are well handled, even the shots showing Kong making goo-goo eyes." *The New Movie Magazine* liked Little Kong better than his old man: "*Son of Kong* is a far, far better picture from the point of view of the general public.... It is sheer melodrama of the wildest type, but where *King Kong* was pure horror, *The Son of Kong* offers excitement and thrills with only those who deserve it meeting their just deserts." *Variety* termed the sequel "fair entertainment," adding, "Same technical advantages which put *King Kong* over as a novelty smash were dished up for the sequel, the same sets and mechanical apparatus obviously playing a repeat. But the punch is no longer there, and in this rehash the same qualities that thrilled on the first trip are likely to impress now as being too much for anybody to swallow." *The New York Herald-Tribune* noted, "If you liked *King Kong*, doubtless you will like his son. The picture is full of thrills, the comic, but very little sense." *The New York Journal* declared, "It's all pretty absurd, but absurdity of this sort makes for amusing entertainment, since it isn't planned to be taken seriously. *Son of Kong* makes no attempt to be a hair-raiser." *The New York Mirror* felt Little Kong "a captivating little monster." "This sequel doesn't begin to come up to the level of the first Kong picture, not in rapidity of action, drama, suspense or daring technical achievement," assessed *The New York Sun*. *The New York Times* termed *Son of Kong* "low melodrama with a number of laughs that are loud and satisfying, although the comical intent of the producers is open to argument.... [It] is not the masterpiece of mechanical ingenuity that *King Kong* was." *The New York World-Telegram* opined, "It is pretty silly and a bad movie, really, but if you accept it for what it is—either a conscious or unconscious burlesque of its predecessor—it will afford you some gleeful moments."

Over the years a misconception about *The Son of Kong* has persisted in some quarters: that it was called *Jamboree* to hide the fact it was a sequel to *King Kong*. If this is true, the charade was short-lived for in the May 4, 1933, issue of *The Hollywood Reporter* an item on *Jamboree* notes it "is a sequel to *King Kong*." This was eight months prior to the film's release.

Son of Sinbad (1955; 91 minutes; Color)

PRODUCER: Robert Sparks. PRESENTER–EXECUTIVE PRODUCER: Howard Hughes. DIRECTOR: Ted Tetzlaff. SCREENPLAY: Jack Pollexfen & Aubrey Wisberg. PHOTOGRAPHY: William Snyder. EDITORS: Roland Gross & Frederick Knudtson. MUSIC: Victor Young. MUSIC DIRECTOR: C. Bakaleinikoff. ART DIRECTORS: Albert S. D'Agostino & Walter E. Keller. SOUND: Clem Portman & Francis Sarver. SET DECORATIONS: Darrell Silvera & John Sturtevant. COSTUMES: Michael Woulfe. MAKEUP: Mel Berns. HAIR STYLIST: Larry Germain. CHOREOGRAPHER: Olga Lunick. TECHNICOLOR CONSULTANT: James Gooch. ASSISTANT DIRECTOR: James Casey.

CAST: Dale Robertson (Sinbad), Sally Forrest (Ameer), Lili St. Cyr (Nerissa), Vincent Price (Omar Khayyam), Mari Blanchard (Kristina), Leon Askin (Khalif), Jay Novello (Jiddah), Raymond Greenleaf (Simon Aristides), Nejla Ates (Market Dancer), Kalatan (Desert Dancer), Ian MacDonald (Murad), Donald Randolph (Councillor), Larry J. Blake (Samit), Edwina Hazard (Lota), Fred Aldrich (Torturer), John Merton, Woody Strode, George Sherwood, Michael Ross, M.U. Smith (Guards), George Barrows (Khalif's Officer), Marilyn Bonney (Veronica), Janet Comerford (Latisse), Alyce Cronin (Helena), Mary Ann Edwards (Rosine), Maryleen Prentice (Zaza), Joan Pastin (Camilla), Judy Ulian (Dalya), Randy Allen, Nancy Westbrook (Wenches), Joan Jordan (Ghenia), Wayne Berk (Gondra), James Griffith (Arab Guide), Robert Wilke (Musa), Tom Moore, Peter Ortiz (Cutthroats), Virginia Bates, Catherine Cassidy, Sally

Musick, Honey King (Trumpeters), Leonteen Danier, Elaine Dupont, Gilda Fontane, Joy Lee, La Rue Mal-ouf, Anna Navarra, Paula Velnay (Slave Girls), Paul Frees (Mahmud), Bob Hopkins (Slave Auctioneer), Michael Mark (Caravan Merchant), Gus Schilling (Beggar Jaffir), Jack Chefe (Seer), Max Wagner, John George (Market Merchants), Irene Barbour, Irene Boulton, Joy Langstaff, Eileen Maxell, Arline Hunter, Elizabeth Smith, Louise Von Kories, Annabelle Thiele, Claire De Witt, Carolea Cole, Pat D'Arcy, Nancy Dunn, Donna Hall, Ann Ford, Zanne Shaw, Judy Jorell, Betty Sabor, Dee Gee Sparks, Libby Vernon, Evelyn Bernard (Tartar Girls), Kenneth Terrell, Charles Horvath (Killed Tartars), Dawn Oney (Alicia), Frank Mills (Prisoner), Marilyn [Kim] Novak, Joi Lansing, Dolores Michaels, Sue Casey, Bobette Bentley, Joanne Arnold, Bette Arlen, Marjorie Holliday, Carol Brewster, Naura Hayden, Mary Ellen Gleason, Anna Lee Carroll, Chris Fortune, Shirley Buchanan, Laurie Carroll, Jane Easton, Claire De Witt, Gerri Patterson, Keith Kerrigan, Suzanne Alexander, Betty Onge, Nancy Moore, Diana Mumby, Dede Moore, Barbara Lohrman, Doreen Woodbury, Jeanne Shores, Joan Whitney, Mary Langan, Maureen Stephenson, Gloria Watson Charlotte Alpert (Harem Girls), Jeanne Evans, Roxanne Delman, Eleanor Bender, Jonni Paris (Arab Women), Dan Bernaducci (Arab), Diane James (Raider).

Not strictly a sequel to *Sinbad the Sailor* (1947) [q.v.], *Son of Sinbad* was a pet project of executive producer Howard Hughes, the owner of RKO Pictures at the time. It began filming early in 1953 and was done in 3-D without SuperScope but when finally released by RKO in the summer of 1955 it was in flat widescreen. The Breen Office objected to some of the dances and the skimpy costumes worn by the 250+ women in the cast. In fact, some sources claim Hughes made the film in order to give screen time to the multitude of pretty starlets he had under contract. Among the *Son of Sinbad* harem girls are future stars Kim Novak, Dolores Michaels, Joi Lansing and Sue Casey. Prior to its release, the Legion of Decency gave the film a condemned rating but all the hoopla resulted in a box office return of over one million dollars after the picture had been in release for only two months. Besides the suggestive dances and scantily clad females, some quarters objected to the casting of ex-striptease dancer Lili St. Cyr in one of the leading roles.

Son of Sinbad is a tongue-in-cheek takeoff of the Arabian Nights tales with Dale Robertson in the title role and Vincent Price as Omar Khayyam obviously having a good time while the story itself is only passable. Besides the obvious eye candy (the famous Forty Thieves are all female), the production is rather wooden plot-wise and almost completely eschews any fantasy elements. The magic "Open Sesame" to the Forty Thieves' cave is shown as a donkey named Sesame who opens its door and the "Greek fire" weapon is a concoction made up of an alchemist's compounds. The lack of magic carpets and other Arabian Nights lore may be one of the reasons the picture is not particularly appealing.

Poet Omar Khayyam (Price) searches for his friend Sinbad (Robertson), son of the famous gallant, in ancient Bagdad, and locates him near the great palace. A reward has been offered by the Khalif (Leon Askin) for Sinbad's capture but he disobeys Omar's warning and enters the palace, reciting his friend's poems. Sinbad flirts with harem girl Nerissa (St. Cyr) but is turned in by Ameer (Sally Forrest), a slave girl in love with him. Captured by the guards, Sinbad and Omar are to be sentenced along with his childhood friend Kristina (Mari Blanchard) and her father, Simon Aristides (Raymond Greenleaf), who have been accused of theft. The Khalif sentences Sinbad and Omar to death. Jiddah (Jay Novello), the ruler's counsel, advises him to see Tartar leader Tamerlane's ambassador Murad (Ian MacDonald) to avoid an invasion of the city. Murad tells the Khalif the Tartars will soon attack Bagdad. Hoping to save Kristina, Sinbad informs the Khalif that her father can make "Greek fire" to be used against the invaders. While the Khalif refuses to free his prisoners, Simon and Kristina show the Khalif the power of the weapon. To insure their safety, Simon makes sure that Kristina can only reveal its formula when under hypnosis. Jiddah and his cohort Murad secretly listen as the demonstration takes place but they cannot figure out what is used to make the Greek fire. The display is successful and the

Sally Forrest, Jay Novello and Leon Askin in *Son of Sinbad* (1955).

Khalif agrees to set Sinbad and Omar free. That night Kristina tells Ameer she loves Sinbad and asks her to tell him of his release. After doing so, Ameer finds Kristina gone and her father killed. Seeing Kristina and her father's scientific compounds with Murad, Ameer uses a carrier pigeon to send a message before being arrested by Jiddah. When he tortures Ameer about the missive, Jiddah finds her tattooed with a Forty Thieves brand. A group once led by Sinbad's father, the Forty Thieves, is being carried on by their female descendants; Jiddah reckons that Ameer's message was sent to them. When they find out they are to be executed, Sinbad and Omar escape from the dungeon and make their way to the Khalif's quarters where Sinbad offers to return Kristina for their freedom, plus riches and the position of the city's second-in-command. The Khalif goes along with the demands not knowing Jiddah has overheard and plans to warn Murad. Ameer meets Sinbad and Omar in the desert and informs them the Forty Thieves will attack a merchant's caravan carrying Murad and his men traveling incognito. Sinbad and Omar go to the caravan's camp where Sinbad has Omar bury him in the sand where he anticipates Kristina's tent will be set. He keeps alive by breathing through a reed. When Murad pulls it out of the ground, he breaks through the sand and finds Kristina, setting her free. Sinbad, Omar and Kristina escape from the camp which is attacked by the Forty Thieves, who retrieve the chemicals needed to make Greek fire. The three escapees are admitted to the Forty Thieves' cave by the donkey Sesame, and Sinbad consults with the band's leader Ghenia (Joan Jordan). Ameer is also in the cave but she refuses to have anything to do with Sinbad when he will not promise himself to her. When Murad's army attacks the cave, Sinbad hypnotizes Kristina and is able to concoct the Greek fire needed to defeat them. Sinbad and Murad fight with swords and Sinbad wins. Sinbad leads the

Forty Thieves to Bagdad for a truce with the Khalif not knowing that the ruler, under the influence of Jiddah, plans to kill him. Upon his arrival at the palace, Sinbad is greeted by the Khalif who turns on Jiddah and orders his tongue cut out. The Forty Thieves are exonerated, Omar is designated the royal poet and Sinbad is made the Khalif's second-in-command. Sinbad proposes marriage to Ameer.

The New York Times dubbed *Son of Sinbad* "merely a routine action adventure with a more than normal complement of diaphanously clad young women doing some cool dances." *Boxoffice* reported, "It's offered as a fairy tale, and all stops are pulled wide in its motivation as such." Ruth Waterbury noted in *The Los Angeles Examiner*, "If for one split second you take *Son of Sinbad* seriously, you'll go out of your mind.... The story doesn't make a lick of sense—but never have I seen so many pretty girls on the screen in one single film." James Robert Parish and Steven Whitney opined in *Vincent Price Unmasked* (1974), "After the contrived censorship hullabaloo raised over the alleged improprieties to be savored in *Son of Sinbad*, viewing the film is a distinct disappointment." On the other hand, Lucy Chase Williams in *The Complete Films of Vincent Price* (1995) called it "a funny, exciting and entertaining romp."

Son of Sinbad was reissued in 1961 by Excelsior Pictures as *Nights in a Harem*.

Song of the South (1946; 94 minutes; Color)

PRODUCER: Walt Disney. ASSOCIATE PRODUCER: Perce Pearce. DIRECTOR: Harve Foster. ANIMATION DIRECTOR: Wilfred Jackson. SCREENPLAY: Dalton Raymond, Morton Grant & Maurice Rapf. CARTOON STORIES: Bill Peet, Ralph Wright & George Stallings, from *Tales of Uncle Remus* by Joel Chandler Harris. PHOTOGRAPHY: Gregg Toland. EDITOR: William M. Morgan. MUSIC: Daniele Amfitheatrof & Charles Wolcott. CARTOON MUSIC: Paul J. Smith. MUSIC DIRECTOR: Charles Wolcott. ORCHESTRATIONS: Edward H. Plumb. VOCAL SUPERVISOR: Ken Darby. SONGS: Sam Coslow, Arthur Johnston, Eliot Daniel, Hy Heath, Johnny Lange, Charles Wolcott, Ray Gilbert, Ali Wrubel, Foster Carling & Robert MacGimsey. ART DIRECTOR: Perry Ferguson. CARTOON ART DIRECTORS: Kenneth Anderson, Charles Philippi, Hugh Hennesy, Harold Doughty & Philip Barber. SOUND: Fred Lau & Harold Steck. SOUND DIRECTOR: C.O. Slyfield. COSTUMES: Mary Wills. ART TREATMENT: Elmer Plummer. SPECIAL PROCESSES: Ub Iwerks. EFFECTS ANIMATORS: George Rowley, Blaine Gibson, Brad Case & Joshua Meador. DIRECTING ANIMATORS: Milt Kahl, Eric Larson, Oliver M. Johnston, Jr., Les Clark, Marc Davis & John Lounsbery. ANIMATORS: Don Lusk, Tom Massey, Murray McClellan, Jack Campbell, Hal King, Harvey Toombs, Ken O'Brien, Al Coe, Hal Ambro, Cliff Nordberg & Rudy Lirriva. BACKGROUND & COLOR STYLISTS: Claude Coats & Mary Blair. BACKGROUND ARTISTS: Ralph Hulett, Brice Mack, Ray Huffine, Edgar Starr & Albert Dempster. TECHNICOLOR DIRECTOR: Natalie Kalmus. ASSOCIATE TECHNICOLOR DIRECTOR: Mitchell Kovaleski.

CAST: Ruth Warrick (Sally), Bobby Driscoll (Johnny), James Baskett (Uncle Remus/Voice of Br'er Fox), Luana Patten (Ginny), Lucile Watson (Miz Doshy), Hattie McDaniel (Aunt Tempy), Eric Rolf (John), Glenn Leedy (Toby), Mary Field (Mrs. Favers), Anita Brown (Chloe), George Nokes (Jake Favers), Gene Holland (Joe Favers), Nicodemus Stewart (Voice of Br'er Bear), Johnny Lee (Voice of Br'er Rabbit), The De Castro Sisters [Babette, Cherie, Peggy] (Voices of Birds).

Song of the South, released by RKO on November 1, 1946, marked the real beginning of Walt Disney's use of live action over animation in making feature films. While Disney included actors in three previous outings, *The Reluctant Dragon*, *Saludos Amigos* and *The Three Caballeros* [qq.v.], *Song of the South* is dominated by live action with the animation used only in a trio of "Uncle Remus" stories. The result is a successful feature film that grossed $2.5 million, making a $500,000 profit in its initial run. While the animated sequences are very well done and quite amusing, the film's highlight is James Baskett's touching performance as Uncle Remus, a role that netted him a special Academy Award. Future Disney regulars Bobby Driscoll and Luana Patten more than adequately portrayed the two children who fall under the spell of Uncle Remus' tales of the adventures of Br'er Rabbit and his adversaries Br'er Fox and Br'er Bear. These animated tales were based on the popular "Uncle Remus" stories by Joel Chandler Harris. The ending with the children and Uncle Remus being joined by Br'er Rabbit and his friends from nature give a satisfying fantasy finale to this heartwarming production. The National Screen Council chose *Song of the South* for the Boxoffice Blue Ribbon Award in February 1947.

In addition to the entertaining story and the enjoyable animated sequences, *Song of the South* also has eight delightful songs, including the Academy Award winner "Zip-a-Dee Doo-Dah." A musical highlight is the baking day scene with Aunt Tempy (Hattie McDaniel) singing "Sooner or Later" as she makes pies and gives one to a wood-toting Uncle Remus. The film's soundtrack has been issued three times on Disneyland Records, first as an extended play 45 rpm album (DBR-28) in 1956 and in the same year as an LP (WDL-4001). It was reissued as a long-playing album (DQ-1205) in 1963.

Except for a Japanese laserdisc, *Song of the South* has not been available on home video in recent years. Despite successful theatrical reissues in 1972 and 1986, the film since been unseen thanks to the political correctness crowd.

In Georgia in the 1890s, John (Eric Rolf) and his wife Sally (Ruth Warrick) travel to the plantation of her grandmother, Miz Doshy (Lucile Watson), with their young son Johnny (Driscoll). With them is their housekeeper and nursemaid, Aunt Tempy (McDaniel). Johnny wants to meet Uncle Remus (Baskett), an elderly black man who told his mother stories when she was a little girl. After arriving at the plantation, Miz Doshy charges Toby (Glenn Leedy), a black boy about Johnny's age, to keep an eye on her grandson so he will not get into mischief. Johnny is brokenhearted when his father, whose newspaper career has brought about marital discord, returns to Atlanta. That night Johnny runs away intent on being with his father but comes across Uncle Remus telling stories to a group of children, including Toby. Aunt Tempy and another house worker, Chloe (Anita Brown), come looking for Johnny; Uncle Remus, who has spied the boy hiding behind a tree, tells them he is with him. Uncle Remus tells Johnny he will travel to Atlanta with him but they need to go to his cabin for provisions. There he entices the boy with the story of Br'er Rabbit (voice of Johnny Lee), who decides to leave home and is caught in a trap by Br'er Fox (voice of Baskett), who plans to cook him. The wily rabbit convinces the dimwitted Br'er Bear (voice of Nicodemus Stewart) that he is working at a high wage as a scarecrow and offers him the job. Thus Br'er Rabbit is able to escape back to the safety of his briar patch home. Sally is upset with Johnny being out so late and reprimands Uncle Remus. The next morning Toby brings Johnny a frog and sneaks it out of his room when Sally arrives with a laced collar suit for her son to wear. When Johnny and Toby return the frog to a nearby pond, they run into Jake (George Nokes) and Joe (Gene Holland) Favers, the sons of a sharecropper. The brothers make fun of Johnny's clothes and then promise to drown a pup belonging to their younger sister Ginny (Patten). Ginny tells Johnny the dog's name is Teechie and she gives it to him and he presents her with his lace collar and then takes her for a boat ride. Sally refuses to let Johnny keep the dog so he takes it to Uncle Remus although the Faver boys threaten him unless he returns the dog to them. Ginny tells Johnny her mother said the dog belonged to her. Uncle Remus recites to Johnny the story of how Br'er Fox dressed up a tar baby in order to entice Br'er Rabbit into fighting it. When he does, Br'er Rabbit gets caught in the tar and Br'er Fox starts a fire in order to cook the rabbit. Br'er Bear wants to kill Br'er Rabbit with a club and the captive tells him to do so but begs not to be thrown into the briar patch. Thinking Br'er Rabbit will he killed by the sharp briars, Br'er Fox tosses him into the patch, not knowing the rabbit was raised there. Br'er Rabbit once more uses his brain to outsmart Br'er Fox and Br'er Bear. When Johnny and Toby are on their way home, the Favers boys accost them and Johnny adopts the strategy of Br'er Rabbit and tells them to do anything they want but not to inform their mother. When Jake and Joe tell Mrs. Favers (Mary Field) about Ginny giving Johnny the pup, she spanks them. The angry boys then complain to Sally, who orders Uncle Remus not to tell Johnny any more stories. Johnny becomes upset when he finds out Uncle Remus has returned Teechie to Jake and Joe. Sally tells Johnny she is going to give him a birthday party and he asks to invite Ginny. The day of the party Johnny goes to fetch Ginny but the brothers make fun of her dress and push her into the mud. The distraught little girl runs crying to the mill. Uncle Remus spies the two children and relates to them how everyone has a laughing place. He says Br'er Rabbit was a prisoner in Br'er Fox's den and was about to be eaten by him and Br'er Bear when he convinces them there is a laughing place and they demand to see it. Br'er Rabbit leads them to a thicket where there is a beehive and Br'er Fox and Br'er Bear are attacked by the bees, letting Br'er Rabbit escape again. The children then look for their laughing place, with Sally finding it at home when her father returns from work. Johnny realizes his laughing place is Uncle Remus' cabin. Sally is upset with Johnny for missing his party, and when she finds out he was with Uncle Remus she tells the old man not to see her son again. The dejected Uncle Remus goes to his cabin and packs a carpetbag, planning to depart to Atlanta. When Johnny goes to Uncle Remus' cabin, he finds it empty and asks his mother about his best friend. Sally tells Johnny what happened and he sees Uncle Remus leaving in a wagon. Trying to stop Uncle Remus from going, Johnny, who is wearing a red suit, runs across a pasture inhabited by a large bull. The beast becomes angry at the sight of Johnny and runs after him, goring the boy. John returns from Atlanta when he hears the news. The boy calls for Uncle Remus. Aunt Doshy brings Uncle Remus to the boy's bedside and the old man talks and revives him. The boy is happy to see his father, who promises to remain on the plantation with him and his mother. Later the recovered Johnny plays with Ginny, Toby and Teechie as Uncle Remus is astounded to see them joined by Br'er Rabbit and his nature friends.

According to *Variety*, "Some of the immortal Uncle Remus 'Brer Rabbit' stories have been set down with a great deal of charm by Walt Disney in this combined live-and-cartoon characterization.... Some excellent Technicolor effects heighten the picture of an idealized romanticized South.... [The] cartoon sequences are great stuff." Bosley Crowther complained in *The New York Times*, "Apparently the Disney wonder-workers are just a lot of conventional hacks when it comes to telling a story with actors instead of cartoons. At least, that's the woeful indication of two-thirds of *Song of the South*." After detailing the plot, Crowther resumed, "In contrast to this mawkish romance, the cartoon episodes, when they do intrude, assume refreshing proportions which they probably do not actually have. Seen by themselves, they would likely be just moderately good Disney shorts, cleverly conceived and animated in an amusingly rambunctious mood.... [T]hey come at such moments when the humans have so completely candyfied the screen that they seem sublime salvations, avenues into fresh, song-laden air." *Boxoffice* felt the film was "one of Disney's all-time best," adding, "It possesses that rare blending of ingredients which equips it with a wide appeal for both adult and juvenile audiences and there can be little doubt that its popularity and profits will press those established by other features from the Disneyan ink pots." *The Film Daily* felt it "a stirring gem ... a delight to the young 'uns and a poignantly sentimental memento to grownups.... The songs are gay and the Technicolor treatment one of the pleasantest jobs of the season." Leonard Maltin noted in *The Disney Films, 3rd Edition* (1995), "There is no denying that it is the cartoon segments that make this film.... The color in these sequences is probably the most bright and vivid ever seen in motion pictures, a quality characteristic of most of Disney's 1940s cartoon output."

The Spiral Staircase (1946; 83 minutes)

PRODUCER: Dore Schary. DIRECTOR: Robert Siodmak. SCREENPLAY: Mel Dinelli, from the novel *Some Must Watch* by Ethel Lina White. PHOTOGRAPHY: Nicholas Musuraca. EDITORS: Harry Marker & Harry Gerstad. MUSIC: Roy Webb. MUSIC DIRECTOR: C. Bakaleinikoff. ART DIRECTORS: Albert S. D'Agostino & Jack Okey. SOUND: John L. Cass & Terry Kellum. SET DECORATIONS: Darrell Silvera. GOWNS: Edward Stevenson. SPECIAL EFFECTS: Vernon L. Walker. ASSISTANT DIRECTOR: Harry Scott.

CAST: Dorothy McGuire (Helen), George Brent (Professor Albert Warren), Ethel Barrymore (Mrs. Warren), Kent Smith (Dr. Brian Perry), Rhonda Fleming (Blanche), Gordon Oliver (Steven Warren), Elsa Lanchester (Mrs. Oates), Sara Allgood (Nurse Barker), Rhys Williams (Alvin Oates), James Best (Constable), Erville Alderson (Dr. Harvey), Charles Wagenheim (Desk Clerk), Myrna Dell (Lame Murder Victim), Dickie Tyler (Freddy Stover), Ellen Corby (Excited Roomer), Larry Wheat (Minister), Stanley Price (Starry-Eyed Man), Irene Mack (Piano Player), Les Raymaster (Projectionist).

From 1931 to 1933 David O. Selznick was RKO's head of production and in 1946 his Vanguard Films joined with RKO in a series of co-production ventures, the first being *The Spiral Staircase*. Released late in 1946, the film is both dramatically and visually compelling with most of its story taking place in an ornate gaslight era mansion full of shadows and dark places. Nearly all the action occurs during a thunderstorm. Its plot of a psychotic killer on the loose in a small New England town is well constructed and the only clue to the culprit is a close-up of an eye as the murderer spies on intended victims. Some sources claim director Robert Siodmak used his own eye in these scenes.

The acting in *The Spiral Staircase* is superb, especially Dorothy McGuire in the difficult role of a mute young woman caught in a killer's web because of her affliction. Her work is nicely matched by Ethel Barrymore as her stern but very ill employer, George Brent as a kindly professor, and Kent Smith as the doctor who loves McGuire. Barrymore was nominated for an Academy Award as Best Supporting Actress for her performance. The rest of the cast is also quite good, especially Rhonda Fleming as the ravishing secretary romanced by stepbrothers, Sara Allgood as a no-nonsense nurse and Elsa Lanchester as the family's drink-prone cook. Erville Alderson contributes a very satisfying cameo as a jealous small town doctor. Matching the acting are the technical aspects of the production. Nicholas Musuraca's photography is the highlight of the movie and it is his ability to capture the menacing atmosphere of the old mansion that brings out the best in the other elements of the melodrama. Albert S. D'Agostino and Jack Okey's art direction and set decoration by Darrell Silvera further facilitate the cinematography as does Roy Webb's low-key, highly effective music score. *The Spiral Staircase* was very successful at the box office, netting RKO nearly a $900,000 profit, and it is one of the best horror films of the 1940s.

In a 1906 bucolic New England community, Helen (McGuire), the mute companion of wealthy bedridden Mrs. Warren (Barrymore), watches a film called *The Kiss* being projected in one of the ground floor rooms of the local hotel. While the flicker is being shown, upstairs a lame young woman (Myrna Dell) is strangled. Hearing a disturbance, the hotel clerk (Charles Wagenheim) finds the body and calls the constable (James Best). This is the third recent homicide. Dr. Brian Parry (Smith) arrives to investigate but finds his more established rival, Dr. Harvey (Alderson), is already on the case. Harvey chides Brian for trying to take some of his practice. Brian offers Helen a ride to the Warren house in his buggy and along the way tells her she must strive to be cured of her affliction in order to have a profession like a teacher or a nurse. A boy (Dickie Tyler) stops the buggy and asks Brian to attend to his sick father, one of Dr. Harvey's patients. Making sure Helen can get home all right, Brian leaves with the boy. Just as Helen gets to the Warren house, it starts to storm, and she is not aware that she is being watched by a black-clad figure. Entering the house, Helen is informed by the cook, Mrs. Oates (Lanchester), that she might have been the victim since the killer targets young women with physical afflictions. When

Helen stops to look in a hallway mirror, someone hides in the shadows and envisions her with no mouth. Mrs. Warren warns Helen to leave the house immediately as she is not safe there. The constable stops by and informs Mrs. Warren's stepson, research scientist Dr. Albert Warren (Brent), that the killer has been placed in the vicinity and Albert assures Helen that she will be protected. Steven Warren (Gordon Oliver), Albert's half-brother, who has just returned from Europe, tries to make time with lovely Blanche (Fleming), Albert's secretary. Albert tells Helen to be especially cautious for the next few days and not to trust anyone. Mrs. Warren, who detests her nurse Barker (Allgood) and makes her sit in the hall, has a relapse and Helen goes for Steven, who rouses her with ether. When he leaves, Mrs. Warren relates to Helen that trouble follows Steven and she wishes he had not come back home. Albert and Steven argue, Albert telling his half-brother he does not like him. Steven says Albert is jealous of him because of Blanche. Mrs. Oates' husband, Alvin (Rhys Williams), who also works for the Warrens, arrives out of the storm and tells Helen he will protect her. Mrs. Warren wants Brian to tend to her; when he arrives, she tells him he reminds her of her late husband, who disliked both his sons. She also informs the doctor that she knows he loves Helen and orders him to get her out of the house that very night. Brian agrees to take Helen away but when he calls for more ether, he finds there is none in the house although Helen had gotten it for Steven three hours before. Since no ether is available locally, Albert sends a disgruntled Alvin out into the storm to go to a nearby town to get the medication. Before leaving, Alvin tells his wife, who likes to drink, to stay sober until he returns. Since no ether is immediately available, Brian suggests brandy and Albert takes Mrs. Oates with him to the cellar to get a bottle. While there, she intentionally drops the candle she is carrying and while Albert looks for it, Mrs. Oates pilfers a bottle for herself. When Mrs. Warren is resting comfortably, Brian talks with Helen and tells her he knows she lost the ability to talk as a child after seeing her parents die in a house fire. He says he plans to take her to a specialist in Boston and that he wants to marry her. Overhearing Brian, the cynical Steven suggests to him that Helen has adapted to her affliction. He also makes snide remarks about Brian's interest in the young woman. They are interrupted by a telephone call asking Brian to attend to a sick boy. He writes down a phone number where he can be reached and gives it to Helen. As he leaves, Brian kisses Helen goodbye. Helen daydreams about marrying Brian but during the ceremony cannot say "I do." Albert informs Helen that if the specialist cannot help her, she can always return and work for his family. Steven walks into Blanche's room and finds her crying and taunts her after she confides that she is unhappy. Blanche orders Steven out of her room and goes to Helen, asking if she can leave with her that night. After Helen agrees, Blanche descends into the dark cellar for a small trunk and is strangled by someone she recognizes. Mrs. Warren and Barker have another row and the nurse quits. Albert asks Steven, who just walked into the house claiming he was out for a walk, to hitch a wagon for her so she can drive to town. Mrs. Warren informs Helen that ten years ago she saw a simple-minded girl murdered in the yard and her body thrown down a well. She implores Helen to leave that night with Blanche or hide under a bed. Albert tells Helen to find Blanche; when she goes into the cellar, Helen sees that Blanche has been murdered. Just then Steven arrives in the cellar, finds the body and tells Helen to forget what she has seen and that he will handle the situation. Thinking Steven is the murderer, Helen locks him in the wine cellar and then goes upstairs and tries unsuccessfully to revive Mrs. Oates, who has passed out drunk in the kitchen. Helen tries to call Brian but is unable to speak. Running into Albert, Helen writes him a note saying Steven is a murderer and he escorts her to his stepmother's room. When they get in front of the hallway mirror, Albert informs Helen he saw her there earlier that day and that in his mind she had no mouth. He tells her he has learned to be strong and is getting rid of all weaklings as his late father would have wanted since he believed there is no room in

Poster for *The Spiral Staircase* (1946).

the world for imperfection. Albert admits hiding the ether so he could sent Alvin away and purposely letting the cook steal the brandy in order to get her drunk. He had to murder Blanche because he loved her and she did not love him and therefore had to die. Helen runs into Mrs. Warren's room and tries unsuccessfully to find the old lady's gun. The constable arrives and informs Albert that Brian will be unable to come for Helen that night because of his sick patient. Helen tries various methods to get the lawman's attention but he drives away as Albert stalks her on the stairs. Mrs. Warren appears at the head of the stairs and shoots Albert, causing Helen to scream. Mrs. Warren collapses and tells Helen to bring Steven, whom she frees from the wine cellar. Before dying, Mrs. Warren tells Steven she thought he was the murderer because Albert only killed when Steven returned home. Steven orders Helen to call Brian and in making the call she realizes she can speak again.

Variety reported, "This is a smooth production of an obvious though suspenseful murder thriller, ably acted and directed. Mood and pace are well set, and story grips throughout." *Boxoffice* called *The Spiral Staircase* "a chiller that will have spectators on the edges of their seats and at the same time [it remains] within the bounds of plausible theater." *The New York Times* stated, "This is a shocker, plain and simple, and whatever pretentions it has to psychological drama may be considered merely as a concession to a currently popular fancy. It is quite evident by the technique director Robert Siodmak has employed to develop and sustain suspense—brooding photography and ominously suggestive settings—that he is at no time striving for narrative subtlety." *The Film Daily* reported, "A striking melodrama possessed of considerable force.... Siodmak has contributed some of his best work in a field in which he specializes, keeping the action always tense and suspense-laden and allowing developments to remain ever on the interesting side.... Siodmak has made of *The Spiral Staircase* a gripping and satisfying production of its class." Phil Hardy wrote in *The Encyclopedia of Horror Movies* (1986), "This is a superb thriller.... Although Hollywood's current enthusiasm for Freud runs a little wild ... any excesses are kept perfectly in check by Siodmak's direction, which turns different levels of the house into areas of light and shadow, not always correctly identified by McGuire as she negotiates the traumatic reef of the spiral staircase between safety and danger. The film is one of the undoubted gothic masterpieces."

Although *The Spiral Staircase* takes place in 1906, the silent movie shown at its beginning is the 1912 Biograph release *The Sands of Dee*, directed by D.W. Griffith and starring Mae Marsh, Robert Harron and Charles Hill Mailes.

On November 25, 1949, Dorothy McGuire reprised the role of Helen in "The Spiral Staircase" on NBC radio's *Screen Directors Playhouse*. A dozen years later (October 4, 1961), the NBC-TV series *Theatre '62* telecast a version of "The Spiral Staircase" with Lillian Gish, Elizabeth Montgomery, Gig Young, Eddie Albert and Edie Adams, directed by Boris Sagal. *The Spiral Staircase* was remade theatrically in Great Britain in 1975 by Columbia-Warner and directed by Peter Collinson. Never issued in the U.S., it starred Jacqueline Bisset, Christopher Plummer, Sam Wanamaker, John Philip Law, Mildred Dunnock, Gayle Hunnicutt and Elaine Stritch. In 2000 the Fox Family Channel did a television movie of *The Spiral Staircase* starring Nicollette Sheridan, Judd Nelson and Alex McArthur.

A native of Germany and brother of writer-director Curt Siodmak, Robert Siodmak also directed the genre efforts *Son of Dracula* (1943), *Cobra Woman* and *Phantom Lady* (both 1944), *The Suspect* and *The Strange Affair of Uncle Harry* (both 1945), *The Dark Mirror* (1946), *Der Schatz der Aztecan* (The Treasure of the Aztecs) and *Die Pyramide des Sonnengottes* (The Pyramid of the Sun God) (both 1965).

Stranger on the Third Floor (1940; 64 minutes)

PRODUCER: Lee Marcus. DIRECTOR: Boris Ingster. SCREENPLAY: Frank Partos. PHOTOGRAPHY: Nicholas Musuraca. EDITOR: Harry Marker. MUSIC: Roy Webb. ART DIRECTORS: Van Nest Polglase & Albert D'Agostino. SOUND: Bailey Fraser. WARDROBE: Renie. SPECIAL EFFECTS: Vernon Walker.

CAST: Peter Lorre (Stranger), John McGuire (Mike Ward), Margaret Tallichet (Jane), Charles Waldron (District Attorney), Elisha Cook, Jr. (Joe Briggs), Charles Halton (Albert Meng), Ethel Griffies (Mrs. Kane), Cliff Clark (Martin), Oscar O'Shea (Judge), Alec Craig (Defense Attorney), Otto Hoffman (Dr. Charles Evans), Henry Roquemore (Mr. McLean), Herbert Vigran (Loud Reporter), Charles Judels (Nick Nanbajan), Bobby Barber (Giuseppe), Dell Henderson, Jack Cheatham (Detectives), Al Ferguson (Guard in Dream), Harry C. Bradley (Court Clerk), Gladden James (Reporter Tom), Jane Keckley (Angry Landlady), Paul McVey (Detective Lieutenant Jones), Ralph Sanford (Truck Driver), Frank Yaconelli (Jack), Emory Parnell (Interrogator in Dream), Ray Cooke (Counterman Phil), Greta Granstedt (Housekeeper), Robert Weldon, Lee Bonnell (Reporters), Bud Osborne (Bartender), Bess Wade (Court Cleaning Woman), Frank O'Connor, Bruce Mitchell, Jim Farley, Don Kelly (Policemen), Lynton Brent (Cab Driver), Max Hoffman, Jr. (Cab Driver Charlie), William Edmunds (Gardener), Broderick O'Farrell (Minister in Dream), Lee Phelps (Waiting Cab Driver), Robert Dudley (Postman), Donald Kerr, Betty Farrington (Lunch Counter Customers), John Harmon (Pedestrian).

Some films grow in stature as time passes and one of these is *Stranger on the Third Floor*, an RKO program feature issued in the late summer of 1940 to little appreciable interest. Highbrow Bosley Crowther in the *New York Times* pontificated that first-time director Boris Ingster's experiment fell flat: "The notion seems to have been that the way to put a psychological melodrama across is to pile on the sound effects and trick up the photography." *Harrison's Reports* stated after seeing the film, "[O]ne feels as if one had gone through a nightmare." Reviewers in the hinterlands were a bit kinder, with the *London* (Pennsylvania) *Daily News* calling it "a vivid portrait of the plight in which an innocent young man finds himself when he is suspected of murder" and the *Oakland* (California) *Tribune* saying there was "gripping action [in] this unusual drama of peril and retribution." *The Film Daily* wrote, "Revolving around an unusual theme, this murder mystery meller should hold the attention of audiences from beginning to end. It is suspenseful throughout, and it has been competently played by an able cast."

New York Star reporter Mike Ward (John McGuire) is the district attorney's (Charles Waldron) only witness to the robbery and murder of café owner Nick Nanbajan (Charles Judels). Mike saw Joe Briggs (Elisha Cook, Jr.) hovering over the body and then running away. Briggs claims he came to the café to repay Mike thirty cents but admits he threatened to kill Nick, who accused him of being a freeloader. Mike wants to marry secretary Jane (Margaret Tallichet) and finds out he will be able to do so with the raise his employer gave him from the publicity he generated from the trial. Jane is not sure of Joe's guilt and becomes upset with Mike when the jury brings in a verdict that calls for execution. Going back to his tacky apartment, Mike sees a scarf-wearing stranger (Peter Lorre) in front of the building. Later he sees the same man in the hall near his room but when he goes after him the stranger runs away. Mike frets over his testimony and also thinks about his rude neighbor Albert Meng (Charles Halton), who is always trying to get him in trouble with their landlady (Ethel Griffies). He recalls how one rainy night Jane came to his room and Meng informed the landlady, causing Mike to threaten to kill his neighbor. Mike dreams he is accused of murdering Meng and is found guilty on circumstantial evidence. Later he finds Meng has had his throat slit, just like Nick, and asks Mary meet him in the park where he tells her he has to go away before he is accused of the killing. She convinces him to go to the police so he can help Joe get a reprieve. The district attorney doubts Mike's premonition of Meng's murder and has him taken to police headquarters as a material witness since he found both victims. When Jane finds out that Mike has been detained by the law, she tries to find the

Lobby card for *Stranger on the Third Floor* (1940) picturing Peter Lorre and Margaret Tallichet.

stranger whom he describes has having thick lips, bulging eyes and wearing a long scarf. The next day she questions dozens of people without success but when she goes to a lunch room for coffee the man comes in and orders two raw hamburgers. She follows him outside and finds him feeding a stray dog. Jane talks to the man and as they walk through the neighborhood she learns he is an escapee from a mental institution. She tries to call the police and he attempts to kill her. She runs away and as the stranger follows her he steps in front of a truck and is killed, but before dying he exonerates Mike and Joe. Mike later takes Jane to city hall to get married—and they are driven there by cabbie Joe.

While hardly a classic, *Stranger on the Third Floor* is an interesting psychological horror film that some sources consider the first *film noir*. Particularly memorable is its harrowing dream sequence in which the reporter finds himself facing the same situation he initiated by his testimony against another man. Lorre's brief appearances as the stranger are not especially memorable, but leads John McGuire and beautiful Margaret Tallichet give solid performances as a young couple caught in the web of circumstantial evidence. Director Boris Ingster, a Russian who worked on the script for *The Last Days of Pompeii* (q.v.), helmed only two more features, *The Judge Steps Out* (1949), for RKO, and *Southside 1-000* (1950). He also co-wrote both movies. During the 1950s and 1960s he produced a number of successful television series.

Don Miller, in *B Movies* (1973), dissected the attributes of *Stranger on the Third Floor*, calling it "a highly original, brooding little gem" with Ingster's directorial debut being "auspicious, especially for a low-budget film." He felt the Frank Partos script (which some claim was augmented by an uncredited Nathanael West) was "obviously a homage to Dostoyevsky." He added, "It's a carefully wrought screenplay but it's likely that, good as it is, it would be far less effective in the hands of an ordinary director. Ingster contributes immeasurably to its success." He noted the director "collaborated with photographer Nicholas Musuraca and special effects man Vernon L. Walker for some striking camera images, all the more unusual to be on display in a limited budget B film.... The fantasy sequences imagined by McGuire also contain examples of Musuraca's agility with balancing light and shadow for effect." Miller felt that another asset was "Roy Webb's quietly evocative music score. Webb, RKO's house composer, used themes from the score a few years later for the Dick Powell detective story, *Murder My Sweet*."

Super-Sleuth (1937; 70 minutes)

PRODUCER: Edward Small. DIRECTOR: Ben Stoloff. SCREENPLAY: Gertrude Purcell & Ernest Pagano. STORY: Harry Segall. PHOTOGRAPHY: Joseph H. August. EDITOR: William Hamilton. ART DIRECTORS: Van Nest Polglase & Al Herman. SOUND: Earl A. Wolcott. GOWNS: Edward Stevenson. SPECIAL EFFECTS: Vernon L. Walker.

CAST: Jack Oakie (Bill Martin), Ann Sothern (Mary Strand), Eduardo Ciannelli (Professor Herman), Alan Bruce (Larry Frank), Edgar Kennedy (Lieutenant Garrison), Joan Woodbury (Doris Duane), Bradley Page (Ralph Waring), Paul Guilfoyle (Gibbons), Willie Best (Warts), William Corson (Beckett), Richard Lane (Barker), Paul Hurst (Motorcycle Policeman), Fred Kelsey (Jailer), Robert Emmett O'Connor (Casey), Alec Craig (Doorman Eddie), Philip Morris (Sullivan), Dick Rush (Grimes), George Rosener (Policeman), Dewey Robinson (Movie Gangster), Ann Hovey (Script Girl), Marie Marks (Hairdresser), Al Klein, Bert Moorhouse (Cameramen), Leona Roberts (Mrs. Effington), Bud Jamison (Burning Beard), Leyland Hodgson (Movie Butler), Wally Albright (Teenage Fan), Benny Burt (Actor), Harland Tucker (Newsman Hugo), Donald Haines, Buster Slaven (Newsboys), Bobby Barber (Battling Photographer), Ronald R. Rondell (Battling Headwaiter), Frank Mills, Buddy Messinger (Suspects), Frank O'Connor (Nightclub Law Officer), John George (Panhandler), Frank M. Thomas (Voice of A.J.), Bud Flanagan [Dennis O'Keefe], Larry Steers (Nightclub Patrons).

A madman using the moniker "Poison Pen" is murdering celebrities. Brash movie star Bill Martin (Jack Oakie), who plays detectives on the screen, vows he is more capable of catching the fiend than the law. This not only upsets police Lieutenant Garrison (Edgar Kennedy), who is heading the effort to find the killer, but also studio publicity chief Mary Strand (Ann Sothern), who secretly loves the egotistical star. The Poison Pen threatens to kill Bill in revenge for his latest screen sleuthing opus, and tries to shoot him at a Hollywood night spot. Bill and Mary consult noted criminal investigator Professor Herman (Eduardo Ciannelli), who also runs the "Crimes Doesn't Pay" horrors exhibit. Unknown to them, Herman is the Poison Pen. While shooting a scene for his new movie the following day, Bill's co-star Ralph Waring (Bradley Page) is accidentally killed during a chase sequence by Herman, who was trying to get Bill. Waring's stand-in, Larry Frank (Alan Bruce), is arrested by Garrison since he and the dead man had recently quarreled. Knowing Larry is innocent, Bill tries to learn the Poison Pen's identity while the madman persists in his attempts to kill the star. To protect the man she loves, Mary gets Bill put in jail, but Bill has Herman post his bail. Realizing the Poison Pen's true identity, Mary takes Bill's valet, Warts (Willie Best), to the horror exhibit after alerting Garrison. Now in the clutches of Herman, Bill is almost killed but Mary saves him and the Poison Pen is arrested.

Released in the summer of 1937, *Super-Sleuth* gave audiences a chance to view the RKO back lot as it told its brisk comedy-horror story. Rudy Behlmer and Tony Thomas noted in *Hollywood's Hollywood: The Movies About the Movies* (1975), "Most of the scenes in this better-than-average programmer take place inside the studio, with a location unit of camera cars and sound trucks also prominent in the action." The success of the picture rests upon whether or not one can stomach the verbose acting of star Jack Oakie. Certainly his screen persona fits the part of self-centered star Bill Martin. Ann Sothern as his loyal, but exasperated girlfriend, compliments the duo. *Modern Movies* wrote, "The team of Oakie and Sothern is an excellent one. Both turn in delightful performances and Miss Sothern is unusually beautiful." *The New York Times* dubbed the feature "an amusing bit of nonsense" while Leonard Maltin in *Film Fan Monthly* (July–August 1973) declared, "Inconsequential, but very funny, outing.... Edgar Kennedy has a plum role as the police detective on the case; at one point Oakie persuades the movie-struck cop to try wearing a toupee." *Variety* noted, "Jack Oakie gives a fine comedy performance in this one and the film, which is excellently written and directed, will please everywhere.... [It's] a real laugh provoker.... Ben Stoloff directs at a rapid pace and keeps melodramatic suspense and comedy situations building rapidly to a hokey and hilarious finale." *Boxoffice* predicted, "Audiences will love this farcical-murder mystery. It's a real laugh romp from start to finish, and if the patrons don't die from fright they'll guffaw themselves to death." According to *The Film Daily*, "It is worked out in such a manner as to be a very hilarious comedy which can well be classed as top flight program material. Yet in viewing the proceedings one is continually outguessed by the twists the writer have supplied." "Jack Oakie is ingenuously funny throughout all the mayhem," said *The New Yorker*, while *Motion Picture* wrote, "It is a ridiculous sort of farce at the expense of Hollywood life and characters, sometimes verging on the slapstick, not an unpleasant picture and all in good fun." The *Monthly Film Bulletin* stated, "The last section in the Chamber of Horrors is rather too wild and lengthy to be as funny as it might have been, but the film provides excellent entertainment."

In 1946 RKO remade *Super-Sleuth* as *Genius at Work* (q.v.), dividing Jack Oakie's role in two to accommodate the comedy team of Alan Carney and Wally Brown.

Tangled Evidence (1934; 57 minutes)

PRODUCER: Julius Hagen. DIRECTOR: George A. Cooper. SCREENPLAY: H. Fowler Mear, from the novel by Mrs. Champion de Crespigny. PHOTOGRAPHY: Ernest Palmer. EDITOR: Lister Laurance. SOUND: Carlisle Mounteney. ASSISTANT DIRECTOR: Fred Merrick.

CAST: Sam Livesey (Inspector Drayton), Joan Marion (Anne Wilmot), Michael Hogan (Ingram Underhill), Michael Shepley (Gilbert Morfield), Reginald Tate (Ellaby), Dick Francis (Frame), Edgar Norfolk (Dr. Ackland), John Turnbull (Moore), Davina Craig (Faith), Gillian Maude (Paula).

Following the murder of her occultist uncle, pretty Anne Wilmot (Joan Marion) is suspected of the crime. Inspector Drayton (Sam Livesey) is assigned to the case and eventually discovers the killer committed the crime fearing the contacts the victim may have had with the occult world.

Like *Excess Baggage* (q.v.) and the 1932 version of *The Face at the Window* (q.v.), *Tangled Evidence* was made by producer Julius Hagen's Real Art Products in cooperation with Radio Pictures, which released it in England. Also, as with the other two films, it is thought to be lost. In *British Sound Films: The Studio Years 1928–1959* (1984), David Quinlan noted, "Somber thriller just about kills and hour."

Tarzan and the Amazons (1945; 76 minutes)

PRODUCER: Sol Lesser. ASSOCIATE PRODUCER: Kurt Neumann. DIRECTOR: William Thiele & (uncredited) Kurt Neumann. SCREENPLAY: John Jacoby & Marjorie L. Pfaelzer. PHOTOGRAPHY: Archie Stout. EDITOR: Robert O. Crandall. ART DIRECTOR: Walter Koessler. SOUND: Jean L. Speak. PRODUCTION DESIGN: Phil Paradise. MAKEUP: Norbert Miles. WARDROBE: Earl Moser. INTERIORS: James E. Altwies. ASSISTANT DIRECTOR: Scott R. Beal.

CAST: Johnny Weissmuller (Tarzan), Brenda Joyce (Jane), Johnny Sheffield (Boy), Henry Stephenson

(Sir Guy Henderson), Maria Ouspenskaya (Amazon Queen), Barton MacLane (Ballister), Don Douglas (Anders), Steven Geray (Brenner), J.M. Kerrigan (Splivens), Shirley O'Hara (Athena), Lionel Royce (Basov), Frederic Burton (LaTour), Frank Darien (Boat Pilot), Christine Forsyth (Amazon Warrior).

Johnny Weissmuller's third appearance as Tarzan for RKO, *Tarzan and the Amazons* was released by the studio in the spring of 1945. It debuted Brenda Joyce in her first of five films as Jane, replacing Maureen O'Sullivan who left the series when it moved to RKO from Metro-Goldwyn-Mayer three years before. This intriguing outing found the jungle man involved with a lost civilization of Amazon women whose leader is portrayed by horror film favorite Maria Ouspenskaya. The very attractive Joyce makes a fine Jane and Weissmuller and Johnny Sheffield continue to carry out their roles as Tarzan and Boy in good form. Barton MacLane, Don Douglas and J.M. Kerrigan fare well as the villains, although Kerrigan's character is somewhat redeemed by his concern for Boy once they are captured by the Amazons. The lost city is impressive. Kurt Neumann, who was associate producer for the previous series entry *Tarzan's Desert Mystery* [q.v.], returned in that capacity on *Tarzan and the Amazons*, also taking over the reins as director. He would continue in those jobs for the next two series outings *Tarzan and the Leopard Woman* [q.v.] and *Tarzan and the Huntress* (1947), before returning to direct *Tarzan and the She-Devil* [q.v.]. He also helmed the genre efforts *Secret of the Blue Room* (1933), *The Unknown Guest* (1943), *Rocketship X-M* (1950), *She Devil* and *Kronos* (both 1957) and *The Fly* (1958).

As they sail on a river, Tarzan (Weissmuller) and Boy (Sheffield) hear a woman, Athena (Shirley O'Hara), scream and they see her jump off a cliff in order to escape leopards and a panther. Tarzan finds her as Cheetah takes a gold bracelet she lost in the fall. Since she cannot walk due to a sprained ankle, Tarzan takes Athena home but warns Boy and Cheetah not to follow. They disobey him. Tarzan and Athena go to Palmyra, the forbidden city of the Amazons where the queen (Ouspenskaya) says all intruders must die although she trusts Tarzan. The jungle man gets back home to meet his mate, Jane (Joyce), who returns from wartime service in England accompanied by Sir Guy Henderson (Henry Stephenson), his fellow archaeologist Anders (Douglas) and zoologist Brenner (Steven Geray), who have come to investigate local tribes. They meet at a trading post run by Ballister (MacLane) and his associate Splivens (Kerrigan). Cheetah presents the bracelet to Jane. The scheming Ballister convinces the scientists to look for Palmyra, hoping to steal its riches. They try to get Tarzan to lead the foray but after Ballister kills a mother lion the jungle man rescues her cubs and refuses to help them. Boy, who has become intrigued by the expedition's scientific paraphernalia, is upset that Tarzan will not help the newcomers and agrees to lead them to Palmyra. When Tarzan is hunting, Jane goes looking for Boy and a windstorm knocks down a tree, pinning her underneath. The expedition reaches the secret city and the queen sentences them to die but when Sir Henry tells her of their peaceful intentions she spares their lives but says they must work the kingdom's quarries. Tarzan returns home and rescues Jane, who has been stalked by a lion. Boy tells Cheetah to bring Athena and enlists her aid in helping him and his friends escape from Palmyra. As they start to leave, Ballister orders the men to pillage the kingdom's riches. When Athena objects, he throws a knife, mortally wounding her. Before dying, the girl strikes a gong that alerts her sister warriors as the objecting Sir Henry is murdered by Ballister. Cheetah goes to get Tarzan while Ballister and Anders escape over a mountain pass that leads from the city. They are pursued by the Amazon women. Ballister uses dynamite to destroy a stone bridge over a chasm, killing Splivens, who tried to protect Boy. Captured by the Amazons, Boy is sentenced to die as Cheetah returns home for Tarzan. On his way to Palmyra, the jungle man sees Ballister and Anders with their plunder and lures them into quicksand, taking their gold treasure back to the Amazons. He uses a fallen tree to span the gap back to the city, returns the booty and takes Boy home.

The Film Daily reported, "Sol Lesser has turned out another entertaining pic ... with sufficient variety to whet the satisfaction of young and old alike.... Complemented by such seasoned performers as Madame Ouspenskaya and Henry Stephenson, director Kurt Neumann has injected enough jungle business into the somewhat mild, however fantastic, screenplay to add the required pace and action." According to *Variety*, "All three stars do some good swimming and Cheetah is very engaging." *Boxoffice* rated it "among the all-time best of the long line of Tarzan films.... Juvenile audiences will find the offering a delightful morsel of pure escapist entertainment, while adults will view it with tolerance and amusement." *The New York Times*, complained that Tarzan and the film "turn out to be very tired specimens indeed. For this time our hero and, possibly, the scenarists, plainly show the ennui stemming from their long application to the same job.... This fantasy, it turns out, is a little on the ludicrous side." *Motion Picture Daily* disagreed: "Packed with action and thrills, *Tarzan and the Amazons* is one of the best of the Tarzan pics, not only in its original story content, but because of an excellent supporting cast, able direction and photography, all of which make the film good box office."

Tarzan and the Leopard Woman (1946; 72 minutes)

PRODUCER: Sol Lesser. ASSOCIATE PRODUCER–DIRECTOR: Kurt Neumann. STORY & SCREENPLAY: Carroll Young. PHOTOGRAPHY: Karl Struss. EDITOR: Robert O. Crandall. MUSIC: Paul Sawtell. ART DIRECTOR: Lewis Creber. SOUND: John R. Carter. MAKEUP: Irving Berns. PRODUCTION DESIGN: Phil Paradise. UNIT MANAGER: Clem Beauchamp. WARDROBE: Robert Martien. DANCE DIRECTOR: Lester Horton. ASSISTANT DIRECTOR: Scott Beal.

CAST: Johnny Weissmuller (Tarzan), Brenda Joyce (Jane), Johnny Sheffield (Boy), Acquanetta (High Priestess Lea), Edgar Barrier (Dr. Ameer Lazar), Dennis Hoey (Commissioner), Tommy Cook (Kimba), Anthony Caruso (Mongo), George J. Lewis (Corporal), Doris Lloyd (Miss Wetherby), Georges Renavent (Ivory Merchant), Louis Mercier (Snake Charmer), Kay Solinas, Lillian Molieri, Iris Flores, Helen Gerald (Zambesi Maidens), Abe "King Kong" Kashey (Tongolo the Terrible), John Shay, Neyle Morrow (Soldiers), Kenneth Terrell, Robert Strong, John Roth, Charles Regan, Cy Schindell (Leopard Men), Bobby Frasco, Bobby Samrich, Ray Dolciame (Bagandi Boys), Robert Barron (Man in Caravan), Ted Billings (Native).

Tarzan and the Leopard Woman features a deadly tribe of Caucasian leopard worshippers. A strong entry in the series, it gives Tarzan (Johnny Weissmuller) a chance to show off his wrestling skills against a brute played by professional grappler "King Kong" Kashey, as well as fight the ferocious leopard men, their queen (Acquanetta) and her half-breed physician consort (Edgar Barrier). Tommy Cook provides Johnny Sheffield's Boy with some competition as the evil-minded younger brother of the queen, set on becoming a warrior by bringing in the hearts of Jane (Brenda Joyce) and Boy. The antics of Cheetah the chimp also highlight the feature as noted by Gabe Essoe in *Tarzan of the Movies* (1968): "In the old Metro days, Tarzan's predicament of being prepared for sacrifice to the leopard god would have been solved by throwing back his head and heralding his trusty elephant herd to the rescue. [Producer Sol] Lesser, however, was more inclined to use Cheetah as the saving grace. The chimp was always employed for comedy business as well as to be direct agent in many of the key situations. The way the chimp was so continuously depended upon to get the troops out of a tight scrape became an obsession with Lesser." Placed in theaters at the beginning of 1946, *Tarzan and the Leopard Woman* was the fourth feature in the series to be released by RKO under Lesser's production auspices. Its working title was *Tarzan and the Leopard Men*.

At an African Zambesi village, Dr. Ameer Lazar (Barrier) comes to see the commissioner (Dennis Hoey) and is offered a promotion that he declines. In the same locale, Tarzan wrestles and defeats Tongolo the Terrible (Abe "King Kong" Kashey) and then helps Jane (Joyce) pick

Advertisement for *Tarzan and the Leopard Woman* (1946).

out a gift for her English relations. With Boy (Sheffield) they go to a local girls' school and talk
with the superintendent (Doris Lloyd), whose students go into the jungle as teachers. When a
dying villager rides into town on a elephant and announces that his caravan was attacked by leopards, Tarzan says his scratches prove the attack was not by leopards who use both teeth and claws.
Tarzan agrees to accompany an expedition led by the commissioner in trying to find the supposed
killer leopards. Lazar, a half-breed, owes allegiance to a secret Bagandi tribe that worships a leopard god and whose warriors wear leopard skins and use claws as weapons. He is the lover of the
tribe's high priestess, Lea (Acquanetta), although he is detested by her younger brother Kimba
(Cook). His henchman Mongo (Anthony Caruso) and their men use real leopards to attack the
expedition. Tarzan kills several of the big cats but still doubts that they attacked the caravan
although he is ridiculed for his belief. Kimba watches the fray and, wanting to become a warrior,
vows to bring in the hearts of Jane and Boy. He goes to Tarzan's lair pretending to be lost and
hungry and is taken in by Jane. Tarzan and Boy are skeptical of his motives. When Tarzan and
Boy leave to get bamboo to fix the family shower, Kimba puts on a leopard outfit preparing to
kill Jane but Tarzan and Boy return. Later Jane becomes suspicious of Kimba when she sees a
fleeting figure of a leopard in the underbrush as Lazar has his warriors attack a caravan carrying
four young teachers (Iris Flores, Helen Gerald, Kay Solinas, Lillian Molieri). Boy finds Kimba's
leopard skin in a cave and puts it on and is captured by the warriors. Cheetah alerts Tarzan, who

saves him. As Tarzan tries to rescue the maidens, Kimba attempts to kill Jane and Boy but is hit by Cheetah and locked in a bamboo storehouse. Tarzan is captured by the leopard men and strapped to a mast in their cave. When Lea learns Kimba's whereabouts, she orders her men to rescue him. The leopard men free Kimba and capture Jane and Boy, taking them to the cave. The commissioner and his corporal (George J. Lewis) are near the area with their men hunting for killer leopards as Tarzan, Jane and Boy are sentenced to be sacrificed to the leopard god. Cheetah unties Tarzan and helps Jane and Boy to escape. When they are free, Tarzan pulls down the mast, causing the ceiling of the cave to collapse, killing Lea and most of her warriors. Lazar and Kimba survive but the injured boy kills Lazar before dying. With the cult destroyed and the commissioner convinced that leopards did not attack the caravans, Tarzan returns home with Jane and Boy.

The Film Daily opined, "It is apparent that Carroll Young was hard put to it to assemble worthwhile material for the newest of the Tarzan series adventure pictures.... The picture is strictly for kids, being much too obvious and unoriginal for the grown-ups." *Variety* carped, "Tarzan is growing old. After all these years of swinging through the trees and giving out with an occasional blood-curdling yell to thrill the kids in the front row, he's finally showing signs of age. Latest Tarzan film is bogged down by stock situations, unimaginative production and direction, indicating Sol Lesser ... is having difficulty keeping up the standard.... Brawny Weissmuller still makes a presentable Tarzan but he, too, shows signs of age, with a growing waistline and a minimum of athletic antics." On the other hand, *Boxoffice* declared it "a field day for juveniles and action addicts—the film has all the standard ingredients, backgrounds, clever trick photography, flora and fauna. The film is impressively produced and boasts an exceptionally good supporting cast."

Tarzan and the Mermaids (1948; 68 minutes)

PRODUCER: Sol Lesser. ASSOCIATE PRODUCER: Joe Noriega. DIRECTOR: Robert Florey. ASSOCIATE DIRECTOR: Miguel M. Delgado. STORY & SCREENPLAY: Carroll Young. PHOTOGRAPHY: Jack Draper. PHOTOGRAPHY ASSOCIATES: Gabriel Figueroa & Raul Martinez Solares. EDITORS: Merrill White & John Sheets. MUSIC: Dimitri Tiomkin. ART DIRECTOR: McClure Capps. ASSOCIATE ART DIRECTOR: Gunther Gerszo. PRODUCTION MANAGER: Ray Heinz. SOUND: James Fields. ASSOCIATE PRODUCTION MANAGERS: Antonio Guerrero Tello & John Mari. COSTUMES: Norma. ASSISTANT DIRECTOR: Bert Briskin. ASSOCIATE ASSISTANT DIRECTORS: Jaime Contreras & Moises Delgado.

CAST: Johnny Weissmuller (Tarzan), Brenda Joyce (Jane), George Zucco (High Priest Palanth), Linda Christian (Mara), Andrea Palma (Mara's Mother), Fernando Wagner (Varga), Edward Ashley (Commissioner), John Lauenz (Benji), Gustavo Rojo (Tiko), Matthew Boulton (British Inspector-General/Narrator).

After making 11 screen appearances as Tarzan since 1932, Johnny Weissmuller bade farewell to the role after *Tarzan and the Mermaids*, which RKO released in the spring of 1948. Costing over $1 million, it was the most expensive Tarzan film to date with filming at the Churubusco Studios near Mexico City along with Acapulco, Pier de la Cuesta, Puerto Marques, La Quebrada and San Juan de Teotihuacan's Aztec ruins. In addition to its scenic locales, the feature offered a music score by Dimitri Tiomkin that included Calypso songs. Its horror aspect is a lost island civilization ruled by a high priest (George Zucco) whose cohort (Fernando Wagner) masquerades as a supernatural god so they can control the populace, forcing them to dive for priceless pearls. Near the end, Tarzan does battle with a giant octopus.

While visually satisfying, *Tarzan and the Mermaids* was rife with problems. Director Robert Florey thought Carroll Young's script unacceptable, and so Albert DePina was called in to make revisions. Florey found it difficult working with both U.S. and Mexican crews and Miguel M. Delgado is credited as associate director. Johnny Weissmuller's stunt double, Angel Garcia, was killed making a cliff dive, producer Sol Lesser had a heart attack during the shooting and a hurricane wreaked havoc with some exterior sets. The loud music and overlong dancing numbers get in the way of the plot, which is somewhat baffling since its locale of the lost island of Aquatania is off the African coast yet populated by Mexicans except for high priest George Zucco with a British accent. Even more incredible is the character of a white singing African mailman, played by radio singer John Laurenz. One of his numbers is "I'm Taking a Letter to My Friend." The film also contained too much filler material with jousting and high diving.

Weissmuller acquits himself well in his last time out as Tarzan, appearing more youthful and energetic than in previous series entries. Brenda Joyce, in her fourth of five appearances as Jane, is as fetching and believable as ever, but the script omitted the part of Boy by having him at school in England. Linda Christian, Gustavo Rojo, Fernando Wagner and Andrea Palma, all popular Mexican players, are prominently featured. For horror fans there is a frail-looking Zucco as the evil high priest, whose costume looks like it is covered with marshmallows.

In a remote area of Africa, the Aquatanians, a strange cult, live an exotic existence diving for fabulous pearls which they give to the god Balu. Their dictator priest, Palanth (Zucco), and a corrupt trader, Varga (Wagner), fool the people into thinking Balu lives while in reality Varga impersonates the deity wearing royal robes and an ornate mask. Beautiful Mara (Christian) is chosen to be the bride of Balu and her mother Luana (Palma) warns her not to defy the gods. Mara loves Tiko (Rojo), who has been banished from the tribe. During the wedding ceremony, Mara jumps from a cliff into the sea and escapes her pursuers. Later she is caught in a fishing net by Tarzan (Weissmuller), who takes her home to his mate Jane (Joyce). The local singing postman Benji (Laurenz) has brought the couple a letter from Boy, who is attending school in England. Varga orders Palanth to find Mara, who tells her story to her protectors and gives Jane a beautiful black pearl. Jane presents it to the commissioner (Edward Ashley) to get money for new homes, a school and a hospital in the community of Nyaga. Palanth's men abduct Mara and take her back to Aquatania but Tarzan follows and that night he enters the forbidden temple on top of a rocky island, finding the Balu costume. Benji delivers the pearl to the commissioner and takes him to Tarzan's home, where Tiko has arrived looking for Mara. After hearing Tiko's story, the commissioner goes in search of Mara accompanied by Jane and Benji. They are captured at Aquatania, and Palanth plans to have them sacrificed to Balu. The god appears, silently orders them freed and sanctions the marriage of Mara and Tiko. Jane recognizes Tarzan as he impersonates Balu. The thwarted Palanth is later confronted by Tarzan, who tells him that if his people find out Balu is just a man they will destroy him. During the wedding festivities, Tarzan agrees to jump from a high rock as Varga returns with his men. The henchmen try to kill Tarzan after he dives but he eludes them and escapes from a giant octopus. Varga impersonates Balu and orders death for the strangers. Tarzan unmasks Varga and the natives turn on him and Palanth. Mara and Tiko are united in marriage.

Independent Exhibitors Film Bulletin noted, "The picture lacks smooth continuity, but does contain some effective spots." *The Film Daily* called *Tarzan and the Mermaids* a "top number in the series.... Full complement of action deriving from colorful fiction in script." *Harrison's Reports* called the feature "fairly entertaining.... [A]side from the usual heroics, the picture ... offers some fascinating seacoast backgrounds, as well as several aquatic sequences, some of which have been photographed under water." *Boxoffice* declared it "one of the better of the line and its reception by audiences generally should be resultantly enthusiastic." While *Variety* called the film "standard," the reviewer added, "Robert Florey gets credit for keeping an implausible story moving swiftly with a minimum of dull, hokey situations.... [There is] some spectacular camera work, probably the best on any Tarzan film."

Tarzan and the She-Devil (1953; 75 minutes)

PRODUCER: Sol Lesser. ASSOCIATE PRODUCER: Lloyd Richards. DIRECTOR: Kurt Neumann. SCREEN-PLAY: Karl Lamb & Carroll Young. PHOTOGRAPHY: Karl Struss. EDITOR: Leon Barsha. MUSIC: Paul Sawtell. MUSIC EDITOR: Audrey Granville. ART DIRECTOR: Carroll Clark. SOUND: Jean L. SPEAK. COS-TUMES: Wesley V. Jeffries. MAKEUP: Gustaf M. Norin. ASSISTANT DIRECTOR: Emmett Emerson.

CAST: Lex Barker (Tarzan), Joyce MacKenzie (Jane), Raymond Burr (Vargo), Monique Van Vooren (Lyra), Tom Conway (Fidel), Michael Grainger (Philippe Lavarre), Henry Brandon (M'Tara), Robert Bice (Maka), Michael Ross (Salim), Mara Corday (Laikopos Women's Leader), Lee Miller (Lyra's Guard), Ethan Laidlaw, Ted Hecht (Guards), Fred Aldrich (Slave), Al Kikume (Native at Dance), Frank Mills (Dance Spectator).

After playing Tarzan in five films since 1949, Lex Barker called it quits after *Tarzan and the She-Devil*, released in June 1953. This somewhat dour affair has Tarzan in a state of depression during much of its screen time and about the only humor involves the chimp Cheetah. In one amusing sequence Cheetah has a confrontation with an angry ostrich after he steals one of her eggs and in another scene he has trouble with a boomerang. Joyce MacKenzie makes a comely Jane but it is the villains who carry the film. Monique Van Vooren is sultry in the title role of the She-Devil while Raymond Burr excels as an oily, greedy ivory poacher and Tom Conway is equally good as the She-Devil's consort. Michael Grainger and Robert Bice make the most of their parts as a French poacher and expedition guide, respectively. The exotic Van Vooren was an actress and internationally known chanteuse who recorded the best-selling record album *Mink in Hi-Fi* (RCA LPM-1553) in 1958. Conway previously appeared in *Tarzan's Secret Treasure* (1941). Much of the "perils of the jungle" footage used in *Tarzan and the She-Devil* was from the 1934 RKO box office blockbuster *Wild Cargo*.

The feature was filmed as *Tarzan and the Ivory Hunters* and *Tarzan Meets the Vampire*. The latter title referred to Van Vooren's siren role as there is nothing horrific about the feature other than the needless slaughter of elephants for their ivory tusks. During scenes in which Jane is delirious, she dreams of a giant octopus (from *Tarzan and the Mermaids*) and a monstrous black spider (from *Tarzan's Desert Mystery*).

Tarzan (Barker) defends the animals of Africa, especially elephants who are hunted and killed to satisfy the greed of ivory hunters for "white gold." Ruthless poachers Vargo (Burr) and Philippe Lavarre (Grainger) lead natives carrying elephant tusks to Dagar when Tarzan stampedes a nearby herd. Although Lavarre says they have plenty of tusks, Vargo states there are never enough. Complaining about the quality of the bearers supplied to him by his employers Lyra (Van Vooren) and Fidel (Conway), Vargo suggests to Lavarre they capture the men of the Laikopos tribe and use them to build a stockade so the elephants cannot escape. Lavarre heads into Laikopos country to establish a site for their venture while Vargo takes the tusks to Dagar where he tells Lyra and Fidel of his plan, saying there is a fortune awaiting them. Fidel declares that Laikopos country is dangerous and he wants Lyra to quit the ivory trade. Lyra likes Vargo's idea and orders her guide Maka (Bice) to prepare the expedition. He warns her that the Laikopos and Tarzan are friends. Maka and his men ambush the Laikopos and capture all the tribesmen, including their chief M'Tara (Henry Brandon). The women of the tribe escape and seek out Tarzan and his mate Jane (MacKenzie) and Tarzan goes to Dagar to free the Laikopos tribesmen, accompanied by his pet chimp Cheetah. That night while guards watch a native girl dance, Tarzan sneaks into the courtyard where the men are kept prisoners, frees them and drops a cache of rifles down a well. As the tribesmen escape, an alarm is sounded and Tarzan is forced to fight Lyra's servant Salim (Michael Ross) but escapes after defeating him. Lyra, Fidel and Vargo lead a foray after the tribesmen but run into Tarzan and Jane near their treetop home. Tarzan refuses Lyra's offer

Poster for *Tarzan and the She-Devil* (1953).

to guide her expedition to capture the elephants and tells the intruders to go back to Dagar. Lyra orders Vargo to recapture the tribesmen while Fidel takes Jane prisoner. Tarzan is captured along with the tribesmen but Fidel and his men bungle their attempt to get Jane. As Jane swings away on a vine, it catches fire and breaks, causing her to drop to the ground unconscious. Tarzan is able to get free and returns home to find Jane missing. Thinking she is dead, Tarzan does not fight when Vargo and is men recapture him. Jane comes to but cannot endure the horrors of the jungle and collapses again. She is found by an elephant who carries her to a friendly tribe but she becomes delirious. Vargo whips Tarzan but it has no effect on the jungle man. When Lyra again tries to get Tarzan to help her with the elephant drive, he asks her why she killed Jane. Vargo and his men again capture the Laikopos tribesmen and take them to Lavarre's camp to start building the stockade. After having terrible dreams, Jane recovers and calls for Tarzan, who wakes and yells her name, with Vargo chaining him in a cell. As Vargo and Lavarre eat, Cheetah steals their water gourd and takes it to Tarzan. As the stockade is being assembled, Fidel is forced to shoot a rogue elephant, causing the herd to stampede. An angry Vargo tells Fidel to go back to Dagar but before leaving Fidel overhears Vargo and Lavarre plan to steal his and Lyra's share of the ivory sale. Jane returns to Dagar and is told by Lyra that Tarzan is deep in the jungle and she leaves to hunt for him. She meets the returning Fidel, who informs Lyra of Vargo and Lavarre's treachery. Lyra orders Jane captured again and she and Fidel take her to Lavarre's camp where Tarzan is hanging by his wrists, still refusing to help the poachers. Lyra orders him cut down and then shows him that Jane is alive and tells Tarzan that if he helps her, he and Jane can go free. Lyra orders Fidel to have Vargo and Lavarre tied up. Tarzan agrees to Lyra's offer but when he calls the elephants, he signals M'Tara and his tribe to close the stockade gates. The elephants charge the stockade and break through as Tarzan rescues Jane. Fidel attempts to shoot Tarzan but when Lyra tries to stop him, he accidentally shoots her before they are trampled by the elephants. Vargo manages to break his bonds and run away while Lavarre is killed by the elephants. Jane, Tarzan and Cheetah take refuge from the rampaging elephants, who trample Vargo. With the ivory poachers dead and the elephant herd safe, Tarzan, Jane and Cheetah return home.

Boxoffice described *Tarzan and the She-Devil* as "neither better nor worse than the average run of features released during the past several seasons top-lining that hardy perennial among jungle adventures, Tarzan...." *Variety* called it "a tedious affair for a goodly portion of its 75 minutes.... Lex Barker looks like a Tarzan should, and consequently comes across okay in the lead, while Joyce MacKenzie is acceptable as his vis-à-vis.... Kurt Neumann's direction ... is on the slow side, but then he wasn't given much to work with."

Tarzan and the Slave Girl (1950; 74 minutes)

PRODUCER: Sol Lesser. DIRECTOR: Lee Sholem. SCREENPLAY: Hans Jacoby & Arnold Belgard. PHOTOGRAPHY: Russell Harlan. EDITOR: Christian Nyby. MUSIC: Paul Sawtell. PRODUCTION DESIGN: Harry Horner. SOUND: John Tribby. PRODUCTION SUPERVISOR: Glenn Cook. ASSISTANT DIRECTOR: James Casey.

CAST: Lex Barker (Tarzan), Vanessa Brown (Jane), Robert Alda (Neil), Hurd Hatfield (Prince of Lionians), Arthur Shields (Dr. E.E. Campbell), Anthony Caruso (Sengo), Denise Darcel (Lola), Robert Warwick (High Priest), Mary Ellen Kay (Moana), Alfonso Pedroza (Nagasi Chief), Tito Renaldo (Chief's Son), Satini Puajloa (Medicine Man), Tom Hern (Molo), Tiny McClure (Wadi Chief), Paul Burns (Elephant Keeper), Freddy Ridgeway (Prince's Son), Martin Wilkins (Serum Bearer), Russ Conklin, Fred Carson, Tom Famarez, Vincent Romaine, Charles Mauu (Nagasi Warriors), Blue Washington, Dook McGill (Randini Bearers), Mona Knox, Jackee Waldron, Rosemary Bertrand, Shirley Ballard, Martha Clemons, Gwen Caldwell, Josephine Parra (Slave Girls), Peter Virgo, Peter Mamakos, Philip E. Harron, Allan Church (Lionian Henchmen), Gene Gary, Gene East (Lionian Guards), Sheldon Jett (Fat Eunuch), George Magrill, Victor Romito (Lionian Warriors).

Lex Barker's second outing as Tarzan for producer Sol Lesser was *Tarzan and the Slave Girl*, issued theatrically in the summer of 1950. It gave him a new Jane, Vanessa Brown in her solo effort in the role, plus more dialogue than usual for his jungle man character. The production moves at a pretty good clip and its plot includes a lost sect of lion worshippers and their hidden city with its Egyptian appearance. The royal tomb set is impressive. The film is not overburdened with animal stock footage or the antics of chimp Cheetah. Its highlight is the appearance of Denise Darcel as a sharp-tongued, flirtatious nurse and her cat fight with Jane over Tarzan. The plot also includes the fierce Wadi warriors, some of the scariest of Tarzan's many movie adversaries. On the other hand, *Tarzan and the Slave Girl* is a retread in that the lost civilization angle was used previously in *Tarzan and the Amazons*, *Tarzan and the Leopard Woman*, *Tarzan and the Mermaids* and *Tarzan's Magic Fountain* (qq.v.), and Tarzan and company crossing a deep gorge to get to a hidden city was done before in *Tarzan and the Amazons*. In past Tarzan films the jungle man would call on a herd of elephants to come to his aid but in *Tarzan and the Slave Girl* he is only given one obviously aged pachyderm on which to rely.

As Tarzan (Barker) and Jane (Brown) ride an elephant followed by chimps Cheetah and Coco, they exchange greetings with several women of the Nagasi tribe, including Moana (Mary Ellen Kay), who is engaged to marry the chief's (Alfonso Pedroza) son (Tito Renaldo). Soon they hear a scream and learn that Moana has disappeared. As Tarzan and Jane take separate paths in investigating the disappearance, Jane is carried away by several men. Tarzan hears Jane call to him and follows, capturing one of the abductors, Molo (Tom Hern), and cutting the face of another, Sengo (Anthony Caruso), in a fight. After the men knock out Tarzan, they escape via the river. After coming to, Tarzan takes Molo to the Nagasi village where he is questioned. Jane realizes that the man is ill and tells Tarzan to go to Randini for a doctor. After a lengthy journey, Tarzan arrives in Randini and informs Dr. Campbell (Arthur Shields) of Molo's symptoms. The doctor fears it might be a very contagious disease. After ordering his nurse Lola (Darcel) to give reluctant Tarzan a hypo, Campbell plans to accompany Tarzan back to the Nagasi village. Lola begs to go along since she is attracted to Tarzan. In the village, Campbell inoculates the Nagasis and then tells Tarzan they must find the abductors since he believes they are the source of the disease. Lola's lazy American hunter boyfriend Neil (Robert Alda) is enlisted to organize the safari. Although Lola wants to go with Tarzan and Campbell, Tarzan tells Jane to take her to their tree house and stay there until he returns. When they get to the tree house, Lola taunts Jane about Tarzan being attracted to her and the two women fight with the angry Lola running into the jungle. There she is captured by Sengo and his men, who also abduct Jane when she tries to come to Lola's rescue. The two women are herded into the jungle to be taken to Sengo's tribe, the Lionians, a sect of lion worshippers. Lola apologizes to Jane for causing trouble. As Tarzan, Campbell, Neil and the Nagasi chief's son and their bearers track the abductors, they are surrounded by warriors of the fierce Wadi tribe who camouflage themselves as foliage and kill with poison darts. Earlier Sengo had told his Wadi allies to kill Tarzan and the members of his safari. After an extended fight with the Wadis in which several of the bearers die, Tarzan and his colleagues cross a deep ravine on a fallen tree and Tarzan pushes the tree into the ravine, thwarting their pursuers. Neil injures his leg and lags behind with Cheetah as the rest of the group goes on to the Lionians' city. Along the way one of the bearers accidentally drops the serum needed to fight the disease but Cheetah finds it and gives it to Neil. Sengo and his men arrive in the city where he tells the prince (Hurd Hatfield) that the young women they have brought are needed to rebuild their civilization because of the disease that just killed his father, their king. When the high priest (Robert Warwick) objects and says the women must be returned to their homes, Sengo convinces the prince to get rid of the high priest by throwing him into a lion's den. Lola is attracted to the prince and tells Sengo she will soon be his queen and he orders her to be beaten. When he confronts her again, Lola grabs Sengo's knife and stabs him. Jane and Lola escape but end up in the royal tomb which is being prepared for the prince's father. Sengo realizes they are in the tomb and orders the queen's chamber, where the women are hiding, to be sealed. Tarzan, Campbell and the Nagasi chief's son arrive in the city and the doctor informs the prince he can cure his little son (Freddy Ridgeway) who also has the disease. Tarzan escapes from the group since he heard Jane call to him upon his arrival in the city. When Campbell realizes he does not have the needed serum, Sengo convinces the prince to feed him to the lions. The prince orders his father's funeral to take place and the late king's coffin is sealed in the crypt. Unknown to the Lionians, Tarzan is hiding in the coffin and manages to move a heavy stone and free Jane and Lola from the queen's chamber. Neil and Cheetah arrive with the serum and Campbell saves the prince's son's life. As Sengo is about to execute the high priest, Tarzan calls to an elephant who breaks down the stone door of the tomb, and he and Jane and Lola emerge. Sengo tells the tribesmen that Tarzan and his group desecrated the king's tomb and orders them captured. Tarzan, with the help of Cheetah and the elephant, fight off the Lionians. After a scuffle with Sengo, Tarzan throws him into the lion pit. The prince orders his warriors to cease fighting and as the new king he asks Lola to stay but Cheetah chains her to Neil.

The New York Times commented, "There is no point in throwing any poisoned critical darts at *Tarzan and the Slave Girl*.... The adventures of the jungle athlete have been going on for a long time now and probably will continue so long as little boys go to the movies.... About the only novelty the picture offers is Cheetah's encounter with a bottle of whisky, and even that isn't very funny." *Variety* felt the film "figures out as a neat entry for this long-lived series market. The casting is apt, the production design good and the action pace just right to sustain the adventuring." Gabe Essoe in *Tarzan of the Movies* (1968) zeroed in on Denise Darcel's assets: "As a half-breed nurse with a yen for men and an immediate fancy for Tarzan, Denise Darcel added a lot of spice to the film, especially when attired in a revealing sarong. Pictures of her holding on to Barker's leg appeared in many girlie magazines."

Tarzan Triumphs (1943; 76 minutes)

PRODUCER: Sol Lesser. DIRECTOR: William Thiele. SCREENPLAY: Roy Chanslor & Carroll Young. STORY: Carroll Young. PHOTOGRAPHY: Harry Wild. EDITOR: Hal Kern. MUSIC: Paul Sawtell. MUSIC DIRECTOR: C. Bakaleinikoff. ART DIRECTOR: Hans Peters. SOUND: John P. Grubb. PRODUCTION DESIGN: Harry Horner. WARDROBE: Elmer Ellsworth. ASSISTANT DIRECTOR: Clem Beauchamp.

CAST: Johnny Weissmuller (Tarzan), Johnny Sheffield (Boy), Frances Gifford (Zandra), Stanley Ridges (Colonel von Reichart), Sig Ruman (Sergeant), Philip Van Zandt (Captain Bausch), Rex Williams (Lt. Reinhardt Schmidt), Pedro de Cordoba (Oman), Otto Reichow (Gruber), Stanley Brown (Achmet), Sven Hugo Borg (Heinz), Manuel Paris (Omar), Wilhelm von Brincken (General Hoffman), George Lynn (Pilot), William Yetter (Guard).

When Metro-Goldwyn-Mayer decided to drop its lucrative Tarzan series following *Tarzan's New York Adventure* in 1942, producer Sol Lesser bought the rights to the character and made a deal with RKO to release a new series of films based on the Edgar Rice Burroughs character. Johnny Weissmuller and Johnny Sheffield continued in their roles of Tarzan and Boy. The character of Jane does not appear in the first RKO outing, *Tarzan Triumphs*, which the studio released theatrically in February 1943. Lesser complied with the request of the State Department to depict Tarzan in a patriotic manner and Carroll Young's original story has the jungle man at odds with Nazis in Central Africa. Gorgeous Frances Gifford enacts the feminine lead as the daughter of a ruler of a lost city whose mineral riches are coveted by the Axis powers. In 1941 Gifford played the title role in the Republic serial *Jungle Girl*, based on the novel by Edgar Rice Burroughs, the creator of Tarzan. *Tarzan Triumphs* greatly benefits from her presence since the villainous characters are presented as typically arrogant Aryans. In one scene the Nazi colonel (Stanley Ridges) calls one of his men a "clumsy oaf" when he trips. The propaganda piece also includes a classic phrase delivered by Tarzan: "Jungle people fight to live. Civilized people live to fight." Being the first Tarzan film in over a year and with its patriotic trappings, *Tarzan Triumphs* proved to be a huge moneymaker for RKO and served as a good springboard for the 11 others that followed it. Of the 12 Tarzan movies released by RKO, only *Tarzan and the Huntress* (1947) and *Tarzan's Savage Fury* (1952) did not have horror or fantasy elements. *Tarzan Triumphs* was re-released to theaters by RKO in 1949.

While exploring the African jungle, Boy (Sheffield) and his pet chimp Cheetah come across the hidden city of Pallandria. Boy falls off a cliff and lands on a tree branch and is saved by beautiful Zandra (Gifford) with the trio being rescued by Tarzan (Weissmuller). Back in their jungle home, Tarzan tells Boy that outside people always bring trouble and then has him read a letter from his mate Jane, who is in London tending to her ill mother and contending with the Nazi blitz of the city. German planes fly over the jungle searching for a place to build a landing field so the Nazis can exploit the area's oil and mineral reserves. Several of the soldiers parachute into the jungle; Schmidt (Rex Williams) is hurt when he lands and uses his radio to get help but his rescuers are blinded by a flock of flamingos and their plane crashes. Tarzan rescues Schmidt from a crocodile and takes him to his jungle home where the German claims to be an English explorer named Sheldon. A convoy of Germans lead by Colonel von Reichart (Ridges) and Captain Bausch (Philip Van Zandt) arrives in Pallandria and are greeted by Zandra, the daughter of Oman (Pedro de Cordoba), the city's ruler. Zandra once saved Bausch when she found him injured in the jungle and introduces the Germans to her father, who makes them welcome. The next day Reichart orders his men to take over the city, and begins using its men as slaves. He also tries to seduce Zandra but she rejects him. When he attempts to force himself on her, Achmet (Stanley Brown), her brother, comes to her rescue and is shot. At Tarzan's tree house, Schmidt tries to use his radio to reach Berlin but Cheetah steals its coil. Zandra escapes from Pallandria but is pursued through the jungle by a German sergeant (Sig Rumann) and his men. She is rescued by Tarzan and all the Germans except the sergeant are killed by flesh-devouring fish. When Cheetah again steals Schmidt's radio coil, the German tries to shoot the chimp but is killed when Tarzan's pet elephant pushes him off a cliff. Zandra tries to convince Tarzan to help her people but he wants to remain neutral. The sergeant returns to Pallandria and informs Reichart and Bausch that Tarzan has their radio and he is ordered to return it. Zandra attempts to go home but Tarzan follows and convinces her to come back with him. When they arrive at his tree house, they find the Germans torturing Boy. Tarzan is shot by the soldiers, who take Boy prisoner. Zandra is led to Tarzan by Cheetah and she remains with him until he has recovered. Once he is well, Tarzan goes to Pallandria but is taken prisoner by the occupiers and sentenced to be shot the next day. Zandra returns home and again rejects Reichart's advances. When she tries to shoot him, she too is sentenced to die. The people attempt a revolt and Reichart orders one in ten be shot along with Tarzan and Zandra. Cheetah shows up with the radio coil, steals the sergeant's knife and cuts Tarzan loose. Seeing Tarzan free, the sergeant attempts to shoot him but the jungle man kills him with his own knife. Tarzan destroys the German's machine gun and frees their captives, who retake Pallandria. Cheetah shoots Bausch, and Reichart escapes into the jungle with the radio. Tarzan plays a game of cat and mouse with Reichart, who tries to call Berlin, but ends up being killed when he falls into a trap and is devoured by a lion.

"Quite a measure of suspense accrues during the development" of *Tarzan Triumphs*, stated *The Motion Picture Herald*. The reviewer added, "William Thiele's direction maintains plausibility [and] the production measures up to expectations." Bosley Crowther in *The New York Times* thought it "pretty much of a piece with the previous Tarzan fables.... It may please a lot of people to see Tarzan banging Nazis right and left. But the jest is decidedly hollow. Cheta [*sic*] the Chimp still has the best brain in the film." *Boxoffice* felt the film "adds up to excellent entertainment for theaters with a fair quota of juvenile attendance and action fans. The excellence of the photography, the antics of the trained baboon and a young elephant, with a few wild animals to add to the menace, keep the action moving at a fast pace, and the story hangs together with more plausibility than might be expected." *Photoplay* noted, "The one-man blitz put on by Tarzan is a piparoo, bringing loads of cheering from the kids in the balcony." *Variety* said the feature "will catch strong attention from the juvenile trade, otherwise it's a dual supporter generally." *The Hollywood Reporter* stated, "The script and its excellent direction by William Thiele mixes enough plausible incident to balance the more extravagant flights of pure fancy...."

Tarzan's Desert Mystery (1943; 70 minutes)

EXECUTIVE PRODUCER: Sol Lesser, Associate Producer: Kurt Neumann. DIRECTOR: William Thiele (& uncredited Kurt Neumann). SCREENPLAY: Edward T. Lowe & Carroll Young. PHOTOGRAPHY: Russ Harlan & Harry Wild. EDITOR: Ray Lockert. MUSIC: Paul Sawtell. MUSIC DIRECTOR: C. Bakaleinikoff. ART DIRECTORS: Ralph Berger & Hans Peters. SOUND: Jean L. Speak & Bailey Fesler. SET DECORATIONS: Victor Gangelin & Stanley Murphy. WARDROBE: Elmer Ellsworth. ASSISTANT DIRECTOR: Derwin Abrahams.

CAST: Johnny Weissmuller (Tarzan), Nancy Kelly (Connie Bryce), Johnny Sheffield (Boy), Otto Kruger (Paul Hendrix), Joe Sawyer (Karl Straeder), Lloyd Corrigan (Sheik Abdul El Khim), Robert Lowery (Prince Selim), Frank Puglia (Magistrate), Philip Van Zandt (Kushmet), Edward Ashley (Sheik Omar), Frank Faylen (Achmed Nogash Segali), George J. Lewis (Ali Baba Hassan), Nestor Paiva (Guard), John Berkes (Charlie), Syd Saylor (Nomad with Camel), Dorothy Adams (Complaining Woman), Bobby Barber (Turban Vendor), Dice (Jaynar).

In an attempt to duplicate the impressive box office success of *Tarzan Triumphs* [q.v.], producer Sol Lesser's second RKO series release, *Tarzan's Desert Mystery*, continued the initial's outings path of the jungle man (Johnny Weissmuller) opposing Nazis. As more box office bait it added a prehistoric locale inhabited by giant lizards, man-eating plants and a monstrous black spider. Again the character of Jane is missing; this time the leading lady (Nancy Kelly) is a magician trying to alert a desert sheik (Lloyd Corrigan) that a Nazi (Otto Kruger) is working in the area. Originally titled *Tarzan Against the Sahara*, the feature did not satisfy Lesser and he had associate producer Kurt Neumann do retakes with the monster sequences tacked onto the end of the production. The result is a very uneven outing that looks like two films sewn together. Further lessening the movie's quality, the dinosaurs were the blown-up lizards from *One Million B.C.* (1940) with Weissmuller superimposed into the footage. Despite its dissimilar plot ploys, *Tarzan's Desert Mystery* proved to be another financial winner for RKO. It was issued late in 1943 with most of its playdates coming the next year. RKO reissued it theatrically in 1949.

After an airplane drops a mail pouch near the jungle home of Tarzan (Weissmuller), Boy (Johnny Sheffield) reads a letter from Jane who is working a as a wartime nurse in London. She requests that Tarzan send her a supply of a medicine that will combat jungle fever. As Tarzan, Boy and Cheetah trek through the jungle to the edge of a desert, Sheik Abdul El Khim (Lloyd Corrigan) and his son Prince Selim (Robert Lowery) return to their home in Bir Herari and are greeted by trader Paul Hendrix (Kruger), who instructs his henchman Karl Straeder (Joe Sawyer) to capture a wild stallion as a gift for the sheik. When Straeder and his men abuse the horse Jaynar (Dice), Tarzan stops them. The steed allows Boy to ride him to an oasis where entertainer Connie Bryce (Kelly) has stopped with her three native bearers (Frank Faylen, Philip Van Zandt, John Berkes). Connie is bringing a message concealed in a bracelet from Sheik Omar (Edward

Ashley) for his fellow Yale graduate Selim, warning him that Hendrix is a German spy out to arm local tribesmen. When the bearers ask Connie to show them her magic act in which she gets sawed in half, she does so but her fake screams causes Tarzan to intervene, scaring off the nomads. To make amends, Tarzan offers to accompany Connie to Bir Herari but when they arrive, Hendrix accuses the jungle man of stealing Jaynar and he is put in jail. Hendrix gives the horse to the grateful sheik but Selim does not trust the trader and warns his father against him. As Cheetah does a wire act to amuse the locals, Connie sings a Yale song, alerting Selim she has a message from Omar. That night she gives him the bracelet while Hendrix and Straeder spy on them. After Connie leaves, they murder Selim; Cheetah escapes with the bracelet. Hendrix accuses Connie of killing Selim and she is found guilty by the magistrate (Frank Puglia) and sentenced to hang. Boy and Cheetah help Tarzan escape from his prison cell by ambushing a guard (Nestor Paiva) and making a rope out of turbans. As Connie is about to be hung, Tarzan rides to her rescue on Jaynar and they go back into the desert with Boy and Cheetah, heading to the jungle where the fever medicine plants grow. They get stranded in a camel driver's hut during a sandstorm but elude Hendrix, Straeder and their men, who have followed them. Tarzan leaves Connie, Boy, Cheetah and Jaynar on the edge of the jungle as he goes in search of the plants. The Germans chase the quartet into the jungle where Straeder is killed by a lion. A giant lizard chases Connie and Boy into a cave inhabited by a huge spider. Boy gets caught in its web as Cheetah goes for Tarzan, who is snared by a man-eating plant. He calls to a herd of elephants who free him and he arrives at the cave in time to stop Hendrix from shooting Connie. The spider devours Hendrix. Tarzan rescues Boy and Connie and they go back to Bir Herari where Connie presents the sheik with the message from Omar. As she leaves, Tarzan gives her the medicine for Jane.

The Film Daily called *Tarzan's Desert Mystery* "strictly kid stuff.... The picture is one long string of events designed to stir up the youngsters no end. This happens so fast and furiously that Tarzan is scarcely is given time to draw a deep breath." According to *The Hollywood Reporter*, "[E]ntertainment falls below standard for the perennial series. It makes too many compromises and wanders too far from the domain where Tarzan is seen to his best advantage." *The New York Times* snidely reported, "Watching *Tarzan's Desert Mystery*, one can almost believe himself back in the declining heyday of Pearl White and *The Perils of Pauline*." *Variety* wrote, "*Tarzan's Desert Mystery* doesn't miss a thing with its quota of Nazi agents and gruesome animals plus the usual Tarzan jungle scenes...." *Boxoffice* predicted that the picture "will probably be popular with juveniles who like their adventure stuff raw and undiluted."

Tarzan's Hidden Jungle (1955; 72 minutes)

PRODUCER: Sol Lesser. DIRECTOR: Harold Schuster. SCREENPLAY: William Lively. PHOTOGRAPHY: William Whitney. EDITOR: Leon Barsha. MUSIC: Paul Sawtell. ART DIRECTOR: William Flannery. SOUND: Jean L. Speak. WARDROBE: Henry West. MAKEUP: Jack Byron. CONTINUITY: Winifred K. Thackrey. ASSISTANT DIRECTOR: Harry Templeton.

CAST: Gordon Scott (Tarzan), Vera Miles (Jill Hardy), Peter Van Eyck (Dr. Bob Celliers), Jack Elam (Burger), Charles Fredericks (DeGroot), Richard Reeves (Reeves), Don Beddoe (Mr. Johnson), Ike Jones (Malenki), Rex Ingram (Sukulu Makuma), Jester Hairston (Witch Doctor), Maidie Norman (Suma), Zippy (Cheetah), Lucky the Chimp.

Gordon Scott took over the role of Tarzan in *Tarzan's Hidden Jungle*, released by RKO Radio early in 1955. Unfortunately producer Sol Lesser spared every expense in putting together this lackluster production, whose only asset is its lead players. Scott makes a convincing Tarzan and Scott's future wife Vera Miles an appealing leading lady. Peter Van Eyck is fine as a good Samaritan doctor while Jack Elam, Charles Fredericks and Richard Reeves are appropriately oily villains. Zippy, from NBC-TV's *Howdy Doody*, took over the role of Cheetah in this outing and is given a romantic interest in another chimp, Lucky. There is little here to recommend to horror fans other than a lost tribe of animal worshippers who toss condemned hunters into a lion pit. The film is overburdened with stock footage, much of it too grainy to match the new scenes filmed on location at Thousand Oaks, California's, World Animal Jungle Compound. *Tarzan's Hidden Jungle* proved to be RKO's final association with the jungle man as Lesser moved the property to Metro-Goldwyn-Mayer. Scott starred in four more series outings, all with increased production values and in color: *Tarzan and the Lost Safari* (1957), *Tarzan's Fight for Life* (1958), *Tarzan's Greatest Adventure* (1959) and *Tarzan the Magnificent* (1960). In addition, Scott played the jungle man in three episodes of an unsold Tarzan television series that were cobbled together as *Tarzan and the Trappers* (1958) and issued to theaters in Europe and shown on television in the U.S.

Hunters DeGroot (Fredericks) and Reeves (Reeves) complain about the lack of game as they shoot a baby elephant and a fawn. Tarzan (Scott) scares off their beaters, who are trying to herd animals in order for them to be shot, and then uses tree sap to stop the elephant's bleeding. The natives return to DeGroot and Reeves, who suggest the best herds are in Sukulu country across the river. The head porter, Malenki (Ike Jones), warns the men that it is taboo and the Sukulus are a lost tribe of animal worshippers who kill anyone who kills an animal. DeGroot scoffs at Malenki's claims and tells Reeves to scout the area or they will not have enough animals

Vera Miles and Gordon Scott in *Tarzan's Hidden Jungle* (1955).

to get paid by their boss, Burger (Elam). The reluctant Reeves crosses the river and spots a large elephant herd, shooting a bull. He is captured by the tribesman, with Tarzan's pet chimp Cheetah stealing his watch, and taken to their village where the chief (Rex Ingram) sentences him and he is thrown into a lion pit. When DeGroot brings in the day's slim kill, Burger has to face his employer, Johnson (Don Beddoe), who demands he fulfill his contract in ten days. Malenki tells Burger about Tarzan, saying he is a friend of all animals. When Burger sees Cheetah with Reeves' pocket watch around his neck, he tells DeGroot they must go to Sukulu country and find Reeves as well as get their quota of animals to satisfy Johnson. On the way to the river, the two men are confronted by Tarzan and demand the return of the baby elephant but he refuses. Tarzan informs Burger and DeGroot that he is taking the animal to a clinic run by Dr. Robert Celliers (Van Eyck) for medical attention and they decide to follow him there. Since Celliers is the only white man the Sukulu tribe trusts, the two hunters formulate a plan to accompany him into Sukulu territory by pretending to be documentary filmmakers. Once there they plan to herd the elephants across the river and capture them. On his way to the clinic with the elephant, Tarzan sees a beautiful woman bathing in the river. She turns out to be Dr. Cellier's nurse, Jill Hardy (Miles). Dr. Cellier removes a bullet from the elephant and is amazed at the healing power of the tree sap Tarzan used on the elephant and asks for more, hoping it will help his human patients. Tarzan leaves to get more of the liquid as Burger and DeGroot arrive at the clinic and try to convince Dr. Cellier to take them with him to see the Sukulus. The physician refuses, but changes his mind when Jill tells him his work needs to be publicized. When the doctor and the two hunters leave for Sukulu country, Malenki follows DeGroot's orders and tries to take the elephant, with Jill stopping him. She learns from Malenki that Burger and DeGroot are hunters and not filmmakers. Tarzan finds out about Jill going to warn Dr. Cellier and follows. Jill drives into the jungle but her car quits and she finds herself entangled in thick flora and menaced by wild creatures. Frightened by a large snake, Jill gets stuck in quicksand but Tarzan pulls her out. Dr. Celliers is welcomed by the Sukulu chief but is scorned by the witch doctor (Jester Hairston). Burger and DeGroot spot an elephant herd and remove the muffler from their Jeep. The noise from the Jeep causes the elephants to stampede across the river. Tarzan and Jill reach the village, and Jill tells Dr. Cellier that Burger and DeGroot deceived him. When tribesmen inform the chief that the elephants have been stampeded, he orders the witch doctor to evoke the spirits that say Dr. Cellier and Jill are to die. Tarzan escapes from the village and calls to the elephants, causing them to reverse their charge. Returning home, they trample Burger and DeGroot. Getting back to the village just as Dr. Cellier and Jill are tossed into the lion pit, Tarzan tames the beasts and his friends are set free.

Variety felt *Tarzan's Hidden Jungle* "a stock entry in the Edgar Rice Burroughs apeman marathon produced by Sol Lesser," adding that Gordon Scott "is a well muscled man but seldom convincing in the part." *The Hollywood Reporter* declared it "sub-standard Tarzan filmfare.... The William Lively screenplay has practically no action...."

Tarzan's Magic Fountain (1949; 73 minutes)

PRODUCER: Sol Lesser. DIRECTOR: Lee Sholem. SCREENPLAY: Curt Siodmak & Harry Chandlee. PHOTOGRAPHY: Karl Struss. EDITOR: Merrill White. MUSIC: Alexander Laslo. ART DIRECTORS: McClure Capps & Phil Paradise. SOUND: Franklin Hansen. WARDROBE: Frank Beeston. MAKEUP: Norbert Miles. ASSISTANT DIRECTOR: Bert Briskin.

CAST: Lex Barker (Tarzan), Brenda Joyce (Jane), Albert Dekker (Trask), Evelyn Ankers (Gloria James), Charles Drake (Dodd), Alan Napier (Douglas Jessup), Ted Hecht (Pasco), Henry Brandon (Siko), Henry Kulky (Vredak), David Bond (The High One), Rory Mallinson (Henchman), Elmo Lincoln (Fisherman),

Rick Vallin (Mountain Leader), Suzanne Ridgeway (Blue Valley Girl), Blue Washington (Beaten Workman).

Lex Barker took over the role of Tarzan in *Tarzan's Magic Fountain*, released by RKO in February 1949. He proved to be well cast as the Lord of the Jungle and would make four more Tarzan features for producer Sol Lesser. Brenda Joyce, who played Jane in the four previous entries, left the series after this outing. The plot of *Tarzan's Magic Fountain* was similar to *She* (q.v.), although it is rejuvenating waters instead of fire that keeps its lovely protagonist (Evelyn Ankers) young. Obvious cost-cutting measures has the film's lost city set being the same one used in *Tarzan and the Leopard Woman* (q.v.); there is also footage from *Tarzan and the Amazons* (q.v.) and a plethora of back screen projection. In addition to the fountain of youth fantasy angle, the film offers horror film favorite Evelyn Ankers, whose character ages without the youth-restoring elixir. Between 1941 and 1945 Ankers appeared in 11 genre efforts for Universal, making her the most popular horror heroine of that era. Villain Albert Dekker was in the horror outings *Dr. Cyclops* (1940), *She Devil* (1957) and *Gamera the Invincible* (1966), as well as RKO's *Experiment Perilous* (q.v.). Overall, *Tarzan's Magic Fountain* proved to be an auspicious Tarzan debut for Barker.

Cheetah, the pet chimpanzee of Tarzan (Barker) and Jane (Joyce), plays with an old cigarette case she found and Jane notices it carries the inscription "To Gloria from Douglas" and is dated October 1928. As Jane wonders about the origin of the object, Cheetah and another chimp go to a hidden airplane crash site with its three skeletons. Cheetah retrieves a pouch housing a diary and takes it home. Jane learns it was written by famous flier Gloria James (Ankers), who disappeared in the African jungles two decades before on an around-the-world flight. While Tarzan refuses to discuss the matter with Jane, he later takes the diary to Air Service Operator owner-pilot Dodd (Charles Drake) in Nyaga and asks him to mail it to Gloria's family in England. Trask (Dekker), who operates a trading post, overhears the conversation and recalls there is a substantial reward for any information on the missing aviatrix offered by Douglas Jessup (Alan Napier), who is serving a life sentence for murder although he claims Gloria can clear him. Knowing Gloria is still alive, Tarzan goes to remote Blue Valley where he is greeted by the High One (David Bond) who permits the woman to depart with him. Rebellious tribesmen Pasco (Ted Hecht) and Siko (Henry Brandon) fear that her leaving will bring outsiders to their land, whose waters have the power to heal the sick and restore youth. When Tarzan returns home with Gloria, Jane is surprised by her youthful appearance. In Nyaga, Dodd agrees to fly Gloria to Nairobi as he recalls a local legend about a fountain of youth. Although Trask scoffs at the idea, he hires Vredak (Henry Kulky), a thug whom Tarzan has whipped twice, once for beating a mule and for doing the same thing to a workman (Blue Washington). Vredak and his henchman (Rory Mallinson) eventually stumble onto the rocky path leading to Blue Valley but the Mountain Leader (Rick Vallin) pins him to a tree with a fiery arrow as the rest of his party runs away. Seeing the incident, Pasco declares death for Tarzan, and Siko vows to carry it out. An airplane drops a mail packet near Tarzan and Jane's home and in it is a letter from Gloria, stating she has married the now freed Douglas and they are coming back to Africa. When Trask and Dodd learn of this news, they make a bargain to follow Tarzan and Gloria to Blue Valley. Siko attacks Tarzan but is thwarted, with the jungle man telling him he is a friend to his people and will never reveal their whereabouts. When Gloria arrives with her new husband, she has aged 20 years and Jane urges Tarzan to take them to Blue Valley but he refuses. Dodd and Trask flew the couple to Tarzan's home but Dodd says engine trouble forces them to remain. Jane tells the group that she and Cheetah can find Blue Valley and leads Gloria, Douglas, Trask and Dodd into the jungle with Tarzan trailing them. Running out of water, the quartet get caught in a gorge during a violent storm and nearly drown

Poster for *Tarzan's Magic Fountain* (1949).

before being rescued by Tarzan. He announces they will go back the next morning but later sneaks away with Gloria and Douglas. When Trask finds out the trio is gone, he threatens to shoot Cheetah unless Jane leads him and Dodd to Blue Valley. Tarzan arrives with Gloria and Douglas; the High One welcomes them, giving the newlyweds the secret elixir. The angry Pasco and Siko vow to burn out Tarzan's eyes so he can never lead anyone there again. Jane, Trask and

Dodd find the rocky path to the valley and come across Vredak's skeleton. As they proceed, the Mountain Leader shoots flaming arrows that kill the two men and trap Jane, who sends Cheetah for Tarzan. The jungle man is knocked out by Pasco, Siko and their comrades are tied to a cave wall as they prepare hot pokers to put out his eyes. Tarzan escapes, followed by Pasco and Siko. Tarzan saves Jane as Cheetah causes a rock slide that kills their pursuers. When they return to their jungle home, Cheetah partakes of a vial of the elixir and reverts to infancy.

The Hollywood Reporter stated that Barker's Tarzan "is equal to any within memory of this reviewer and we're afraid that goes back to Elmo Lincoln." (The screen's first Tarzan, Elmo Lincoln had a bit part in *Tarzan's Magic Fountain* as a fisherman; he first played the jungle man in 1918's *Tarzan of the Apes*.) *The New York Times* liked Barker as Tarzan: "[H]e seems to be just what the witch-doctor ordered for this tattered series." Regarding the feature, however, the reviewer called it "a matter of stale peanuts at the same old jungle stand. Instead of resorting to new ideas and treatment and a timely overhauling job, the studio has dragged out a moldy script, the same sheepish-looking extras, and the wheezing chimpanzee, Cheetah, who isn't getting any younger, either." *Boxoffice* felt the feature "follows in general pattern its predecessors, one which leans a little more on fantasy than most. But the same flora and fauna are there and, again, the animal actors carry a good share of the Thespian burden, most especially its comedy quotient." *Variety* reported, "Lee Sholem's direction has a number of slow spots, particularly in dialog scenes between the humans, but otherwise furnishes a good pace to the action moments...."

Tarzan's Peril (1951; 79 minutes)

PRODUCER: Sol Lesser. DIRECTOR: Byron Haskin. SCREENPLAY: Samuel Newman & Francis Swann. ADDITIONAL DIALOGUE: John Cousins. PHOTOGRAPHY: Karl Struss & Phil Brandon. EDITOR: John Murray. MUSIC: Michel Michelet. ART DIRECTOR: John Meehan. SOUND: Fred Lau. WARDROBE: Wesley Jeffries. MAKEUP: Don Cash. PRODUCTION SUPERVISOR: Fred Ahern. PRODUCTION ASSISTANTS: Peter Colemore & Tony Dean. SECOND UNIT DIRECTOR: Phil Brandon. SECOND UNIT PHOTOGRAPHY: Jack Whitehead. ASSISTANT DIRECTOR: James Paisley. LOCATION UNIT ASSISTANT DIRECTOR: Cliff Brandon.

CAST: Lex Barker (Tarzan), Virginia Huston (Jane), George Macready (Radijeck), Douglas Fowley (Herbert Trask), Glenn Anders (Andrews), Dorothy Dandridge (Melmendi), Alan Napier (Commissioner Peters), Edward Ashley (Connors), Walter Kingsford (Barney), Frederick O'Neal (Balum), James Moultrie (Nessi), Stanley Logan (Governor), Joel Fluellen (Attendant), Bruce Lester (Warden), Davis Roberts (Emissary), Wesley Gale (Native Boss), Florence Robertson (Maiden), Juanita Moore, Lawrence Lamarr, Chester Jones (Natives), Buster Cooke (African White Hunter), Milton Wood (Bulam's Attendant), Maxie Thrower, Jack Williams, Bill Washington, Martin Wilkins, James Frazier (Guards), Frances Driver (Mother), Evelyn Burwell (Woman).

The third of Lex Barker's RKO five Tarzan features, *Tarzan's Peril* is an average outing in the series buoyed by footage shot in Kenya, Tanganyika and Uganda and nicely interpolated with lensing done at the company's Culver City studios and in Mexico City's Chapultepec Park. Made as *Tarzan's Mate in Peril*, the feature was released in March 1951. Its only fantasy aspect is a scene where Tarzan becomes engulfed in a large plant that tries to devour him. After Tarzan cuts himself free, he also saves a young elephant caught in the long leaves and appendages of the killer flora.

As one of his last duties as commissioner in the jungles of British East Africa, Peters (Alan Napier), along with his successor Connors (Edward Ashley), observes the crowning of Ashuba tribe queen Melmendi (Dorothy Dandridge). The elaborate ceremony includes native dancers and simulated warfare. Peters introduces Connors to young tribe member Nessi (James Moultrie). Members of the Yorango tribe, led by their cruel king Bulam (Frederick O'Neal), arrive and Melmendi rejects the king's offer of a chest of jewels in return for marriage. Peters warns Connors to keep strong drink and guns out of the hands of the natives and then bids farewell to Melmendi and her tribe, who want him to stay. A caravan of three trucks moves through the area lead by Radijeck (George Macready), a slave trader and gunrunner. He is in cahoots with Trask (Douglas Fowley) and Andrews (Glenn Anders), smuggling rifles to Bulam and his tribe. Jungle drums bring news that Radijeck has escaped execution; when Tarzan (Barker) learns of this, he finds Peters and tells him the news. Tarzan then goes to his tree house home to inform his wife Jane (Virginia Huston), who once nursed Radijeck back to health after a bout with malaria but later denounced him. Tarzan finds that Cheetah has stolen Peters' notebook, and he and Jane go by boat to Randini to return it to him. When one of Radijeck's caravan's trucks breaks down, he orders his native bearers to carry the boxes with the rifles. Along the way they run into Peters and Connors. Trask pretends to be a missionary taking Bibles to the natives but when Peters tries to inspect his cargo, he and Connors are shot and killed by Radijeck. After Radijeck gives Andrews a pocket watch belonging to Peters, the safari continues. At a riverbank stop, Radijeck deliberately pushes a heavy box onto Andrews, breaking his leg. Although he begs them not to desert him, Radijeck and Trask leave Andrews behind and he crawls into the river, drifting downstream holding onto a large tree limb. Tarzan rescues the man from hungry crocodiles with Cheetah finding the pocket watch. Realizing that the time piece belongs to Peters, Tarzan and Jane take Andrews to Randini for medical help and then go to see the governor (Stanley Logan). When the governor says he does not have the authority to hunt for the missing commissioner, Tarzan decides to do so himself and tells Jane to return to their jungle home. At the Yorango village, Radijeck barters with Bulam for the rifles as Tarzan realizes that the two British officials have been murdered. After observing Radijeck with Bulam and his tribesmen, Tarzan swings through the treetops to the Yorango village where he collects some of the rifles and throws them in the river. He is spotted by Radijeck and the tribesmen and after a terrific fight Tarzan is hit on the head. Radijeck wants to shoot him but Bulam insists he be thrown in the river to drown. Tarzan manages to get entangled in some debris and is swept over a waterfall, eventually being washed ashore. Cheetah gets an elephant to remove the debris on top of Tarzan. After receiving payment for the rifles in precious jewels, Radijeck and Trask, along with four Yorango guides, leave the area as Bulam and his tribesmen go to attack the Ashuba village. Melmendi and her defenseless village are overwhelmed by the Yorangos and she is taken prisoner. Tarzan revives but Cheetah discovers a bevy of carnivorous plants and the jungle man gets entangled in one of them, but manages to cut himself free with his knife. He finds a baby elephant entrapped by one of the killer plants and disentangles it before heading to the Yorango village. When he sees a warrior about to kill Nessi, he rescues the boy and sends him to the Ashuba village to free his people. After rescuing Melmendi, Tarzan distributes weapons to the Ashuba warriors who have arrived with Nessi. When Bulam finds Melmendi gone, he arouses his drunken men but it is too late and his village is attacked by the Ashubas. The Yorangos are routed and Bulam is killed in a fight with Tarzan, who goes to find Radijeck. When their guides desert them, Radijeck and Trask quarrel with Radijeck shooting Trask and going alone on foot through the hostile jungle. He comes upon Tarzan and Jane's tree house. Radijeck informs Jane he wants her to guide him to the river and then hits her. Tarzan arrives and Radijeck threatens to shoot Jane but uses his last bullet to try and kill the jungle man. Tarzan knocks Radijeck from the treehouse and he dies in the fall. Cheetah swallows the pocket watch which can be heard ringing in her stomach as Tarzan and Jane are reunited.

Lex Barker is a more articulate Tarzan than Johnny Weissmuller and holds *Tarzan's Peril* together in good form. The trio of villains played by George Macready, Douglas Fowley and

Poster for *Tarzan's Peril* (1951).

Glenn Anders are more interesting, as is the evil, cunning native chief portrayed by Frederick O'Neal. As the ninth actress to play the role, Virginia Huston is a plain Jane in her solo outing as the jungle man's spouse. Dorothy Dandridge has a few good scenes as a tribal queen.

Boxoffice commented that producer Lesser "dipped extensively into his coffers to provide backgrounds and a productional framework that are definitely on the opulent side.... [T]he story is a bit slow in getting under way, but it winds up with a slambang finish that is sure to titillate the juveniles...." *Variety* reported it was "sturdy fare for the action market," adding, "John Murray's neat editing keeps the film tight and expertly cuts in the location footage with that manufactured in the studio.... [T]here's interesting use of native dances and primitive music in the film's opening sequences." Gabe Essoe noted in *Tarzan of the Movies* (1968), "The plans to make *Peril* the first Tarzan feature in color were discarded when a large portion of the color footage was spoiled on location. At that point, the film was converted to black and white. Some of those Technicolor background sequences, however, did turn up in later Tarzan pictures when Lesser began using color in 1957."

Tembo (1952; 80 minutes; Color)

PRODUCER-DIRECTOR-SCRIPT: Howard Hill. ASSOCIATE PRODUCERS: James Leicester & Bud McKinney. PHOTOGRAPHY: Arthur E. Phelps. EDITOR: Thomas P. Pratt. MUSIC: Claude Sweeten. ASSISTANT DIRECTOR: Carl Mikule.

CAST: Howard Hill, C. Edwin Hill, the Rev. Howard Bigelow (Themselves), Westbrook Van Voorhis (Narrator).

Tembo derives its title from the name of a killer elephant which is brought down by four arrows fired by noted archer and explorer Howard Hill at the movie's climax. The film is a documentary account of Hill's expedition into the Belgian Congo in search of the fierce Leopard Men tribe. Like most of its ilk it is mainly a travelogue that covers the people and animals of the equatorial African jungles. The safari took nine months and covered over 30,000 miles. It contains scenes of Hill hunting various animals with his long bow as well as human interest scenes such as a clown monkey dubbed Spike and the adoption of a baby gazelle whose mother has been killed by a lion. One exciting scene has the safari leader (C. Edwin Hill) being attacked by a python who is dispatched by Hill. About the only genre offering the film contains is the Leopard Men, who adorn themselves with leopard skins and claws, and their belief that the safari has brought a curse down upon them since a bull elephant has attacked the tribe. To make amends, Hill agrees to kill the beast. Following his success, the safari ends with a village celebration.

Boxoffice termed *Tembo* a "well-edited and frequently engrossing subject"; the reviewer also noted "Hill's remarkable prowess with the bow, and the wealth of flora and fauna captured by the Ansco Color cameras...." *Variety* wrote, "Subject is fairly interesting, and would have been more so had the footage been trimmed considerably and more excitement worked into the sequences. Ansco color used does a very good job of showing off the African terrain, natives and animal life."

Their Big Moment (1934; 68 minutes)

EXECUTIVE PRODUCERS: Pandro S. Berman & Cliff Reid. DIRECTOR: James Cruze. SCREENPLAY: Arthur Caesar & Marion Dix, from the play *Afterwards* by Walter C. Hackett. PHOTOGRAPHY: Harold Wenstrom. EDITOR: William Hamilton. MUSIC DIRECTOR: Max Steiner. ART DIRECTOR: Van Nest Polglase. SOUND: P.J. Faulkner, Jr.

CAST: ZaSu Pitts (Tillie Whim), Slim Summerville (Bill Ambrose), William Gaxton (The Great La

Salle), Bruce Cabot (Lane Franklin), Kay Johnson (Eve Farrington), Julie Haydon (Fay Harley), Ralph Morgan (Dr. Portman), Huntley Gordon (John Farrington), Tamara Geva (Lottie/Madame Marvo), Wallace MacDonald (Theater Manager), Edward [Ed] Brady (Stage Manager), Frank O'Connor (Detective), Frank Mills (Pilot).

In *B Movies* (1973), Don Miller wrote, "ZaSu Pitts was in demand in 1933, and indications are that she was instrumental in keeping Universal's head above the financial waters." Among the actress' most popular films for that studio were a half-dozen with Slim Summerville between 1932 and 1934; they worked together for the seventh time in a loan-out to RKO for *Their Big Moment*, issued in the summer of 1934. RKO seemed to have a penchant for stories revolving around spiritualism and this was the gist of *Their Big Moment*'s plot, which had the two comedians as assistants to a fake medium, the Great La Salle, played by stage star William Gaxton in his feature debut. The film proved to be the final 1930s teaming of Pitts and Summerville; they were reunited for three 1941 outings, *Uncle Joe*, *Niagara Falls* and *Miss Polly*, the last two being Hal Roach featurettes. *Their Big Moment* was based on the 1933 London stage play *Afterwards* by Walter C. Hackett and was filmed under that title.

Beautiful widow Fay Harley (Julie Haydon), a Long Island socialite, becomes entranced with fake medium-physician Dr. Portman (Ralph Morgan) after the death of her husband in an airplane crash. Out to bilk Fay, Portman says he has an important message for her from Arthur. Eve Farrington (Kay Johnson), Fay's sister, who had a secret affair with her brother-in-law, is determined to break Portman's spell on her sibling and enlists the aid of a faded vaudeville illusionist, the Great La Salle (Gaxton), and his mind reader associate Madame Marvo (Tamara Geva), whose real name is Lottie. When Lottie becomes jealous of Eve, she leaves the act and is replaced by Tillie Whim (Pitts), a fluttery woman who assists La Salle along with her boyfriend, Bill Ambrose (Summerville). Eve pays the trio $6,000 to pretend to be in an airplane accident near Fay's estate and then set up a séance to expose Portman, who has been tormenting the widow with aircraft noises from a hidden audio device. Portman is suspicious of Tillie's powers and insists she undergo a test which she manages to pass with help from Bill and La Salle. During her trance, Tillie announces that Fay's husband was murdered and warns her not to sign any papers. Eve and her husband John (Huntley Gordon) think La Salle and his assistants have betrayed them and order the trio to leave the estate, but La Salle believes Tillie is a real medium and says they will stay to solve the murder. Portman, who has Fay's power of attorney, is suspicious of Lane Franklin (Bruce Cabot), the dead man's lawyer, and accuses him of tampering with the plane, causing his client's death. He says Franklin had embezzled funds from his late client. To make it appear that Portman poisoned Fay, Franklin obtains a toxin from the fakir's medical bag and places it in a drink intended for the widow. Fay does not touch the drink and La Salle realizes what Franklin planned. He tricks the lawyer into thinking he drank the poison and with Tillie's help gets him to confess. Bill finds Portman's audio machine, thus exposing him to Fay. Franklin and Portman are taken to jail and the grateful sisters thank La Salle, Tillie and Bill for saving them from the two crooks.

Unlike most films dealing with phony mediums, *Their Big Moment* contains the plot ploy of having Tillie actually meeting the victim on an astral plane while in a trance, thus revealing he was murdered. Outside of that, the film is basically a typical comedy-mystery molded to fit the talents of stars Pitts and Summerville. Both are somewhat overshadowed by William Gaxton's brash illusionist and the convoluted murder plot.

The New York Times proclaimed "Mr. Summerville, a comic fellow when properly staged, is lost in the general welter of iniquity and hysteria, and Miss Pitts does what she can with her butterfly hands and moonstruck expression." *The Film Daily* opined, "Fairly good comedy drama with clairvoyant theme.... While there's nothing especially new or outstanding about the yarn, it's the type of fare that generally gets by all right in the neighborhood houses. ZaSu Pitts and Slim Summerville are the chief attractions." *Variety* noted, "The laughs are never heavy but they're abundant. Plus the suspense of the mystery narrative picture should have fairly good audience strength...." The Detroit Council of Catholic Organizations labeled the film as unsuitable for children and adolescents.

The Thing from Another World (1951; 87 minutes)

PRODUCER: Howard Hawks. ASSOCIATE PRODUCER: Edward Lasker. DIRECTOR: Christian Nyby. SCREENPLAY: Charles Lederer, from the story "Who Goes There?" by John W. Campbell, Jr. PHOTOGRAPHY: Russell Harlan. EDITOR: Roland Gross. MUSIC: Dimitri Tiomkin. ART DIRECTORS: Albert S. D'Agostino & John J. Hughes. SOUND: Clem Portman & Phil Brigandi. SET DECORATIONS: Darrell Silvera & William Stevens. SPECIAL EFFECTS: Donald Steward. SPECIAL PHOTOGRAPHIC EFFECTS: Linwood Dunn. MAKEUP: Lee Greenway. HAIR STYLIST: Larry Germain.

CAST: Margaret Sheridan (Nikki Nicholson), Kenneth Tobey (Captain Pat Hendry), Robert Cornthwaite (Dr. Arthur Carrington), Douglas Spencer (Ned "Scotty" Scott), James Young (Lieutenant Eddie Dykes), Dewey Martin (Crew Chief Bob), Robert Nichols (Lieutenant Ken "Mac" MacPherson), William Self (Corporal Barnes), Eduard Franz (Dr. Stern), Sally Creighton (Mrs. Chapman), James Arness (The Thing), Edmund Breon (Dr. Ambrose), John Dierkes (Dr. Chapman), Everett Glass (Professor Wilson), William Neff (Bill Stone), Paul Frees (Dr. Vorhees), Norbert Schiller (Dr. Laurentz), George Fenneman (Dr. Redding), David McMahon (Brigadier General Fogarty), Robert Stevenson (Captain Fred Smith), Robert Gutknecht (Corporal Hause), Ted Cooper, Allan Ray (Lieutenants), Nicholas Byron (Tex Richards), Robert Bray (Captain), Lee Tung Foo (Lee the Cook), Walter Ng (Cook), Milton Kibbee, Ray McDonald, William J. O'Brien, H.B. Newton (Scientists), King Kong, Charles K. Opunui, Riley Sunrise (Eskimos), Billy Curtis (small version of the Thing).

One of the all-time great science fiction pictures, *The Thing from Another World* ranks second only to *King Kong* (q.v.) as RKO's finest genre achievement. Released by RKO Radio in the spring of 1951, the feature was co-produced by the studio and producer Howard Hawks' Winchester Pictures Corporation. Mainly filmed at the RKO Ranch in Encino, California, it also had location filming in Cut Bank and Lewiston, Montana, and a Los Angeles ice house, California Consumers. Scientific equipment was borrowed from Cal Tech for the feature and three electronics companies were consulted before filming. Christian Nyby, who was editor of some of Hawks' previous films, is credited as the director although he closely collaborated with Hawks on most of the filming. Costing $1.1 million, the film grossed $2 million during its initial release. Hawks cast unknown players in the film's lead roles. Kenneth Tobey later appeared in such genre efforts as *The Beast from 20,000 Fathoms* (1953), *It Came from Beneath the Sea* (1955), *The Vampire* (1957) and *The Howling* (1981). James Arness played the title role, four years before winning everlasting fame as Marshal Matt Dillon on *Gunsmoke* (CBS-TV, 1955–75). Makeup supervisor Lee Greenway took three months to perfect the Thing's makeup at a cost of $40,000. Several scenes of Arness as the creature were cut by Hawks so as not to overkill the alien's appearance. For the same reason Hawks kept news people off the set during filming to avoid exposing the title creature's looks before the movie's release.

The Thing from Another World is based on a 1938 short story, "Who Goes There?" by John W. Campbell, Jr., written under the pen name Don A. Stuart. Hawks only used the framework of the story and made it more topical by tapping into the then-current UFO-sighting phenomenon. The picture pokes fun at the military, government and science with the by-the-book military man (Tobey) shown to have more common sense than his superiors and a Nobel Prize–winning scientist (Robert Cornthwaite) who wants to save the vampire alien at any cost, even giving up

Lobby card for *The Thing from Another World* (1951).

the lives of the personnel at the polar scientific base he supervises. Perfectly paced, wonderfully acted and establishing just the right balance between the horrors it presents and the protagonists who must deal with them, the movie was perfect for its time and retains great entertainment value. On the lighter side, the romantic give and take between the characters played by Tobey and Margaret Sheridan is straight out of other Howard Hawks movies like *His Girl Friday* (1940). *The Thing from Another World* was reissued in 1954 and 1957, six minutes shy of its original 87 minute running time.

At an Army military club in Anchorage, Alaska, newsman Ned "Scotty" Scott (Douglas Spencer) joins Captain Pat Hendry (Tobey), Lieutenant Eddie Dykes (James Young) and Lieutenant Ken "Mac" MacPherson (Robert Nichols), saying he is looking for a good story. Pat is ordered by Brigadier General Fogarty (David McMahon) to investigate an air crash near a North Pole scientific base, Polar Expedition 6, supervised by Nobel Prize winner Dr. Arthur Carrington (Cornthwaite). Scotty asks to go along. During the flight, Pat gets a call from the base's radio operator, Tex Richards (Nicholas Byron), saying something is disturbing instrument readings. Upon arrival, Pat seeks out Carrington's secretary, Nikki Nicholson (Sheridan), and jokingly chides her for suddenly leaving after their date in Anchorage. Carrington informs Pat that something landed 48 miles due east of the base and that radar shows it lifted up just before crashing and he estimates it to be over 20 thousand tons of steel. Pat, Carrington, Scotty, Eddie, Mac and Crew Chief Bob (Dewey Martin) fly within one-half mile of the crash site and then take dog sleds to the very spot. The men see what appears to be an air foil protruding from the ice and by standing around the buried-in-ice aircraft's outline, determine that it is round and declare it a flying saucer. Pat and Carrington agree on using a thermite bomb to get access to the object but when they set off the bomb it causes a second explosion which demolishes the craft. Just as Pat, Carrington and Scotty deplore the loss of the object, one of the men spies an eight-foot man encased in the ice. Since a storm is rapidly developing, Pat orders the ice around the man cut and placed on a dog sled and taken to the plane. The expedition returns to the base as the storm hits and Pat has the ice-bound alien placed in a store room while he awaits orders from Fogarty. Carrington wants to thaw the creature to study it but Pat refuses and orders Mac to stand guard over it. Pat attempts to contact Fogarty but the storm has blocked out communications. Nikki asks Pat what the boogie man in ice really is. After a couple of hours Mac wants to be relieved of watching the alien and Corporal Barnes (William Self) is assigned the task. In order to avoid looking at the thing, Barnes throws a blanket over it, not realizing it is an electric blanket. The ice thaws and Barnes sees the living alien and shoots at it before hysterically running to tell Pat. Going to the store room, Pat and his men realize the creature has gone outside, where it is attacked by sled dogs. It kills two of the animals before escaping. Part of its arm is found under one of the dogs. Examining the arm, Carrington and his colleagues find it has no animal tissue and that the creature is basically a very intelligent vegetable which Scotty dubs a "super-carrot." Seed pods are found under the hand of the alien and Carrington says it is superior to humans in every way. The hand begins to move and the scientists theorize that it has been revitalized by absorbing the blood of the dog that severed it. When Pat orders his men to use axes to destroy the creature, Carrington objects. In the greenhouse, Carrington tells his colleagues the alien has been there and they find the body of a dog with all its blood drained. Since Carrington wants to communicate with the creature, he asks his colleagues to guard the greenhouse as he thinks it will return there. When Pat tries again to reach Fogarty, Dr. Stern (Eduard Franz), one of the men left on guard in the greenhouse, arrives in an injured state and says two of his colleagues were attacked by the alien and left hanging with their throats cut. Pat and some men approach the greenhouse and when he opens the door the creature, whose arm has re-grown, swings at him. They quickly close and bolt the door. The exhausted Carrington informs his colleagues that he has taken the seed pods, placed them in soil and fed them blood plasma and shows them they are growing. Nikki is repulsed by the sight of the pulsating pods and asks to be excused. Finding out there is an unexplained loss of blood plasma, Pat asks Nikki what Carrington is doing and she lets him read the typed notes. Pat confronts Carrington, who is adamant that the alien be studied. A radio message from Fogarty orders Pat to watch over the alien until weather allows him (Fogarty) to come to the base. When the storm causes temperatures to become dangerously low, Pat orders the alien be destroyed, telling Carrington he is willing to face a court martial. As Pat and his men discuss how to kill the alien, Nikki suggests boiling, baking or frying it since it is made of vegetable matter. When the creature invades the compound, the men use kerosene and flame throwers to set it on fire but it escapes through a window. Dr. Redding (George Fenneman), one of Carrington's colleagues, suggests using electricity to destroy the thing. Time becomes of the essence after the alien shuts off the compound's heat system. Carrington argues that they owe it to science to die in order to protect the alien. Pat and his men rig a wired walkway down a long corridor and lure the creature to the generator room. To stop the Army men, Carrington shuts off the generator and brandishes a gun, but he is thwarted. As the Thing makes its way along the corridor, Carrington attempts to communicate with it but he is knocked down. When the alien gets to the right spot, the power is turned on and the electric bolts causes it to disintegrate into ashes. Pat orders the alien pods destroyed. As he and Nikki look to the future together, Scotty sends a radio message to the rest of the world of the events, along with an ominous plea to watch the skies.

Reviewed as *The Thing*, the movie was called "an exploitation special" by *Variety*; the reviewer said it "lacks genuine entertainment values but hep hoopla should help it pay off." *The New York Times* felt, "Not since Dr. Frankenstein wrought his mechanical monster has the screen had such a good time dabbling in scientific-fiction," but also warned, "Adults and children can have a lot of old-fashioned movie fun at *The Thing*, but parents should understand their children and think twice before letting them see this film if their emotions are not properly conditioned." Chris Steinbrunner and Burt Goldblatt wrote in *Cinema of the Fantastic* (1972), "*The Thing from Another World* marked a milestone in intelligent, literate, realistic science fiction. Just as Hawks had predicted, it was an enormous financial success." Noting the film's combination of horror and sci-fi, Denis Gifford stated in *A Pictorial History of Horror Movies* (1973), "*The Thing*, for all its dazzling direction, fast-paced cutting, overlapping acting and authentic setting, was beneath its cinematic surface set securely in the mold of Universal Gothic. Howard Hughes and Christian Nyby used the classic horror film formula.... The Thing is, of course, the Monster: in looks, in power, yet not in soul. There is no spark of even man-made humanity in this man-shaped monster: It is a creature of fury, of violence, of hate." Philip Strick in *Science Fiction Movies* (1976) wrote, "The most memorable science fiction movie dealing with the resuscitation of aliens remains *The Thing*.... [It] is as splendid to listen to as to watch, for the sheer pace and enthusiasm of its dialogue." In *Films of Science Fiction and Fantasy* (1988), Baird Searles wrote, "Adding to

Advertisement for *The Thing from Another World* (1951).

the *verismo* are Howard Hawks' (uncredited) direction, and the realistic, overlapping dialogue that gave a near documentary feel to much of the action. These factors, plus the claustrophobic device of the isolated circumstances, make for a truly scary film." "This is one of the best alien invasion movies ever made," said C.J. Henderson in *The Encyclopedia of Science Fiction Movies* (2001). "Tension builds evenly throughout this incredibly well-made film. The audience dreads each opening door, staring unblinking, waiting for the creature to strike. The romantic subplot is well handled, never cloying or getting in the way of the main events, but often helping the plot along nicely. The characters are far more complex than is standard for such films."

In 1982 Universal released *The Thing*, director John Carpenter's remake of the 1951 film; here the plot sticks closer to the short story. Although well-made with top-notch, state-of-the-art special effects, it lacks the endearing, and enduring, quality of the Howard

Hawks production and is saddled with sickening monster effects. The 2011 film *The Thing* was a prequel to Carpenter's.

RKO/Turner Home Entertainment released a colorized version of *The Thing from Another World* in 1993.

Thirteen Women (1932; 73 minutes)

EXECUTIVE PRODUCER: David O. Selznick. DIRECTOR: George Archainbaud. SCREENPLAY: Bartlett Cormack & Samuel Ornitz. PHOTOGRAPHY: Leo Tover. EDITOR: Charles L. Kimball. MUSIC: Max Steiner. ART DIRECTOR: Carroll Clark. SOUND: Hugh McDowell, Jr.

CAST: Irene Dunne (Laura Stanhope), Ricardo Cortez (Sergeant Crane), Jill Esmond (Jo Turner), Myrna Loy (Ursula Georgi), Mary Duncan (June Raskob), Kay Johnson (Helen Dawson Frye), Florence Eldridge (Grace Coombs), C. Henry Gordon (Swami Yogadachi), Peg Entwistle (Hazel Clay Cousins), Harriet Hagman (May Raskbo), Edward Pawley (Burns), Blanche Frederici (Miss Kirsten), Wally Albright (Bobby Stanhope), James Donlan (Detective Mike), Elsie Prescott (Nan), Edward LeSaint (Chief of Detectives), Lloyd Ingraham, Mitchell Lewis (Detectives), Marjorie Gateson (Hazel's Friend), Lew Meehan, Bob Reeves (Policemen), Clarence Geldart (Coroner), Louis Matheaux (Police Chemist), Eric Wilton (Butler Henry), Lee Phelps (Train Conductor), Oscar Smith (Porter), Allen Pomeroy (Ringmaster), Aloha Porter, Audrey Scott (Horse Back Performers), Eddie Viera, Buster Bartell, Clayton Behee, Eddie De Coma (Trapeze Performers), Teddy Mangean (High Wire Performer), Cliff Herbert (Circus Performer), Kenneth Thomson (Mr. Cousins).

Hazel Clay Cousins (Peg Entwistle) and her traveling companion (Marjorie Gateson) visit Hazel's St. Albans Seminary sorority sisters, June (Mary Duncan) and May Raskbo (Harriet Hagman), siblings who are stars of the Joe E. Marvel Circus and perform a death-defying high wire act. June has received horoscopes from a New York City astrologist, Swami Yogadachi (C. Henry Gordon), and due to his dire predictions, she fears for her sister's life. During their next performance, May falls to her death, resulting in June's insanity. Hazel later receives a similar horoscope from the swami and suddenly shoots her husband (Kenneth Thomson). The swami is under the spell of beautiful Ursula Georgi (Myrna Loy), a half-caste who has vowed to destroy all the coeds at St. Albans who prevented her from crossing the color line. Unknown to the swami, who predicted optimistic futures for the women, Ursula changed the horoscopes to predict their deaths. Another sorority sister living in California, Grace Coombs (Florence Eldridge), gets a horoscope from the swami not only predicting her death but his own. The same day the swami goes to board a subway train but Ursula hypnotizes him into jumping in front of it, causing his death. Wealthy Beverly Hills divorcee Laura Stanhope (Irene Dunne) calls Helen Frye (Kay Johnson) and invites her to come for a reunion of the sorority sisters. Helen, who has just lost her small daughter, takes a train west and runs into Ursula. After the two reminisce, Ursula mesmerizes Helen into shooting herself. While another sorority sister, Jo Turner (Jill Esmond), is visiting Laura, they are informed of Helen's suicide by Sergeant Clive (Ricardo Cortez), who is investigating the case. Earlier he observed Ursula getting off the train and questioned her and she told him she was Miss Clemons. Laura becomes upset because she received a horoscope from the swami predicting a dire fate for her little boy Bobby (Wally Albright) on his upcoming birthday. As Clive brings Helen's luggage to Laura's home, Grace arrives and proclaims that the swami's predictions will come true. Laura asks her to leave. Unknown to Laura, her chauffeur, Burns (Edward Pawley), is in love with Ursula, as he once worked for the swami. Ursula sends Bobby a box of poisoned chocolates but Laura becomes suspicious and has Clive analyze them. Intrigued by Laura's sorority pin, Clive travels to St. Albans where he talks with the headmistress, Miss Kirsten (Blanche Frederici), who tells him about the close-knit sorority sisters and the outcast

Advertisement for *Thirteen Women* (1932).

Ursula. Clive sends to New York City for a photograph of Ursula as the newspapers play up the "Horoscope Murders." While Ursula forces Burns to take a ball containing a bomb to Bobby for his birthday, Clive gets word that she worked for the swami and her photograph reveals she is Miss Clemons. Laura has Burns drive her to the police station so Bobby's gifts can be checked. Clive and his associate Mike (James Donlan) trail them. Burns escapes by jumping out of the car

Myrna Loy and Ricardo Cortez in *Thirteen Women* (1932).

which Laura and Clive manage to stop. The bomb explodes when the gifts are thrown out of the vehicle. Clive tells Laura to take a train to New York City and on board he sets a trap to capture Ursula. After Bobby is asleep, Laura is confronted by Ursula, who hypnotizes her. When Ursula attempts to kill Bobby, Clive stops her and the madwoman jumps off the train, fulfilling the swami's prophecy of her demise.

Surviving prints of *Thirteen Women* run 59 minutes, supposedly the length of the feature's 1935 reissue, although some initial review sources also give that running time (others list it at 73 minutes). Several loose ends dangle, such as June becoming insane over her sister's death, the somewhat sudden exit of Jo and Grace, and Hazel's shooting of her husband. While the title says 13 women, only ten are shown in the film. Footage of the other three, played by Julie Haydon, Betty Furness and Phyllis Fraser, was deleted before the film's release. An extended scene between Hazel and her husband was mostly excised with Kenneth Thomson making only a fleeting appearance as the murdered man. Myrna Loy dominates the proceedings as the serpent-like, sexy Ursula, while top-billed Irene Dunne is not attractively presented, especially her hair style. When Ursula confronts Laura at the finale she asks, "Do you know what it means to be half caste in a world ruled by whites?" Loy replaced Zita Johann as Ursula. Peg Entwisle, who played Hazel, committed suicide on September 18, 1932, two days after the film premiered.

Thirteen Women is an intriguing, well-acted horror drama although its premise of miscegenation is archaic by today's standards. *Harrison's Reports* looked into *their* crystal ball and prognosticated, "[T]the material cannot make an acceptable picture. It is too horrible." Later it announced, "It turned out exactly as predicted." The same source also stated that the feature performed only "fair to poor" at the box office based on exhibitors' response. *The New York Times* reported, "It is horror without laughter, horror that is too awful to be modish and too stark to save itself from a headlong plunge into hokum.... There is an uncomfortable absence of hearty male chatter in this demoniacal intrigue. Ricardo Cortez ... appears too late and too briefly to brighten the gloom." The film does hint at a budding romance between the detective and divorcee Laura at its finale.

The (Huntingdon, Pennsylvania) *Daily News* wrote, "This is intellectually planned entertainment full of suspense and powerful situations.... A fine shading of humanness and understanding is injected into Cortez's portrayal." *Motion Picture* decreed that the film "carries a kick," and added, "A feeling of suppressed excitement runs through the picture which is not a bad substitute for continuity of plot. You may be dazed." *Photoplay* termed it a "gripping picture" while *Picture Play* called it "the most confused and incredible picture of the month." *Variety* thought Tiffany Thayer's novel "fast, light reading, thanks to the writing, but on celluloid it deteriorates into an unreasonably farfetched wholesale butcher shop drama which no amount of good acting could save.... Myrna Loy, constantly under the handicap of being an unbelievable person, makes the best of the killer role." *The Film Daily* felt *Thirteen Women* a "good drama showing influence of astrology and the power of suggestion on women.... This feature's greatest asset is suspense.... [It] should particularly interest the women." In *Film Fan Monthly* (September 1973), Leonard Maltin called it "a flimsy piece of tripe that handled differently might have made a terrific thriller.... The script is so full of holes, and some of the acting so ludicrous, that the film's possibilities quickly go down the drain, leaving a fairly interesting but absurd piece of melodrama behind."

The Three Caballeros (1944; 71 minutes; Color)

PRODUCER: Walt Disney. DIRECTOR–PRODUCTION SUPERVISOR: Norman Ferguson. LIVE ACTION DIRECTOR: Harold Young. SEQUENCE DIRECTORS: Clyde Geronimi, Jack Kinney & Bill Roberts. STORY: Homer Brightman, Ernest Terrazas, Ted Sears, Bill [Peet] Peed, Ralph Wright, Elmer Plummer, Roy Williams, Bill Cottrell, Del Connell & James Bodrero. LIVE ACTION PHOTOGRAPHY: Ray Rennahan. LIVE ACTION EDITOR: Don Halliday. LIVE ACTION ART DIRECTOR: Richard Irvine. MUSIC: Charles Wolcott, Edward H. Plumb & Paul J. Smith. SONGS: Manuel Esperon, Ray Gilbert, Ernesto Cortezar, Ary Barroso, Agustin Lara, E. Santos, Dorival Cayymi, Benedicto Lacerda, Joao de Barro, Carlo Braga & Charro Gil. ART SUPERVISORS: Ken Anderson, Robert Cormack & Mary Blair. LIVE ACTION SOUND: C.O. Slyfield. ASSISTANT PRODUCTION SUPERVISOR: Larry Lansburgh. LIVE ACTION PRODUCTION MANAGER: Dan Keefe. ANIMATORS: Ward Kimball, Eric Larson, Fred Moore, John Lounsbery, Les Clark, Milt Kahl, Hal King, Franklin Thomas, Harvey Toombs, Bob Carlson, John Sibley, Bill Justice, Oliver M. Johnston, Jr. Milt Neil, Marvin Woodward & John Patterson. SPECIAL EFFECTS ANIMATORS: Josh Meador, George Rowley, John McManus & Edwin Aardal. LIVE ACTION PROCESS EFFECTS: Ub Iwerks. LIVE ACTION PROCESS TECHNICIAN: Richard Jones. LIVE ACTION TECHNICAL ADVISOR: Gail Papineau. LIVE ACTION COLOR CONSULTANT: Phil Dike. TECHNICOLOR DIRECTOR: Natalie Kalmus. TECHNICOLOR ASSOCIATE DIRECTOR: Morgan Padelford. BACKGROUNDS: Albert Dempster, Art Riley, Ray Huffine, Don Douglass & Claude Coats. LAYOUT: Donald Da Gradi, Hugh Hennesy, McLaren Stewart, Yale Gracey, Herbert Ryman, John Hench & Charles Philippi. CHOREOGRAPHY: Billy Daniels, Aloysio Oliveira & Carmelita Maacci.

CAST: Aurora Miranda (Brazilian Singer), Carmen Molina (Mexican Dancer), Dora Luz (Mexican Singer), Sterling Holloway (Voice of Professor Holloway), Clarence Nash (Voice of Donald Duck), Jose Oliveira (Voice of Joe Carioca), Joaquin Garay (Voice of Panchito), Frank Graham, Fred Shields (Narrators), Nestor Amarale, Almirante, Trio Calaveras, Ascencio Del Rio Trio (Musicians), Padua Hills Players (Actors), Pinto Colvig (Voice of Aracuan Bird), Billy Daniels (Brazilian Dancer), Carlos Ramirez (Singer).

Work on *The Three Caballeros* began in the early 1940s but it was not completed until 1944 because of the Walt Disney Studios' involvement in World War II propaganda films and the lack of Technicolor stock. It premiered in Mexico City late in 1944 but RKO Radio did not release it in the U.S. until early in 1945. Like the earlier *Saludos Amigos* (q.v.) it was a mixture of animation and live action that attempted to consolidate relations between the U.S. and its Latin American neighbors. Although a favorite of Disney enthusiasts, *The Three Caballeros* basically falls flat. Its biggest assets are non-stop action and two lovely songs, "You Belong to My Heart" and "Baia," which produced a top ten platter for Bing Crosby on Decca Records (23413). For all its music and comedy and its achievements technically, the feature visually lacks the necessary ingredients to make it anything other than a pleasant time passer. Thanks to the South American market, the feature turned a profit but did not get reissued theatrically until 1976, then in a shortened version. To commemorate the 50th anniversary of the feature, in 1994 the Disney Company produced the video *The Making of* The Three Caballeros, narrated by Corey Burton.

For his Friday the 13th birthday, Donald Duck (voice of Clarence Nash) gets a package from South America and when he opens it he finds several gifts. A movie projector and a film reel is in the first thing Donald opens and the movie, narrated by Professor Holloway (voice of Sterling Holloway), is about Aves Raras (Strange Birds) and first tells of Pablo, an Antarctic penguin who dreams of living in a tropical clime. After several failed attempts to leave home, Pablo fashions an ice boat and sails north. When he reaches the equator his craft melts but he makes a speedboat from his bathtub and reaches the Galapagos Island where he becomes a bird in paradise. Next exotic birds are shown, including Aracuan (voice of Pinto Colvig), who runs on and off the film. An elderly Uruguayan gaucho tells of hunting for condors when he was a boy called Gauchito and his discovery of a flying donkey, Burrito. He is able to tame the animal and decides to get rich by entering him in a race at the local fiesta. It takes awhile for Gauchito to untie Burrito's wings but when he does, the two fly around the track and win the race—only to be disqualified and run out of town. Opening another gift, Donald finds a book entitled *Brasil* and out pops his pal Joe Carioca (voice of Jose Oliveira), a parrot. When Joe finds out that Donald has never been to Baia, he hits him with a mallet, shrinking the duck in size, and takes him there. They meet a lovely cookie vendor (Aurora Miranda) and join her and her friends in a song and dance before she kisses Donald. Back at Donald's house, Joe returns the duck to normal size so Donald can open another gift. This one is entitled *Mexico* and houses a charro rooster, Panchito (voice of Joaquin Garay). The three sing "The Three Caballeros" and Panchito presents Donald with a pinata which he says is full of surprises. Panchito then recounts *Las Posadas* which is the very spirit of Christmas. It is a re-enactment of Joseph and Mary's nine-day journey to Bethlehem by village children who keep being turned away when they ask for lodgings. Finally they are admitted to a friendly house where they are fed and then open a pinata. Donald tries to break open his pinata but Joe and Panchito keep it moving out of his way until at last he smashes it and all kinds of things come out including a flying serape. Donald, Joe and Panchito jump on the serape and go to the fishing area of Patzcuaro where they enjoy the night life. Next they stop in Vera Cruz where dancers do the "Lilongo," with the three travelers joining the festivities. Landing in Acapulco, Donald plays on the beach with dozens of beautiful girls, and in Mexico City he falls for a beautiful woman (Carmen Molina) who sings "You Belong to My Heart." Donald then joins a lovely dancer (Dora Luz) who does the "Zandunga" and "Jesusita" before Joe and Panchito get him involved in a fake bullfight. When the angry Donald runs head first into the bull, which is filled with firecrackers, it explodes, ending his adventures.

Variety reported, "Walt Disney in *The Three Caballeros* reveals a new form of cinematic entertainment wherein he blends live action and animation into a socko feature production.... There's no question that Disney has brought to the screen a technique of combining live action with cartoon animation which is revolutionary and significant." *Boxoffice* concurred, calling the feature "another milestone," adding, "The film carries fantasy to a new and almost unbelievable high. It demonstrates tricks of color, camera and paint pot which absolutely defy description. Sequence after sequence, breathtakingly beautiful in their Technicolor lushness and utterly baffling in their technique, follow in such rapid succession that the effect is nigh vertiginous." Leonard Maltin in *The Disney Films, 3rd Edition* (1995) called it "a bright, fast-moving, and often brilliant melange of sights and sounds. Somewhat like *Fantasia*, it was the cause of considerable controversy among critics in 1945, and only recently has become one of the most admired Disney features among film buffs." In *The Animated Movie Guide* (2005), Martin Goodman wrote, "*The Three Caballeros* is the wildest, most surrealistic film ever produced by the Disney studio. At times it resembles a Latino version of *Fantasia*, at other times a weak *Silly Symphony*, and in still other moments a psychedelic head trip where reality warps at a moments notice. The film actually seems to speed up as it progresses.... Between the hyperkinetic animated characters, the constant dancing, and the surrealistic interludes, *The Three Caballeros* is a head-spinning experience best enjoyed by Disney fans who want an alternative to the sedate symphonies of *Snow White and the Seven Dwarfs* or *Bambi*."

Tomorrow at Seven (1933; 62 minutes)

PRODUCERS: Samuel Ziergler & Joseph I. Schnitzer. DIRECTOR: Ray Enright. SCREENPLAY: Ralph Spence. PHOTOGRAPHY: Charles Schoenbaum. EDITOR: Rose Loewinger. MUSIC: David Broekman. MUSIC DIRECTOR: Abe Meyer. ART DIRECTOR: Edward Jewell. SOUND: Lodge Cunningham. ASSISTANT DIRECTOR: Gaston Glass.

CAST: Chester Morris (Neil Broderick), Vivienne Osborne (Martha Winters), Frank McHugh (Detective Clancy), Allen Jenkins (Detective Dugan), Henry Stephenson (Thornton Drake), Grant Mitchell (Austin Winters), Charles Middleton (Coroner), Oscar Apfel (Asa Marsden), Virginia Howell (Mrs. Quincy), Cornelius Keefe (Pilot Henderson), Edward LeSaint (Real Coroner), Gus Robinson (Pompey), Bud Geary (Co-Pilot).

One of four feature films made by Jefferson Pictures Corporation in 1932–33, *Tomorrow at Seven* is a good, old-fashioned dark house thriller with lots of that genre's standbys, including a "clutching hand" phantom character, a mysterious mute housekeeper, a fiend who leaves a calling card and a strange murder weapon. RKO Pictures distributed the feature in the summer of 1933. While obviously made on a tight budget (there are only three sets: a Chicago home, an airplane and a Louisiana plantation house), the picture is briskly directed by Ray Enright and never lacks interest. The cast is especially good, including leads Chester Morris and Vivienne Osborne. Morris earlier appeared in a similar role in *The Bat Whispers* (1930). On loan from Warner Bros., Frank McHugh and Allen Jenkins provide the comedy relief as two thick-headed Chicago detectives, with Jenkins quite amusing in the scenes where he gives out with incomprehensible slang. The rest of the performers also excel, notably Henry Stephenson as the capitalist out to unmask a serial killer, Grant Mitchell as his taciturn secretary and Charles Middleton, cast against type as a G-man. Virginia Howell makes a good substitute for Martha Mattox portraying a mysterious, mute housekeeper. *Tomorrow at Seven* was reissued in 1948 by M&A Alexander Productions.

Chicago millionaire Asa Marsden (Oscar Apfel) unveils his latest find, a genuine unlisted Old Master he bought for $50,000, to an old friend who murders him and leaves the calling card of the Black Ace on his chest. On a train to Chicago, mystery writer Neil Broderick (Morris) meets Martha Winters (Osborne), the daughter of Austin Winters (Mitchell), secretary to businessman Thornton Drake (Stephenson). Broderick is writing a book about the Black Ace and wants to interview Drake, who has spent a fortune trying to uncover the egomaniac's identity. When Neil makes derogatory remarks about Winters, Martha informs him that Winters is her father. At Drake's mansion, Neil asks his help in capturing the Black Ace and Drake accedes.

Winters disagrees with his employer's decision to work with Neil, whom he dislikes. While Martha, Drake and Neil are having drinks, Winters works a jigsaw puzzle sent to Drake earlier in the day and finds it contains the words TOMORROW AT SEVEN within an outline of the Black Ace. Two police detectives, Clancy (McHugh) and Dugan (Jenkins), arrive and Winters tells them about the Black Ace's warning to Drake. Martha suggests that Drake charter a plane to his Louisiana plantation to get away from the Black Ace and he agrees, requesting that the detectives accompany his party, although Dugan is afraid of flying. After four hours in the air, the plane lights go out; when they come back on, Winters is found murdered, the wound caused by a thin, sharp instrument, the same as with the Black Ace's other victims. Clancy says someone on the plane killed Winters and after they arrive at the plantation he begins questioning the passengers and pilot. Neil demands that a coroner be

His strength helpless to defend her against the unseen terror!

"TOMORROW AT SEVEN"

A sensational crime drama with a startling climax

CHESTER MORRIS
VIVIENNE OSBORNE
FRANK McHUGH
ALLEN JENKINS
Henry Stephenson
Grant Mitchell
Directed by Ray Enright

Advertisement for *Tomorrow at Seven* (1933).

called from nearby Benville and when he makes the phone call, he also signals to someone outside the house. When the pilot (Cornelius Keefe) attempts to telephone his company, the wires are cut. Neil informs Martha that her father was killed deliberately as the coroner (Middleton) arrives to examine Winters' body. He finds a letter written by Winters which he gives to Clancy, who is reading it aloud when the lights go out. When Martha turns on the light switch, the letter is missing. Clancy and Dugan search the men and find nothing so Clancy orders everyone locked in their rooms for the night as he and Dugan stand guard outside Drake's bedroom door. A mysterious figure searches the living room; hearing a noise, Clancy and Dugan go downstairs to investigate. There is a knock at the door and a newcomer (Edward LeSaint) tells them *he* is the coroner. Clancy deduces that the fake coroner was the Black Ace, who took the letter. Neil goes to Martha's room and demands to know why she took the letter and where she hid it. She admits to placing the letter on the mantel in the living room. When they go to get it, they find blank paper along with the Black Ace's card. Clancy and Dugan catch them and Clancy accuses Neil of being the Black Ace. Clancy takes Neil to Drake and tells him Neil is the killer, leaving Dugan to guard Martha. As Dugan gabs about liking the South, a clutching hand reaches for Martha.

Dugan and Clancy search the grounds for Martha as Drake watches Neil at gunpoint. Martha wakes up outside, having been brought there by Drake's mute housekeeper (Howell) and the fake coroner. Drake tells Neil that he demands to know where Martha is and who is working as Neil's accomplice. The fake coroner disarms Drake, and Neil reveals that the man is really Jerry Simons of the Bureau of Criminal Investigation. Neil finds the missing letter on Drake; in it, Winters names his employer as the Black Ace. As Neil tells Drake he has suspected him for some time, Drake's gardener Pompey (Gus Robinson) gets the drop on him and Jerry. When Clancy and Dugan knock at the door, the noise gives Neil and Jerry time to jump Drake and Pompey and a fight ensues. Neil knocks down Pompey, who picks up Drake's cane, which contains a hidden knife at its bottom, and throws it at Neil. Neil dodges the weapon which goes through the door and kills Drake, who is on the other side. After subduing Pompey, Neil shows the confession letter to Clancy, who claims he always thought Neil was innocent.

Hollywood Filmograph called *Tomorrow at Seven* a "splendid feature.... [H]ere is a picture the kids will go wild about, for it has all the creepy mystery stuff and the grownups will give it a hand at the finish." *Motion Picture* termed it "a mystery yarn that is all in fun, with excitement and comedy balancing neatly." On the other hand, *The New York Times* felt, "As a semi-humorous murder mystery the film is neither very funny nor very mysterious. It is—to use a world that should never be juxtaposed with homicide—mild." *Variety* reported, "Low pressure murder mystery which doesn't move as fast as it should." *The Hollywood Reporter* wrote, "Minus most of the usual cheap tricks, and plus one of the best opening sequences seen in some time, *Tomorrow at Seven* is a mystery thriller with the accent on the mystery.... [E]ven if the plot doesn't at all times hold water, it holds enough to give any audience a large dose of cold chills."

Tomorrow at Seven was the product of prolific script writer Ralph Spence, the author of the 1925 play *The Gorilla* which was filmed in 1927, 1930 and 1939.

Later in 1933, a master villain also called the Black Ace appeared in the 12-chapter Mascot serial *The Mystery Squadron*.

Two in the Dark (1936; 74 minutes)

ASSOCIATE PRODUCER: Zion Myers. DIRECTOR: Ben Stoloff. SCREENPLAY: Seton I. Miller, from the novel by Gelett Burgess. PHOTOGRAPHY: Nicholas Musuraca. EDITOR: George Crone. MUSIC DIRECTOR: Alberto Colombo. ART DIRECTORS: Van Nest Polglase & Al Herman. SOUND: John E. Tribby. GOWNS: Bernard Newman.

CAST: Walter Abel (Ford Adams), Margot Grahame (Marie Smith), Wallace Ford (Harry Hillyer), Gail Patrick (Irene Lassiter), Alan Hale (Police Inspector Florio), Leslie Fenton (Stuart Eldredge), Eric Blore (Edmund Fish), Erin O'Brien-Moore (Olga Konar), Erik Rhodes (Carlo Gheet), J. Carrol Naish (Burt Mansfield), Addison [Jack] Randall (Duke Reed), Forbes Murray (Richard Denning), Arthur Hoyt (Mr. Pegley), Thelma White (Dolly), Pierre Watkin (City Editor), Nora Cecil (Mrs. Potter), Russell Hicks (Officer McCord), Richard Howard (Officer O'Brien), Fern Emmett (Housekeeper), Frank Mayo (Desk Clerk), Gaston Glass (Headwaiter), Ward Bond (Park Policeman), Hector Sarno (Diner Owner), Harry Bowen (Taxi Driver), Tom McGuire (Doorman), Ernie Alexander (Messenger).

In the mid–1930s RKO tried to make a screen team of Walter Abel and Margot Grahame and first paired them in a respectable version of *The Three Musketeers* (1935), followed by *Two in the Dark*, which was based on Gelett Burgess' 1934 novel *Two O'Clock Courage*. This intriguing thriller about amnesia and murder was a good showcase for its two stars although Wallace Ford stole the show as a wisecracking, pugnacious newshound. Its minor horrific touch is that the protagonist fears having committed a killing while unaware of his past. Moving at a steady clip, the feature keeps the identity of the guilty party a secret until its tense finale. Ben Stoloff's steady direction accounts for much of the film's success as do the supporting players, especially Alan Hale as a bombastic police inspector, Eric Blore as a befuddled butler, J. Carrol Naish portraying a jealous actor, and Nora Cecil as a grim landlady. Despite good critical response, *Two in the Dark* failed to click with the public and *Harrison's Reports* deemed its box office performance "Poor." It proved to be the end of the Abel-Grahame combination. Nevertheless, nine years later RKO remade the property and released it under its source name, *Two O'Clock Courage* (q.v.), with Stoloff serving as producer.

One early Boston morning, a man (Abel) standing under a street light is suffering from a head injury and amnesia, has blood on his hands and $500 in his pocket. He is seen by Marie Smith (Grahame), an actress who has been evicted from her lodgings. She comes to the aid of the hurt man and, after hearing that Richard Denning (Forbes Murray), a theatrical producer, has been murdered, they suspect the man might have committed the crime. Trying to keep the stranger away from the law, Marie takes him to her former residence, a boarding house run by severe Mrs. Potter (Nora Cecil); he takes a room using the name David Robbins, since the initials D.R. are on his hat band. He and Marie learn that Denning's chauffeur, Duke Reed (Addison [Jack] Randall), is a suspect; they go to the man's residence and are found there by Police Inspector Florio (Hale) and newsman Harry Hillyer (Ford). Both of them think the man is Reed but he tells them he is Jimmy Smith, another reporter investigating the case. The four travel to Denning's home where his butler, Edmund Fish (Blore), does not say the man is Duke. While there, the man notices the manuscript of a play written by Kenneth Orme on Denning's desk. Since he possesses a matchbook from the Yorkshire Arms Hotel, the man and Marie go there but are followed

Nora Cecil and Wallace Ford in *Two in the Dark* (1936).

by the suspicious Hillyer. At the hotel the man is greeted by Irene Lassiter (Gail Patrick) and as they talk, playwright Stuart Eldredge (Leslie Fenton) arrives and calls the man Jitney, implying they attended school together. Stuart has an altercation with actor Burt Mansfield (Naish), who accuses him of bothering his girlfriend Olga Konar (Erin O'Brien-Moore), the star of Eldredge's play. Later Eldredge has the man join him in his suite and he learns his name is Ford Adams. Eldredge also mentions their mutual friend Kenneth Orme, who is now deceased. Since he is registered at the Yorkshire, Ford searches his own room and locates a letter from Orme's mother giving him authority to sell her son's work. When he returns to Denning's office to get the manuscript he is shot, but it is only a flesh wound. As a result, Ford's memory returns and he realizes that Eldredge plagiarized Orme's play and tried to steal the only remaining copy from Denning. Florio believes Ford is the killer and follows him to Stuart's rooms where Ford confronts Stuart, who admits to his charges. Florio arrests Stuart, who goes to his bedroom for a coat and is shot. Hillyer finds Olga in another room and she confesses to killing Denning and Stuart as both of them had been blackmailing her over letters she had written to Denning before falling in love with Mansfield. With his memory returned and exonerated of murder, Ford looks forward to the future with Marie.

The New York Times said the feature "merits the attention of cinemagoers who take an especial interest in mystery stories liberally sprinkled with comedy.... [It's] consistently entertaining." *Boxoffice* termed it an "exceptionally fine mystery thriller packed with surprising situations and suspense.... Direction has been handled with a deft hand guiding plot development through a series of tense situations." *Photoplay* opined, "[T]his plot is as clean-cut and easy to follow as it is novel and fast-moving, the perfect score for this kind of thing." *Variety* wrote, "While not a powerful contribution to the murder mystery cycle, *Two in the Dark* has several notable virtues which combine to establish it as pretty good entertainment.... Unique from start to finish, the plot not only manages to successfully pique the interest but it also carefully maintains suspense as to the facts which underlie the murder." *The Film Daily* declared, "The clever unraveling of the mystery holds you tense to the final scene. The honors go to the author for a very unusual plot, ably seconded by smart direction and a very competent cast throughout." "A fairly good murder melodrama.... Good for adults," said *Harrison's Reports*. *The Weekly Guide* asserted, "A mystery story that is really mysterious, with many unexpected and sometimes amusing twists and a surprise outcome. Well written and directed." *Hollywood* dubbed the feature an "extremely mystifying mystery film ... a thoroughly entertaining program."

The storyline of a plagiarized play, blackmail and murder were also used in RKO's *Forty Naughty Girls* (q.v.), released 20 months after *Two in the Dark*.

Two O'Clock Courage (1945; 65 minutes)

PRODUCER: Ben Stoloff. EXECUTIVE PRODUCER: Sid Rogell. DIRECTOR: Anthony Mann. SCREENPLAY: Robert E. Kent, from the novel by Gelett Burgess. ADDITIONAL DIALOGUE: Gordon Kahn. PHOTOGRAPHY: Jack MacKenzie. EDITOR: Philip Martin, Jr. MUSIC: Roy Webb. ART DIRECTORS: Albert S. D'Agostino & L.O. Croxton. SOUND: James A. Stewart & Bailey Fesler. SET DECORATIONS: Darrell Silvera & William Stevens. GOWNS: Renie. SPECIAL EFFECTS: Vernon L. Walker. ASSISTANT DIRECTOR: Clem Beauchamp.

CAST: Tom Conway (Ted Allison), Ann Rutherford (Patty Mitchell), Richard Lane (Al Haley), Lester Matthews (Mark Evans), Roland Drew (Steve Maitland), Emory Parnell (Inspector Bill Brenner), Bettejane [Jane] Greer (Helen Carter), Jean Brooks (Barbara "Babs" Borden), Bryant Washburn (Robert Dilling), Harold De Becker (Wilbur Judson), Chester Clute (Mr. Daniels), Almira Sessions (Mrs. Daniels), Charles C. Wilson (City Editor Brandt), Sarah Edwards (Mrs. Tuttle), Carl Kent (Dave Rennick), Maxine Semon

(Housekeeper), Edmund Glover (O'Brien), Philip Morris (Officer McCord), Jack Norton (Drunk), Guy Zanette (Headwaiter), Elaine Riley (Cigarette Girl), Tom Coleman (Waiter), Chris Drake (Assistant Editor), Nancy Marlow (Hat Check Girl), Eddie Dunn, Bob Robinson (Policemen), Bob Alden (Newsboy), Jason Robards (Man in Picture).

A remake of *Two in the Dark* (q.v.), *Two O'Clock Courage* takes a lighter look at the tale of an amnesiac (Tom Conway) and his quest to not only find his true identity but also to clear himself of a murder charge. Much of the underplayed but well done comedy is handled by Richard Lane as a harried reporter and Emory Parnell as his sarcastic police inspector nemesis. Conway nicely carries off the difficult role of a man with memory loss while attractive Ann Rutherford adds zest to the proceedings as the cabbie who has faith in him. Director Anthony Mann made his RKO debut in this outing, as did actress Jane Greer, billed here as Bettejane Greer. Although her part is small, she makes a good impression. Jean Brooks is wasted in a role that only shows off her beauty and histrionic abilities at the finale. Thanks to Mann's steady direction through a somewhat convoluted plot, *Two O'Clock Courage* is a more-than-adequate programmer. The opening scene of Conway's dark figure coming out of the fog and nearly hit by Rutherford's cab and his later semi-conscious dream sequence give the film a bit of a horrific twist. The feature was produced by Ben Stoloff, who directed its predecessor *Two in the Dark*.

On a foggy night in Ocean View, Patty Mitchell (Rutherford) almost runs down a man (Conway) who steps in front of her cab. At first she thinks he is drunk and then realizes the man has been slugged because of a cut on his head. As the man tries to clear his mind, he realizes he is suffering from amnesia and finds he has a hatband with the initials R.D., two Imperial Theatre tickets and a matchbook from the Regency Hotel's Blue Room. Patty talks the man into going to the police but when they get there they learn someone matching his description and wearing a pin-stripe suit is wanted for questioning in the murder of Robert Dilling (Bryant Washburn), a theatrical producer. For his protection, Patty takes the man to a tailor (Chester Clute) for a new suit and hat and there they hear a radio bulletin naming Dave Rennick (Carl Kent), Dilling's chauffeur, as a suspect in the homicide. Although Patty wants the man to leave Ocean View he takes her to Rennick's apartment and finds a copy of the play *Menace* by Mark Evans (Lester Matthews) and learns that the playwright has been paying Dilling $400 a week, one-half of his royalties. Police Inspector Bill Brenner (Parnell) arrives at the apartment as the same time as newshound Al Haley (Lane) and the two find Patty and her new friend there. Patty claims they are Clarence Smith and wife and have just been married but their honeymoon was interrupted when her Dayton, Ohio, reporter husband learned of Dilling's murder and decided to investigate. Both Brenner and Haley are wary of the claim and take them to the Dilling home where the British butler, Wilbur Judson (Harold De Becker), informs Brenner that the man is not Rennick. While searching Dilling's desk the man finds a manuscript to a play called *Two O'Clock Courage* by Lawrence Tenny. Brenner gets a call saying a tailor had seen a man wearing a dark pin-stripe suit in his shop and since Judson is wearing such an outfit he is arrested and taken to headquarters. The man and Patty drive to her boarding house so she can change clothes to go with him to the Regency Hotel's Blue Room and they have a run-in with her nosy landlady (Sarah Edwards) with Patty informing her they are newlyweds. At the Blue Room, Haley talks with his editor (Charles C. Wilson) on the telephone and informs him that Judson has been released by the police and he suspects the killer is named Harry. The man and Patty arrive at the Blue Room where a drunk (Jack Norton) calls the man Step, as does lovely Helen Carter (Greer). As they have drinks, Helen tells Step she is surprised to see him since he had an argument with Dilling the night before. Playwright Evans comes by and also refers to the man as Step, mentioning they were friends since college. After Evans and Helen leave to dance, Patty and the man also start to dance

Tom Conway and Emory Parnell in *Two O'Clock Courage* (1945).

when they see Evans engaged in a fight with actor Steve Maitland (Roland Drew). Sending Patty home, the man goes to Evans' room and is told that Maitland is unhappy because Evans tried to keep him out of his play. The man learns his given name is Theodore or Ted and that he was dubbed Step in college because of his football prowess by their mutual friend Lawrence Tenny, who later killed himself. Ted starts to leave but when he goes back into the apartment he finds Evans with Patty and Evans calls him Ted Allison. Ted returns to Patty's rooms where he hears a radio bulletin that he is being sought in Dilling's murder. When Brenner and Haley show up, he escapes through a window. Later Ted and Patty call all the hotels in town and find he is registered in room 312 at the Regency. Telling Patty to return to her lodgings, Ted goes to the Regency while Brenner arrests Rennick for killing his boss; the chauffeur says it was Maitland who threatened Dilling. Upon questioning by Brenner, Maitland admits having an altercation with Dilling for bothering his girlfriend, Barbara Borden (Brooks), the star of *Menace*. Barbara informs Brenner that Dilling had an argument with Ted Allison. Ted finds a letter in his room from Lawrence Tenny's mother telling him to represent her in negotiations involving her son's play. Haley goes to Ted's room and the two fight, with Ted escaping and returning to Dilling's house to get the copy of Tenny's play. He finds the manuscript but is knocked out after being grazed by a bullet to his head. Half-conscious, Ted recalls a showdown with Evans over Tenny's play with Evans giving him $500 before he is shot. Coming to, Ted is found by a policeman (Bob Robinson) who takes him to Brenner. Ted informs the inspector that Dilling was blackmailing Evans for plagiarizing Tenny's work. When they go to see Evans, Ted accuses him of killing Dilling when he tried to stop him from stealing the last copy of Tenny's manuscript. Admitting he shot Dilling, Evans goes to his bedroom for a coat and a shot is heard. Evans is found dead with a revolver by his side but Ted deduces the weapon has not been fired. Hearing another shot, Ted and Brenner search nearby rooms and locate Barbara, who has shot herself. Before dying, the actress tells Ted, Brenner and Haley that she murdered Dilling because he was blackmailing her over letters she had written him before she fell in love with Maitland. Barbara also says she shot Evans because he knew why she was being blackmailed by Dilling. Haley, who has given his harried editor too many wrong story leads, loses out on a bonus for bungling the Dilling murder story. Ted and Patty return to her rooms, and this time they show her landlady their marriage license.

The New York Times called the plot of *Two O'Clock Courage* "the somewhat bizarre complication from which a minimum of humor is derived.... There is not much cause here for caring whether Mr. Conway did it or not." *Boxoffice* noted, "The film probably was designed to serve as nothing more than the second feature on routine dual programs and in such niche it will satisfy the average customer, and do slightly better by those fans who like their murders laced with laughs." *Variety* complained that the film "has less guts than its title. Film is a slow-paced, drab mystery." *The Film Daily* called it "long on dialogue and short on action.... [T]he production insults the intelligence far more than necessary.... Conway does well under the handicap of a poor script. Miss Rutherford does the best she can with her role."

Two Weeks to Live (1943; 76 minutes)

PRODUCER: Ben Hersh. EXECUTIVE PRODUCER: Jack William Votion. DIRECTOR: Malcolm St. Clair. SCREENPLAY: Michael L. Simmons & Roswell Rogers. PHOTOGRAPHY: Jack MacKenzie. EDITOR: Duncan Mansfield. MUSIC DIRECTOR: Lud Gluskin. ART DIRECTOR: F. Paul Sylos. SOUND: Ferol Redd. SET DECORATIONS: Ben Berk. UNIT MANAGER: John E. Burch. ASSISTANT DIRECTOR: Charles Kerr.

CAST: Lum [Chester Lauck] (Lum Edwards), Abner [Norris Goff] (Abner Peabody), Franklin Pangborn (Mr. Pickney), Kay Linaker (Madge Carmen), Irving Bacon (Omar Tennyson Gimpel), Herbert Rawlinson (J.J. Stark), Ivan Simpson (Professor Albert Frisby), Rosemary LaPlanche (Miss LaPlanche), Danny Duncan (Ulysses), Evelyn Knapp (Miss Morris), Charles Middleton (Elmer Kelton), Luis Alberni (The New Dr. Jekyll), Jack Rice (Hotel Clerk), Tim Ryan (Thrill-a-Minute Higgins), Oscar O'Shea (Squire Skimp), Edward Earle (Dr. J.J. O'Brien), Frank Jaquet (Dr. Leach), Nora Cecil (Grandma Masters), Si Jenks (Station Agent), Ben Erway (Mr. Fleming), Hank Mann (Janitor), Lynton Brent, Bert Moorhouse (FBI Agents), Jerry Hausner (Reporter), Charles Gemora (Plato the Gorilla), Donald Kerr (Plato's Owner), Lane Bradford (Rocket Loader), Cyril Ring (Pilot), Frank Mills (Mechanic), John Sheehan (Harp Delivery Man), Roger Neury (Hotel Waiter), Harry Tenbrook (Wheelchair Pusher), Billy Bletcher (Classified Advertising Collector), Gil Frye (Stark's Assistant), Jack Carr (Airfield Attendant), Jack Gardner (Elevator Operator), Jim Farley (Gossip), Tiny Jones (Pine Ridge Citizen).

Chester Lauck and Norris Goff played Pine Ridge, Arkansas' Lum Edwards and Abner Peabody, co-owners of the Jot 'em Down Store, on radio for 23 years. *Lum and Abner* started in 1931 on station KTHS in Hot Springs, Arkansas, and later in the year went national on NBC as a summer replacement series. The show proved so successful that NBC brought it back early in 1932. In 1934 it moved to Mutual. In 1935 the series was on the NBC Blue network and remained there until 1938 when it was broadcast by CBS. From 1941 to 1945 *Lum and Abner* was on ABC before returning to CBS in 1947 where it remained until 1953. It had its final season back on ABC, ending its lengthy run in the spring of 1954. Given the RKO penchant for making films centered on radio stars, the studio partnered with Jack William Votion Productions for a half-dozen Lum and Abner features between 1940 and 1946. In 1943 RKO released two genre-related Lum and Abner pictures, *Two Weeks to Live* in February, followed seven months later by *So This Is Washington* (q.v.).

Two Weeks to Live retained such Pine Ridge denizens as Squire Skimp (Oscar O'Shea), postman Ulysses (Danny Duncan) and Grandma Masters (Nora Cecil). Among its screwy plot ploys are a bungled medical diagnosis (thus the title), a harried office building manager (Franklin Pangborn), a poem-spouting window washer (Irving Bacon) with his invisible dog, a mad scientist (Luis Alberni) and his Jekyll-Hyde potion, a dancing gorilla (Charles Gemora), an attractive but homicidal insurance swindler (Kay Linaker) and her haunted house, a fast-talking airplane daredevil promoter (Tim Ryan), foreign spies and an addled inventor (Ivan F. Simpson) with a rocket which he plans to send to Mars. All these subplots are nimbly directed by comedy veteran Malcolm St. Clair, thus the picture is never dull. In one somewhat underplayed but highly amusing scene, downhearted Abner (Goff) having just learned he has two weeks to live, tries to take his mind off his troubles—but in succession he sees a newspaper article on death and taxes, a book entitled *One Foot in the Grave* and, turning on the radio, he hears a funeral dirge. For genre fans, Charles Gemora reprises his gorilla outfit originally used in *Ingagi* (q.v.), Luis Alberni portrays a wide eyed Jekyll and Hyde and Ivan F. Simpson is grand as the muddled Mars rocket inventor. The briefly seen missile is well done.

Chicago lawyer J.J. Stark (Herbert Rawlinson) of the Stark & Stark law firm sends an airmail special delivery letter to Abner Peabody (Goff) in Pine Ridge, Arkansas. Postman Ulysses (Duncan) brings the letter, several days late, to the Jot 'em Down Store which Abner runs with his best friend Lum Edwards (Lauck). Abner has Ulysses read the letter which informs him he has inherited the C&O Railroad due to the death of his Uncle Ernest. Abner wants to be the railroad's conductor so Lum appoints himself the C&O's president and tells Abner they need to run a spur line from Pine Ridge to the county seat, obtain rights-of-way to do so and sell stock in the railroad. To get the needed funds for the rights-of-way, Lum and Abner convince the locals to invest in the enterprise and they raise nearly $10,000. The duo goes to see Stark at his office in Chicago's Bar Building. When they find that Stark is not in his office, they take a train to Gold City to see the C&O and learn from the station agent (Si Jenks) that Uncle Ernest's gold mine there petered out years ago. They find the train in a ruined condition. Stark informs Lum and Abner that a salvage dealer will pay $200 for the railroad. On their way from the lawyer's office, Abner, who distrusts elevators, falls on a wet, soapy floor. The building's janitor (Hank Mann) informs the manager, Mr. Pinckney (Pangborn), about Abner's fall and Pinkney insists Abner see a doctor. At the doctor's (Edward Earle) office, his love-struck nurse (Rosemary LaPlanche) mixes up patient cards and Abner is mistakenly told by the secretary (Evelyn Knapp) that he has only two weeks to live. When they return to their hotel, Lum and Abner get a message from Squire Skimp (O'Shea) in Pine Ridge saying all the money has been paid for the rights-of-way. While they try to think of ways to raise the funds to repay the people of Pine Ridge, Lum and Abner meet window washer Gimpel (Bacon), who spouts made-up poems and whose sidekick is an unseen dog. Hearing of their woes and that Abner has only a short time to live, Gimpel suggests he make $500 by painting a nearby flag pole atop a skyscraper. After much objecting, Abner takes the job but bungles it by falling on Lum. Gimpel then suggests the two men run an advertisement for Abner's services which reads "Human Daredevil—Days Numbered." A line of people answer the ad, including the New Dr. Jekyll (Alberni), who wants Abner to take his formula to see if he turns into Mr. Hyde. When Abner declines, Lum takes the doctor into another room and Plato the Gorilla (Gemora) and his owner (Donald Kerr) appear hoping Abner will become Plato's new dancing partner. When he sees Plato, Abner thinks Lum drank Jekyll's formula. When Lum and the doctor re-appear, they think Abner has swallowed the elixir and turned into Plato. Rejecting both offers, Lum and Abner are then approached by Madge Carmen (Linaker), who wants to give Abner $1,000 to spend the night in her house to prove it is not haunted. She says she will pay Abner if he lives until morning since she wants to sell the place. While Mrs. Carmen's offer is refused, Lum and Abner accept a $5,000 deal with Thrill-A-Minute Higgins (Ryan), who hires Abner to go from one midair airplane into another. The reluctant Abner successfully performs the stunt only to learn Higgins ran off with the money. Lum and Abner then accept Gimpel's suggestion that they sue the hotel over Abner's fall. Lum negotiates with Pinkney and his lawyer (Ben Erway) and ends up with only $60, nearly all of which is claimed by a collector (Billy Bletcher) to pay for their newspaper advertisement. Lum has lunch with Mrs. Carmen, who tells him her mother is very ill and that she must sell her house so he promises he will talk with Abner about staying the night there. The woman plans to blow up the house while Abner is there and collect on her husband's insurance since she will claim Abner was her spouse. Elmer Kelton (Charles Middleton) from Pine Ridge arrives in Chicago and informs Lum and Abner that the people there think they have swindled them and plan to take them to court to get their money back. Lum convinces Abner to take Mrs. Carmen's job and

Chester Lauck as Lum and Norris Goff as Abner, the stars of *Two Weeks to Live* (1943).

she gives Abner a violin case to take back to the house. The case contains a time bomb. She also has him wear a bracelet to keep ghosts away although it really contains her husband's identification. On the way to the house on Laurel Street, Abner stops to help a boy fix his bicycle and ends up going to Elm Street to a rundown house used as a headquarters by foreign saboteurs. When Abner sees one of the spies, he thinks he is a ghost and runs away, leaving the violin case behind. The bomb explodes as Abner makes a getaway back to the hotel. Lum and Abner are visited by Professor Albert Frisby (Simpson) who offers Abner $10,000 to ride in his rocket and take a message to Mars. Accepting the offer, Abner is about to board the rocket when he realizes his death date is here and he goes back to the hotel. Lum and Frisby follow. Since Lum has a bad cold, the desk clerk (Jack Rice) sends a doctor (Frank Jaquet) to see him. After examining Abner, the doctor declares he is in good health. When the doctor announces Lum is in a bad way, he agrees to ride in the rocket. Stark, who has sold their railroad rights-of-ways for $20,000, learns from Gimple that Lum and Abner are headed for the Mars Airport and follows them by taxi. As Lum waits in the rocket, Abner has second thoughts about sending his friend on the trip and accidentally sits on the launcher, shooting the craft into the air. The rocket ship crashes near a sign saying NINE MILES FROM MARS and Lum heads in that direction, not realizing he has landed in Iowa.

   Photoplay termed *Two Weeks to Live* "fun, homespun and homegrown," while *Variety* commented, "Lum & Abner swing through their usual rural antics here, and whatever radio voltage the homespun pair enjoys with hinterland audiences will be required to give this more than passing attention...."

"*Two Weeks to Live* should have little difficulty pleasing Lum and Abner fans. In fact, it should have little trouble pleasing any one who relishes hokum and plenty of it," said *The Film Daily*. Regarding the movie's change of locale from Pine Ridge to Chicago, *Boxoffice* reported, "The switch develops broad, even slapstick, comedy rather than the homely, philosophical kind which won them their ether popularity. Their fans probably will not mind the change too much— for the intrinsic L & A appeal still asserts itself, despite the wild scripting."

The Whip Hand (1951; 82 minutes)

PRODUCER: Lewis J. Rachmil. DIRECTOR–PRODUCTION DESIGNER: William Cameron Menzies. SCREENPLAY: George Bricker & Frank L. Moss. STORY: Roy Hamilton. PHOTOGRAPHY: Nicholas Musuraca. EDITOR: Robert Golden. MUSIC: Paul Sawtell. MUSIC DIRECTOR: C. Bakaleinikoff. ART DIRECTORS: Carroll Clark & Albert S. D'Agostino. SOUND: Clem Portman & Earl Wolcott. SET DECORATIONS: James Altwies & Darrell Silvera.

CAST: Carla Balenda (Janet Keller), Elliott Reid (Matt Corbin), Edgar Barrier (Dr. Edward Keller), Raymond Burr (Steve Loomis), Otto Waldis (Dr. Wilhelm Bucholtz), Michael Steele (Chick), Lurene Tuttle (Molly Loomis), Peter Brocco (Nate Garr), Lewis Martin (Peterson), Frank Darien (Luther Adams), Olive Carey (Mabel Turner), Leonid Snegoff (Russian General), Billy Nelson (Delivery Man Ed), Milton Kibbee (Grocery Company Owner), Mary Baer (Miss Price), Gregory Gay (Sweitart), Douglas Evans (Carstairs), George Chandler (Jed), Donald Dillaway (McIntyre), William Challee, Robert Foulk (Guards), G. Pat Collins (Gate Guard Nelson), Roy Darmour (Harry Jones), Tom Greenway, Brick Sullivan, Bob Thorn (FBI Agents), Frank Wilcox (Bradford), Jameson Shade (Sheriff), Art Dupuis (Speedboat Pilot), Stanley Blystone (Pier Guard), Elizabeth Flournoy (Secretary), Eddie Borden (Experiment Patient).

The Whip Hand is one of the more obscure works of legendary director–production designer William Cameron Menzies; it was one of his features. (He went on to direct the interesting genre efforts *The Maze* and *Invaders from Mars* in 1953.) Made as *The Man He Found*, *The Whip Hand* was released in the fall of 1951 after extensive retakes. The film originally told how Adolf Hitler (Bobby Watson) was in hiding in New England, planning a new world order, but Howard Hughes, the owner of RKO, insisted the plot be changed to the Soviets trying to pollute America's water supply. A Nazi scientist, now working for the Reds, was retained. The shift to Communists as the bad guys did not go over well with some of the cast members, including leading man Elliott Reid, later the host of the left-leaning TV satire *That Was the Week That Was* (1964). The locale of the feature was also changed to rural Wisconsin, with filming in California's San Bernadino Mountains. While Hughes was correct in believing the Communist theme was more topical than a "Hitler lives" retread, the new scenes eventually sent the feature into the red (pun intended), grossing only $150,000 at the box office against a cost of $376,000.

While fishing at Lake Winnoga in Wisconsin, journalist Matt Corbin (Reid) hits his head on a rock during a fall in a sudden thunderstorm. He drives to a nearby lodge but he is refused entrance. Driving to the town of Winnoga, he is directed to the home of Dr. Edward Keller (Edgar Barrier) by gas station worker Nate Garr (Peter Brocco). Matt is treated by Dr. Keller and he meets the man's sister Janet (Carla Balenda). The physician informs him that the owner of the lodge, Peterson (Lewis Martin), does not like strangers. The doctor escorts Matt to the Winnoga Inn, where he is told by owner Steve Loomis (Raymond Burr) that the town is practically deserted because five years before a virus killed off the lake's trout. Matt thinks the town's story would make a fine article for *American View* magazine. Matt talks with store owner Luther Adams (Frank Darien), who says he refused to sell out after outsiders bought up most of the area. Luther quits talking when Garr appears. Matt sees Janet going to the town's movie house and follows her. Janet is friendly with Matt but suggests he leave Winnoga. The next day Matt

Elliott Reid, Edgar Barrier and Carla Balenda in *The Whip Hand* (1951).

tells Steve he plans to stay and write his article. After Matt sets out to explore the locale, Steve orders his helper Chick (Michael Steele) to shadow him. Matt goes to the lodge and takes a few photographs before again being ordered off the property. Janet warns Matt that he will not be able to communicate with the outside world since Steve's wife Molly (Lurene Tuttle) controls the telephone switchboard. After noticing some books by Dr. Wilhelm Bucholtz (Otto Waldis) on Janet's shelf, Matt plans to drive to the next town but his car will not start. He is also shown his destroyed camera by Chick. Matt gets Luther to send a message to his editor, Bradford (Frank Wilcox), in a coded note but Steve and Molly find out and have Dr. Keller give Luther a drug that kills him. Steve takes Matt to the lodge to meet Peterson, who gives him a tour and invites him to stay. Later Peterson orders Dr. Keller to get rid of his sister because he fears she may have revealed too much to Matt. Bradford gets Matt's message and believes he has found Nazi war criminal Buchlotz. Matt locates Janet, who says her brother has asked her to bring a lethal drug to the lodge. Fearing for her life, Matt convinces her to leave with him. As she waits in a canoe, Matt goes back to the lodge where Bucholtz brags of his plans to contaminate Chicago's water supply for his new bosses, the rulers of the Soviet Union. He shows off his human guinea pigs as a manhunt begins for Matt and Janet. The two escape detection by hiding under a rock ledge but are spotted by Chick, who is killed by Matt. The couple goes into the forest and come upon Mabel Turner's (Olive Carey) cabin. She agrees to take them to the sheriff (Jameson Shade) but instead drives them to Loomis and his cohorts. At the lodge, Bucholtz tells Matt and Janet of his plans and Peterson orders Dr. Keller to eliminate his sister. The doctor shoots Peterson but is killed. Government agents alerted by Bradford arrive at the lodge and attempt to arrest Bucholtz. He takes refuge in a bulletproof room and announces he will destroy the lodge with a device that will saturate the air with killer germs. Matt, who has received a key to the room from Dr. Keller, takes the weapon away from him. The scientist's experimental subjects take revenge on the madman. Later Matt's article, accompanied by a photo of him and his fiancée Janet, is published by Bradford.

Variety reported, "This is an above-average thriller, strong on suspense.... William Cameron Menzies' direction keeps the tension boiling along the tightly developed unfoldment.... Suspense gains from Menzies' production design, which makes good use of the outdoor locale...." In *Science Fiction* (1984), Phil Hardy called *The Whip Hand* a "science fiction thriller, full of suspense, ingeniously made from an unreleased film, *The Man He Found*.... [I]t was one of the best received anti-communist films of the fifties, probably because of the skillful way Menzies put together [George] Bricker and [Frank L.] Moss' re-workings of the old material." He also said the film was "highly atmospheric."

The use of germ warfare was such a novel concept in the early 1950s as to place *The Whip Hand* in the sci-fi genre, along with Otto Waldis' mad scientist (a Nazi turned Communist!) and his swathed guinea pigs, the results of the madman's terrible experiments.

You'll Find Out (1940; 97 minutes)

PRODUCER-DIRECTOR: David Butler. SCREENPLAY: James V. Kern. STORY: David Butler & James V. Kern. SPECIAL MATERIAL: Monte Brice, Andrew Bennison & R.T.M. Scott. PHOTOGRAPHY: Frank Redman. EDITOR: Irene Morra. MUSIC DIRECTOR: Roy Webb. MUSIC ARRANGER: George Duning. SONGS: Jimmy McHugh & Johnny Mercer. ART DIRECTORS: Van Nest Polglase & Carroll Clark. SOUND: Earl A. Wolcott. SET DECORATIONS: Darrell Silvera. GOWNS: Edward Stevenson. SONOVOX EFFECTS: Gilbert Wright. ASSISTANT DIRECTOR: Fred A. Fleck.

CAST: Kay Kyser (Himself), Boris Karloff (Judge Spencer Mainwaring), Peter Lorre (Professor Karl Fenninger), Helen Parrish (Janis Bellacrest), Dennis O'Keefe (Chuck Deems), Bela Lugosi (Prince Saliano), Alma Kruger (Margo Bellacrest), Joseph Eggenton (Jurgen), Kay Kyser's Band (Themselves), Harry Babbitt, Ginny Simms, Ish Kabibble, Sully Mason (Themselves), Louise Currie (Marion), Mary Martha Wood (Georgia), Dorothy Moore (Penny), Mimi Montaye (Mimi), Joan Warner (Joan), Mary Bovard (Mary), Jane Patten (Jane), Jeanne Houser (Jean), Jeff Corey (Mr. Corey), Eleanor Lawson (Gaby Lawson), Bill Telaak (Bus Driver), Leonard Mudie (Real Karl Fenninger), Joe North (Servant), Eugenia Rafee (French Maid), Frank Mills (Cab Driver), Bess Flowers (Taxi Passenger), Beulah Parkington (Radio Listener), Guy Webster (Infant), Larry McGrath (Complainer), Frank O'Connor (Kay Kyser Fan).

The only screen teaming of film terror titans Boris Karloff, Peter Lorre and Bela Lugosi came in *You'll Find Out*, the second film vehicle for popular bandleader Kay Kyser. His first cinema outing, *That's Right—You're Wrong* (1939), proved so successful that producer-director David Butler re-teamed with Kyser for *You'll Find Out*, which RKO Radio issued in November 1940. Kyser first broadcast on radio over Mutal in 1937 and the next year headlined *Kay Kyser's Kollege of Musical Knowledge* which ran on NBC from 1938 to 1948 before the show had its final season on ABC, ending in the summer of 1949. During that time Kyser had a large radio following and his recordings for Columbia Records were big sellers. An acquired taste, Kyser's mainstay was silly comedy combined with big band music and he developed an ensemble of popular vocalists that included Harry Babbitt, Ginny Simms, Sully Mason, Ish Kabibble and, later, Mike Douglas.

At 97 minutes, *You'll Find Out* gave audiences an overdose of Kyser and not enough of Boris Karloff, Bela Lugosi or Peter Lorre. Five musical numbers, in addition to Kyser's theme song "Thinking of You," inflate the running time; they're all lesser compositions of Jimmy McHugh and Johnny Mercer. One of them, "You Got Me This Way," reached the Top Twenty and provided bestselling platters for Kyser (vocal by Harry Babbitt) on Columbia Records (35762) and Tommy Dorsey and His Orchestra and the Pied Pipers on Victor Records (26770) in 1941. Lovely Ginny Simms sings two songs, "I'd Know You Anywhere" and "I've Got a One Track Mind," the latter with Babbitt. In the film she somewhat upstages leading lady Helen Parrish, who was borrowed from Universal. Dennis O'Keefe, as Kyser's manager, is basically the co-star of the production as he and his boss try to find out who is trying to kill off his fiancée, played by Parrish. Although the film starts out with one of Kyser's radio shows and its silly shenanigans, it mainly takes place in a Massachusetts manor house filled with a plethora of exotic (and often horrifying) memorabilia. The film proved to be a box office winner, earning a profit of nearly $170,000.

Despite sixth billing in the opening credits, Bela Lugosi comes off best of the trio of horror stars. Karloff has little to do besides appear sinister and Peter Lorre acts as a good guy most of the time despite being in cahoots with Karloff and Lugosi in wanting to dispatch the leading lady. Lugosi has the best role of the three, that of a fake swami who is bilking a rich old woman with phony spiritualism. Although his screen time is limited, Lugosi makes the most of it, especially in the scene where he ogles Ginny Simms. All the trappings of an old house murder mystery are present in *You'll Find Out*, including a thunderstorm, séances, ghostly voices, floating faces, secret panels and an underground tunnel filled with horrific items, including a life-size gorilla and an Egyptian statue.

Despite the dull and inane Kay Kyser and the multitude of musical numbers, including the ridiculous "Bad Humor Man," *You'll Find Out* is a fair mystery-comedy worth seeing because of its villains Karloff, Lugosi and Lorre. It is a handsomely made production with excellent art direction by Van Nest Polglase and Carroll Clark and set decoration by Darrell Silvera. Besides Kyser, its main annoyance is a device called Sonovox which amplifies throat sounds into music. It is almost unbearable when Harry Babbitt uses it in a duet with Ginny Simms at the finale on "I've Got a One Track Mind."

You'll Find Out was filmed as *The Old Professor*, Kay Kyser's radio moniker, and shown in Spanish-language countries as *El Castillo de los Misterios* (The Castle of the Mysteries).

Kay Kyser's radio show *The Kollege of Musical Knowledge* does a program in which two contestants (Jeff Corey, Eleanor Lawson) compete for a prize. After the broadcast, Kay's manager Chuck Deems (O'Keefe) introduces him to his fiancée, Janis Bellacrest (Parrish), who has just graduated from finishing school. For her 21st birthday party, the Kyser band is going to appear at Janis' remote country home, Bellacrest Manor. As Chuck and Janis are leaving the broadcast

Peter Lorre, Bela Lugosi and Boris Karloff in *You'll Find Out* **(1940).**

studio, she is almost hit by a car. She tells Chuck it was deliberate, her third near-accident in two weeks. The band travels to Bellacrest Manor by bus with one of the members, Ish Kabbible (himself), bringing his dog Prince. Upon their arrival, Kay and the band members find the mansion is full of exotic memorabilia brought there by its builder, explorer Elmer Bellacrest, Janis' late father. Janis introduces Kay to her aunt, Margo Bellacrest (Alma Kruger), who dabbles in spiritualism. Margo tells the bandleader they are kindred souls. A thunderstorm develops as the band members settle in. Judge Spencer Mainwaring (Karloff) is introduced by Janis as one of her dearest friends. The butler (Joseph Eggenton) informs Kay that Elmer was killed by natives while on an expedition and that Elmer's friend Mainwaring, who was with him, barely escaped with his life. When Kay gets to his room he is visited by Margo's medium, Prince Saliano (Lugosi), who says the house is haunted and that Elmer's spirit is in the room. A mysterious man climbs a tree next to the house and observes Janis and band singer Ginny Simms (herself) in Janis' bedroom. Janis screams at seeing a face at the window. As she and Ginny run from the room, the singer is nearly killed by the dart from a blow gun. Kay says he wants to leave immediately but Chuck tries to convince him they should stay and protect Janis. A group of society girls led by Marion (Louise Currie) arrive for the party. Just as Kay tries to inform Janis he is leaving, a lightning bolt destroys the bridge leading to the house and knocks out the telephone. After the band entertains the young women, Janis tells Kay, Chuck and Mainwaring that she has hired Professor Karl Fenninger (Lorre) to expose Prince Saliano, who she says is bilking her aunt. Just then Mainwaring introduces Fenninger, who reveals that he arrived before the bridge was destroyed. He also tells Janis it was his face she saw at the window. When the others leave the room, Mainwaring and Fenninger makes plans to get rid of Janis at Saliano's next séance. Janis wants Saliano to conduct another séance in order to expose him. When Kay and Fenninger argue with Saliano, Margo demands an apology. During the séance, in which flowers move in the air, a horn materializes and three death masks appear, Elmer's head talks. Seeing her late father, Janis faints and slumps to the floor just as Fenninger causes the chandelier over her chair to drop. Fenninger informs the group that Saliano is not faking and is really in a trance. Margo calls Kay a disturbing influence. That night Kay and Chuck see a waving white light in their room which turns out to be Prince with phosphorous on his tail. Finding a secret panel in the fireplace, the two men follow the dog into a stone cellar filled with grotesque mementos, including a stuffed gorilla that falls on Kay. They follow the tunnel which leads outside. While searching the garden, Kay and Chuck see a lurking figure that turns out to be Ish looking for Prince. When Kay sits on a stone seat, Ish messes with a sundial, sending Kay back into the tunnel. There he finds Saliano's work room, including the three death masks and a sound effects machine. Kay hides when Saliano returns, but when he leaves Kay escapes from the tunnel into the ballroom. He goes back to his room where he tells Chuck, Ish, singer Harry Babbitt (himself) and bandsman Sully Mason (himself) that someone is trying to kill Janis, having found Elmer's will in the workshop. Kay suggests another séance to expose Saliano and gets approval from Fenninger. When Saliano, Mainwaring and Fenninger discuss the matter, Saliano opposes another séance but Mainwaring says during it Fenninger will electrocute Janis. Saliano uses the effects machine to call to Margo claiming to be Elmer and wanting to speak to Janis. Kay arranges for Janis and Ginny to be locked in Janis' bedroom, guarded by Ish and Sully. When Ish sees a large lancet emerge from the wall and try to kill Janis, he yells and they all run downstairs just as the séance is about to start. Kay sneaks back into the tunnel and catches Saliano working his fake spiritualism tricks. He knocks out the fraud just as Fenninger prepares to electrocute Janis, but is stopped when Kay speaks through the effects machine. Mainwaring gets the drop on the group and runs to the work room where he fights with Kay but gets knocked out. Back upstairs, Kay tells Fenninger to bring up Saliano and Mainwaring and then reports that the codicil in Elmer's will left his estate to Janis and not Margo, the reason the crooks wanted Janis out of the way. A disheveled man (Leonard Mudie) arrives claiming to be the real Fenninger as the crooks return with guns, throw explosives into the ballroom and depart. Prince grabs the dynamite, which Kay manages to get away from him and throw in the garden. The dog again takes the dynamite and chases Saliano, Mainwaring and the fake Fenninger and an explosion follows. As Ish laments the loss of his pet, Prince returns with Saliano's turban.

Regarding *You'll Find Out*, *Photoplay* stated, "There are plenty of laughs.... Kay is natural and pleasing on the screen." On the other hand, Bosley Crowther in *The New York Times* called it "one of those silly shudder-comedies.... Apparently the script writers were scared out of their wits by their own ideas, for the dialogue and plot developments indicate that little was devoted to them.... [O]n the whole, the picture is just routine and dull." *Boxoffice* reported, "Adept showmanship is spelled out all over this musical-mystery-comedy in capital letters. The combination of Kay Kyser and his renowned musical aggregation with the screen's three most villainous bad men ... stamps the effort as a resounding box office hit...." *The Film Daily* wrote, "Liberally sprinkled with hokum, lots of laughs and the 'smooth' music of Kay Kyser and his orchestra, this new RKO offering emerges as a surprise package of swell popular entertainment.... There are laughs aplenty from beginning to end and the picture even kids itself before it is over with amusing results." *Variety* declared, "Kay Kyser's second film starrer is solid comedy entertainment.... Story is a lively admixture of comedy, music, and eerie thrills, with accent on the comedy side." *The*

New York Post asserted, "The picture is silly (intentionally), lively, and full of all the tricks of the thriller trade...."

Zombies on Broadway (1945; 68 minutes)

PRODUCER: Ben Stoloff. EXECUTIVE PRODUCER: Sid Rogell. DIRECTOR: Gordon Douglas. SCREEN-PLAY: Lawrence Kimble. ADAPTATION: Robert E. Kent. STORY: Robert Faber & Charles Newman. PHOTOGRAPHY: Jack MacKenzie. EDITOR: Philip Martin, Jr. MUSIC: Roy Webb. MUSIC DIRECTOR: C. Bakaleinikoff. ART DIRECTORS: Albert S. D'Agostino & Walter E. Keller. SOUND: Richard Van Hessen & Terry Kellum. SET DECORATIONS: Darrell Silvera & Al Greenwood. DANCE DIRECTOR: Charles O'Curran. GOWNS: Edward Stevenson. MAKEUP: Maurice Seiderman. ASSISTANT DIRECTOR: Sam Ruman.

CAST: Wally Brown (Jerry Miles), Alan Carney (Mike Strager), Bela Lugosi (Dr. Paul Renault), Anne Jeffreys (Jean LaDance), Sheldon Leonard (Ace Miller), Frank Jenks (Gus), Russell Hopton (Benny), Joseph Vitale (Joseph), Ian Wolfe (Professor Hopkins), Louis Jean Heydt (Douglas Walker), Darby Jones (Kalaga the Zombie), Sir Lancelot (Calypso Singer), Harold Herskind (Stenga the Zombie), Emory Parnell (Ship Captain), Carl Kent (Hot-Foot Davis), Martin Wilkins (Sam), Nicodemus [Nick] Stewart (Worthington), Walter Soderling (Dr. Robertson), Virginia Lyndon, Betty Yeaton (Dancers), Bob St. Angelo (Steward), Jason Robards (Club Manager), Rosemary LaPlanche (Sarong-Wearing Show Girl), Robert Clarke (Wimp), Bill Williams (Serum Smuggler), Augie Gomez (Knife Thrower), Dick Botiller (Café Boss), Max Wagner (Café Waiter), Rudolph Adrian (High Priest), Matthew Jones (Fat Native), Bess Flowers, Norman Mayes (Club Patrons), Eddie Hall (Man on Gangplank).

Hoping to emulate the success of Bud Abbott and Lou Costello at Universal, RKO teamed two of its contract players, vaudevillians Wally Brown and Alan Carney, and starred them in *Adventures of a Rookie* in 1944. The feature proved successful enough for the studio to launch a

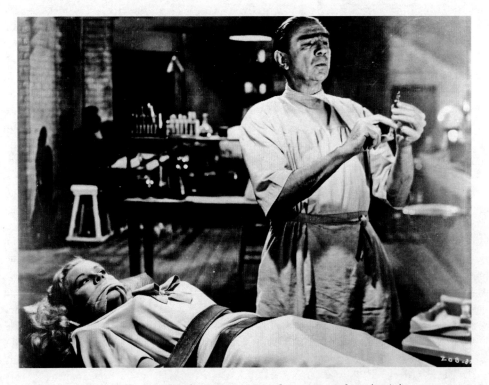

Anne Jeffreys and Bela Lugosi in *Zombies on Broadway* (1945).

Lobby card for *Zombies on Broadway* (1945).

series with Brown and Carney via *Seven Days Ashore* and *Girl Rush* (both 1944) and *Radio Stars on Parade* (1945), plus having them in supporting roles in *Step Lively* (1944). Unfortunately the team appeared to be running out of steam so RKO fell back on the dependable ploy of having its comic stooges opposite Bela Lugosi in a horror comedy, *Zombies on Broadway*, which came to theaters in May 1945. In some ways, the feature is little more than a spoof of *I Walked with a Zombie* (q.v.), replete with Darby Jones (as a zombie) and calypso singer Sir Lancelot repeating their roles from that thriller; the zombie scenes in both films take place on the Caribbean island of San Sebastian. Overall, *Zombies on Broadway* is passably entertaining with Brown and Carney fairly easy to take, their wheezy gags not too annoying among the movie's horror trappings. The latter includes Ian Wolfe as a slightly addled museum curator (one of the props is the same stuffed gorilla used to frighten Kay Kyser in *You'll Find Out* [q.v.]), Lugosi's mad scientist experimenting with scientifically creating zombies, his castle laboratory and two zombies (Jones, Harold Herskind). Makeup artist Maurice Seiderman created the five zombie masks used in the film in 20 days. Blonde Anne Jeffreys makes an enticing leading lady and she briefly gets to sing and dance. Sheldon Leonard has some good moments as a gangster trying to open a night club called the Zombie Hut and Frank Jenks and Russell Hopton do well as his thick-headed stooges. Of course, the highlight of the picture is Lugosi as the mad scientist. While his screen time is short, Lugosi dominates the film and without him it would most certainly have been less entertaining. The film's jungle scenes were shot on the jungle set used to make the studio's Tarzan series. *Zombies on Broadway* proved successful enough for RKO to put Brown and Carney into another scare comedy, *Genius at Work* (q.v.), which re-teamed them with Lugosi and Jeffreys.

Hoping to start a legitimate business, a night club called the Zombie Hut, one-time gangster Ace Miller (Leonard) discusses his plans with henchmen Gus (Jenks) and Benny (Hopton). Press agents Jerry Miles (Brown) and Mike Strager (Carney) have promised him they will produce a real zombie for the club's opening. When Ace demands to see the attraction, they show him black boxer Sam (Martin Wilkins) in whiteface makeup. For years radio commentator Douglas Walker (Louis Jean Heydt) has been trying to put Ace behind bars and he arrives at the club with his assistant Wimp (Robert Clarke). Walker tells Ace he had better produce a real zombie for the opening or he will expose him on his radio show. Ace informs Jerry and Mike they must come up with a zombie or he will have Gus and Benny take care of them. The two press agents go to see Professor Hopkins (Wolfe) at the International Museum and Mike tells him they are scientists doing research on zombies. Hopkins says zombies are the living dead and that he went to school with Dr. Paul Renault (Lugosi), who studied the subject. Since over 25 years has passed, Hopkins is not sure if Renault is still alive but he suggests they try to find him on the island of San Sebastian. Mike tells Jerry they are going to California but when they go back to their apartment to pack, Ace is there and has Gus and Benny put them on a steamer headed to the island. Upon arrival, Jerry and Mike are serenaded by a calypso singer (Sir Lancelot) and observed by Renault's henchman Joseph (Joseph Vitale), who buys a bottle of serum needed by his boss from a smuggler sailor (Bill Williams). Joseph tells Renault about the newcomers but the doctor is more interested in having his zombie Kalaga (Jones) obtain new recruits for his experiments, since all the others have died. Renault laments to Joseph that in 20 years he has not been able to do with science what the natives have done with voodoo in creating zombies. Jerry and Mike go to the Café San Sebastian where they watch beautiful singer-dancer Jean La Danse (Jeffreys) perform. When they ask the waiter (Max Wagner) and café boss (Dick Botiller) where they can obtain a zombie, both tough guys run away screaming. Jean hears Jerry and Mike inquire about zombies and tells them she will find one for them if they will get her off the island where she has been stranded for two years. Jean takes Jerry and Mike into the jungle, unaware that Kalaga is following them. As they come upon a native voodoo ceremony, Kalaga knocks down Jerry and gets Mike out of the way long enough to abduct Jean and take her to Renault. Hiding in a village hut, Mike gets into a trunk while Jerry puts soot on his face and pretends to be a native. When the natives jab the trunk with spears, Mike runs away followed by Jerry and they end up climbing a tree by a high wall overlooking San Sebastian Castle, Renault's home. There they are spotted by Joseph, who takes them to see Renault. When Jerry and Mike asks Renault about zombies, he decides to use them in his next experiment instead of Jean. He tells Joseph to have them dig two graves in case the experiment fails. As they are digging, Mike's shovel hits a trap door and he falls into a tunnel where he spies Kalaga in his coffin. Running back to Jerry, Mike tells him what happened but his friend scoffs. Renault orders Kalaga to bring him Mike. That night Jerry and Mike get ready for bed and Kalaga carries off Mike and takes him to Renault's laboratory where the mad scientist turns him into a zombie. Jean tries to help Mike and Jerry but Joseph ties her up as Renault orders Kalaga to bring Jerry to the laboratory. Jean escapes and knocks out Joseph. A monkey who has followed Mike and Jerry from the jungle hides Renault's syringe when he is ready to inject Jerry. As Renault tries to get the syringe from the monkey, Jean unties Jerry and they run upstairs. Renault follows Jean and Jerry. Jean mistakenly knocks out Jerry and then revives him, and he fights with the scientist. Renault orders Kalaga to kill Jerry but the zombie murders his master, takes him outside and throws him into one of the newly dug graves. Jean and Jerry take Mike to the boat which is surrounded by angry natives. When the natives see Mike in a zombie state they let him pass so Jerry, Jean and the monkey also pretend to be zombies and get on the boat. When they dock in New York, Jerry, Mike and Jean are met by Gus and Benny, who are skeptical about Mike being a zombie. When they are unable to cause Mike any pain, Gus and Benny tell Ace that Mike has become one of the walking dead. Walker, Hopkins and another scientist (Walter Soderling) are among the opening night crowd at Ace's club awaiting a zombie's appearance. Mike sees a pretty entertainer (Rosemary LaPlanche) in a sarong and he returns to his normal self. When Ace finds out, he prepares to shoot Jerry and Mike. Jean, who has spotted Renault's syringe kit in the monkey's possession, turns out the lights. When the zombie is presented on stage it turns out to be Ace, who has been given the serum by Jean. As Mike watches the show, Jerry and Jean go off together to be alone but Jerry mistakenly sits on the syringe.

As would be expected *The New York Times* did not care for *Zombies on Broadway*, calling it a "minor comedy item [that] comes up with very few laughs." According to *Variety*, "[A]bout half of it punched hard for laughs, some of which fail to materialize.... Picture moves faster than previous entries in the 'zombie' cycle, with Gordon Douglas' direction mainly responsible. It's lots better than the script." Regarding Lugosi, the reviewer said he "is as menacing as ever." *The Film Daily* noted, "Comedy is the chief ingredient of *Zombies on Broadway*, which dishes out mystery and horror stuff to set off the laugh-getting situations in which the clowning abilities of Wally Brown and Alan Carney are unleashed with moderate effect. Audiences partial to slapstick will find the attraction suited to their tastes, but considered generally the footage is pretty much run-of-the-mime." *The New York Herald Tribune* dubbed it "an appalling little film."

Selected Short Subjects

Bested by a Beard (1940; 20 minutes)

PRODUCER: Lou Brock. DIRECTOR: Charles E. Roberts. SCREENPLAY: George Jeske & Charles E. Roberts. PHOTOGRAPHY: Frank Redman. EDITOR: John Lockert. SOUND: Hugh McDowell.

CAST: Leon Errol (Leon Errol), Anita Garvin (Vivian Errol), Sally Payne (Maisie), Arthur O'Connell (Phil), Mervin Williams (Professor Zinko), Stanley Blystone (Macready), Frank O'Connor (Morrison), Perry Ivins (Doctor).

Between 1934 and 1951, Leon Errol starred in 89 two-reel comedies for RKO, a few of which were spook comedies, including *Bested by a Beard*, issued in February 1940. This two-reeler's minor connection to the horror genre has Leon involved with a fake spiritualist (Mervin Williams), who is played for laughs rather than chills. There is not a dull moment in the short's 20-minute running time although the plot is mundane at best. *Bested by a Beard* features an early film appearance by Arthur O'Connell who was later nominated for Best Supporting Actor Academy Awards for *Picnic* (1955) and *Anatomy of a Murder* (1959).

Morrison (Frank O'Connor) of the Confidential Loan Company tells Leon Errol (himself) that he is going to repossess his furniture if he does not come up with $150 to repay a loan. Adding to Leon's troubles, his wife Vivian's (Anita Garvin) sister Maisie (Sally Payne) and husband Phil (O'Connell) arrive for a visit. Leon tells Phil he can get the money by pawning Vivian's watch but when the sisters start to go shopping, the Errols' baby cries and is only placated by playing with the watch. Trying to get the watch, Leon and Phil sing the baby to sleep but also doze off themselves. When Vivian and Maisie return, Vivian wants to know the whereabouts of her watch. Leon suggests the baby swallowed it and Vivian calls in a doctor (Perry Ivins) whose x-rays show the infant is fine. Phil takes the watch but instead of pawning it he places a bet on a horse race. Maisie proposes bringing in spiritualist Professor Zinko (Williams), who wears a turban and a fake beard. Phil tells Leon he will pretend to be Zinko but has a flat tire and returns to the Errol house. Zinko starts to reveal to Vivian the location of her watch when Phil knocks him out from behind. Phil and Leon then carry Zinko into a bedroom. Seeing Zinko has a phony beard, Phil has Leon dress as the seer and inform Vivian that someone stole

Leon Errol, the star of several RKO scare comedy shorts.

the watch. Leon's horse wins $372, Vivian takes the money and Leon, as Zinko, announces that the watch was taken by someone reaching through the window. Macready (Stanley Blystone) arrives looking for Zinko, who told his wife he is cheating on her, although it is Zinko who is having an affair with Macready's wife. As Macready chases Leon thinking he is Zinko, Morrison and his men come for the furniture. Leon and Phil hide under two mattresses and end up being carted away in the Confidential Loan Company truck.

Cooks and Crooks (1942; 18 minutes)

PRODUCER: Bert Gilroy. DIRECTOR: Henry James [Harry Edwards]. STORY & SCREENPLAY: Harry Darcy & Henry James [Harry Edwards]. PHOTOGRAPHY: Nicholas Musuraca. EDITOR: Les Milbrook. SOUND: John C. Grubb.

CAST: Edgar Kennedy (Edgar Kennedy), Sally Payne (Sally Kennedy), Dot Farley (Mother), Jack Rice (Brother), Ann Summers (Vi), Marten Lamont (Danny), John McGuire (Police Detective), Lew Kelly (Client), Lillian Randolph (Beulah Jackson).

RKO's most prolific short subject series starred Edgar Kennedy, who headlined 103 two-reel comedies for the studio between 1931 until his death in 1948. The series was dubbed "Mr. Average Man" and in it the perennially put-upon Kennedy faced an uphill battle against the world, burdened by a feather-headed wife, an overbearing mother-in-law and a freeloading brother-in-law. Like the Leon Errol series, the Kennedy shorts contained a few spook comedies, with *Cooks and Crooks* being issued in June 1942. As with most of the Kennedy series it has a good share of laughs although it is hardly one of the better outings.

Mail order private eye Edgar Kennedy (himself) listens in as his wife Sally (Sally Payne) hears her mother (Dot Farley) complain about Edgar not buying her a new coat and her brother (Jack Rice) whining about not getting a new car. Edgar tells them to go to work just as a client (Lew Kelly) arrives offering him $5,000 to find $50,000 hidden in the kitchen wall of the Colby residence, which he claims to own. Jewel thieves Vi (Ann Summers) and Danny (Marten Lamont) are using the place as a hideout and refuse to admit Edgar when he shows up pretending to be the gas man. Beulah Jackson (Lillian Randolph) arrives to apply for a cook's job and Edgar scares her away by telling her the place is haunted. He dresses in her clothes and puts on blackface makeup, getting the job. Edgar starts looking for the money by breaking up the kitchen wall as Danny tells Vi he thinks the cook is a phony. A police detective (John McGuire) and his men arrive as Edgar breaks through the wall and gets punched by Danny. The detective thinks Edgar is part of the gang and to prove his innocence Edgar takes him to his client, who is painting an invisible fence.

Extra! Extra! (1932; 20 minutes)

SUPERVISOR: Lew Lipton. DIRECTOR: Harry Sweet. SCREENPLAY: Ralph Cedar. STORY: Lex Neal. EDITOR: Fred Maguire.

CAST: Frank McHugh, Ralph Ince, Frank Austin, Jerry Mandy.

In 1931 and 1932, Frank McHugh headlined four comedy short subjects for RKO along with appearing in a couple of the studio's Masquers Club two-reelers. *Extra! Extra!*, released in the spring of 1932, cast McHugh as a tipsy newspaper reporter who gets fired and tries to reinstate himself since his editor is out to expose a phony spiritualist. The newsman goes to the medium's headquarters, thinking it is a speakeasy, and has all kinds of trouble with the fakir's gang until he finally unmasks the fraud, writes a big story and gets his job back.

The Film Daily reported, "Very good newspaper comedy.... Some very funny gags happen." *New England Film News* stated, "Frank McHugh ... is a wow in this number and makes it a real hit."

Ghost Buster (1952; 17 minutes)

PRODUCER: George Bilson. DIRECTOR: Hal Yates. SCREENPLAY: Elwood Ullman. PHOTOGRAPHY: Frank Redman. EDITOR: Edward W. Williams. ART DIRECTOR: Feild Gray.

CAST: Gil Lamb (Slim Patterson), Carol Hughes (Betty Ames), Donald MacBride (J.R. Lynch), Donna Martell (Laura), Jim Hayward (Bigelow), Edward Clark (Oswald), George Wallace (Chuck Dixon), Barbara Pepper (Mrs. Nolan).

Released in March 1952, *Ghost Buster* was RKO's last spook comedy and one of its best. Part of a brief series headlining limber Gil Lamb, it is fast-paced and quite atmospheric in its second half, which takes place in a remote mansion during a howling wind storm. The place is plagued with slamming shutters, lights going on and off, strange noises, secret panels and a monstrous presence. Lamb makes the most of his role of a love-struck window washer who wants to impress his girl by becoming a slick reporter and solving the disappearance of a missing heir. He is particularly amusing when he takes on the guise of a gangly nurse in order to get admission to the estate. His pratfalls and other physical comedy are a delight. *Boxoffice* called it "an engaging comedy with enough material for a full-length feature."

Window washer Slim Patterson (Lamb) is in love with Betty Ames (Carol Hughes), secretary to newspaper city editor J.R. Lynch (Donald MacBride). Slim nearly falls out of a window trying to give Betty a box of smashed chocolates but his rival, smart-alecky reporter Chuck Dixon (George Wallace), brings her a bigger box. Lynch assigns Dixon to find Lionel, the missing heir to the Bigelow estate, and the two overhear Slim trying to impress Betty by telling her he plans to someday run the newspaper. After being scolded by Lynch and told to wash the windows, Slim decides to solve the Bigelow case himself. He goes to the remote mansion and claims to be a reporter but is thrown out by Oswald the butler (Edward Clark). Mrs. Nolan (Barbara Pepper), Bigelow's (Jim Hayward) nurse, leaves, complaining about noises in the night. That evening Slim returns in a cab during a wind storm dressed as nurse Aggie Patterson. Oswald tries to stop Aggie from staying but Bigelow hires her. That night a hand comes out of the wall and tries to stab the nurse. Slim calls Betty and tells her he is at Bigelow's place and she warns him not to take any chances. After a terrible scream is heard, pretty maid Laura (Donna Martell) wants to stay with Aggie but after she sees a monster in her master's bed, Bigelow turns up missing. While searching for Bigelow under his bed, Aggie hears the butler and a man wearing a monster mask talking about her. Aggie falls through a secret panel and fights both men in a hidden room as Betty, Lynch and Chuck arrive with the police. Slim beats up both men, and the monster turns out to be the missing nephew, Lionel. Bigelow is set free and Lynch agrees to hire Slim as his new reporter.

Goodness! A Ghost (1940; 16 minutes)

PRODUCER: Lou Brock. ASSOCIATE PRODUCER: Clem Beauchamp. DIRECTOR: Harry D'Arcy. SCREENPLAY: Harry Langdon. STORY: George Jeske & Arthur V. Jones. PHOTOGRAPHY: Harry Wild. EDITOR: John Lockert. SOUND: Earl Mounge.

CAST: Harry Langdon (O'Toole), Robert Stanton [Kirby Grant], Harold Daniels (Actors), Diane Hunter (Maisie), Herbert Clifton (Grandfather O'Toole), Tiny Sanford, Jim Morton, Carl Freemason (Thugs), Jack Rice (Jackson).

Harry Langdon is considered one of the top comedy stars of the 1920s, in a league with

Charles Chaplin, Harold Lloyd and Buster Keaton. A series of misfortunes, some of which he brought on himself, left Langdon floundering in the sound era but he continued to work and between 1929 and his death in 1945 he appeared in a number of feature films and 43 short subjects. He made sound shorts for Hal Roach–MGM, Educational, Paramount and from 1934 to 1945 for Columbia. Sandwiched between the Columbia two-reelers was a solo RKO effort, *Goodness! A Ghost*, released in March 1940. Langdon wrote the screenplay for this miserable short subject, possibly the nadir of his career. Laughs are few and far between in this forced effort which looks like something strung together at the beginning of the sound era instead of the usual slick RKO production.

O'Toole (Langdon), the sound effects man for a theatrical troupe putting on the play *Love Conquers All*, wants the part of a policeman when the actor (Jack Rice) playing the part quits due to too many unexplained mishaps. O'Toole says the uniform worn in the role belonged to his grandfather (Herbert Clifton) and he gets the part. As the company breaks for lunch, O'Toole works on his lines but is scared when the ghost of his grandfather tells him to respect the uniform and not fail a call to duty. A young woman (Diane Hunter) who thinks O'Toole is a real policeman begs him to go to an apartment and capture three thugs (Tiny Sanford, Jim Morton, Carl Freemason) while she goes for reinforcements. O'Toole busts in on the trio and they decide to have a poker game to see who wins the right to kill him. O'Toole tries to save himself as his grandfather's ghost flies a model airplane around the room, harassing the thugs, who take refuge in a wall bed. The police arrive and arrest the crooks and O'Toole runs back to the theater only to learn he missed the performance.

Unlike most scare comedies, *Goodness! A Ghost* did have an actual ghost, albeit a pesky one. Harry Langdon made two other scare comedies, *Shivers* (1934) and *To Heir Is Human* (1944), both for Columbia.

High and Dizzy (1950; 17 minutes)

PRODUCER: George Bilson. DIRECTOR: Hal Yates. SCREENPLAY: Earl Baldwin. PHOTOGRAPHY: J. Roy Hunt. EDITOR: Edward W. Williams. ART DIRECTOR: Walter E. Keller.

CAST: Leon Errol (Leon Errol), Dorothy Granger (Dorothy Errol), Betty Underwood (Irma), Willie Best (Wesley), Marlo Dwyer (Tenant with Dog), Irmatrude (Itself).

Dorothy Errol (Dorothy Granger) awakens to find her husband Errol (Leon Errol) has not been to bed. She finds him asleep on the divan in the next room and deduces that he stayed out all night although he tells her his taxi broke down and he walked home. Going to fix breakfast, Dorothy finds a chicken (Irmatrude) in the kitchen and Leon says he won it in a turkey raffle. The chicken squawks "Home on the Range" as Irma (Betty Underwood), an entertainer at the Hotsie Totsie Club, calls and demands that Leon return her bird. She tells him it works with her in an act and it is worth $5,000 and took three years to train. Leon attempts to catch the chicken to return it to Irma but Dorothy tells him to get ready for work. Cleaning man Wesley (Willie Best), who claims he is about to have a nervous breakdown, arrives to wash windows and is unnerved by the singing chicken. Dorothy offers Wesley fifty cents to take the bird to the basement and kill it. As he is about to behead the chicken with a hatchet, it sings a funeral dirge and he lets it go. The chicken gets on the elevator and scares another tenant (Marlo Dwyer) and her dog. Leon captures the bird but Irma shows up and he runs away with it. They are chased by the dog. The chicken escapes from Leon and walks on the fourteenth floor ledge of the building. Leon crawls after the bird and the dog follows him. Irma goes to Leon's apartment and finds a trail of feathers. When she sees Leon and the bird on the ledge, she goes into the apartment's bedroom and rescues her chicken. Dorothy confronts Irma and the chicken and finds out about Leon's escapades at the club the night before, cornering him on the ledge. Trying to save himself, Leon ends up dangling from the building's flagpole.

Released in February 1950, *High and Dizzy* rates as a fantasy film due to its singing chicken. Otherwise it is a typical Leon Errol misadventure with Leon caught by his wife in another philandering situation. Although shorts like *High and Dizzy* showed budget constraint, the Leon Errol series continued to be popular with exhibitors and audiences. This one was more harried than funny but it fared well with his fans.

Host to a Ghost (1947; 17 minutes)

PRODUCER: George Bilson. DIRECTOR: Hal Yates. SCREENPLAY: Charles E. Roberts & Hal Yates. EDITOR: Edward W. Williams.

CAST: Edgar Kennedy (Edgar Kennedy), Florence Lake (Florence Kennedy), Dot Farley (Mother), Jack Rice (Brother), Chester Clute (John Parkhurst), Ida Moore (Mrs. Parkhurst).

Florence (Florence Lake) and Mother (Dot Farley) look into a crystal ball as Mother tries to bring back her first husband. Brother (Jack Rice) brags to his brother-in-law Edgar (Edgar Kennedy) that he made $400 in real estate by selling the house Edgar has been renting. Brother tries to sell Edgar a house for $160 but Edgar says they are going to move into the Parkhurst house, which is said to be haunted. The four of them go there and find it rundown as someone watches them through a hole in the wall. In the bedroom Florence sees a hand with a knife and later someone cuts off Edgar's tie. As Edgar runs downstairs in fright, Brother has flour poured over his head while he is in the kitchen. When Edgar and Brother bump into each other, Edgar thinks he is a ghost. Mrs. Parkhurst (Ida Moore) arrives looking for her dead husband, who she claims was murdered but the body was never found. Footsteps are heard and John Parkhurst (Chester Clute) admits he faked his own death, with the help of his pals, in order to have some fun. He orders Edgar, Florence, Mother and Brother off the property and Edgar agrees to buy the other house from Brother, only to find out the price has gone up $1,000.

Host to a Ghost was also the title of a 1941 two-reel Andy Clyde spook comedy for Columbia Pictures. The RKO effort is a typical entry in the Edgar Kennedy series with Edgar not only having to deal with freeloading Mother and Brother but also a nettling fake ghost. *The Film Daily* announced, "Kennedy fans will knock themselves out at this one."

Indian Signs (1943; 17 minutes)

PRODUCER: Bert Gilroy. DIRECTOR-SCREENPLAY: Charles E. ROBERTS. PHOTOGRAPHY: Robert De Grasse. EDITOR: Robert Swink. EDITOR: John C. GRUBB.

CAST: Edgar Kennedy (Edgar Kennedy), Irene Ryan (Irene Kennedy), Dot Farley (Mother), Jack Rice (Brother), Harry Harvey (Harry), Eddie Gribbon, Frank O'Connor, Charles Doherty (Policemen).

This rather involved entry in RKO's Edgar Kennedy series finds Edgar pretending to be the ghost of an Indian in order to dissuade his wife (Irene Ryan) and mother-in-law (Dot Farley) from dabbling in the occult. The quick-moving short is fairly amusing but not one of Kennedy's best. The scenes in which he has trouble with an electric shaver are quite entertaining.

Mother (Farley) and Brother (Jack Rice) show up at the Kennedy home for an unwanted visit, Mother announcing that her Indian spirit guide Anawanda told them to come. Edgar's co-worker Harry (Harry Harvey) suggests he hold a séance to prove the spirit is an illusion. That night Edgar pretends to be a medium and puts on a tribal head mask but runs into trouble when spotted by a policeman (Frank O'Connor). Edgar finally appears as the spirit and tells Mother and Brother to go home. When Edgar's wife Irene helps him take off the Indian makeup, he ends up covered with iodine.

Lost in Limehouse; Or Lady Esmerelda's Predicament (1933; 21 minutes)

PRODUCER: Lou Brock. DIRECTOR: Otto Brower. SCREENPLAY: Walter Weems & Harrington Reynolds. PHOTOGRAPHY: Nicholas Musuraca. EDITOR: Sam White. SOUND: P.J. Faulkner.

CAST: Laura LaPlante (Lady Esmerelda), Walter Byron (Harold Heartright), John Sheehan (Sir Marmaduke Rakes), Olaf Hytten (Sheerluck Jones), Charles McNaughton (Hotson), William Burress (Hop Tup), Maurice Black (Hoo Flung), Stuart Holmes (Ah Tee), Richard Carle (Earl of Dunkwell), Ivan F. Simpson (Duke of Dunkwell), Helen Bolton (Duchess of Dunkwell), Nola Luxford (Diana), Crauford Kent (Effingwell the Butler), Dell Henderson (The Masque).

Between 1931 and 1933 the Masquers Club, a professional acting fraternity, turned out a series of two-reel comedies co-produced by RKO Radio Pictures. These all-star affairs were broad spoofs of various genres and themes and had the flavor of Victorian melodramas played for laughs. Released in the spring of 1933, *Lost in Limehouse; or Lady Esmerelda's Predicament* was a fairly tame burlesque of drawing room dramas, the Yellow Peril and Sherlock Holmes. Olaf Hytten played all-knowing detective Sheerluck Jones, assisted by the thick-headed Hotson (Charles McNaughton). The short mainly holds interest for its cast and as viewing for Holmes fanciers.

At Dunkwell Castle, the duke (Ivan F. Simpson) and duchess (Helen Bolton) lament that their daughter Esmerelda (Laura LaPlante) has been abducted. Sir Marmaduke Rakes (John Sheehan) assures them he will find her although she spurned him. Adventurer Harold Heartright (Walter Byron) arrives with a letter he was handed by a young woman he saw with a group of villainous Chinese. The letter from Esmerelda informs her parents that she is being held prisoner in Limehouse by Hoo Flung (Maurice Black). Harold promises to save Esmerelda and goes to Pike Street to see detective Sheerluck Jones (Hytten) and his associate Hotson (McNaughton). Unknown to the trio, Esmerelda is really in the hands of Marmaduke. Going to Limehouse disguised as Chinese, Sheerluck, Hotson and Harold are mistaken for hatchet men hired by Hoo Flung to carry out a Tong war. Harold finds the bound Esmerelda with both admitting they have secretly loved the other for years. When Hoo Flung learns Sheerluck and Hotson are imposters, a fight ensues, starting a worldwide Tong conflict. Harold rescues Esmerelda but he is knocked out by Marmaduke, who carries off the girl. Coming to, Harold tells Sheerluck and Hotson that Marmaduke has Esmerelda and a second fight ensues between Harold and Marmaduke, who is defeated. The duke and duchess arrive in the Limehouse dive and find their daughter in the arms of Harold. Just as they are all about to be blown up, Harold throws the bomb out a window, demolishing most of the area.

No More Relatives (1948; 18 minutes)

PRODUCER: George Bilson. DIRECTOR-SCREENPLAY: Hal Yates. STORY: Scott Darling. PHOTOGRAPHY: Frank Redman. EDITOR: Edward W. Williams. SOUND: John Tribby.

CAST: Edgar Kennedy (Edgar Kennedy), Florence Lake (Florence Kennedy), Dot Farley (Mother), Jack Rice (Brother), Walter Long (Joe).

One of the last films in RKO's long-running two-reel comedy series starring Edgar Kennedy, *No More Relatives* is only average although it is somewhat brightened by Walter Long as an imposter who terrorizes Kennedy, and the appearance of a gorilla that Edgar mistakes for his brother-in-law (Jack Rice). Kennedy's tussle with the simian is somewhat amusing but overall the short is pretty flat. It does have the surprise ending of Edgar getting a kiss from his usual nemesis, Mother (Dot Farley).

After Mother (Farley) and Brother (Rice) promise never to return to the Kennedy household, Edgar (Kennedy) and his wife Florence (Florence Lake) make a pact not to have relatives live with them again. When freeloading Mother and Brother abruptly return, Florence tells them about the deal she made with Edgar. In order to void it, Brother suggests they get someone to pretend to be Edgar's rich Uncle Jim, whom he has never seen. Borrowing $50 from Florence, Brother hires Joe (Long) to play the part. When he arrives at the Kennedy home, Edgar invites him to stay. Florence reminds Edgar of their pact just as Mother and Brother arrive and demand to remain if Uncle Jim stays. When Edgar and his fake uncle go shopping, the imposter spends a lot of money, costing Edgar over $300. Florence, Mother and Brother decide that Joe has to go and Florence tells Edgar the truth. When Edgar confronts Joe, he gets knocked down; Joe says he plans to stay. Brother suggests borrowing a neighbor's gorilla outfit to scare off Joe, unaware that a real gorilla is on the loose. When the gorilla shows up, Edgar thinks it is Brother and tries to get it to go into the house to scare Joe. Edgar ends up wrestling the gorilla until he sees Brother and then tries to jump through a window into the house only to lose his pants. The gorilla comes into the house and confronts Joe, who jumps through a window and runs away. When the gorilla goes into the kitchen, Mother knocks it out with a chair. As she and Brother start to leave, Edgar tells them to stay.

One Live Ghost (1936; 21 minutes)

PRODUCER: Lee Marcus. ASSOCIATE PRODUCER: Bert Gilroy. DIRECTOR: Leslie Goodwins. SCREENPLAY: Monte Collins & Leslie Goodwins. PHOTOGRAPHY: Jack MacKenzie. EDITOR: Edward Mann. SOUND: W.C. Moore.

CAST: Leon Errol (Henry Morton/Philpot the Valet/Henry Morton's Ghost), Vivian Oakland (Ethel Morton), Robert Graves (Bert), Delmar Watson (Sonny Morton), Lucille Ball (Maxine), Alan Curtis (Alan), Donald Kerr (Chauffeur).

Henry Morton (Leon Errol) wants a little relaxation by going on a fishing trip. His wife Vivian (Vivian Oakland) takes the car for shopping, their boy Sonny (Delmar Watson) makes a mess and Maxine (Lucille Ball), the maid, is noisy. Harry's friend Bert (Robert Graves) suggests he fake suicide and reappear as his own valet to see if his family misses him. Sonny overhears the plan and tells his mother but no one informs Maxine. To get even with Henry, Vivian gives the valet, Philpot (Errol), his room and pretends to be romantic while complaining about her "late" husband. Henry gets upset and Bert suggests they hold a séance and bring him back to haunt his family for their behavior.

An early installment in RKO's long-running Leon Errol series of two-reel comedies, *One Live Ghost* is best known today for the appearance of Lucille Ball as a giddy maid. In actuality, she has little to do as practically all the slapstick comedy is performed by Errol in an atypical role as a man who is unappreciated by his family. The short seems to have two plots. First Leon wants to go on a fishing trip and in its second half be becomes a valet and then a ghost to get even with his brazen wife and son, not realizing they are aware of his trickery. Overall this is only a mild spook comedy since even the ghost is bogus.

Sham Poo, the Magician (1932; 17 minutes)

SUPERVISOR: Lou Brock. DIRECTOR: Harry Sweet. SCREENPLAY: Harry Sweet & Hugh Cummings. EDITOR: Daniel Mandell.

CAST: Hugh Herbert, Roscoe Ates, Dorothy Granger.

Released in late November 1932, *Sham Poo, the Magician* was one of RKO's two-reel "Headliner" series shorts. It was a spoof of the radio series *Chandu the Magician* which was broadcast from 1932 to 1936 before being revived from 1948 to 1950. One month before *Sham Poo*'s release, Fox issued the feature film *Chandu the Magician* starring Edmund Lowe and Bela Lugosi. The two-reeler has two zanies (Hugh Herbert, Roscoe Ates) invading an Oriental café and harassing the famous magician Sham Poo. *The Film Daily* said the short has "a wealth of gags that are sure fire laugh-getters.... There is plenty of slapstick and a wow of a finish." Leonard Maltin in *The Great Movie Shorts* (1972) called it "bizarre."

The Song of the Voodoo (1931; 9 minutes)

CAST: Tom Terris (Narrator).

White Zombie, released theatrically by United Artists in the summer of 1932, is credited with being the first film to use voodoo as part of its story. It was, however, preceded in theaters by the RKO-Pathé short subject *The Song of the Voodoo*, part of the studio's "Vagabond Adventure" series, produced by the Van Beuren Corporation. A voodoo ceremony is pictured in the documentary along with a overview of Haiti, where residents are shown in various activities, plus a tour of sculptor Charles Normil's studio. *Exhibitors' Forum* termed it "another of the popular Vagabond Adventure series which is always interesting.... The description of the voodoo ceremony by Tom Terris is vividly told in his usual accomplished manner." *The Film Daily* called it an "interesting travel talk" and concluded, "The descriptive matter of the voodoo ceremony is more interesting than the photographs."

Spinning Mice (1935; 8 minutes; Color)

DIRECTORS: Burt Gillett & Tom Palmer. MUSIC: Winston Sharples.

Released in April 1935, this sixth entry in RKO–Van Beuren Corporation's "Rainbow Parade" series combines live action and animation and is filmed in color. Its story has two young children playing with spinning mice. One of the mice is asked why he keeps spinning and he explains that one should not tamper with nature. The story proceeds to relate the tale of an aged alchemist who tries to make the ugly beautiful with tragic results. *Boxoffice* dubbed it "Entertaining."

The Spook Speaks (1947; 19 minutes)

PRODUCER: George Bilson. SCREENPLAY-DIRECTOR: Hal Yates. PHOTOGRAPHY: Jack MacKenzie. EDITOR: Edward R. WILLIAMS. SOUND: Phil Brigand.

CAST: Leon Errol (Leon Errol), Dorothy Granger (Dorothy Errol), Steven Flagg [Michael St. Angel] (Nephew), Harry Harvey (Harry), Suzi Crandall, Phil Warren, Donald Kerr, Mickey Simpson.

Tired of his drinking, Leon's (Leon Errol) wife Dorothy (Dorothy Granger) decides to teach him a lesson when their nephew (Steven Flagg), thought killed in action, returns home safe and well. Leon comes home intoxicated and wakes up to see the nephew, who tells him they are both dead with Heaven putting them on probation as they cannot be seen or heard. Dorothy and everyone else goes along with the gag and she pretends to marry Leon's best friend Harry (Harry Harvey) and talks constantly about how Leon neglected her. Feeling remorse for his attitude toward his wife, Leon decides to take her with him but when he is hit over the head with a vase he wakes up vowing to reform.

The Spook Speaks is a *Topper* (1937) takeoff and a fine vehicle for Errol's comedic talents. It relies less on slapstick and more on dialogue and amusing situations. In his career study of Leon

Errol in *Film Fan Monthly* (July–August 1970), Leonard Maltin stated, "Although laced with oddball, black humor, *The Spook Speaks* is one of the most entertaining, offbeat entries in the Errol series."

Spooky Wooky (1950; 17 minutes)

PRODUCER: George Bilson. SCREENPLAY-DIRECTOR: Hal Yates. PHOTOGRAPHY: J. Roy Hunt. EDITOR: Edward R. Williams. ART DIRECTOR: Walter E. Keller.

CAST: Leon Errol (Leon Errol), Dorothy Granger (Dorothy Errol), Wendy Waldron (Susan Errol), Ralph Hodges (Jerry), Edward Gargan, Charlie Hall (Movers), Ray Cooke (Messenger).

Coming near the end of RKO's Leon Errol two-reel comedy series, *Spooky Wooky* is a pretty good scare comedy. A partial remake of the Edgar Kennedy 1947 short *Host to a Ghost* (q.v.), it includes the scary Indian tribal mask used in another Kennedy two-reeler, *Indian Signs* (q.v.). Much of the action takes place in a remote haunted house: Once the Errol family arrives there, the action is non-stop as they are harassed by various frightening characters like someone in a skeleton suit, a supposed ghost and a figure wearing the tribal mask. Edward Gargan and Charlie Hall are amusing as superstitious moving men who describe how a man was murdered in the house, his body never found, and how he still haunts it.

Leon Errol (Errol) gets a special delivery letter from an insurance company and his wife Dorothy (Dorothy Granger) and daughter Susan (Wendy Waldron) steam it open and find it contains a check for $5,000. Both women start talking about what they will buy with the money but Leon informs them he is using it to purchase a house in the country to get away from apartment living and Susan's many boyfriends. They get to the house, the Errols find it is rundown and old. Susan's boyfriend Jerry (Ralph Hodges) arrives and she tells him they have to find a way to get her father to return to the city. Two movers (Gargan, Hall) tell the family a murder was committed in the house and it is haunted. When Susan hears them, she faints. That night the wind causes the house to make creepy noises. Leon is forced to get up to hush a howling dog and Susan screams, claiming she saw a ghost. Something wearing an Indian fright mask scares Leon, as does a ghostly figure. Leon denies to Dorothy that he saw a ghost but when they hear the sound of rattling chains he goes downstairs to investigate and the ghost frightens Dorothy. The lights go out, Leon ignites what he thinks is a candle but it turns out to be a flare and he sees a floating candle. Something wearing a skeleton outfit chases Leon who hides in a chest where he hears Susan and Jerry discuss their pranks to get him out of the house. After he confronts them, Leon decides to scare one of his tormenters but it turns out to be Dorothy, who faints.

Thru Thin and Thicket; or, Who's Zoo in Africa (1933; 17 minutes)

SUPERVISING PRODUCER: Lou Brock. DIRECTOR: Mark Sandrich. SCREENPLAY: Ben Holmes & Walter Weems. PHOTOGRAPHY: Nicholas Musuraca. EDITOR: Sam White.

CAST: Eddie Borden (Scoop Skinner), Dorothy Granger (Tarkana), James Finlayson (Trader Cohen), Grayce Hampton (Mrs. Chuzzlebottom), Dell Henderson (The Masque); Crauford Kent, Zack Williams, Curtis Benton, Max Davidson, Lou Gottschalk, Eddie Sturgis, Donald Reed, Tom Brower, Tony Merlo, Lou Payne, Rex Barnett, E.H. Calvert, Russell Simpson, Charles McNaughton.

One of a series of two-reel spoofs produced by the Masquers Club in cooperation with RKO, this is a takeoff of jungle pictures, chiefly MGM's *Trader Horn* (1931) and *Tarzan the Ape Man* (1932) along with RKO's 1932 smash hit *Bring 'em Back Alive*. The silliness involves famed white hunter Trader Cohen (James Finlayson) leading Mrs. Chuzzlebottom's (Grayce Hampton) heavy-drinking expedition into the African jungle where reporter Scoop Skinner (Eddie Borden) vies with other members of the group in romancing the beautiful jungle girl Tarkana (Dorothy Granger). Like the other entries in the series, the short hardly takes itself seriously and is good fun.

Westward Ho-Hum (1941; 16 minutes)

PRODUCER: Bert Gilroy. DIRECTOR: Clem Beauchamp. SCREENPLAY: George Jeske & Clem Beauchamp. PHOTOGRAPHY: Nicholas Musuraca. EDITOR: Les Millbrook. SOUND: Earl Mounce.

CAST: Edgar Kennedy (Edgar Kennedy), Sally Payne (Sally Kennedy), Jack Rice (Brother), Ernie Adams (Red), Ethan Laidlaw (Rusty Gordon), Glenn Strange (Sheriff).

Edgar Kennedy out West in a spooky ghost town should have provided a good quota of laughs, but *Westward Ho-Hum* is pretty well summed up by its title. Released in the fall of 1941, it falls short in the mirth department; especially tiresome is Kennedy's mishaps with a loose board while stalking supposed phantoms in the Gold Nugget Restaurant. The scene with Brother (Jack Rice) driving a flivver in the desert at night with Edgar perched on the front holding a flashlight is amusing, but there is little else noteworthy in this tired two-reeler. Sorely missed is Dot Farley as Edgar's troublesome mother-in-law. *The Film Daily* noted, "Situations are not particular [*sic*] bright and should produce a few chuckles."

Two outlaws (Ernie Adams, Ethan Laidlaw) hide out in the ghost town of Gold Nugget, Nevada, as Edgar (Kennedy), his wife Sally (Sally Payne) and brother-in-law (Rice) drive through the desert to take possession of a restaurant which Edgar bought sight unseen. As Edgar and Brother argue, Edgar runs into a tall cactus, knocking down a sign post. That night they stop to camp and the next day find they are in the middle of Gold Nugget. When Edgar goes to look over the restaurant, he plays a game of hide-and-seek with the outlaws who think he is a lawman. Finding out Edgar is unarmed, they force him to drive them out of town but quick-thinking Sally lassoes the bad men. A sheriff (Glenn Strange) and his posse arrive, take the outlaws into custody and tell Sally she will get a $500 reward. When Edgar informs the sheriff he owns the restaurant, he is told that Gold Nugget is a ghost town.

Chronology

Feature Films

• 1929 •
Seven Keys to Baldpate (December)

• 1930 •
Ingagi (March)
Midnight Mystery (June)
Check and Double Check (October)

• 1931 •
The Public Defender (April)
The Perfect Alibi (August)

• 1932 •
Ghost Valley (May)
Bird of Paradise (August)
The Sign of Four (August)
The Most Dangerous Game (September)
Thirteen Women (September)
The Phantom of Crestwood (October)
The Face at the Window (October)
The Penguin Pool Murder (December)
Secrets of the French Police (December)
The Black Ghost

• 1933 •
The Monkey's Paw (January)
The Great Jasper (March)
Excess Baggage (March)
King Kong (April)
Deluge (April)
India Speaks (April)
Tomorrow at Seven (July)
Before Dawn (August)
The Ghost Camera (August)
A Shot in the Dark (November)
The Son of Kong (December)

• 1934 •
The Lost Patrol (February)
The Crime Doctor (March)
Tangled Evidence (March)
Murder on the Blackboard (June)
Their Big Moment (August)
Adventure Girl (August)
Lord Edgware Dies (August)
Dangerous Corner (December)
The Pointing Finger (December)
The Black Abbot

• 1935 •
Murder on a Honeymoon (February)
The Nitwits (June)
She (July)
The Return of Peter Grimm (September)
The Rainmakers (October)
The Last Days of Pompeii (October)
Seven Keys to Baldpate (December)

• 1936 •
Two in the Dark (January)
Murder on a Bridle Path (April)
Mummy's Boys (October)
The Plot Thickens (December)

• 1937 •
Riding on Air (June)
Super-Sleuth (July)
Forty Naughty Girls (September)

• 1938 •
Snow White and the Seven Dwarfs (February)
Crime Ring (July)

• 1939 •
Bad Lands (August)

The Flying Deuces (November)
The Hunchback of Notre Dame (December)

• 1940 •
Fantasia (January)
Pinocchio (February)
The Saint's Double Trouble (February)
Beyond Tomorrow (May)
Stranger on the Third Floor (August)
You'll Find Out (November)

• 1941 •
The Devil and Miss Jones (April)
The Reluctant Dragon (June)
Dumbo (October)
All That Money Can Buy (October)

• 1942 •
A Date with the Falcon (January)
Mexican Spitfire Sees a Ghost (June)
Bambi (August)
Scattergood Survives a Murder (October)
Cat People (December)

• 1943 •
Tarzan Triumphs (February)
Two Weeks to Live (February)
Saludos Amigos (February)
I Walked with a Zombie (April)
The Leopard Man (May)
The Ghost Ship (July)
So This Is Washington (August)
The Seventh Victim (August)
The Falcon and the Co-eds (November)
Tarzan's Desert Mystery (December)

• 1944 •
The Curse of the Cat People (March)
Gildersleeve's Ghost (June)
Experiment Perilous (December)

• 1945 •
The Falcon in Mexico (February)
The Three Caballeros (February)
Tarzan and the Amazons (April)
Having Wonderful Crime (April)
The Enchanted Cottage (April)
Two O'Clock Courage (April)
The Body Snatcher (May)

Zombies on Broadway (May)
Isle of the Dead (September)
The Brighton Strangler (September)
Man Alive (November)
A Game of Death (November)
The Spiral Staircase (December)
Dick Tracy (December)

• 1946 •
Tarzan and the Leopard Woman (January)
The Falcon's Alibi (April)
Bedlam (May)
Make Mine Music (August)
Genius at Work (October)
Song of the South (November)
Dick Tracy vs. Cueball (December)
The Falcon's Adventure (December)

• 1947 •
It's a Wonderful Life (January)
Sinbad the Sailor (January)
Dick Tracy's Dilemma (May)
Seven Keys to Baldpate (June)
Fun and Fancy Free (September)
Dick Tracy Meets Gruesome (September)
The Secret Life of Walter Mitty (September)

• 1948 •
The Miracle of the Bells (March)
Tarzan and the Mermaids (May)
Melody Time (May)
Guns of Hate (June)
The Boy with the Green Hair (November)

• 1949 •
Tarzan's Magic Fountain (February)
Mighty Joe Young (August)
The Mysterious Desperado (September)
The Adventures of Ichabod and Mr. Toad (October)

• 1950 •
Cinderella (March)
Tarzan and the Slave Girl (August)
Bunco Squad (September)
Experiment Alcatraz (November)

• 1951 •
Tarzan's Peril (March)
The Thing from Another World (April)

Jungle Headhunters (June)
Alice in Wonderland (July)
The Whip Hand (October)

• 1952 •
Tembo (January)
Captive Women (October)
Angel Face (December)

• 1953 •
Peter Pan (February)
Port Sinister (April)
Tarzan and the She-Devil (June)

• 1954 •
Killers from Space (January)
Quest for the Lost City (May)
Hansel and Gretel (December)

• 1955 •
Tarzan's Hidden Jungle (February)
Son of Sinbad (June)
Pearl of the South Pacific (October)
Breakaway

• 1956 •
The Brain Machine (February)
Murder on Approval (May)
Rodan (August)

• 1958 •
From the Earth to the Moon (November)

• 1959 •
The Mysterians (May)

Short Subjects

• 1931 •
Song of the Voodoo (October)

• 1932 •
Extra! Extra! (April)
Sham Poo, the Magician (November)

• 1933 •
Lost in Limehouse; or, *Lady Esmerelda's Predicament* (April)
Thru Thin and Thicket; or, *Who's Zoo in Africa*

• 1935 •
Spinning Mice (April)

• 1936 •
One Live Ghost (November)

• 1940 •
Bested by a Beard (February)
Goodness! A Ghost (March)

• 1941 •
Westward Ho-Hum (September)

• 1942 •
Cooks and Crooks (June)

• 1943 •
Indian Signs (March)

• 1947 •
Host to a Ghost (July)
The Spook Speaks (December)

• 1948 •
No More Relatives (February)

• 1950 •
High and Dizzy (February)
Spooky Wooky (December)

• 1952 •
Ghost Buster (March)

Bibliography

Books

Barnes, David. *Sherlock Holmes on the Screen: The Complete Film and TV History*. London: Reynolds and Hearn, 2002.

Beck, Jerry, with Martin Goodman, Andrew Leal, W.R. Miller and Fred Patten. *The Animated Movie Guide*. Chicago: Chicago Review Press, 2001.

Bojarski, Richard. *The Films of Bela Lugosi*. Secaucus, NJ: Citadel, 1980.

_____, and Kenneth Beale. *The Films of Boris Karloff*. Secaucus, NJ: Citadel, 1974.

Brooks, Tim, and Earl Marsh. *The Complete Directory to Prime Time Network TV Shows, 1946–Present*. New York: Ballantine, 1988.

Davies, David Stuart. *Holmes at the Movies: The Screen Career of Sherlock Holmes*. New York: Bramhall House, 1976.

DeAndrea, William L. *Encyclopedia Mysteriosa*. New York: Prentice Hall General Reference, 1997.

Essoe, Gabe. *Tarzan of the Movies*. Secaucus, NJ: Citadel, 1968.

Everman, Welch. *Cult Science Fiction Films*. New York: Citadel/Carol, 1995.

Everson, William K. *The Films of Laurel and Hardy*. Secaucus, NJ: Citadel, 1967.

Garbicz, Adam, and Jacek Klimowski. *Cinema, The Magic Vehicle: A Guide to the Achievement, Journey Two: The Cinema in the Fifties*. Metuchen, NJ: Scarecrow, 1979.

Gifford, Denis. *British Cinema*. London: A. Zwemmer/New York: A.S. Barnes, 1968.

_____. *The British Film Catalogue 1895–1985*. New York: Facts on Film, 1986.

_____. *Karloff: The Man, the Monster, the Movies*. New York: Curtis, 1973.

_____. *A Pictorial History of Horror Movies*. London: Hamblyn, 1973.

Glut, Donald F. *Classic Movie Monsters*. Metuchen, NJ: Scarecrow, 1978.

Haining, Peter. *Agatha Christie: Murder in Four Acts*. London: Virgin, 1990.

Hardy, Phil, ed. *The Encyclopedia of Horror Movies*. New York: Harper and Row, 1986.

_____. *Science Fiction*. New York: William Morrow, 1984.

Haydock, Ron. *Deerstalker! Holmes and Watson on Screen*. Metuchen, NJ: Scarecrow, 1978.

Henderson, C.J. *The Encyclopedia of Science Fiction Movies*. New York: Checkmark, 2001.

Hickerson, Jay. *The New, Revised Ultimate History of Network Radio Programming and Guide to All Circulating Shows*. Hamden, CT: Jay Hickerson, 1997.

Jacobs, Stephen. *Boris Karloff: More Than a Monster*. Sheffield, England: Tomahawk, 2011.

Jewell, Richard B., with Vernon Harbin. *The RKO Story*. London: Octopus, 1982.

Lee, Walt. *Reference Guide to Fantastic Films* (3 vols.). Los Angeles: Chelsea-Lee, 1972–74.

Lentz, Harris M., III. *Science Fiction, Horror & Fantasy Film and Television Credits. 2nd Ed.* Jefferson, NC: McFarland, 2001.

Leonard, William Tolbert. *Theatre: Stage to Screen to Television*. Metuchen, NJ: Scarecrow, 1985.

London, Rose. *Zombie: The Living Dead*. New York: Bounty, 1976.

Maltin, Leonard. *The Disney Films, 3rd Ed*. New York: Hyperion, 1995.

_____. *The Great Movie Shorts*. New York: Crown, 1972.

_____. *Leonard Maltin's 2008 Movie Guide*. New York: Signet, 2007.

_____. *Movie Comedy Teams*. New York: New American Library, 1985.

Marrill, Alvin H. *Samuel Goldwyn Presents*. South Brunswick, NJ: A.S. Barnes, 1976.

Miller, Don. *B Movies*. New York: Curtis, 1973.

Naha, Ed. *From Screen to Scream*. New York: Avon, 1975.

Neibaur, James L. *The RKO Features*. Jefferson, NC: McFarland, 1994.

Osborne, Jerry. *Official Price Guide to Movie/TV Soundtracks and Original Cast Albums, 2nd Ed*. New York: House of Collectibles, 1997.

Palmer, Scott. *The Films of Agatha Christie*. London, B.T. Batsford, 1993.

_____. *A Who's Who of British Film Actors*. Metuchen, NJ: Scarecrow, 1981.

Parish, James Robert. *The Hollywood Celebrity Death Book*. Las Vegas: Pioneer, 1993.

_____, and Michael R. Pitts. *The Great Detective Pictures*. Metuchen, NJ: Scarecrow, 1990.

_____, and _____. *The Great Science Fiction Pictures*. Metuchen, NJ: Scarecrow, 1977.

_____, and _____. *The Great Science Fiction Pictures II*. Metuchen, NJ: Scarecrow, 1990.

Parish, James Robert, and Stephen Whitney. *Vincent Price Unmasked: A Biography*. New York: Drake, 1974.

Pitts, Michael R. *Famous Movie Detectives*. Metuchen, NJ: Scarecrow, 1979.

_____. *Famous Movie Detectives II*. Metuchen, NJ: Scarecrow, 1991.

_____. *Famous Movie Detectives III*. Lanham, MD: Scarecrow, 2004.

_____. *Horror Film Stars, 3rd Ed*. Jefferson, NC: McFarland, 2002.

_____. *Radio Soundtracks: A Reference Guide, 2nd Edition*. Metuchen, NJ: Scarecrow, 1986.

Price, Michael H., with George E. Turner. *Forgotten Horrors 2*. Baltimore, MD: Midnight Marquee Press, 2001.

_____, and John Wooley, with George E. Turner. *Forgotten Horrors 3*. Baltimore, MD: Luminary Press, 2003.

Quinlan, David. *British Sound Films: The Studio Years, 1928–1959*. Totowa, NJ: Barnes and Noble, 1985.

_____. *Quinlan's Film Directors: The Ultimate Guide to the Directors of the Big Screen*. London: B.T. Batsford, 1999.

_____. *Quinlan's Film Stars: The Ultimate Guide to the Stars of the Big Screen, 5th Ed*. Washington, DC: Brassey's, 2000.

Radosh, Ronald, and Allis Radosh. *Red Star Over Hollywood: The Film Colony's Long Romance with the Left*. San Francisco: Encounter, 2005.

Rainey, Buck. *Serials and Series: A World Filmography, 1912–1956*. Jefferson, NC: McFarland, 1999.

Rhodes, Gary D., and Bill Kaffenberger. *No Traveler Returns: The Lost Years of Bela Lugosi*. Duncan, OK: BearManor Media, 2012.

Richards, Jeffrey (ed.). *The Unknown 30s: An Alternative History of the British Cinema, 1929–1939*. London and New York: I.B. Tauris, 1998.

Scheuer, Steven H., ed. *TV Movie Almanac & Ratings, 1958 and 1959*. New York: Bantam, 1958.

Searles, Baird. *Films of Science Fiction and Fantasy*. New York: AFI/Harry N. Abrams, 1988.

Senn, Bryan. *Golden Horrors: An Illustrated Critical Filmography, 1931–1939*. Jefferson, NC: McFarland, 1996.

Steinbrunner, Chris, and Burt Goldblatt. *Cinema of the Fantastic*. New York: Galahad, 1972.

Steinbrunner, Chris, and Norman Michaels. *The Films of Sherlock Holmes*. Secaucus, NJ: Citadel, 1978.

Strick, Philip. *Science Fiction Movies*. London: Octopus, 1976.

Terrace, Vincent. *The Complete Encyclopedia of Television Programs, 1947–1976* (2 vols.). Cranbury, NJ: A.S. Barnes, 1976.

Turner, George E., and Michael H. Price. *Forgotten Horrors: The Definitive Edition*. Baltimore, MD: Midnight Marquee, 1999.

Tuska, Jon. *The Detective in Hollywood*. Garden City, NJ: Doubleday, 1978.

TV Feature Film Sourcebook (2 vols.). New York: Broadcast Information Bureau, 1978.

Van Hise, James. *Calling Tracy! Six Decades of Dick Tracy*. Las Vegas: Pioneer, 1990.

Webb, Graham. *The Animated Film Encyclopedia: A Complete Guide to American Shorts, Features, and Sequences, 1900–1979*. Jefferson, NC: McFarland, 2000.

Williams, Lucy Chase. *The Complete Films of Vincent Price*. New York: Citadel/Carol, 1995.

Willis, Donald C. *Horror and Science Fiction Films: A Checklist*. Metuchen, NJ: Scarecrow, 1972.

Young, R.G. *Encyclopedia of Fantastic Films: Ali Baba to Zombies*. New York: Applause, 2000.

Periodicals

British Weekly Kinema Guide
Christian Science Monitor
The Cinema
Exhibitor's Forum
Film Bulletin
The Film Daily
Film Fan Monthly
Filmfax
Films in Review
Focus on Film
Harrison's Reports
Hollywood
Hollywood Filmograph
The Hollywood Reporter
The Hollywood Spectator
Independent Exhibitors Film Bulletin
The International Photographer
Kinematograph Weekly
Motion Picture
Motion Picture Daily
Motion Picture Herald
Motion Picture News
Motion Picture Times
Movie Action
Movie Classic
The Nation
New England Film News
The New Movie Magazine
Photoplay
PM

Picture Play Magazine
Picture Show
Screen Facts
Time
Variety
Views & Reviews

Websites

American Film Institute (www.afi.com)
Boxoffice (www.boxoffice.com)
Internet Movie Database (www.imdb.com)
Media History Digital Library (www.archive.org)
Newspaper Archive (www.newspaperarchive.com)
You Tube (www.youtube.com)

Index